Situated on the east coast of the South Island, the city of Christchurch lies between the braided Waimakariri River and the spectacular Banks Peninsula. The latter was formed by the erosion of two ancient volcanic cones by glaciers and their subsequent inundation by the sea. *(Image courtesy Fugro NPA Ltd)*

PHILIP'S

MODERN SCHOOL ATLAS

97TH EDITION

IN ASSOCIATION WITH
THE ROYAL GEOGRAPHICAL SOCIETY
WITH THE INSTITUTE OF BRITISH GEOGRAPHERS

MAP SYMBOLS

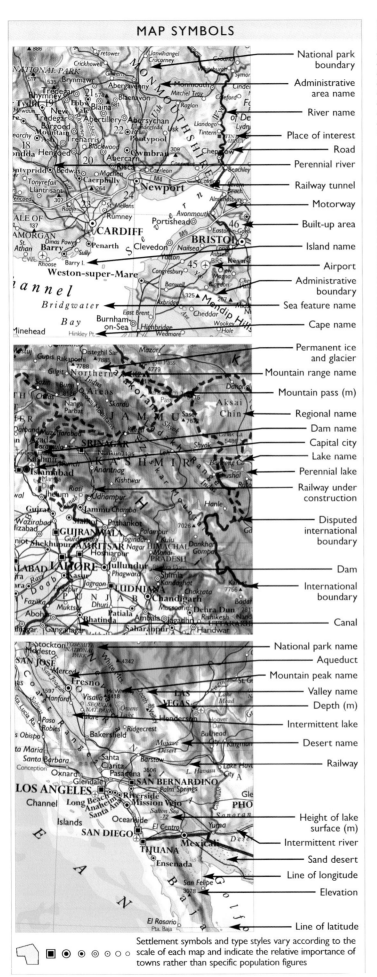

- National park boundary
- Administrative area name
- River name
- Place of interest
- Road
- Perennial river
- Railway tunnel
- Motorway
- Built-up area
- Island name
- Airport
- Administrative boundary
- Sea feature name
- Cape name
- Permanent ice and glacier
- Mountain range name
- Mountain pass (m)
- Regional name
- Dam name
- Capital city
- Lake name
- Perennial lake
- Railway under construction
- Disputed international boundary
- Dam
- International boundary
- Canal
- National park name
- Aqueduct
- Mountain peak name
- Valley name
- Depth (m)
- Intermittent lake
- Desert name
- Railway
- Height of lake surface (m)
- Intermittent river
- Sand desert
- Line of longitude
- Elevation
- Line of latitude

Settlement symbols and type styles vary according to the scale of each map and indicate the relative importance of towns rather than specific population figures

SUBJECT LIST

Acid rain	37
Agriculture	38, 136–7
Aid (international)	152
AIDS and HIV	61, 153
Air travel	42, 61, 142
Alternative energy	139
Arctic ice cap	130
Armed conflicts	153
Biomes	58, 74, 92, 100, 106, 118, 134–5
BRIC countries	151
Bush fires	101
Carbon dioxide emissions	37, 61, 130
Climate	34–5, 58, 74, 92, 100, 106, 118, 128–9, 132–3
Climate change	35, 130–1
Coal	41, 61, 101, 138
Conservation	37
Continental drift	124
Crime rates	48
Debt (international)	152
Deforestation	131
Desertification	131
Drought	10, 101
Drug traffic	153
Earthquakes	12, 81, 83, 115, 125
Education	48, 61, 145
Electricity generation	41, 139
El Niño	129
Employment	39, 80, 140
Energy	40–1, 61, 101, 138
Ethnic groups	47
European Union (EU)	60–1
Eurozone	60
Exports	39, 141
Family size	149
Fishing	38, 136–7
Flood risk	36
Food production	38, 136–7
Forestry	136–7
Fuel	40–1, 138
Gender Inequality Index (GII)	145
Geology	32, 124
Global warming	35, 130
Greenhouse gases	37, 130
Gross National Income (GNI)	61, 144
Group of Eight (G8)	151
Health care	48, 61, 145
Heatwaves	101
Human Development Index (HDI)	144
Hurricanes	116
Hydroelectricity	41, 61, 80, 101, 139
Illiteracy	145
Imports	39
Industry	39, 80
Infant mortality	
Internet	48
Inter-tropical convergence zone (ITCZ)	
Languages	60
La Niña	
Latitude and longitude	
LEDCs	
Life expectancy	
Literacy	
Manufacturing	39, 80
Map projections	
Maternal mortality	
MEDCs	
Migration	47
Minerals	101
Monsoon	
National parks	
Natural vegetation	37, 1
Nuclear power	12, 41, 61
Ocean conveyor belt	
Ocean currents	
Oil and gas	40–1, 61, 88, 101
Plate tectonics	1
Population	46–7, 59, 75, 93, 107, 119, 1
Refugees	
Religions	
Remote sensing	
Renewable energy	41
Research and development	
Satellite imagery	
Scale	
Services	39
Soils	37, 1
Standards of living	48, 61
Telecommunications	
Time zones	
Tourism	43, 61, 113
Trade	39
Transport	4
Travel	42–3
Tsunamis	12, 8
Unemployment	
United Nations (UN)	
Urban population	
Volcanoes	81, 115
Waste recycling	
Water supply	36, 88
Wealth	48, 61
Wind power	
World Heritage Sites	37

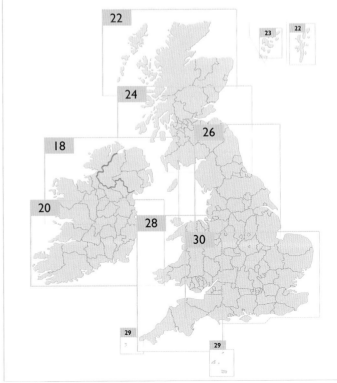

CONTENTS

LE, LATITUDE AND LONGITUDE 4
PROJECTIONS 5
RODUCTION 6–7

REMOTE SENSING 6–16

OUR COMPOSITES 8
ETATION AND LANDFORMS 9
BAL MONITORING 10–11
RONMENTAL MONITORING 12–13
LOGICAL INTERPRETATION 14
THETIC APERTURE RADAR 15
URBAN ENVIRONMENT 16

UNITED KINGDOM AND IRELAND 17–48

AND – NORTH 18–19
AND – SOUTH 20–21
THERN SCOTLAND 22–23
THERN SCOTLAND 24–25
THERN ENGLAND 26–27
ES AND SOUTH-WEST ENGLAND 28–29
TH AND SOUTH-EAST ENGLAND 30–31
ND IRELAND: GEOLOGY 32
ND IRELAND: RELIEF OF LAND 33
ND IRELAND: CLIMATE 34–35
ND IRELAND: ENVIRONMENT 36–37
ND IRELAND: AGRICULTURE,
DUSTRY AND TRADE 38–39
ND IRELAND: ENERGY 40–41
ND IRELAND: TRANSPORT
ID TOURISM 42–43
ND IRELAND: COUNTIES AND
GIONS 44–45
ND IRELAND: POPULATION TRENDS 46–47
ND IRELAND: STANDARDS OF LIVING 48

THE WORLD 49–122

WORLD: RELIEF OF LAND 50–51
WORLD: COUNTRIES 52–53
TIC OCEAN AND ANTARCTICA 54–55

EUROPE: RELIEF OF LAND 56
EUROPE: COUNTRIES 57
EUROPE: CLIMATE AND BIOMES 58
EUROPE: POPULATION 59
EUROPEAN UNION 60–61
UK AND IRELAND 62
SCANDINAVIA AND THE BALTIC LANDS 63
CENTRAL EUROPE 64–65
FRANCE 66
SPAIN AND PORTUGAL 67
ITALY AND THE BALKAN STATES 68–69
EASTERN EUROPE AND TURKEY 70–71
ASIA: RELIEF OF LAND 72
ASIA: COUNTRIES 73
ASIA: CLIMATE AND BIOMES 74
ASIA: POPULATION AND WEALTH 75
RUSSIA AND NORTHERN ASIA 76–77
CHINA AND THE FAR EAST 78–79
CHINA: INDUSTRY AND HYDROELECTRICITY 80
JAPAN 81
SOUTH-EAST ASIA 82–83
SOUTH ASIA 84–85
THE MIDDLE EAST 86–87
THE MIDDLE EAST: OIL AND WATER 88
ARABIA AND THE HORN OF AFRICA 89
AFRICA: RELIEF OF LAND 90
AFRICA: COUNTRIES 91
AFRICA: CLIMATE AND BIOMES 92
AFRICA: POPULATION AND WEALTH 93
NORTHERN AFRICA 94–95
CENTRAL AND SOUTHERN AFRICA 96–97
OCEANIA 98–99
OCEANIA: CLIMATE AND POPULATION 100–101
PACIFIC OCEAN 102–103
NORTH AMERICA: RELIEF OF LAND 104
NORTH AMERICA: COUNTRIES 105
NORTH AMERICA: CLIMATE AND BIOMES 106
NORTH AMERICA: POPULATION AND
WEALTH 107
CANADA 108–109

UNITED STATES 110–111
NORTH-EAST UNITED STATES AND
THE ST LAWRENCE 112–113
MEXICO, CENTRAL AMERICA AND
THE CARIBBEAN 114–115
CARIBBEAN: HURRICANES 116
SOUTH AMERICA: RELIEF OF LAND 117
SOUTH AMERICA: CLIMATE AND BIOMES 118
SOUTH AMERICA: POPULATION AND
WEALTH 119
SOUTH AMERICA 120–121
SOUTH-EAST BRAZIL 122

WORLD THEMES 123–160

THE WORLD: VOLCANOES
AND EARTHQUAKES 124–125
THE WORLD: TEMPERATURE AND
OCEAN CURRENTS 126
THE WORLD: PRESSURE, WINDS
AND PRECIPITATION 127
THE WORLD: CLIMATE 128–129
THE WORLD: CLIMATE CHANGE 130–131
THE WORLD CLIMATE STATISTICS 132–133
THE WORLD: BIOMES 134–135
THE WORLD: AGRICULTURE 136–137
THE WORLD: ENERGY AND MINERALS 138–139
THE WORLD: INDUSTRY AND TRADE 140–141
THE WORLD: TRAVEL AND TOURISM 142–143
THE WORLD: STANDARDS OF LIVING 144–145
THE WORLD: POPULATION DISTRIBUTION 146–147
THE WORLD: POPULATION TRENDS 148–149
THE WORLD: LANGUAGES AND RELIGION 150
THE WORLD: INTERNATIONAL
ORGANIZATIONS 151
THE WORLD: HUMAN CONCERNS 152–153
THE WORLD: SOCIAL AND
ECONOMIC STATISTICS 154–159
THE WORLD: PHYSICAL DIMENSIONS 160

INDEX 161–184

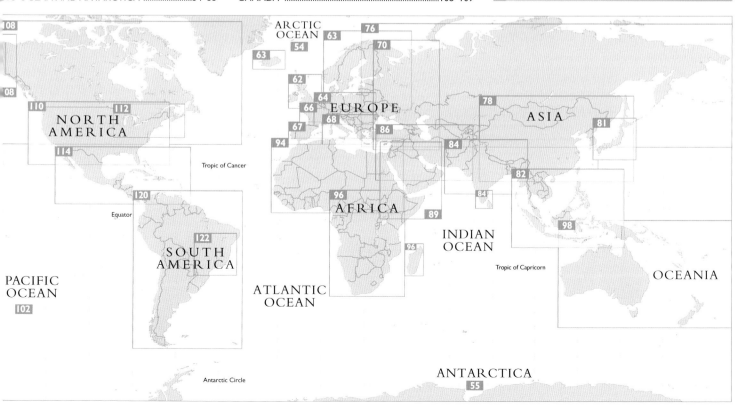

SCALE

The scale of a map is the relationship of the distance between two points shown on the map and the distance between the same two points on the Earth's surface. For instance, 1 inch on the map represents 1 mile on the ground, or 10 kilometres on the ground is represented by 1 centimetre on the map.

Instead of saying 1 centimetre represents 10 kilometres, we could say that 1 centimetre represents 1 000 000 centimetres on the map. If the scale is stated so that the same unit of measurement is used on both the map and the ground, then the proportion will hold for any unit of measurement. Therefore, the scale is usually written 1:1 000 000. This is called a 'representative fraction' and usually appears at the top of the map page, above the scale bar.

Calculations can easily be made in centimetres and kilometres by dividing the second figure in the representative fraction by 100 000 (i.e. by deleting the last five zeros). Thus at a scale of 1:5 000 000, 1 cm on the map represents 50 km on the ground. This is called a 'scale statement'. The calculation for inches and miles is more laborious, but 1 000 000 divided by 63 360 (the number of inches in a mile) shows that 1:1 000 000 can be stated as 1 inch on the map represents approximately 16 miles on the ground.

Many of the maps in this atlas feature a scale bar. This is a bar divided into the units of the map – miles and kilometres – so that a map distance can be measured with a ruler, dividers or a piece of paper, then placed along the scale bar, and the distance read off. To the left of the zero on the scale bar there are usually more divisions. By placing the ruler or dividers on the nearest rounded figure to the right of the zero, the smaller units can be counted off to the left.

The map extracts below show Los Angeles and its surrounding area at six different scales. The representative fraction, scale statement and scale bar are positioned above each map. Map 1 is at 1:27 000 and is the largest scale extract shown. Many of the individual buildings are identified and most of the streets are named, but at this scale only part of central Los Angeles can be shown within the given area. Map 2 is much smaller in scale at 1:250 000. Only a few important buildings and streets can be named, but the whole of central Los Angeles is shown. Maps 3, 4 and 5 show how greater areas can be depicted as the map scale decreases, down to Map 6 at 1:35 000 000. At this small scale, the entire Los Angeles conurbation is depicted by a single town symbol and a large part of the south-western USA and part of Mexico is shown.

The scales of maps must be used with care since large distances on small-scale maps can be represented by one or two centimetres. On certain projections scale is only correct along certain lines, parallels or meridians. As a general rule, the larger the map scale, the more accurate and reliable will be the distance measured.

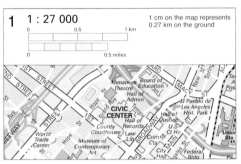

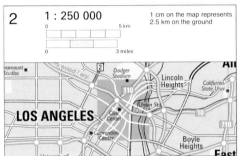

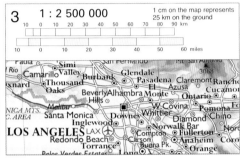

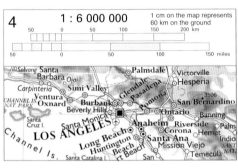

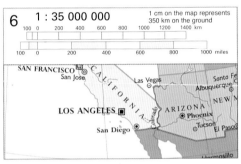

LATITUDE AND LONGITUDE

Accurate positioning of individual points on the Earth's surface is made possible by reference to the geometric system of latitude and longitude.

Latitude is the distance of a point north or south of the Equator measured at an angle with the centre of the Earth, whereby the Equator is latitude 0 degrees, the North Pole is 90 degrees north and the South Pole 90 degrees south. Latitude parallels are drawn west–east around the Earth, parallel to the Equator, decreasing in diameter from the Equator until they become a point at the poles. On the maps in this atlas the lines of latitude are represented by blue lines running across the map in smooth curves, with the degree figures in blue at the sides of the maps. The degree interval depends on the scale of the map.

Lines of longitude are meridians drawn north–south, cutting the lines of latitude at right angles on the Earth's surface and intersecting with one another at the poles. Longitude is measured by an angle at the centre of the Earth from the prime meridian (0 degrees), which passes through Greenwich in London. It is given as a measurement east or west of the Greenwich Meridian from 0 to 180 degrees. The meridians are normally drawn north–south vertically down the map, with the degree figures in blue in the top and bottom margins of the map.

In the index each place name is followed by its map page number, its letter-figure grid reference, and then its latitude and longitude. The unit of measurement is the degree, which is subdivided into 60 minutes. An index entry states the position of a place in degrees and minutes. The latitude is followed by N(orth) or S(outh) and the longitude E(ast) or W(est).

For example:
Helston, U.K.   29 G3   50 7N   5 17W
Helston is on map page 29, in grid square G3, and is 50 degrees 7 minutes north of the Equator and 5 degrees 17 minutes west of Greenwich.

McKinley, Mt., U.S.A.   108 C4   63 4N   151 0W
Mount McKinley is on map page 108, in grid square C4, and is 63 degrees 4 minutes north of the Equator and 151 degrees 0 minutes west of Greenwich.

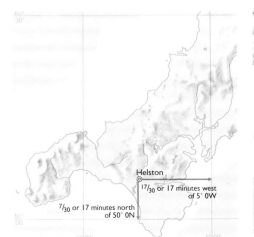

HOW TO LOCATE A PLACE OR FEATURE

The two diagrams (left) show how to estimate the required distance from the nearest line of latitude or longitude on the map page, in order to locate a place or feature listed in the index (such as Helston in the UK and Mount McKinley in the USA, as detailed in the above example).

In the left-hand diagram there are 30 minutes between the lines and so to find the position of Helston an estimate has to be made: 7 parts of the 30 minutes north of the 50 0N latitude line, and 17 parts of the 30 minutes west of the 5 0W longitude line.

In the right-hand diagram it is more difficult to estimate because there is an interval of 10 degrees between the lines. In the example of Mount McKinley, the reader has to estimate 3 degrees 4 minutes north of 60 0N and 1 degree west of 150 0W.

MAP PROJECTIONS

A map projection is the systematic depiction of the imaginary grid of lines of latitude and longitude from a globe on to a flat surface. The grid of lines is called the 'graticule' and it can be constructed either by graphical means or by mathematical formulae to form the basis of a map. As a globe is three dimensional, it is not possible to depict its surface on a flat map without some form of distortion. Preservation of one of the basic properties listed below can only be secured at the expense of the others and thus the choice of projection is often a compromise solution.

Correct area

In these projections the areas from the globe are to scale on the map. This is particularly useful in the mapping of densities and distributions. Projections with this property are termed 'equal area', 'equivalent' or 'homolographic'.

Correct distance

In these projections the scale is correct along the meridians, or, in the case of the 'azimuthal equidistant', scale is true along any line drawn from the centre of the projection. They are called 'equidistant'.

Correct shape

This property can only be true within small areas as it is achieved only by having a uniform scale distortion along both the 'x' and 'y' axes of the projection. The projections are called 'conformal' or 'orthomorphic'.

Map projections can be divided into three broad categories – **'azimuthal'**, **'conic'** and **'cylindrical'**. Cartographers use different projections from these categories depending on the map scale, the size of the area to be mapped, and what they want the map to show.

AZIMUTHAL OR ZENITHAL PROJECTIONS

These are constructed by the projection of part of the graticule from the globe on to a plane tangential to any single point on it. This plane may be tangential to the equator (equatorial case), the poles (polar case) or any other point (oblique case). Any straight line drawn from the point at which the plane touches the globe is the shortest distance from that point and is known as a 'great circle'. In its 'gnomonic' construction any straight line on the map is a great circle, but there is great exaggeration towards the edges and this reduces its general uses. There are five different ways of transferring the graticule on to the plane and these are shown below. The diagrams below also show how the graticules vary, using the polar case as the example.

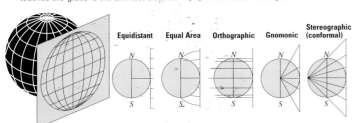

Equidistant   Equal Area   Orthographic   Gnomonic   Stereographic (conformal)

Polar case

The polar case is the simplest to construct and the diagram on the right shows the differing effects of all five methods of construction, comparing their coverage, distortion, etc, using North America as the example.

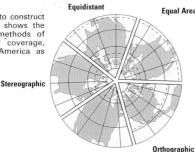

Oblique case

The plane touches the globe at any point between the Equator and poles. The oblique orthographic uses the distortion in azimuthal projections away from the centre to give a graphic depiction of the Earth as seen from any desired point in space.

Equatorial case

The example shown here is Lambert's Equivalent Azimuthal. It is the only projection which is both equal area and where bearing is true from the centre.

CONICAL PROJECTIONS

These use the projection of the graticule from the globe on to a cone which is tangential to a line of latitude (termed the 'standard parallel'). This line is always an arc and scale is always true along it. Because of its method of construction, it is used mainly for depicting the temperate latitudes around the standard parallel, i.e. where there is least distortion. To reduce the distortion and include a larger range of latitudes, the projection may be constructed with the cone bisecting the surface of the globe so that there are two standard parallels, each of which is true to scale. The distortion is thus spread more evenly between the two chosen parallels.

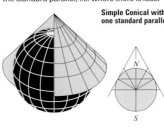

Simple Conical with one standard parallel

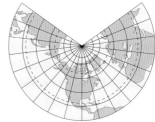

Bonne

This is a modification of the simple conic, whereby the true scale along the meridians is sacrificed to enable the accurate representation of areas. However, scale is true along each parallel but shapes are distorted at the edges.

Albers Conical Equal Area

This projection uses two standard parallels. The selection of these relative to the land area to be mapped is very important. It is equal area and is especially useful for large land masses oriented east–west, such as the USA.

CYLINDRICAL AND OTHER WORLD PROJECTIONS

This group of projections are those which permit the whole of the Earth's surface to be depicted on one map. They are a very large group of projections and the following are only a few of them. Cylindrical projections are constructed by the projection of the graticule from the globe on to a cylinder tangential to the globe. Although cylindrical projections can depict all the main land masses, there is considerable distortion of shape and area towards the poles. One cylindrical projection, Mercator, overcomes this shortcoming by possessing the unique navigational property that any straight line drawn on it is a line of constant bearing ('loxodrome'). It is used for maps and charts between 15° either side of the Equator. Beyond this, enlargement of area is a serious drawback, although it is used for navigational charts at all latitudes.

Mercator

Simple Cylindrical

Cylindrical with two standard parallels

Eckert IV
(pseudo-cylindrical equal area)

Hammer
(polyconic equal area)

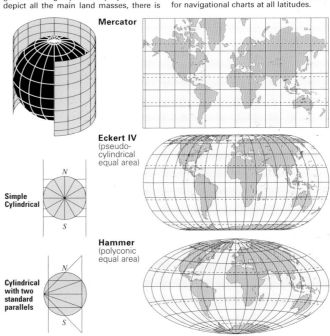

The first satellite to monitor our environment systematically was launched as long ago as April 1961. It was called TIROS-1 and was designed specifically to record atmospheric change. The first of the generation of Earth resources satellites was Landsat-1, launched in July 1972.

The succeeding decades have seen a revolution in our ability to survey and map our global environment. Digital sensors mounted on satellites now scan vast areas of the Earth's surface day and night. They collect and relay back to Earth huge volumes of geographical data which is processed and stored by computers.

Satellite imagery and remote sensing

Continuous development and refinement, and freedom from national access restrictions, have meant that sensors on these satellite platforms are increasingly replacing surface and airborne data-gathering techniques. Twenty-four hours a day, satellites are scanning and measuring the Earth's surface and atmosphere, adding to an ever-expanding range of geographic and geophysical data available to help us identify and manage the problems of our human and physical environments. Remote sensing is the science of extracting information from such images.

Satellite orbits

Most Earth-observation satellites (such as the Landsat, SPOT and IRS series) are in a near-polar, Sun-synchronous orbit (*see diagram opposite*). At altitudes of around 700–900 km the satellites revolve around the Earth approximately every 100 minutes and on each orbit cross a particular line of latitude at the same local (solar) time. This ensures that the satellite can obtain coverage of most of the globe, replicating the coverage typically within 2–3 weeks. In more recent satellites, sensors can be pointed sideways from the orbital path, and 'revisit' times with high-resolution frames can thus be reduced to a few days.

Exceptions to these Sun-synchronous orbits include the geostationary meteorological satellites, such as Meteosat. These have a 36,000 km high orbit and rotate around the Earth every 24 hours, thus remaining above the same point on the Equator.

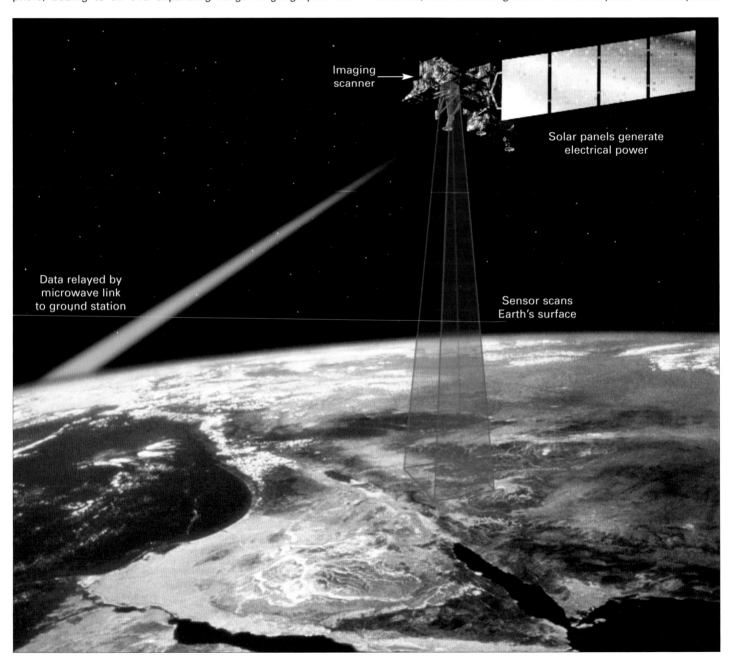

Imaging scanner

Solar panels generate electrical power

Data relayed by microwave link to ground station

Sensor scans Earth's surface

Landsat-7

This is the latest addition to the Landsat Earth-observation satellite programme, orbiting at 705 km above the Earth. With onboard recorders, the satellite can store data until it passes within range of a ground station. Basic geometric and radiometric corrections are then applied before distribution of the imagery to users.

These satellites acquire frequent images showing cloud and atmospheric moisture movements for almost a full hemisphere.

In addition, there is the Global Positioning System (GPS) satellite 'constellation', which orbits at a height of 20,200 km, consisting of 24 satellites. These circle the Earth in six different orbital planes, enabling us to fix our position on the Earth's surface to an accuracy of a few centimetres. Although developed for military use, this system is now available to individuals through hand-held receivers and in-car navigation systems. The other principal commercial uses are for surveying and air and sea navigation.

Digital sensors

Early satellite designs involved images being exposed to photographic film and returned to Earth by capsule for processing, a technique still sometimes used today. However, even the first commercial satellite imagery, from Landsat-1, used digital imaging sensors and transmitted the data back to ground stations (*see diagram opposite*).

Passive, or optical, sensors record the radiation reflected from the Earth for specific wavebands. Active sensors transmit their own microwave radiation, which is reflected from the Earth's surface back to the satellite and recorded. The SAR (Synthetic Aperture Radar) images on page 15 are examples of the latter.

Whichever scanning method is used, each satellite records image data of constant width but potentially several thousand kilometres in length. Once the data has been received on Earth, it is usually split into approximately square sections or 'scenes' for distribution.

Spectral resolution, wavebands and false-colour composites

Satellites can record data from many sections of the electromagnetic spectrum (wavebands) simultaneously. Since we can only see images made from the three primary colours (red, green and blue), a selection of any three wavebands needs to be made in order to form a picture that will enable visual interpretation of the scene to be made. When any combination other than the visible bands are used, such as near or middle infrared, the resulting image is termed a 'false-colour composite'. An example of this is shown on page 8.

The selection of these wavebands depends on the purpose of the final image – geology, hydrology, agronomy and environmental requirements each have their own optimum waveband combinations.

GEOGRAPHIC INFORMATION SYSTEMS

A Geographic Information System (GIS) enables any available geospatial data to be compiled, presented and analysed using specialized computer software.

Many aspects of our lives now benefit from the use of GIS – from the management and maintenance of the networks of pipelines and cables that supply our homes, to the exploitation or protection of the natural resources that we use. Much of this is at a regional or national scale and the data collected from satellites form an important part of our interpretation and understanding of the world around us.

GIS systems are used for many aspects of central planning and modern life, such as defence, land use, reclamation, telecommunications and the deployment of emergency services. Commercial companies can use demographic and infrastructure data within a GIS to plan marketing strategies, identifying where their services would be most needed, and thus decide where best to locate their businesses. Insurance companies use GIS to determine premiums based on population distribution, crime figures and the likelihood of natural disasters, such as flooding or subsidence.

Whatever the application, all the relevant data can be prepared in a GIS so that a user can extract and display the information of particular interest on a map, or compare it with other material in order to help analyse and resolve a specific problem. From analysis of the data that has been acquired it is often possible to use a GIS to create a computer 'model' of possible future situations and see what impact various actions may have. A GIS can also monitor change over time, aiding the interpretation of long-term trends.

A GIS may also use satellite data to extract useful information and map large areas, which would otherwise take many man-years using other methods. For applications such as hydrocarbon and mineral exploration, forestry, agriculture, environmental monitoring and urban development, these developments have made it possible to undertake projects on a global scale unheard of before.

To find out more about how GIS works and how it affects our lives, why not go the Ordnance Survey's Mapzone website at: http://mapzone.ordnancesurvey.co.uk/mapzone/giszone.html

SELECTED REMOTE SENSING SATELLITES			
Year Launched	Satellite	Country	Pixel Size (Resolution) (b&w/colour)
Passive Sensors (Optical)			
1972	Landsat-1 MSS	USA	80 m
1978	NOAA AVHRR	USA	1.1 km
1981	Cosmos TK-350	Russia	10 m
1982	Landsat-4 TM	USA	30 m
1986	SPOT-1	France	10 / 20 m
1988	IRS-1A	India	36 / 72 m
1989	Cosmos KVR-1000	Russia	2 m
1991	IRS-1B	India	36 / 72 m
1995	IRS-1C	India	5.8 / 23.5 m
1997	IRS-1D	India	5.8 / 23.5 m
1999	Landsat-7 ETM	USA	15 / 30 m
1999	UoSAT-12	UK	10 / 32 m
1999	IKONOS-2	USA	1.0 / 4 m
1999	ASTER	USA	15 m
2000	Hyperion	USA	30 m
2000	EROS-A1	International	1.8 m
2001	Quickbird	USA	0.61 / 2.4 m
2002	SPOT-5	France	2.5 / 5 / 10 m
2002	DMC AlSat-1	Algeria (UK)	32 m
2003	DMC UK	UK	32 m
2003	DMC NigeriaSat-1	Nigeria (UK)	32 m
2003	DMC BilSat	Turkey (UK)	32 m
2003	OrbView-3	USA	1.0 / 4 m
2004	Formosat-2	Taiwan	2.0 / 8 m
2004	KOMPSAT-2	South Korea	1.0 / 4 m
2006	ALOS PRISM & AVNIR	Japan	2.5 m
2007	WorldView-1	USA	0.5 m*
2008	GeoEye-1	USA	0.4* / 1.6 m
2008	RapidEye	Germany	6.5 m
2009	WorldView-2	USA	0.4* / 1.6 m
2011	DMC NigeriaSAT-2	Nigeria (UK)	2.5 / 5 m
Active Sensors (Synthetic Aperture Radar)			
1991	ERS-1	Europe	25 m
1992	JERS-1	Japan	18 m
1995	ERS-2	Europe	25 m
1995	RADARSAT	Canada	8–100 m
2002	ENVISAT	Europe	25 m
2006	ALOS PALSAR	Japan	10 m
2007	RADARSAT-2	Canada	3 m
2007	TERRASAR-X	Germany	1 m
2007	COSMO-SkyMed	Italy	1 m

* Distribution of satellite image resolutions better than 0.5 m are restricted.

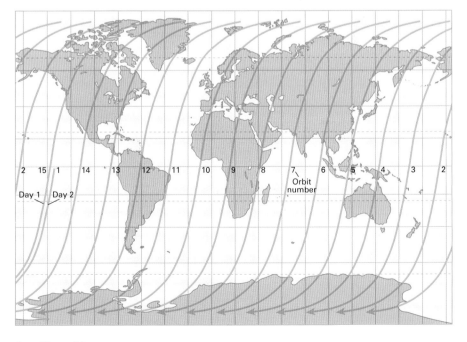

Satellite orbits

Landsat-7 makes over 14 orbits per day in its Sun-synchronous orbit. During the full 16 days of a repeat cycle, coverage of the areas between those shown is achieved.

Natural-colour and false-colour composites

These images show the salt ponds at the southern end of San Francisco Bay, which now form the San Francisco Bay National Wildlife Refuge. They demonstrate the difference between 'natural colour' (*top*) and 'false colour' (*bottom*) composites.

The top image is made from visible red, green and blue wavelengths. The colours correspond closely to those one would observe from an aircraft. The salt ponds appear green or orange-red due to the colour of the sediments they contain. The urban areas appear grey and vegetation is either dark green (trees) or light brown (dry grass).

The bottom image is made up of near-infrared, visible red and visible green wavelengths. These wavebands are represented here in red, green and blue, respectively. Since chlorophyll in healthy vegetation strongly reflects near-infrared light, this is clearly visible as red in the image.

False-colour composite imagery is therefore very sensitive to the presence of healthy vegetation. The bottom image thus shows better discrimination between the 'leafy' residential urban areas, such as Palo Alto (south-west of the Bay), and other urban areas by the 'redness' of the trees. The high chlorophyll content of watered urban grass areas shows as bright red, contrasting with the dark red of trees and the brown of natural, dry grass. *(EROS)*

Western Grand Canyon, Arizona, USA

This false-colour image shows in bright red the sparse vegetation on the limestone plateau, including sage, mesquite and grasses. Such imagery is used to monitor this and similar fragile environments. The sediment-laden river, shown as blue-green, can be seen dispersing into Lake Mead to the north-west. Side canyons cross the main canyon in straight lines, showing where erosion along weakened fault lines has occurred. *(EROS)*

Har Nuur, Mongolia

'Har Nuur' means 'Black Lake'. It is situated in a remote inland basin in the west of Mongolia. The yellow areas are sand-desert dune fields, which are being blown eastwards on the prevailing westerly winds. This image, from the International Space Station, shows a spur of sand pushing across the south-west shore of the lake. *(NASA EO-1 team)*

Washington State, USA

The chequerboard pattern shows the square or rectangular land parcels used for commercial forestry. Brown or orange indicates bare earth, light green represents grassland or young trees, and dark green shows mature woodland. Used over time, images such as this allow scientists to monitor deforestation and new planting, and their consequent effects on the carbon cycle. *(EROS)*

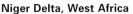

Niger Delta, West Africa

The River Niger is the third longest river in Africa after the Nile and Congo, and this false-colour image shows the different vegetation types. Deltas are by nature constantly evolving sedimentary features and often contain many ecosystems within them. In the case of the Niger Delta, there are also vast hydrocarbon reserves beneath it with associated wells and pipelines. Satellite imagery helps to plan activity and monitor this fragile and changing environment. *(EROS)*

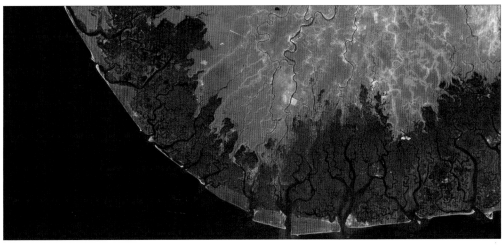

Puyehue-Cordón Volcano, Chile
Part of the ash plume from the June 2011 major eruption from this strato-volcano in the Andes can be seen drifting eastwards at high altitude across the coast of Argentina, to the north of the distinctive shape of the Valdés Peninsula. The ash eventually travelled in the upper atmosphere as far as Australia and New Zealand, causing disruption to commercial flights. *(Jeff Schmaltz, MODIS Rapid Response Team at NASA GSFC)*

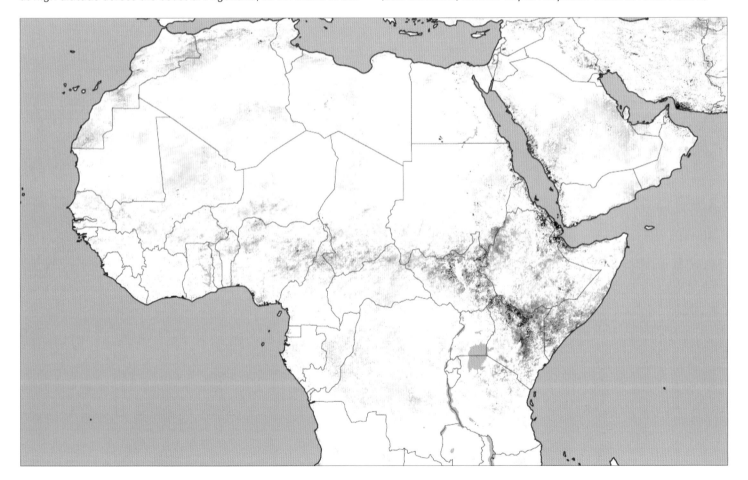

East African drought
The colours on the image represent the 'vegetation anomaly', i.e. the deviation from what would be considered normal growth, between April and June 2011. Brown indicates poor plant growth and highlights the severe drought in Somalia, South Sudan and northern Kenya. *(NASA GIMMS Group at GSFC)*

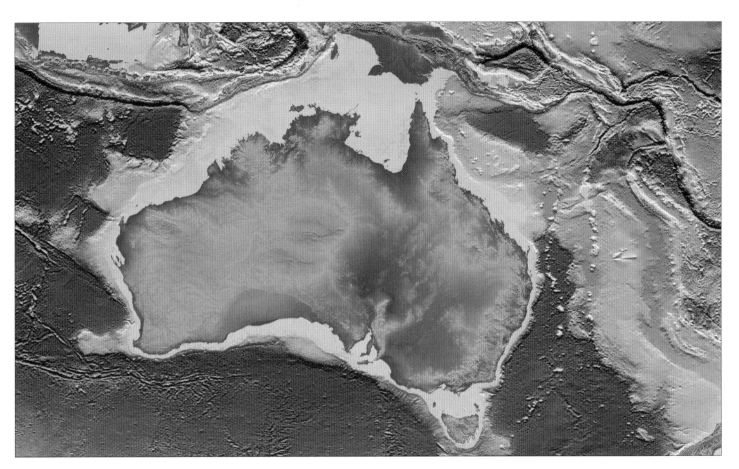

Mapping the ocean floors
The accurate global mapping of whole ocean floors has only been possible since the advent of satellite radar altimetry. From a precisely known orbit, microwave pulses measure the ocean surface. The effects of tides, waves and currents can mathematically be removed from these measurements and the resultant ocean-surface shape reflects that of the ocean floor beneath, due to the gravitational effects of the water over the sea-floor topography. However, for large-scale navigational charts, shipboard echo soundings are still used. *(Fugro NPA Ltd)*

Weather monitoring
Geostationary and polar orbiting satellites monitor the Earth's atmospheric movements, giving us an insight into the global workings of the atmosphere and permitting us to predict weather change. *(NASA image courtesy GOES Project Science Office)*

Tropical Cyclone 'Billy'
On Christmas Day 2008 the storm approaches Western Australia from the Indian Ocean. Such images aid in monitoring the development and track of weather systems. *(Jeff Schmaltz, MODIS Rapid Response Team at NASA GSFC)*

Zhugpu, China
On 10 August 2010, after intense monsoon rains, this remote region suffered disastrous flooding, followed by a series of landslides, which together claimed over 1,500 lives. Access to the area was very difficult and satellite imagery helped focus and direct rescue efforts, using scarce resources. *(WorldView-2 courtesy DigitalGlobe)*

Fukushima Nuclear Power Station, Japan
This image was captured by the GeoEye-1 satellite, travelling at 6 km/sec and 680 km above the Earth. In front of the pylons, in the centre of the image, the damaged reactors in the heart of the irradiated area can be seen, following the March 2011 Japanese earthquake and tsunami. It allowed initial assessment of a very dangerous area to take place with minimum risk to human life. *(Image courtesy GeoEye)*

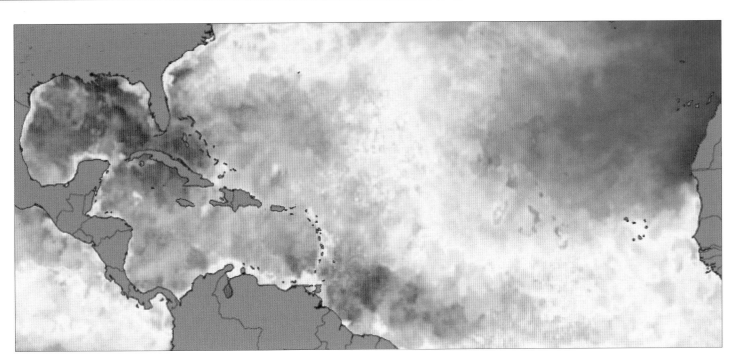

Ocean temperature monitoring

Part of a global dataset, the central Atlantic Ocean from West Africa across to Central America is shown during the hurricane season in Central and North America, in August 2011. The yellow and orange colours indicate surface water temperatures over 27.8°C, the critical temperature above which tropical storms are fuelled and intensified. The powerful Hurricane Irene hit the eastern United States later in the month. (NASA image created by Jesse Allen, using merged AMSR-E/MODIS data)

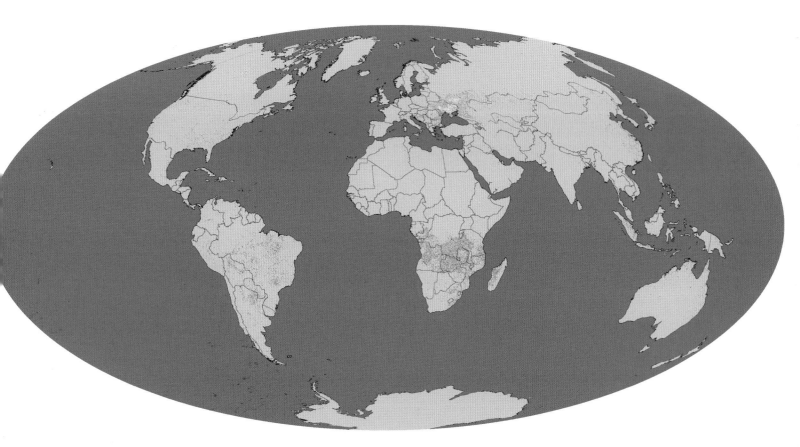

World fires

This image shows all the fires worldwide that were burning during August 2008, whether they were man-made to clear ground for crops, for example, or occurred naturally from, say, lightning strikes. The orange tint indicates where fires are at their fiercest. Over any given year the areas affected by the fires move with the seasons, February being the month with most fires in the tropics. Acquiring this data from satellites allows efficient management of scarce resources in remote and environmentally threatened areas. (NASA image by Reto Stockli and Jesse Allen using data courtesy of the MODIS Land Science Team at NASA GSFC)

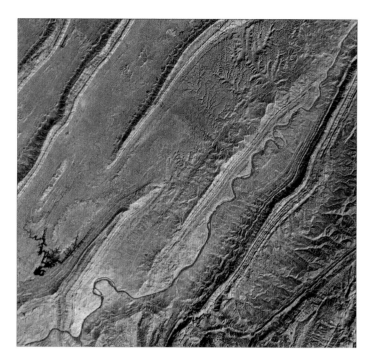

Sichuan Basin, China

The north-east/south-west trending ridges in this image are anticlinal folds developed in the Earth's crust as a result of plate collision and compression. Geologists map these folds and the lowlands between them formed by synclinal folds, as they are often the areas where oil or gas are found in commercial quantities. The river shown in this image is the Yangtse, near Chongqing. *(China RSGS)*

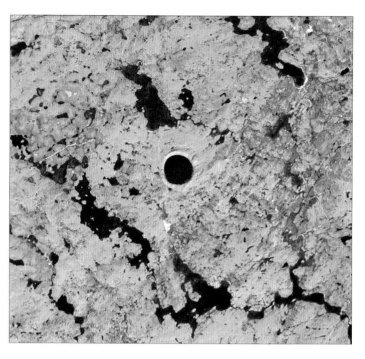

Pingualuit Crater, Canada

The circular feature is a meteorite crater in the Ungava Peninsula, Québec, formed by an impact over 1.4 million years ago. It is 3.4 km wide and the lake within is 264 m deep. The lake has no link to any water sources and has been formed only by rain and snow. Thus the water is very pure and among the world's clearest and least saline. Sediments at the bottom have been unaffected by ice sheets and are important for scientific research. *(Fugro NPA Ltd)*

Wadi Hadramaut, Yemen

Yemen is extremely arid – however, in the past it was more humid and wet, enabling large river systems to carve out the deep and spectacular gorges and dried-out river beds (*wadis*) seen in this image. The erosion has revealed many contrasting rock types. The image has been processed to exaggerate this effect, producing many shades of red, pink and purple, which make geological mapping easier and more cost-effective. *(EROS)*

Zagros Mountains, Iran

These mountains were formed as Arabia collided with Southern Eurasia. The upper half of this colour-enhanced image shows an anticline that runs east–west. The dark grey features are called *diapirs*, which are bodies of viscous rock salt that are very buoyant and sometimes rise to the surface, spilling and spreading out like a glacier. The presence of salt in the region is important as it stops oil escaping to the surface. *(EROS)*

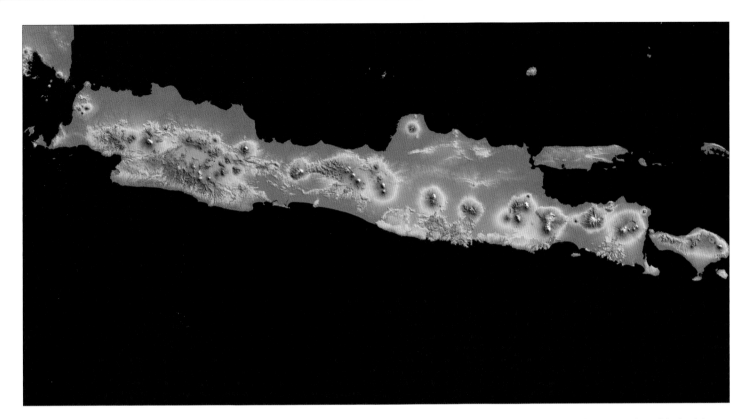

Topographic surveys

In February 2000 the Shuttle Radar Topography Mission (SRTM) was launched. Over 11 days, using specially developed radar equipment, it captured the topography of 80% of the Earth's land area at high resolution. This was the first time that this had been done on a consistent basis globally and for many inaccessible areas was the first survey. The image above shows the volcanic cones of the Indonesian islands of Java and Bali. *(Fugro NPA Ltd)*

Environmental monitoring

Synthetic Aperture Radar (SAR) uses microwaves to penetrate cloud and needs no solar illumination, so is ideal for monitoring remote and difficult areas. In the middle of this image the David Glacier in Antarctica is seen flowing to the sea. Here it floats onwards and is known as the Drygalski Ice Tongue. At its end, a tabular iceberg is breaking off, or 'calving', whilst to the right is part of a 120 km long iceberg that almost collided with it. *(ESA)*

Lidar surveying
Lasers based on aircraft or satellites can be used to scan surface elevations to an accuracy of a few centimetres. This extract from a survey of the whole of London shows the City of London from St Paul's Cathederal in the north-west to the Tower of London and Tower Bridge in the south-east. The very narrow and deep urban canyons and atriums in this area clearly demonstrate the advantages of airborne laser scanning (Lidar), which only requires a single line-of-sight to obtain precise measurements. A basic variant of this technology has been used for several years from satellites to acquire elevation profiles of the surface of Mars. Sensors capable of more detailed scanning are currently under development for Earth-orbiting satellites. *(Precision Terrain Surveys Ltd – www.precisionterrain.com)*

Dubai, United Arab Emirates
The long shadow of the the Burj Khalifa, currently the world's tallest free-standing structure at 848 metres, falls across this image. Completed in September 2009, it has 160 floors and the world's fastest elevators, which travel at 64 km/h. Dubai has expanded from a small fishing settlement to a modern city of over 1.5 million people in less than 50 years. *(Image courtesy GeoEye)*

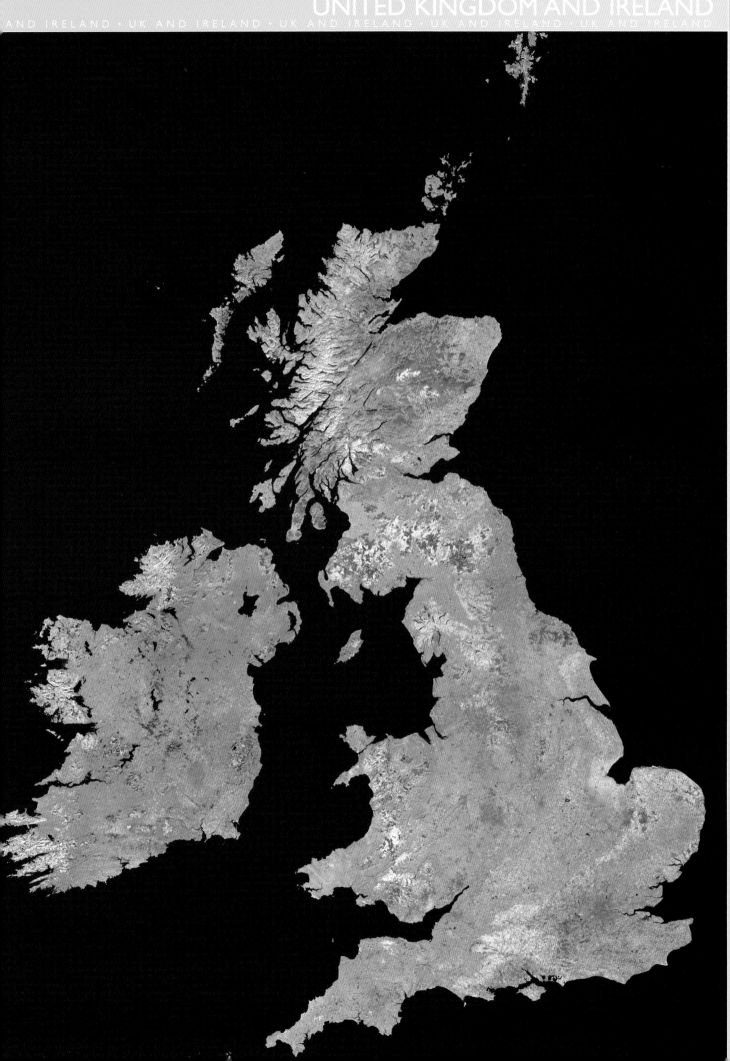

ATLANTIC

OCEAN

Malin He

Trawbreaga

Tory Island
Horn Hd.
Mulroy Bay
Fanad Hd.
Dunaff Hd.
Clonmany

Inishbofin
Dunfanaghy
Portsalon
Lough Swilly
In

Bloody Foreland
Falcarragh
Cloghaneely
Creeslough
Carrickart
Milford
Rathmullen

Inishfree B.
Gola I.
Bunbeg
Gweedore
GLENVEAGH NAT. PARK
752 Errigal
L. Beagh
Kilmacrenan
Rathmelton

The Rosses
Burtonport
Crolly
Dunglow
Church Hill
Letterkenny (Leitir Ceanainn)
Derry/Londond
Newtown
Cunningham

Arranmore

Crohy Hd.
683
Derryveagh Mts.
Kingarrow
Swilly
Newmills
St. Johnstown

D O N E G A L

Gweebarra Bay
Lettermacaward
Fintown
Cloghan
Convoy
Raphoe
Ba

Dawros Hd.
Maas
Glenties
Stranorlar
Ballybofey
Castlefinn
Lifford
St.

Loughros More Bay
Ardara
Blue Stack Mts.
676 Lavagh More
Finn
Sion

Glen B.
444 Slieve Tooey
Glencolumbkille
N O T
U I

Rossan Point
Slieve League
601
Carrick
Dunkineely
Inver
Donegal
Derg
Lough Derg
Castlederg
Newtown

Rathlin O'Birne I.
Killybegs
Mountcharles
Laghy
Drumquin

Carrigan Hd.
Muckros Hd.
Mc Swyne's Bay
St. John's Point
Donegal Harbour
Ballintra
Coolmore
Pettigo
Ederny

Donegal Bay
Ballyshannon
Belleek
Kesh
Ederny
Pettigo

Inishmurray
Bundoran
Erne
Lower Lough Erne
Boa I.
Irvinestown
Trillic

Cliffony
Kinlough
Garrison
Derrygonnelly
Ballinamallard

Sligo Bay
Grange
Lough Melvin
Glenade
FERMANAGH
Enniskillen
CASTLE COOLE

Downpatrick Head
Rosses Point
Carney
644 Truskmore
Lisbellaw
Brooke

CEIDE FIELDS
Ballycastle
Killala Bay
Drumcliff
Manorhamilton
Lough Macnean
Letterbreen
Arney
Magu

Maumakeogh 380
RATHFRANPARK
Killala
Easky
Sligo (Sligeach)
LEITRIM
Glenfarne
Upper Lough Erne
Dowra
Swanlinbar

Broad Haven
Belderg
Inishcrone
Dromore West
Lough Gill
Dromahair
Lackagh Hills
667 Cuilcagh
Derrylin
Newte

Benwee Hd.
Portacloy
Glenamoy
MOYNE ABBEY
Crockets Town
Drumkeeran
Bawnbo

Broad Haven
Belmullet
An Geata Mór (Binghamstown)
Carrowmore Lough
Killala
544 Knockalongy
Beltra
Ballysadare
Collooney
Corry Mt. 391
Lough Allen
Keadew
587 Slieve Anierin
Ballyconnell

Erris Head
Annagh Hd.
Bangor
Owenmore
BALLYCROY NAT. PARK
Crossmolina
Coolaney
S L I G O
Ballymote
Arigna
Drumshanbo
Ballinamore
Newtown Gore
Killashandra

Inishkea North
Inishkea South
Fallmore
Blacksod Pt.
Saddle Hd.
Ridge Pt.
Ballycroy
722
Castlehill
Lahardaun
806 Nephin
Deel
Lough Conn
Mullanys Cross
Aclare
Bunnanaddan
Lough Arrow
Fenagh
Leitrim
Drumsna
Cloone
Carrigallen
Lough Oughter

Achill Head
Croaghaun 665
Dooagh
Keel
Slievemore 672
Nephin Beg Range
627
714 L. Feeagh
L. Cullin
Beltra
Pontoon
Foxford
Callow
Charlestown
Tobercurry
Bunnaddan
Ballaghaderreen
Croghan
Lough Key
Boyle
Carrick-on-Shannon
Drumod
Mohill
Arvagh

Achill I.
Dooega Hd.
Corraun Peninsula
Mallaranny
Beltra L.
Bellavary
Strade Friars
Swinford
Tawnyinah
Carracastle
Frenchpark
Ballinameen
Elphin
Roosky
Drumlish
Corn Hill 279
Ballinalee
Granard

Achill Sd.
Achillbeg I.
Newport
Newport B.
TURLOUGH PARK HOUSE
Castlebar (Caislean an Bharraigh)
Kiltamagh
Bohola
Bohola
Charlestown
Ballaghaderreen
Croghan
Bellanagare
Ballinameen
Elphin
Lough Forbes
Newtown Forbes
Longford (An Longfort)

Clare Island
461
Clew Bay
Westport
Westport B.
M A Y O
Balla
Knock
Ballyhaunis
Ballinlough
Castlerea
Tulsk
R O S C O M M O N
Strokestown
Scramoge
Lanesborough
L O N G F O R D
Edgeworthstown
Castle

Inishturk
Caher I.
Killadoon
Louisburgh
Croagh Patrick
Kilmaine
Manulla
Kilkelly
Knock
Ballyglass
Claremorris
Ballinlough
Ballymoe
Oran
Ballintober
Roscommon (Ros Comáin)
Kilteevan
Knockcroghery
Ballymurray
Lough Ree
Ballymahon
Ballynacarrigy
WES

Inishbofin
Inishshark
Killary Harbour
Mweelrea 819
683
Sheeffry Hills
Partry Mts.
392
Lough Carra
Lough Mask
Ballindine
Cloonfad
Williamstown
Fuerty
Glennamaddy
Mount Talbot
Athleague
Ballygar
Mount Talbot
Keenagh
Carrickboy
Lough Owel
Mullin
(Muila
gCean

Tully Cross
KYLEMORE ABBEY
Letterfrack
CONNEMARA NAT. PARK
Leenaun
763
Maumturk Mts.
730 Benbaun
Sheeffry Hills
Ballinrobe
Hollymount
Kilmaine
Milltown
Dunmore
Barnaderg
Mayloagh
Mount Bellew Bridge
Thomas Street
Ballyforan
Ballinasloe (Béal Átha Sluaighe)
Moate
Roscrea

Clifden B.
Clifden
Recess
Joyce Country
Maum
The Bens
Lough Corrib
Kilbennan Church
Tuam (Tuaim)
Castleblakeney
Glentane
Athlone (Baile Átha Luain)
Ballynahown
Horseleap
Clard

Ballyconneely
Roundstone
660 Maam
Maam Cross
Oughterard
Rosscahill
Headford
Clonbur
Cong
Shrule
Kilconnell
Aughrim
Shannonbridge
CLONMACNOISE
Durrow Abbey

Slyne Head
Ballyconneely B.
Kilkieran Bay
Cashel
Glinsk
Screeb
G A L W A Y
Clare
Moycullen
Claregalway
Athenry
Attymon
Monivea
Aughrim
Suck
Killtullagh
Clodiagh

Bertraghboy Bay
Lettermore
Carraroe
Costelloe
Rossaveel
Galway (Gaillimh)
Killtullagh
Ahascragh
Clonmacnoise
Clodagh

Scale (ft / m)

ft	m
2250	750
1500	500
600	200
300	100
0	0

m	ft
20	60
50	150
100	300
200	600
500	1500
1000	3000
2000	6000

Projection : Conical with two standard parallels

West from Greenwich

SCOTLAND

NORTHERN IRELAND

ISLE OF MAN

IRISH SEA

WALES

DUBLIN (Baile Átha Cliath)

COPYRIGHT PHILIP'S

1:1 000 000

Map: Ireland – South

ATLANTIC OCEAN

MAYO

GALWAY

CLARE

LIMERICK

KERRY

CORK

TIPPERARY

ROS-COMMON

Munster

CONNEMARA NAT. PARK

BURREN NAT. PARK

KILLARNEY NAT. PARK

Inishshark, Inishbofin, Cleggan, Tully Cross, Letterfrack, KYLEMORE ABBEY, Leenaun, Joyce Country, Lough Mask, Ballinrobe, Dunmore, Roscommon (Ros Comáin) Fuerty, Ballymurray, Keen

Clifden B., Clifden, Ballyconneely, Recess, Benbaun 730, The Bens, Maumturk Mts., Maum, Cong, Shrule, Kilmaine, Milltown, Glennamaddy, Kilkerrin, Athleague, Mount Talbot, Lough Ree

CONNEMARA, Toombeola, Roundstone, Maam Cross, Screeb, Oughterard, Rosscahill, Clonbur, Headford, Belclare, Tuam (Tuaim), Barnaderg, Mayloogh, Ballinmore Bridge, Kiltoom

Slyne Head, Derryrush, Glinsk, Kilkieran, Carna, Lettermore, Costelloe, Rossaveel, Inveran, Spiddle, Barna, Salthill, Galway (Gaillimh), Oranmore, Clarinbridge, Craughwell, TUROE STONE, Mullagh, Laurencetown, Banagher

Bertraghboy Bay, Gorumna I., Lettermullan, Cashla B., North Sound, Black Hd., Murroogh, Burren, Ballyvaghan, AILLWEE CAVE, Slieve Elbhe 345, Lisdoonvarna, Kilfenora, Corrofin, Crusheen, Feakle, Scarriff, Woodford, 358, Derrybrien, Slieve Aughty, 297, Whitegate, Abbey, Portumna

Inishmore, Kilmurvy, Kilronan, Inishmaan, Aran Islands, South Sd., BALLYNALACKAN CASTLE, Inisheer, Cliffs of Moher, Liscannor, Ennistimon, Hags Hd., Lehinch, Ennis (Inis), Tulla, Tuamgraney, L. Graney, 376, Cloghjordan, Roscrea

Liscannor Bay, Spanish Pt., Mal Bay, Milltown Malbay, Slievecallan 391, Quilty, Kilmurry, Darragh, Clarecastle, Quin, Newmarket-on-Fergus, Kilkishen, Sixmilebridge, Broadford, O'Briensbridge, Killaloe, Keeper Hill 694, Silvermine Mts., Borrisoleigh, Templederry, Templemore

Mutton I., Creegh, Liscasey, Ballynacally, Kildysart, SNN Shannon (Sionainn), Bunratty, Ardnacrusha, Castleconnell, Newport, Silvermines, Dolla, Templederry, Holycross

Donegal Pt., Doonbeg, Kilmihil, Moyasta, Kilrush, Labasheeda, Foynes, Limerick (Luimneach), Ballycummin, Cappamore, Slievefelim 466, Upperchurch

Carrigaholt, Scattery I., Shannon, Tarbert, Glin, Shanagolden, Askeaton, Patrickswell, Caherconlish, Pallas Green, Golden Vale, Dundrum, Tipperary (Tiobraid Árann), Golden (Caiseal)

Loop Hd., Kilbaha, Mouth of the Shannon, Astee, Ballylongford, Ballyhahill, Creeves, Newbridge, Rathkeale, Adare, Croom, Fedamore, Bruff, Hospital, Emly, Limerick Junction

Kerry Hd., Ballybunion, Newtown Sands, Lisselton, Listowel, Athea, Ardagh, Newcastle West, Ballingarry, Bruree, Kilmallock, Galbally, Galty Mts., Galtymore 920, Knockeven

Ballyheige, Causeway, Lixnaw, Lerrig, Feale, Abbeyfeale, Broadford, Newtownshandrum, Charleville (Ráth Luirc), Kilfinnane, Ballylanders, Ballyporeen, Clogheen

Seven Hogs, Rough Pt., Ardfert, Fenit, Tralee B., Tralee (Trá Lí), Stacks Mts. 357 334, Glanaruddery Mts., Killinlea, Abbeyfeale, Milford, Dromcolliher, Liscarroll, Kildorrery, Mitchelstown, Knockmealdown Mts. 795

Brandon Pt., Ballydavid Hd., 953, Brandon Mt., Stradbally, Castlegregory, Camp, 827, Slieve Mish 853, Castlemaine, CRAG CAVE, Castleisland, Buttevant, Doneraile, Rockmills, Kilworth Mts. 302, Araglin, Knockmealdown

Smerwick Harbour, Ballyferriter, GALLARUS ORATORY, Sybil Pt., Milltown, Dingle (An Daingean), Anascaul, Maine, Farranfore, Kishkeam, Kanturk, Castletownroche, Glanworth, Kilworth, Ballyduff, Cappoquin

Inishtooskert, Ventry, Killorglin, Milltown, Rathmore, Millstreet, Mallow (Mala), Killavullen, Fermoy, Blackwater, Tallowbridge, Lismore, Tallow

Great Blasket I., Slea Hd., Dingle Bay, Castlemaine Harbour, Laune, Beaufort, Killarney (Cill Airne), Muckross, The Paps 696, Banteer, Nagles Mts. 429, Knocknaskagh, Rathcormack, Aghern, Conna

Dingle Peninsula, 46, Iveragh, Glenbeigh, L. Caragh, ROSS CASTLE, L. Leane, MacGillycuddy's Reeks, 835, Carrauntoohil 1041, KILLARNEY NAT. PARK, The Paps, Donoughmore, Carrignavar, Watergrasshill

Inishvickillane, 52, Valencia Harbour, Cahersiveen (Cathair Saidhbhín), Killarney, Mangerton Mt. 840, Derrynasaggart Mts. 650, Ballyvourney, Macroom, Coachford, Blarney, BLARNEY CASTLE, Cork (Corcaigh), Midleton (Mainistir an Corann), Killeagh, Youghal (Eochaill)

Valencia I., Bray Hd., Portmagee, Moyle, Lissatinnig Bridge, Templenoe, Kenmare, Kilgarvan, Inchigeelagh, Kilmichael, Crookstown, Ballincollig, Douglas, Passage West, Carrigtohill, Ballynacorra, Castlemartyr

Puffin I., St. Finan's Bay, Waterville, Ballinskelligs, Ardkearagh, New Chapel Cross, Derriana L., Sneem, Parknasilla, Knockboy 707, Inchigeelagh, Lee, GARRANES RING FORT, Carrigaline, Cobh (An Cobh), Cloyne, Aghada, Whitegate, Ballycotton

Great Skellig (Skellig Michael) 73, Bolus Hd., Ballinskelligs B., Hog's Hd., Lamb's Hd., Kenmare River, Lauragh, Ardgroom, Bunaw, Adrigole, Glengarriff, Shehy Mts., Kealkill, 537, Nowen Hill, Drimoleague, Bandon (Droichead na Bandan), Kilbrittain, Inishannon, Belgooly, Crosshaven

Scariff I., Coulagh B., Slieve Miskish, Hungry Hill 686, Caha Mts., Curryglass, Bantry, Dunmanway, Ballineen, Enniskean, Kinsale, Cork Harbour, 38

Cods Hd., Ballydonegan B., Allihies, Castletown Bearhaven, Bear I., Whiddy I., Bantry Bay, Durrus, Kilcrohane, Ballydehob, Kilcoe, Skull, Castletownshend, KNOCKDRUM FORT, Glandore, Rosscarbery, Clonakilty, Timoleague, Courtmacsherry, Barry's Pt., Seven Heads, Kinsale Harbour, Courtmacsherry B., Old Head of Kinsale

Dursey I., Dursey Hd., Crow Hd., Sheeps Hd., Dunmanus B., Toormore, Goleen, Crookhaven, Mizen Hd., Long I., Roaringwater B., Baltimore, Clear I., C. Clear, Sherkin I., Toe Hd., Galley Hd., Glandore Harbour, Carbery, Leap, Connonagh, Ross, DROMBEG, Galley Hd., 66

Elevation scale

ft	m
2250	750
1500	500
1200	400
600	200
300	100
0	0
20	60
50	150
100	300

Projection : Conical with two standard parallels

West from Greenwich

1:1 000 000

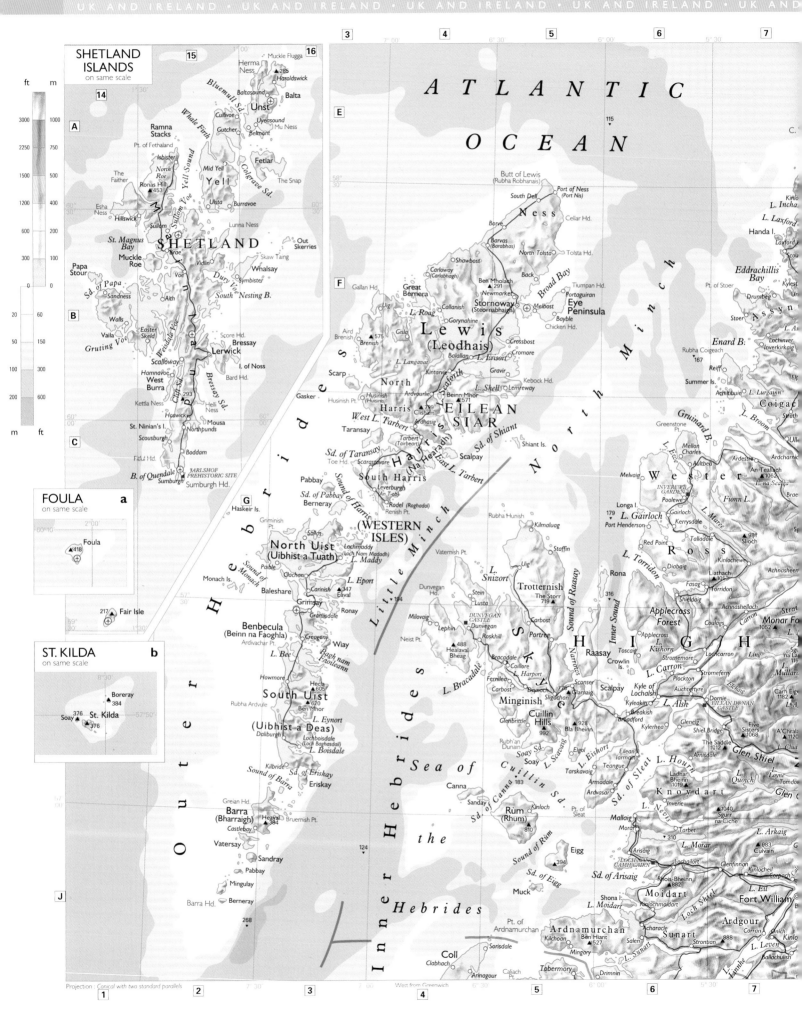

ORKNEY
ISLANDS
on same scale

NORTH SEA

Pentland Firth

Caithness

Sutherland

Easter Ross

Moray Firth

MORAY

Buchan

Formartine

Garioch

ABERDEENSHIRE

Mar

Kincardine

Cairngorm Mts.

Grampian Mountains

CAIRNGORMS NAT. PARK

Braemar

Braes of Angus

PERTH AND KINROSS

ANGUS

Strathmore

Howe of the Mearns

Inverness

Aberdeen

COPYRIGHT PHILIP'S

1: 1 000 000

5   0   10   20   30   40   50 km

5   0   5   10   15   20   25   30   35 miles

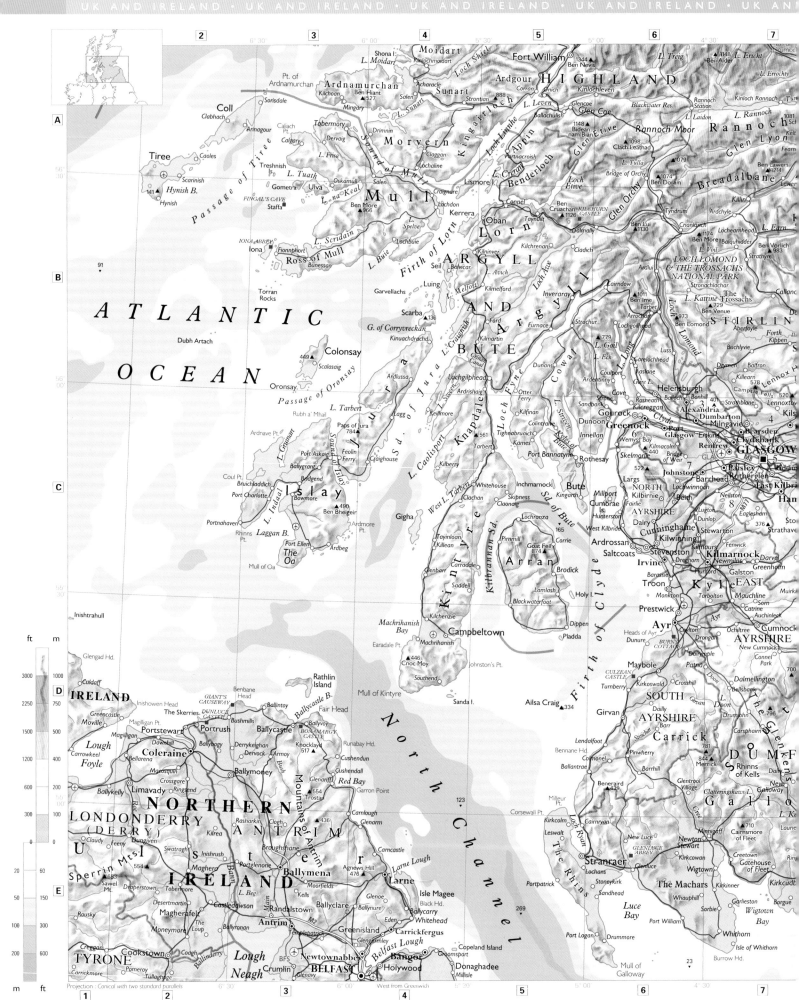

Key to Scottish unitary
authorities on map
2 DUNDEE CITY   9 NORTH LANARKSHIRE
3 WEST DUNBARTONSHIRE   10 FALKIRK
4 EAST DUNBARTONSHIRE   11 CLACKMANNANSHIRE
5 CITY OF GLASGOW   12 WEST LOTHIAN
6 INVERCLYDE   13 CITY OF EDINBURGH
7 RENFREWSHIRE   14 MIDLOTHIAN
8 EAST RENFREWSHIRE

NORTH

SEA

1:1 000 000

COPYRIGHT PHILIP'S

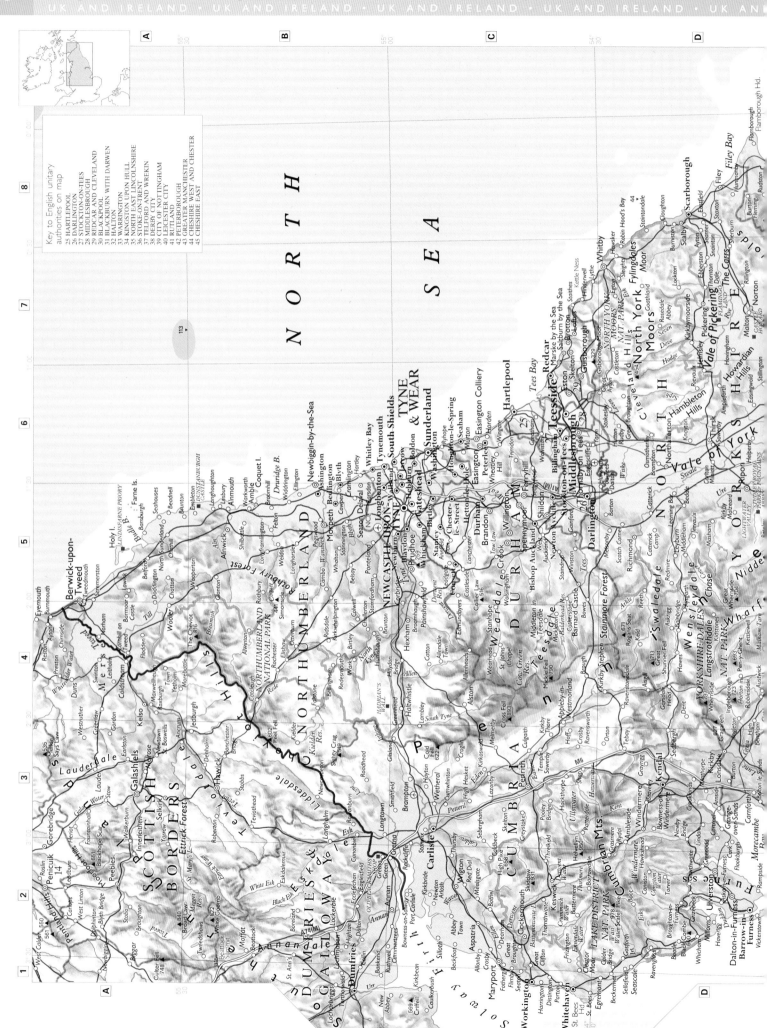

1:1 000 000

Projection: Conical with two standard parallels

| | km |
| 5 0 | 10 20 30 40 50 |

| | miles |
| 5 0 5 | 10 15 20 25 30 35 |

| m | 750 | 500 | 400 | 200 | 100 | 60 | 0 |
| ft | 2250 | 1500 | 1200 | 600 | 300 | 150 | 0 |

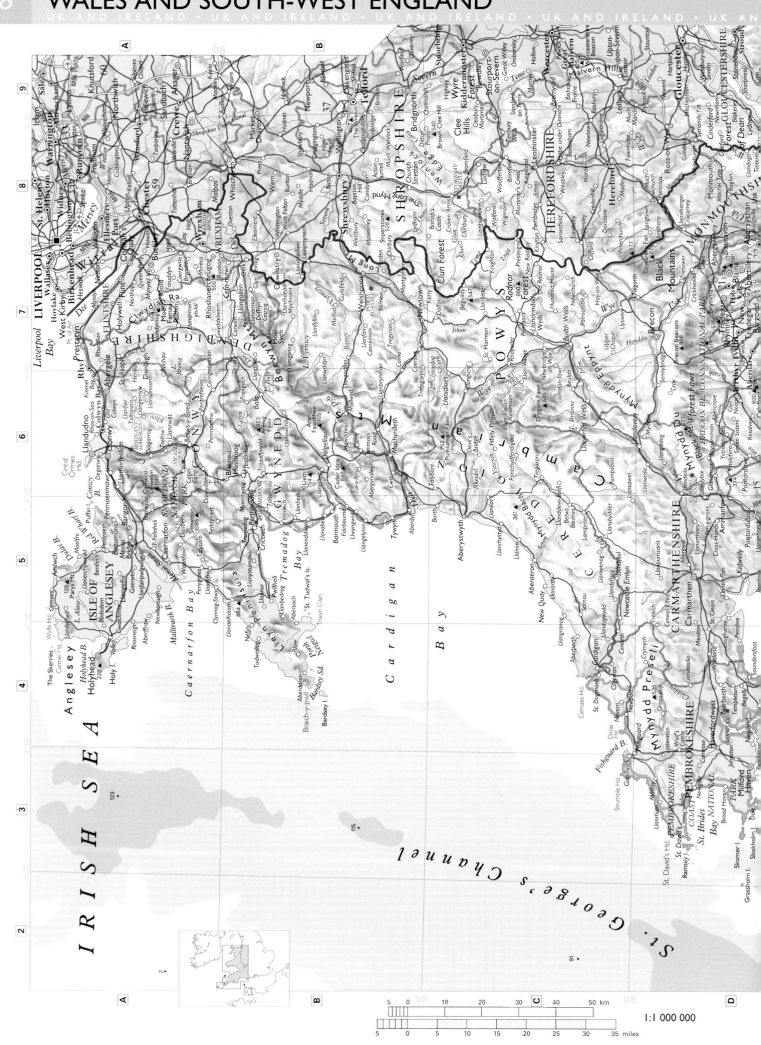

IRISH SEA

Liverpool Bay

Caernarfon Bay

Cardigan Bay

St. George's Channel

ANGLESEY
Isle of Anglesey
Holyhead

GWYNEDD
SNOWDONIA NATIONAL PARK
Snowdon 1085

LIVERPOOL
Birkenhead
Chester

FLINTSHIRE
DENBIGHSHIRE
Llandudno
Colwyn Bay
Rhyl

WREXHAM
Wrexham

SHROPSHIRE
Shrewsbury
Telford
Bridgnorth

POWYS
Welshpool
Newtown

HEREFORDSHIRE
Hereford
Leominster

CEREDIGION
Aberystwyth

CARMARTHENSHIRE
Carmarthen

PEMBROKESHIRE
PEMBROKESHIRE COAST NATIONAL PARK
Fishguard
Milford Haven
St. David's

BRECON BEACONS NATIONAL PARK
Brecon

MONMOUTHSHIRE
Monmouth
Abergavenny

GLOUCESTERSHIRE
Gloucester

WORCESTERSHIRE
Worcester
Malvern

5 0 5 10 20 30 40 50 km

5 0 5 10 15 20 25 30 35 miles

1:1 000 000

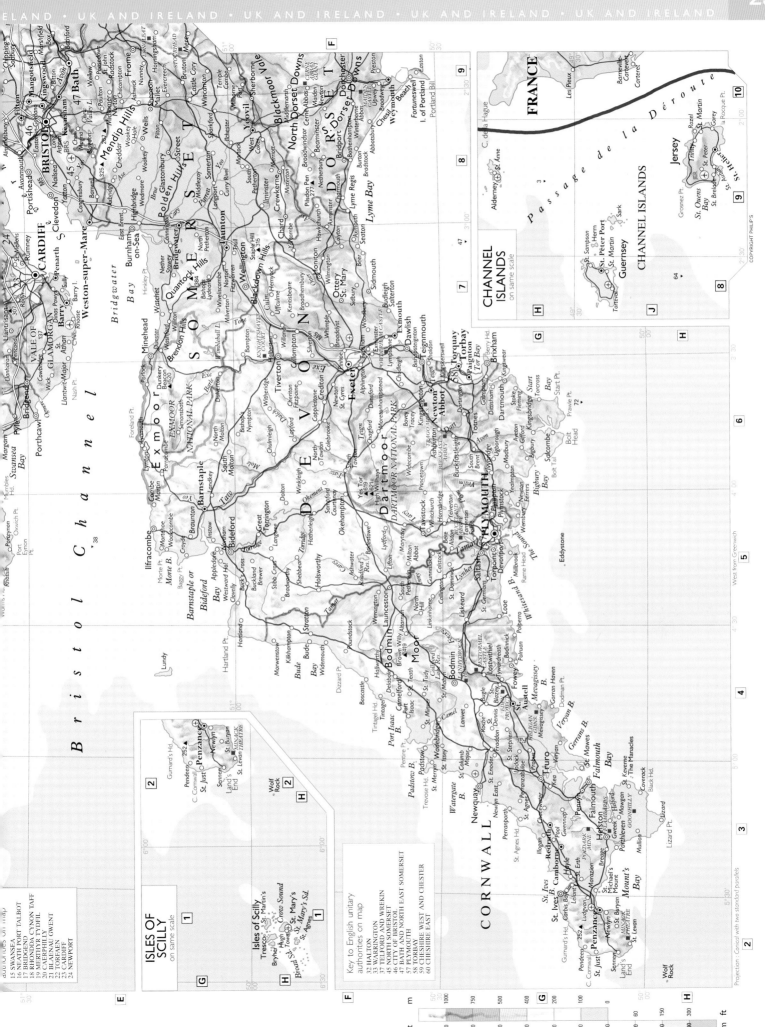

FRANCE

Passage de la Déroute

CHANNEL ISLANDS

Jersey

CHANNEL ISLANDS
on same scale

Guernsey

COPYRIGHT PHILIP'S

Bristol Channel

ISLES OF SCILLY
on same scale

Isles of Scilly

Key to English unitary
authorities on map

15 SWANSEA
16 NEATH PORT TALBOT
17 BRIDGEND
18 RHONDDA CYNON TAFF
19 MERTHYR TYDFIL
20 CAERPHILLY
21 BLAENAU GWENT
22 TORFAEN
23 CARDIFF
24 NEWPORT

32 HALTON
33 WARRINGTON
37 TELFORD AND WREKIN
45 NORTH SOMERSET
46 CITY OF BRISTOL
47 BATH AND NORTH EAST SOMERSET
57 PLYMOUTH
58 TORBAY
59 CHESHIRE WEST AND CHESTER
60 CHESHIRE EAST

Projection: Conical with two standard parallels

West from Greenwich

6

2 3 4 5

A

B

C

D

E

POWYS

SHROPSHIRE

STAFFORDSHIRE

WEST MIDLANDS

BIRMINGHAM

WOLVERHAMPTON

COVENTRY

WARWICKSHIRE

HEREFORDSHIRE

WORCESTERSHIRE

CARMARTHENSHIRE

GLOUCESTERSHIRE

OXFORDSHIRE

Oxford

Cheltenham

Gloucester

Swindon

WEST BERKSHIRE

WILTSHIRE

MONMOUTHSHIRE

Newport

CARDIFF

GLAMORGAN

VALE OF GLAMORGAN

Swansea

Bristol Channel

Bridgwater Bay

BRISTOL

Bath

Salisbury Plain

HAMPSHIRE

EXMOOR

EXMOOR NATIONAL PARK

SOMERSET

Taunton

DEVON

Exeter

DORSET

Mendip Hills

Blackmoor Vale

Yeovil

North Dorset Downs

South Dorset Downs

Poole

BOURNEMOUTH

SOUTHAMPTON

New Forest NATIONAL PARK

ISLE OF WIGHT

Newport

Winchester

Salisbury

Andover

Lyme Bay

Bristol Channel

Cotswold Hills

Berkshire Downs

Vale of White Horse

NOTTINGHAM

DERBY

LEICES

ft m

2250 750
1500 500
1200 400
600 200
300 100
0 0
20 60
50 150

m ft

Projection: Conical with two standard parallels

West from Greenwich

1 2 3

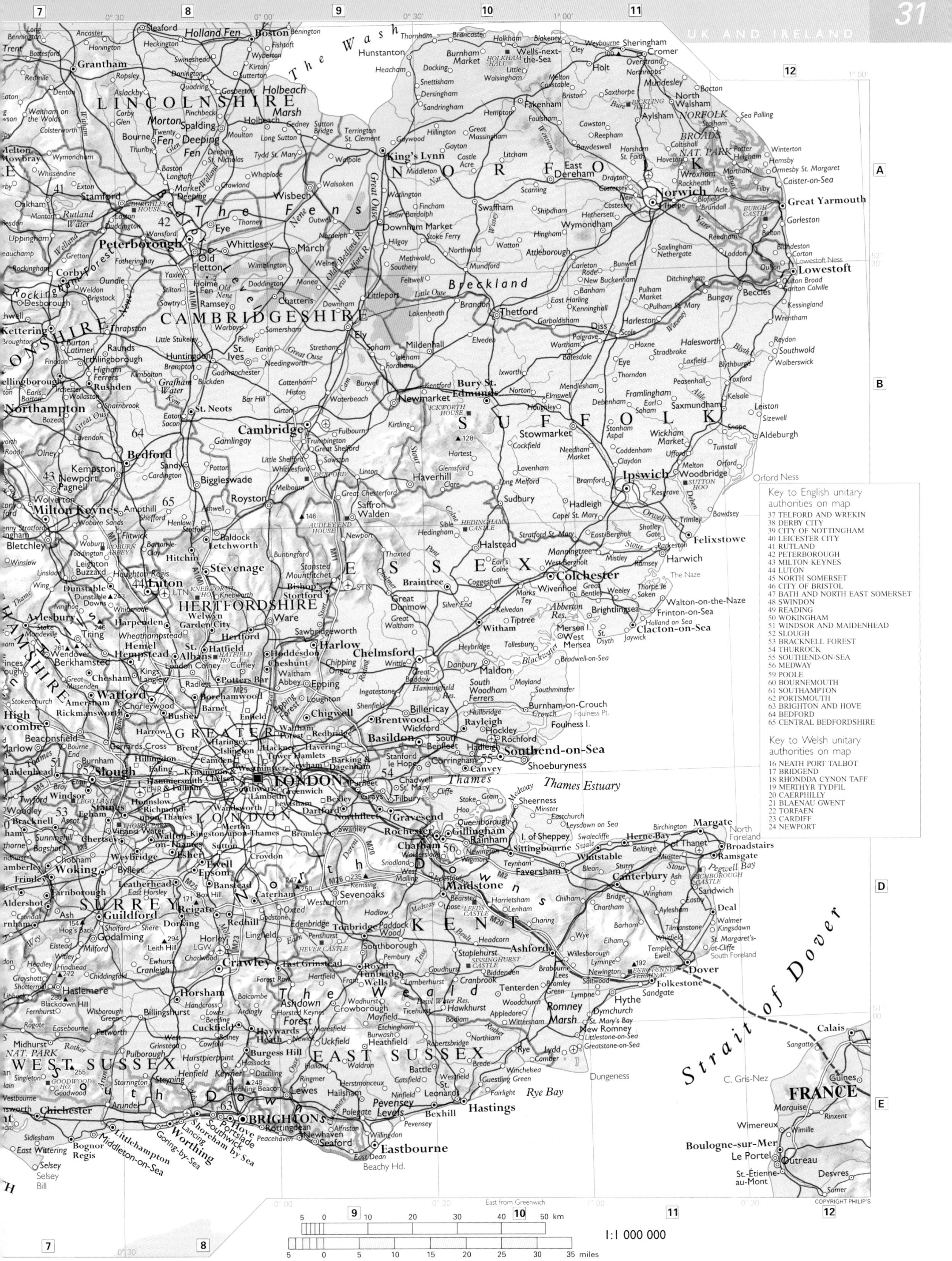

LINCOLNSHIRE

NORFOLK

CAMBRIDGESHIRE

SUFFOLK

ESSEX

HERTFORDSHIRE

GREATER LONDON

KENT

SURREY

WEST SUSSEX

EAST SUSSEX

The Wash

The Fens

Breckland

NORFOLK BROADS NAT. PARK

Thames Estuary

North Downs

South Downs

The Weald

Ashdown Forest

Romney Marsh

Strait of Dover

FRANCE

Key to English unitary authorities on map

37 TELFORD AND WREKIN
38 DERBY CITY
39 CITY OF NOTTINGHAM
40 LEICESTER CITY
41 RUTLAND
42 PETERBOROUGH
43 MILTON KEYNES
44 LUTON
45 NORTH SOMERSET
46 CITY OF BRISTOL
47 BATH AND NORTH EAST SOMERSET
48 SWINDON
49 READING
50 WOKINGHAM
51 WINDSOR AND MAIDENHEAD
52 SLOUGH
53 BRACKNELL FOREST
54 THURROCK
55 SOUTHEND-ON-SEA
56 MEDWAY
59 POOLE
60 BOURNEMOUTH
61 SOUTHAMPTON
62 PORTSMOUTH
63 BRIGHTON AND HOVE
64 BEDFORD
65 CENTRAL BEDFORDSHIRE

Key to Welsh unitary authorities on map

16 NEATH PORT TALBOT
17 BRIDGEND
18 RHONDDA CYNON TAFF
19 MERTHYR TYDFIL
20 CAERPHILLY
21 BLAENAU GWENT
22 TORFAEN
23 CARDIFF
24 NEWPORT

East from Greenwich

1:1 000 000

0 5 10 20 30 40 50 km

5 0 5 10 15 20 25 30 35 miles

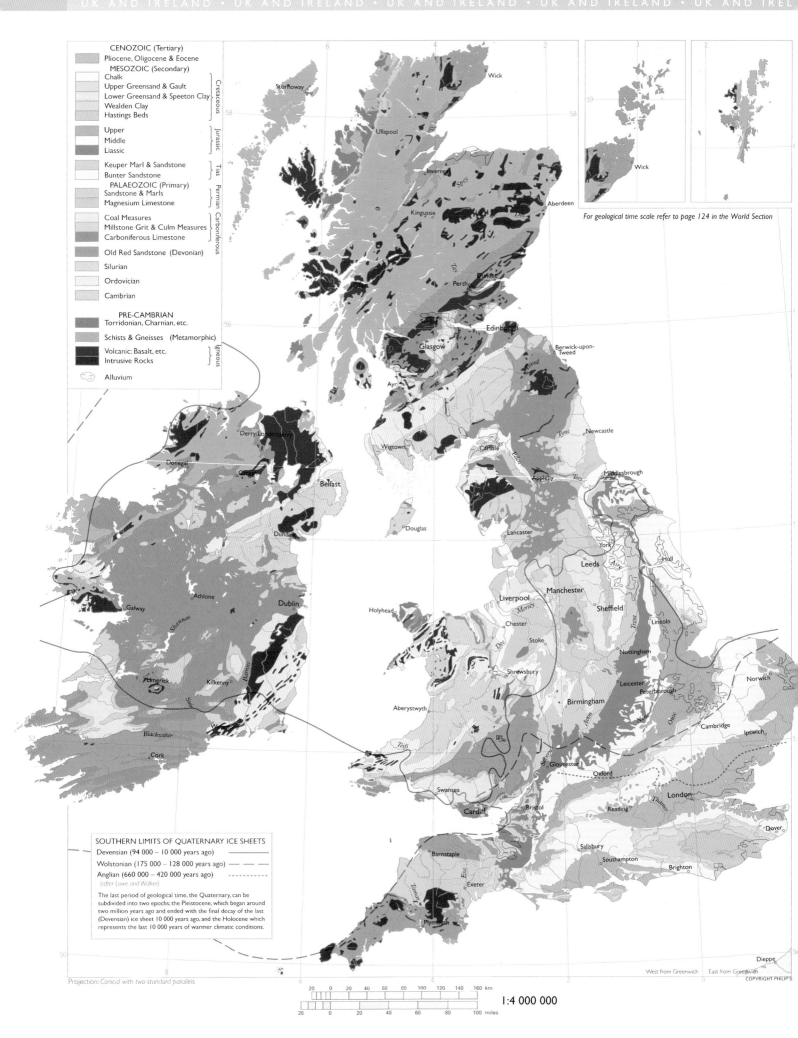

CENOZOIC (Tertiary)
Pliocene, Oligocene & Eocene
MESOZOIC (Secondary)
Chalk
Upper Greensand & Gault
Lower Greensand & Speeton Clay
Wealden Clay
Hastings Beds

Upper
Middle
Liassic

Keuper Marl & Sandstone
Bunter Sandstone
PALAEOZOIC (Primary)
Sandstone & Marls
Magnesium Limestone

Coal Measures
Millstone Grit & Culm Measures
Carboniferous Limestone

Old Red Sandstone (Devonian)

Silurian

Ordovician

Cambrian

PRE-CAMBRIAN
Torridonian, Charnian, etc.

Schists & Gneisses (Metamorphic)

Volcanic: Basalt, etc.
Intrusive Rocks

Alluvium

Cretaceous / *Jurassic* / *Trias* / *Permian* / *Carboniferous* — *Igneous*

For geological time scale refer to page 124 in the World Section

SOUTHERN LIMITS OF QUATERNARY ICE SHEETS
Devensian (94 000 – 10 000 years ago)
Wolstonian (175 000 – 128 000 years ago)
Anglian (660 000 – 420 000 years ago)
(after Lowe and Walker)

The last period of geological time, the Quaternary, can be
subdivided into two epochs; the Pleistocene, which began around
two million years ago and ended with the final decay of the last
(Devensian) ice sheet 10 000 years ago, and the Holocene which
represents the last 10 000 years of warmer climatic conditions.

Projection: *Conical with two standard parallels*

20 0 20 40 60 80 100 120 140 160 km
20 0 20 40 60 80 100 miles

1:4 000 000

West from Greenwich East from Greenwich
COPYRIGHT PHILIP'S

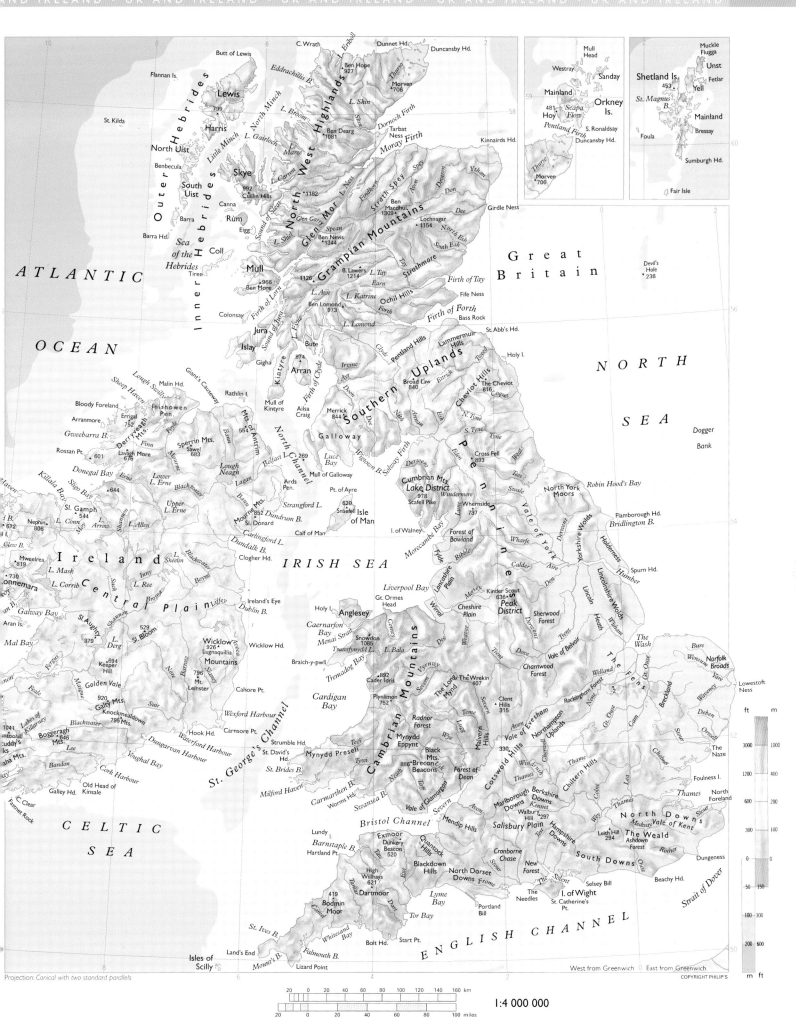

Projection: Conical with two standard parallels

COPYRIGHT PHILIP'S

West from Greenwich   East from Greenwich

1:4 000 000

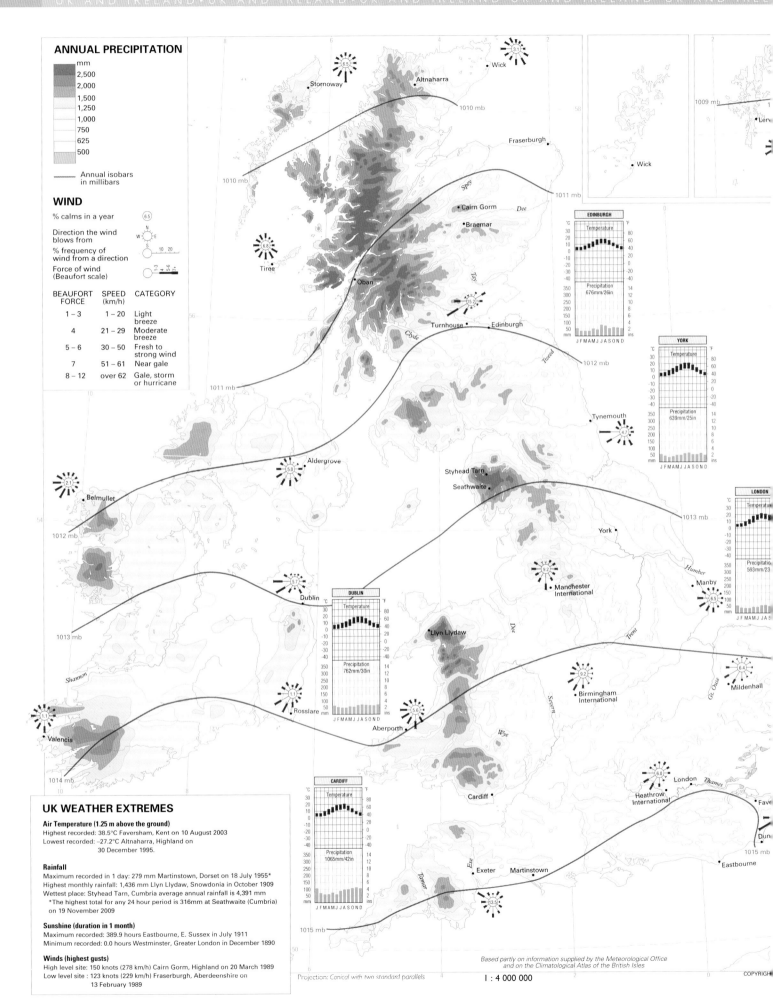

ANNUAL PRECIPITATION

mm
- 2,500
- 2,000
- 1,500
- 1,250
- 1,000
- 750
- 625
- 500

Annual isobars
in millibars

WIND

% calms in a year (6.5)

Direction the wind
blows from

% frequency of
wind from a direction

Force of wind
(Beaufort scale)

BEAUFORT FORCE	SPEED (km/h)	CATEGORY
1 – 3	1 – 20	Light breeze
4	21 – 29	Moderate breeze
5 – 6	30 – 50	Fresh to strong wind
7	51 – 61	Near gale
8 – 12	over 62	Gale, storm or hurricane

UK WEATHER EXTREMES

Air Temperature (1.25 m above the ground)
Highest recorded: 38.5°C Faversham, Kent on 10 August 2003
Lowest recorded: –27.2°C Altnaharra, Highland on
30 December 1995.

Rainfall
Maximum recorded in 1 day: 279 mm Martinstown, Dorset on 18 July 1955*
Highest monthly rainfall: 1,436 mm Llyn Llydaw, Snowdonia in October 1909
Wettest place: Styhead Tarn, Cumbria average annual rainfall is 4,391 mm
    *The highest total for any 24 hour period is 316mm at Seathwaite (Cumbria)
on 19 November 2009

Sunshine (duration in 1 month)
Maximum recorded: 389.9 hours Eastbourne, E. Sussex in July 1911
Minimum recorded: 0.0 hours Westminster, Greater London in December 1890

Winds (highest gusts)
High level site: 150 knots (278 km/h) Cairn Gorm, Highland on 20 March 1989
Low level site: 123 knots (229 km/h) Fraserburgh, Aberdeenshire on
    13 February 1989

EDINBURGH
Temperature
Precipitation
676mm/26in

YORK
Temperature
Precipitation
639mm/25in

LONDON
Temperature
Precipitation
593mm/23

DUBLIN
Temperature
Precipitation
762mm/30in

CARDIFF
Temperature
Precipitation
1065mm/42in

1010 mb
1010 mb
1011 mb
1012 mb
1011 mb
1012 mb
1013 mb
1013 mb
1013 mb
1014 mb
1015 mb
1015 mb
1009 mb

Stornoway
Wick
Altnaharra
Fraserburgh
Spey
Cairn Gorm
Dee
Braemar
Tiree
Oban
Tay
Turnhouse
Edinburgh
Clyde
Tweed
Tynemouth
Aldergrove
Styhead Tarn
Seathwaite
York
Belmullet
Manby
Manchester International
Dublin
Dee
Humber
Llyn Llydaw
Trent
Birmingham International
Shannon
Severn
Gt. Ouse
Mildenhall
Rosslare
Aberporth
Wye
Valencia
London
Thames
Heathrow International
Faver
Cardiff
Eve
Exeter
Martinstown
Tamar
Eastbourne
Dun
Wick
Lerv

Based partly on information supplied by the Meteorological Office
and on the Climatological Atlas of the British Isles

Projection: Conical with two standard parallels

1 : 4 000 000

COPYRIGH

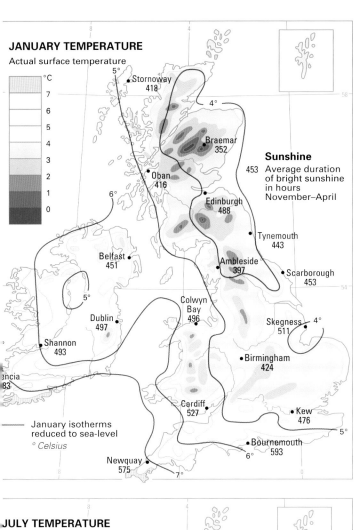

JANUARY TEMPERATURE

Actual surface temperature

°C
7
6
5
4
3
2
1
0

Sunshine

453 Average duration of bright sunshine in hours November–April

— January isotherms reduced to sea-level
° Celsius

Stornoway 418
Braemar 352
Oban 416
Edinburgh 488
Tynemouth 443
Belfast 451
Ambleside 397
Scarborough 453
Colwyn Bay 496
Skegness 511
Dublin 497
Shannon 493
Birmingham 424
Cardiff 527
Kew 476
Bournemouth 593
Newquay 575

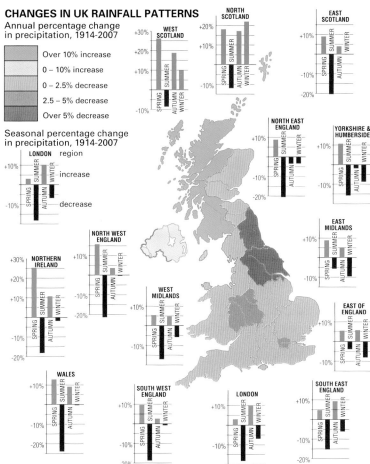

CHANGES IN UK RAINFALL PATTERNS

Annual percentage change in precipitation, 1914-2007

Over 10% increase
0 – 10% increase
0 – 2.5% decrease
2.5 – 5% decrease
Over 5% decrease

Seasonal percentage change in precipitation, 1914-2007

region
increase
decrease

WEST SCOTLAND
NORTH SCOTLAND
EAST SCOTLAND
NORTH EAST ENGLAND
YORKSHIRE & HUMBERSIDE
LONDON
NORTH WEST ENGLAND
EAST MIDLANDS
NORTHERN IRELAND
WEST MIDLANDS
EAST OF ENGLAND
WALES
SOUTH WEST ENGLAND
LONDON
SOUTH EAST ENGLAND

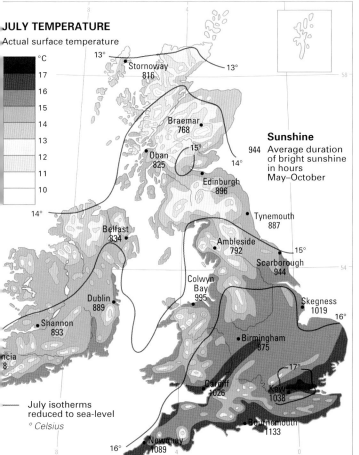

JULY TEMPERATURE

Actual surface temperature

°C
17
16
15
14
13
12
11
10

Sunshine

944 Average duration of bright sunshine in hours May–October

— July isotherms reduced to sea-level
° Celsius

Stornoway 816
Braemar 768
Oban 825
Edinburgh 896
Tynemouth 887
Belfast 834
Ambleside 792
Scarborough 944
Colwyn Bay 995
Skegness 1019
Dublin 889
Shannon 893
Birmingham 875
Cardiff 1026
Kew 1038
Bournemouth 1133
Newquay 1089

COPYRIGHT PHILIP'S

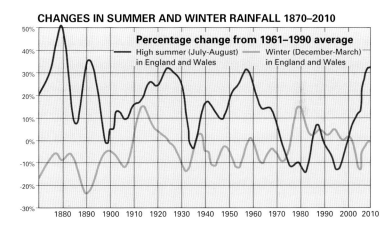

CHANGES IN SUMMER AND WINTER RAINFALL 1870–2010

Percentage change from 1961–1990 average

— High summer (July-August) in England and Wales
— Winter (December-March) in England and Wales

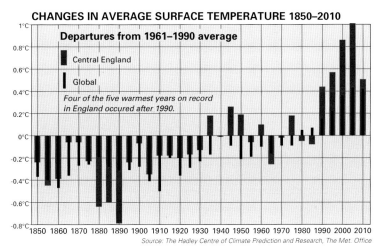

CHANGES IN AVERAGE SURFACE TEMPERATURE 1850–2010

Departures from 1961–1990 average

Central England

Global

Four of the five warmest years on record in England occured after 1990.

Source: The Hadley Centre of Climate Prediction and Research, The Met. Office

WATER SUPPLY

Regions of reliably high rainfall (more than 1,250 mm in at least 70% of the years)

③ Major reservoirs (capacity over 20 million cubic metres, see list opposite for details)

→ Existing inter-regional transfers of water (by pipeline and river)

→ Proposed inter-regional transfers of water (by pipeline and river)

□ Proposed estuary storage site

▽ Proposed groundwater storage site

Principal sources of groundwater (porous and jointed aquifers)

THAMES WATER Water supply and sewerage companies in the UK

There are no water authorities in Ireland, each county and urban borough is responsible for its own water supply

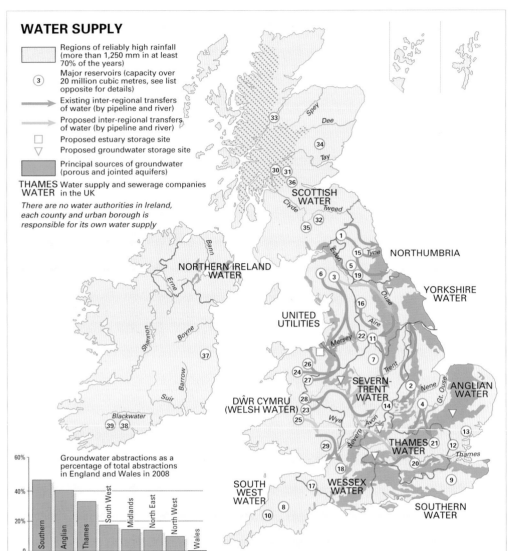

Groundwater abstractions as a percentage of total abstractions in England and Wales in 2008

MAJOR RESERVOIRS (with capacity in millio

England
1	Kielder Reservoir	198
2	Rutland Water	123
3	Haweswater	85
4	Grafham Water	59
5	Cow GreenReservoir	41
6	Thirlmere	41
7	Carsington Reservoir	36
8	Roadford Reservoir	35
9	Bewl Water Reservoir	31
10	Colliford Lake	29
11	Ladybower Reservoir	28
12	Hanningfield Reservoir	27
13	Abberton Reservoir	25
14	Draycote Water	23
15	Derwent Reservoir	22
16	Grimwith Reservoir	22
17	Wimbleball Lake	21
18	Chew Valley Lake	20
19	Balderhead Reservoir	20
20	Thames Valley (linked reservoirs)	
21	Lea Valley (linked reservoirs)	
22	Longendale (linked reservoirs)	

Wales
23	Elan Valley
24	Llyn Celyn
25	Llyn Brianne
26	Llyn Brenig
27	Llyn Vyrnwy
28	Llyn Clywedog
29	Llandegfedd Reservoir

Scotland
30	Loch Lomond
31	Loch Katrine
32	Megget Reservoir
33	Loch Ness
34	Blackwater Reservoir
35	Daer Reservoir
36	Carron Valley Reservo.

Ireland
37	Poulaphouca Reservoir
38	Inishcarra Reservoir
39	Carrigadrohid Reservo

WATER SUPPLY IN ENGLAND AND WALES

Total water abstraction in England and Wales in . was approximately 55,000 million litres a day.

The pie graph represents the almost 15,000 millic litres a day that were supplied by the water supp companies in England and Wales in 2008.

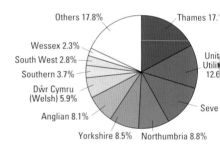

Others 17.8%
Thames 17.
Wessex 2.3%
South West 2.8%
Southern 3.7%
Dŵr Cymru (Welsh) 5.9%
Anglian 8.1%
Yorkshire 8.5%
Northumbria 8.8%
Unit Utili 12.6
Seve

WASTE RECYCLING

The percentage of total household waste recycled in 2010

Over 45%
40 – 45%
35 – 40%
Under 35%

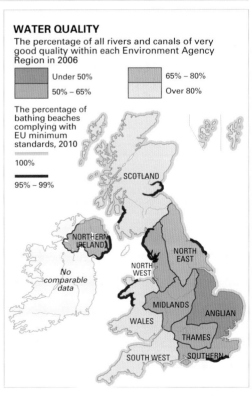

WATER QUALITY

The percentage of all rivers and canals of very good quality within each Environment Agency Region in 2006

Under 50%
50% – 65%
65% – 80%
Over 80%

The percentage of bathing beaches complying with EU minimum standards, 2010

100%
95% – 99%

FLOOD RISK IN ENGLAND AND WALES

Areas at greatest risk from flooding (as designated by the Environment Agen

△ Counties worst affected by flooding in summer 2007

AIR QUALITY
Greenhouse gas emissions for selected EU countries 1998-2009

	million tonnes of CO_2 equivalent			Share of total EU 27 emissions (2009)
	1998	2003	2009	
27	5,192.5	5,177.4	4,614.5	100%
...gium	151.0	145.9	124.4	2.7%
...mark	75.2	73.6	61.0	1.3%
...nce	585.6	565.7	517.2	11.2%
...many	1,077.6	1,030.6	919.7	19.9%
...ece	122.4	130.9	122.5	2.7%
...and	64.8	67.8	62.4	1.4%
...y	540.8	573.5	491.1	10.6%
...herlands	225.5	215.4	198.9	4.3%
...and	413.1	384.6	376.7	8.2%
...tugal	74.9	81.7	74.6	1.6%
...in	337.9	403.7	367.5	8.0%
...eden	73.8	70.9	60.0	1.3%
...ted Kingdom	700.2	657.6	566.2	12.3%

OILS

- Calcareous brown earth
- Brown earth
- Acid brown earth
- Podsol
- Peaty podsol
- Grey-brown podsol
- Gley
- Basin peat and alluvial gleys
- Peaty gley and blanket peat

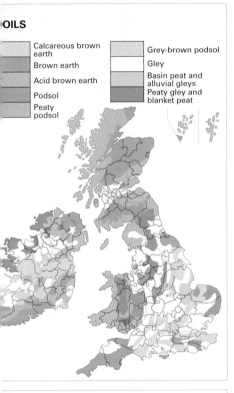

NATURAL VEGETATION
...he plant cover associated with a particular ...nvironment if it was unaffected by human activity

- Oak
- Beech and oak
- Ash and oak
- Birch and oakwood
- Scots pine
- Heath, moorland, water meadows, fen, bog and marsh

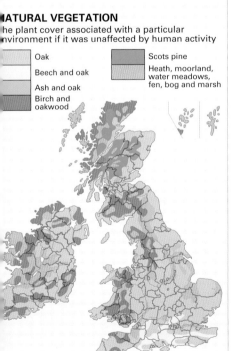

ACID RAIN
Average acidity of precipitation in the UK (pH scale)

- 4.29 and under (most acidic)
- 4.30 – 4.39
- 4.40 – 4.49
- 4.50 – 4.59
- 4.60 – 4.69
- 4.70 – 4.79
- 4.80 and over (least acidic)

ESAs
Environmentally Sensitive Areas in the UK

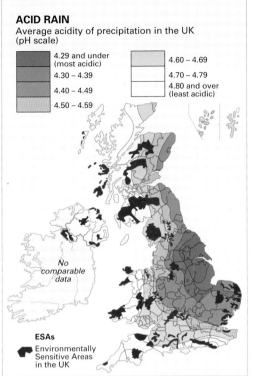

No comparable data

GREENHOUSE GAS EMISSIONS
CO_2 emissions in tonnes per capita 2008

- Over 20
- 12 – 20
- 10 – 12
- 8 – 10
- 6 – 8
- Under 6

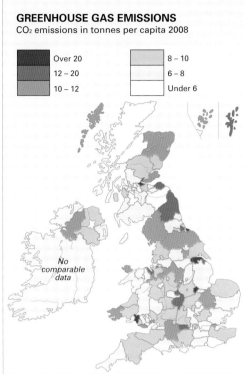

No comparable data

CONSERVATION

- National Parks
- Areas of Outstanding Natural Beauty (AONBs)
- National Scenic Areas (NSAs)
- Forest Parks, Regional Parks in Scotland and Special Protection Areas (SPAs)
- Green Belts (and the urban areas they surround)
- Heritage Coast (England and Wales)

✳ World Heritage Sites in the UK and Ireland

Other designated UK sites not shown:
St. Kilda, Atlantic Ocean
Henderson I., Pacific Ocean
Gough I. and Inaccessible I., Atlantic Ocean
St. George, Bermuda

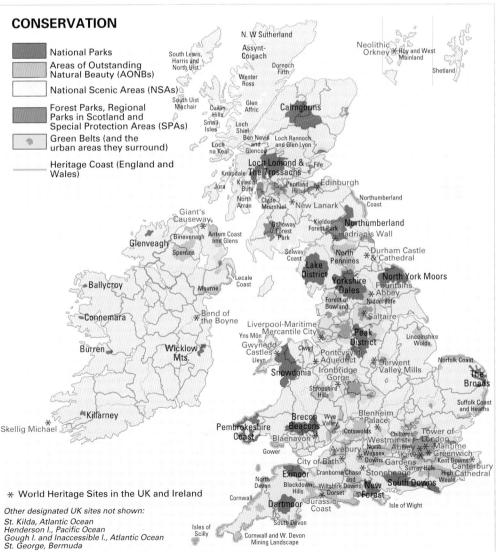

TYPES OF FARM

- Dairy cattle
- Beef cattle
- Sheep
- ● Pigs and/or poultry
- Mixed farming
- Market gardening (fruit and vegetables)
- Cereals
- Other crops (mainly potatoes, sugar beet)
- —— Northern limit of 9 month growing season
- Forests
- Built-up areas
- Areas with over 1,000 mm rainfall per year

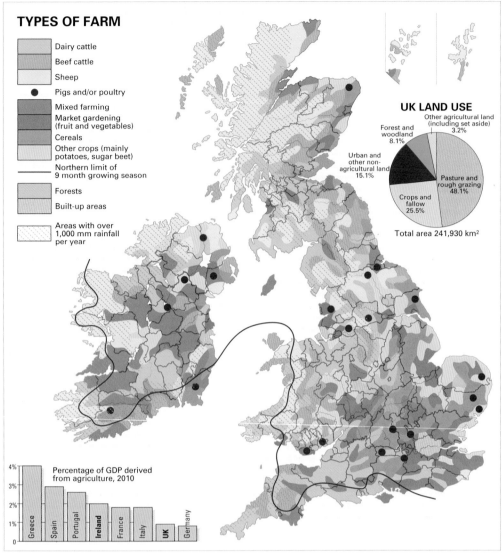

UK LAND USE

Other agricultural land (including set aside) 3.2%
Forest and woodland 8.1%
Urban and other non-agricultural land 15.1%
Pasture and rough grazing 48.1%
Crops and fallow 25.5%

Total area 241,930 km²

Percentage of GDP derived from agriculture, 2010

Greece, Spain, Portugal, Ireland, France, Italy, UK, Germany

CEREAL FARMING
The percentage of the total farmland used for growing cereals in 2009

- Over 40
- 25 – 40
- 10 – 25
- 5 – 10
- 0 – 5

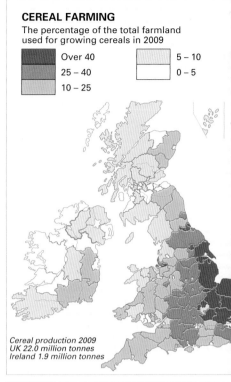

*Cereal production 2009
UK 22.0 million tonnes
Ireland 1.9 million tonnes*

DAIRY FARMING
The number of dairy cows per 100 hectares of farmland in 2009

- Over 40
- 30 – 40
- 20 – 30
- 10 – 20
- 0 – 10
- No data

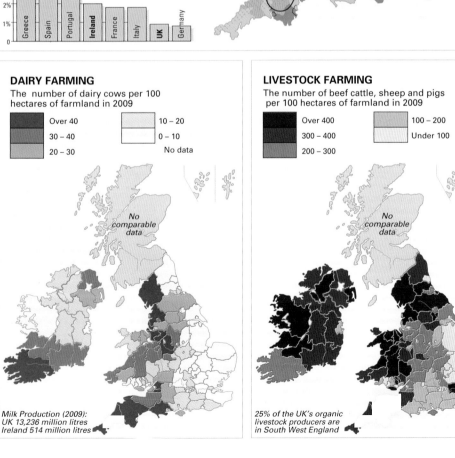

No comparable data

*Milk Production (2009):
UK 13,236 million litres
Ireland 514 million litres*

LIVESTOCK FARMING
The number of beef cattle, sheep and pigs per 100 hectares of farmland in 2009

- Over 400
- 300 – 400
- 200 – 300
- 100 – 200
- Under 100

No comparable data

25% of the UK's organic livestock producers are in South West England

West Coast of Scotland 366,569 tonnes
Scalloway Lerw
Scrabster
Kinlochbervie
Ullapool Fraserburgh
Mallaig Peterhe
North Sea 295,367 tonn
Killybegs Kirkcudbright
Portavogie
Kilkeel Ardglass
Rossaveel
Howth Penrhyn
Holyhead
Dunmore East
Castletown Bearhaven Milford Haven
Bristol Channel and Celtic Sea 25,384 tonnes
Shoreham
Brixham Newha
Newlyn Plymouth
English Channel 49,507 tonnes
West Ireland and Sole Bank 34,378 tonnes

FISHING
Major fishing ports by size of catch landed

- ▽ Demersal e.g. cod (Deep sea fish)
- ▼ Pelagic e.g. mackerel (Shallow sea fish)
- ▽ Shellfish e.g. lobster

The most importar inshore fishing gro

North Sea 295,367 tonnes
Total amount caught i each fishing region 201

1000 500 200 100 50 m
Depth of sea in metres

EMPLOYMENT IN SERVICES

The percentage of the workforce employed in the service industry in 2010

- Over 85%
- 80 – 85%
- 75 – 80%
- 70 – 75%
- Under 70%

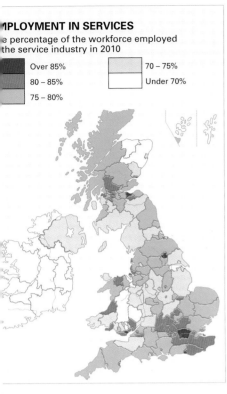

EMPLOYMENT IN MANUFACTURING

The percentage of the workforce employed in the manufacturing in 2010

- Over 15%
- 12.5 – 15%
- 10 – 12.5%
- 7.5 – 10%
- 5 – 7.5%
- Under 5%

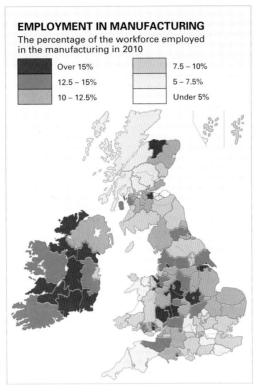

MOTOR MANUFACTURING IN ENGLAND AND WALES

- Car manufacturing sites
- Commercial vehicle manufacturing sites
- Selected engine manufacturing sites

Source: SMMT 2011

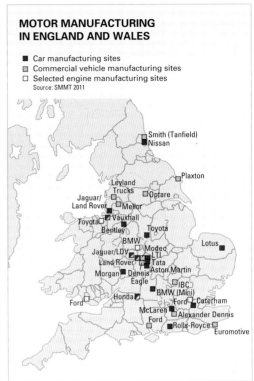

CHANGES IN EMPLOYMENT IN THE UK

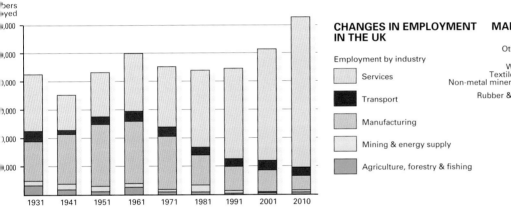

Employment by industry

- Services
- Transport
- Manufacturing
- Mining & energy supply
- Agriculture, forestry & fishing

MANUFACTURING OUTPUT IN THE UK

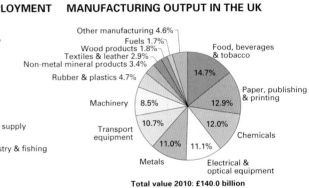

- Other manufacturing 4.6%
- Fuels 1.7%
- Wood products 1.8%
- Textiles & leather 2.9%
- Non-metal mineral products 3.4%
- Rubber & plastics 4.7%
- Machinery 8.5%
- Transport equipment 10.7%
- Metals 11.0%
- Electrical & optical equipment 11.1%
- Chemicals 12.0%
- Paper, publishing & printing 12.9%
- Food, beverages & tobacco 14.7%

Total value 2010: £140.0 billion

UK FOREIGN TRADE

TOP TEN TRADING PARTNERS One container represents 1% of the total value of imports or 1% of the total value of exports in 2010

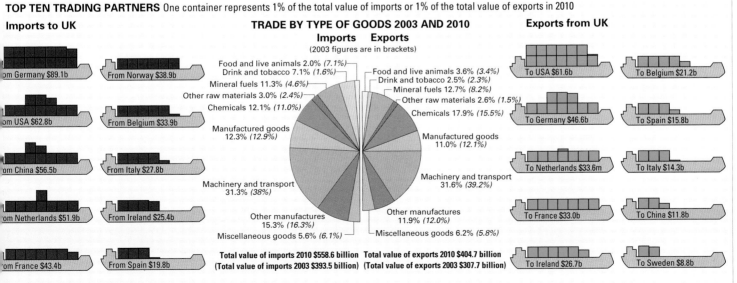

Imports to UK

- From Germany $89.1b
- From USA $62.8b
- From China $56.5b
- From Netherlands $51.9b
- From France $43.4b
- From Norway $38.9b
- From Belgium $33.9b
- From Italy $27.8b
- From Ireland $25.4b
- From Spain $19.8b

TRADE BY TYPE OF GOODS 2003 AND 2010

Imports   Exports
(2003 figures are in brackets)

Imports:
- Food and live animals 2.0% (7.1%)
- Drink and tobacco 7.1% (1.6%)
- Mineral fuels 11.3% (4.6%)
- Other raw materials 3.0% (2.4%)
- Chemicals 12.1% (11.0%)
- Manufactured goods 12.3% (12.9%)
- Machinery and transport 31.3% (38%)
- Other manufactures 15.3% (16.3%)
- Miscellaneous goods 5.6% (6.1%)

Exports:
- Food and live animals 3.6% (3.4%)
- Drink and tobacco 2.5% (2.3%)
- Mineral fuels 12.7% (8.2%)
- Other raw materials 2.6% (1.5%)
- Chemicals 17.9% (15.5%)
- Manufactured goods 11.0% (12.1%)
- Machinery and transport 31.6% (39.2%)
- Other manufactures 11.9% (12.0%)
- Miscellaneous goods 6.2% (5.8%)

Total value of imports 2010 $558.6 billion
(Total value of imports 2003 $393.5 billion)
Total value of exports 2010 $404.7 billion
(Total value of exports 2003 $307.7 billion)

Exports from UK

- To USA $61.6b
- To Germany $46.6b
- To Netherlands $33.6m
- To France $33.0b
- To Ireland $26.7b
- To Belgium $21.2b
- To Spain $15.8b
- To Italy $14.3b
- To China $11.8b
- To Sweden $8.8b

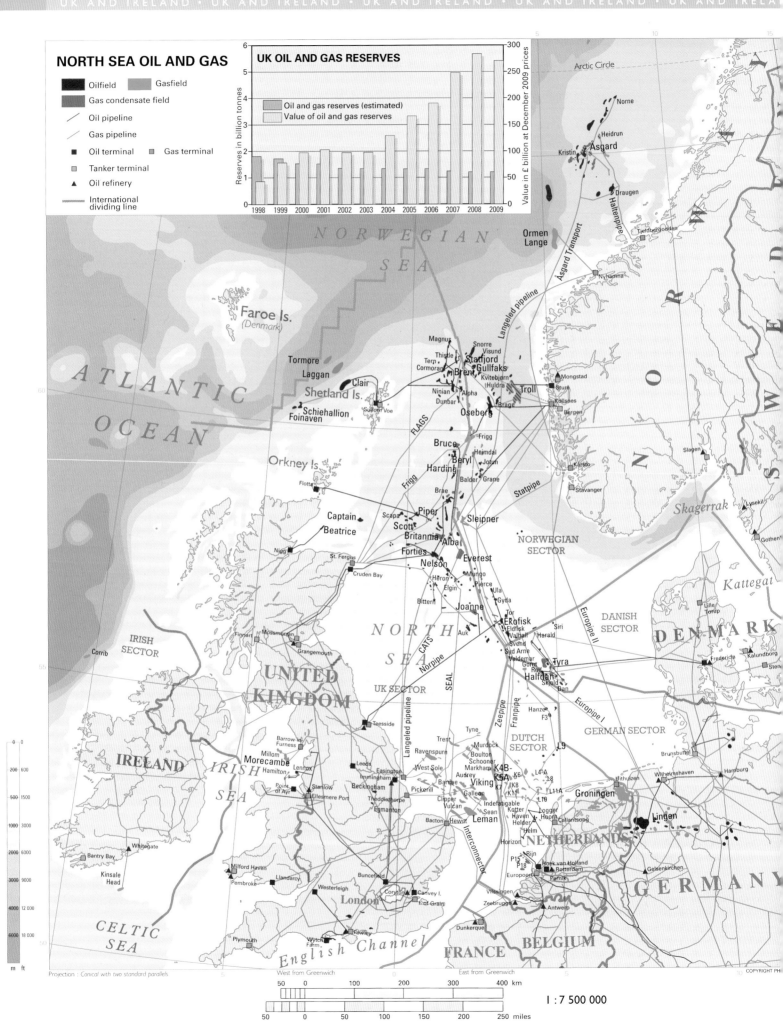

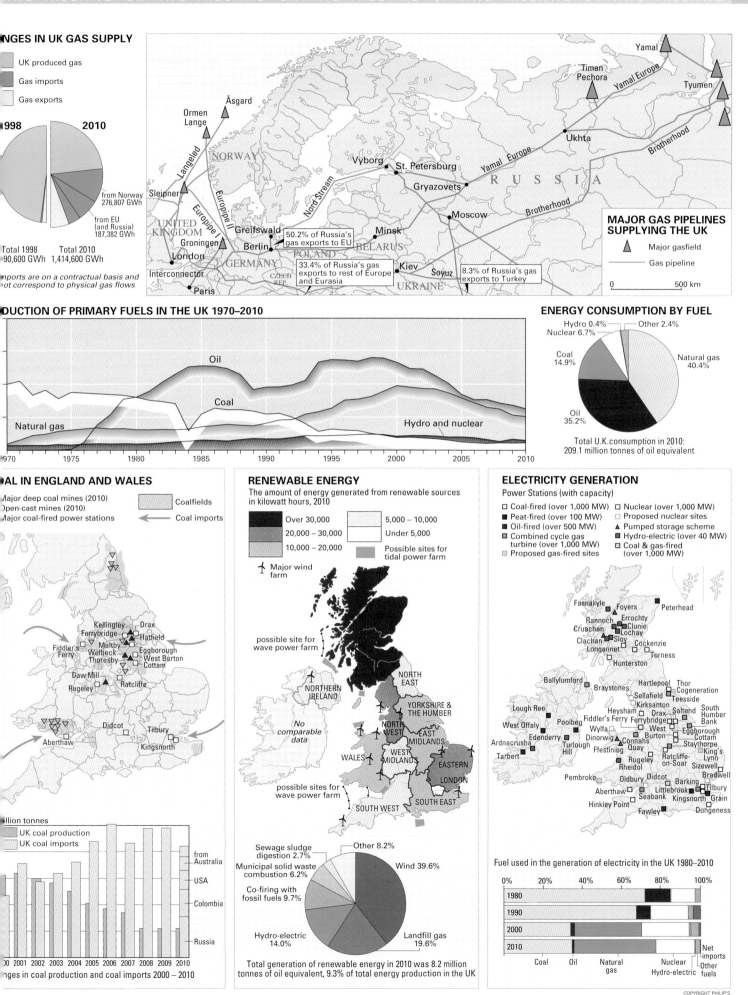

NGES IN UK GAS SUPPLY

- UK produced gas
- Gas imports
- Gas exports

1998   2010

from Norway 276,807 GWh

from EU (and Russia) 187,382 GWh

Total 1998   Total 2010
90,600 GWh   1,414,600 GWh

mports are on a contractual basis and ot correspond to physical gas flows

MAJOR GAS PIPELINES SUPPLYING THE UK

▲ Major gasfield
— Gas pipeline

0   500 km

50.2% of Russia's gas exports to EU

33.4% of Russia's gas exports to rest of Europe and Eurasia

8.3% of Russia's gas exports to Turkey

DUCTION OF PRIMARY FUELS IN THE UK 1970–2010

Oil
Coal
Natural gas
Hydro and nuclear

1970 1975 1980 1985 1990 1995 2000 2005 2010

ENERGY CONSUMPTION BY FUEL

- Hydro 0.4%
- Other 2.4%
- Nuclear 6.7%
- Coal 14.9%
- Natural gas 40.4%
- Oil 35.2%

Total U.K. consumption in 2010: 209.1 million tonnes of oil equivalent

AL IN ENGLAND AND WALES

Major deep coal mines (2010)
Open-cast mines (2010)
Major coal-fired power stations

Coalfields
← Coal imports

llion tonnes

- UK coal production
- UK coal imports

from Australia
USA
Colombia
Russia

00 2001 2002 2003 2004 2005 2006 2007 2008 2009 2010

nges in coal production and coal imports 2000 – 2010

RENEWABLE ENERGY

The amount of energy generated from renewable sources in kilowatt hours, 2010

- Over 30,000
- 20,000 – 30,000
- 10,000 – 20,000
- 5,000 – 10,000
- Under 5,000
- Possible sites for tidal power farm

✈ Major wind farm

possible site for wave power farm

NORTHERN IRELAND

No comparable data

NORTH EAST
YORKSHIRE & THE HUMBER
NORTH WEST
EAST MIDLANDS
WEST MIDLANDS
WALES
EASTERN
LONDON
SOUTH EAST
SOUTH WEST

possible sites for wave power farm

- Sewage sludge digestion 2.7%
- Other 8.2%
- Municipal solid waste combustion 6.2%
- Wind 39.6%
- Co-firing with fossil fuels 9.7%
- Hydro-electric 14.0%
- Landfill gas 19.6%

Total generation of renewable energy in 2010 was 8.2 million tonnes of oil equivalent, 9.3% of total energy production in the UK

ELECTRICITY GENERATION

Power Stations (with capacity)

- ☐ Coal-fired (over 1,000 MW)
- ■ Peat-fired (over 100 MW)
- ■ Oil-fired (over 500 MW)
- ■ Combined cycle gas turbine (over 1,000 MW)
- ▨ Proposed gas-fired sites
- ☐ Nuclear (over 1,000 MW)
- ☐ Proposed nuclear sites
- ▲ Pumped storage scheme
- ■ Hydro-electric (over 40 MW)
- ☐ Coal & gas-fired (over 1,000 MW)

Fuel used in the generation of electricity in the UK 1980–2010

0% 20% 40% 60% 80% 100%

1980
1990
2000
2010

Coal Oil Natural gas Nuclear Hydro-electric Net imports Other fuels

COPYRIGHT PHILIP'S

ROADS AND FERRIES

M6 Motorways
Other main roads
Principal car ferry routes

56 Average 24 hour flow of vehicles for major sections of motorway network. Figures are given in thousands for 2010

RAILWAYS

Electrified lines
Other main lines
High-speed rail link
Planned high-speed rail link (HSR 2)

Furthest distances from London reached within a journey time of

	3 hours	6 hours
1950	○	○
2010	●	●

CHANNEL TUNNEL AND HIGH-SPEED RAIL LINKS IN EUROPE

Estimated journey times between London and other selected European cities

London–Berlin
London–Amsterdam
London–Paris
London–Brussels

5   10   15   20 hours

1990 — Best time achievable before opening of Channel Tunnel

2002 — Opening of Channel Tunnel in 1994 and completion of high-speed links in Europe

2010 — Journey time on completion of high speed rail link from London St. Pancras to Folkestone

MEANS OF TRANSPORTATION WITHIN THE UK

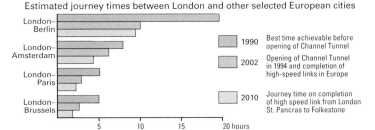

GOODS
250 225 200 175 150 125 100 75 50 25 0
billion tonne km

1980
1990
2000
2009

Pipelines Rail Water Road

PASSENGE
0 100 200 300 400 500 600 700
billion passenger k

Private Transport (cars)   Public Transport (buses and coaches)

SEAPORTS

Goods traffic by port in thousand tonnes (2010)

50,000
25,000
10,000
5,000

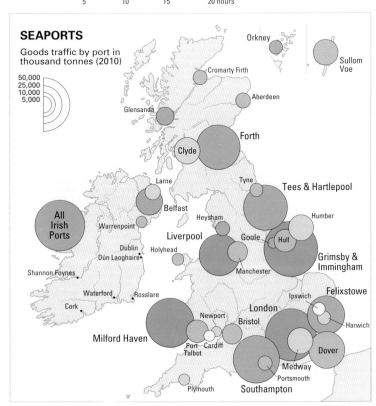

AIRPORTS

Passenger traffic in thousands (2010)

60,000
30,000
5,000
1,000

(34.6%) International Passengers as a percentage of the total for busiest airports

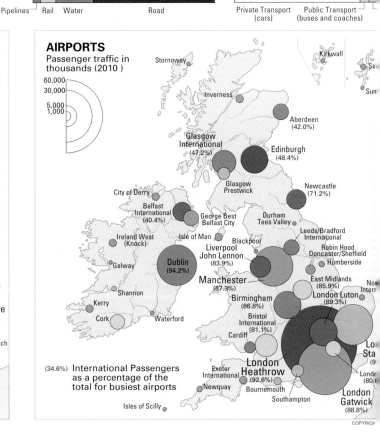

COPYRIGH

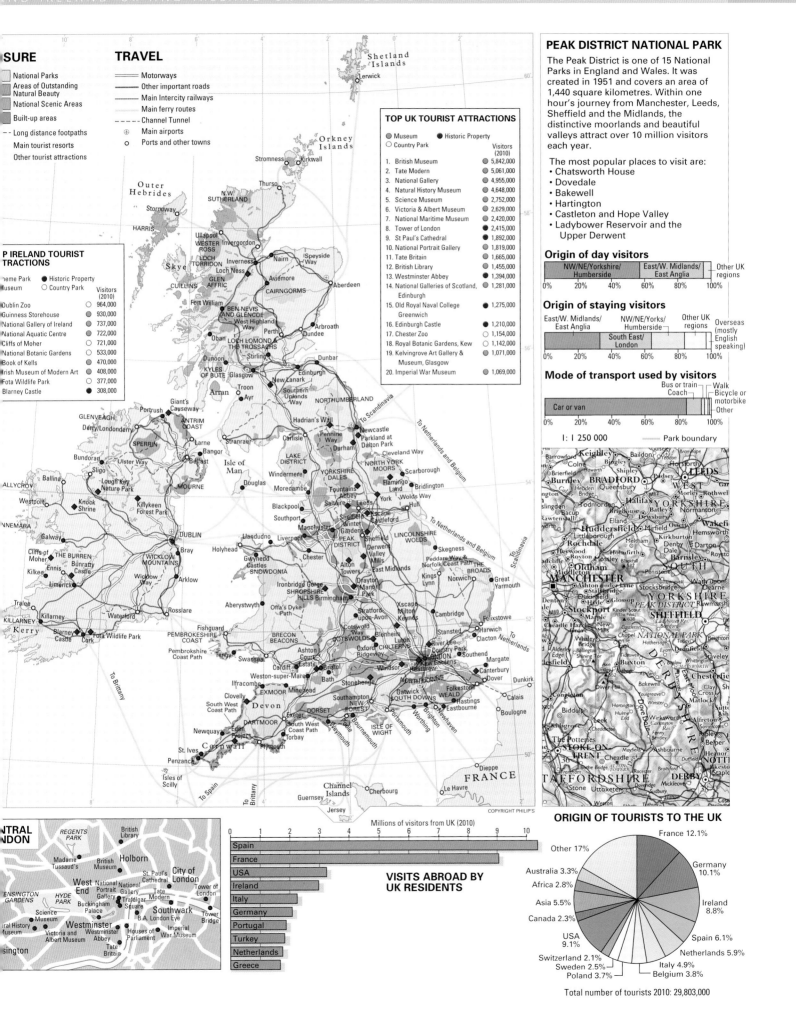

SURE

- National Parks
- Areas of Outstanding Natural Beauty
- National Scenic Areas
- Built-up areas
- Long distance footpaths
- Main tourist resorts
- Other tourist attractions

TRAVEL

- Motorways
- Other important roads
- Main Intercity railways
- Main ferry routes
- Channel Tunnel
- ⊕ Main airports
- ○ Ports and other towns

P IRELAND TOURIST TRACTIONS

- ● heme Park ● Historic Property
- ● useum ○ Country Park

	Visitors (2010)
Dublin Zoo	○ 964,000
Guinness Storehouse	● 930,000
National Gallery of Ireland	● 737,000
National Aquatic Centre	● 722,000
Cliffs of Moher	○ 721,000
National Botanic Gardens	● 533,000
Book of Kells	● 470,000
Irish Museum of Modern Art	● 408,000
Fota Wildlife Park	○ 377,000
Blarney Castle	● 308,000

TOP UK TOURIST ATTRACTIONS

- ● Museum ● Historic Property
- ○ Country Park

		Visitors (2010)
1. British Museum	●	5,842,000
2. Tate Modern	●	5,061,000
3. National Gallery	●	4,955,000
4. Natural History Museum	●	4,648,000
5. Science Museum	●	2,752,000
6. Victoria & Albert Museum	●	2,629,000
7. National Maritime Museum	●	2,420,000
8. Tower of London	●	2,415,000
9. St Paul's Cathedral	●	1,892,000
10. National Portrait Gallery	●	1,819,000
11. Tate Britain	●	1,665,000
12. British Library	●	1,455,000
13. Westminster Abbey	●	1,394,000
14. National Galleries of Scotland, Edinburgh	●	1,281,000
15. Old Royal Naval College Greenwich	●	1,275,000
16. Edinburgh Castle	●	1,210,000
17. Chester Zoo	○	1,154,000
18. Royal Botanic Gardens, Kew	○	1,142,000
19. Kelvingrove Art Gallery & Museum, Glasgow	●	1,071,000
20. Imperial War Museum	●	1,069,000

PEAK DISTRICT NATIONAL PARK

The Peak District is one of 15 National Parks in England and Wales. It was created in 1951 and covers an area of 1,440 square kilometres. Within one hour's journey from Manchester, Leeds, Sheffield and the Midlands, the distinctive moorlands and beautiful valleys attract over 10 million visitors each year.

The most popular places to visit are:
- Chatsworth House
- Dovedale
- Bakewell
- Hartington
- Castleton and Hope Valley
- Ladybower Reservoir and the Upper Derwent

Origin of day visitors

NW/NE/Yorkshire/Humberside	East/W. Midlands/East Anglia	Other UK regions

0%   20%   40%   60%   80%   100%

Origin of staying visitors

East/W. Midlands/East Anglia	NW/NE/Yorks/Humberside	Other UK regions	Overseas (mostly English speaking)
	South East/London		

0%   20%   40%   60%   80%   100%

Mode of transport used by visitors

Bus or train — Walk
Coach — Bicycle or motorbike
Car or van — Other

0%   20%   40%   60%   80%   100%

1: 1 250 000   — Park boundary

COPYRIGHT PHILIP'S

ORIGIN OF TOURISTS TO THE UK

- France 12.1%
- Germany 10.1%
- Ireland 8.8%
- Spain 6.1%
- Netherlands 5.9%
- Italy 4.9%
- Belgium 3.8%
- Poland 3.7%
- Sweden 2.5%
- Switzerland 2.1%
- USA 9.1%
- Canada 2.3%
- Asia 5.5%
- Africa 2.8%
- Australia 3.3%
- Other 17%

Total number of tourists 2010: 29,803,000

VISITS ABROAD BY UK RESIDENTS

Millions of visitors from UK (2010)

0 1 2 3 4 5 6 7 8 9 10

- Spain
- France
- USA
- Ireland
- Italy
- Germany
- Portugal
- Turkey
- Netherlands
- Greece

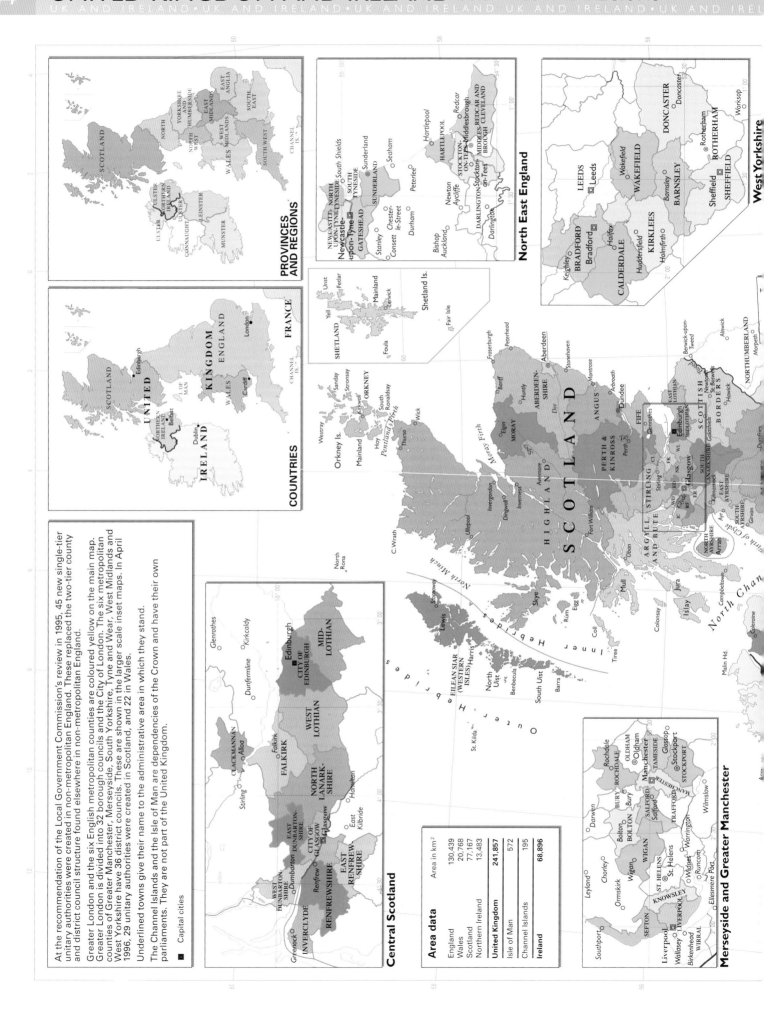

PROVINCES AND REGIONS

SCOTLAND

NORTH

YORKSHIRE AND HUMBERSIDE

EAST MIDLANDS

EAST ANGLIA

NORTH WEST

WEST MIDLANDS

SOUTH EAST

WALES

SOUTH WEST

CHANNEL IS.

ULSTER

ULSTER

NORTHERN IRELAND

ULSTER

CONNAUGHT

LEINSTER

MUNSTER

COUNTRIES

SCOTLAND

NORTHERN IRELAND

Belfast

IRELAND

Dublin

I. OF MAN

UNITED KINGDOM

ENGLAND

Edinburgh

London

WALES

Cardiff

CHANNEL IS.

FRANCE

North East England

NORTH TYNESIDE

NEWCASTLE UPON TYNE

Newcastle-upon-Tyne

SOUTH TYNESIDE

South Shields

GATESHEAD

SUNDERLAND

Sunderland

Seaham

Peterlee

Chester-le-Street

Stanley

Consett

Durham

Bishop Auckland

Redcar

Hartlepool

HARTLEPOOL

REDCAR AND CLEVELAND

MIDDLES-BROUGH

Middlesbrough

STOCKTON-ON-TEES Stockton-on-Tees

Newton Aycliffe

DARLINGTON

Darlington

Shetland Is.

Unst

Fetlar

Yell

Mainland

Lerwick

SHETLAND

Foula

Fair Isle

West Yorkshire

DONCASTER

Doncaster

Worksop

Rotherham

ROTHERHAM

SHEFFIELD

Sheffield

LEEDS

Leeds

WAKEFIELD

Wakefield

BARNSLEY

Barnsley

Keighley

BRADFORD

Bradford

KIRKLEES

Huddersfield

Holmfirth

CALDERDALE

Halifax

At the recommendation of the Local Government Commission's review in 1995, 45 new single-tier unitary authorities were created in non-metropolitan England. These replaced the two-tier county and district council structure found elsewhere in non-metropolitan England.

Greater London and the six English metropolitan counties are coloured yellow on the main map. Greater London is divided into 32 borough councils and the City of London. The six metropolitan counties of Greater Manchester, Merseyside, South Yorkshire, Tyne and Wear, West Midlands and West Yorkshire have 36 district councils. These are shown in the larger scale inset maps. In April 1996, 29 unitary authorities were created in Scotland, and 22 in Wales.

Underlined towns give their name to the administrative area in which they stand.

The Channel Islands and the Isle of Man are dependencies of the Crown and have their own parliaments. They are not part of the United Kingdom.

■ Capital cities

Orkney Is.

Westray

Sanday

Stronsay

ORKNEY

Mainland

Kirkwall

Hoy

South Ronaldsay

Pentland Firth

North Rona

C. Wrath

Thurso

Wick

Ullapool

Dingwall

Inverness

Aviemore

HIGHLAND

SCOTLAND

Fraserhead

Peterhead

Fraserburgh

Banff

Huntly

ABERDEEN-SHIRE

Aberdeen

Stonehaven

Elgin

MORAY

Dee

ANGUS

Montrose

Arbroath

Dundee

PERTH & KINROSS

Perth

FIFE

Glenrothes

Invergordon

Fort William

Oban

Stirling

STIRLING

Glasgow

Edinburgh

MIDLOTHIAN

EAST LOTHIAN

Dunbar

SCOTTISH BORDERS

St Boswells

Hawick

Berwick-upon-Tweed

Alnwick

NORTHUMBERLAND

Morpeth

Moray Firth

EILEAN SIAR (WESTERN ISLES)

Lewis

Stornoway

Harris

North Uist

Benbecula

South Uist

Barra

St. Kilda

Skye

Rum

Eigg

Coll

Tiree

Mull

Colonsay

Jura

Islay

ARGYLL AND BUTE

NORTH AYRSHIRE

Arran

SOUTH AYRSHIRE

Ayr

Kilmarnock

LANARKSHIRE

Campbeltown

Firth of Clyde

North Minch

Inner Hebrides

Outer Hebrides

The Minch

North Chan

Malin Hd.

Coleraine

Central Scotland

Glenrothes

Kirkcaldy

Dunfermline

Edinburgh

CITY OF EDINBURGH

MID-LOTHIAN

WEST LOTHIAN

Falkirk

FALKIRK

CLACKMANNAN

Alloa

Stirling

NORTH LANARK-SHIRE

Hamilton

East Kilbride

Glasgow

CITY OF GLASGOW

EAST DUNBARTON-SHIRE

Dumbarton

WEST DUNBARTON-SHIRE

Renfrew

Greenock

INVERCLYDE

EAST RENFREWSHIRE

RENFREWSHIRE

Area data

	Area in km²
England	130,439
Wales	20,768
Scotland	77,167
Northern Ireland	13,483
United Kingdom	**241,857**
Isle of Man	572
Channel Islands	195
Ireland	**68,896**

Merseyside and Greater Manchester

Darwen

Rochdale

ROCHDALE

OLDHAM

Oldham

Glossop

BURY

Bury

TAMESIDE

Manchester

MANCHESTER

SALFORD

Salford

TRAFFORD

STOCKPORT

Stockport

Bolton

BOLTON

WIGAN

Wigan

Warrington

Wilmslow

Leyland

Chorley

Ormskirk

ST. HELENS

St. Helens

Widnes

Runcorn

Ellesmere Port

KNOWSLEY

SEFTON

Southport

Liverpool

LIVERPOOL

Wallasey

Birkenhead

WIRRAL

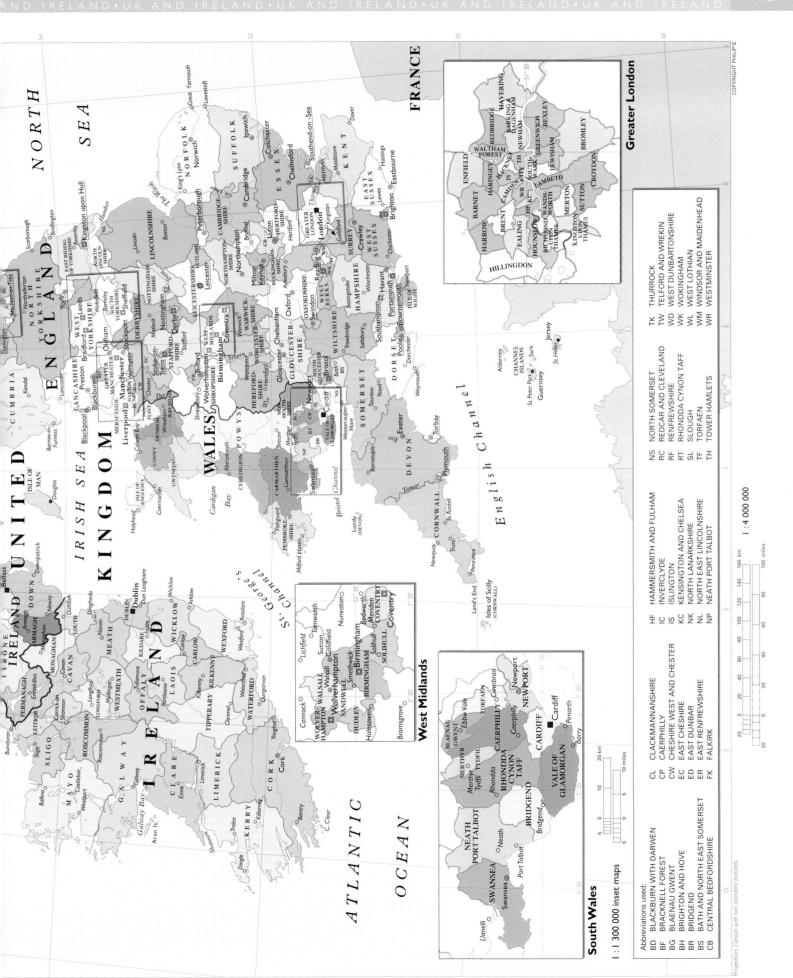

Greater London

TK	THURROCK
TW	TELFORD AND WREKIN
WD	WEST DUNBARTONSHIRE
WK	WOKINGHAM
WL	WEST LOTHIAN
WM	WINDSOR AND MAIDENHEAD
WR	WESTMINSTER

NS	NORTH SOMERSET
RC	REDCAR AND CLEVELAND
RF	RENFREWSHIRE
RT	RHONDDA CYNON TAFF
SL	SLOUGH
TF	TORFAEN
TH	TOWER HAMLETS

HF	HAMMERSMITH AND FULHAM
IC	INVERCLYDE
IS	ISLINGTON
KC	KENSINGTON AND CHELSEA
NK	NORTH LANARKSHIRE
NL	NORTH EAST LINCOLNSHIRE
NP	NEATH PORT TALBOT

1 : 4 000 000

Abbreviations used:
BD	BLACKBURN WITH DARWEN
BF	BRACKNELL FOREST
BG	BLAENAU GWENT
BH	BRIGHTON AND HOVE
BR	BRIDGEND
BS	BATH AND NORTH EAST SOMERSET
CB	CENTRAL BEDFORDSHIRE

CL	CLACKMANNANSHIRE
CP	CAERPHILLY
CW	CHESHIRE WEST AND CHESTER
EC	EAST CHESHIRE
ED	EAST DUNBAR
ER	EAST RENFREWSHIRE
FK	FALKIRK

West Midlands

South Wales

1 : 300 000 inset maps

COPYRIGHT PHILIP'S

Projection: Conical with two standard parallels

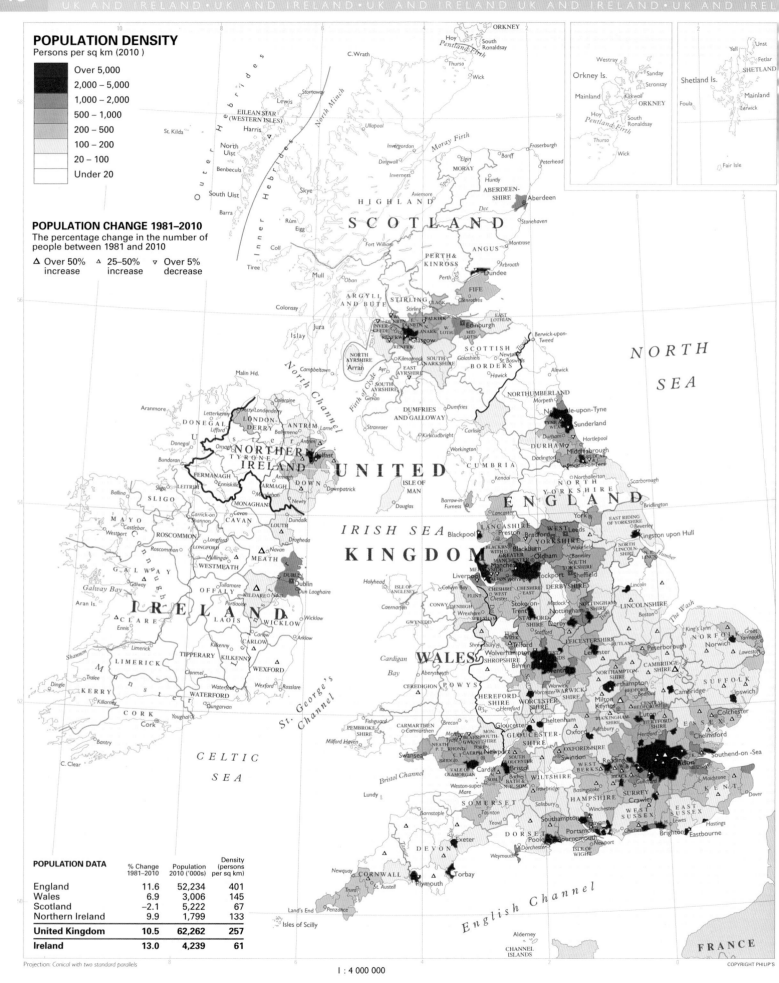

POPULATION DENSITY
Persons per sq km (2010)

Over 5,000
2,000 – 5,000
1,000 – 2,000
500 – 1,000
200 – 500
100 – 200
20 – 100
Under 20

POPULATION CHANGE 1981–2010
The percentage change in the number of people between 1981 and 2010

△ Over 50% increase   △ 25–50% increase   ▽ Over 5% decrease

POPULATION DATA

	% Change 1981–2010	Population 2010 ('000s)	Density (persons per sq km)
England	11.6	52,234	401
Wales	6.9	3,006	145
Scotland	–2.1	5,222	67
Northern Ireland	9.9	1,799	133
United Kingdom	**10.5**	**62,262**	**257**
Ireland	**13.0**	**4,239**	**61**

Projection: Conical with two standard parallels

1 : 4 000 000

COPYRIGHT PHILIP'S

POPULATION DENSITY IN 1891

Persons per sq km

- Over 1,000
- 500 – 1,000
- 200 – 500
- 100 – 200
- 50 – 100
- 25 – 50
- Under 25

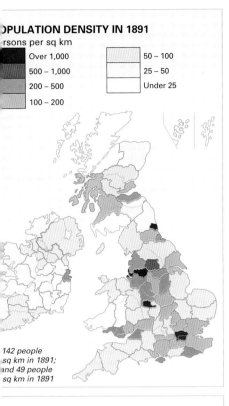

142 people
sq km in 1891;
nd 49 people
sq km in 1891

ETHNIC GROUPS

Ethnic minorities as a percentage of total
population in 2010

- Over 25%
- 10 – 25%
- 5 – 10%
- 0 – 5%

Ethnic minority groups

138 000 Total number of
ethnic minority
people in each
region

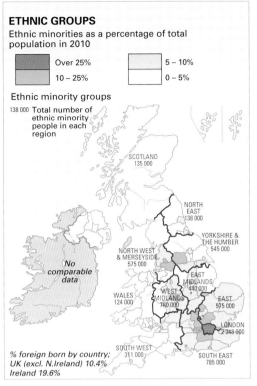

SCOTLAND
135 000

NORTH
EAST
138 000

YORKSHIRE &
THE HUMBER
545 000

NORTH WEST
& MERSEYSIDE
575 000

*No
comparable
data*

EAST
MIDLANDS
440 000

WALES
124 000

WEST
MIDLANDS
780 000

EAST
575 000

LONDON
2 348 000

SOUTH WEST
311 000

SOUTH EAST
785 000

*% foreign born by country;
UK (excl. N.Ireland) 10.4%
Ireland 19.6%*

MIGRATION

The difference between the number moving in and
the number moving away per 1,000 inhabitants 2010

- Over 10 moved in
- 1 – 10 moved in
- 0 – 1 moved in
- 0 – 1 moved away
- 1 – 10 moved away
- Over 10 moved away

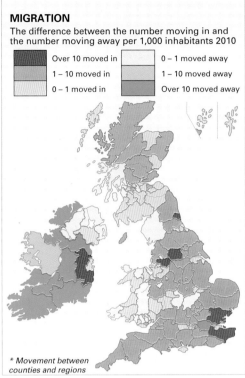

** Movement between
counties and regions*

NATURAL POPULATION CHANGE

The difference between the number of births and the
number of deaths per thousand inhabitants in 2010

- Over 10 more births
- 5 – 10 more births
- 2.5 – 5 more births
- 1 – 2.5 more births
- 0 – 1 more births
- 0 – 1 more deaths

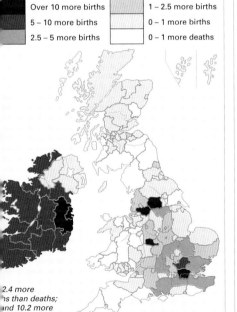

2.4 more
hs than deaths;
nd 10.2 more
hs than deaths

YOUNG PEOPLE

The percentage of the population
under 15 years old in 2010

- Over 22%
- 20 – 22%
- 18 – 20%
- 16 – 18%
- 14 – 16%

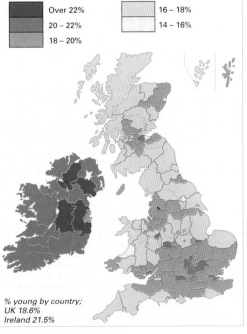

*% young by country;
UK 18.6%
Ireland 21.5%*

OLD PEOPLE

The percentage of the population
aged 65 and over in 2010

- Over 22%
- 20 – 22%
- 18 – 20%
- 16 – 18%
- 14 – 16%
- Under 14%

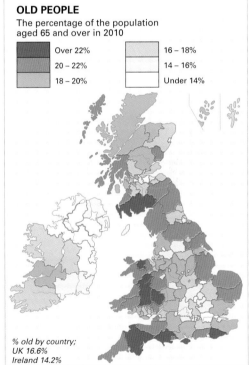

*% old by country;
UK 16.6%
Ireland 14.2%*

VITAL STATISTICS (1900–2010)

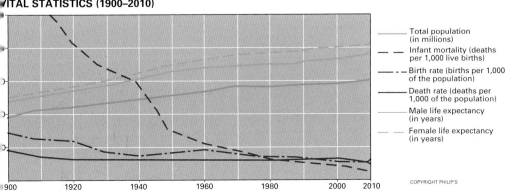

— Total population
(in millions)

– – Infant mortality (deaths
per 1,000 live births)

–·– Birth rate (births per 1,000
of the population)

— Death rate (deaths per
1,000 of the population)

— Male life expectancy
(in years)

—·— Female life expectancy
(in years)

1900   1920   1940   1960   1980   2000   2010

COPYRIGHT PHILIP'S

AGE STRUCTURE OF THE UK

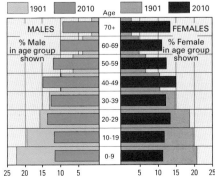

1901   2010   Age   1901   2010

MALES   70+   FEMALES
% Male   60-69   % Female
in age group   50-59   in age group
shown   40-49   shown
               30-39
               20-29
               10-19
               0-9

25 20 15 10 5   5 10 15 20 25

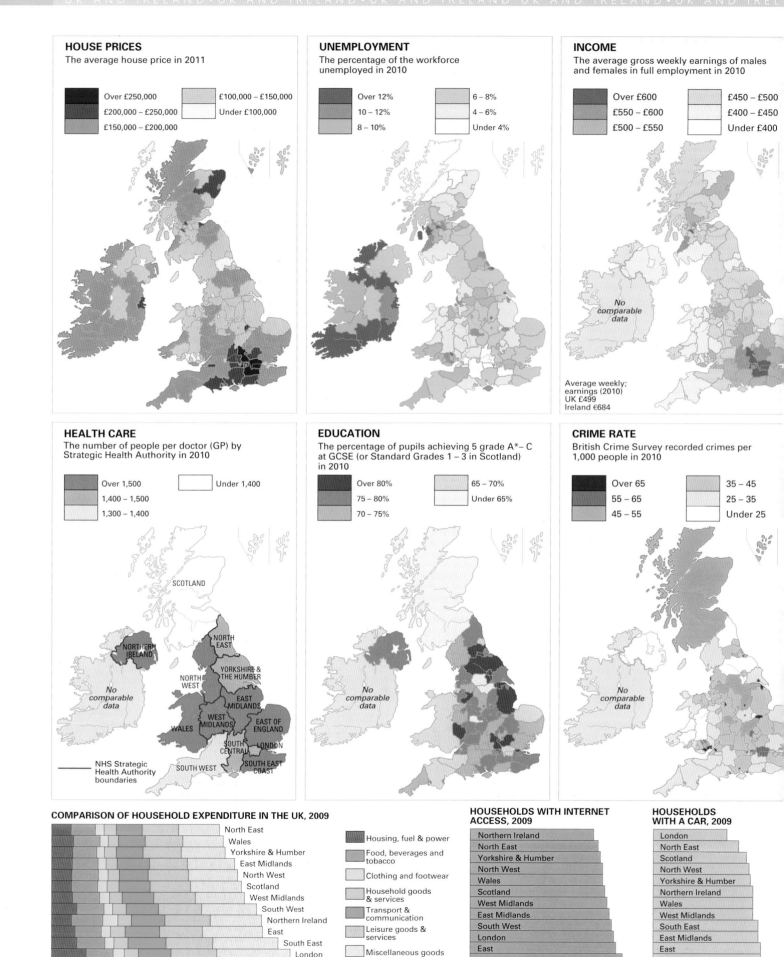

HOUSE PRICES
The average house price in 2011

- Over £250,000
- £200,000 – £250,000
- £150,000 – £200,000
- £100,000 – £150,000
- Under £100,000

UNEMPLOYMENT
The percentage of the workforce unemployed in 2010

- Over 12%
- 10 – 12%
- 8 – 10%
- 6 – 8%
- 4 – 6%
- Under 4%

INCOME
The average gross weekly earnings of males and females in full employment in 2010

- Over £600
- £550 – £600
- £500 – £550
- £450 – £500
- £400 – £450
- Under £400

No comparable data

Average weekly; earnings (2010)
UK £499
Ireland €684

HEALTH CARE
The number of people per doctor (GP) by Strategic Health Authority in 2010

- Over 1,500
- 1,400 – 1,500
- 1,300 – 1,400
- Under 1,400

No comparable data

SCOTLAND
NORTHERN IRELAND
NORTH EAST
YORKSHIRE & THE HUMBER
NORTH WEST
EAST MIDLANDS
WEST MIDLANDS
EAST OF ENGLAND
WALES
SOUTH CENTRAL
LONDON
SOUTH WEST
SOUTH EAST COAST

—— NHS Strategic Health Authority boundaries

EDUCATION
The percentage of pupils achieving 5 grade A*– C at GCSE (or Standard Grades 1 – 3 in Scotland) in 2010

- Over 80%
- 75 – 80%
- 70 – 75%
- 65 – 70%
- Under 65%

No comparable data

CRIME RATE
British Crime Survey recorded crimes per 1,000 people in 2010

- Over 65
- 55 – 65
- 45 – 55
- 35 – 45
- 25 – 35
- Under 25

No comparable data

COMPARISON OF HOUSEHOLD EXPENDITURE IN THE UK, 2009

North East
Wales
Yorkshire & Humber
East Midlands
North West
Scotland
West Midlands
South West
Northern Ireland
East
South East
London

0   £100   £200   £300   £400   £500   £600 per week
Average household expenditure per week in UK in 2009: £461.70

- Housing, fuel & power
- Food, beverages and tobacco
- Clothing and footwear
- Household goods & services
- Transport & communication
- Leisure goods & services
- Miscellaneous goods

COPYRIGHT PHILIP'S

HOUSEHOLDS WITH INTERNET ACCESS, 2009

Northern Ireland
North East
Yorkshire & Humber
North West
Wales
Scotland
West Midlands
East Midlands
South West
London
East
South East

0   10%   20%   30%   40%   50%   60%   70%

HOUSEHOLDS WITH A CAR, 2009

London
North East
Scotland
North West
Yorkshire & Humber
Northern Ireland
Wales
West Midlands
South East
East Midlands
East
South West

0   20%   40%   60%   80%   10

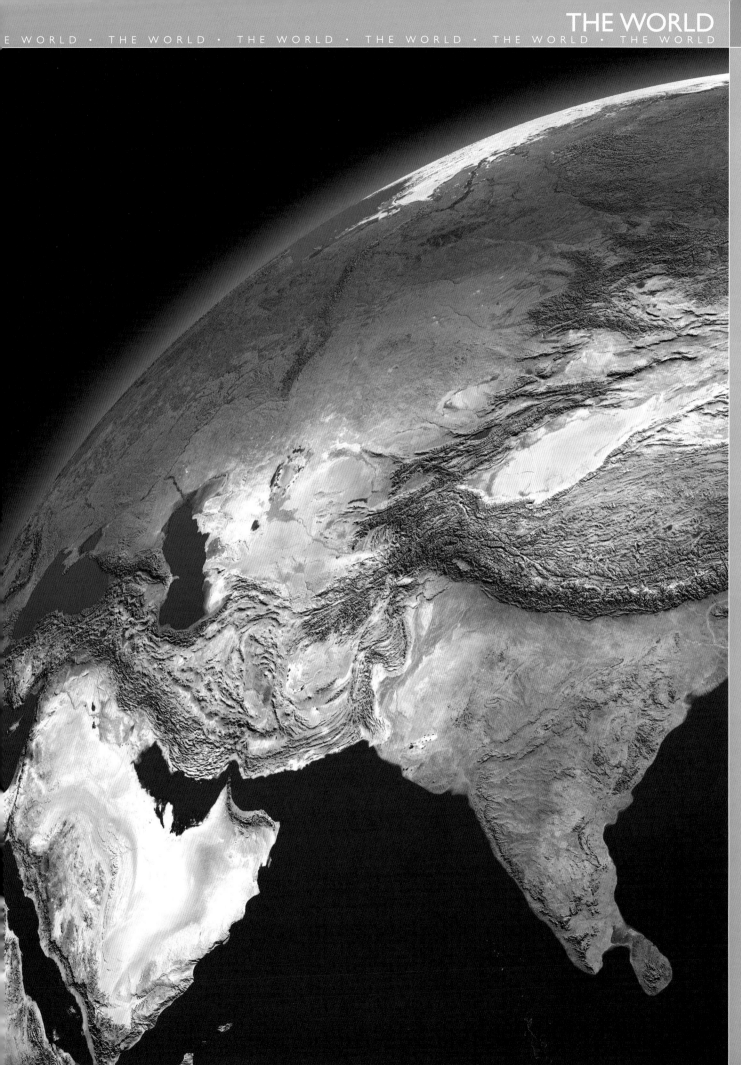

Equatorial Scale 1:95 000 000

Projection: Winkel III

West from Greenwi

Map labels (North America / Arctic):
Pt. Barrow, Beaufort Sea, North Magnetic Pole, Queen Elizabeth Is., Ellesmere I., Greenlan Sea, Jan Mayen, Norwe Sea, Arctic Circle, Denmark Str., Iceland, Faroe Is., Bering Str., Alaska, Mt. McKinley 6194 (Denali), Yukon, Gr. Bear L., Victoria I., Baffin Island, Hudson Str., C. Farewell, Bering Sea, Aleutian Is., Gulf of Alaska, Gr. Slave L., Hudson Bay, Labrador, Labrador Sea, Ireland, Great Britain, Queen Charlotte Is., Vancouver I., Peace, Nelson, L. Winnipeg, Great Lakes, St. Lawrence, Newfoundland, C. Race, Nova Scotia, B. of Biscay, Pic d'A, Coast Mts., Rocky Mountains, North America, Great Plains, Laurentian Plateau, G. of St. Lawrence, Iberian Pen., C. Mendocino, Columbia, Missouri, Mt. Elbert 4399, Arkansas, Mississippi, Ohio, C. Cod, Azores, Cascade Mts., Great Basin, Sierra Nevada, Mt. Whitney 4418, Death Valley 86, Appalachian Mts., Mt. Mitchell 2037, C. Hatteras, Bermuda, Madeira, J. Toubkal 4165, Atlas Mts., Maghre, Hawaiian Is., Mauna Kea 4205, Lower California, G. of California, Rio Grande, Florida, Gulf of Mexico, Florida Str., Sargasso Sea, ATLANTIC OCEAN, Canary Is., Tropic of Cancer, Revilla Gigedo Is., Popocatepetl 5452, Pico de Orizaba 5610, Yucatan, Cuba, Bahamas, Hispaniola, Milwaukee Deep 8605, C. Verde Is., C. Verde, Senegal, Jamaica, Greater Antilles, Puerto Rico, Lesser Antilles, Caribbean Sea, Central America, Trinidad, Isthmus of Panama, Orinoco, Llanos, Guiana Highlands, Mt. Roraima 2810, Equator, Gulf of Gui, C. Palmas, Galapagos Is., Negro, Japurá, Amazon, Selvas, C. de São Roque, Chimborazo 6267, Marañón, South America, Purus, Madeira, Tapajós, Xingu, Tocantins, São Francisco, Ascension, Marquesas Is., Plateau of Mato Grosso, St. Helena, Society Is., Tuamotu Is., Tahiti, L. Titicaca, Bolivian Plateau, Brazilian Highlands, Tropic of Capricorn, Cook Is., Tubuai Is., Pitcairn I., Easter I., C. Frio, ATLANTIC OCEAN, Chile Trench 8050, Cerro Ojos del Salado 6863, Gran Chaco, Paraguay, Paraná, Arch. de Juan Fernández, Cerro Aconcagua 6962, Pampas, R. de la Plata, Tristan da Cunha, Negro, OCEAN, Patagonia, Falkland Is., S. Georgia, South Sandwich Is., Magellan's Str., Tierra del Fuego, C. Horn, Scotia Sea, Drake Passage, South Orkney Is., South Shetland Is., Antarctic Circle, Antarctic Peninsula, Weddell Sea, Thurston I., Alexander I., Palmer Land, Caird Coast, Coats Land, Marie Byrd Land, Ellsworth Land, Vinson Massif 4897, Ronne Ice Shelf, Berkner I., Roosevelt I., Ross Sea, PACIFIC OCEAN, Polynesia, Line Is., Kiritimati

Cross-section profile:

8000m	PACIFIC OCEAN	NORTH AMERICA		ATLANTIC OCEAN			
6000m		Sierra Nevada	Rocky Mountains			Canary Basin	Pie
4000m	Hawaiian Is.	Mt. Whitney 4418	Mt. Elbert 4399	Appalachian Mts.		Mid-Atlantic Ridge	Ib
2000m	Mauna Kea 4205		Great Plains	Mt. Mitchell 2037	North American Basin	Azores	Pe
40°N	North Pacific Basin						
2000m		Mendocine Fracture Zone	Mississippi				
4000m			NORTH AMERICAN PLATE				

11 12 13 14 15 16 17 18 19

A R C T I C   O C E A N

Barents Sea · Novaya Zemlya · Kara Sea · Severnaya Zemlya · C. Chelyuskin · New Siberian Is. · Taimyr Pen. · Laptev Sea · Wrangel I. · Deshneva

N. Cape · whit... · Narodnaya 1894 · Ob · Central Siberian Plateau · Lower Tunguska · Verkhoyansk Ra. · Cherski Ra. · Kolyma Ra.

A

Gulf of Bothnia · L. Onega · L. Ladoga · West Siberian Plain · Yenisey · Angara · Stanovoy Ra. · Sea of Okhotsk · Klyuchevskaya 4750 · Bering Sea · Aleutian Is.

B

North European Plain · Central Russian Uplands · Volga · Aral Sea · Syrdarya · L. Balkhash · Baikal · Sakhalin · Kuril Is. · ▼7822 Aleutian Trench

Carpath... · Danube · Dnieper · Don · Sayan Mts. · Altai · Gobi Desert · Manchuria · Amur · Kuril Trench ▼10 542 · Hokkaido

B

Black Sea · Elbrus 5642 · −28 Caspian Sea · Aral Sea · Antoharya · Tian Shan · Tarim Basin · Hwang · Sea of Japan (East Sea) · 40

nean Sea · Anatolia · Mt. Ararat 5165 · Pamirs · Qilian Shan · China · Korea · Japan · Mt. Fuji 3776

C

Middle East · Mesopotamia · Elburz Mts. · 4604 · Kunlun Shan · Plateau of Tibet · Gongga Shan 7556 · East China Sea · Shikoku · Kyushu · Japan Trench ▼10 554 · P A C I F I C · Midway Is.

Dead Sea · Isthmus of Suez · Euphrates · Persian Gulf · K2 8611 · Karakoram · Himalaya · Mt. Everest 8850 · Si · Ryukyu Is.

Libyan Desert · Arabia · Red Sea · Thar Desert · Ganges · Deccan · Taiwan · 20

...besti · Arabian Sea · Bay of Bengal · E. Ghats · W. Ghats · India · Hainan · Wake

ca · Chad · Rub' al Khali · G. of Aden · Socotra · Andaman Is. · Indo-China · Luzon · Philippine Is. · Guam · Mariana Is. · O C E A N · M i c r o n e s i a · Marshall Is.

D

Blue Nile · Ethiopian Highlands · Somali Peninsula · C. Guardafui · C. Comorin · Ceylon · Nicobar Is. · Isthmus of Kra · South China Sea · Mindanao · Belau · Caroline Is. · Gilbert Is.

Congo · Ruwenzori 5100 · Mt. Kenya 5199 · Maldives · Malay Pen. · G. of Thailand · Sulu Sea · Kinabalu 4101 · Celebes Sea · Nauru · Phoenix Is.

Congo Basin · L. Victoria · 5895 · Kilimanjaro · Seychelles · I N D I A N · Borneo · Celebes · Molucca · Banda Sea · Bismarck Arch. · Solomon Is. · Ellice Is. · Tokelau Is.

E

Katanga · L. Tanganyika · Sumatra · Java Sea · Puncak Jaya 4884 · New Guinea · New Britain

Rift Valley · L. Malawi · Comoros · O C E A N · 7450 Java Trench · Christmas I. · Timor · Arafura Sea · Torres Str. · C. York · New Hebrides · Samoa Is.

Zambezi · Madagascar · Cocos Is. · Timor Sea · Arnhem Land · Cape York Pen. · Coral Sea · New Caledonia · Fiji Is. · 20

Kalahari Desert · Pic Boby 2658 · Réunion · Mauritius · Rodrigues · Kimberley Plateau · Tanami Desert · Great Barrier Reef · New Caledonia · Tonga Is. · 10 822 ▼

Limpopo · Orange · Mozambique Channel · Hamersley Ra. · MacDonnell Ra. · Great Dividing Ra. · Lord Howe I. · Kermadec Is. · ▼10 047

F

e of Hope · Amsterdam I. · Australia · Great Victoria Desert · L. Eyre 16 · Murray · Mt. Kosciuszko 2228 · North I. · ft m · 12 000 4000

Prince Edward Is. · Crozet Is. · Kerguelen · Nullarbor Plain · Great Australian Bight · C. Leeuwin · Darling · Bass Str. · Tasman Sea · South I. · New Zealand · 9000 3000 · 6000 2000

Heard I. · Tasmania · 3753 Aoraki Mt Cook · Chatham Is. · 3000 1000 · 1500 500 · 600 200

G

S O U T H E R N   O C E A N · Auckland Is. · Macquarie I. · 0 0

South Magnetic Pole · 600 200 · 6000 2000 · 12 000 4000

Land · Amery Ice Shelf · Enderby Land · Queen Mary Coast · Wilkes Land · Victoria Land · Balleny Is. · 15 000 5000 · 18 000 6000

H

A n t a r c t i c a · Mt. Erebus 3743 · Ross Sea · 80 · 24 000 8000

East from Greenwich · ft m

11 12 13 14 15 16 17 18 19

J R O P E · A · S · K2 8611 · I · Mt. Everest 8850 · A · Gongga Shan 7556 · P A C I F I C   O C E A N

Tyrrhenian Sea · Ægean Sea · Elbrus 5642 · Tian Shan · Yellow Sea · Sea of Japan

Balkan Peninsula · Anatolia · Caucasus · Caspian Sea · Pamirs · Tarim Basin · Qilian Shan · Korea · Honshū

Apennines · 40°N

Japan Trench · Emperor Seamount Chain

E U R A S I A N   P L A T E

B

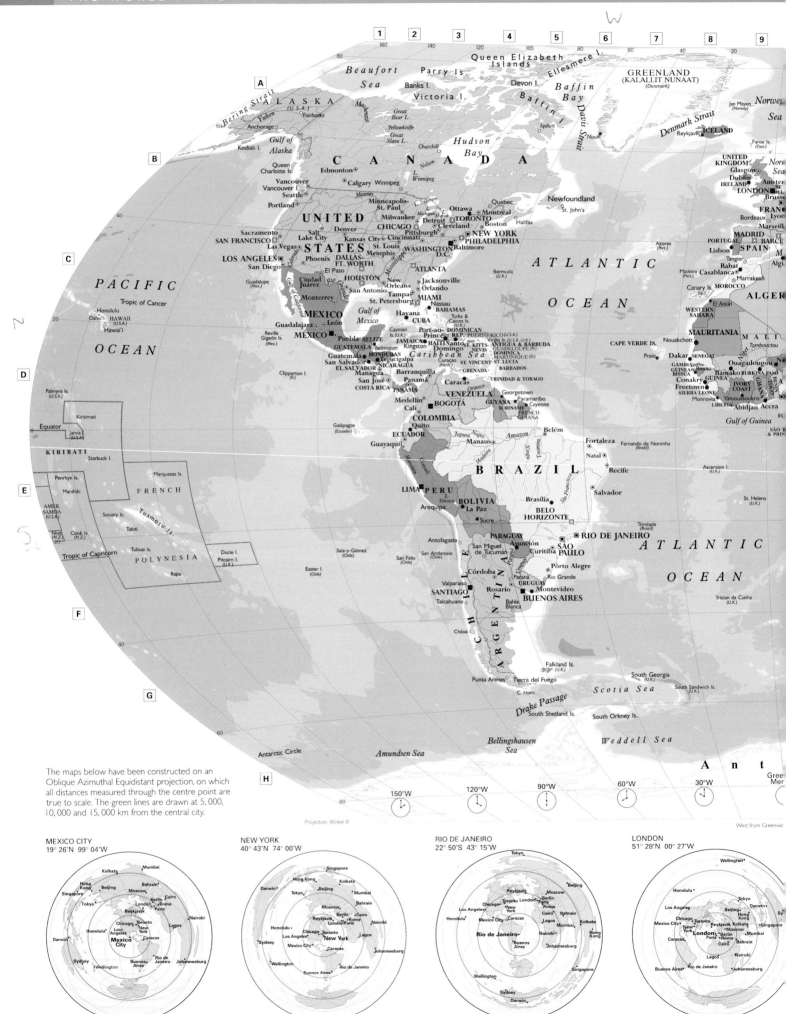

The maps below have been constructed on an Oblique Azimuthal Equidistant projection, on which all distances measured through the centre point are true to scale. The green lines are drawn at 5,000, 10,000 and 15,000 km from the central city.

Projection: Winkel III

West from Greenwic

MEXICO CITY
19° 26'N 99° 04'W

NEW YORK
40° 43'N 74° 00'W

RIO DE JANEIRO
22° 50'S 43° 15'W

LONDON
51° 28'N 00° 27'W

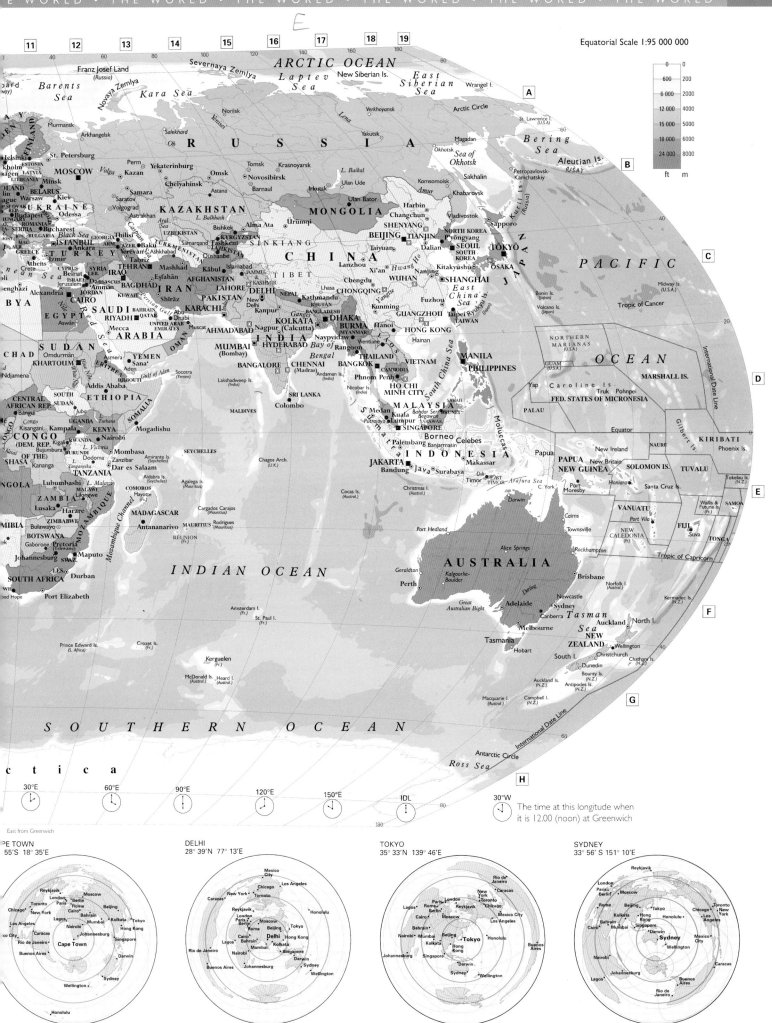

Equatorial Scale 1:95 000 000

ft	m
0	0
600	200
6 000	2000
12 000	4000
15 000	5000
18 000	6000
24 000	8000

11 12 13 14 15 16 17 18 19

A B C D E F G H

ARCTIC OCEAN
Franz Josef Land (Russia)
Severnaya Zemlya
Laptev Sea
New Siberian Is.
East Siberian Sea
Wrangel I.
Barents Sea
Novaya Zemlya
Kara Sea
Norilsk
Salekhard
Ob
Yenisey
Lena
Verkhoyansk
Arctic Circle
St. Lawrence I. (U.S.A)
Bering Sea
Magadan
Yakutsk
Okhotsk
Sea of Okhotsk
Petropavlovsk-Kamchatskiy
Aleutian Is. (U.S.A)

Murmansk
Arkhangelsk
Helsinki
St. Petersburg
RUSSIA
Tomsk
Krasnoyarsk
Komsomolsk
Sakhalin
Khabarovsk

MOSCOW
Volga
Perm
Yekaterinburg
Omsk
L. Baikal
Ulan Ude
Irkutsk
Amur
Vladivostok
Kuril Is. (Russia)

Kazan
Samara
Chelyabinsk
Novosibirsk
Barnaul
Harbin
Changchun
Sapporo
Saratov
Volgograd
Astana
KAZAKHSTAN
MONGOLIA
SHENYANG
NORTH KOREA
Pyongyang
SEOUL
SOUTH KOREA
TŌKYŌ
JAPAN

Astrakhan
Aral Sea
L. Balkhash
Ulan Bator
BEIJING
TIANJIN
Dalian
OSAKA
Kitakyūshū

Caspian Sea
UZBEKISTAN
Bishkek
Alma Ata
Ürümqi
Taiyuan
SINKIANG
CHINA
Hwang Ho
Nanjing
SHANGHAI
East China Sea

Tbilisi
GEORGIA
KYRGYZSTAN
Samarqand
Tashkent
Lanzhou
Xi'an
WUHAN
Midway Is. (U.S.A)
Bonin Is. (Japan)

Baku
ARM
AZER
TURKMENISTAN
Dushanbe
Chengdu
CHONGQING
Yangtze
Fuzhou
Volcano Is. (Japan)
Tropic of Cancer

Ankara
Yerevan
Ashkhabad
TIBET
Lhasa
Kunming
GUANGZHOU
Taipei
TAIWAN

Mashhad
TEHRĀN
Kābul
Islamabad
JAMMU & KASHMIR
NEPAL
Kathmandu
BHUTAN
HONG KONG
Hainan

ISTANBUL
TURKEY
CYPRUS
SYRIA
Eşfahān
AFGHANISTAN
New Delhi
DELHI
Kanpur
BANGLADESH
DHAKA
NORTHERN MARIANAS (U.S.A)

Athens
Izmir
Beirut
Damascus
IRAQ
IRAN
LAHORE
PAKISTAN
Ganges
KOLKATA (Calcutta)
BURMA (MYANMAR)
GUAM (U.S.A)

Crete
ISRAEL
Jerusalem
Amman
BAGHDAD
Shīrāz
KARACHI
Naypyidaw
Rangoon
PACIFIC OCEAN

LEB
JORDAN
KUWAIT
BAHRAIN
AHMADABAD
INDIA
HYDERABAD
THAILAND
LAOS
Vientiane
Hanoi
Caroline Is.

Alexandria
CAIRO
SAUDI
QATAR
Abu Dhabi
MUMBAI (Bombay)
Bay of Bengal
BANGKOK
VIETNAM
Yap
Truk
Pohnpei
FED. STATES OF MICRONESIA

LIBYA
EGYPT
RIYADH
UNITED ARAB EMIRATES
Muscat
BANGALORE
CHENNAI (Madras)
Andaman Is. (India)
CAMBODIA
Phnom Penh
PALAU
MARSHALL IS.

Aswān
Mecca
OMAN
Lakshadweep (India)
HO CHI MINH CITY
MANILA
PHILIPPINES

Red Sea
ARABIA
BAHRAIN
Nicobar Is. (India)
SRI LANKA
Colombo
MALDIVES
South China Sea
SABAH
MALAYSIA
Equator
KIRIBATI

CHAD
SUDAN
KHARTOUM
Omdurmān
YEMEN
Sana'
Aden
Gulf of Aden
Socotra (Yemen)
Medan
SARAWAK
BRUNEI
Bandar Seri Begawan
NAURU
Gilbert Is.
Phoenix Is.

Ndjamena
Asmara
ERITREA
DJIBOUTI
Kuala Lumpur
SINGAPORE
Borneo
Celebes
Moluccas
Papua
PAPUA NEW GUINEA
New Ireland
New Britain
SOLOMON IS.
TUVALU
Tokelau Is. (N.Z.)

CENTRAL AFRICAN REP.
SOUTH SUDAN
Addis Ababa
ETHIOPIA
Palembang
INDONESIA
Banjarmasin
Makassar
Honiara
Santa Cruz Is.

Bangui
UGANDA
KENYA
Nairobi
SOMALIA
Mogadishu
JAKARTA
Bandung
Java
Surabaya
Dili
EAST TIMOR
VANUATU
Port Vila
WALLIS & FUTUNA Is. (Fr.)
SAMOA

CONGO
(DEM. REP. OF THE)
Kigali
RWANDA
BURUNDI
L. Victoria
Mombasa
Zanzibar
Christmas I. (Austral.)
C. York
Port Moresby
NEW CALEDONIA
FIJI
Suva
TONGA

SHASA
Kanaga
Kisangani
Kampala
Dodoma
SEYCHELLES
Amirante Is. (Seychelles)
Cocos Is. (Austral.)
Arafura Sea
Cairns
Townsville

Kasai
Congo
TANZANIA
Dar es Salaam
Aldabra Is. (Seychelles)
Darwin
Port Hedland
Rockhampton
Norfolk I. (Austral.)

Lubumbashi
L. Malawi
Agalega Is. (Mauritius)
Cargados Carajos (Mauritius)
Alice Springs
Brisbane
Kermadec Is. (N.Z.)

ANGOLA
ZAMBIA
MALAWI
COMOROS
Mayotte (Fr.)
MADAGASCAR
AUSTRALIA
Geraldton
Kalgoorlie-Boulder
Newcastle
Tropic of Capricorn

Lusaka
Harare
MOZAMBIQUE
Antananarivo
MAURITIUS
Rodrigues (Mauritius)
RÉUNION
Perth
Sydney
Canberra
Auckland
North I.

ZIMBABWE
Bulawayo
Mozambique Channel
INDIAN OCEAN
Great Australian Bight
Adelaide
Melbourne
Tasman Sea
NEW ZEALAND
Wellington

BOTSWANA
Gaborone
Pretoria (Tshwane)
SWZ
LES
Maputo
Amsterdam I. (Fr.)
St. Paul I. (Fr.)
Tasmania
Hobart
South I.
Christchurch
Chatham Is. (N.Z.)

SOUTH AFRICA
Johannesburg
Durban
Port Elizabeth
Prince Edward Isds. (S. Africa)
Crozet Is. (Fr.)
Dunedin
Bounty Is. (N.Z.)
Antipodes Is. (N.Z.)

Good Hope
Kerguelen (Fr.)
McDonald Is. (Austral.)
Heard I. (Austral.)
Macquarie I. (Austral.)
Campbell I. (N.Z.)

SOUTHERN OCEAN
Antarctic Circle
Ross Sea
International Date Line

c t i c a

30°E 60°E 90°E 120°E 150°E IDL 30°W

The time at this longitude when it is 12.00 (noon) at Greenwich

East from Greenwich

CAPE TOWN
33° 55'S 18° 35'E

DELHI
28° 39'N 77° 13'E

TOKYO
35° 33'N 139° 46'E

SYDNEY
33° 56'S 151° 10'E

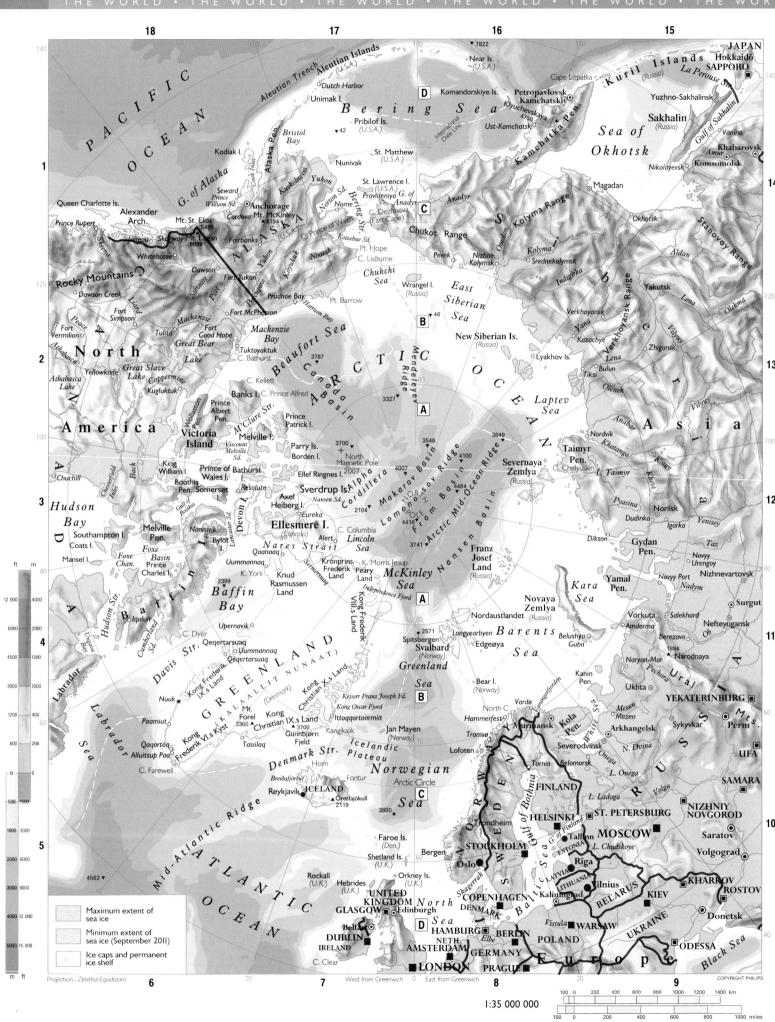

Projection : Zenithal Equidistant

West from Greenwich   East from Greenwich

COPYRIGHT PHILIPS

1:35 000 000

Maximum extent of sea ice

Minimum extent of sea ice (September 2011)

Ice caps and permanent ice shelf

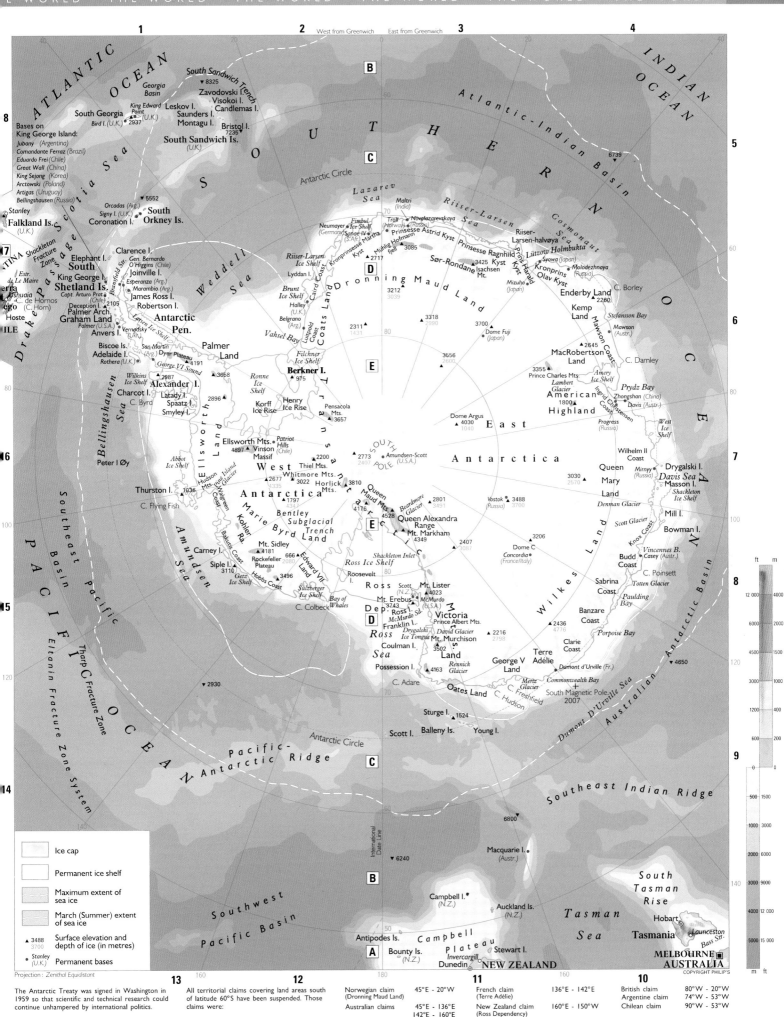

1:20 000 000

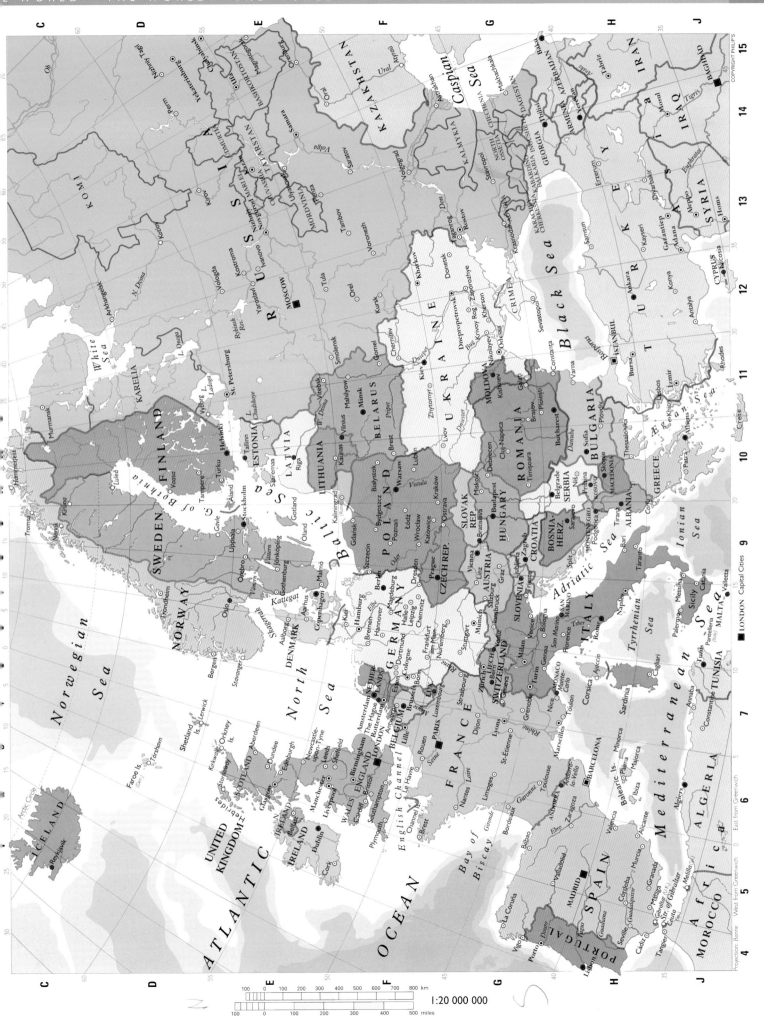

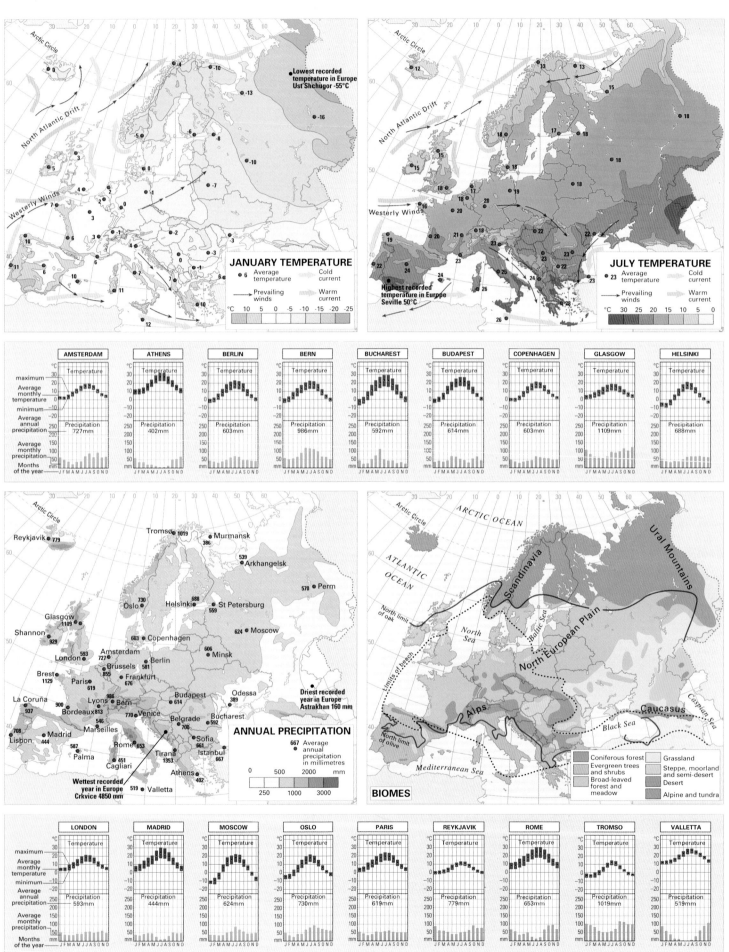

JANUARY TEMPERATURE

Lowest recorded temperature in Europe Ust'Shchugor -55°C

	Average temperature		Cold current
6	Average temperature		Cold current
	Prevailing winds		Warm current

°C 10 5 0 -5 -10 -15 -20 -25

JULY TEMPERATURE

Highest recorded temperature in Europe Seville 50°C

| 23 | Average temperature | | Cold current |
| | Prevailing winds | | Warm current |

°C 30 25 20 15 10 5 0

North Atlantic Drift
Westerly Winds

AMSTERDAM Temperature — Precipitation 727mm

ATHENS Temperature — Precipitation 402mm

BERLIN Temperature — Precipitation 603mm

BERN Temperature — Precipitation 986mm

BUCHAREST Temperature — Precipitation 592mm

BUDAPEST Temperature — Precipitation 614mm

COPENHAGEN Temperature — Precipitation 603mm

GLASGOW Temperature — Precipitation 1109mm

HELSINKI Temperature — Precipitation 688mm

maximum
Average monthly temperature
minimum
Average annual precipitation
Average monthly precipitation
Months of the year

ANNUAL PRECIPITATION

Tromsø 1019, Murmansk 386, Reykjavik 779, Arkhangelsk 539, Perm 570, Oslo 730, Helsinki 688, St Petersburg 559, Glasgow 1109, Shannon 929, Moscow 624, Copenhagen 603, Minsk 606, London 593, Amsterdam 727, Berlin 581, Brussels 855, Frankfurt 676, Brest 1129, Paris 619, Lyons 986, Bern 813, Budapest 614, Odessa 389, La Coruña 900, Bordeaux 937, Venice 770, Belgrade 700, Bucharest 592, Marseilles 546, Sofia 661, Lisbon 708, Madrid 444, Rome 653, Istanbul 667, Palma 587, Tirana 1353, Cagliari 451, Athens 402, Valletta 519

Driest recorded year in Europe Astrakhan 160 mm

Wettest recorded year in Europe Crkvice 4850 mm

| 667 | Average annual precipitation in millimetres |

0   500   2000   mm
250   1000   3000

BIOMES

ARCTIC OCEAN, ATLANTIC OCEAN, Arctic Circle, Scandinavia, Ural Mountains, North European Plain, North Sea, Baltic Sea, Alps, Caucasus, Black Sea, Caspian Sea, Mediterranean Sea

North limit of oak
Limits of beech
North limit of olive

	Coniferous forest		Grassland
	Evergreen trees and shrubs		Steppe, moorland and semi-desert
	Broad-leaved forest and meadow		Desert
			Alpine and tundra

LONDON Temperature — Precipitation 593mm

MADRID Temperature — Precipitation 444mm

MOSCOW Temperature — Precipitation 624mm

OSLO Temperature — Precipitation 730mm

PARIS Temperature — Precipitation 619mm

REYKJAVIK Temperature — Precipitation 779mm

ROME Temperature — Precipitation 653mm

TROMSO Temperature — Precipitation 1019mm

VALLETTA Temperature — Precipitation 519mm

maximum
Average monthly temperature
minimum
Average annual precipitation
Average monthly precipitation
Months of the year

Projection: Bonne

COPYRIGHT PHILIP'S

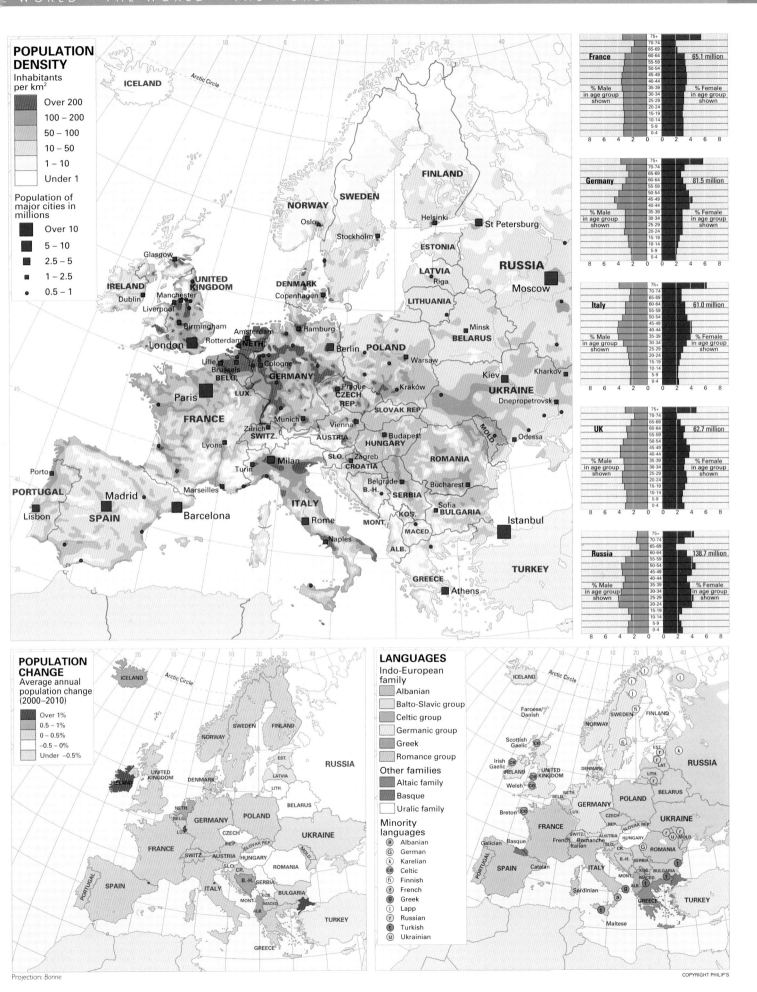

POPULATION DENSITY

Inhabitants per km²

- Over 200
- 100 – 200
- 50 – 100
- 10 – 50
- 1 – 10
- Under 1

Population of major cities in millions

- Over 10
- 5 – 10
- 2.5 – 5
- 1 – 2.5
- 0.5 – 1

France 65.1 million
% Male in age group shown / % Female in age group shown

Germany 81.5 million
% Male in age group shown / % Female in age group shown

Italy 61.0 million
% Male in age group shown / % Female in age group shown

UK 62.7 million
% Male in age group shown / % Female in age group shown

Russia 138.7 million
% Male in age group shown / % Female in age group shown

POPULATION CHANGE

Average annual population change (2000–2010)

- Over 1%
- 0.5 – 1%
- 0 – 0.5%
- –0.5 – 0%
- Under –0.5%

LANGUAGES

Indo-European family

- Albanian
- Balto-Slavic group
- Celtic group
- Germanic group
- Greek
- Romance group

Other families

- Altaic family
- Basque
- Uralic family

Minority languages

- (a) Albanian
- (G) German
- (k) Karelian
- (ce) Celtic
- (fi) Finnish
- (f) French
- (g) Greek
- (l) Lapp
- (r) Russian
- (t) Turkish
- (u) Ukrainian

Projection: Bonne

COUNTRIES OF THE EU

- Founder members (Treaty of Rome 1957)
- Admission in 1973
- Admission in 1981
- Admission in 1986
- Admission in 1990 (German unification)
- Admission in 1995
- Admission in 2004
- Admission in 2007

€ Euro-zone ○ HQ of European institutions

EU COUNTRY COMPARISONS	Population (thousands)	Annual Income (US$ per capita)
Germany	82,283	34,100
France	64,768	32,600
United Kingdom	62,348	34,800
Italy	58,091	29,900
Spain	46,506	33,600
Poland	38,464	17,900
Romania	21,959	11,500
Netherlands	16,783	39,500
Greece	10,750	31,000
Portugal	10,736	21,700
Belgium	10,423	36,800
Czech Republic	10,202	24,900
Hungary	9,992	18,800
Sweden	9,074	36,600
Austria	8,214	39,200
Bulgaria	7,149	12,500
Denmark	5,516	36,000
Slovakia	5,470	21,100
Finland	5,255	34,100
Ireland	4,623	55,600
Lithuania	3,545	15,500
Latvia	2,218	14,400
Slovenia	2,003	27,700
Estonia	1,291	18,500
Cyprus	1,103	21,000
Luxembourg	498	79,600
Malta	407	24,300
Total EU 2010 (27 countries)	**499,671**	**29,207**

REGIONS OF THE EU

Austria (States)
1 Niederösterreich
2 Oberösterreich
3 Burgenland
4 Kärnten
5 Salzburg
6 Steiermark
7 Tirol
8 Wien
9 Vorarlberg

Belgium (Regions)
1 Bruxelles
2 Vlaanderen
3 Wallonie

Bulgaria (Regions)
1 Severen tsentralen
2 Severoiztochen
3 Severozapaden
4 Yugoiztochrn
5 Yugozapaden
6 Yuzhen tsentralen

Cyprus (member state with no corresponding division)

Czech Republic (Kraje)
1 Jihovychod
2 Jihozapad
3 Moravskoslezsko
4 Praha
5 Severovychod
6 Severozapad
7 Stredni Cechy
8 Stredni Morava

Denmark (member state with no corresponding division)

Estonia (member state with no corresponding division)

Finland (Provinces)
1 Åland
2 Itä-Suomi
3 Väli-Suomi
4 Pohjois-Suomi
5 Uusimaa (Suuralu
6 Etelä-Suomi

France (Regions)
1 Alsace
2 Aquitaine
3 Auvergne
4 Bourgogne
5 Bretagne
6 Centre
7 Champagne-Ardenne
8 Corse
9 Franche-Comté
10 Ile-de-France
11 Languedoc-Roussillon
12 Limousin
13 Loire (Pays de la)
14 Lorraine
15 Midi-Pyrénées
16 Nord-Pas-de-Calais
17 Normandie (Basse
18 Normandie (Haute
19 Picardie
20 Poitou-Charentes
21 Provence-Alpes-Côte d'Azur
22 Rhône-Alpes

Germany (Länder)
1 Baden-Württemberg
2 Niedersachsen
3 Bayern
4 Berlin
5 Brandenburg
6 Bremen
7 Hamburg
8 Hessen
9 Mecklenburg-Vorpommern
10 Nordrhein-Westfalen
11 Rheinland-Pfalz
12 Saarland
13 Sachsen
14 Sachsen-Anhalt
15 Schleswig-Holstei
16 Thüringen

Greece (Regions)
1 Anatoliki Makedonia kai Thraki
2 Kriti
3 Voreio Aigaio
4 Notio Aigaio
5 Epiros
6 Attiki
7 Sterea Ellas
8 Dytiki Ellas
9 Ionioi Nisoi
10 Dytiki Makedonia
11 Kentriki Makedoni
12 Peloponnese
13 Thessaly

Hungary (Megyék)
1 Del-Alfold
2 Del-Dunantul
3 Eszak-Alfold
4 Eszak-Magyarorszag
5 Kozep-Dunantul
6 Kozep-Magyarorszag
7 Nyugat-Dunantul

Ireland (Regions)
1 Border, Midlands & Western
2 Southern & Eastern

Italy (Regions)
1 Abruzzo
2 Basilicata
3 Calábria
4 Campánia
5 Emilia-Romagna
6 Friuli-Venézia Giulia
7 Lazio
8 Liguria
9 Lombardia
10 Marche
11 Molise
12 Umbria
13 Piemonte
14 Puglia
15 Sardegna
16 Sicilia
17 Toscana
18 Trentino-Alto Adig
19 Valle d'Aosta
20 Venéto

Latvia (member state with no corresponding division)

Lithuania (member state with no corresponding division)

Luxembourg (member state with no corresponding division)

Malta (member state with no corresponding division)

Netherlands (Regions)
1 Noord-Nederland
2 Oost-Nederland
3 West-Nederland
4 Zuid-Nederland

Poland (Voivodships)
1 Dolnosląskie
2 Kujawsko-Pomorskie
3 Łódzkie
4 Lubelskie
5 Lubuskie
6 Mafopolskie
7 Mazowieckie
8 Opolskie
9 Podkarpackie
10 Podlaskie
11 Pomorskie
12 Śląskie
13 Swietokrzyskie
14 Warmińsko-Mazur
15 Wielkopolskie
16 Zachodniopomors

Portugal (Autonomous regions)
1 Alentejo
2 Algarve
3 Centro
4 Lisboa-Vale do Tejo
5 Norte

Romania (Regions)
1 Bucureşti
2 Centru
3 Nord-Est
4 Nord-Vest
5 Sud
6 Sud-Est
7 Sud-Vest
8 Vest

Slovak Republic (Kraj)
1 Bratislavsky Kraj
2 Stredne Slovensko
3 Vychodne Slovensko
4 Zapadne Slovensko

Slovenia (member state with no corresponding division)

Spain (Autonomous communities)
1 Andalucía
2 Aragon
3 Asturias
4 Islas Baleares
5 Pais Vasco
6 Islas Canarias
7 Cantabria
8 Castilla y Léon
9 Castilla-La Mancha
10 Cataluña
11 Extremadura
12 Galicia
13 Madrid
14 Murcia
15 Navarra
16 Rioja (La)
17 Valencia

Sweden (Regions)
1 Stockholm
2 Östra Mellansverige
3 Sydsverige
4 Västsverige
5 Norra Mellansverige
6 Mellersta Norrland
7 Övre Norrland
8 Småland med öarr

United Kingdom (Regions)
1 North East
2 North West
3 Yorkshire & The Humber
4 East Midlands
5 West Midlands
6 East
7 London
8 South East
9 South West
10 Wales
11 Scotland
12 Northern Ireland

Projection: Bonne

COPYRIGH

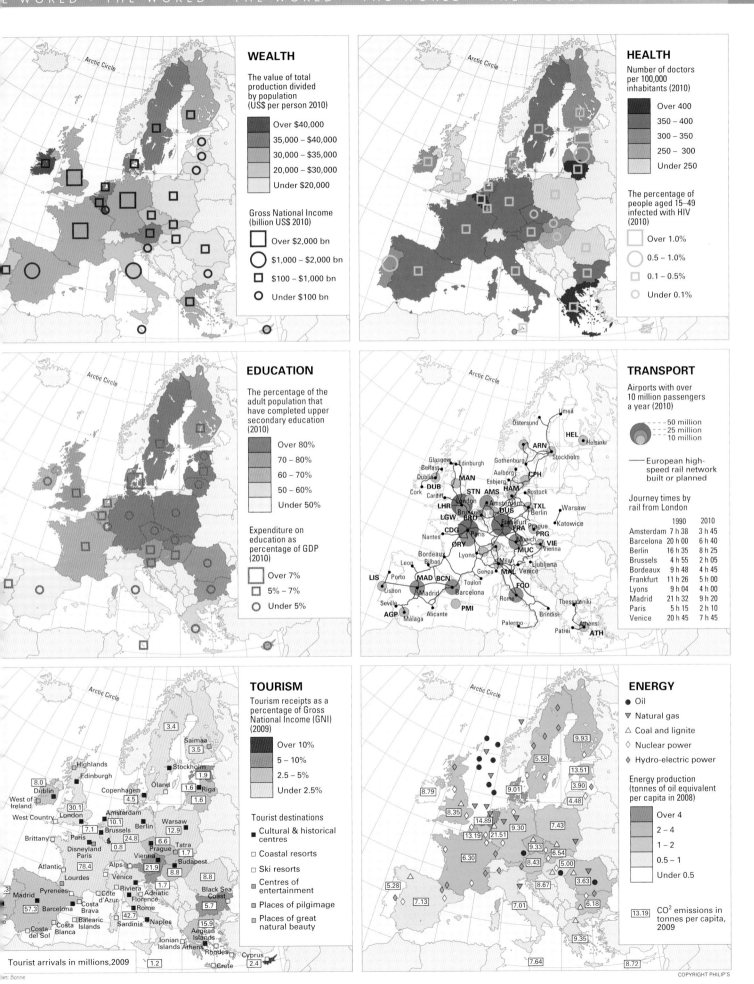

WEALTH

The value of total production divided by population (US$ per person 2010)

- Over $40,000
- 35,000 – $40,000
- 30,000 – $35,000
- 20,000 – $30,000
- Under $20,000

Gross National Income (billion US$ 2010)

- ☐ Over $2,000 bn
- ◯ $1,000 – $2,000 bn
- ☐ $100 – $1,000 bn
- ◯ Under $100 bn

HEALTH

Number of doctors per 100,000 inhabitants (2010)

- Over 400
- 350 – 400
- 300 – 350
- 250 – 300
- Under 250

The percentage of people aged 15–49 infected with HIV (2010)

- ☐ Over 1.0%
- ◯ 0.5 – 1.0%
- ☐ 0.1 – 0.5%
- ◯ Under 0.1%

EDUCATION

The percentage of the adult population that have completed upper secondary education (2010)

- Over 80%
- 70 – 80%
- 60 – 70%
- 50 – 60%
- Under 50%

Expenditure on education as percentage of GDP (2010)

- ☐ Over 7%
- ☐ 5% – 7%
- ◯ Under 5%

TRANSPORT

Airports with over 10 million passengers a year (2010)

- 50 million
- 25 million
- 10 million

— European high-speed rail network built or planned

Journey times by rail from London

	1990	2010
Amsterdam	7 h 38	3 h 45
Barcelona	20 h 00	6 h 40
Berlin	16 h 35	8 h 25
Brussels	4 h 55	2 h 05
Bordeaux	9 h 48	4 h 45
Frankfurt	11 h 26	5 h 00
Lyons	9 h 04	4 h 00
Madrid	21 h 32	9 h 20
Paris	5 h 15	2 h 10
Venice	20 h 45	7 h 45

Airport codes: Östersund, HEL, Helsinki, ARN, Stockholm, Glasgow, Edinburgh, Gothenburg, Belfast, Aalborg, CPH, Dublin, Esbjerg, MAN, STN, AMS, HAM, Rostock, Cork, Cardiff, London, Amsterdam, TXL, Berlin, Warsaw, LHR, Brussels, DUS, LGW, BRU, Frankfurt, Prague, PRG, Katowice, CDG, Paris, FRA, Nantes, Munich, VIE, Vienna, ØRY, MUC, Bordeaux, Lyons, Milan, Bilbao, Ljubljana, Leon, Genoa, MXP, Venice, LIS, MAD, BCN, Toulon, FCO, Lisbon, Madrid, Barcelona, Rome, Seville, Thessaloniki, AGP, Alicante, PMI, Brindisi, Málaga, Palermo, Patrai, Athens, ATH

TOURISM

Tourism receipts as a percentage of Gross National Income (GNI) (2009)

- Over 10%
- 5 – 10%
- 2.5 – 5%
- Under 2.5%

Tourist destinations

- ■ Cultural & historical centres
- ☐ Coastal resorts
- ☐ Ski resorts
- ▣ Centres of entertainment
- ▣ Places of pilgimage
- ▣ Places of great natural beauty

Tourist arrivals in millions, 2009

Labels: 3.4, Saimaa 3.5, Highlands, Stockholm, Edinburgh, 1.9, Öland, Copenhagen 4.5, 1.6, Riga, 8.0, Dublin, 1.6, West of Ireland, London 30.1, Amsterdam 10.1, Berlin 12.9, Warsaw, West Country, Brussels 7.1, Brittany, Paris, Disneyland Paris 78.4, 0.8, Prague 6.6, Tatra 1.7, Vienna 21.9, Budapest 8.8, Atlantic, Alps, Lourdes, Venice, Riviera 1.7, 8.8, Black Sea Coast, Pyrenees, Côte d'Azur, Adriatic, Madrid, Florence, 57.3, Barcelona, Rome, 5.7, Costa Brava, Balearic Islands, Sardinia, Naples, Costa del Sol, Costa Blanca, 15.9, Aegean Islands, Ionian Islands, Athens, Rhodes, Cyprus 2.4, Crete 1.2

м: Bonne

ENERGY

- ● Oil
- ▽ Natural gas
- △ Coal and lignite
- ◇ Nuclear power
- ◆ Hydro-electric power

Energy production (tonnes of oil equivalent per capita in 2008)

- Over 4
- 2 – 4
- 1 – 2
- 0.5 – 1
- Under 0.5

☐ 13.19 CO^2 emissions in tonnes per capita, 2009

Labels: 9.93, 5.58, 13.51, 3.90, 8.79, 9.01, 4.48, 8.35, 14.89, 9.30, 7.43, 13.19, 21.51, 9.33, 6.54, 6.30, 8.43, 5.00, 5.28, 8.67, 3.63, 7.13, 7.01, 6.18, 9.35, 7.64, 8.72

COPYRIGHT PHILIP'S

Projection: Conical with two standard parallels

1:5 000 000

East from Greenwich
COPYRIGHT PHILIP'S

West from Greenwich

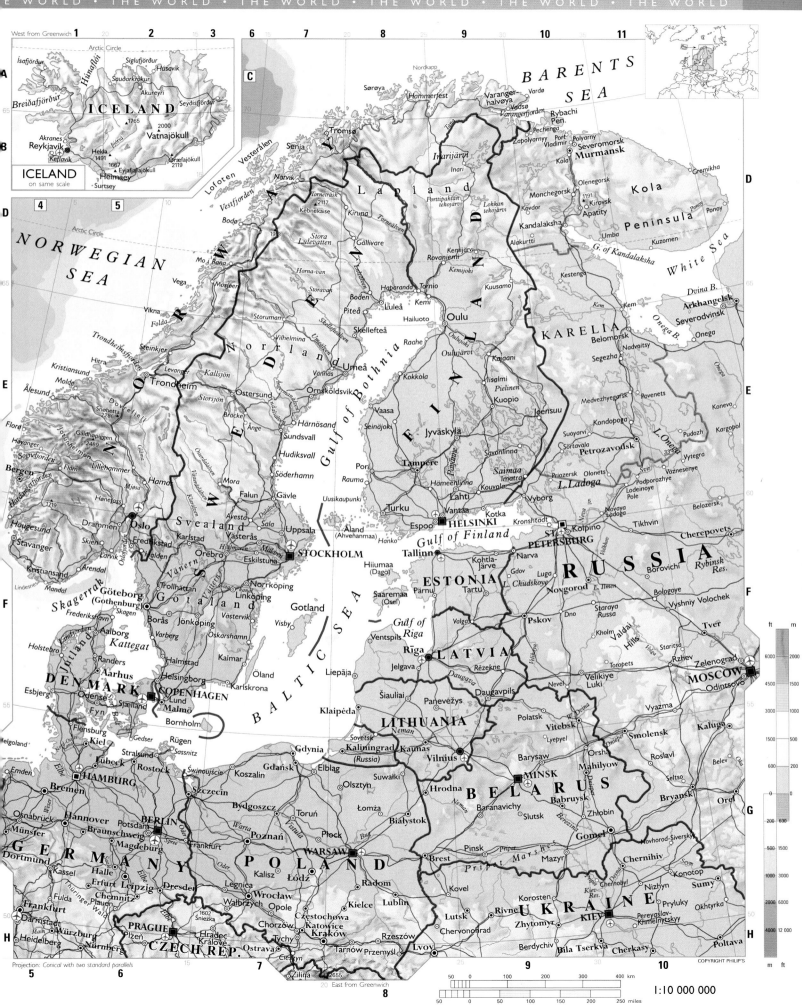

ICELAND

ICELAND on same scale

Reykjavik
Keflavik
Akranes
Breiðafjörður
Ísafjörður
Hunaflói
Siglufjörður
Sauðárkrókur
Akureyri
Húsavík
Seyðisfjörður
Hekla 1491
Þórisjökull
1765
2000 Vatnajökull
1667
Öræfajökull 2119
Eyjafjallajökull
Heimaey
Surtsey

West from Greenwich
Arctic Circle

NORWEGIAN SEA

BARENTS SEA

Nordkapp
Søroya
Hammerfest
Tromsø
Nordkyn
Vardø
Vadsø
Varanger-halvøya
Varangerfjorden
Rybachi Pen.
Pechenga
Zapolyarnyy
Vladimir
Port Vladimir
Polyarny
Severomorsk
Murmansk
Gremikha
Kola
Monchegorsk
Olenegorsk
1191 Kirovsk
Kovdor
Apatity
Kandalaksha
G. of Kandalaksha
White Sea
Umba
Ponoy
Kuzomen
Peninsula

Senja
Vesterålen
Lofoten
Narvik
Vestfjorden
Bodø
Mo i Rana
Mosjøen
Vega
Vikna
Folda
Namsos
Steinkjer
Levanger
Trondheim
Trondheimsfjorden
Hitra
Kristiansund
Molde
Ålesund
Florø
Høyanger
Sognefjorden
Bergen
Hardangerfjorden
Haugesund
Stavanger
Kristiansand
Mandal
Lindesnes
Arendal
Larvik
Skien
Drammen
OSLO
Fredrikstad
Halden
Hønefoss
Hamar
Lillehammer
Mjøsa
Flåm
Jostedalsbreen 2469
Jotunheimen
Galdhøpiggen 2469
Dovrefjell
Snøhetta 2286
1719

Lapland
Torneträsk 2117
Kebnekaise
Kiruna
Torneälven
Gällivare
Stora Lulevatten
Storavan
Horna-van
Vilhelmina
Storuman
Vännäs
Umeå
Örnsköldsvik
Härnösand
Sundsvall
Hudiksvall
Söderhamn
Ljusdal
Mora
Falun
Gävle
Avesta
Sala
Uppsala
Västerås
Eskilstuna
STOCKHOLM
Örebro
Karlstad
Norrköping
Linköping
Vänern
Vättern
Trollhättan
Göteborg (Gothenburg)
Borås
Jönköping
Varberg
Halmstad
Helsingborg
Västervik
Oskarshamn
Kalmar
Öland
Karlskrona
Visby
Gotland
Svealand
Götaland
Norrland
Skagerrak
Kattegat

Inari
Inarijärvi
Porttipahlan tekojärvi
Lokkan tekojärvi
Kemijärvi
Rovaniemi
Kemijoki
Kuusamo
Alakurtti
Kestenga
Kem
Belomorsk
Segezha
Medvezhyegorsk
Povenets
Kargopol
Konevo
Pudozh
L. Onega 330
Onega B.
Onega
Vytegra

KARELIA
FINLAND
Kajaani
Iisalmi
Oulu
Oulujärvi
Oulujoki
Raahe
Kokkola
Vaasa
Seinäjoki
Pielinen
Kuopio
Joensuu
Jyväskylä
Savonlinna
Saimaa
Imatra
Tampere
Pori
Rauma
Hämeenlinna
Lahti
Kouvola
Kotka
Vantaa
HELSINKI
Espoo
Turku
Åland (Ahvenanmaa)
Hanko
Uusikaupunki
Suoyarvi
Sortavala
Petrozavodsk
Priozersk
Olonets
Podporozhye
Lodeinoye Pole
Voznesenye
Novaya Ladoga
L. Ladoga
Vyborg
Kronstadt
Kolpino
ST. PETERSBURG
Neva
Tikhvin
Belozersk
Cherepovets

Gulf of Bothnia
Haparanda
Tornio
Kemi
Boden
Luleå
Piteå
Skellefteå
Skellefteälven
Hailuoto

BALTIC SEA

Gulf of Finland
Tallinn
Narva
Kohtla-Järve
Hiiumaa (Dago)
Saaremaa (Ösel)
Pärnu
Tartu
L. Chudskoye
Gdov
ESTONIA
Valga
Gulf of Riga
Ventspils
RIGA
Jelgava
Liepāja
LATVIA
Rēzekne
Daugava
Daugavpils
Šiauliai
Panevėžys
Klaipeda
Sovetsk
LITHUANIA
Neman
Kaliningrad (Russia)
Kaunas
VILNIUS
Gdynia
Gdańsk
Elbląg
Suwałki
Koszalin
Olsztyn
Łomża
Białystok
Hrodna
Barysaw
MINSK
BELARUS
Babruysk
Slutsk
Slonim
Baranavichy
Zhlobin

Pskov
Luga
Novgorod
L. Ilmen
Staraya Russa
Dno
RUSSIA
Borovichi
Rybinsk Res.
Vyshniy Volochek
Tver
Rzhev
Zelenograd
MOSCOW
Odintsovo
Vyazma
Kaluga
Belev
Smolensk
Orsha
Mahilyow
Vitebsk
Lyepyel
Polatsk
Velikiye Luki
Nevel
Kholm
Valday Hills
Toropets
Staritsa

GERMANY
Hamburg
Bremen
Hannover
Braunschweig
Magdeburg
Potsdam
BERLIN
Dortmund
Münster
Osnabrück
Kassel
Halle
Leipzig
Erfurt
Dresden
Chemnitz
Plauen
Frankfurt
Würzburg
Nürnberg
Heidelberg
Darmstadt
Fulda
Thüringer Wald

POLAND
Szczecin
Świnoujście
Bydgoszcz
Toruń
Poznań
Warta
Płock
WARSAW
Łódź
Kalisz
Legnica
Wrocław
Opole
Częstochowa
Katowice
Kraków
Tychy
Ostrava
Cieszyn
Žilina
Kielce
Radom
Lublin
Rzeszów
Tarnów
Przemyśl
Sniezka 1602
Walbrzych

CZECH REP.
PRAGUE
Plzeň
Hradec Králové

UKRAINE
KIEV
Zhytomyr
Lutsk
Rivne
Korosten
Chernobyl
Kiev Res.
Chernihiv
Nizhyn
Sumy
Konotop
Okhtyrka
Pryluky
Pereyaslav-Khmelnytskyy
Bila Tserkva
Cherkasy
Poltava
Lvov
Chervonohrad
Berdychiv
Kovel
Brest
Pinsk
Pripet Marshes
Mazyr
Gomel
Novhorod-Siverskyy
Bryansk
Orel
Roslavl
Seltso

Bornholm
Rügen
Sassnitz
Stralsund
Rostock
Lübeck
Kiel
Flensburg
Gedser
DENMARK
COPENHAGEN
Malmö
Lund
Helsingør
Aarhus
Odense
Aalborg
Randers
Holstebro
Esbjerg
Fredericia
Sjælland
Fyn
Jutland
Kattegat
Little Belt
Great Belt

Projection: Conical with two standard parallels

km
0 50 100 200 300 400 km
0 50 100 150 200 250 miles

Projection: Conical with two standard parallels

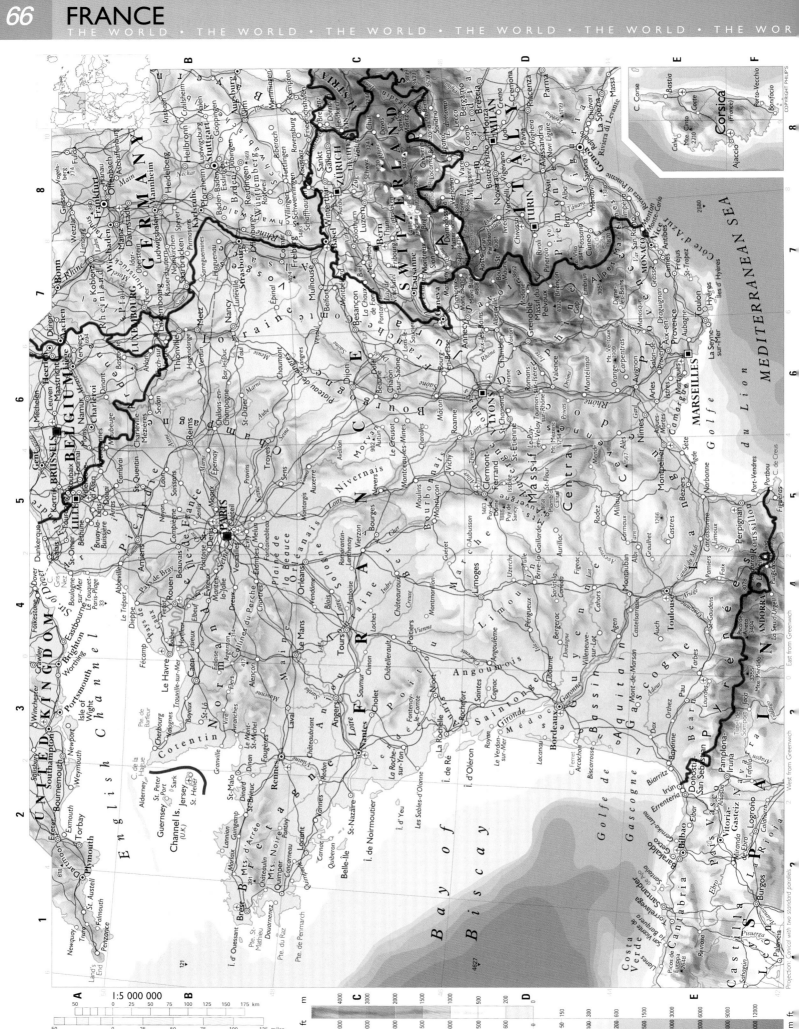

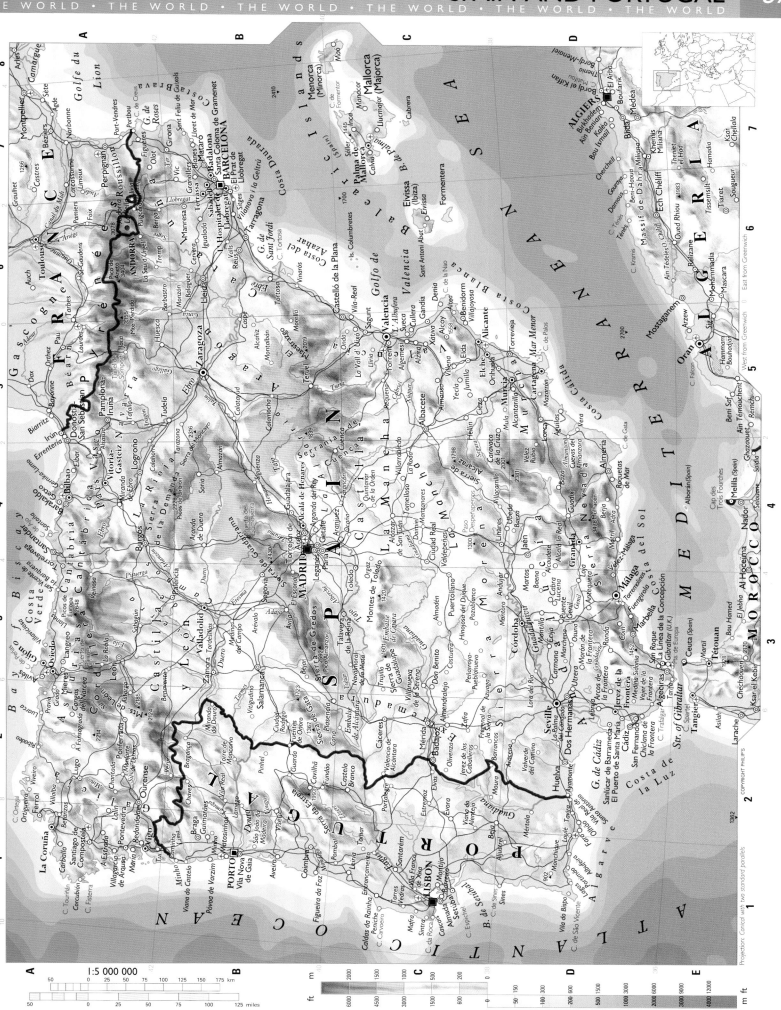

1:5 000 000

A   B   C   D   E

m   ft

ft   6000   4500   3000   1500   600   200   0   50   150   300   600   1200   1800   2400   3000   4000   m
      2000   1500   1000   500   200   0

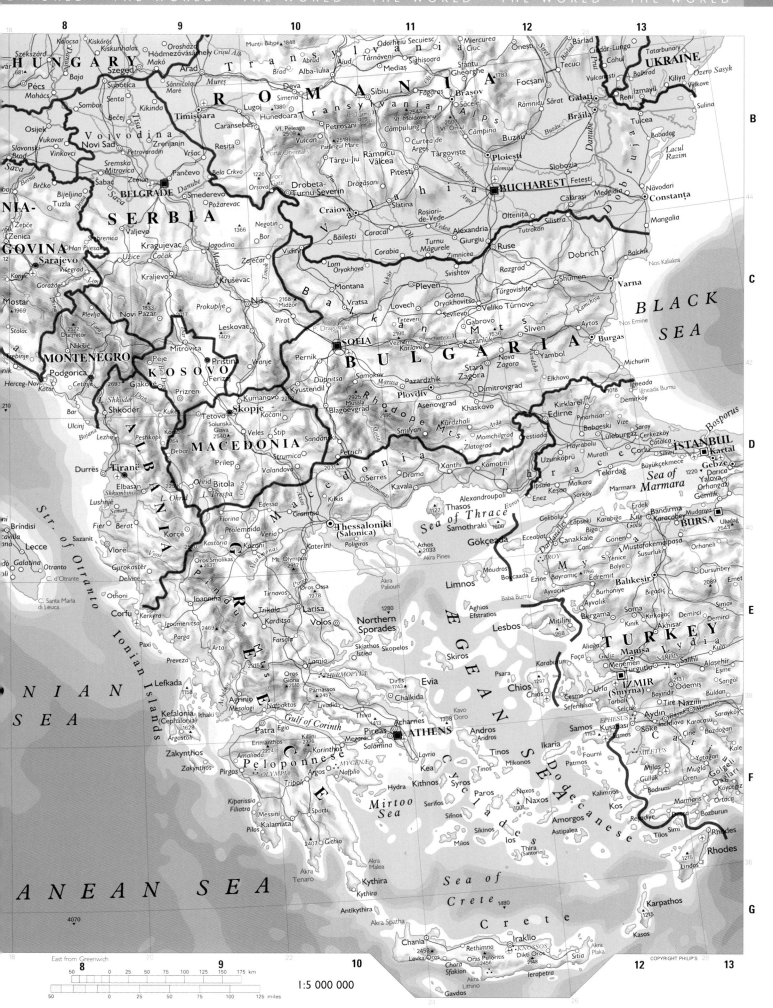

East from Greenwich

8   9   10   12   13

50   0   25   50   75   100   125   150   175 km

50   0   25   50   75   100 miles

1:5 000 000

COPYRIGHT PHILIP'S

1:10 000 000

Projection: Conical with two standard parallels

East from Greenwich

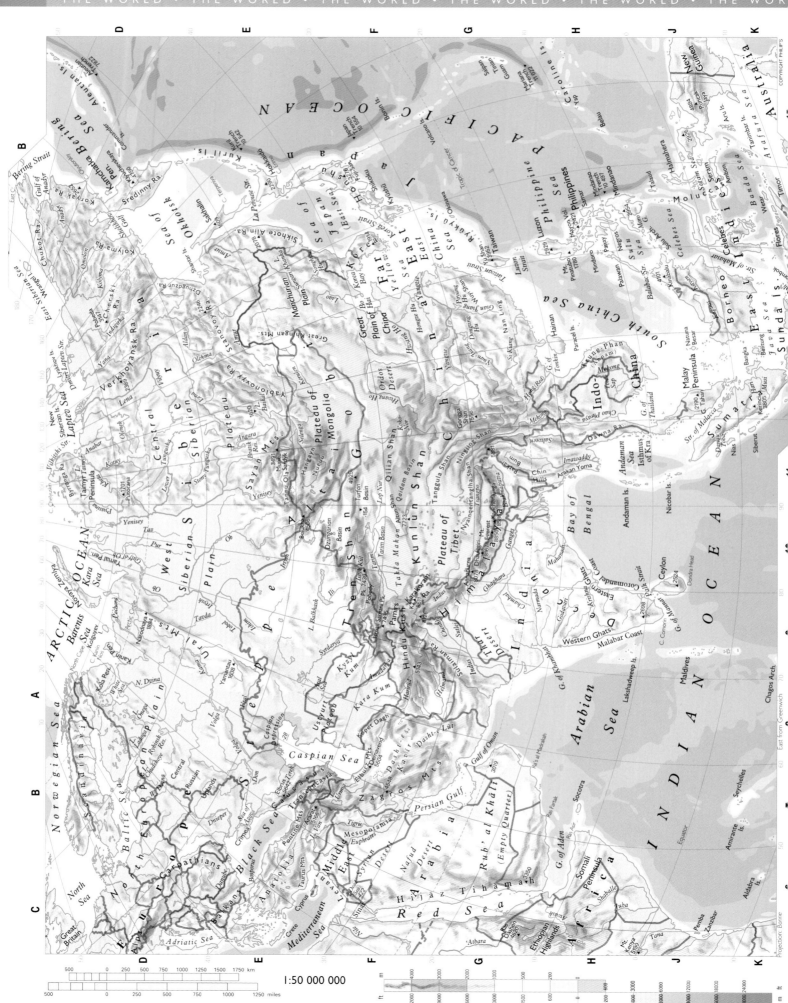

1:50 000 000

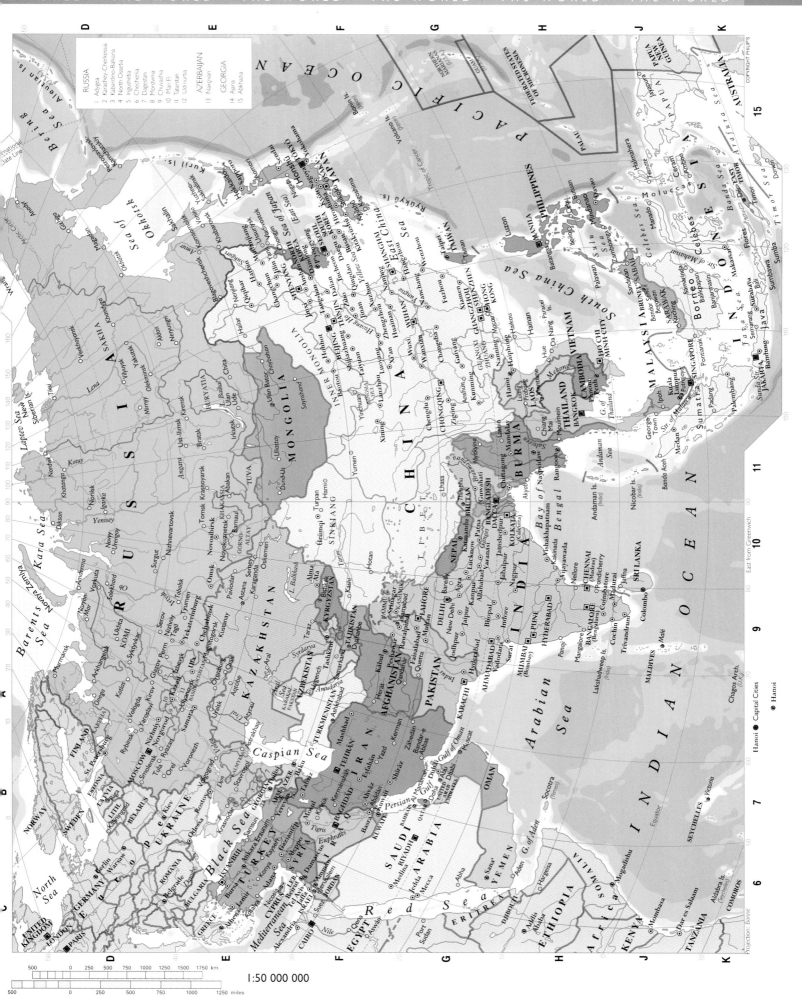

RUSSIA
1 Abgea
2 Karachey-Cherkessia
3 Kabardino-Balkara
4 North Ossetia
5 Ingushetia
6 Chechenia
7 Dagestan
8 Mordovia
9 Chuvashia
10 Mari El
11 Tatarstan
12 Udmurtia

AZERBAIJAN
13 Naxçıvan

GEORGIA
14 Ajaria
15 Abkhazia

COPYRIGHT PHILIP'S

Hanoi ● Capital Cities

● Hanoi

Projection: Zone

1:50 000 000

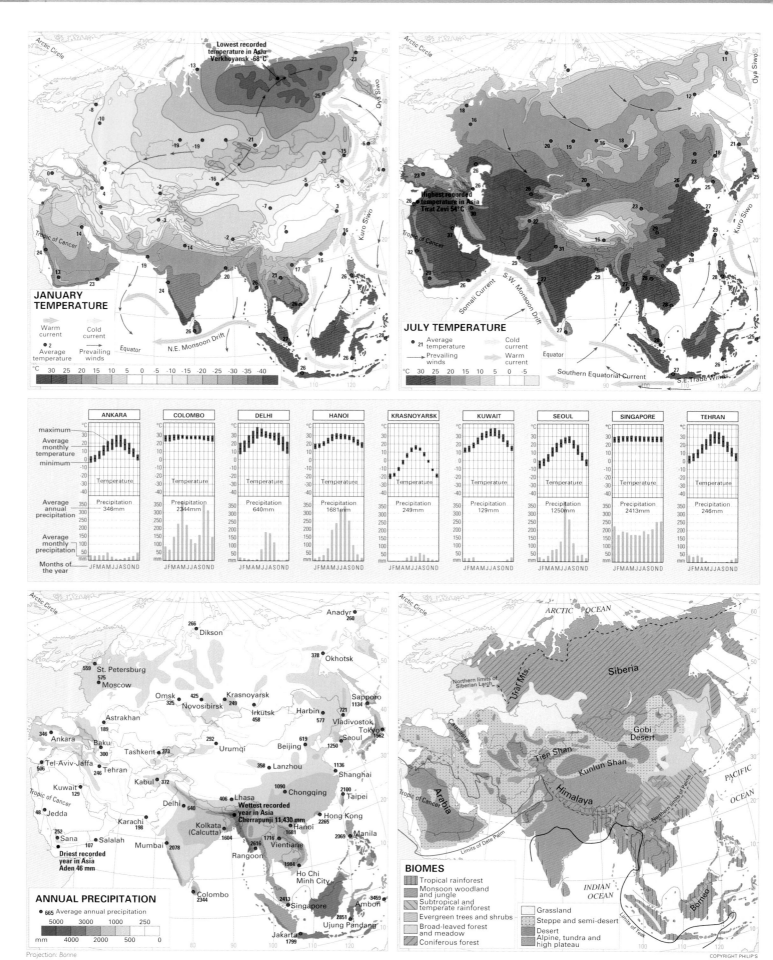

JANUARY TEMPERATURE

Lowest recorded temperature in Asia Verkhoyansk -68°C

→ Warm current
→ Cold current
• 2 Average temperature
⇒ Prevailing winds
Equator
N.E. Monsoon Drift

°C 30 25 20 15 10 5 0 -5 -10 -15 -20 -25 -30 -35 -40

JULY TEMPERATURE

Highest recorded temperature in Asia Tirat Zevi 54°C

• 21 Average temperature
→ Prevailing winds
⇒ Cold current
⇒ Warm current
Equator
Somali Current
S.W. Monsoon Drift
Southern Equatorial Current
S.E. Trade Winds

°C 30 25 20 15 10 5 0 -5

Climate graphs (average monthly temperature / precipitation):

City	Average annual precipitation
ANKARA	346mm
COLOMBO	2344mm
DELHI	640mm
HANOI	1681mm
KRASNOYARSK	249mm
KUWAIT	129mm
SEOUL	1250mm
SINGAPORE	2413mm
TEHRAN	246mm

maximum — Average monthly temperature — minimum
Average annual precipitation
Average monthly precipitation
Months of the year: J F M A M J J A S O N D

ANNUAL PRECIPITATION

Wettest recorded year in Asia Cherrapunji 11,430 mm
Driest recorded year in Asia Aden 46 mm

• 665 Average annual precipitation

mm 5000 4000 3000 2000 1000 500 250 0

Dikson 266
Anadyr 260
Okhotsk 378
St. Petersburg 559
Moscow 575
Omsk 325
Novosibirsk 425
Krasnoyarsk 249
Irkutsk 458
Sapporo 1134
Harbin 577
Vladivostok 721
Tokyo 1562
Astrakhan 189
Ankara 346
Baku 300
Tashkent 373
Urumqi 292
Beijing 619
Seoul 1250
Tel-Aviv-Jaffa 506
Tehran 246
Kabul 372
Lanzhou 358
Shanghai 1136
Kuwait 129
Delhi 640
Lhasa 406
Chongqing 1090
Taipei 2100
Jedda 48
Karachi 198
Kolkata (Calcutta) 1604
Hanoi 1681
Hong Kong 2265
Manila 2069
Sana 252
Salalah 107
Mumbai 2078
Vientiane 1716
Rangoon 2616
Ho Chi Minh City 1984
Colombo 2344
Singapore 2413
Ambon 3459
Ujung Pandang 2851
Jakarta 1799

Projection: Bonne

BIOMES

Northern limits of Siberian Larch
Siberia
Ural Mts.
Caucasus
Gobi Desert
Tien Shan
Kunlun Shan
Arabia
Himalaya
Northern limits of Palms
Limits of Date Palm
Tropic of Cancer
Limits of Teak
Borneo
ARCTIC OCEAN
PACIFIC OCEAN
INDIAN OCEAN

- Tropical rainforest
- Monsoon woodland and jungle
- Subtropical and temperate rainforest
- Evergreen trees and shrubs
- Broad-leaved forest and meadow
- Coniferous forest
- Grassland
- Steppe and semi-desert
- Desert
- Alpine, tundra and high plateau

COPYRIGHT PHILIP'S

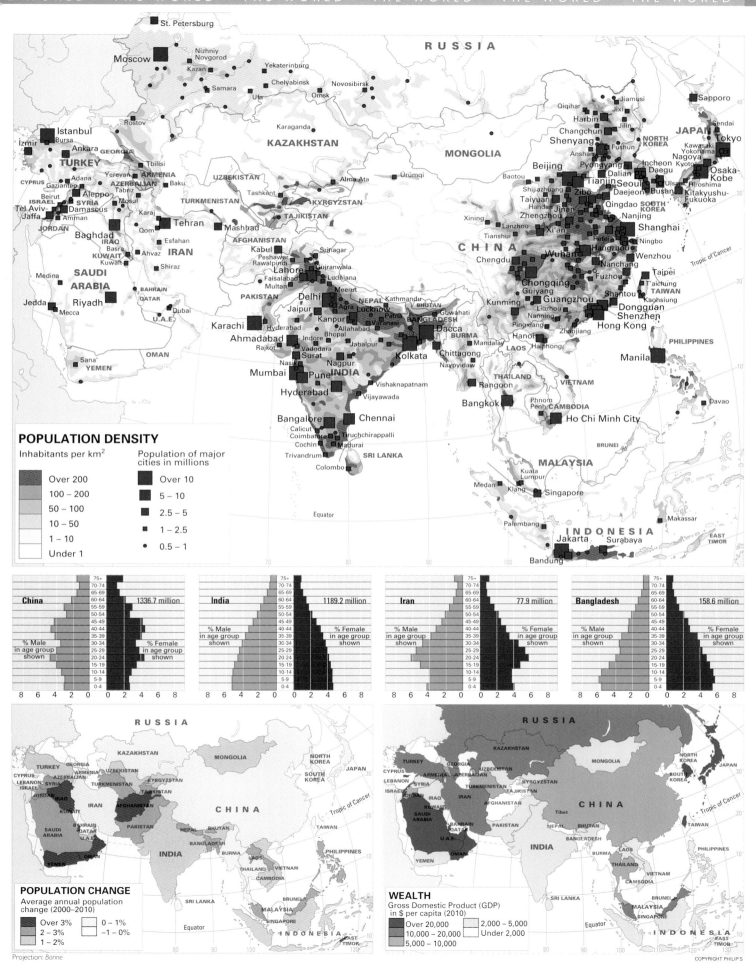

POPULATION DENSITY

Inhabitants per km²

- Over 200
- 100 – 200
- 50 – 100
- 10 – 50
- 1 – 10
- Under 1

Population of major cities in millions

- Over 10
- 5 – 10
- 2.5 – 5
- 1 – 2.5
- 0.5 – 1

China 1336.7 million

India 1189.2 million

Iran 77.9 million

Bangladesh 158.6 million

% Male in age group shown / % Female in age group shown

POPULATION CHANGE

Average annual population change (2000–2010)

- Over 3%
- 2 – 3%
- 1 – 2%
- 0 – 1%
- –1 – 0%

WEALTH

Gross Domestic Product (GDP) in $ per capita (2010)

- Over 20,000
- 10,000 – 20,000
- 5,000 – 10,000
- 2,000 – 5,000
- Under 2,000

Projection: Bonne

COPYRIGHT PHILIP'S

RUSSIA
1 Adygea
2 Karachey Cherkessia
3 Kabardino-Balkaria
4 North Ossetia
5 Ingushetia
6 Chechenia
7 Dagestan
8 Mordvinia
9 Chuvashia
10 Mari El
11 Tatarstan
12 Udmurtia
13 Khakassia
AZERBAIJAN
14 Naxçivan
GEORGIA   UKRAINE
15 Ajaria   17 Crimea
16 Abkhazia

Projection: Conical Orthomorphic with two standard parallels   East from Greenwich

OCEAN

Severnaya Zemlya

Ostrov Komsomolets
Ostrov Oktyabrskoy Revolyutsii
965
Ostrov Bolshevik

Vilkitski Strait
C. Chelyuskin

Byrranga Ra.
1146
Taimyr Peninsula
621

Laptev Sea
New Siberian Islands
Ostrova Delonga
Ostrov Faddeyevskiy
Ostrov Novaya Sibir

East Siberian Sea

Wrangel I.
1096

Chukchi Sea

C. Dezhneva (East C.)
Uelen
553

Chukot Range
1194
Providemiya
Beringovskiy

St. Lawrence I. (USA)

Bering Sea

Gulf of Anadyr
Anadyr

Koryak Range
2453

Sredinnyy Range

Kamchatka Peninsula
Petropavlovsk-Kamchatskiy
Vilyuchinsk
2359

Sea of Okhotsk

Kuril Islands

Sakhalin

RUSSIA

Verkhoyansk Range
Cherski Range
Stanovoy Range
Yablonovyy Range

Yakutsk
Lena
Vilyuy

Irkutsk
Lake Baikal
Ulan Ude

Bratsk
Krasnoyarsk
Sayan Mountains

MONGOLIA

Ulan Bator

Hangayn Nuruu
Hentiyn Nuruu

Gobi

Aerhtai Shan (Altay)

CHINA

BEIJING
BAOTOU HOHHOT ZHANGJIAKOU
TANGSHAN
DALIAN

SHENYANG
ANSHAN
FUSHUN
CHANGCHUN
JILIN
HARBIN
QIQIHAR
DAQING
JIAMUSI
JIXI
MUDANJIANG
Manchuria

NORTH KOREA
PYONGYANG
NAMPO
Hamhŭng
Wŏnsan
Ch'ŏngjin
Kimch'aek

SOUTH KOREA
SEOUL
INCHEON
DAEJEON
DAEGU
BUSAN
GWANGJU

Sea of Japan (East Sea)

JAPAN
SAPPORO
HOKKAIDŌ
Hakodate
Aomori
Akita
Niigata
Kanazawa
KYOTO
KOBE
OSAKA
HONSHŪ

Vladivostok
Khabarovsk
Komsomolsk-na-Amur
Amur

1:20 000 000

100 0 100 200 300 400 500 600 700 800 km
100 0 100 200 300 400 500 miles

COPYRIGHT PHILIP'S

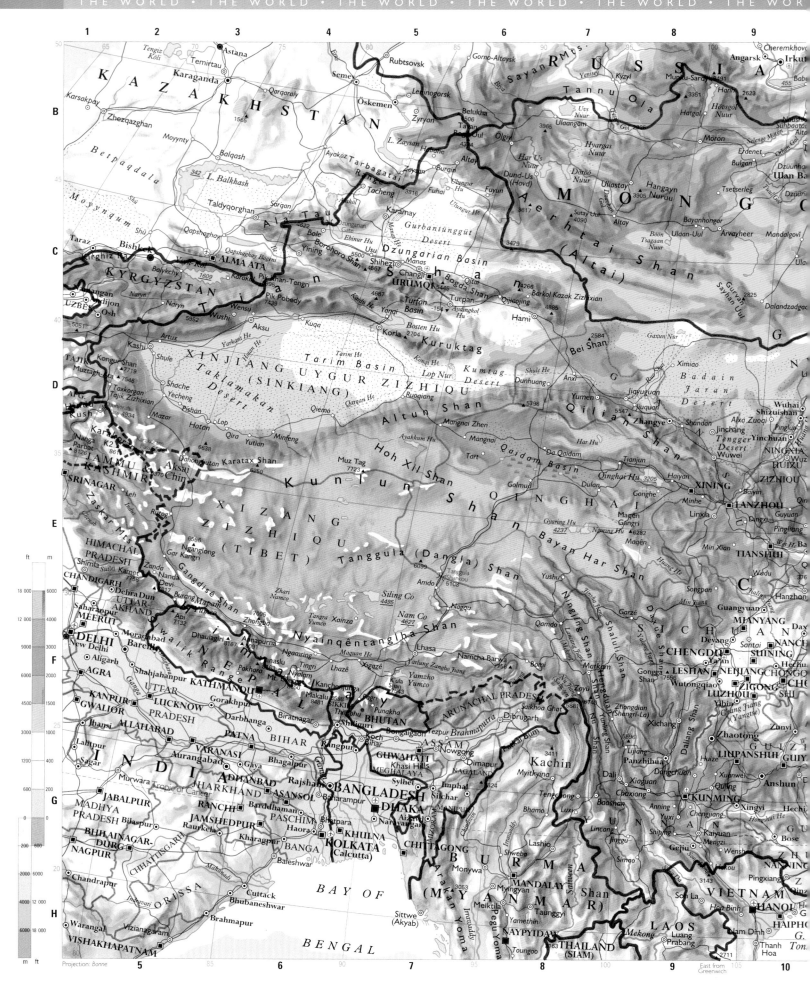

RUSSIA

Baikal

Yablonovyy
Range

Ulan Ude

Chita

Bukachacha

Nerchinsk

Sretensk

Shilka

Onon

Ergun He

Gulian

Shimanovsk

Zeya

Svobodnyy

Chegdomyn

Amur

Aleksandrovsk-
Sakhalinskiy

1609

Poronaysk

Sakhalin

Dolinsk

Komsomolsk-
na-Amur

Yuzhno-Sakhalinsk

Kholmsk

Tatar
Strait

Vanino

Ostrov
Kunashir

SEA OF

JAPAN

(EAST SEA)

HONG KONG, MACAU
AND SHENZHEN
1:770 000

EAST CHINA

SEA

PACIFIC

OCEAN

SOUTH CHINA

SEA

PHILIPPINES

1:15 000 000

COPYRIGHT PHILIP'S

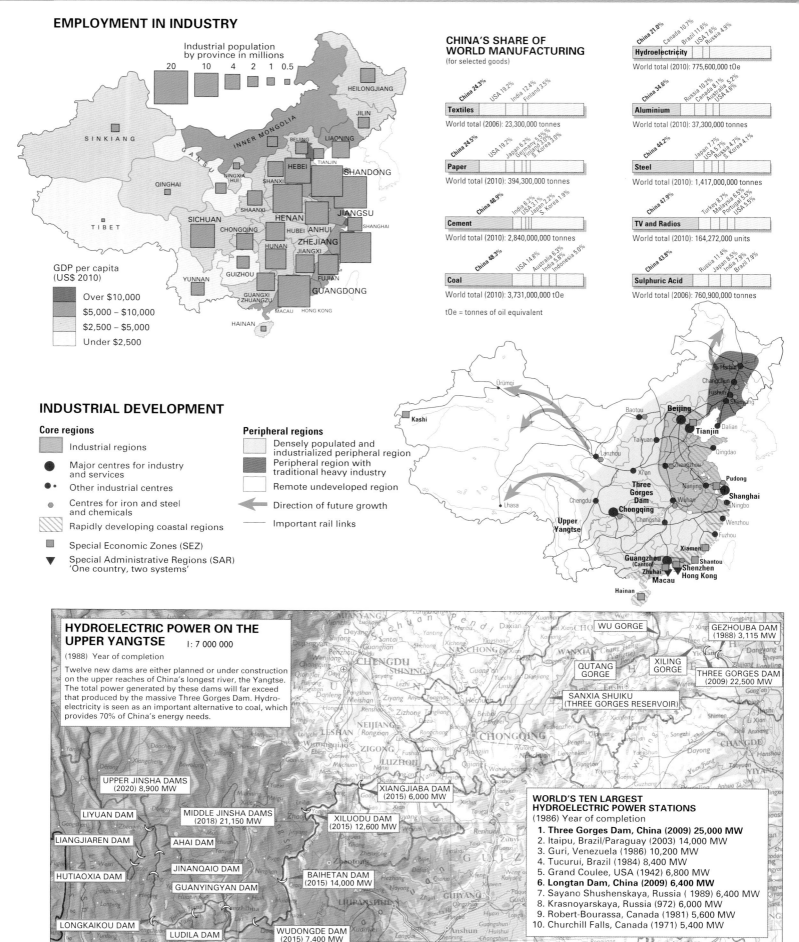

EMPLOYMENT IN INDUSTRY

Industrial population by province in millions
20 10 4 2 1 0.5

HEILONGJIANG
JILIN
SINKIANG
INNER MONGOLIA
GANSU
BEIJING
LIAONING
TIANJIN
HEBEI
NINGXIA HUI
SHANXI
SHANDONG
QINGHAI
SHAANXI
JIANGSU
TIBET
SICHUAN
HENAN
CHONGQING
HUBEI ANHUI
SHANGHAI
ZHEJIANG
HUNAN
JIANGXI
YUNNAN
GUIZHOU
FUJIAN
GUANGXI ZHUANGZU
GUANGDONG
MACAU HONG KONG
HAINAN

GDP per capita
(US$ 2010)

Over $10,000
$5,000 – $10,000
$2,500 – $5,000
Under $2,500

CHINA'S SHARE OF WORLD MANUFACTURING
(for selected goods)

Textiles — China 24.3%, USA 19.2%, India 12.4%, Finland 3.5%
World total (2006): 23,300,000 tonnes

Paper — China 24.5%, USA 19.2%, Japan 6.2%, Germany 5.5%, Finland 3.0%, S. Korea 3.0%
World total (2010): 394,300,000 tonnes

Cement — China 48.9%, India 6.2%, USA 3.1%, Japan 2.2%, S. Korea 1.9%
World total (2010): 2,840,000,000 tonnes

Coal — China 48.3%, USA 14.8%, Australia 6.3%, India 5.8%, Indonesia 5.0%
World total (2010): 3,731,000,000 tOe

Hydroelectricity — China 21.0%, Canada 10.7%, Brazil 11.6%, USA 7.6%, Russia 4.9%
World total (2010): 775,600,000 tOe

Aluminium — China 34.6%, Russia 10.2%, Canada 8.1%, Australia 5.2%, USA 4.6%
World total (2010): 37,300,000 tonnes

Steel — China 44.2%, Japan 7.7%, USA 5.5%, Russia 4.7%, S. Korea 4.1%
World total (2010): 1,417,000,000 tonnes

TV and Radios — China 47.9%, Turkey 8.7%, Malaysia 6.5%, Portugal 5.5%, USA 5.5%
World total (2010): 164,272,000 units

Sulphuric Acid — China 43.8%, Russia 11.4%, Japan 8.5%, India 7.9%, Brazil 7.9%
World total (2006): 760,900,000 tonnes

tOe = tonnes of oil equivalent

INDUSTRIAL DEVELOPMENT

Core regions

Industrial regions

● Major centres for industry and services

●• Other industrial centres

○ Centres for iron and steel and chemicals

Rapidly developing coastal regions

■ Special Economic Zones (SEZ)

▼ Special Administrative Regions (SAR) 'One country, two systems'

Peripheral regions

Densely populated and industrialized peripheral region

Peripheral region with traditional heavy industry

Remote undeveloped region

← Direction of future growth

— Important rail links

Ürümqi
Kashi
Baotou
Beijing
Tianjin
Dalian
Taiyuan
Qingdao
Lanzhou
Xi'an
Zhengzhou
Pudong
Nanjing
Shanghai
Three Gorges Dam
Wuhan
Ningbo
Chengdu
Chongqing
Changsha
Wenzhou
Upper Yangtse
Lhasa
Fuzhou
Xiamen
Guangzhou (Canton)
Shantou
Zhuhai
Shenzhen
Macau Hong Kong
Hainan
Harbin
Changchun
Fushun
Shenyang

HYDROELECTRIC POWER ON THE UPPER YANGTSE 1: 7 000 000

(1988) Year of completion

Twelve new dams are either planned or under construction on the upper reaches of China's longest river, the Yangtse. The total power generated by these dams will far exceed that produced by the massive Three Gorges Dam. Hydro-electricity is seen as an important alternative to coal, which provides 70% of China's energy needs.

WU GORGE
GEZHOUBA DAM (1988) 3,115 MW
QUTANG GORGE
XILING GORGE
THREE GORGES DAM (2009) 22,500 MW
SANXIA SHUIKU (THREE GORGES RESERVOIR)

UPPER JINSHA DAMS (2020) 8,900 MW
LIYUAN DAM
MIDDLE JINSHA DAMS (2018) 21,150 MW
LIANGJIAREN DAM
AHAI DAM
HUTIAOXIA DAM
JINANQAIO DAM
GUANYINGYAN DAM
LONGKAIKOU DAM
LUDILA DAM
XIANGJIABA DAM (2015) 6,000 MW
XILUODU DAM (2015) 12,600 MW
BAIHETAN DAM (2015) 14,000 MW
WUDONGDE DAM (2015) 7,400 MW

WORLD'S TEN LARGEST HYDROELECTRIC POWER STATIONS
(1986) Year of completion

1. **Three Gorges Dam, China (2009) 25,000 MW**
2. Itaipu, Brazil/Paraguay (2003) 14,000 MW
3. Guri, Venezuela (1986) 10,200 MW
4. Tucurui, Brazil (1984) 8,400 MW
5. Grand Coulee, USA (1942) 6,800 MW
6. **Longtan Dam, China (2009) 6,400 MW**
7. Sayano Shushenskaya, Russia (1989) 6,400 MW
8. Krasnoyarskaya, Russia (972) 6,000 MW
9. Robert-Bourassa, Canada (1981) 5,600 MW
10. Churchill Falls, Canada (1971) 5,400 MW

COPYRIGHT PHILIP'S

JAPAN EARTHQUAKE AND TSUNAMI 2011

1:15 000 000

Epicentre of earthquake
11 March 2011
(magnitude 9.0)

Observed tsunami heights

Over 8 metres

Over 4 metres

Over 2 metres

Over 1 metre

Epicentres of previous earthquakes (magnitude 7.0 or more since AD 1600)

Plate boundary

Destructive plate boundary (plates colliding)

Direction of movement

Active volcanoes

NORTH AMERICAN PLATE

6,742 dead, or missing in Iwate Prefecture

13,818 dead, or missing in Miyagi Prefecture

1,957 dead, or missing in Fukushima Prefecture

Epicentre 11 March 2011

Fukushima Daiichi Nuclear Power Station

Tokyo

EURASIAN PLATE

PACIFIC PLATE

TOTAL JAPAN
22,589 dead, or missing

PHILIPPINE PLATE

Wakkanai
Rebun-Tō
Rishiri-Tō
Esashi
Otoineppu
Ōmu
Mombetsu
Abashiri-Wan
Rausu-Dake
1661
Kunashir
Teshio
Nayoro
Yūbetsu
Abashiri
Shari
Nakashibetsu
Embetsu
Engaru
Kitami
Shari
Nemuro
Haboro
Shibetsu
Asahikawa
2290
Daisetsu-Zan
Tokachi-Dake
2077
Shibecha
Akkeshi
Rumoi
Takikawa
Bibai
HOKKAIDŌ
Honbetsu
Kushiro
Ishikari-Wan
Iwamizawa
Ebetsu
Obihiro
Poroshiri-Dake
2052
Atsuta
SAPPORO
Otaru
Kamui-Misaki
Iwanai
Shikotsu-Ko
Suttsu
Toya-Ko
Tomakomai
Hiroo
Setana
Uchiura-Wan
Muroran
Samani
Okushiri-Tō
Yakumo
Erimo-misaki
Esashi
Hakodate
Esan-Misaki
Matsumae-Hantō
Matsumae
Ohata
Shiriya-Zaki
Shiragami-Misaki
Kanagi
Mutsu-Wan
Mutsu
Shimokita-Hantō
Goshogawara
Aomori
Hakkōda-San
1585
Towada
Hachinohe
Henashi-Misaki
Hirosaki
Ōdate
Towada-Ko
Kuji
Noshiro
Oga
Iwate-San
2041
Morioka
Miyako
Oga-Hantō
Akita
Ōmagari
1914
Tōhoku
Kamaishi
Yurihonjō
Hanamaki
Kesennuma
Chōkai-San
2230
Ichinoseki
Sakata
Ōsaki
Ishinomaki
Tsuruoka
Megami
1980
Oshika-Hantō
Yamagata
SENDAI
Sendai-Wan
Chūbu
Sado
Ryōtsu
Niigata
Sōma
Minamisōma
Aikawa
Shibata
Fukushima
Honshū
Niitsu
Higashiiajima-San
2024
Kōriyama
Iwaki
Sanjo
Aizuwakamatsu
Sukagawa
Kitaibaraki
Nagaoka
Minamiaizu
Hitachi
Noto-Hantō
Suzu-Misaki
Tōkamachi
2578
Wajima
Suzu
Toyama-Wan
Utsunomiya
Mito
Nanao
Himi
Jōetsu
Nagano
Tsuchiura
Takaoka
Toyama
Maebashi
Kiryū
Oyama
Kanazawa
Hodaka-Dake
Asama
2542
Takasaki
Kantō
Komatsu
3190
Matsumoto
Kumagaya
SAITAMA
Kawaguchi
Haku-San
Takayama
Ina
Kōfu
Kawagoe
Funabashi
Fukui
2702
3063
3192
TOKYO
Chiba
Echizen
Fuji-San
Ichihara
Tsuruga
Gifu
Iida
3776
KAWASAKI
Ichinomiya
Toyota
Shizuoka
YOKOHAMA
Kyō-ga-Saki
Tottori
Toyooka
Maizuru
Ogaki
Numazu
Yokosuka
Wakasa-Wan
Ayabe
NAGOYA
Fuji
Itō
Tateyama
Chūgoku
Matsue
Yonago
Fukuchiyama
Yokkaichi
Okazaki
Toyohashi
Izu-Hantō
Ō-Shima
Izumo
Tsuyama
KYŌTO
Ōtsu
Iwata
Hamamatsu
Nojima-Zaki
Ōda
1712
Biwa-Ko
Matsusaka
Irō-Zaki
Nii-Jima
Sanchi
Himeji
Amagasaki
Higashiosaka
Suruga-Wan
Izu-Shotō
Hamada
Fuchū
Okayama
KOBE
OSAKA
Ise-Wan
Miyake-Jima
Masuda
Izumi-Sano
Daiō-Misaki
HIROSHIMA
Fukuyama
Takamatsu
Naruto
Awaji-Shima
Wakayama
Owase
Hagi
Iwakuni
Kure
Marugame
1915
Yamaguchi
Ube
Shunan
Imabari
Ikeda
Tokushima
Tanabe
Shingū
Hachijō-Jima
Shimonoseki
Matsuyama
1955
Anan
Mugi
Kushimoto
Iki
Nōgata
KITAKYŪSHŪ
Kōchi
Muroto
Shio-no-Misaki
Karatsu
FUKUOKA
Buzen
Beppu
Yawatahama
Muroto-Misaki
Imari
Saga
Kurume
Ōita
Uwajima
Tosa-Wan
Aoga-Shima
Sasebo
Isahaya
Unzen-Dake
Ōmuta
Kumamoto
Saiki
1359
1787
Shimanto
Sukumo
Nagasaki
Yatsushiro
Minamata
Nobeoka
Ashizuri-Zaki
Amakusa-Shotō
Hyūga
Ushibuka
Kyūshū
Miyazaki
Koshikijima-Rettō
Satsuma-Sendai
Miyakonojō
Nichinan
Sakurajima
1118
Kagoshima
Kanoya
Ibusuki
Makurazaki
Sata-Misaki

SEA OF JAPAN (EAST SEA)
JAPAN

SOUTH KOREA
Yeongdeok
Pohang
ULSAN
Ulleungdo (S. Korea)
Dokdo (Takeshima)
Oki-Shotō (Japan)
Korea Strait
Tsushima (Japan)

PACIFIC OCEAN
Inland Sea

8412
9076

Projection: Conical with two standard parallels

East from Greenwich

COPYRIGHT PHILIP'S

1:6 400 000

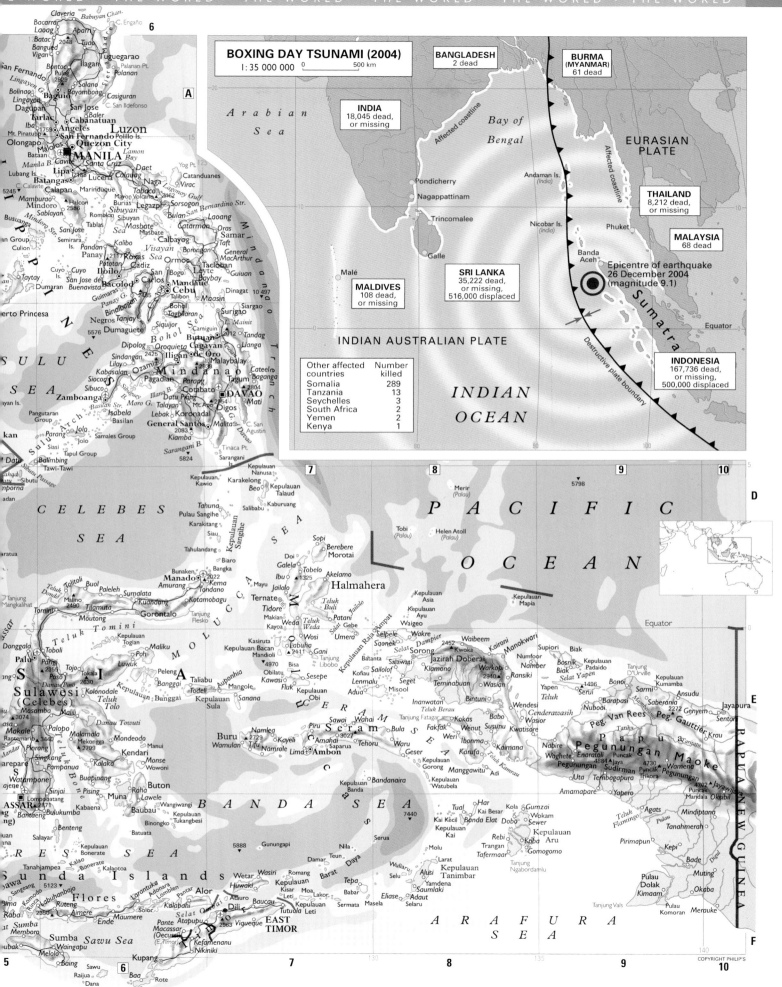

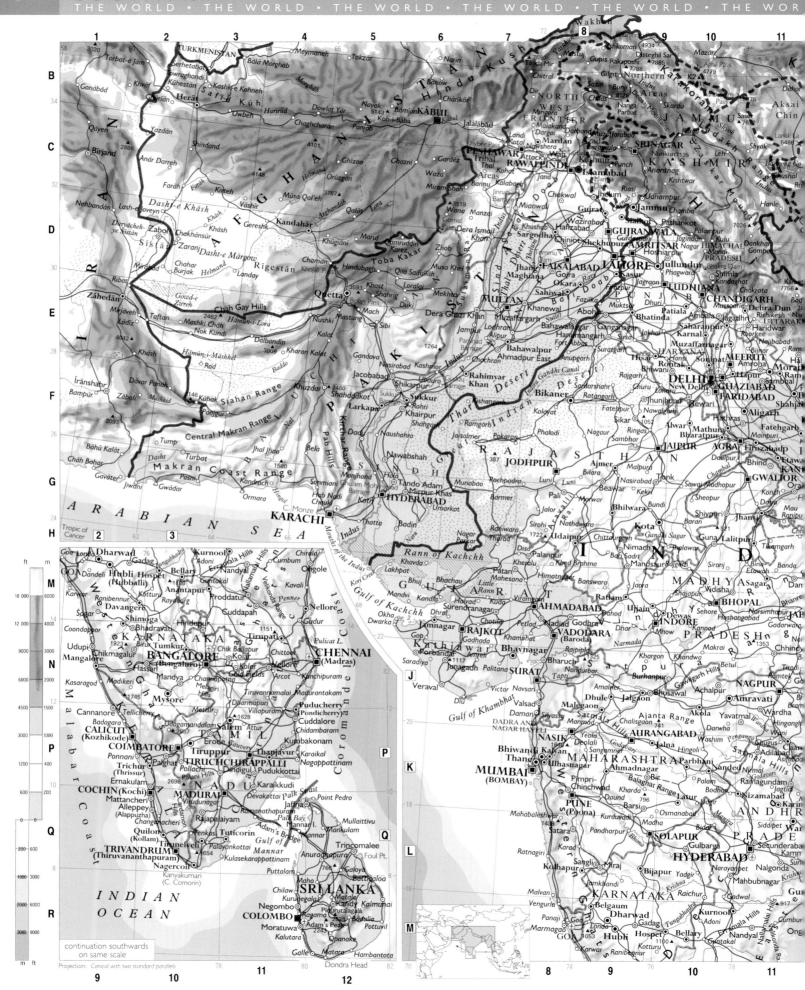

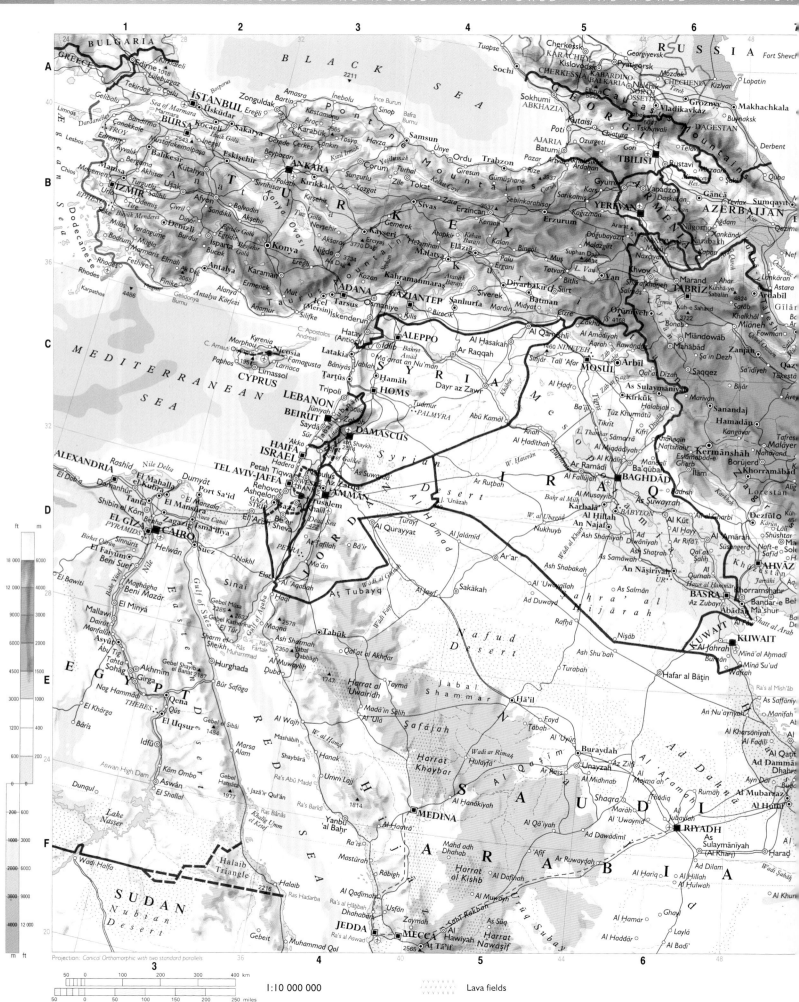

Projection: Conical Orthomorphic with two standard parallels

1:10 000 000

Lava fields

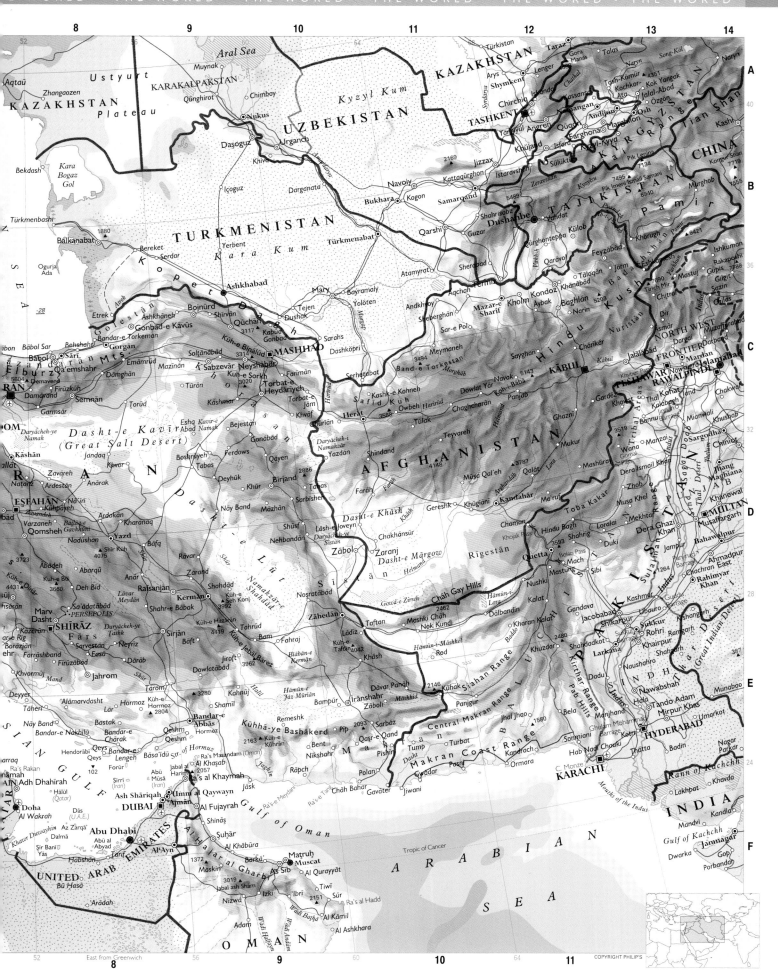

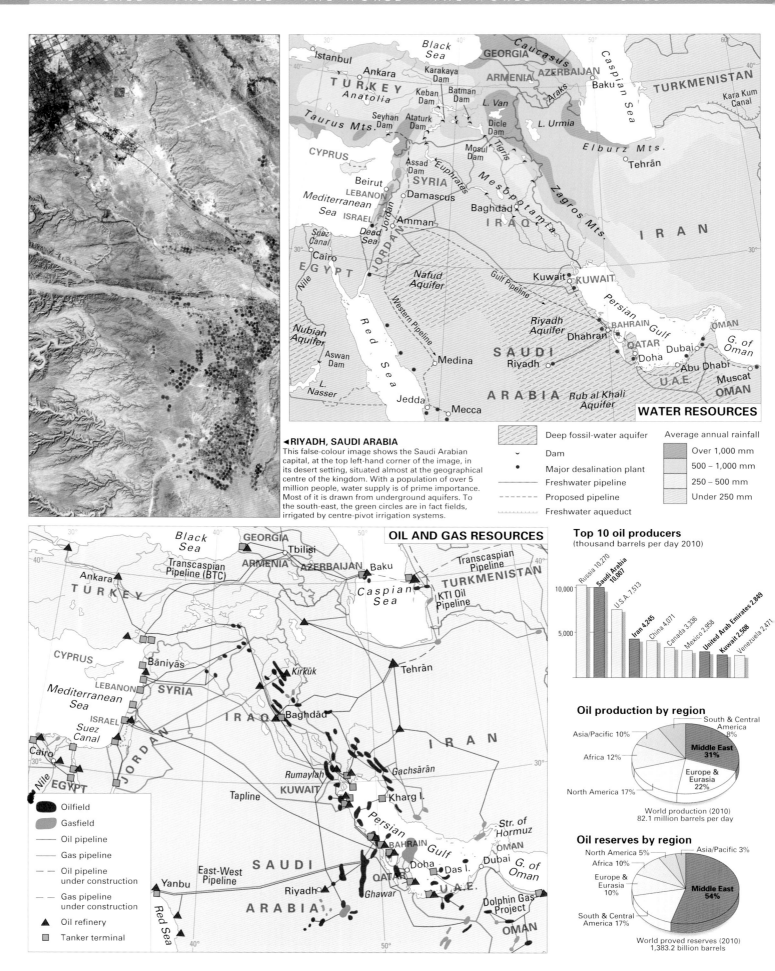

WATER RESOURCES

◄ **RIYADH, SAUDI ARABIA**
This false-colour image shows the Saudi Arabian capital, at the top left-hand corner of the image, in its desert setting, situated almost at the geographical centre of the kingdom. With a population of over 5 million people, water supply is of prime importance. Most of it is drawn from underground aquifers. To the south-east, the green circles are in fact fields, irrigated by centre-pivot irrigation systems.

Deep fossil-water aquifer
∨ Dam
• Major desalination plant
—— Freshwater pipeline
– – – Proposed pipeline
⁙⁙⁙⁙ Freshwater aqueduct

Average annual rainfall
Over 1,000 mm
500 – 1,000 mm
250 – 500 mm
Under 250 mm

OIL AND GAS RESOURCES

Oilfield
Gasfield
—— Oil pipeline
—— Gas pipeline
– – – Oil pipeline under construction
– – – Gas pipeline under construction
▲ Oil refinery
■ Tanker terminal

Top 10 oil producers
(thousand barrels per day 2010)

Russia 10,270
Saudi Arabia 10,007
U.S.A. 7,513
Iran 4,245
China 4,071
Canada 3,336
Mexico 2,958
United Arab Emirates 2,849
Kuwait 2,508
Venezuela 2,471

Oil production by region

Asia/Pacific 10%
Africa 12%
North America 17%
Europe & Eurasia 22%
Middle East 31%
South & Central America 8%

World production (2010)
82.1 million barrels per day

Oil reserves by region

North America 5%
Africa 10%
Europe & Eurasia 10%
South & Central America 17%
Middle East 54%
Asia/Pacific 3%

World proved reserves (2010)
1,383.2 billion barrels

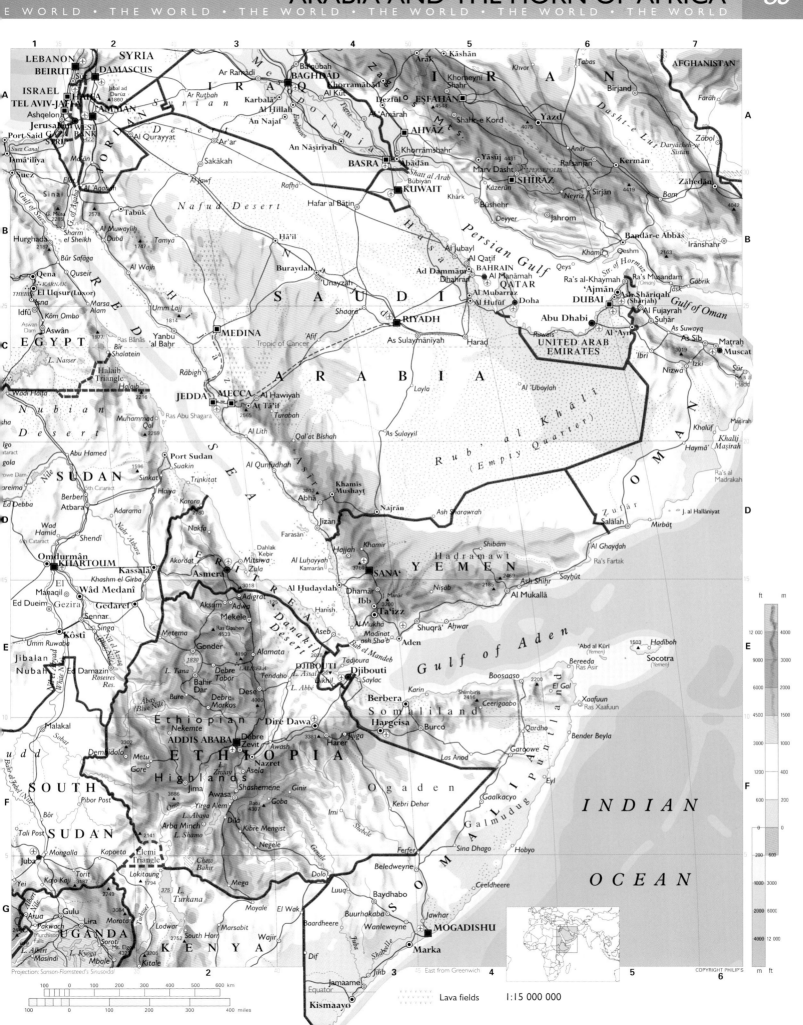

Projection: Sanson-Flamsteed's Sinusoidal

Lava fields

1:15 000 000

COPYRIGHT PHILIP'S

East from Greenwich

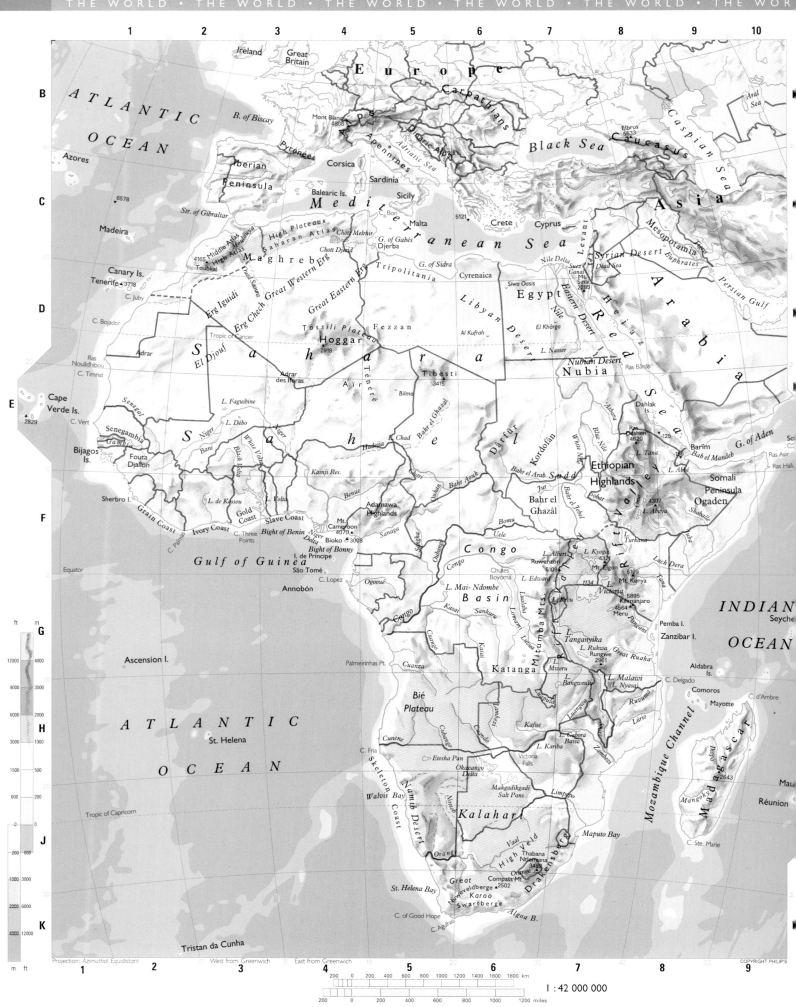

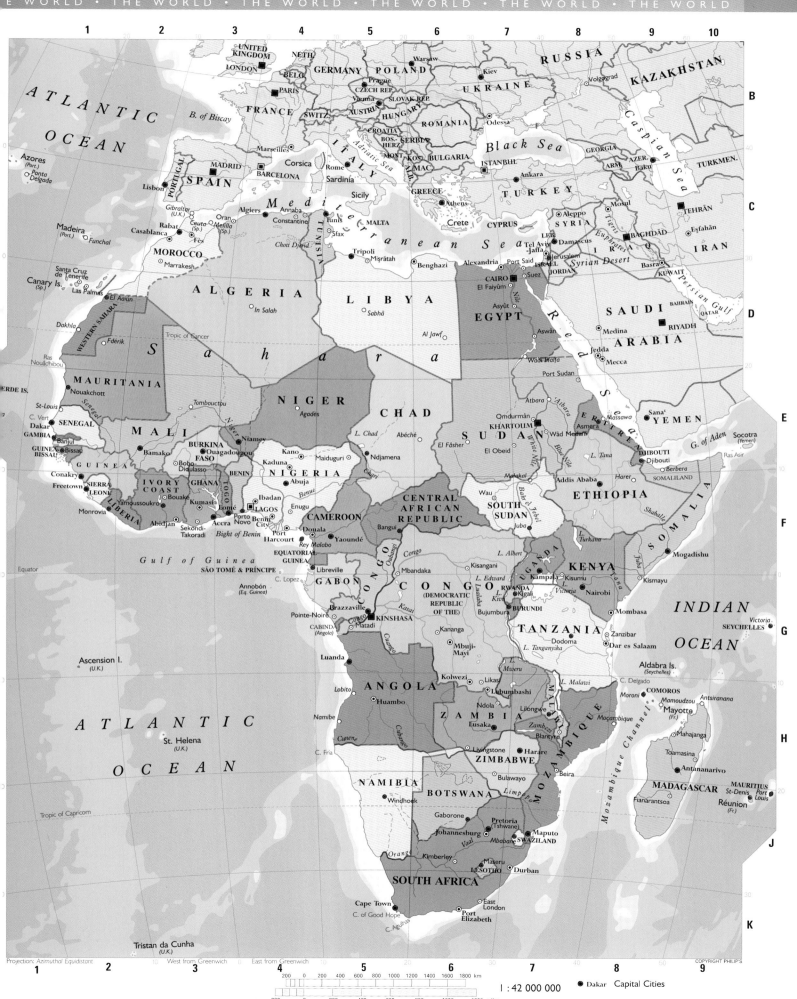

Projection: Azimuthal Equidistant

West from Greenwich   East from Greenwich

COPYRIGHT PHILIP'S

1 : 42 000 000

200   0   200 400 600 800 1000 1200 1400 1600 1800 km

200   0   200   400   600   800   1000   1200 miles

● Dakar   Capital Cities

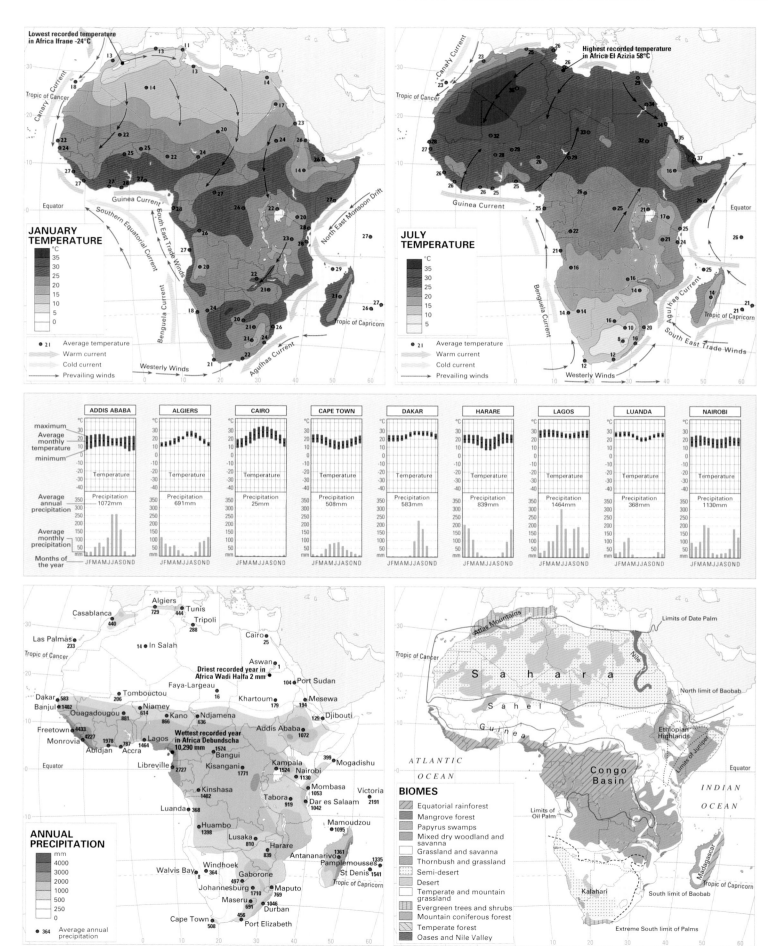

Lowest recorded temperature in Africa Ifrane -24°C

JANUARY TEMPERATURE

°C
35
30
25
20
15
10
5
0

- 21 Average temperature
- Warm current
- Cold current
- Prevailing winds

Highest recorded temperature in Africa El Azizia 58°C

JULY TEMPERATURE

°C
35
30
25
20
15
10
5

- 21 Average temperature
- Warm current
- Cold current
- Prevailing winds

ADDIS ABABA — Precipitation 1072mm
ALGIERS — Precipitation 691mm
CAIRO — Precipitation 25mm
CAPE TOWN — Precipitation 508mm
DAKAR — Precipitation 583mm
HARARE — Precipitation 839mm
LAGOS — Precipitation 1464mm
LUANDA — Precipitation 368mm
NAIROBI — Precipitation 1130mm

maximum
Average monthly temperature
minimum

Average annual precipitation

Average monthly precipitation

Months of the year

ANNUAL PRECIPITATION

mm
4000
3000
2000
1000
500
250
0

- 364 Average annual precipitation

Driest recorded year in Africa Wadi Halfa 2 mm

Wettest recorded year in Africa Debundscha 10,290 mm

BIOMES

- Equatorial rainforest
- Mangrove forest
- Papyrus swamps
- Mixed dry woodland and savanna
- Grassland and savanna
- Thornbush and grassland
- Semi-desert
- Desert
- Temperate and mountain grassland
- Evergreen trees and shrubs
- Mountain coniferous forest
- Temperate forest
- Oases and Nile Valley

Limits of Date Palm
North limit of Baobab
Limits of Juniper
Limits of Oil Palm
South limit of Baobab
Extreme South limit of Palms

Sahara
Sahel
Guinea
Atlas Mountains
Ethiopian Highlands
Congo Basin
Kalahari
Nile

ATLANTIC OCEAN
INDIAN OCEAN

Projection: Zenithal Equidistant

COPYRIGHT PHILIP'S

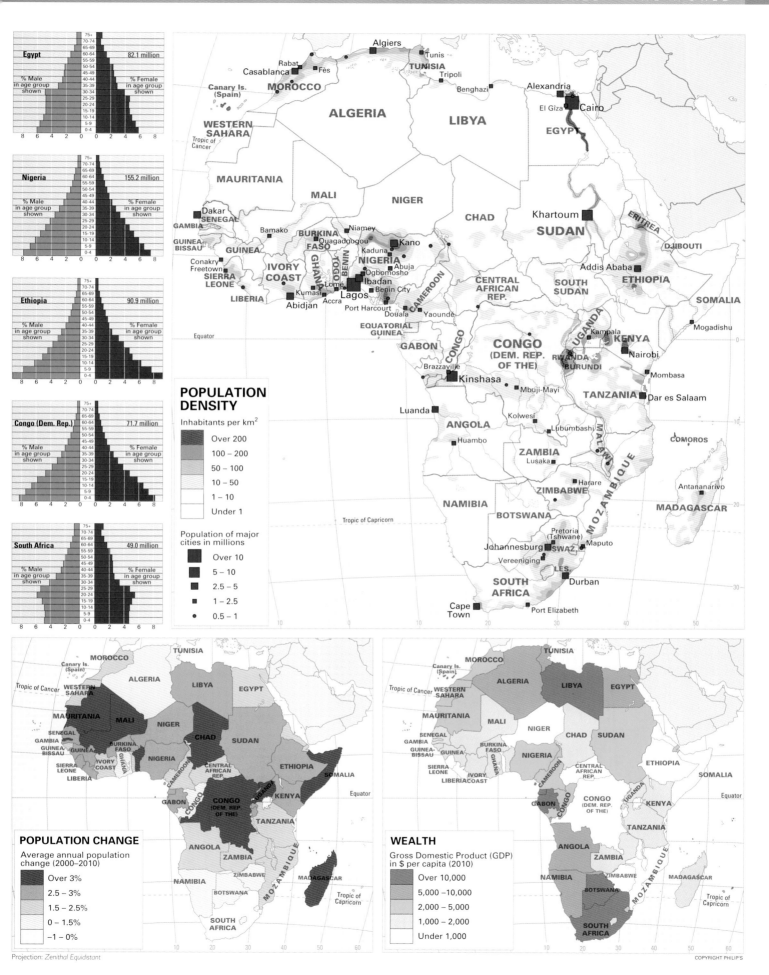

Egypt 82.1 million

75+
70-74
65-69
60-64
55-59
50-54
45-49
% Male 40-44 % Female
in age group 35-39 in age group
shown 30-34 shown
25-29
20-24
15-19
10-14
5-9
0-4
8 6 4 2 0 2 4 6 8

Nigeria 155.2 million

75+
70-74
60-64
55-59
50-54
45-49
% Male 40-44 % Female
in age group 35-39 in age group
shown 30-34 shown
25-29
20-24
15-19
10-14
5-9
0-4
8 6 4 2 0 2 4 6 8

Ethiopia 90.9 million

75+
70-74
65-69
60-64
55-59
50-54
45-49
% Male 40-44 % Female
in age group 35-39 in age group
shown 30-34 shown
25-29
20-24
15-19
10-14
5-9
0-4
8 6 4 2 0 2 4 6 8

Congo (Dem. Rep.) 71.7 million

75+
70-74
65-69
60-64
55-59
50-54
45-49
% Male 40-44 % Female
in age group 35-39 in age group
shown 30-34 shown
25-29
20-24
15-19
10-14
5-9
0-4
8 6 4 2 0 2 4 6 8

South Africa 49.0 million

75+
70-74
65-69
60-64
55-59
50-54
45-49
% Male 40-44 % Female
in age group 35-39 in age group
shown 30-34 shown
25-29
20-24
15-19
10-14
5-9
0-4
8 6 4 2 0 2 4 6 8

POPULATION DENSITY

Inhabitants per km²

- Over 200
- 100 – 200
- 50 – 100
- 10 – 50
- 1 – 10
- Under 1

Population of major cities in millions

- Over 10
- 5 – 10
- 2.5 – 5
- 1 – 2.5
- 0.5 – 1

POPULATION CHANGE

Average annual population change (2000–2010)

- Over 3%
- 2.5 – 3%
- 1.5 – 2.5%
- 0 – 1.5%
- –1 – 0%

Projection: *Zenithal Equidistant*

WEALTH

Gross Domestic Product (GDP) in $ per capita (2010)

- Over 10,000
- 5,000 – 10,000
- 2,000 – 5,000
- 1,000 – 2,000
- Under 1,000

COPYRIGHT PHILIP'S

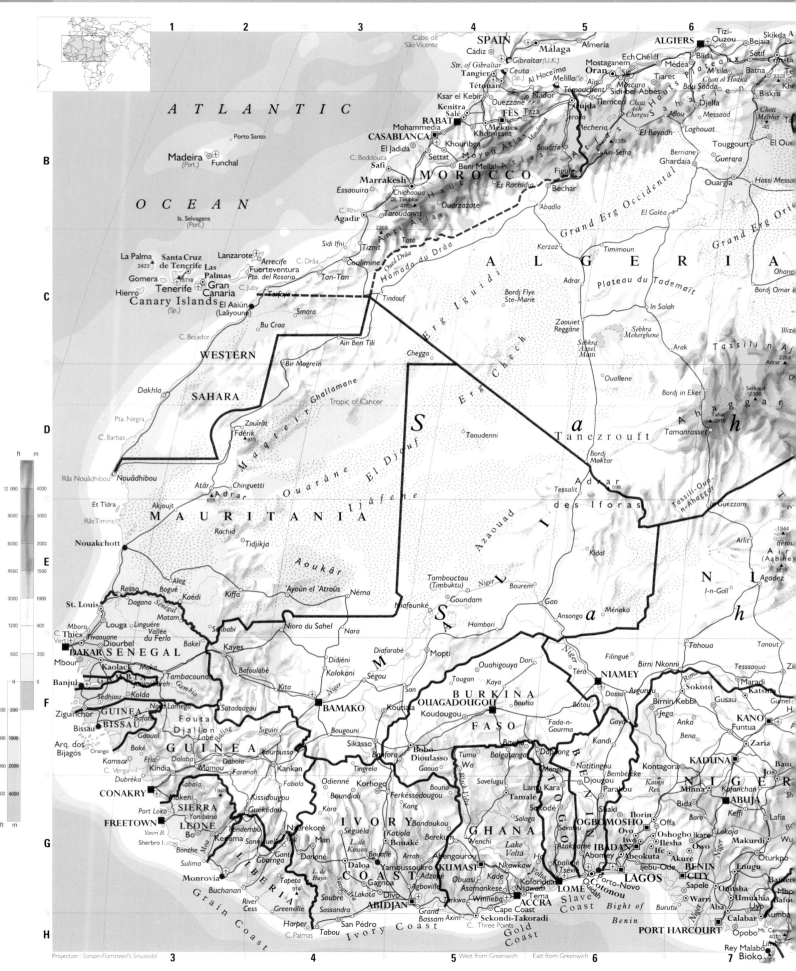

Bizerte
Ra's at Tib (C. Bon)
CARTHAGE
TUNIS
Beja
Nabeul
Sousse
Pantelleria (It.)
Msaken
Monastir
Mahdia
Lampedusa (It.)
Sfax
Golfe de Gabès
Djerba
Zarzis
Ben Gardane
enine
Zuwārah
Az Zāwiyah
Gharyān
Mizdah
Al Khums
Misrātah
TRIPOLI
Daraj
Al Hamādah al al Hamrā'
Tripolitania
mis
Idehan Awbārī
Awbārī
Sabhā
Birāk
Al Harūj al Aswad
Marzūq
W. Barju
Fezzan
Idehan Marzūq
Al Qatrūn
Waw al Kabīr

ITALY
Sicily
MALTA
Valletta (It.)

MEDITERRANEAN SEA

Peloponnese
GREECE
Cyclades
Rhodes
Rhodes
Chania
Iraklio
Crete

Pantelleria

Surt
Khalīj Surt
Ajdābiyā
BENGHAZI
Al Marj
Al Bayda
Sūsah
Darnah
Bumbah
Tubruq
Bardīyah
Salūm
Cyrenaica

CYRENE
Suluq
Al 'Uqaylah
Marādah
Awjilah
Zillah
Sarīr Calanscio
Tazerbo
Al Jaghbūb
Siwa
Qattara Depression
Western Desert
Ed Déffa
Marsa Matrūh
El Alamein

LIBYA
Libyan Desert

Rebiana Desert
Al Jawf
Al Kufrah
Hadabat el Gilf el Kebīr

EGYPT
ALEXANDRIA
El Mahalla el Kubra
Damanhûr
Dumyât
Port Said
Tantā
Zagazig
El Mansûra
Ismâ'iliya
Suez Canal
EL GIZA
PYRAMIDS
CAIRO
Helwân
Suez
El Faiyûm
Beni Suef
Maghâgha
Sinai
El Minyâ
Mallawi
Eastern Desert
Manfalût
Asyût
Tahta
Sohâg
Girga
Qena
Qasr Farâfra
El Wâhât el Dakhla
Isna
Idfû
Kôm Ombo
El Wâhât el Khârga
Aswân
Aswan High Dam
L. Nasser
Toshka Lakes
ABU SIMBEL
Wadi Halfa

TURKEY
Antalya
Alanya
Anamur
İçel
ADANA
Hatay (Antioch)
Nicosia
Latakia
CYPRUS
Limassol
Paphos
Tripoli
Hamâh
HOMS
ALEPPO
SYRIA
Euphrates
Ar Rutbah
IRAQ
BEIRUT
DAMASCUS
LEBANON
Sûr
Jabal ad Durūz
ISRAEL
TEL AVIV-JAFFA
Ashqelon
JERUSALEM
WEST BANK
AMMAN
Syrian
JORDAN
Al Qurayyat
Ma'ān
Al 'Aqaba
Sakākah
Al Jawf
Desert
Tabūk
SAUDI
ARABIA
Al Muwaylih
Al Wajh
Umm Lajj
Yanbu al Bahr
Marsa Alam
Bûr Safâga
Hurghada
Sharm el Sheikh
Gulf of Suez
Gulf of Aqaba

RED SEA
Ras Bânâs
Halaib Triangle
Halaib
Ras Hadarba
Rābigh
Ras Abu Shagara
Muhammad Qol
Port Sudan
Suakin
Trinkitat

Idehan Awbārī
LIBYA
Sahara

Sarīr Tibasti
Aozou Strip
Tibesti
Zouar
Emi Koussi
Bardai
Pic Toussidé
Tarso Emissi
Aozou
Bikkū Bittī
Toummo
Madama
Chirfa
Bilma
Grand Erg de Bilma
Borkou
Faya-Largeau
Ounianga Kébir
Dépression du Mourdi
Fada
Ennedi
Zagaoua
Erg du Djourab
Dépression du Bodélé
CHAD
Ziguéy
Biltine
Mao
Bahr el Ghazal
Moussoro
Ati
Abéché
Oum Hadjer
L. Chad
Massakory
Ndjamena
Bokoro
Mongo
Goz Beïda
Massenya
Bitkine
Abou-Deïa
Am Timan
Bousso
Bongor
Guider
Chari
Maroua
Garoua
Lagone
Laï
Sarh
Moundou
Doba
Goré
Batangafo
Kaga Bandoro
CENTRAL AFRICAN REPUBLIC
Bossangoa
Bozoum
Bouar
Baboua
Carnot
Bossembélé
Berbérati
Bangui
Bimbo
Mbaïki

Nubian Desert
Selima
Kosha
3rd Cataract
Delgo
Abu Hamed
Dongola
Kareima
Merowe Dam
5th Cataract
Ed Debba
Berber
Atbara
Ed Dâmer
Adarama
Khartûm Bahri
KHARTOUM
Omdurmân
El Manaqil
Wâd Medanî
Gedaref
Kassalâ
Khashm el Girba
ERITREA
Nakfa
Akordat
Karora
Metema
Gonder
Bahir Dar
L. Tana
Blue Nile
Abay
Debre Markos
ETHIOPIA
Nekemte
Metu
Gore
Jima
L. Abaya
Arba Minch
L. Shamo

SUDAN
Malha
Kutum
El Fâsher
Umm Keddada
Sodiri
El Wuz
Ed Dueim
El Obeid
Er Rahad
Kôsti
Sennar
Darfûr
Al Junaynah
Zalingei
Nyala
J. Marrah
En Nahud
Umm Ruwaba
Abu Zabad
Kordofân
Jibalan Nubah
Kâdugli
Ed Da'ein
Roseires Res.
Ed Damazin
Singa

SOUTH SUDAN
Abyei
Bahr el Arab
Râga
Aweil
Wau
Gogrial
Tonj
Rumbek
Bôr
Pibor Post
Bahr el Ghazal
Bahr el Jebel (Nile)
Sudd
Sobat
Malakal
Jur
Bahr el Ghazal
Mt. Toussoro
Sa'id Bundas
Massif des Bongos
Ndélé
Birao
Harazé
Yalinga
Bria
Ippy
Bakouma
Bambari
Sibut
Obo
Bangassou
Ouarra
Amadi
Tali Post
Toinya
Equatoria
Kapoeta
Elemi Triangle
Juba
Yambio
Yei
Kajo Kaji
Torit
Lokitaung
L. Turkana
CONGO (DEM. REP. OF THE)

Lava fields

100 0 100 200 300 400 500 600 km
100 0 100 200 300 400 miles

1:15 000 000

COPYRIGHT PHILIPS

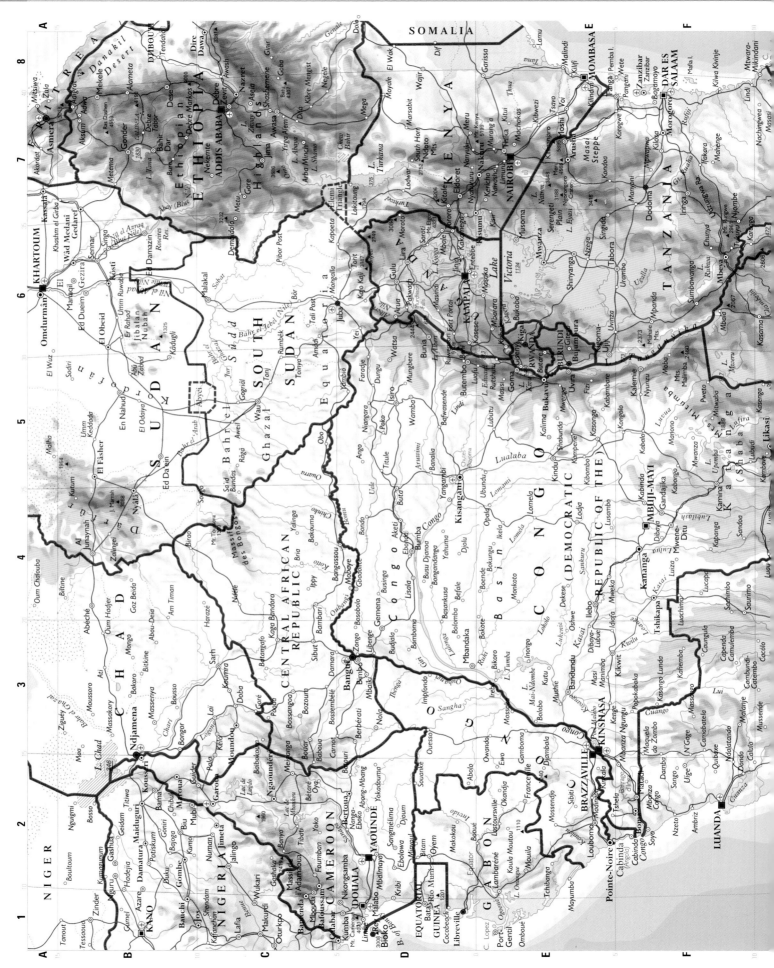

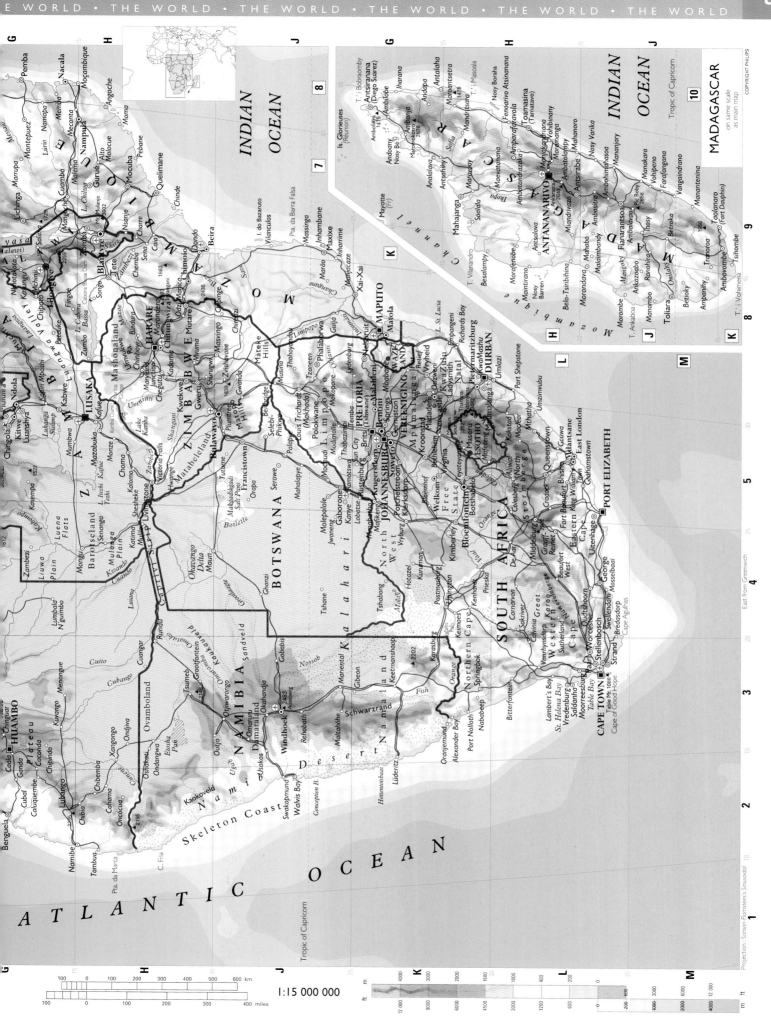

MADAGASCAR
on same scale
as main map

INDIAN OCEAN

INDIAN OCEAN

ATLANTIC OCEAN

SOUTH AFRICA

BOTSWANA

NAMIBIA

ZIMBABWE

ZAMBIA

MOZAMBIQUE

1:15 000 000

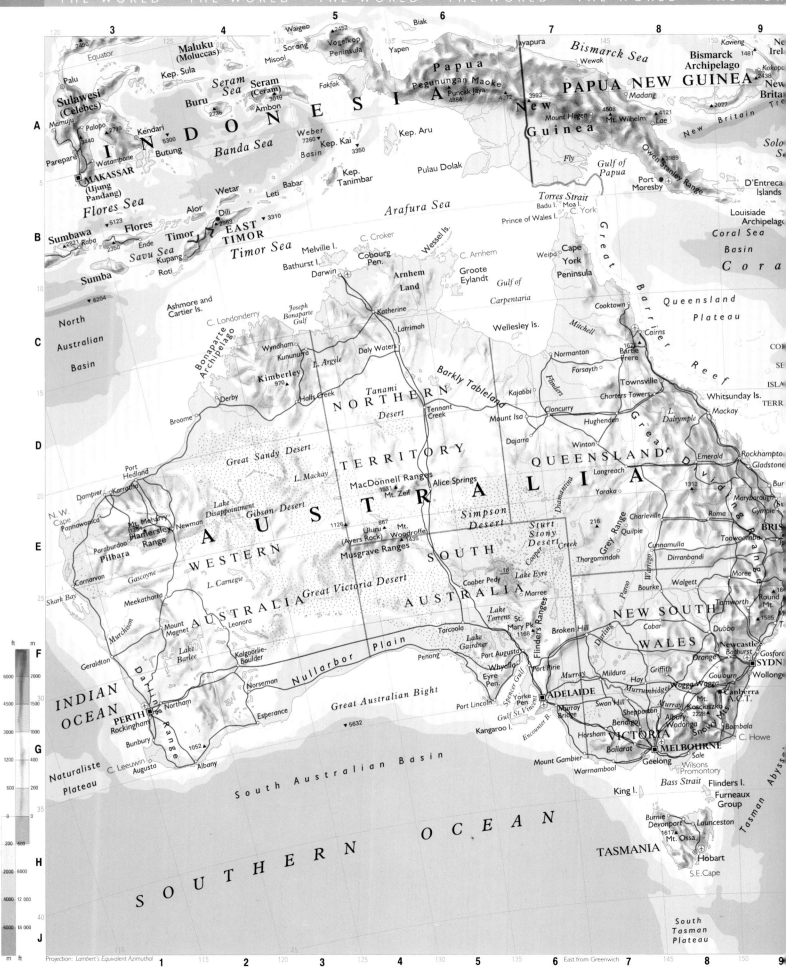

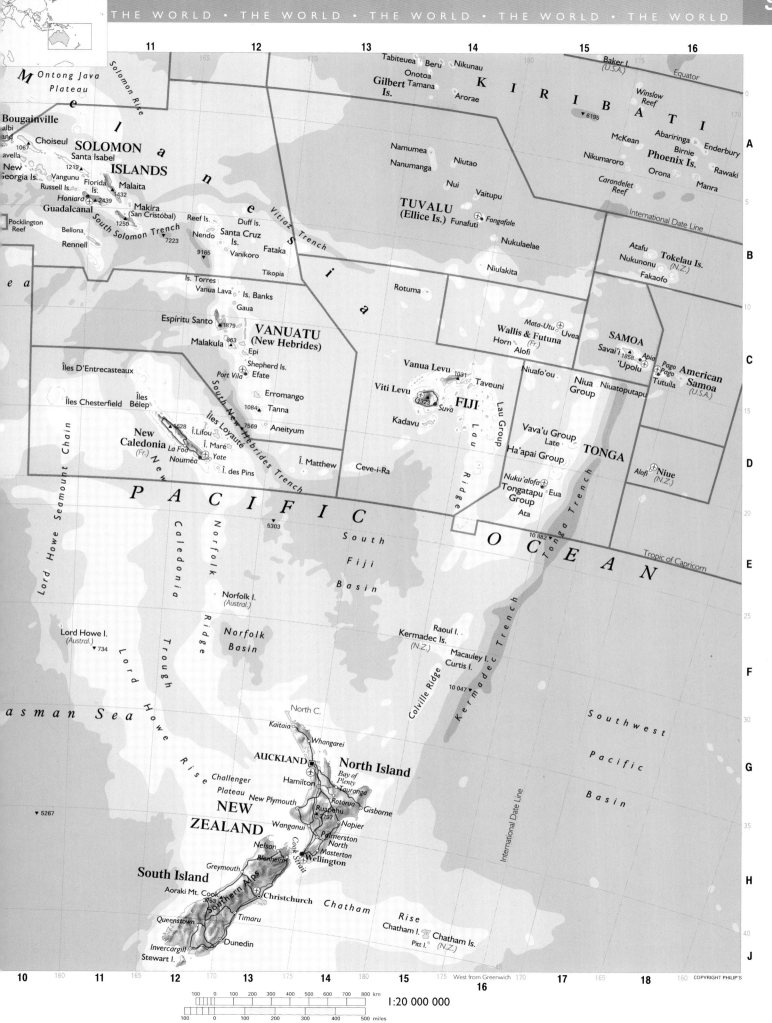

11 12 13 14 15 16

Ontong Java Plateau

Solomon Rise

Bougainville
albi
and
Choiseul
SOLOMON
Santa Isabel
1067
avella
New
Georgia Is.
1219
Vangunu
Russell Is.
Florida
Is.
Malaita
1432
ISLANDS
Honiara
2439
Guadalcanal
Makira
(San Cristóbal)
Bellona
1250
Pocklington
Reef
Rennell

Tabiteuea
Beru
Nikunau
Onotoa
Tamana
Nikumaro
Gilbert
Arorae
Is.
K
I
R
I
B
A
T
I

Baker I.
(U.S.A.)
Equator

6195
Winslow
Reef

Namumea
Niutao
McKean
Abariringa
Birnie
Enderbury
Nanumanga
Nikumaroro
Phoenix Is.
Rawaki
Nui
Vaitupu
Carondelet
Reef
Orona
Manra
TUVALU
(Ellice Is.)
Funafuti
Fongafale
International Date Line

Reef Is.
Duff Is.
Nukulaelae
Santa Cruz
Nendo
Is.
7223
Fataka
9165
Vanikoro
Niulakita
Atafu
Tokelau Is.
Nukunonu
(N.Z.)
Fakaofo

Tikopia

Is. Torres
Vanua Lava
Is. Banks
Rotuma
Mata-Utu
Uvea
Gaua
Wallis & Futuna
(Fr.)
Horn Alofi
SAMOA
Savai'i 1858
Apia
Espíritu Santo
1879
VANUATU
Vanua Levu
'Upolu
Pago
Pago
American
Malakula
863
(New Hebrides)
1031
Taveuni
Niuafo'ou
Niua
Niuatoputapu
Tutuila
Samoa
(U.S.A.)
Epi
Shepherd Is.
Viti Levu
Group
Îles D'Entrecasteaux
Port Vila
Efate
1323
FIJI
Îles Chesterfield
Îles
Erromango
Suva
Bélep
1084
Tanna
Kadavu
Vava'u Group
7569
Aneityum
Late
TONGA
Îles Loyauté
Lau
New
1628
Î. Lifou
Ha'apai Group
Caledonia
La Foa
Î. Mare
Yate
Ridge
Alofi
Niue
(Fr.)
Nouméa
Nuku'alofa
Eua
(N.Z.)
Î. des Pins
Î. Matthew
Ceve-i-Ra
Tongatapu
Group
Ata

P
A
C
I
F
I
C
5303
O
C
E
A
N
10 882

South
Fiji
Basin
Tropic of Capricorn

Norfolk I.
(Austral.)

Lord Howe I.
(Austral.)
Norfolk
Basin
734
Raoul I.
Southwest
Kermadec Is.
(N.Z.)
Macauley I.
Curtis I.
Pacific
10 047
Basin

Tasman Sea
North C.
Kaitaia
Whangarei
AUCKLAND
Hamilton
North Island
Bay of
Plenty
Tauranga
Challenger
Plateau
New Plymouth
Rotorua
Gisborne
5267
NEW
Ruapehu
Wanganui
2797
Napier
ZEALAND
Palmerston
North
Nelson
Masterton
Blenheim
Wellington
South Island
Greymouth
Cook
Strait
Aoraki Mt. Cook
3753
Southern Alps
Christchurch
Chatham
Queenstown
Timaru
Rise
Chatham I.
Chatham Is.
Invercargill
Dunedin
Pitt I.
(N.Z.)
Stewart I.

Melanesia

Vitiaz Trench

Lau Group

Kermadec Trench

Colville Ridge

International Date Line

Cook Strait

New Caledonia

Caledonia Trough

Norfolk Ridge

Lord Howe Rise

Lord Howe Seamount Chain

South New Hebrides Trench

South Solomon Trench

Tonga Trench

A
B
C
D
E
F
G
H
J

0
170
5
10
15
20
25
30
35
40
45

165
170
175
180
175
170
165
160
160

10 11 12 13 14 15 16 17 18

West from Greenwich

COPYRIGHT PHILIP'S

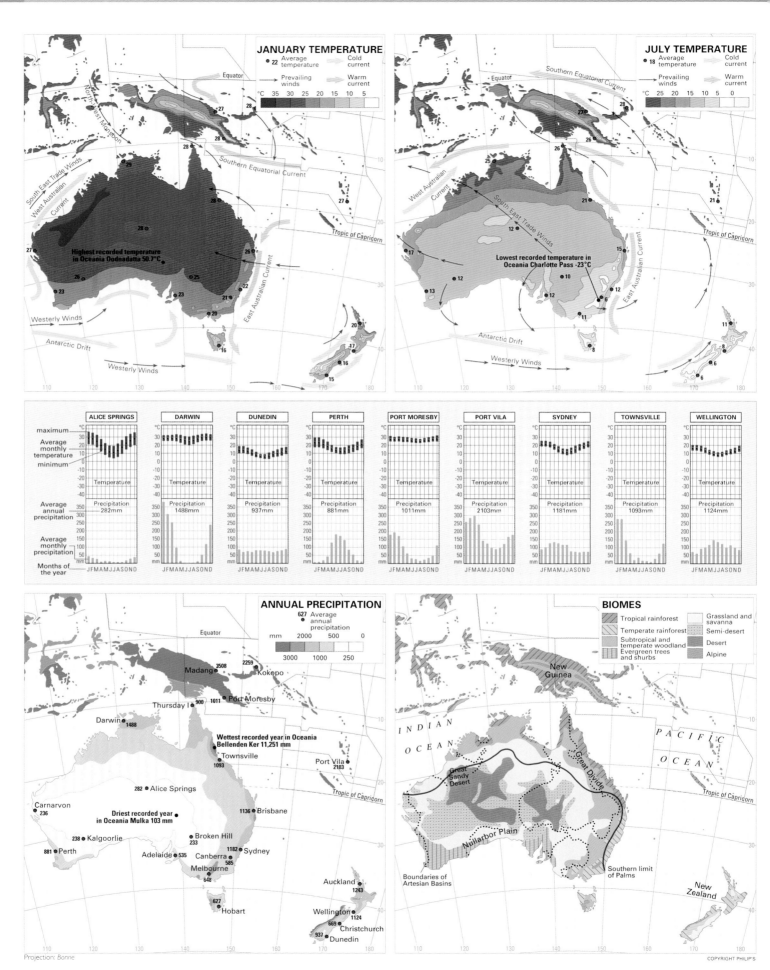

JANUARY TEMPERATURE

• 22 Average temperature
Cold current
Prevailing winds
Warm current

°C 35 30 25 20 15 10 5

Equator

North West Monsoon

South East Trade Winds

South Australian Current

Southern Equatorial Current

Tropic of Capricorn

East Australian Current

Westerly Winds

Antarctic Drift

Westerly Winds

Highest recorded temperature in Oceania Oodnadatta 50.7°C

JULY TEMPERATURE

• 18 Average temperature
Cold current
Prevailing winds
Warm current

°C 25 20 15 10 5 0

Equator

Southern Equatorial Current

West Australian Current

South East Trade Winds

Tropic of Capricorn

East Australian Current

Antarctic Drift

Westerly Winds

Lowest recorded temperature in Oceania Charlotte Pass -23°C

Climate graphs

maximum
Average monthly temperature
minimum

Average annual precipitation

Average monthly precipitation

Months of the year

ALICE SPRINGS	DARWIN	DUNEDIN	PERTH	PORT MORESBY	PORT VILA	SYDNEY	TOWNSVILLE	WELLINGTON
Temperature	Temperature	Temperature	Temperature	Temperature	Temperature	Temperature	Temperature	Temperature
Precipitation 282mm	Precipitation 1488mm	Precipitation 937mm	Precipitation 881mm	Precipitation 1011mm	Precipitation 2103mm	Precipitation 1181mm	Precipitation 1093mm	Precipitation 1124mm
JFMAMJJASOND	JFMAMJJASOND	JFMAMJJASOND	JFMAMJJASOND	JFMAMJJASOND	JFMAMJJASOND	JFMAMJJASOND	JFMAMJJASOND	JFMAMJJASOND

ANNUAL PRECIPITATION

627 Average annual precipitation

mm 2000 500 0
3000 1000 250

Equator

Madang 3508
Kokopo 2259
Port Moresby 1011
Thursday I 900
Darwin 1488

Wettest recorded year in Oceania Bellenden Ker 11,251 mm

Townsville 1093
Port Vila 2103

Alice Springs 282

Tropic of Capricorn

Carnarvon 236

Driest recorded year in Oceania Mulka 103 mm

Brisbane 1136

Kalgoorlie 238
Broken Hill 233
Perth 881
Sydney 1182
Adelaide 535
Canberra 585
Melbourne 648

Auckland 1243

Hobart 627

Wellington 1124
Christchurch 669
Dunedin 937

BIOMES

Tropical rainforest
Temperate rainforest
Subtropical and temperate woodland
Evergreen trees and shurbs
Grassland and savanna
Semi-desert
Desert
Alpine

New Guinea

INDIAN OCEAN

PACIFIC OCEAN

Great Sandy Desert

Great Divide

Tropic of Capricorn

Nullarbor Plain

Southern limit of Palms

Boundaries of Artesian Basins

New Zealand

Projection: Bonne

COPYRIGHT PHILIP'S

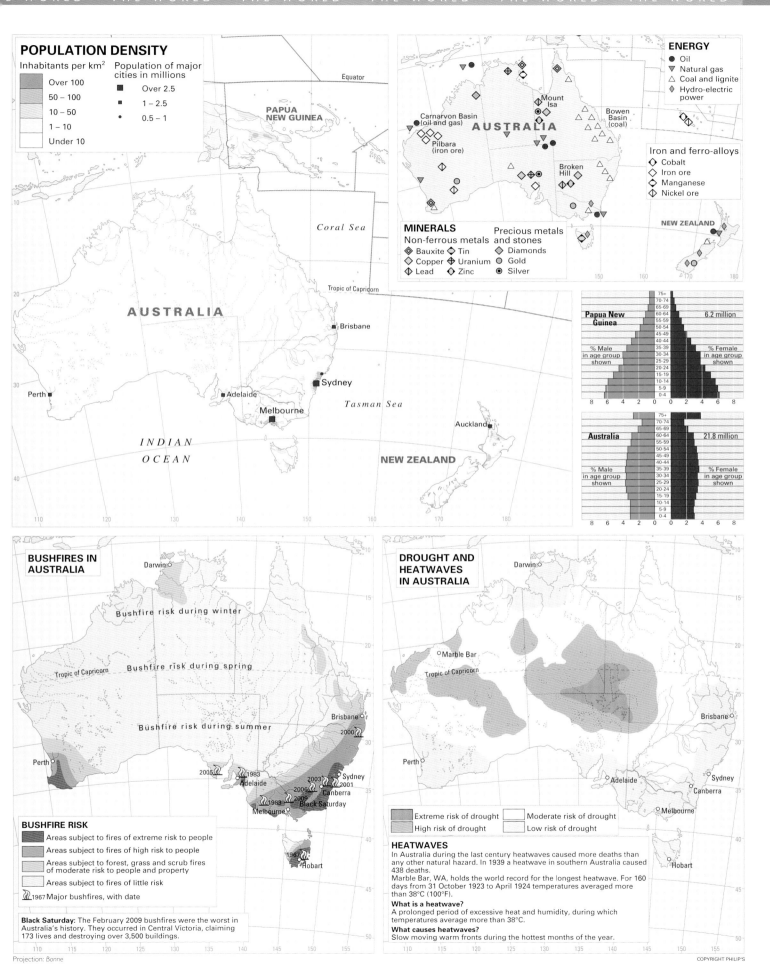

POPULATION DENSITY

Inhabitants per km²

- Over 100
- 50 – 100
- 10 – 50
- 1 – 10
- Under 10

Population of major cities in millions

- ■ Over 2.5
- ■ 1 – 2.5
- • 0.5 – 1

ENERGY

- ● Oil
- ▼ Natural gas
- △ Coal and lignite
- ◆ Hydro-electric power

Iron and ferro-alloys

- ◇ Cobalt
- ◇ Iron ore
- ◇ Manganese
- ◇ Nickel ore

MINERALS

Non-ferrous metals

- ◈ Bauxite
- ◇ Copper
- ◇ Lead
- ◇ Tin
- ✛ Uranium
- ◇ Zinc

Precious metals and stones

- ◇ Diamonds
- ● Gold
- ◉ Silver

Carnarvon Basin (oil and gas)
Pilbara (iron ore)
Mount Isa
Bowen Basin (coal)
Broken Hill
AUSTRALIA
NEW ZEALAND

Population pyramids:
Papua New Guinea — 6.2 million
Australia — 21.8 million
% Male in age group shown / % Female in age group shown

PAPUA NEW GUINEA
Equator
Coral Sea
Tropic of Capricorn
Brisbane
Sydney
Adelaide
Melbourne
Perth
Tasman Sea
Auckland
INDIAN OCEAN
NEW ZEALAND
AUSTRALIA

BUSHFIRES IN AUSTRALIA

Darwin
Bushfire risk during winter
Tropic of Capricorn
Bushfire risk during spring
Bushfire risk during summer
Perth
Brisbane
2000
2005
1983
Adelaide
2003
2001
2006
2009
Canberra
Black Saturday
1983
Sydney
Melbourne
1967
Hobart

BUSHFIRE RISK

- Areas subject to fires of extreme risk to people
- Areas subject to fires of high risk to people
- Areas subject to forest, grass and scrub fires of moderate risk to people and property
- Areas subject to fires of little risk
- ⌇1967 Major bushfires, with date

Black Saturday: The February 2009 bushfires were the worst in Australia's history. They occurred in Central Victoria, claiming 173 lives and destroying over 3,500 buildings.

DROUGHT AND HEATWAVES IN AUSTRALIA

Darwin
Marble Bar
Tropic of Capricorn
Perth
Brisbane
Adelaide
Sydney
Canberra
Melbourne
Hobart

- Extreme risk of drought
- High risk of drought
- Moderate risk of drought
- Low risk of drought

HEATWAVES

In Australia during the last century heatwaves caused more deaths than any other natural hazard. In 1939 a heatwave in southern Australia caused 438 deaths.

Marble Bar, WA, holds the world record for the longest heatwave. For 160 days from 31 October 1923 to April 1924 temperatures averaged more than 38°C (100°F).

What is a heatwave?
A prolonged period of excessive heat and humidity, during which temperatures average more than 38°C.

What causes heatwaves?
Slow moving warm fronts during the hottest months of the year.

Projection: Bonne

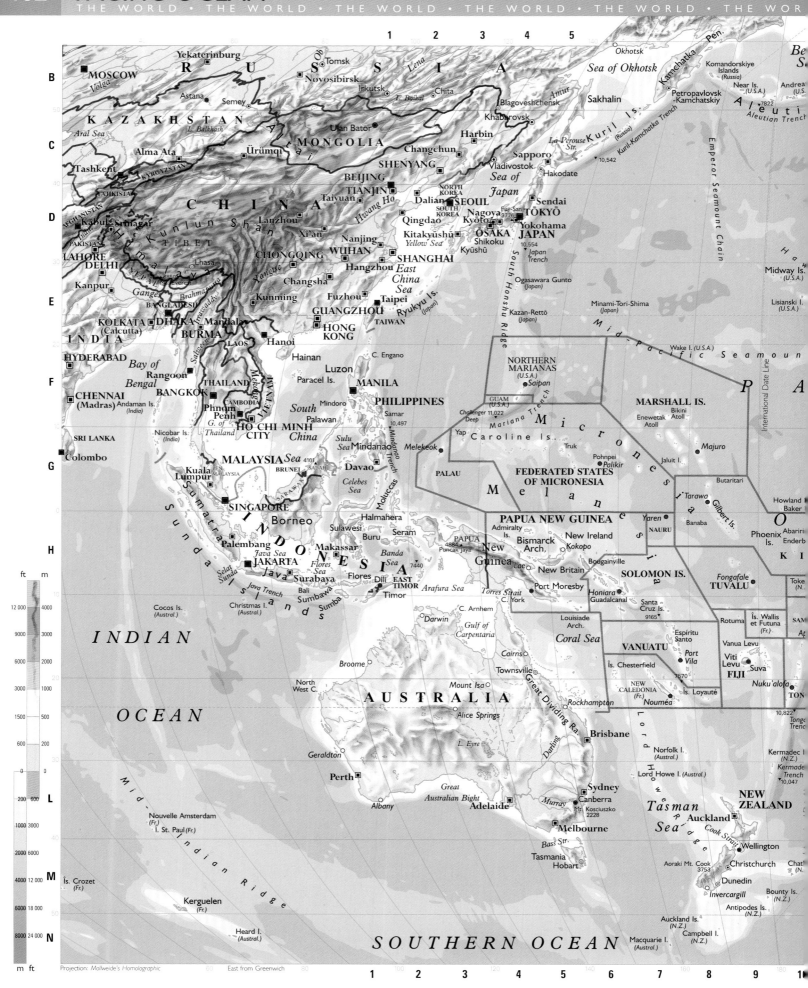

ALASKA
(U.S.A.)
Anchorage
Gulf of Alaska
Juneau
Bristol Bay
s. (U.S.A.)
Prince of Wales I.
(U.S.A.)
Prince Rupert
Queen Charlotte Is.
(Canada)
5959

CANADA

16 17 18 19 20

ROCKY
Edmonton
L. Winnipeg
Newfoundland

Vancouver
Vancouver I.
Calgary
Regina
Winnipeg
St. Lawrence
St. John's
Victoria
Seattle
Québec
Montréal
Portland
L. Superior
Minneapolis
L. Huron
L. Michigan
TORONTO
Ottawa
Boston
Boise
Detroit
Buffalo
L. Erie
Snake
Missouri
Salt Lake
City
Denver
CHICAGO
Pittsburgh
NEW YORK
PHILADELPHIA
C. Mendocino
Colorado
Kansas City
Cincinnati
Baltimore
WASHINGTON D.C.
ATLANTIC
SACRAMENTO
4418
St. Louis
SAN FRANCISCO
UNITED STATES
Oklahoma City
Memphis
ATLANTA
C. Hatteras
Bermuda
(U.K.)
6741
Phoenix
DALLAS
LOS ANGELES
Mississippi
Appalachian Mts.
San Diego
HOUSTON
Jacksonville
Ciudad
Juárez
New
Orleans
Sargasso Sea
Guadalupe
(Mex.)
Golfo de California
San Antonio
Monterrey
Gulf of Mexico
MIAMI
BAHAMAS
OCEAN
Tropic of Cancer
Baja California
Havana
Florida Str.
West Indies
C. San Lucas
MEXICO
Yucatan Channel
CUBA
Honolulu
O'ahu
HAWAI'I
Guadalajara
5610
Mérida
HAITI
8605
DOMINICAN REP.
4205
(U.S.A.)
C. Puebla
JAMAICA
Leeward
Is.
Hawai'i
Is. de Revillagigedo
(Mex.)
BELIZE
7680
Kingston
PUERTO
RICO
(U.S.A.)
Acapulco
GUATEMALA
HONDURAS
Caribbean Sea
BARBADOS
ston I.
CIFIC
Î. Clipperton
(Fr.)
Guatemala
San Salvador
NICARAGUA
Barranquilla
Windward Is.
Palmyra I.
(U.S.A.)
EL SALVADOR
Managua
San José
Maracaibo
Teraina
COSTA
RICA
Colón
Panamá
Caracas
Tabuaeran
Kiritimati
PANAMÁ
Orinoco
VENEZUELA
I. del Coco
(Costa Rica)
Medellín
BOGOTÁ
Jarvis I.
(U.S.A.)
Equator
I. de Malpelo
(Colombia)
Cali
COLOMBIA
Malden I.
Starbuck I.
Galápagos
(Ecuador)
Quito
ECUADOR
Tongareva
Îs. Marquises
Guayaquil
Iquitos
BRAZIL
Pukapuka
Manihiki
Vostok I.
Caroline I.
(Millennium I.)
C. Paliñas
Amazonas
Suwarrow Is.
Flint I.
Îs. de la
Société
Îs. Tuamotu
Trujillo
Cook Is.
(N.Z.)
Tahiti
6369
PERU
FRENCH POLYNESIA
Papeete
LIMA
L. Titicaca
Nevado Ancohuma
6550
Rarotonga
Mururoa
Îs. Tubuaï
Cusco
Arequipa
La Paz
6866
BOLIVIA
Peru-
Tropic of Capricorn
Arica
Iquique
PARAGUAY
Henderson I.
Antofagasta
Asunción
Pitcairn I.
(U.K.)
San Félix
(Chile)
San Ambrosio
(Chile)
8050
San Miguel
de Tucumán
Rapa
Trench
Sala-y-Gómez
(Chile)
Pôrto
Alegre
I. de Pascua
(Chile)
Córdoba
Aconcagua
6962
URUGUAY
Arch. de
Juan Fernández
(Chile)
Valparaíso
Rosario
SANTIAGO
BUENOS
AIRES
Montevideo
Concepción
Río de la Plata
ARGENTINA
ATLANTIC
6212
OCEAN
Pacific-Antarctic Ridge
Punta Arenas
Falkland Is.
(U.K.)
Magellan's Str.
South Georgia
(U.K.)
Tierra del Fuego
C. Horn

Equatorial Scale 1:54 000 000

NORTH AMERICA RELIEF OF LAND

Projection: Bonne

West from Greenwich

COPYRIGHT PHILIP'S

1:35 000 000

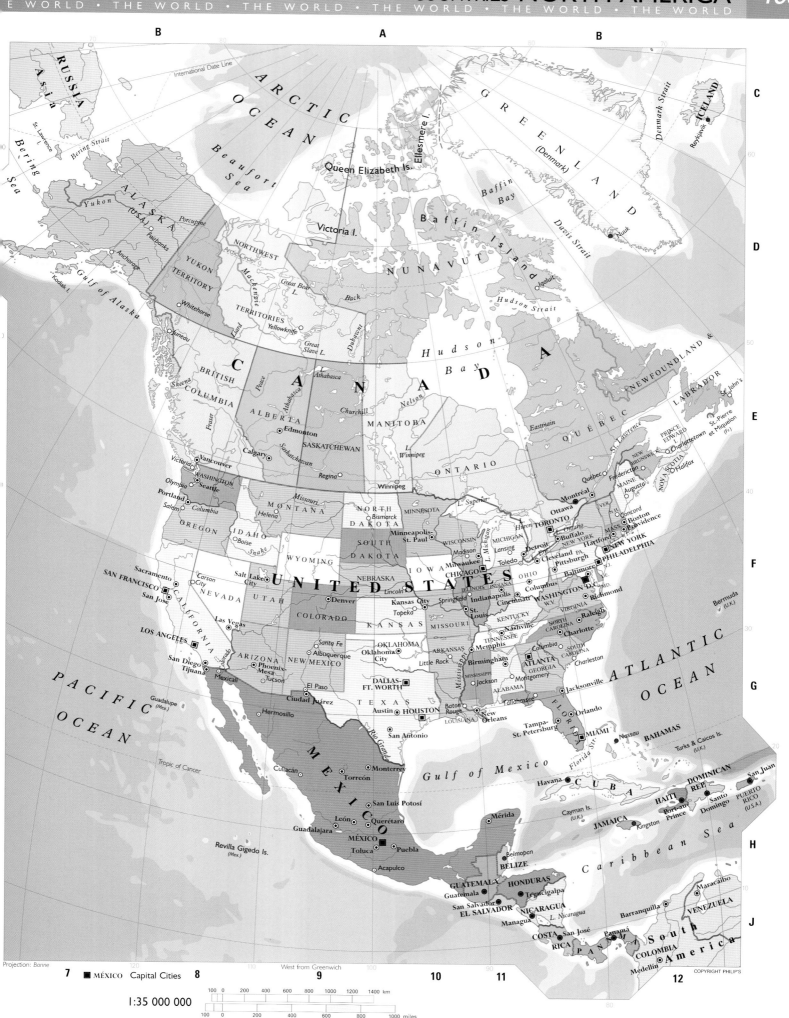

Projection: Bonne

West from Greenwich

MÉXICO Capital Cities

1:35 000 000

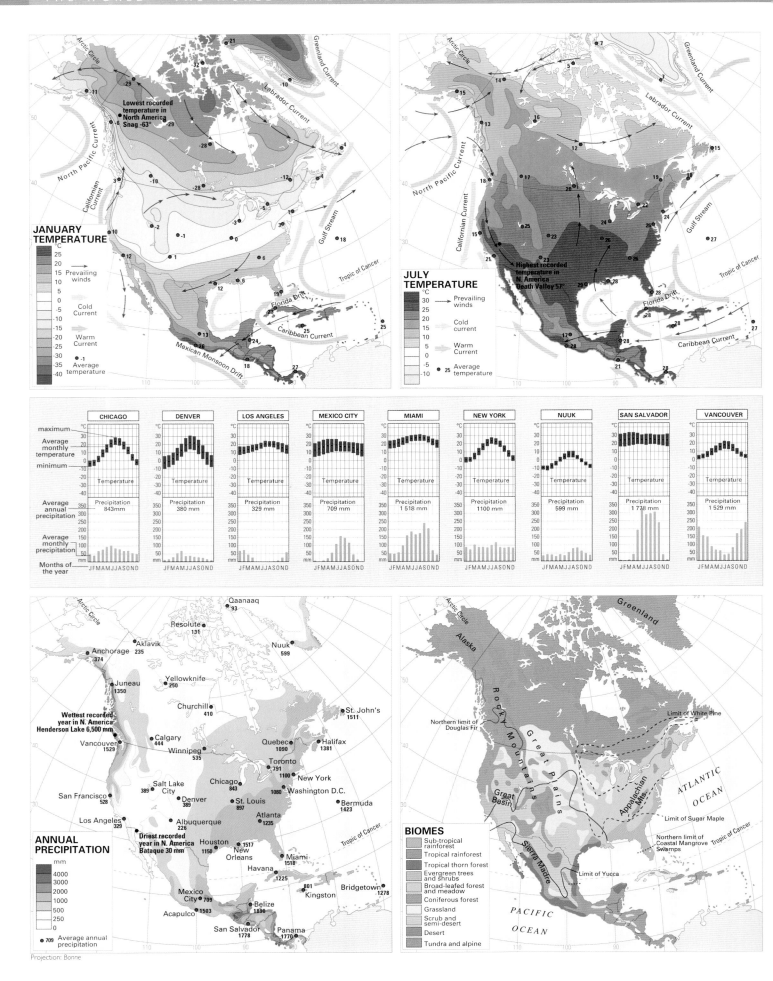

JANUARY TEMPERATURE

°C
25
20
15 → Prevailing winds
10
5
0
-5 → Cold Current
-10
-15
-20 → Warm Current
-25
-30
-35 ● -1 Average temperature
-40

Lowest recorded temperature in North America Snag -63°

Arctic Circle
Greenland Current
Labrador Current
North Pacific Current
Californian Current
Gulf Stream
Tropic of Cancer
Florida Drift
Caribbean Current
Mexican Monsoon Drift

JULY TEMPERATURE

°C
30 → Prevailing winds
25
20
15
10 → Cold current
5
0
-5 → Warm Current
-10
● 25 Average temperature

Highest recorded temperature in N. America Death Valley 57°

Arctic Circle
Greenland Current
Labrador Current
North Pacific Current
Californian Current
Gulf Stream
Tropic of Cancer
Florida Drift
Caribbean Current

Climate graphs

CHICAGO	DENVER	LOS ANGELES	MEXICO CITY	MIAMI	NEW YORK	NUUK	SAN SALVADOR	VANCOUVER

maximum
Average monthly temperature
minimum

Average annual precipitation
Average monthly precipitation
Months of the year

Temperature — Precipitation:
- Chicago 843mm
- Denver 380 mm
- Los Angeles 329 mm
- Mexico City 709 mm
- Miami 1 518 mm
- New York 1100 mm
- Nuuk 599 mm
- San Salvador 1 778 mm
- Vancouver 1 529 mm

JFMAMJJASOND

ANNUAL PRECIPITATION

mm
4000
3000
2000
1000
500
250
0
● 709 Average annual precipitation

Wettest recorded year in N. America Henderson Lake 6,500 mm

Driest recorded year in N. America Bataque 30 mm

- Qaanaaq 93
- Resolute 131
- Aklavik
- Anchorage 374
- Juneau 1350
- Yellowknife 250
- Nuuk 599
- Churchill 410
- St. John's 1511
- Calgary 444
- Vancouver 1529
- Winnipeg 535
- Quebec 1090
- Halifax 1381
- Toronto 791
- San Francisco 528
- Salt Lake City 389
- Chicago 843
- New York 1080
- Washington D.C.
- Denver 389
- St. Louis 897
- Bermuda 1423
- Los Angeles 329
- Albuquerque 226
- Atlanta 1235
- Houston 1150
- New Orleans 1517
- Miami 1518
- Havana 1225
- Kingston 801
- Bridgetown 1278
- Mexico City 709
- Belize 1890
- Acapulco 1503
- San Salvador 1778
- Panama 1770

Arctic Circle
Tropic of Cancer

Projection: Bonne

BIOMES

- Sub-tropical rainforest
- Tropical rainforest
- Tropical thorn forest
- Evergreen trees and shrubs
- Broad-leafed forest and meadow
- Coniferous forest
- Grassland
- Scrub and semi-desert
- Desert
- Tundra and alpine

Greenland
Arctic Circle
Alaska
Rocky Mountains
Great Plains
Great Basin
Sierra Madre
Appalachian Mts.
ATLANTIC OCEAN
PACIFIC OCEAN
Tropic of Cancer

Northern limit of Douglas Fir
Limit of White Pine
Limit of Sugar Maple
Northern limit of Coastal Mangrove Swamps
Limit of Yucca

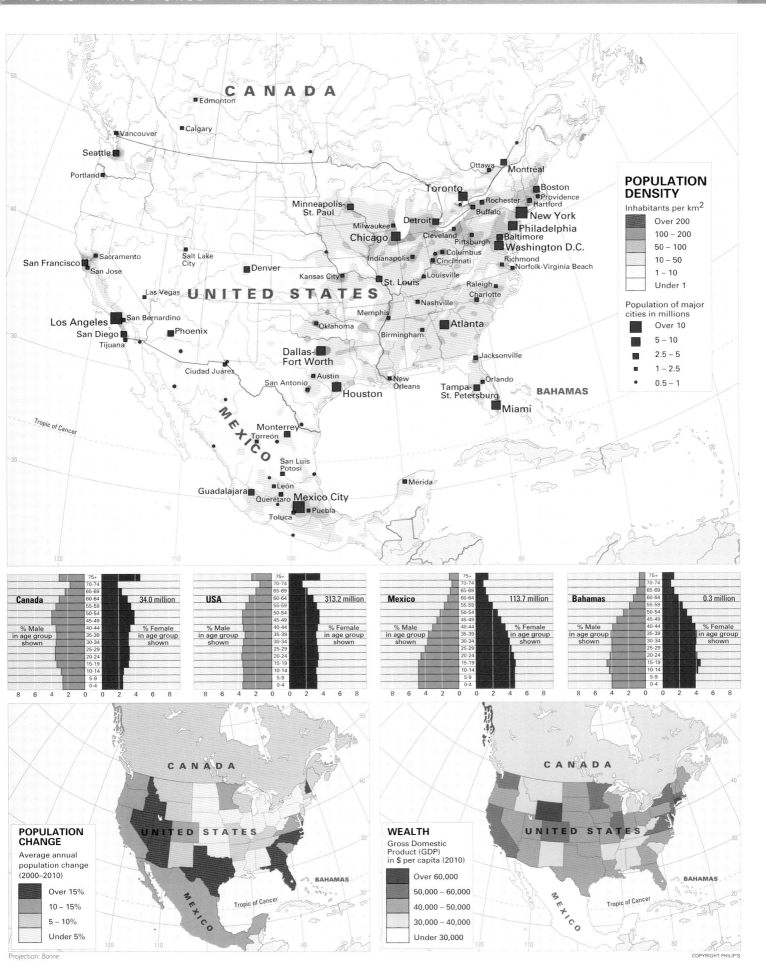

CANADA
Edmonton
Vancouver · Calgary
Seattle
Portland

Ottawa · Montréal
Toronto
Boston
Minneapolis-St. Paul
Rochester · Providence
Hartford
Detroit · Buffalo
New York
Milwaukee
Chicago · Cleveland · Philadelphia
Pittsburgh · Baltimore
Columbus · Washington D.C.
Indianapolis · Cincinnati
Richmond
Norfolk-Virginia Beach

Salt Lake City
Denver
Kansas City
Louisville
Raleigh
St. Louis
Charlotte
Nashville
San Francisco · Sacramento
San Jose
Las Vegas
UNITED STATES
Memphis
Los Angeles · San Bernardino
San Diego
Oklahoma
Birmingham
Atlanta
Tijuana
Phoenix
Jacksonville
Ciudad Juárez
Dallas-Fort Worth
San Antonio · Austin
New Orleans
Orlando
Tampa-St. Petersburg
BAHAMAS
Houston
Miami
Tropic of Cancer
Monterrey
Torreón
San Luis Potosí
MEXICO
Mérida
León
Guadalajara · Querétaro
Mexico City
Toluca · Puebla

POPULATION DENSITY
Inhabitants per km²
Over 200
100 – 200
50 – 100
10 – 50
1 – 10
Under 1

Population of major cities in millions
Over 10
5 – 10
2.5 – 5
1 – 2.5
0.5 – 1

Canada 34.0 million
75+ 70-74 65-69 60-64 55-59 50-54 45-49 40-44 35-39 30-34 25-29 20-24 15-19 10-14 5-9 0-4
% Male in age group shown / % Female in age group shown
8 6 4 2 0 2 4 6 8

USA 313.2 million
% Male in age group shown / % Female in age group shown
8 6 4 2 0 2 4 6 8

Mexico 113.7 million
% Male in age group shown / % Female in age group shown
8 6 4 2 0 2 4 6 8

Bahamas 0.3 million
% Male in age group shown / % Female in age group shown
8 6 4 2 0 2 4 6 8

POPULATION CHANGE
Average annual population change (2000–2010)
Over 15%
10 – 15%
5 – 10%
Under 5%

WEALTH
Gross Domestic Product (GDP) in $ per capita (2010)
Over 60,000
50,000 – 60,000
40,000 – 50,000
30,000 – 40,000
Under 30,000

Projection: Bonne

COPYRIGHT PHILIP'S

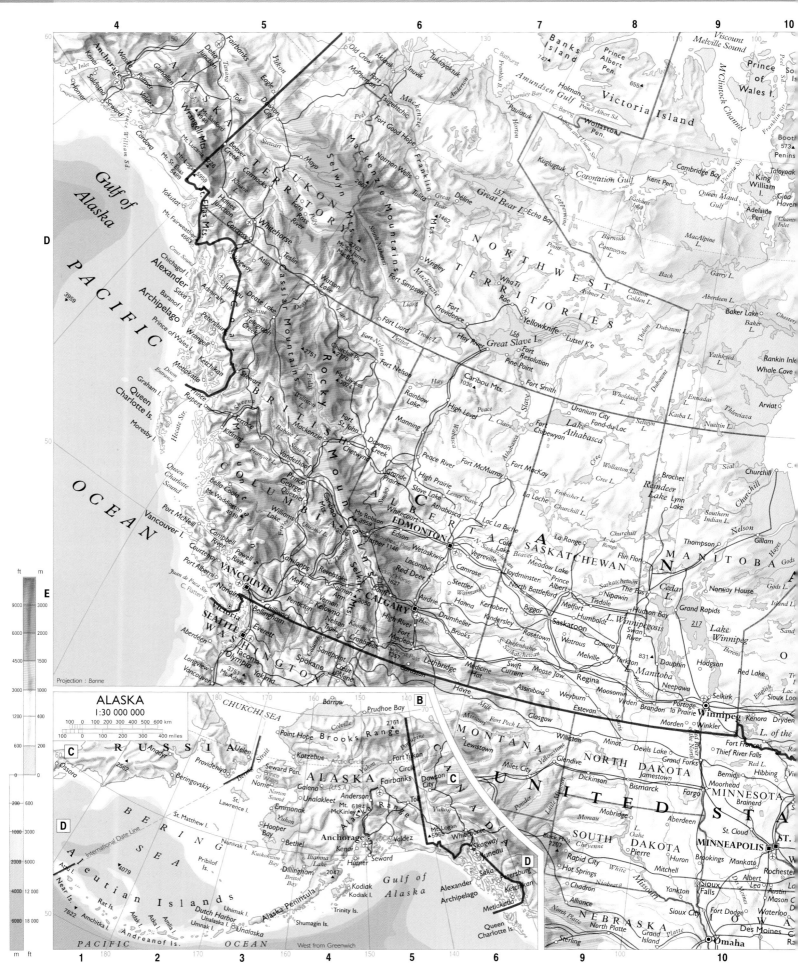

NORTHERN CANADA

Continuation northwards on same scale as main map

1:15 000 000

West from Greenwich

COPYRIGHT PHILIP'S

HAWAI'I

Projection: Albers' Equal Area with two standard parallels

West from Greenwich

Projection: Albers' Equal Area with two standard parallels

1:6 000 000

0   50   100   150   200 km
50   0   50   100   150 miles

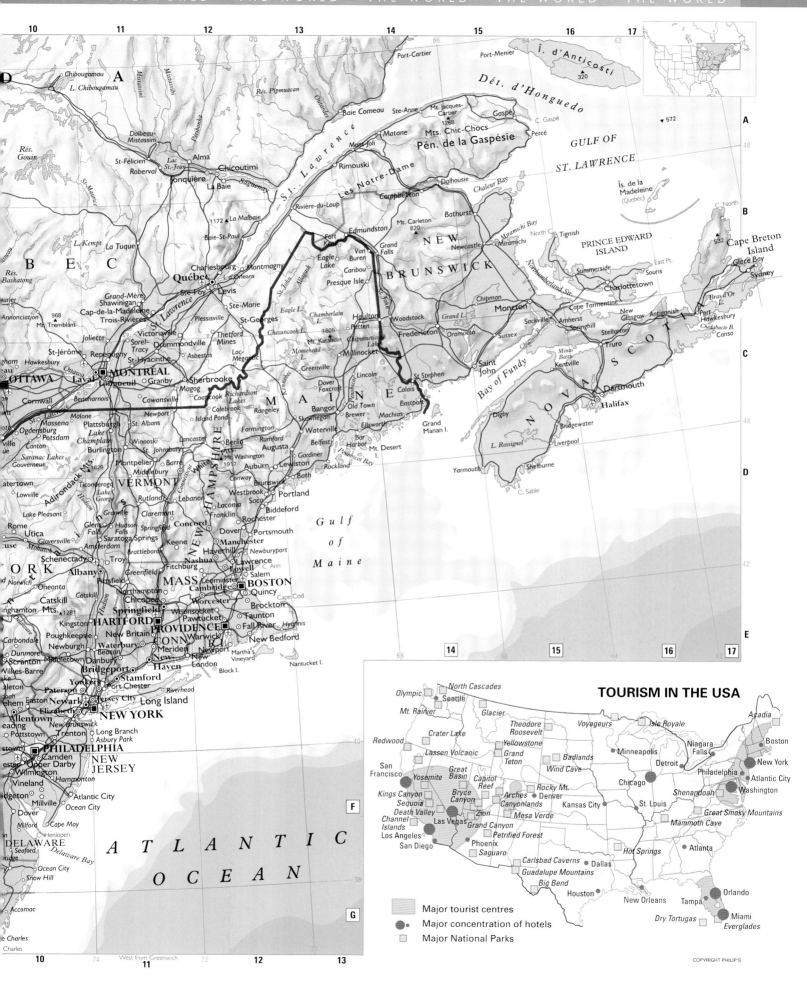

TOURISM IN THE USA

Major tourist centres
Major concentration of hotels
Major National Parks

COPYRIGHT PHILIP'S

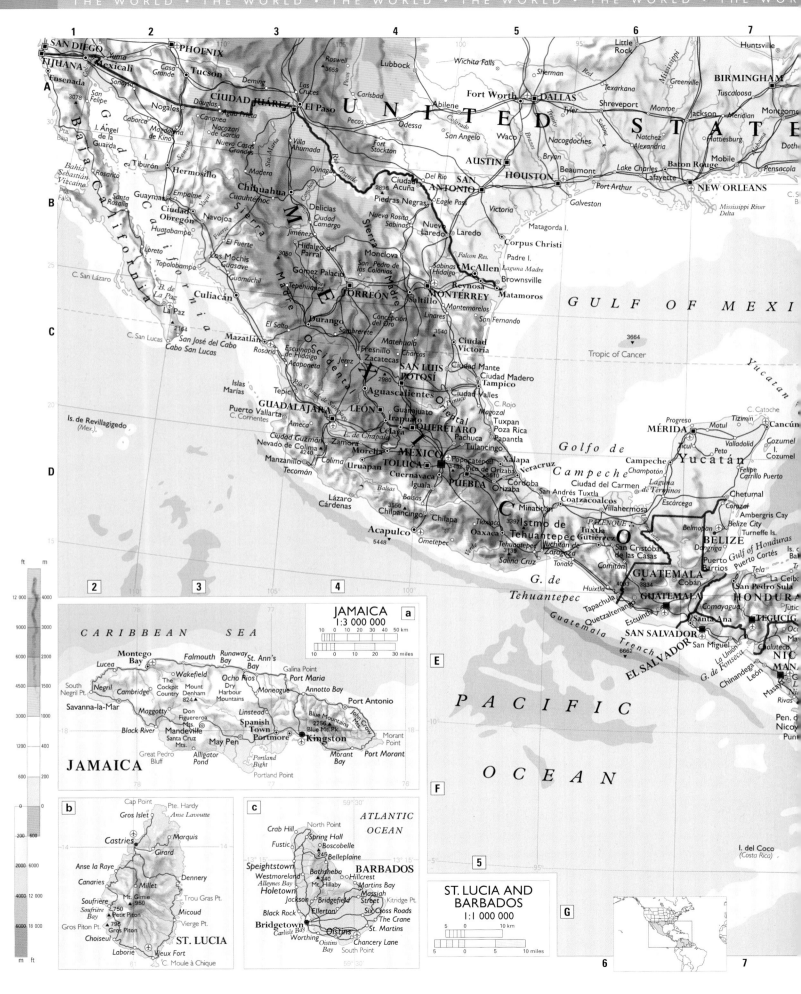

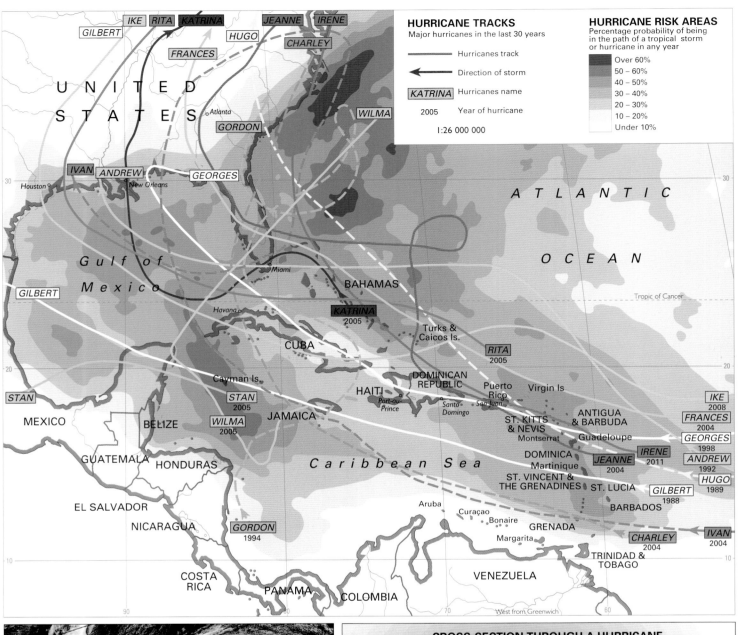

HURRICANE TRACKS
Major hurricanes in the last 30 years

——— Hurricanes track

⟵ Direction of storm

[KATRINA] Hurricanes name

2005 Year of hurricane

1:26 000 000

HURRICANE RISK AREAS
Percentage probability of being in the path of a tropical storm or hurricane in any year

Over 60%
50 – 60%
40 – 50%
30 – 40%
20 – 30%
10 – 20%
Under 10%

IKE RITA KATRINA JEANNE IRENE
GILBERT HUGO
FRANCES CHARLEY

U N I T E D
S T A T E S
Atlanta
WILMA
GORDON

IVAN ANDREW GEORGES
Houston New Orleans

A T L A N T I C

O C E A N

GILBERT
Gulf of
Mexico
Miami
BAHAMAS
Tropic of Cancer

Havana
KATRINA
2005
Turks &
Caicos Is.

CUBA
RITA
2005

Cayman Is.
STAN
2005
DOMINICAN
REPUBLIC
Puerto
Rico
Virgin Is
IKE
2008

STAN
WILMA
2005
HAITI
Port-au-
Prince
Santo
Domingo
San Juan
ANTIGUA
& BARBUDA
FRANCES
2004

MEXICO
BELIZE
JAMAICA
Montserrat
Guadeloupe
GEORGES
1998

GUATEMALA HONDURAS
C a r i b b e a n   S e a
DOMINICA
Martinique
JEANNE
2004
IRENE
2011
ANDREW
1992

ST. VINCENT &
THE GRENADINES
ST. LUCIA
HUGO
1989

EL SALVADOR
Aruba
ST. KITTS
& NEVIS
GILBERT
1988

NICARAGUA
GORDON
1994
Curaçao
Bonaire
GRENADA
Margarita
BARBADOS
CHARLEY
2004
IVAN
2004

COSTA
RICA
PANAMA
COLOMBIA
West from Greenwich
TRINIDAD &
TOBAGO
VENEZUELA

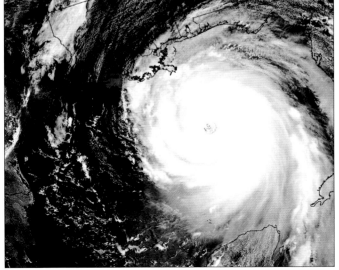

▲ Hurricane Katrina hit the USA's Gulf Coast on 29th August 2005. It was the costliest and one of the five deadliest hurricanes ever to strike the United States. This satellite image shows the storm approaching the US coastline.

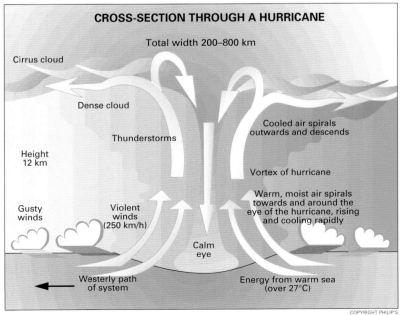

CROSS-SECTION THROUGH A HURRICANE

Total width 200–800 km

Cirrus cloud

Dense cloud

Cooled air spirals
outwards and descends

Thunderstorms

Height
12 km

Vortex of hurricane

Warm, moist air spirals
towards and around the
eye of the hurricane, rising
and cooling rapidly

Gusty
winds

Violent
winds
(250 km/h)

Calm
eye

Westerly path
of system

Energy from warm sea
(over 27°C)

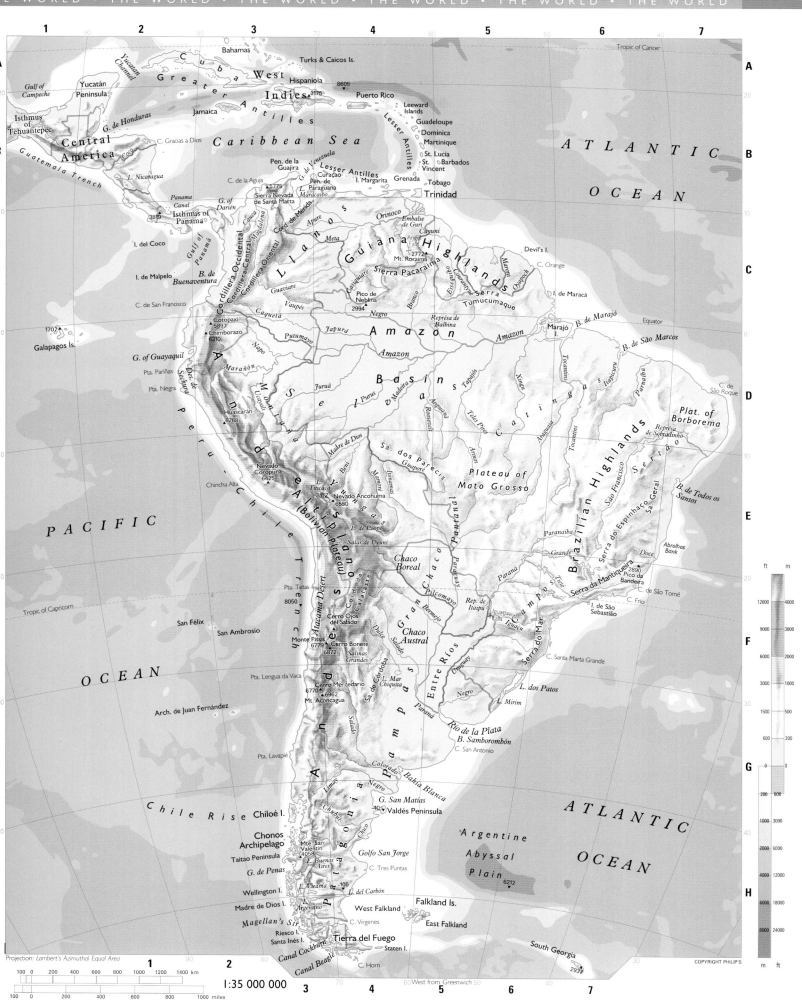

Projection: Lambert's Azimuthal Equal Area

1:35 000 000

COPYRIGHT PHILIP'S

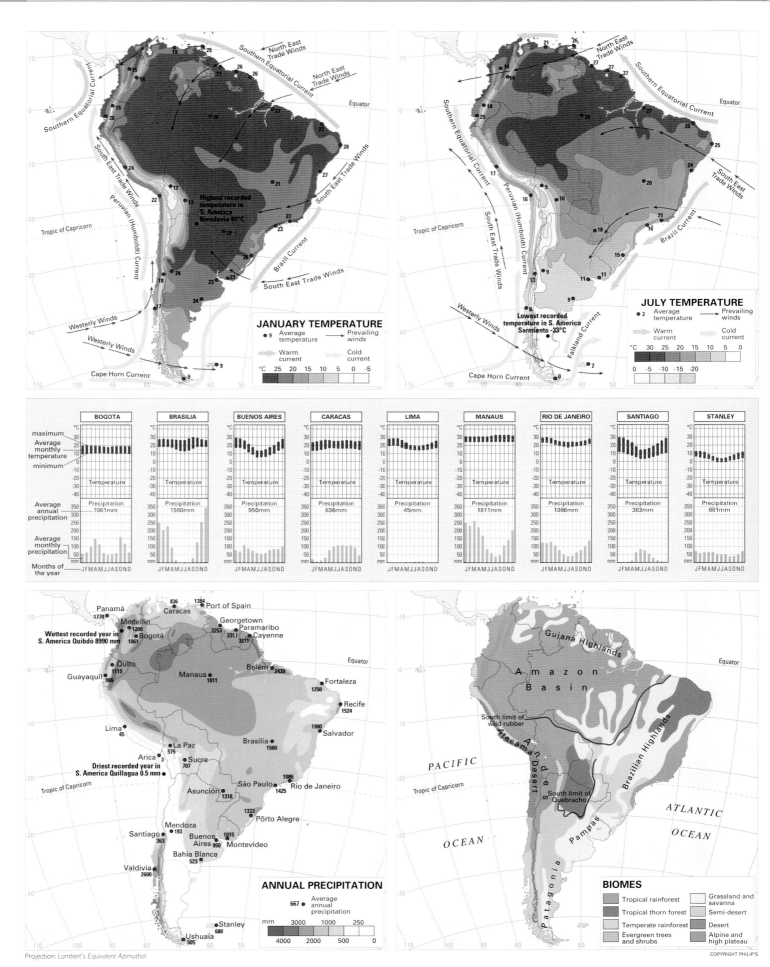

JANUARY TEMPERATURE

Highest recorded temperature in S. America Rivadavia 49°C

- 9 Average temperature
- → Prevailing winds
- Warm current
- Cold current

°C 25 20 15 10 5 0 -5

JULY TEMPERATURE

Lowest recorded temperature in S. America Sarmiento -33°C

- 2 Average temperature
- → Prevailing winds
- Warm current
- Cold current

°C 30 25 20 15 10 5 0

0 -5 -10 -15 -20

BOGOTA — Temperature / Precipitation 1061mm
BRASILIA — Temperature / Precipitation 1560mm
BUENOS AIRES — Temperature / Precipitation 950mm
CARACAS — Temperature / Precipitation 836mm
LIMA — Temperature / Precipitation 45mm
MANAUS — Temperature / Precipitation 1811mm
RIO DE JANEIRO — Temperature / Precipitation 1086mm
SANTIAGO — Temperature / Precipitation 363mm
STANLEY — Temperature / Precipitation 681mm

maximum
Average monthly temperature
minimum
Average annual precipitation
Average monthly precipitation
Months of the year JFMAMJJASOND

ANNUAL PRECIPITATION

Panamá 1770
Medellín 1200
Bogotá 1061
Caracas 836
Port of Spain 1384
Georgetown 2253
Paramaribo 2311
Cayenne 3211
Wettest recorded year in S. America Quibdó 8990 mm
Quito 1115
Guayaquil 886
Manaus 1811
Belém 2439
Fortaleza 1250
Recife 1524
Lima 45
La Paz 575
Arica 3
Sucre 707
Driest recorded year in S. America Quillagua 0.5 mm
Brasília 1560
Salvador 1900
São Paulo 1425
Rio de Janeiro 1086
Asunción 1318
Pôrto Alegre 1333
Mendoza 193
Santiago 363
Buenos Aires 950
Montevideo 1015
Bahía Blanca 523
Valdivia 2600
Stanley 680
Ushuaïa 505

- 667 Average annual precipitation
- mm 3000 1000 250
- 4000 2000 500 0

Projection: Lambert's Equivalent Azimuthal

BIOMES

Guiana Highlands
Amazon Basin
South limit of wild rubber
Andes
Atacama Desert
South limit of Quebracho
Brazilian Highlands
Pampas
Patagonia
PACIFIC OCEAN
ATLANTIC OCEAN

- Tropical rainforest
- Tropical thorn forest
- Temperate rainforest
- Evergreen trees and shrubs
- Grassland and savanna
- Semi-desert
- Desert
- Alpine and high plateau

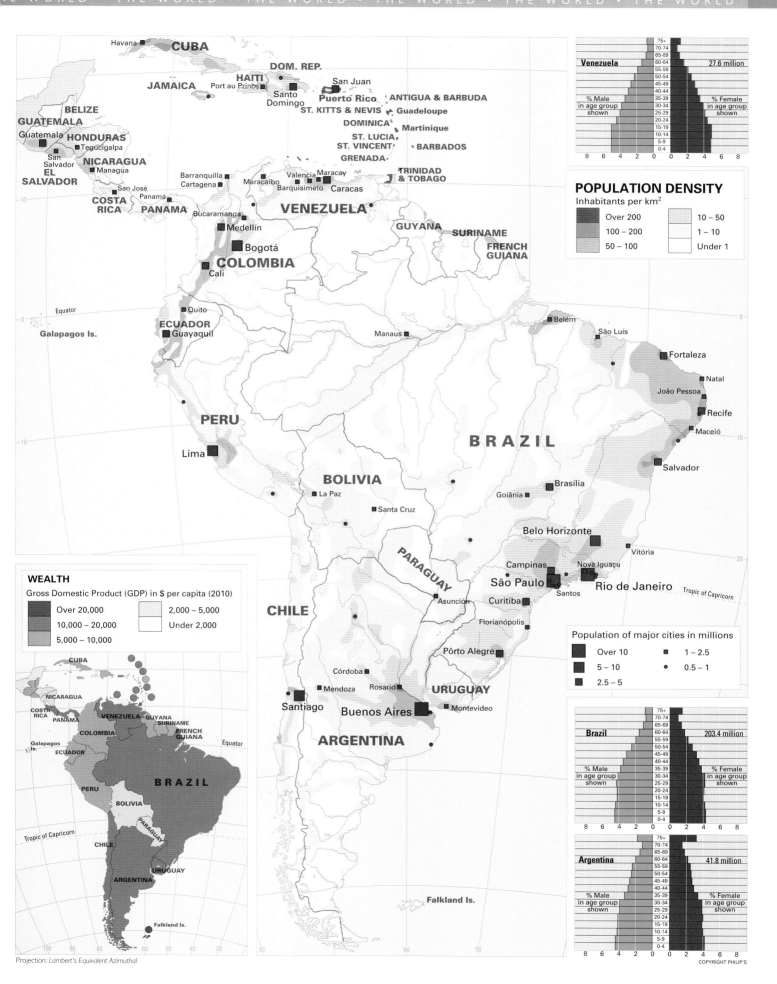

CUBA
Havana

DOM. REP.
HAITI
JAMAICA
Port au Prince
San Juan
Santo Domingo
Puerto Rico
ANTIGUA & BARBUDA
ST. KITTS & NEVIS
Guadeloupe
DOMINICA
Martinique
ST. LUCIA
ST. VINCENT
BARBADOS
GRENADA

BELIZE
GUATEMALA
Guatemala
HONDURAS
Tegucigalpa
San Salvador
EL SALVADOR
NICARAGUA
Managua
COSTA RICA
San José
PANAMA
Panamá

Barranquilla
Cartagena
Maracaibo
Valencia
Barquisimeto
Maracay
Caracas
TRINIDAD & TOBAGO

Bucaramanga
Medellín
Bogotá
COLOMBIA
Cali

VENEZUELA

GUYANA
SURINAME
FRENCH GUIANA

Equator
Quito
ECUADOR
Guayaquil
Galapagos Is.

Belém
Manaus
São Luís
Fortaleza
Natal
João Pessoa
Recife
Maceió

PERU
Lima

BRAZIL

BOLIVIA
La Paz
Santa Cruz

Brasília
Goiânia

Salvador

Belo Horizonte
Vitória

PARAGUAY

Campinas
São Paulo
Santos
Nova Iguaçu
Rio de Janeiro
Curitiba

Asunción

Florianópolis

CHILE

Pôrto Alegre

Córdoba
Mendoza
Rosario
URUGUAY
Santiago
Buenos Aires
Montevideo

ARGENTINA

Falkland Is.

Tropic of Capricorn

POPULATION DENSITY
Inhabitants per km²

Over 200	10 – 50
100 – 200	1 – 10
50 – 100	Under 1

Venezuela 27.6 million
% Male in age group shown % Female in age group shown
75+
70-74
65-69
60-64
55-59
50-54
45-49
40-44
35-39
30-34
25-29
20-24
15-19
10-14
5-9
0-4
8 6 4 2 0 0 2 4 6 8

Brazil 203.4 million
% Male in age group shown % Female in age group shown
75+
70-74
65-69
60-64
55-59
50-54
45-49
40-44
35-39
30-34
25-29
20-24
15-19
10-14
5-9
0-4
8 6 4 2 0 0 2 4 6 8

Argentina 41.8 million
% Male in age group shown % Female in age group shown
75+
70-74
65-69
60-64
55-59
50-54
45-49
40-44
35-39
30-34
25-29
20-24
15-19
10-14
5-9
0-4
8 6 4 2 0 0 2 4 6 8

Population of major cities in millions

Over 10	1 – 2.5
5 – 10	0.5 – 1
2.5 – 5	

WEALTH
Gross Domestic Product (GDP) in $ per capita (2010)

Over 20,000	2,000 – 5,000
10,000 – 20,000	Under 2,000
5,000 – 10,000	

CUBA
NICARAGUA
COSTA RICA
PANAMA
VENEZUELA
GUYANA
SURINAME
FRENCH GUIANA
COLOMBIA
Galapagos Is.
ECUADOR
Equator
PERU
BRAZIL
BOLIVIA
PARAGUAY
Tropic of Capricorn
CHILE
URUGUAY
ARGENTINA
Falkland Is.

Projection: Lambert's Equivalent Azimuthal

COPYRIGHT PHILIP'S

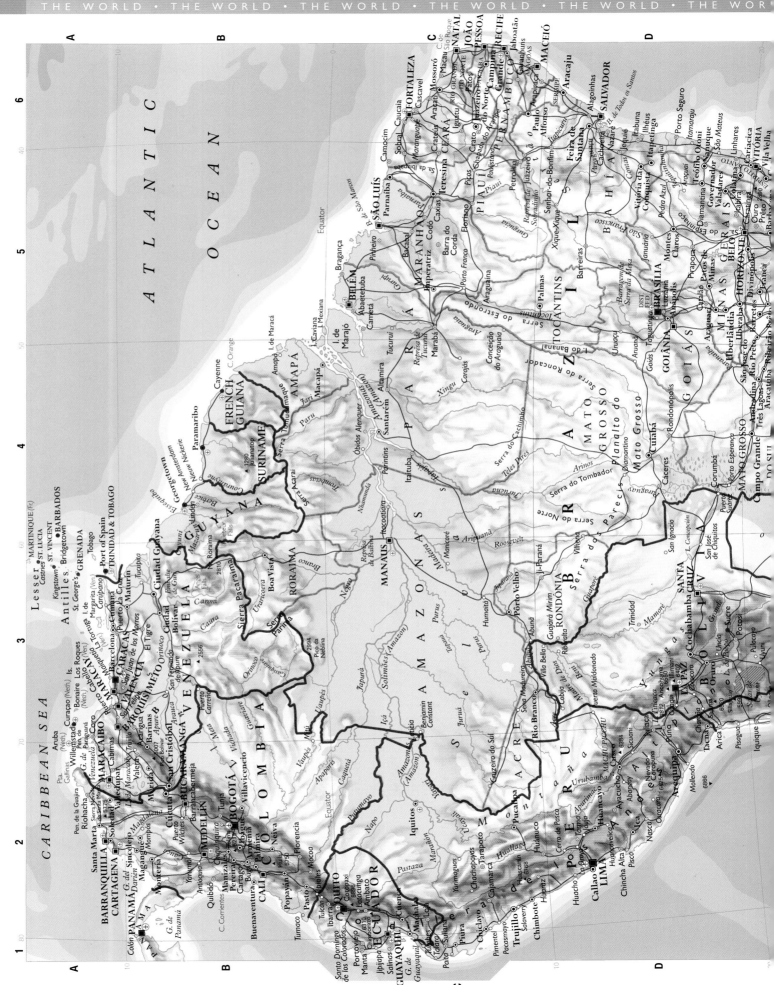

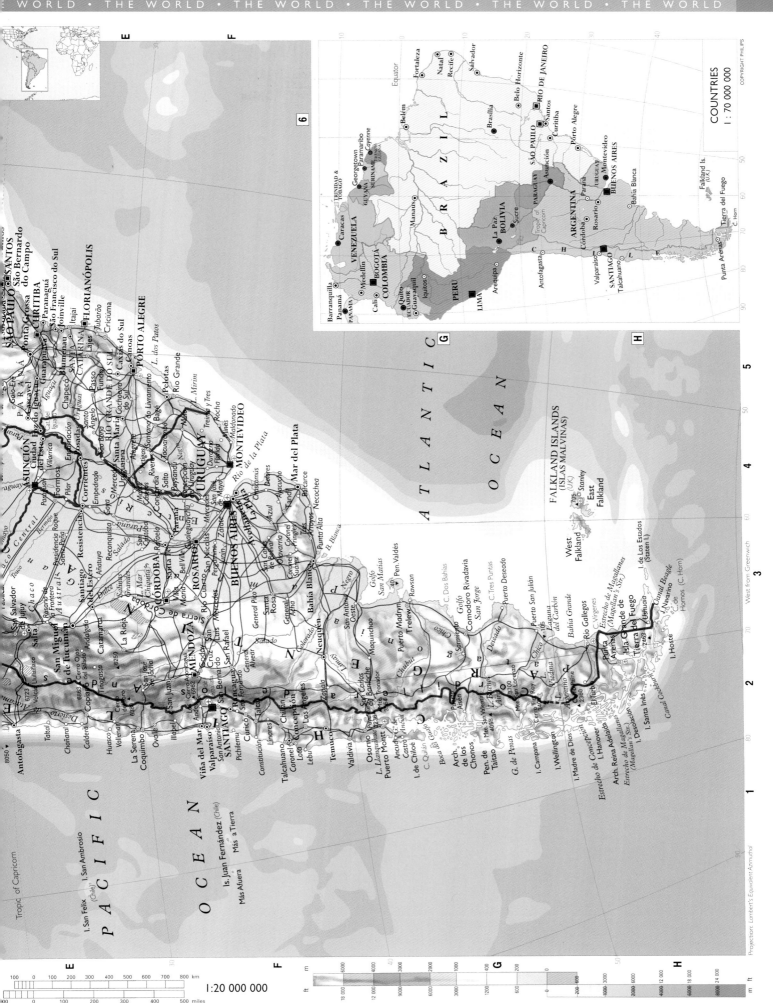

E F 6

COUNTRIES
1 : 70 000 000

COPYRIGHT PHILIPS

Equator

Baranquilla
Panamá
PANAMA
Cali
COLOMBIA
Medellín
BOGOTA
Quito
ECUADOR
Guayaquil
Iquitos
PERU
LIMA
Arequipa

VENEZUELA
Caracas

TRINIDAD &
TOBAGO
Georgetown
GUYANA
Paramaribo
SURINAME
Cayenne
FRENCH
GUIANA

Belém
Fortaleza
Natal
Recife
Salvador

Manaus

B R A Z I L

Brasília
Belo Horizonte
RIO DE JANEIRO
SÃO PAULO
Santos
Curitiba
Pôrto Alegre

La Paz
BOLIVIA
Sucre

PARAGUAY
Asunción

C H I L E

ARGENTINA
Córdoba
Rosario
Paraná
URUGUAY
Montevideo
BUENOS AIRES
Bahía Blanca

Antofagasta
Valparaíso
SANTIAGO
Talcahuano

Tropic of
Capricorn

Punta Arenas
Tierra del Fuego
C. Horn

Falkland Is.
(U.K.)

G H

ATLANTIC OCEAN

PACIFIC OCEAN

SÃO PAULO
SANTOS
São Bernardo
do Campo
CURITIBA
Ponta Grossa
Paranaguá
São Francisco do Sul
Joinville
Itajaí
Blumenau
FLORIANÓPOLIS
CATARINA
Tubarão
Criciúma
L. dos Patos
Lajes
Caxias do Sul
Canoas
PORTO ALEGRE
Rio Grande
Pelotas
L. Mirim

ASUNCIÓN
Ciudad del Este
RIO GRANDE DO SUL
Santa Maria
Santana do Livramento
Bagé
Formosa
Pilar
Resistencia
Corrientes
URUGUAY
Rocha
Maldonado
Treinta y Tres
MONTEVIDEO
Mar del Plata

CÓRDOBA
Santa Fe
ROSARIO
BUENOS AIRES
La Plata
Azul
Tandil
Necochea
Bahía Blanca
Punta Alta

San Miguel
de Tucumán
Salta
San Salvador
de Jujuy
Catamarca
La Rioja
San Juan
MENDOZA
San Rafael
San Luis
General Pico
Santa Rosa
Neuquén
Río Colorado
San Antonio Oeste
Golfo
San Matías
Pen. Valdés
Rawson
Trelew
Puerto Madryn
Golfo San Jorge
Comodoro Rivadavia
Puerto Deseado
Puerto San Julián
Río Gallegos

Antofagasta
Taltal
Chañaral
Caldera
Copiapó
Vallenar
Huasco
La Serena
Coquimbo
Ovalle
Illapel
Valparaíso
Viña del Mar
SANTIAGO
San Antonio
Rancagua
Curicó
Talca
Linares
Chillán
Concepción
Talcahuano
Coronel
Lota
Los Angeles
Lebu
Temuco
Valdivia
Osorno
Puerto Montt
L. Llanquihue
I. de Chiloé
Castro
Arch. de los Chonos
Pen. de Taitao
G. de Penas
I. Campana
I. Wellington
I. Madre de Dios
Arch. Reina Adelaida
Estrecho de Magallanes
(Magellan's Str.)
I. Santa Inés
I. Desolación
I. Hanover

FALKLAND ISLANDS
(ISLAS MALVINAS)
West Falkland
East Falkland
Stanley

Estrecho de Magallanes
(Magellan's Str.)
Punta Arenas
Tierra del Fuego
I. de los Estados
(Staten I.)
Canal Beagle
C. de Hornos (C. Horn)
I. Navarino
I. Hoste

West from Greenwich

Projection: Lambert's Equivalent Azimuthal

E
100 0 100 200 300 400 500 600 700 800 km
0 100 200 300 400 500 miles
1:20 000 000

m
6000
4000
3000
2000
1000
400
200
0

ft
18 000
12 000
9000
6000
3000
1200
600
0
600
3000
6000
12 000
18 000
24 000
ft

m
200
2000
4000
6000
8000
m

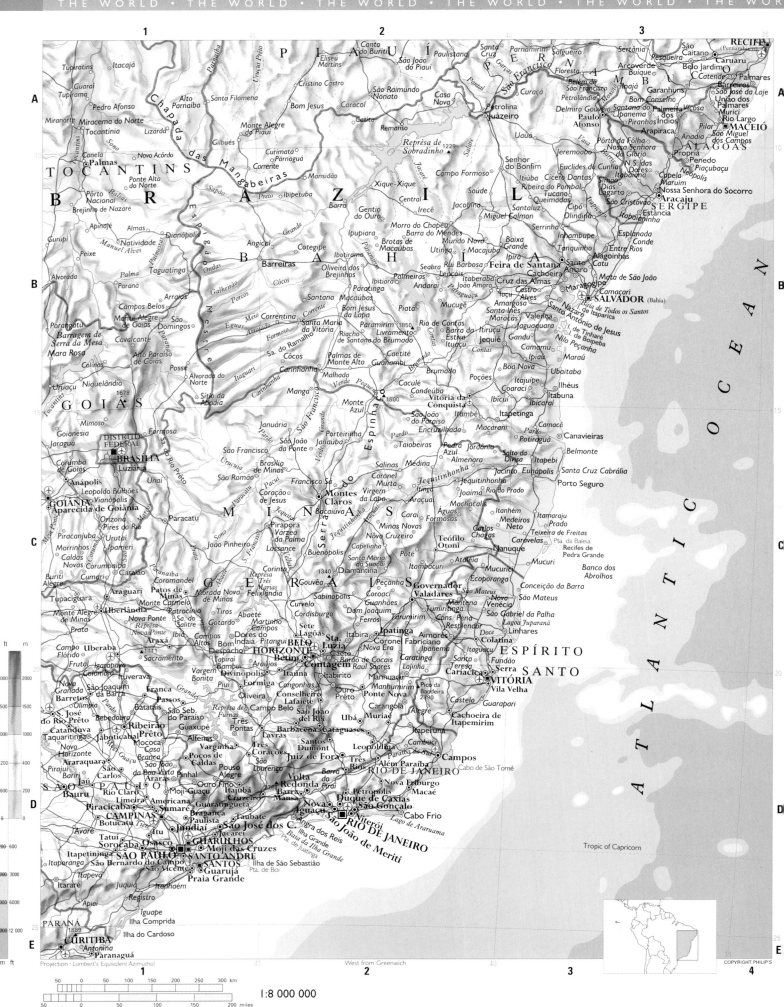

Projection : Lambert's Equivalent Azimuthal

West from Greenwich

1:8 000 000

COPYRIGHT PHILIP'S

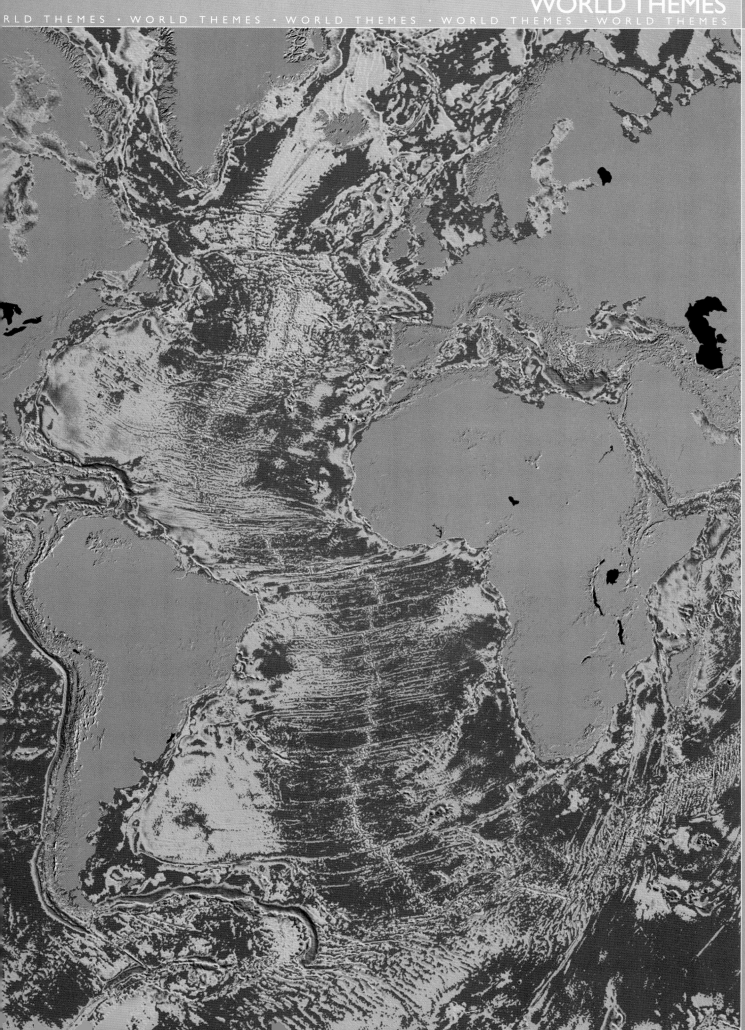

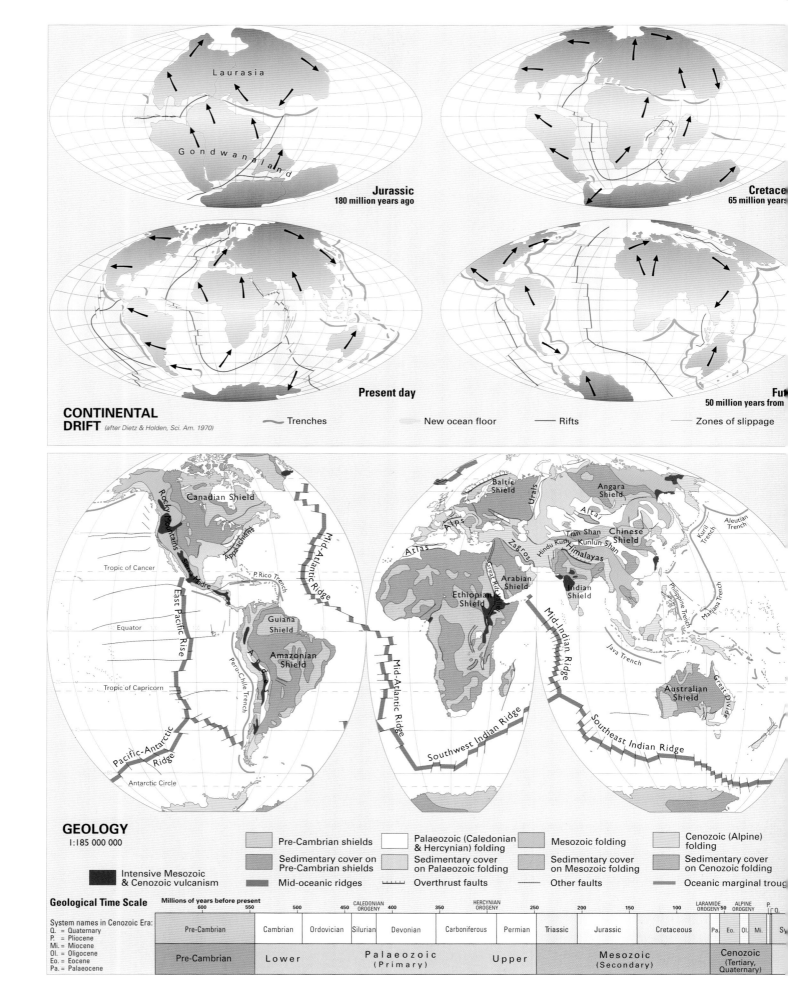

Laurasia

Gondwanaland

Jurassic
180 million years ago

Cretace
65 million years

Present day

Fu
50 million years from

CONTINENTAL DRIFT *(after Dietz & Holden, Sci. Am. 1970)*

— Trenches   New ocean floor   — Rifts   Zones of slippage

GEOLOGY
1:185 000 000

Pre-Cambrian shields	Palaeozoic (Caledonian & Hercynian) folding	Mesozoic folding
		Cenozoic (Alpine) folding
Sedimentary cover on Pre-Cambrian shields	Sedimentary cover on Palaeozoic folding	Sedimentary cover on Mesozoic folding
		Sedimentary cover on Cenozoic folding

Intensive Mesozoic & Cenozoic vulcanism   Mid-oceanic ridges   Overthrust faults   Other faults   Oceanic marginal troug

Geological Time Scale

System names in Cenozoic Era:
Q. = Quaternary
P. = Pliocene
Mi. = Miocene
Ol. = Oligocene
Eo. = Eocene
Pa. = Palaeocene

Millions of years before present

	600	550	500	450	CALEDONIAN OROGENY 400	350	HERCYNIAN OROGENY	250	200	150	100	LARAMIDE OROGENY 50	ALPINE OROGENY	P.	
	Pre-Cambrian		Cambrian	Ordovician	Silurian	Devonian	Carboniferous	Permian	Triassic	Jurassic	Cretaceous	Pa.	Eo.	Ol. Mi.	Sy

Pre-Cambrian	Lower	Palaeozoic (Primary)	Upper	Mesozoic (Secondary)	Cenozoic (Tertiary, Quaternary)

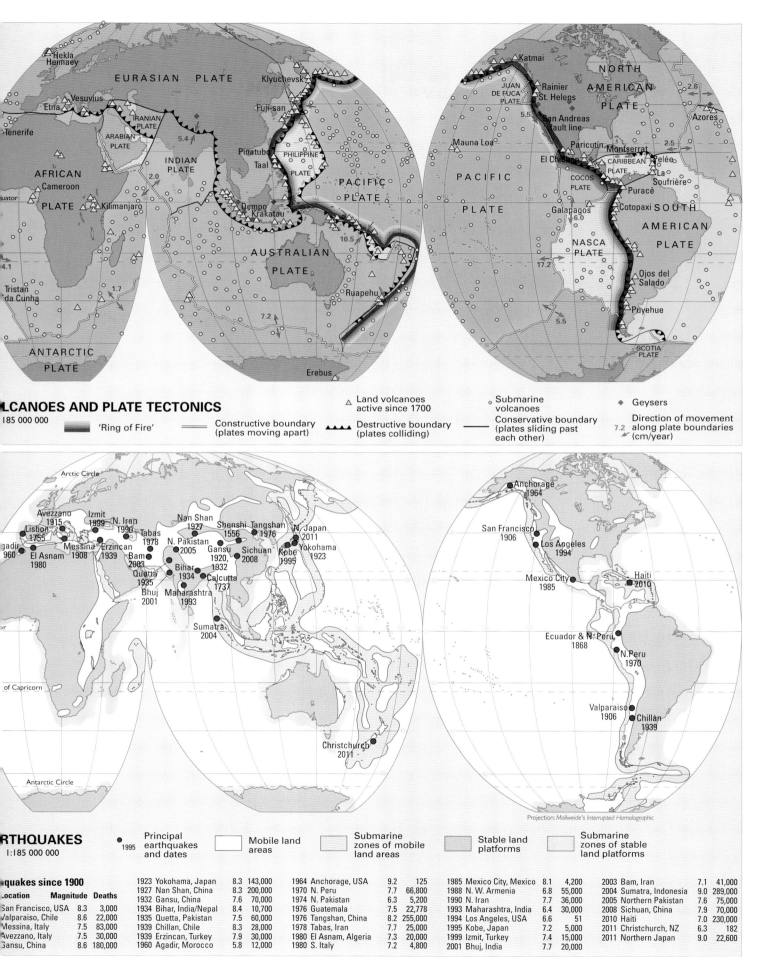

LCANOES AND PLATE TECTONICS

185 000 000

'Ring of Fire'

△ Land volcanoes active since 1700
∘ Submarine volcanoes
✛ Geysers

Constructive boundary (plates moving apart)
▲▲▲ Destructive boundary (plates colliding)
Conservative boundary (plates sliding past each other)
7.2 ⬿ Direction of movement along plate boundaries (cm/year)

RTHQUAKES

1:185 000 000

● 1995 Principal earthquakes and dates
☐ Mobile land areas
☐ Submarine zones of mobile land areas
☐ Stable land platforms
☐ Submarine zones of stable land platforms

quakes since 1900

Location	Magnitude	Deaths									
San Francisco, USA	8.3	3,000	1923 Yokohama, Japan	8.3	143,000	1964 Anchorage, USA	9.2	125	1985 Mexico City, Mexico	8.1	4,200
			1927 Nan Shan, China	8.3	200,000	1970 N. Peru	7.7	66,800	1988 N. W. Armenia	6.8	55,000
Valparaiso, Chile	8.6	22,000	1932 Gansu, China	7.6	70,000	1974 N. Pakistan	6.3	5,200	1990 N. Iran	7.7	36,000
Messina, Italy	7.5	83,000	1934 Bihar, India/Nepal	8.4	10,700	1976 Guatemala	7.5	22,778	1993 Maharashtra, India	6.4	30,000
Avezzano, Italy	7.5	30,000	1935 Quetta, Pakistan	7.5	60,000	1976 Tangshan, China	8.2	255,000	1994 Los Angeles, USA	6.6	51
Gansu, China	8.6	180,000	1939 Chillan, Chile	8.3	28,000	1978 Tabas, Iran	7.7	25,000	1995 Kobe, Japan	7.2	5,000
			1939 Erzincan, Turkey	7.9	30,000	1980 El Asnam, Algeria	7.3	20,000	1999 Izmit, Turkey	7.4	15,000
			1960 Agadir, Morocco	5.8	12,000	1980 S. Italy	7.2	4,800	2001 Bhuj, India	7.7	20,000

2003 Bam, Iran	7.1	41,000
2004 Sumatra, Indonesia	9.0	289,000
2005 Northern Pakistan	7.6	75,000
2008 Sichuan, China	7.9	70,000
2010 Haiti	7.0	230,000
2011 Christchurch, NZ	6.3	182
2011 Northern Japan	9.0	22,600

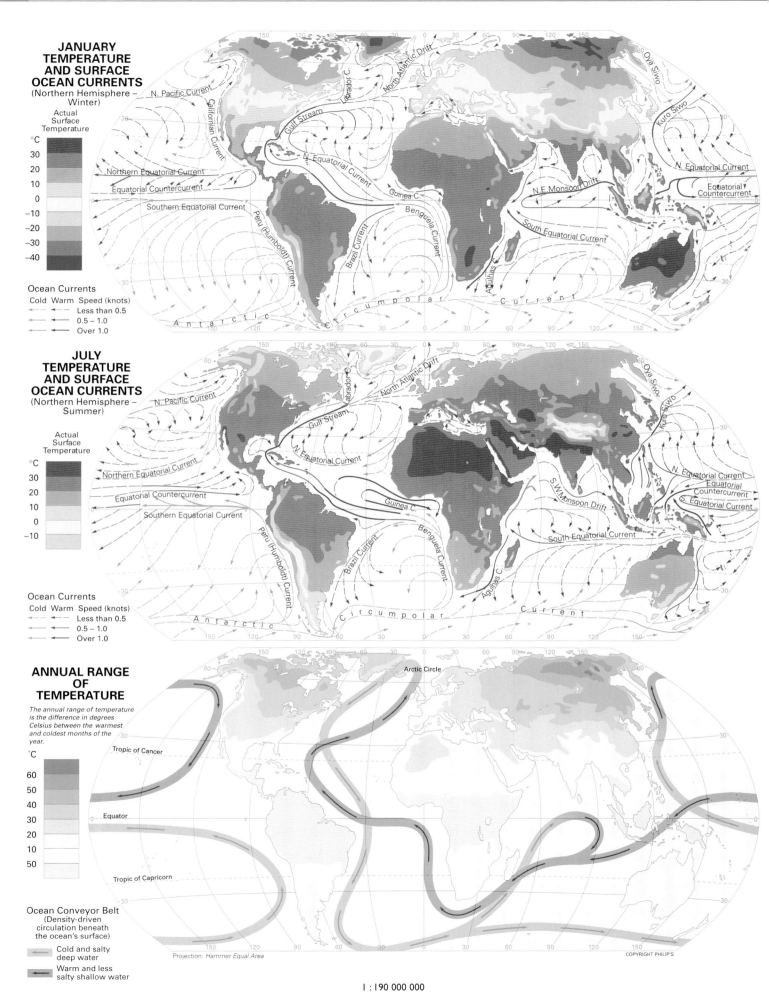

JANUARY TEMPERATURE AND SURFACE OCEAN CURRENTS
(Northern Hemisphere – Winter)

Actual Surface Temperature

°C
30
20
10
0
−10
−20
−30
−40

Ocean Currents

Cold	Warm	Speed (knots)
		Less than 0.5
		0.5 – 1.0
		Over 1.0

JULY TEMPERATURE AND SURFACE OCEAN CURRENTS
(Northern Hemisphere – Summer)

Actual Surface Temperature

°C
30
20
10
0
−10

Ocean Currents

Cold	Warm	Speed (knots)
		Less than 0.5
		0.5 – 1.0
		Over 1.0

ANNUAL RANGE OF TEMPERATURE

The annual range of temperature is the difference in degrees Celsius between the warmest and coldest months of the year.

°C
60
50
40
30
20
10
50

Ocean Conveyor Belt
(Density-driven circulation beneath the ocean's surface)

Cold and salty deep water

Warm and less salty shallow water

Projection: *Hammer Equal Area*

COPYRIGHT PHILIP'S

1 : 190 000 000

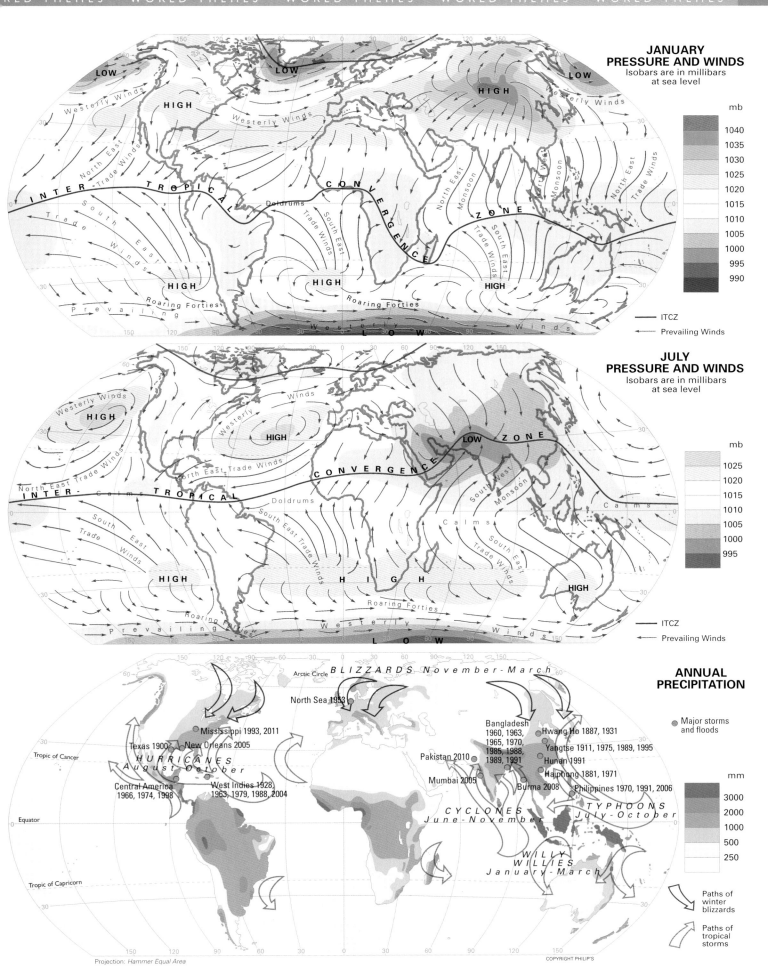

JANUARY PRESSURE AND WINDS
Isobars are in millibars at sea level

LOW
LOW
LOW
HIGH
HIGH
Westerly Winds
Westerly Winds
Westerly Winds
North East Trade Winds
North East Trade Winds
North East Trade Winds
INTER - TROPICAL CONVERGENCE ZONE
Doldrums
Trade
South East Trade Winds
South East Trade Winds
South East Trade Winds
Winds
HIGH
HIGH
HIGH
Roaring Forties
Roaring Forties
Prevailing
Westerly Winds
LOW
North West Monsoon

mb
1040
1035
1030
1025
1020
1015
1010
1005
1000
995
990

—— ITCZ
←— Prevailing Winds

JULY PRESSURE AND WINDS
Isobars are in millibars at sea level

HIGH
HIGH
HIGH
LOW ZONE
Westerly Winds
Westerly
Winds
North East Trade Winds
North East Trade Winds
INTER - Calms TROPICAL CONVERGENCE
Doldrums
South East Trade Winds
South East Trade Winds
Calms
South West Monsoon
Calms
HIGH
HIGH
HIGH
HIGH
Roaring Forties
Roaring Forties
Prevailing
Westerly Winds
LOW

mb
1025
1020
1015
1010
1005
1000
995

—— ITCZ
←— Prevailing Winds

ANNUAL PRECIPITATION

Arctic Circle
BLIZZARDS November-March
North Sea 1953
Mississippi 1993, 2011
Texas 1900
New Orleans 2005
Tropic of Cancer
HURRICANES August-October
Central America 1966, 1974, 1998
West Indies 1928, 1963, 1979, 1988, 2004
Equator
Bangladesh 1960, 1963, 1965, 1970, 1985, 1988, 1989, 1991
Pakistan 2010
Mumbai 2005
Hwang Ho 1887, 1931
Yangtse 1911, 1975, 1989, 1995
Hunan 1991
Haiphong 1881, 1971
Burma 2008
Philippines 1970, 1991, 2006
CYCLONES June-November
TYPHOONS July-October
WILLY WILLIES January-March
Tropic of Capricorn

● Major storms and floods

mm
3000
2000
1000
500
250

⟡ Paths of winter blizzards
⟡ Paths of tropical storms

Projection: Hammer Equal Area
COPYRIGHT PHILIP'S

KEY TO CLIMATE REGIONS MAP

Climate group	Climate	Temperature	Rainfall
A TROPICAL RAINY CLIMATES	**Af** RAIN FOREST CLIMATE / **Am** MONSOON CLIMATE / **Aw** SAVANNA CLIMATE	All mean monthly temperatures above 18°C	*(graph: Rainfall during the driest month (mm) vs Annual rainfall (mm); zones Af, Aw, Am)*
B DRY CLIMATES	**BS** STEPPE CLIMATE / **BW** DESERT CLIMATE	Mean annual temperature; h = above 18°C; k = below 18°C	*(graph: Mean annual temperature °C vs Annual rainfall (mm); BW, BS, BW/BS boundary, BS/Wet Climates Boundary, Wet Climates A,C,D)*
C WARM TEMPERATE RAINY CLIMATES	**Cw** DRY WINTER CLIMATE / **Cs** DRY SUMMER CLIMATE (Mediterranean) / **Cf** CLIMATE WITH NO DRY SEASON	Mean temperature of the coldest month between -3°C to 18°C	**a** Mean temperature of hottest month above 22°C, and with more than 4 months of over 10°C — **w** dry winter Rainfall of the driest month of the cold season is one-tenth or less of the rainfall of the wettest month of the hot season; **b** Mean temperature of hottest month below 22°C and with more than 4 months of over 10°C — **s** dry summer Rainfall of the driest month of the hot season is less than one-third of the rainfall of the wettest month of the cold season and less than 40mm
D COLD TEMPERATE RAINY CLIMATES	**Dw** DRY WINTER CLIMATE / **Df** CLIMATE WITH NO DRY SEASON	Mean temperature of the coldest month below -3°C	**c** Mean temperature of hottest month below 22°C, but with less than 4 months of over 10°C — **f** with no dry season Rainfall does not correspond to **w** or **s** climates; **d** Mean temperature of hottest month above 22°C, and of the coldest month below -38°C
E POLAR CLIMATES	**ET** TUNDRA CLIMATE / **EF** PERPETUAL FROST	Mean temperature of the hottest month between 0°C and 10°C; Mean temperature of the hottest month below 0°C	**H** More than 1500m above sea level

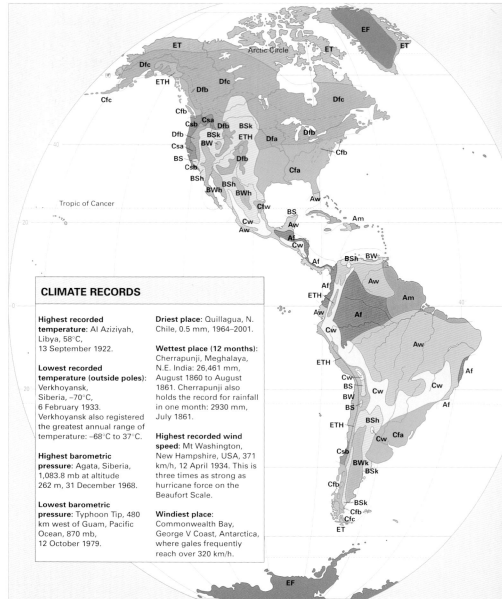

Projection: *Interrupted Mollweide's Homolographic*

CLIMATE RECORDS

Highest recorded temperature: Al Aziziyah, Libya, 58°C, 13 September 1922.

Lowest recorded temperature (outside poles): Verkhoyansk, Siberia, −70°C, 6 February 1933. Verkhoyansk also registered the greatest annual range of temperature: −68°C to 37°C.

Highest barometric pressure: Agata, Siberia, 1,083.8 mb at altitude 262 m, 31 December 1968.

Lowest barometric pressure: Typhoon Tip, 480 km west of Guam, Pacific Ocean, 870 mb, 12 October 1979.

Driest place: Quillagua, N. Chile, 0.5 mm, 1964–2001.

Wettest place (12 months): Cherrapunji, Meghalaya, N.E. India: 26,461 mm, August 1860 to August 1861. Cherrapunji also holds the record for rainfall in one month: 2930 mm, July 1861.

Highest recorded wind speed: Mt Washington, New Hampshire, USA, 371 km/h, 12 April 1934. This is three times as strong as hurricane force on the Beaufort Scale.

Windiest place: Commonwealth Bay, George V Coast, Antarctica, where gales frequently reach over 320 km/h.

THE MONSOON   1:90 000 000

Monthly rainfall

mm		mm	
400		50	→ wind direction
200		25	ITCZ (intertropical convergence zone)
100		0	

In early March, which normally marks the end of the subcontinent's cool season and the start of the hot season, winds blow outwards from the mainland. But as the overhead sun and the ITCZ move northwards, the land is intensely heated, and a low-pressure system develops. The south-east trade winds, which are drawn across the Equator, change direction and are sucked into the interior to become south-westerly winds, bringing heavy rain. By November, the overhead sun and the ITCZ have again moved southwards and the wind directions are again reversed. Cool winds blow from the Asian interior to the sea, losing any moisture on the Himalayas before descending to the coast.

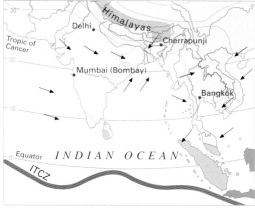

March – Start of the hot, dry season, the ITCZ is over the southern Indian Ocean.

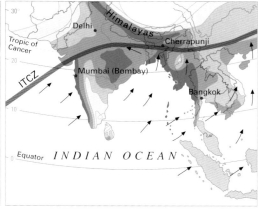

July – The rainy season, the ITCZ has migrated northwards; winds blow onshore.

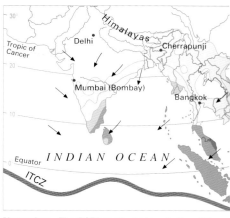

November – The ITCZ has returned south, the offshore are cool and dry.

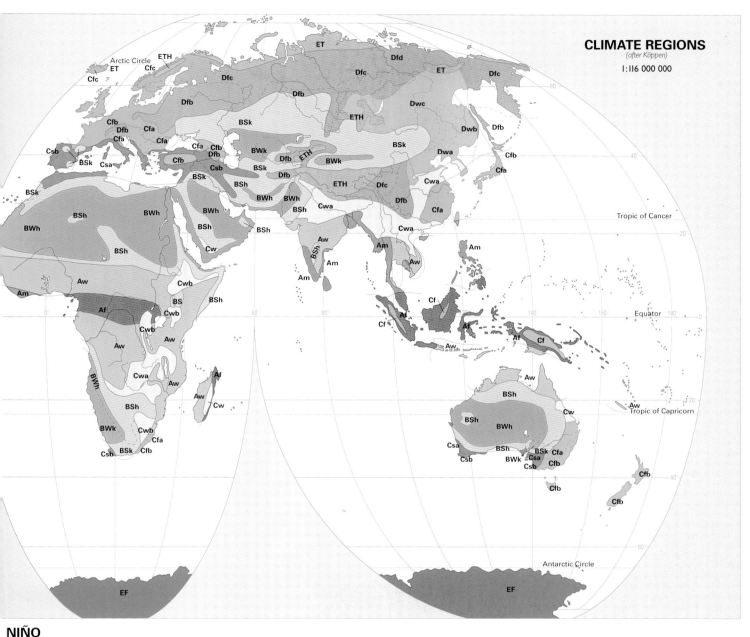

CLIMATE REGIONS
(after Köppen)

1:116 000 000

NIÑO

iño, 'The Little Boy' in Spanish, was originally the name given by local fishermen to the
m current that can appear off the Pacific coast of South America. In a normal year,
th-easterly trade winds drive surface waters westwards off the coast of South America,
wing cold, nutrient-rich water up from below. In an El Niño year, warm water from the
t Pacific suppresses upwelling in the east, depriving the region of nutrients and driving
fish away. The water is warmed by as much as 7°C, disturbing the tropical atmosphere
ulation. During an intense El Niño, the south-east trade winds change direction and
ome equatorial westerlies, resulting in climatic extremes in many regions of the world,
h as drought in parts of Australia and India, and heavy rainfall in south-eastern USA.

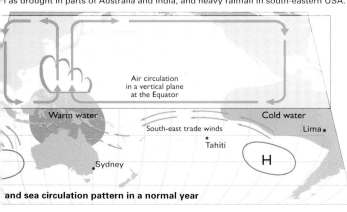

and sea circulation pattern in a normal year

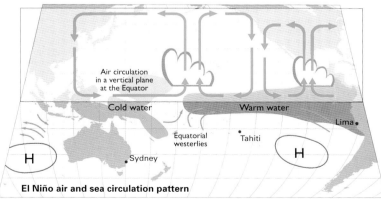

El Niño air and sea circulation pattern

El Niño events occur about every 4 to 7 years and typically last for around 12 to 18
months. El Niño usually results in reduced rainfall across northern and eastern Australia.
This can lead to widespread and severe drought, as well as increased temperatures and
bushfire risk. However, each El Niño event is unique in terms of its strength as well as its
impact. It is measured by the Southern Oscillation Index (SOI) and the changes in ocean
temperatures.
La Niña, or 'The Little Girl', is associated with cooler waters in the central and eastern
Pacific. A La Niña year can result in cooler land temperatures across the tropics and
subtropics and more storms in the North Atlantic.

COPYRIGHT PHILIP'S

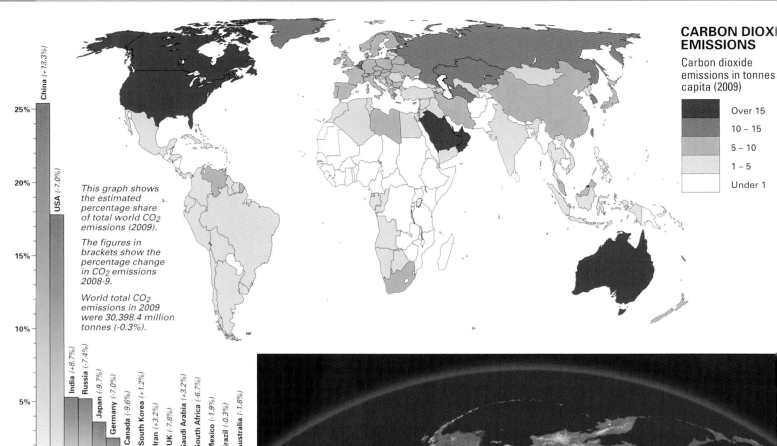

CARBON DIOXIDE EMISSIONS

Carbon dioxide emissions in tonnes capita (2009)

- Over 15
- 10 – 15
- 5 – 10
- 1 – 5
- Under 1

This graph shows the estimated percentage share of total world CO₂ emissions (2009).

The figures in brackets show the percentage change in CO₂ emissions 2008-9.

World total CO₂ emissions in 2009 were 30,398.4 million tonnes (-0.3%).

Bar chart labels:
- China (+13.3%)
- USA (-7.0%)
- India (+8.7%)
- Russia (-7.4%)
- Japan (-9.7%)
- Germany (-7.0%)
- Canada (-9.6%)
- South Korea (+1.2%)
- Iran (+3.2%)
- UK (-7.8%)
- Saudi Arabia (+3.2%)
- South Africa (-6.7%)
- Mexico (-1.9%)
- Brazil (-0.3%)
- Australia (-1.8%)

Arctic Ice Cap

This image shows the extent of sea-ice in the Arctic in September 2008. The sea-ice area expands and contracts seasonally and September, at the end of the northern hemisphere summer, represents its smallest extent. The year 2008 showed the biggest reduction in sea-ice since satellite surveillance began in 1979 and this is believed to be related to climate change and global warming. Although dramatic, the sea-ice itself is thought to be quite thin, on average about 3 m (10 ft) thick. Even large reductions would not in themselves involve any sea-level change since the ice is floating and displaces the sea water. One by-product of this is the opening-up of clear sea. This would enable shipping in the northern hemisphere to move between the Atlantic and Pacific Oceans using the much shorter routes around the north coasts of Canada and of Russia, rather than heading south to do this.

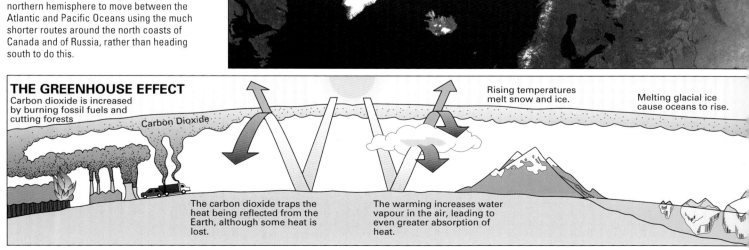

THE GREENHOUSE EFFECT

Carbon dioxide is increased by burning fossil fuels and cutting forests

Carbon Dioxide

Rising temperatures melt snow and ice.

Melting glacial ice cause oceans to rise.

The carbon dioxide traps the heat being reflected from the Earth, although some heat is lost.

The warming increases water vapour in the air, leading to even greater absorption of heat.

PREDICTED CHANGE IN TEMPERATURE

The difference between actual annual average surface air temperature, 1960–90, and predicted annual average surface air temperature, 2070–2100. This map shows the predicted increase, assuming a 'medium growth' of the global economy and assuming that no measures to combat the emission of greenhouse gases are taken.

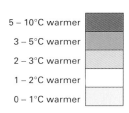

- 5 – 10°C warmer
- 3 – 5°C warmer
- 2 – 3°C warmer
- 1 – 2°C warmer
- 0 – 1°C warmer

Source: The Hadley Centre of Climate Prediction and Research, The Met. Office.

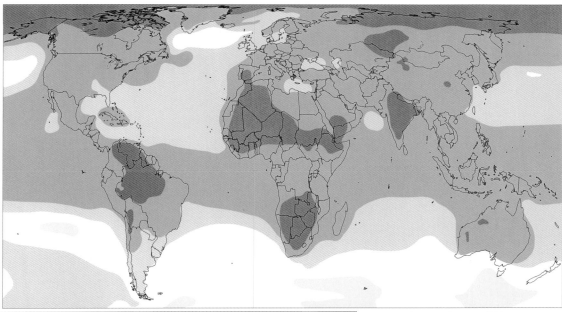

PREDICTED CHANGE IN PRECIPITATION

The difference between actual annual average precipitation, 1960–90, and predicted annual average precipitation, 2070–2100. It should be noted that these predicted annual mean changes mask quite significant seasonal detail.

- Over 2 mm more rain per day
- 1 – 2 mm more rain per day
- 0.5 – 1 mm more rain per day
- 0.2 – 0.5 mm more rain per day
- No change
- 0.2 – 0.5 mm less rain per day
- 0.5 – 1 mm less rain per day
- 1 – 2 mm less rain per day
- Over 2 mm less rain per day

DESERTIFICATION AND DEFORESTATION

- Existing deserts and dry areas
- Areas with a high risk of desertification
- Areas with a moderate risk of desertification
- Former extent of rainforest
- Existing rainforest

Deforestation 1990–2010

	Total forest cover in million ha 1990	Total forest cover in million ha 2010	% change 1990-2010
	574.8	519.5	-9.6
ia	153.4	147.4	-3.9
sia	118.5	90.9	-23.3
	69.9	67.0	-4.1
	62.8	57.2	-8.9
New Guinea	31.5	28.6	-9.2
on	24.3	19.9	-18.1
	22.7	22.3	-1.8
sia	20.4	18.6	-8.8
	17.0	8.7	-48.8
d	16.9	15.0	-11.2
ascar	13.5	12.1	-10.4

COPYRIGHT PHILIP'S

THE WORLD CLIMATE STATISTICS

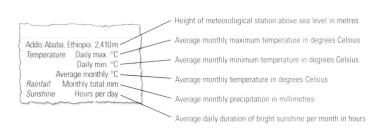

Addis Ababa, Ethiopia 2,410m — Height of meteorological station above sea level in metres
Temperature Daily max. °C — Average monthly maximum temperature in degrees Celsius
Daily min. °C — Average monthly minimum temperature in degrees Celsius
Average monthly °C — Average monthly temperature in degrees Celsius
Rainfall Monthly total mm — Average monthly precipitation in millimetres
Sunshine Hours per day — Average daily duration of bright sunshine per month in hours

	Jan	Feb	Mar	Apr	May	June	July	Aug	Sept	Oct	Nov	Dec	Year
Addis Ababa, Ethiopia 2,410m													
Temperature Daily max. °C	23	24	25	24	25	23	20	20	21	22	23	22	23
Daily min. °C	6	7	9	10	9	10	11	11	10	7	5	5	8
Average monthly °C	14	15	17	17	17	16	16	15	15	15	14	14	15
Rainfall Monthly total mm	13	35	67	91	81	117	247	255	167	29	8	5	1,115
Sunshine Hours per day	8.7	8.2	7.6	8.1	6.5	4.8	2.8	3.2	5.2	7.6	6.7	7	6.4
Alice Springs, Australia 580m													
Temperature Daily max. °C	35	35	32	27	23	19	19	23	27	31	33	35	28
Daily min. °C	21	20	17	12	8	5	4	6	10	15	18	20	13
Average monthly °C	28	27	25	20	15	12	12	14	18	23	25	27	21
Rainfall Monthly total mm	44	33	27	10	15	13	7	8	7	18	29	38	249
Sunshine Hours per day	10.3	10.4	9.3	9.2	8	8	8.9	9.8	10	9.7	10.1	10	9.5
Anchorage, USA 183m													
Temperature Daily max. °C	–7	–3	0	7	13	18	19	17	13	6	–2	–6	–6
Daily min. °C	–15	–12	–9	–2	4	8	10	9	5	–2	–9	–14	–2
Average monthly °C	–11	–7	–4	3	9	13	15	13	9	2	–5	–10	–4
Rainfall Monthly total mm	20	18	13	11	13	25	47	64	64	47	28	24	374
Sunshine Hours per day	2.4	4.1	6.6	8.3	8.3	9.2	8.5	6	4.4	3.1	2.6	1.6	5.4
Athens, Greece 107m													
Temperature Daily max. °C	13	14	16	20	25	30	33	33	29	24	19	15	23
Daily min. °C	6	7	8	11	16	20	23	23	19	15	12	8	14
Average monthly °C	10	10	12	16	20	25	28	28	24	20	15	11	18
Rainfall Monthly total mm	62	37	37	23	23	14	6	7	15	51	56	71	402
Sunshine Hours per day	3.9	5.2	5.8	7.7	8.9	10.7	11.9	11.5	9.4	6.8	4.8	3.8	7.3
Bahrain City, Bahrain 2m													
Temperature Daily max. °C	20	21	25	29	33	36	37	38	36	32	27	22	30
Daily min. °C	14	15	18	22	25	29	31	32	29	25	22	16	23
Average monthly °C	17	18	21	25	29	32	34	35	32	29	25	19	26
Rainfall Monthly total mm	18	12	10	9	2	0	0	0	0	0.4	3	16	70
Sunshine Hours per day	5.9	6.9	7.9	8.8	10.6	13.2	12.1	12	12	10.3	7.7	6.4	9.5
Bangkok, Thailand 10m													
Temperature Daily max. °C	32	33	34	35	34	33	32	32	32	31	31	31	33
Daily min. °C	20	23	24	26	25	25	25	24	24	24	23	20	24
Average monthly °C	26	28	29	30	30	29	28	28	28	28	27	26	28
Rainfall Monthly total mm	9	30	36	82	165	153	168	183	310	239	55	8	1,438
Sunshine Hours per day	8.2	8	8	10	7.5	6.1	4.7	5.2	5.2	6.1	7.3	7.8	7
Brasilia, Brazil 910m													
Temperature Daily max. °C	28	28	28	28	27	27	27	29	30	29	28	27	28
Daily min. °C	18	18	18	17	15	13	13	14	16	18	18	18	16
Average monthly °C	23	23	23	22	21	20	20	21	23	24	23	22	22
Rainfall Monthly total mm	252	204	227	93	17	3	6	3	30	127	255	343	1,560
Sunshine Hours per day	5.8	5.7	6	7.4	8.7	9.3	9.6	9.8	7.9	6.5	4.8	4.4	7.2
Buenos Aires, Argentina 25m													
Temperature Daily max. °C	30	29	26	22	18	14	14	16	18	21	25	28	22
Daily min. °C	17	17	16	12	9	5	6	6	8	10	14	16	11
Average monthly °C	23	23	21	17	13	10	10	11	13	15	19	22	16
Rainfall Monthly total mm	79	71	109	89	76	61	56	61	79	86	84	99	950
Sunshine Hours per day	9.2	8.5	7.5	6.8	4.9	3.5	3.8	5.2	6	6.8	8.1	8.5	6.6
Cairo, Egypt 75m													
Temperature Daily max. °C	19	21	24	28	32	35	35	35	33	30	26	21	28
Daily min. °C	9	9	12	14	18	20	22	22	20	18	14	10	16
Average monthly °C	14	15	18	21	25	28	29	28	26	24	20	16	22
Rainfall Monthly total mm	4	4	3	1	2	1	0	0	1	1	3	7	27
Sunshine Hours per day	6.9	8.4	8.7	9.7	10.5	11.9	11.7	11.3	10.4	9.4	8.3	6.4	9.5
Cape Town, South Africa 44m													
Temperature Daily max. °C	26	26	25	23	20	18	17	18	19	21	24	25	22
Daily min. °C	15	15	14	11	9	7	7	7	8	10	13	15	11
Average monthly °C	21	20	20	17	14	13	12	12	14	16	18	20	16
Rainfall Monthly total mm	12	19	17	42	67	98	68	76	36	45	12	13	505
Sunshine Hours per day	11.4	10.2	9.4	7.7	6.1	5.7	6.4	6.6	7.6	8.6	10.2	10.9	8.4
Casablanca, Morocco 59m													
Temperature Daily max. °C	17	18	20	21	22	24	26	26	26	24	21	18	22
Daily min. °C	8	9	11	12	15	18	19	20	18	15	12	10	14
Average monthly °C	13	13	15	16	18	21	23	23	22	20	17	14	18
Rainfall Monthly total mm	78	61	54	37	20	3	0	1	6	28	58	94	440
Sunshine Hours per day	5.2	6.3	7.3	9	9.4	9.7	10.2	9.7	9.1	7.4	5.9	5.3	7.9

	Jan	Feb	Mar	Apr	May	June	July	Aug	Sept	Oct	Nov	Dec	Year
Chicago, USA 186m													
Temperature Daily max. °C	1	2	6	14	21	26	29	28	24	17	8	2	15
Daily min. °C	–7	–6	–2	5	11	16	20	19	14	8	0	–5	–6
Average monthly °C	–3	–2	2	9	16	21	24	23	19	13	4	–2	4
Rainfall Monthly total mm	47	41	70	77	96	103	86	80	69	71	56	48	844
Sunshine Hours per day	4	5	6.6	6.9	8.9	10.2	10	9.2	8.2	6.9	4.5	3.7	7
Christchurch, New Zealand 5m													
Temperature Daily max. °C	21	21	19	17	13	11	10	11	14	17	19	21	16
Daily min. °C	12	12	10	7	4	2	1	3	5	7	8	11	7
Average monthly °C	16	16	15	12	9	6	6	7	9	12	13	16	11
Rainfall Monthly total mm	56	46	43	46	76	69	61	58	51	51	51	61	669
Sunshine Hours per day	7	6.5	5.6	4.7	4.3	3.9	4.1	4.7	5.6	6.1	6.9	6.3	5.5
Colombo, Sri Lanka 10m													
Temperature Daily max. °C	30	31	31	31	30	30	29	29	30	29	29	30	30
Daily min. °C	22	22	23	24	25	25	25	25	25	24	23	22	24
Average monthly °C	26	26	27	28	28	27	27	27	27	27	26	26	27
Rainfall Monthly total mm	101	66	118	230	394	220	140	102	174	348	333	142	2,368
Sunshine Hours per day	7.9	9	8.1	7.2	6.4	5.4	6.1	6.3	6.2	6.5	6.4	7.8	6.9
Darwin, Australia 30m													
Temperature Daily max. °C	32	32	33	33	33	31	31	32	33	34	34	33	33
Daily min. °C	25	25	25	24	23	21	19	21	23	25	26	26	24
Average monthly °C	29	29	29	29	28	26	25	26	28	29	30	29	28
Rainfall Monthly total mm	405	309	279	77	8	2	0	1	15	48	108	214	1,466
Sunshine Hours per day	5.8	5.8	6.6	9.8	9.3	10	9.9	10.4	10.1	9.4	9.6	6.8	8.6
Harbin, China 175m													
Temperature Daily max. °C	–14	–9	0	12	21	26	29	27	20	12	–1	–11	9
Daily min. °C	–26	–23	–12	–1	7	14	18	16	8	0	–12	–22	–3
Average monthly °C	–20	–16	–6	6	14	20	23	22	14	6	–7	–17	3
Rainfall Monthly total mm	4	6	17	23	44	92	167	119	52	36	12	5	577
Sunshine Hours per day	6.4	7.8	8	7.8	8.3	8.6	8.6	8.2	7.2	6.9	6.1	5.7	7.5
Hong Kong, China 35m													
Temperature Daily max. °C	18	18	20	24	28	30	31	31	30	27	24	20	25
Daily min. °C	13	13	16	19	23	26	26	26	25	23	19	15	20
Average monthly °C	16	15	18	22	25	28	28	28	27	25	21	17	23
Rainfall Monthly total mm	30	60	70	133	332	479	286	415	364	33	46	17	2,265
Sunshine Hours per day	4.7	3.5	3.1	3.8	5	5.4	6.8	6.5	6.6	7	6.2	5.5	5.3
Honolulu, Hawaii 5m													
Temperature Daily max. °C	26	26	26	27	28	29	29	29	30	29	28	26	28
Daily min. °C	19	19	19	20	21	22	23	23	23	22	21	20	21
Average monthly °C	23	22	23	23	24	26	26	26	26	26	24	23	24
Rainfall Monthly total mm	96	84	73	33	25	8	11	23	25	47	55	76	556
Sunshine Hours per day	7.3	7.7	8.3	8.6	8.8	9.1	9.4	9.3	9.2	8.3	7.5	6.2	8.3
Jakarta, Indonesia 10m													
Temperature Daily max. °C	29	29	30	31	31	31	31	31	31	31	30	29	30
Daily min. °C	23	23	23	24	24	23	23	23	23	23	23	23	23
Average monthly °C	26	26	27	27	27	27	27	27	27	27	27	26	27
Rainfall Monthly total mm	300	300	211	147	114	97	64	43	66	112	142	203	1,799
Sunshine Hours per day	6.1	6.5	7.7	8.5	8.4	8.5	9.1	9.5	9.6	9	7.7	7.1	8.1
Kabul, Afghanistan 1,791m													
Temperature Daily max. °C	2	4	12	19	26	31	33	33	30	22	17	8	20
Daily min. °C	–8	–6	1	6	11	13	16	15	11	6	1	–3	5
Average monthly °C	–3	–1	6	13	18	22	25	24	20	14	9	3	12
Rainfall Monthly total mm	28	61	72	117	33	1	7	1	0	1	37	14	372
Sunshine Hours per day	5.9	6	5.7	6.8	10.1	11.5	11.4	11.2	9.8	9.4	7.8	6.1	8.5
Khartoum, Sudan 380m													
Temperature Daily max. °C	32	33	37	40	42	41	38	36	38	39	35	32	37
Daily min. °C	16	17	20	23	26	27	26	25	25	25	21	17	22
Average monthly °C	24	25	28	32	34	34	32	30	32	32	28	25	30
Rainfall Monthly total mm	0	0	0	1	7	5	56	80	28	2	0	0	179
Sunshine Hours per day	10.6	11.2	10.4	10.8	10.4	10.1	8.6	8.6	9.6	10.3	10.8	10.6	10.2
Kingston, Jamaica 35m													
Temperature Daily max. °C	30	30	30	31	31	32	32	32	32	31	31	31	31
Daily min. °C	20	20	20	21	22	24	23	23	23	23	22	21	22
Average monthly °C	25	25	25	26	26	28	28	28	27	27	26	26	26
Rainfall Monthly total mm	23	15	23	31	102	89	38	91	99	180	74	36	801
Sunshine Hours per day	8.3	8.8	8.7	8.7	8.3	7.8	8.5	8.5	7.6	7.3	8.3	7.7	8.2

Kolkata (Calcutta), India 5m		Jan	Feb	Mar	Apr	May	June	July	Aug	Sept	Oct	Nov	Dec	Year
Temperature	Daily max. °C	27	29	34	36	35	34	32	32	32	32	29	26	31
	Daily min. °C	13	15	21	24	25	26	26	26	26	23	18	13	21
	Average monthly °C	20	22	27	30	30	30	29	29	29	28	23	20	26
Rainfall	Monthly total mm	10	30	34	44	140	297	325	332	253	114	20	5	1,604
Sunshine	Hours per day	8.6	8.7	8.9	9	8.7	5.4	4.1	4.1	5.1	6.5	8.3	8.4	7.1

Lagos, Nigeria 40m		Jan	Feb	Mar	Apr	May	June	July	Aug	Sept	Oct	Nov	Dec	Year
Temperature	Daily max. °C	32	33	33	32	31	29	28	28	29	30	31	32	31
	Daily min. °C	22	23	23	23	23	22	22	21	22	22	23	22	22
	Average monthly °C	27	28	28	28	27	26	25	24	25	26	27	27	26
Rainfall	Monthly total mm	28	41	99	99	203	300	180	56	180	190	63	25	1,464
Sunshine	Hours per day	5.9	6.8	6.3	6.1	5.6	3.8	2.8	3.3	3	5.1	6.6	6.5	5.2

Lima, Peru 120m		Jan	Feb	Mar	Apr	May	June	July	Aug	Sept	Oct	Nov	Dec	Year
Temperature	Daily max. °C	28	29	29	27	24	20	20	19	20	22	24	26	24
	Daily min. °C	19	20	19	17	16	15	14	14	14	15	16	17	16
	Average monthly °C	24	24	24	22	20	17	17	16	17	18	20	21	20
Rainfall	Monthly total mm	1	1	1	1	5	5	8	8	8	3	3	1	45
Sunshine	Hours per day	6.3	6.8	6.9	6.7	4	1.4	1.1	1	1.1	2.5	4.1	5	3.9

Lisbon, Portugal 77m		Jan	Feb	Mar	Apr	May	June	July	Aug	Sept	Oct	Nov	Dec	Year
Temperature	Daily max. °C	14	15	17	20	21	25	27	28	26	22	17	15	21
	Daily min. °C	8	8	10	12	13	15	17	17	17	14	11	9	13
	Average monthly °C	11	12	14	16	17	20	22	23	21	18	14	12	17
Rainfall	Monthly total mm	111	76	109	54	44	16	3	4	33	62	93	103	708
Sunshine	Hours per day	4.7	5.9	6	8.3	9.1	10.6	11.4	10.7	8.4	6.7	5.2	4.6	7.7

London (Kew), UK 5m		Jan	Feb	Mar	Apr	May	June	July	Aug	Sept	Oct	Nov	Dec	Year
Temperature	Daily max. °C	6	7	10	13	17	20	22	21	19	14	10	7	14
	Daily min. °C	2	2	3	6	8	12	14	13	11	8	5	4	7
	Average monthly °C	4	5	7	9	12	16	18	17	15	11	8	5	11
Rainfall	Monthly total mm	54	40	37	37	46	45	57	59	49	57	64	48	593
Sunshine	Hours per day	1.7	2.3	3.5	5.7	6.7	7	6.6	6	5	3.3	1.9	1.4	4.3

Los Angeles, USA 30m		Jan	Feb	Mar	Apr	May	June	July	Aug	Sept	Oct	Nov	Dec	Year
Temperature	Daily max. °C	18	18	18	19	20	22	24	24	24	23	22	19	21
	Daily min. °C	7	8	9	11	13	15	17	17	16	14	11	9	12
	Average monthly °C	12	13	14	15	17	18	21	21	20	18	16	14	17
Rainfall	Monthly total mm	69	74	46	28	3	3	0	0	5	10	28	61	327
Sunshine	Hours per day	6.9	8.2	8.9	8.8	9.5	10.3	11.7	11	10.1	8.6	8.2	7.6	9.2

Lusaka, Zambia 1,154m		Jan	Feb	Mar	Apr	May	June	July	Aug	Sept	Oct	Nov	Dec	Year
Temperature	Daily max. °C	26	26	26	27	25	23	23	26	29	31	29	27	27
	Daily min. °C	17	17	16	15	12	10	9	11	15	18	18	17	15
	Average monthly °C	22	22	21	21	18	17	16	19	22	25	23	22	21
Rainfall	Monthly total mm	224	173	90	19	3	1	0	1	1	17	85	196	810
Sunshine	Hours per day	5.1	5.4	6.9	8.9	9	9	9.1	9.6	9.5	9	7	5.5	7.8

Manaus, Brazil 45m		Jan	Feb	Mar	Apr	May	June	July	Aug	Sept	Oct	Nov	Dec	Year
Temperature	Daily max. °C	31	31	31	31	31	31	32	33	34	34	33	32	32
	Daily min. °C	24	24	24	24	24	24	24	24	24	25	25	24	24
	Average monthly °C	28	28	28	27	28	28	28	29	29	29	29	28	28
Rainfall	Monthly total mm	278	278	300	287	193	99	61	41	62	112	165	220	2,096
Sunshine	Hours per day	3.9	4	3.6	3.9	5.4	6.9	7.9	8.2	7.5	6.6	5.9	4.9	5.7

Mexico City, Mexico 2,309m		Jan	Feb	Mar	Apr	May	June	July	Aug	Sept	Oct	Nov	Dec	Year
Temperature	Daily max. °C	21	23	26	27	26	25	23	24	23	22	21	21	24
	Daily min. °C	5	6	7	9	10	11	11	11	11	9	6	5	8
	Average monthly °C	13	15	16	18	18	18	17	17	17	16	14	13	16
Rainfall	Monthly total mm	8	4	9	23	57	111	160	149	119	46	16	7	709
Sunshine	Hours per day	7.3	8.1	8.5	8.1	7.8	7	6.2	6.4	5.6	6.3	7	7.3	7.1

Miami, USA 2m		Jan	Feb	Mar	Apr	May	June	July	Aug	Sept	Oct	Nov	Dec	Year
Temperature	Daily max. °C	24	25	27	28	30	31	32	32	31	29	27	25	28
	Daily min. °C	14	15	16	19	21	23	24	24	24	22	18	15	20
	Average monthly °C	19	20	21	23	25	27	28	28	27	25	22	20	24
Rainfall	Monthly total mm	51	48	58	99	163	188	170	178	241	208	71	43	1,518
Sunshine	Hours per day	7.7	8.3	8.7	9.4	8.9	8.5	8.7	8.4	7.1	6.5	7.5	7.1	8.1

Montreal, Canada 57m		Jan	Feb	Mar	Apr	May	June	July	Aug	Sept	Oct	Nov	Dec	Year
Temperature	Daily max. °C	−6	−4	2	11	18	23	26	25	20	14	5	−3	11
	Daily min. °C	−13	−11	−5	2	9	14	17	16	11	6	0	−9	3
	Average monthly °C	−9	−8	−2	6	13	19	22	20	16	10	3	−6	7
Rainfall	Monthly total mm	87	76	86	83	81	91	98	87	96	84	89	89	1,047
Sunshine	Hours per day	2.8	3.4	4.5	5.2	6.7	7.7	8.2	7.7	5.6	4.3	2.4	2.2	5.1

Moscow, Russia 156m		Jan	Feb	Mar	Apr	May	June	July	Aug	Sept	Oct	Nov	Dec	Year
Temperature	Daily max. °C	−6	−4	1	9	18	22	24	22	17	10	1	−5	9
	Daily min. °C	−14	−16	−11	−1	5	9	12	9	4	−2	−6	−12	−2
	Average monthly °C	−10	−10	−5	4	12	15	18	16	10	4	−2	−8	4
Rainfall	Monthly total mm	31	28	33	35	52	67	74	74	58	51	36	36	575
Sunshine	Hours per day	1	1.9	3.7	5.2	7.8	8.3	8.4	7.1	4.4	2.4	1	0.6	4.4

New Delhi, India 220m		Jan	Feb	Mar	Apr	May	June	July	Aug	Sept	Oct	Nov	Dec	Year
Temperature	Daily max. °C	21	24	29	36	41	39	35	34	34	34	28	23	32
	Daily min. °C	6	10	14	20	26	28	27	26	24	17	11	7	18
	Average monthly °C	14	17	22	28	33	34	31	30	29	26	20	15	25
Rainfall	Monthly total mm	25	21	13	8	13	77	178	184	123	10	2	11	665
Sunshine	Hours per day	7.7	8.2	8.2	8.7	9.2	7.9	6	6.3	6.9	9.4	8.7	8.3	8

Perth, Australia 60m		Jan	Feb	Mar	Apr	May	June	July	Aug	Sept	Oct	Nov	Dec	Year
Temperature	Daily max. °C	29	30	27	25	21	18	17	18	19	21	25	27	23
	Daily min. °C	17	18	16	14	12	10	9	9	10	11	14	16	13
	Average monthly °C	23	24	22	19	16	14	13	13	15	16	19	22	18
Rainfall	Monthly total mm	8	13	22	44	128	189	177	145	84	58	19	13	900
Sunshine	Hours per day	10.4	9.8	8.8	7.5	5.7	4.8	5.4	6	7.2	8.1	9.6	10.4	7.8

Reykjavik, Iceland 18m		Jan	Feb	Mar	Apr	May	June	July	Aug	Sept	Oct	Nov	Dec	Year
Temperature	Daily max. °C	2	3	5	6	10	13	15	14	12	8	5	4	8
	Daily min. °C	−3	−3	−1	1	4	7	9	8	6	3	0	−2	3
	Average monthly °C	0	0	2	4	7	10	12	11	9	5	3	1	5
Rainfall	Monthly total mm	89	64	62	56	42	42	50	56	67	94	78	79	779
Sunshine	Hours per day	0.8	2	3.6	4.5	5.9	6.1	5.8	5.4	3.5	2.3	1.1	0.3	3.7

Santiago, Chile 520m		Jan	Feb	Mar	Apr	May	June	July	Aug	Sept	Oct	Nov	Dec	Year
Temperature	Daily max. °C	30	29	27	24	19	15	15	17	19	22	26	29	23
	Daily min. °C	12	11	10	7	5	3	3	4	6	7	9	11	7
	Average monthly °C	21	20	18	15	12	9	9	10	12	15	17	20	15
Rainfall	Monthly total mm	3	3	5	13	64	84	76	56	31	15	8	5	363
Sunshine	Hours per day	10.8	8.9	8.5	5.5	3.6	3.3	3.3	3.6	4.8	6.1	8.7	10.1	6.4

Shanghai, China 5m		Jan	Feb	Mar	Apr	May	June	July	Aug	Sept	Oct	Nov	Dec	Year
Temperature	Daily max. °C	8	8	13	19	24	28	32	32	27	23	17	10	20
	Daily min. °C	−1	0	4	9	14	19	23	23	19	13	7	2	11
	Average monthly °C	3	4	8	14	19	23	27	27	23	18	12	6	15
Rainfall	Monthly total mm	48	59	84	94	94	180	147	142	130	71	51	36	1,136
Sunshine	Hours per day	4	3.7	4.4	4.8	5.4	4.7	6.9	7.5	5.3	5.6	4.7	4.5	5.1

Sydney, Australia 40m		Jan	Feb	Mar	Apr	May	June	July	Aug	Sept	Oct	Nov	Dec	Year
Temperature	Daily max. °C	26	26	25	22	19	17	17	18	20	22	24	25	22
	Daily min. °C	18	19	17	14	11	9	8	9	11	13	16	17	14
	Average monthly °C	22	22	21	18	15	13	12	13	16	18	20	21	18
Rainfall	Monthly total mm	89	101	127	135	127	117	117	76	74	71	74	74	1,182
Sunshine	Hours per day	7.5	7	6.4	6.1	5.7	5.3	6.1	7	7.3	7.5	7.5	7.5	6.8

Tehran, Iran 1,191m		Jan	Feb	Mar	Apr	May	June	July	Aug	Sept	Oct	Nov	Dec	Year
Temperature	Daily max. °C	9	11	16	21	29	30	37	36	29	24	16	11	22
	Daily min. °C	−1	1	4	10	16	20	23	23	18	12	6	1	11
	Average monthly °C	4	6	10	15	22	25	30	29	23	18	11	6	17
Rainfall	Monthly total mm	37	23	36	31	14	2	1	1	1	5	29	27	207
Sunshine	Hours per day	5.9	6.7	7.5	7.4	8.6	11.6	11.2	11	10.1	7.6	6.9	6.3	8.4

Timbuktu, Mali 269m		Jan	Feb	Mar	Apr	May	June	July	Aug	Sept	Oct	Nov	Dec	Year
Temperature	Daily max. °C	31	35	38	41	43	42	38	35	38	40	37	31	37
	Daily min. °C	13	16	18	22	26	27	25	24	24	23	18	14	21
	Average monthly °C	22	25	28	31	34	34	32	30	31	31	28	23	29
Rainfall	Monthly total mm	0	0	0	1	4	20	54	93	31	3	0	0	206
Sunshine	Hours per day	9.1	9.6	9.6	9.7	9.8	9.4	9.6	9	9.3	9.5	9.5	8.9	9.4

Tokyo, Japan 5m		Jan	Feb	Mar	Apr	May	June	July	Aug	Sept	Oct	Nov	Dec	Year
Temperature	Daily max. °C	9	9	12	18	22	25	29	30	27	20	16	11	19
	Daily min. °C	−1	−1	3	4	13	17	22	23	19	13	7	1	10
	Average monthly °C	4	4	8	11	18	21	25	26	23	17	11	6	14
Rainfall	Monthly total mm	48	73	101	135	131	182	146	147	217	220	101	61	1,562
Sunshine	Hours per day	6	5.9	5.7	6	6.2	5	5.8	6.6	4.5	4.4	4.8	5.4	5.5

Tromsø, Norway 100m		Jan	Feb	Mar	Apr	May	June	July	Aug	Sept	Oct	Nov	Dec	Year
Temperature	Daily max. °C	−2	−2	0	3	7	12	16	14	10	5	2	0	5
	Daily min. °C	−6	−6	−5	−2	1	6	9	8	5	1	−2	−4	0
	Average monthly °C	−4	−4	−3	0	4	9	13	11	7	3	0	−2	3
Rainfall	Monthly total mm	96	79	91	65	61	59	56	80	109	115	88	95	994
Sunshine	Hours per day	0.1	1.6	2.9	6.1	5.7	6.9	7.9	4.8	3.5	1.7	0.3	0	3.5

Ulan Bator, Mongolia 1,305m		Jan	Feb	Mar	Apr	May	June	July	Aug	Sept	Oct	Nov	Dec	Year
Temperature	Daily max. °C	−19	−13	−4	7	13	21	22	21	14	6	−6	−16	4
	Daily min. °C	−32	−29	−22	−8	−2	7	11	8	2	−8	−20	−28	−11
	Average monthly °C	−26	−21	−13	−1	6	14	16	14	8	−1	−13	−22	−4
Rainfall	Monthly total mm	1	1	2	5	10	28	76	51	23	5	5	2	209
Sunshine	Hours per day	6.4	7.8	8	7.8	8.3	8.6	8.6	8.2	7.2	6.9	6.1	5.7	7.5

Vancouver, Canada 5m		Jan	Feb	Mar	Apr	May	June	July	Aug	Sept	Oct	Nov	Dec	Year
Temperature	Daily max. °C	6	7	10	14	17	20	23	22	19	14	9	7	14
	Daily min. °C	0	1	3	5	8	11	13	12	10	7	3	2	6
	Average monthly °C	3	4	6	9	13	16	18	17	14	10	6	4	10
Rainfall	Monthly total mm	214	161	151	90	69	65	39	44	83	172	198	243	1,529
Sunshine	Hours per day	1.6	3	3.8	5.9	7.5	7.4	9.5	8.2	6	3.7	2	1.4	5

Verkhoyansk, Russia 137m		Jan	Feb	Mar	Apr	May	June	July	Aug	Sept	Oct	Nov	Dec	Year
Temperature	Daily max. °C	−47	−40	−20	−1	11	21	24	21	12	−8	−33	−42	−8
	Daily min. °C	−51	−48	−40	−25	−7	4	6	1	−6	−20	−39	−50	−23
	Average monthly °C	−49	−44	−30	−13	2	12	15	11	3	−14	−36	−46	−16
Rainfall	Monthly total mm	7	5	5	4	5	25	33	30	13	11	10	7	155
Sunshine	Hours per day	0	2.6	6.9	9.6	9.7	10	9.7	7.5	4.1	2.4	0.6	0	5.4

Washington, D.C., USA 22m		Jan	Feb	Mar	Apr	May	June	July	Aug	Sept	Oct	Nov	Dec	Year
Temperature	Daily max. °C	7	8	12	19	25	29	31	30	26	20	14	8	19
	Daily min. °C	−1	−1	2	8	13	18	21	20	16	10	4	−1	9
	Average monthly °C	3	3	7	13	19	24	26	25	21	15	9	4	14
Rainfall	Monthly total mm	84	68	96	85	103	88	108	120	100	78	75	75	1,080
Sunshine	Hours per day	4.4	5.7	6.7	7.4	8.2	8.8	8.6	8.2	7.5	6.5	5.3	4.5	6.8

Tropical Rain Forest
Tall broadleaved evergreen forest, trees 30–50m high with climbers and epiphytes forming continuous canopies. Associated with wet climate, 2–3000mm precipitation per year and high temperatures 24–28°C. High diversity of species, typically 100 per ha, including lianas, bamboo, palms, rubber, mahogany. Mangrove swamps form in coastal areas.

Subtropical and Temperate Rain Forest
Precipitation, which is less than in the Tropical Rain Forest, falls in the long wet season interspersed with a season of reduced rainfall and lower temperatures. As a result there are fewer species, thinner canopies, fewer lianas and denser ground level foliage. Vegetation consists of evergreen oak, laurel, bamboo, magnolia and tree ferns.

Monsoon Woodland and Open Jungle
Mostly deciduous trees, because of the long dry season and lower tempera. Trees can reach 30m but are sparser than in the rain forests. There competition for light and thick jungle vegetation grows at lower levels species diversity includes lianas, bamboo, teak, sandalwood, sal and ba

This diagram shows the highly stratified nature of the tropical rain forest. Crowns of trees form numerous layers at different heights and the dense shade limits undergrowth.

Temperate Deciduous and Coniferous Forest
A transition zone between broadleaves and conifers. Broadleaves are better suited to the warmer, damper and flatter locations.

Coniferous Forest (Taiga or Boreal)
Forming a large continuous belt across Northern America and Eurasia with a uniformity in tree species. Characteristically trees are tall, conical with short branches and wax-covered needle-shaped leaves to retain moisture. Cold climate with prolonged harsh winters and cool summers where average temperatures are under 0°C for more than six months of the year Undergrowth is sparse with mosses and lichens. Tree species include pine, fir, spruce, larch, tamarisk.

Mountainous Forest, mainly Coniferous
Mild winters, high humidity and high levels of rainfall throughout the year provide habitat for dense needle-leaf evergreen forests and the largest trees in the world, up to 100m, including the Douglas fir, redwood and giant sequoia.

High Plateau Steppe and Tundra
Similar to arctic tundra with frozen ground for the majority of the year. Very sparse ground coverage of low, shallow-rooted herbs, small shrubs, mosses, lichens and heather interspersed with bare soil.

Arctic Tundra
Average temperatures are 0°C, precipitation is mainly snowfall and the ground remains frozen for 10 months of the year. Vegetation flourishes when the shallow surface layer melts in the long summer days. Underlying permafrost remains frozen and surface water cannot drain away, making conditions marshy. Consists of sedges, snow lichen, arctic meadow grass, cotton grasses and dwarf willow.

Polar and Mountainous Ice Desert
Areas of bare rock and ice with patches of rock-strewn lithosols, low in organic matter and low water content. In sheltered patches only a few mosses, lichens and low shrubs can grow, including woolly moss and purple saxifrage.

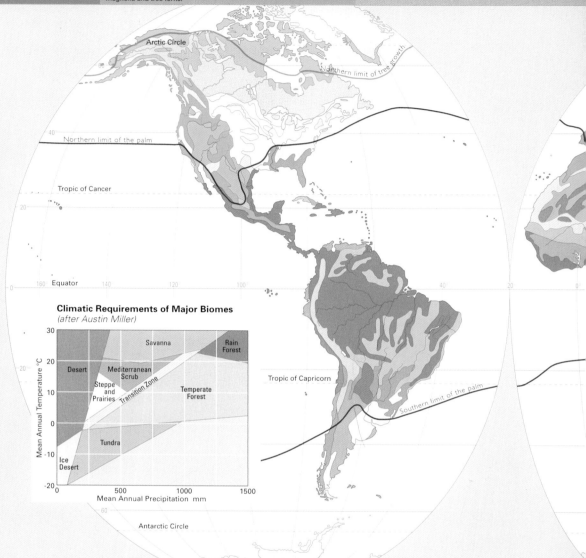

Climatic Requirements of Major Biomes
(after Austin Miller)

SOIL REGIONS
1:220 000 000

- Tundra soil
- Podzols
- Brown forest soil
- Lightly leached dry forest soil
- Red and yellow subtropical forest soil
- Reddish savanna soil and tropical red earths
- Laterites
- Chernozem
- Degraded chernozem
- Black savanna soil
- Chestnut steppe soil
- Desertic (arid) soil
- Alluvium
- Mountain and high plateau soils
- Oases soil
- Tropical and mangrove swamp

(after Glinka, Stremme, Marbut, and others)

Tropical and Temperate Woodland, Scrub and Bush
clearings with woody shrubs and tall grasses. Trees are fire-resistant and deciduous or xerophytic because of long dry periods. Species include eucalyptus, acacia, mimosa and euphorbia.

Tropical Savanna with Low Trees and Bush
Tall, coarse grass with enough precipitation to support a scattering of short deciduous trees and thorn scrub. Vegetation consists of elephant grass, acacia, palms and baobob and is limited by aridity, grazing animals and periodic fires; trees have developed thick, woody bark, small leaves or thorns.

Tropical Savanna and Grassland
Areas with a hot climate and long dry season. Extensive areas of tall grasses often reach 3.5m with scattered fire and drought resistant bushes, low trees and thickets of elephant grass. Shrubs include acacia, baobab and palms.

BIOMES
Classified by Climax Vegetation
1:116 000 000

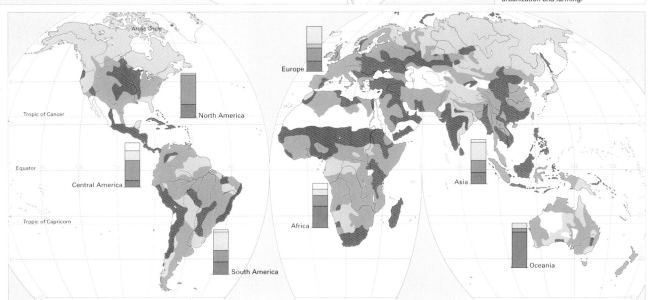

Dry Semi-desert with Shrub and Grass
Xerophytic shrubs with thin grass cover and few trees, limited by a long dry season and short, hot, rainy period. Sagebrush, bunch grass and acacia shrubs are common.

Desert Shrub
Scattered xerophytic plants able to withstand daytime extremes in temperature and long periods of drought. There is a large diversity of desert flora such as cacti, yucca, tamarisk, hard grass and artemisia.

Desert
Precipitation less than 250mm per year. Vegetation is very sparse, mainly bare rock, sand dunes and salt flats. Vegetation comprises a few xerophytic shrubs and ephemeral flowers.

Dry Steppe and Shrub
Semi-arid with cold, dry winters and hot summers. Bare soil with sparsely distributed short grasses and scattered shrubs and short trees. Species include acacia, artemisia, saksaul and tamarisk.

Temperate Grasslands, Prairie and Steppe
Continuous, tall, dense and deep-rooted swards of ancient grasslands, considered to be natural climax vegetation as determined by soil and climate. Average precipitation 250–750mm, with a long dry season, limits growth of trees and shrubs. Includes Stipa grass, buffalo grass, blue stems and loco weed.

Mediterranean Hardwood Forest and Scrub
Areas with hot and arid summers. Sparse evergreen trees are short and twisted with thick bark, interspersed with areas of scrub land. Trees have waxy leaves or thorns and deep root systems to resist drought. Many of the hardwood forests have been cleared by man, resulting in extensive scrub formation – maquis and chaparral. Species found are evergreen oak, stone pine, cork, olive and myrtle.

Temperate Deciduous Forest and Meadow
Areas of relatively high, well-distributed rainfall and temperature favourable for forest growth. The Tall broadleaved trees form a canopy in the summer, but shed their leaves in the winter. The undergrowth is sparse and poorly developed, but in the spring, herbs and flowers develop quickly. Diverse species, with up to 20 per ha, including oak, beech, birch, maple, ash, elm, chestnut and hornbeam. Many of these forests have been cleared for urbanization and farming.

SOIL DEGRADATION
1:220 000 000

Areas of Concern
- Areas of serious concern
- Areas of some concern
- Stable terrain
- Non-vegetated land

Causes of soil degradation (by region)
- Grazing practices
- Other agricultural practices
- Industrialization
- Deforestation
- Fuelwood collection

(after Wageningen)

AGRICULTURAL PRODUCTION

Crops

Wheat
China 16.8% India 11.8% Russia 9.0% USA 8.8% France 5.6% Canada 3.9% Germany 3.7%

World total (2009): 685,614,000 tonnes

Rice
China 28.1% India 19.5% Indonesia 9.4% Bangladesh 7.0% Vietnam 5.7% Birma 4.8% Thailand 4.6%

World total (2009): 685,240,000 tonnes

Cassava
Nigeria 15.7% Thailand 12.9% Brazil 10.4% Indonesia 9.4% Congo (D.R.) 6.4% Ghana 5.2%

World total (2009): 233,796,000 tonnes

Barley
Russia 11.8% France 8.5% Germany 8.1% Ukraine 7.8% Canada 6.3% Australia 5.3%

World total (2009): 152,125,000 tonnes

Maize
USA 40.7% China 20.0% Brazil 6.3%

World total (2009): 818,823,000 tonnes

Potatoes
China 22.2% Russia 10.4% India 9.4% Ukraine 6.0% USA 5.9%

World total (2009): 329,581,000 tonnes

Soybeans
USA 41.0% Brazil 25.7% Argentina 13.9% China 6.7%

World total (2009): 223,185,000 tonnes

Millet
India 33.0% Nigeria 18.3% Niger 10.0% Mali 5.2% China 4.6%

World total (2009): 26,702,000 tonnes

Sugar Cane
Brazil 40.4% India 17.2% China 7.0% Thailand 4.0% Pakistan 3.0% Mexico 3.0%

World total (2009): 1,661,251,000 tonnes

Sugar Beet
France 15.4% USA 11.8% Germany 11.4% Russia 11.0% Turkey 7.6% Poland 4.8% UK 3.3%

World total (2009): 227,158,000 tonnes

Animal Products

Milk
India 16.0% USA 12.7% China 5.7% Pakistan 4.9% Russia 4.6% Brazil 4.2%

World total (2009): 702,137,000 tonnes

Eggs
China 40.8% USA 7.9% India 4.7% Japan 3.7%

World total (2009): 68,034,000 tonnes

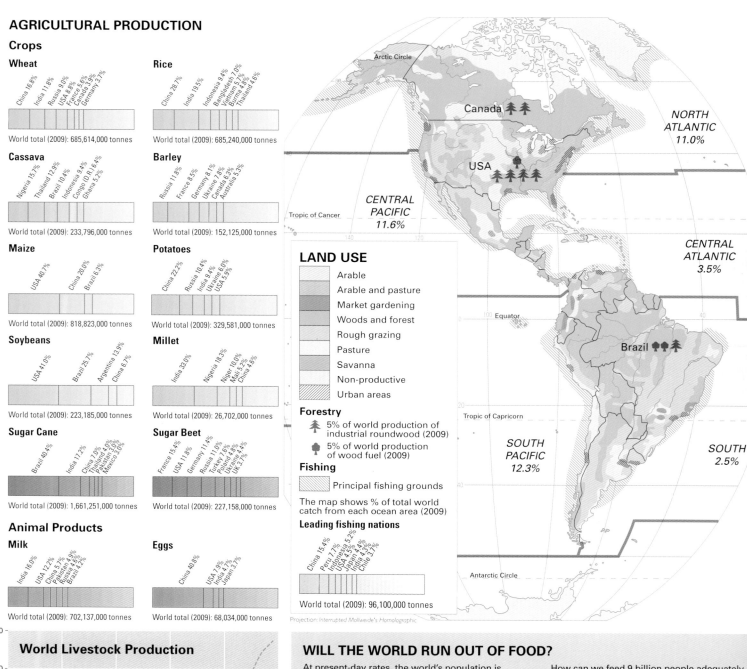

LAND USE

- Arable
- Arable and pasture
- Market gardening
- Woods and forest
- Rough grazing
- Pasture
- Savanna
- Non-productive
- Urban areas

Forestry

- 🌲 5% of world production of industrial roundwood (2009)
- 🌳 5% of world production of wood fuel (2009)

Fishing

- Principal fishing grounds

The map shows % of total world catch from each ocean area (2009)

Leading fishing nations
China 15.4% Peru 7.7% Indonesia 5.2% USA 4.5% Japan 4.4% India 4.3% Chile 3.7%

World total (2009): 96,100,000 tonnes

Projection: Interrupted Mollweide's Homolographic

NORTH ATLANTIC 11.0%

CENTRAL PACIFIC 11.6%

CENTRAL ATLANTIC 3.5%

SOUTH PACIFIC 12.3%

SOUTH 2.5%

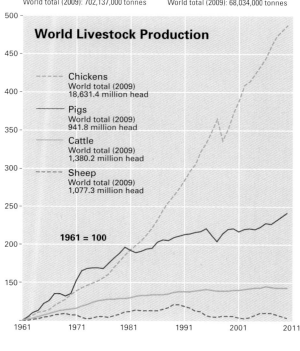

World Livestock Production

- Chickens — World total (2009) 18,631.4 million head
- Pigs — World total (2009) 941.8 million head
- Cattle — World total (2009) 1,380.2 million head
- Sheep — World total (2009) 1,077.3 million head

1961 = 100

WILL THE WORLD RUN OUT OF FOOD?

At present-day rates, the world's population is predicted to reach at least 9 billion people by 2050. To sustain this population there will have to be a 70% increase in food production.

Currently, many people struggle to achieve the minimum food intake to sustain life. Globally, about 1 billion people are malnourished compared with 1 billion who are overweight.

Over 30% of the world's grain is fed to livestock because more and more people like to eat meat. But animals (and humans) are very inefficient in their utilization of nutrients; generally less than 20% of the nitrogen in their food is used; the rest is excreted, causing air and water pollution.

Meat is also very expensive in terms of water consumption: 0.5 kg of beef requires 8,442 litres of water to produce it. By 2030 there will be a 30% increase in water demand. Over 71% of the Earth's surface is covered in water but less than 3% of this is fresh water, of which over two-thirds is frozen in ice-caps and glaciers. Its over-exploitation in developed areas and availability in regions where it is scarce are major problems. For example, China currently has 23% of the world's population, but only 11% of its water.

How can we feed 9 billion people adequately and sustainably? The Royal Society has said that we need 'Sustainable Intensification', that is, to produce more using less and with less of an impact on the environment through good soil management, maintaining or enhancing crop genetic diversity, and introducing pest and disease resistance, as well as better fertiliser use

Some, however, reject technological approach and advocate extensive systems described as 'organic', 'bio-dynamic' or 'ecological', objecting to the reliance on chemical fertilisers and pesticides.

We need to reduce the 30% of the world's crop yield lost to pests, diseases and weeds; protect the fertile soil that irregularly covers only 11% of the global land surface and is a non-renewab asset; and cut back on food waste. In the UK it is estimated that 8.3 million tonnes of food worth £20 billion is sent to landfill each year. Some people now live on the food thrown away by shops – called 'skipping'.

If we adopt appropriate techniques and modify our behaviour, we stand a good chance of feedi the future, predominantly urban, population.

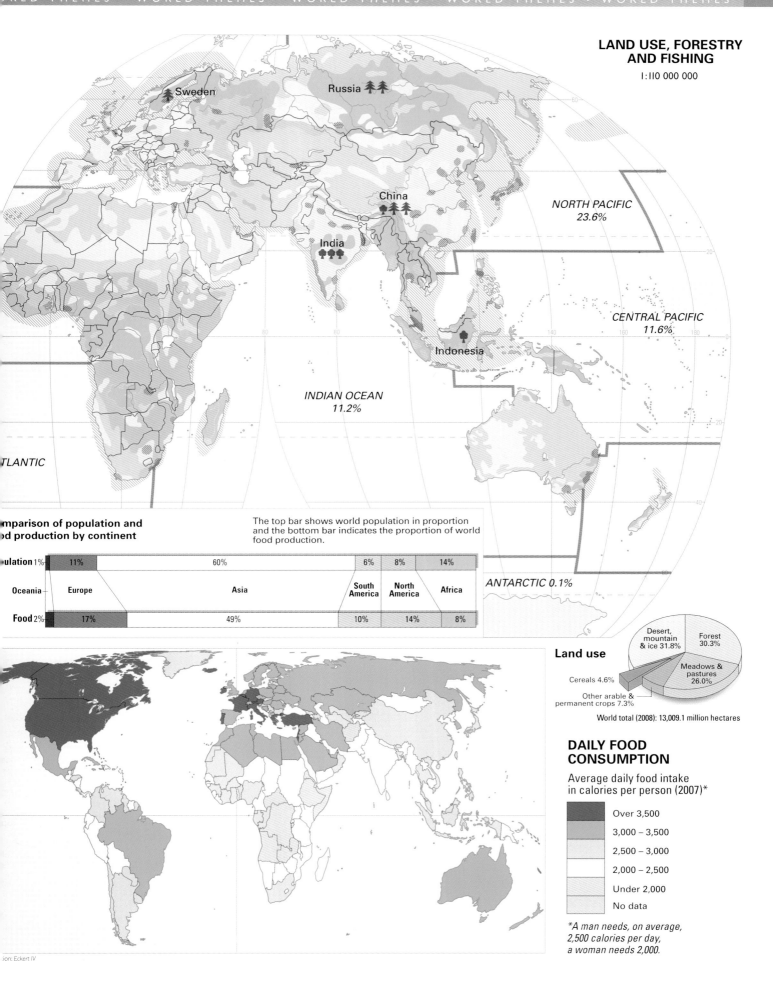

LAND USE, FORESTRY AND FISHING

1:110 000 000

Sweden

Russia

China

India

Indonesia

NORTH PACIFIC
23.6%

CENTRAL PACIFIC
11.6%

INDIAN OCEAN
11.2%

ATLANTIC

ANTARCTIC 0.1%

Comparison of population and food production by continent

The top bar shows world population in proportion and the bottom bar indicates the proportion of world food production.

Population 1%	11%	60%	6%	8%	14%
Oceania	Europe	Asia	South America	North America	Africa
Food 2%	17%	49%	10%	14%	8%

Land use

Desert, mountain & ice 31.8%

Forest 30.3%

Meadows & pastures 26.0%

Cereals 4.6%

Other arable & permanent crops 7.3%

World total (2008): 13,009.1 million hectares

DAILY FOOD CONSUMPTION

Average daily food intake in calories per person (2007)*

	Over 3,500
	3,000 – 3,500
	2,500 – 3,000
	2,000 – 2,500
	Under 2,000
	No data

*A man needs, on average, 2,500 calories per day, a woman needs 2,000.

Projection: Eckert IV

ENERGY BALANCE

Difference between primary energy production and consumption in millions of tonnes of oil equivalent (MtOe) 2008

Over 35 surplus

1 – 35 surplus

1 deficit – 1 surplus (approx. balance)

1 – 35 deficit

Over 35 deficit

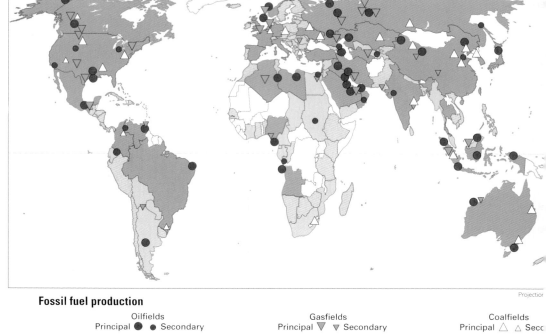

Projection

WORLD OIL RESERVES

World oil reserves by region and country, billion tonnes (2009)

World total 181.7 billion tonnes

Al:	Algeria	No:	Norway
Au:	Australia	Po:	Poland
Br:	Brazil	Ru:	Russia
Cn:	China	SA:	Saudi Arabia
In:	Indonesia	S Af:	South Africa
Iq:	Iraq	UAE:	United Arab Emirates
Ka:	Kazakhstan		
Li:	Libya	USA:	United States of America
Ni:	Nigeria		
		Ve:	Venezuela

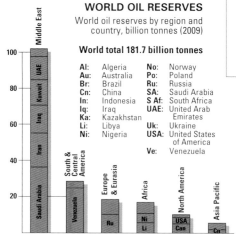

WORLD GAS RESERVES

World natural gas reserves by region and country, billion tonnes of oil equivalent (2009)

World total 172.1 billion tonnes of oil equivalent

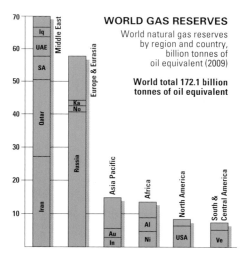

WORLD COAL RESERVES

World coal reserves (including lignite) by region and country, billion tonnes (2009)

World total 826.0 billion tonnes

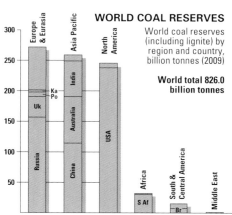

Fossil fuel production

Oilfields
Principal ● Secondary ●

Gasfields
Principal ▽ Secondary ▽

Coalfields
Principal △ Seco

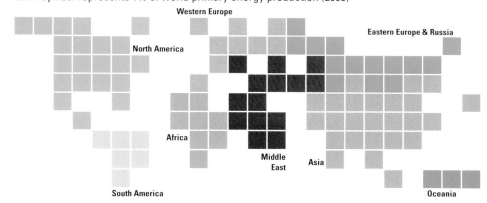

Oil production — Russia 12.9%, Saudi Arabia 12.0%, USA 8.7%, Iran 5.2%, China 5.2%, Canada 4.2%, Mexico 3.7%, UAE 3.3%, Venezuela 3.2%

World total (2010): 3,913,700,000 tonnes

Gas production — USA 19.3%, Russia 18.4%, Canada 5.0%, Iran 4.3%, Norway 3.3%, Saudi Arabia 2.6%

World total (2010): 2,880,900,000 tonnes of oil equivalent

Coal production — China 48.2%, USA 14.8%, Australia 6.2%, India 5.8%, Russia...

World total (2010): 3,731,400,000 tonnes equivalent

ENERGY PRODUCTION BY REGION

Each symbol represents 1% of world primary energy production (2008)

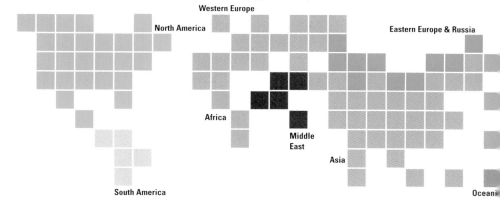

ENERGY CONSUMPTION BY REGION

Each symbol represents 1% of world primary energy consumption (2008)

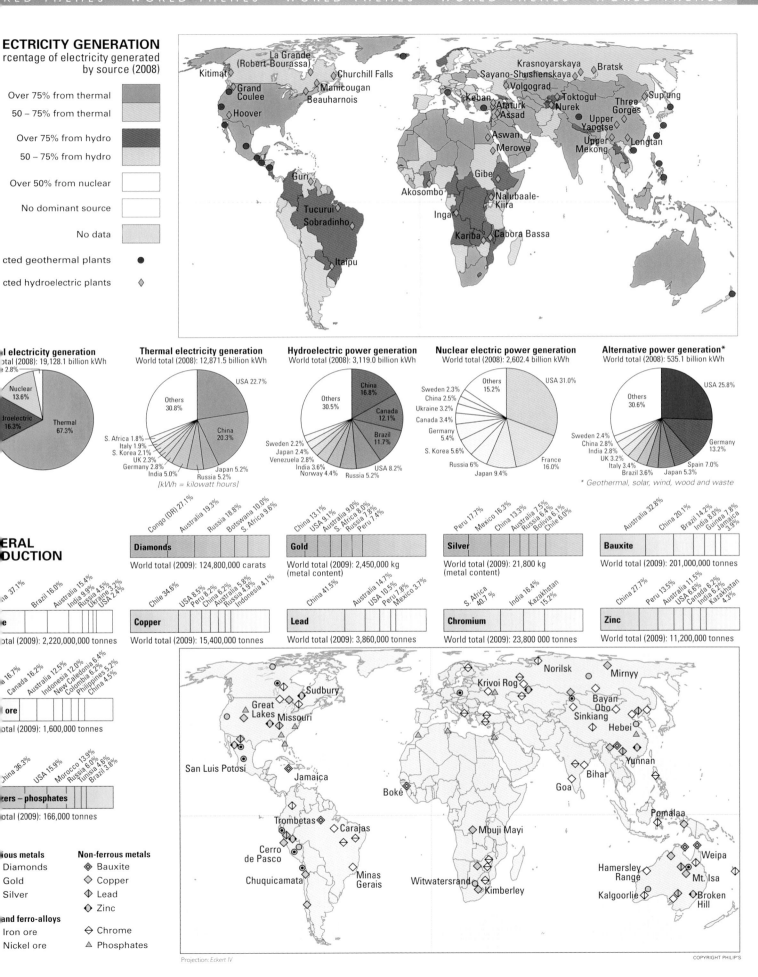

ECTRICITY GENERATION
rcentage of electricity generated by source (2008)

- Over 75% from thermal
- 50 – 75% from thermal
- Over 75% from hydro
- 50 – 75% from hydro
- Over 50% from nuclear
- No dominant source
- No data
- cted geothermal plants ●
- cted hydroelectric plants ◇

Map labels: La Grande (Robert-Bourassa), Kitimat, Grand Coulee, Hoover, Churchill Falls, Manicougan, Beauharnois, Guri, Tucurui, Sobradinho, Itaipu, Krasnoyarskaya, Sayano-Shushenskaya, Volgograd, Bratsk, Sup'ung, Keban, Ataturk, Assad, Toktogul, Nurek, Three Gorges, Longtan, Upper Yangtse, Upper Mekong, Aswan, Merowe, Gibe, Akosombo, Nalubaale-Kiira, Inga, Kariba, Cabora Bassa

l electricity generation
otal (2008): 19,128.1 billion kWh
- Nuclear 13.6%
- Hydroelectric 16.3%
- Thermal 67.3%
- 2.8%

Thermal electricity generation
World total (2008): 12,871.5 billion kWh
- USA 22.7%
- China 20.3%
- Japan 5.2%
- Russia 5.2%
- India 5.0%
- Germany 2.8%
- UK 2.3%
- S. Korea 2.1%
- Italy 1.9%
- S. Africa 1.8%
- Others 30.8%

[kWh = kilowatt hours]

Hydroelectric power generation
World total (2008): 3,119.0 billion kWh
- China 16.8%
- Canada 12.1%
- Brazil 11.7%
- USA 8.2%
- Russia 5.2%
- India 3.6%
- Norway 4.4%
- Venezuela 2.8%
- Japan 2.4%
- Sweden 2.2%
- Others 30.5%

Nuclear electric power generation
World total (2008): 2,602.4 billion kWh
- USA 31.0%
- France 16.0%
- Japan 9.4%
- Russia 6%
- S. Korea 5.6%
- Germany 5.4%
- Canada 3.4%
- Ukraine 3.2%
- China 2.5%
- Sweden 2.3%
- Others 15.2%

Alternative power generation*
World total (2008): 535.1 billion kWh
- USA 25.8%
- Germany 13.2%
- Spain 7.0%
- Japan 5.3%
- Brazil 3.6%
- Italy 3.4%
- UK 3.2%
- India 2.8%
- China 2.8%
- Sweden 2.4%
- Others 30.6%

* Geothermal, solar, wind, wood and waste

ERAL DUCTION

Diamonds — World total (2009): 124,800,000 carats
- Congo (DR) 27.1%, Australia 19.3%, Russia 18.8%, Botswana 10.0%, S. Africa 9.6%

Gold — World total (2009): 2,450,000 kg (metal content)
- China 13.1%, USA 9.1%, Australia 9.0%, S. Africa 8.0%, Russia 7.8%, Peru 7.4%

Silver — World total (2009): 21,800 kg (metal content)
- Peru 17.7%, Mexico 16.3%, China 13.3%, Australia 7.5%, Russia 6.4%, Bolivia 6.1%, Chile 6.0%

Bauxite — World total (2009): 201,000,000 tonnes
- Australia 32.8%, China 20.1%, Brazil 14.2%, India 8.0%, Guinea 7.8%, Jamaica 3.9%

Copper — World total (2009): 15,400,000 tonnes
- Chile 34.6%, USA 8.5%, Peru 8.2%, China 6.2%, Australia 5.8%, Russia 4.9%, Indonesia 4.1%

Lead — World total (2009): 3,860,000 tonnes
- China 41.5%, Australia 14.7%, USA 10.5%, Peru 7.8%, Mexico 3.7%

Chromium — World total (2009): 23,800 000 tonnes
- S. Africa 40.7%, India 16.4%, Kazakhstan 15.2%

Zinc — World total (2009): 11,200,000 tonnes
- China 27.7%, Peru 13.5%, Australia 11.5%, USA 6.6%, Canada 6.2%, India 6.2%, Kazakhstan 4.3%

[Nickel ore?] —
- ina 37.1%, Brazil 16.0%, Australia 15.4%, India 9.9%, Russia 4.5%, Ukraine 3.2%, USA 2.4%
- World total (2009): 2,220,000,000 tonnes

e —
- 16.7%, Canada 16.2%, Australia 12.5%, Indonesia 12.0%, New Caledonia 6.4%, Colombia 6.2%, Philippines 5.2%, China 4.5%

ore — World total (2009): 1,600,000 tonnes

zers – phosphates —
- China 36.3%, USA 15.9%, Morocco 13.9%, Russia 6.0%, Tunisia 4.6%, Brazil 3.8%
- otal (2009): 166,000 tonnes

ious metals
- Diamonds ◈
- Gold
- Silver

Non-ferrous metals
- Bauxite ◈
- Copper ◇
- Lead ◈
- Zinc ◇

and ferro-alloys
- Iron ore ◇
- Nickel ore

- Chrome ◇
- Phosphates △

Mineral map labels: Norilsk, Mirnyy, Krivoi Rog, Bayan Obo, Sinkiang, Hebei, Yunnan, Sudbury, Great Lakes, Missouri, San Luis Potosí, Jamaica, Boké, Bihar, Goa, Pomalaa, Trombetas, Carajas, Mbuji Mayi, Cerro de Pasco, Chuquicamata, Minas Gerais, Witwatersrand, Kimberley, Hamersley Range, Kalgoorlie, Mt. Isa, Weipa, Broken Hill

Projection: Eckert IV

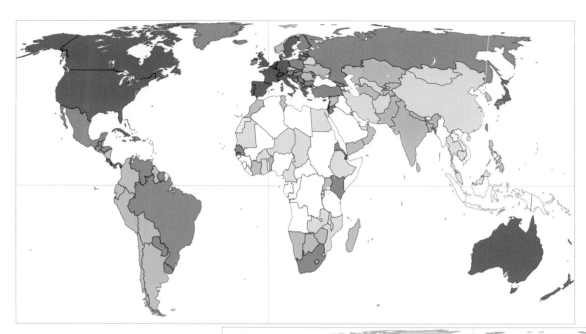

IMPORTANCE OF SERVICE SECTOR

Percentage of total GDP from service sector (2010)

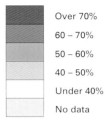

- Over 70%
- 60 – 70%
- 50 – 60%
- 40 – 50%
- Under 40%
- No data

Countries with the highest and lowest percentage of GDP from services

Highest		Lowest	
Monaco	95%	Eq. Guinea	4
Luxembourg	68%	Liberia	18
Bahamas	84%	Sierra Leone	20
Djibouti	82%	Qatar	21
Palau	82%	Angola	25

UK 77% from services

IMPORTANCE OF MANUFACTURING SECTOR

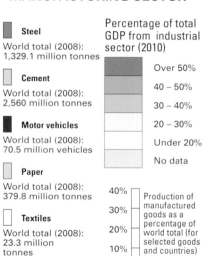

- **Steel**
World total (2008): 1,329.1 million tonnes

- **Cement**
World total (2008): 2,560 million tonnes

- **Motor vehicles**
World total (2008): 70.5 million vehicles

- **Paper**
World total (2008): 379.8 million tonnes

- **Textiles**
World total (2008): 23.3 million tonnes

Percentage of total GDP from industrial sector (2010)

- Over 50%
- 40 – 50%
- 30 – 40%
- 20 – 30%
- Under 20%
- No data

40% / 30% / 20% / 10% Production of manufactured goods as a percentage of world total (for selected goods and countries)

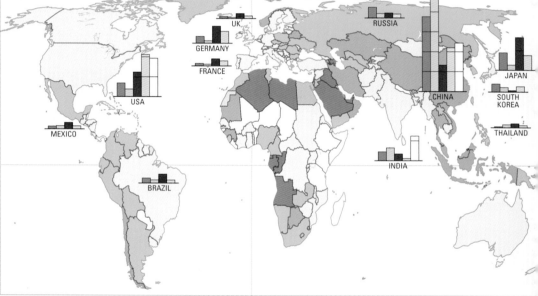

EMPLOYMENT BY ECONOMIC ACTIVITY Selected countries (2008)

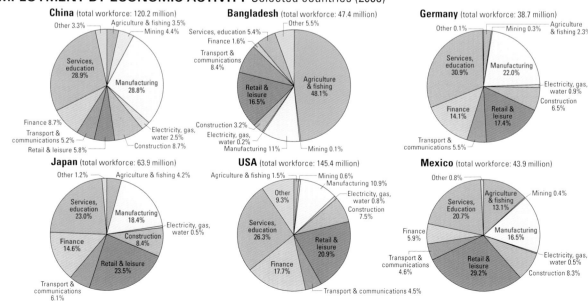

China (total workforce: 120.2 million)
- Other 3.3%
- Agriculture & fishing 3.5%
- Mining 4.4%
- Manufacturing 28.8%
- Services, education 28.9%
- Finance 8.7%
- Transport & communications 5.2%
- Retail & leisure 5.8%
- Electricity, gas, water 2.5%
- Construction 8.7%

Bangladesh (total workforce: 47.4 million)
- Services, education 5.4%
- Finance 1.6%
- Transport & communications 8.4%
- Other 5.5%
- Retail & leisure 16.5%
- Agriculture & fishing 48.1%
- Construction 3.2%
- Electricity, gas, water 0.2%
- Manufacturing 11%
- Mining 0.1%

Germany (total workforce: 38.7 million)
- Other 0.1%
- Mining 0.3%
- Agriculture & fishing 2.3%
- Services, education 30.9%
- Manufacturing 22.0%
- Electricity, gas, water 0.9%
- Construction 6.5%
- Finance 14.1%
- Retail & leisure 17.4%
- Transport & communications 5.5%

Japan (total workforce: 63.9 million)
- Other 1.2%
- Agriculture & fishing 4.2%
- Services, education 23.0%
- Manufacturing 18.4%
- Electricity, gas, water 0.5%
- Finance 14.6%
- Construction 8.4%
- Retail & leisure 23.5%
- Transport & communications 6.1%

USA (total workforce: 145.4 million)
- Agriculture & fishing 1.5%
- Mining 0.6%
- Manufacturing 10.9%
- Other 9.3%
- Electricity, gas, water 0.8%
- Construction 7.5%
- Services, education 26.3%
- Retail & leisure 20.9%
- Finance 17.7%
- Transport & communications 4.5%

Mexico (total workforce: 43.9 million)
- Other 0.8%
- Agriculture & fishing 13.1%
- Mining 0.4%
- Services, Education 20.7%
- Manufacturing 16.5%
- Finance 5.9%
- Transport & communications 4.6%
- Retail & leisure 29.2%
- Electricity, gas, water 0.5%
- Construction 8.3%

RESEARCH & DEVELOPM[ENT]

Expenditure on R&D as a percentage of GDP (2008)

Country	Percentage
Israel	4.9
Sweden	3.8
Finland	3.5
Japan	3.4
South Korea	3.2
USA	2.8
Denmark	2.7
Iceland	2.7
Austria	2.7
Germany	2.5
France	2.0
Belgium	1.9
UK	1.9
Canada	1.8
Luxembourg	1.7
Slovenia	1.7
Netherlands	1.6
Norway	1.6
Portugal	1.5
Czech Republic	1.5
China	1.4
Ireland	1.4
Spain	1.3
Estonia	1.3
New Zealand	1.2

WORLD TRADE

Percentage share of total
world exports by value (2010)

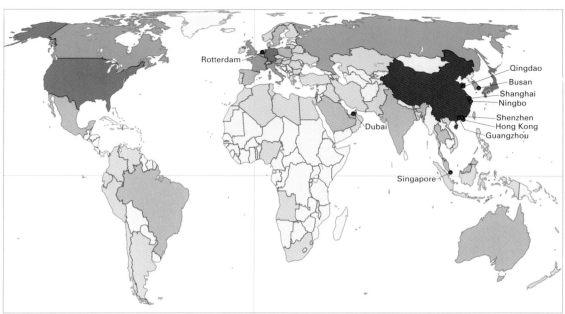

Over 10%

5 – 10%

2.5 – 5%

1.0 – 2.5%

0.1 – 1.0%

Under 0.1%

No data

Top ten container ports •

International trade is dominated by a
handful of powerful maritime nations;
the members of 'G8' (Canada, France,
Germany, Italy, Japan, Russia, UK and
USA) and the 'BRIC' nations (Brazil,
Russia, India and China).

JOR EXPORTS   Leading manufactured items and their exporters (2010)

Motor Vehicles
World total: US$ 3,502,062 million

- Germany 16.6%
- Japan 16.2%
- USA 10.3%
- France 5.8%
- Canada 5.5%
- Belgium 4.7%
- Spain 4.1%
- UK 4.1%
- 3.8%
- 3.3%
- .9%
- 2.1%
- 1.7%
- Other 18.9%

Telecommunications Gear
World total: US$ 1,650,697 million

- China 23%
- USA 8.6%
- Hong Kong 7.8%
- South Korea 7.2%
- Mexico 6.9%
- Japan 4.2%
- Hungary 4%
- Germany 3.9%
- Netherlands 3.8%
- UK 2.3%
- Singapore 2.3%
- Finland 2.2%
- Other 23.7%

Petrol Products
World total: US$ 2,100,016 million

- Russia 11.8%
- USA 8.9%
- Singapore 6.8%
- Netherlands 6%
- Belgium 4.4%
- S. Korea 4%
- India 3.7%
- UK 3.7%
- Germany 3%
- France 2.8%
- Canada 2.8%
- Kuwait 2.7%
- Saudi Arabia 2.7%
- Other 36.8%

Computers
World total: US$ 1,616,793 million

- China 28.7%
- USA 10.6%
- Hong Kong 6.3%
- Netherlands 6%
- Singapore 5.3%
- Germany 5.3%
- Japan 5%
- 4.5%
- 4%
- .7%
- Other 21.8%

Electrical Components
World total: US$ 5,588,630 million

- China 14.9%
- USA 10.8%
- Japan 8.4%
- Germany 7.2%
- Hong Kong 7.1%
- Singapore 5.2%
- S. Korea 4.9%
- Mexico 3.7%
- France 3.2%
- Netherlands 2.3%
- Other 32.3%

Pharmaceuticals
World total: US$ 1,436,679 million

- Belgium 13.9%
- Germany 13%
- USA 11.1%
- France 9%
- Switzerland 8.8%
- UK 8.7%
- Ireland 7.4%
- Italy 3.4%
- Netherlands 2.6%
- Sweden 2.2%
- Other 19.8%

Top Container Ports

Total container traffic,
in million TEU (2010)
('TEU' stands for Twenty-foot
Equivalent Unit, the equivalent
of a standard container)

(Bar chart, values approximate)
- Singapore ~26
- Shanghai ~25
- Hong Kong ~21
- Shenzhen (China) ~18
- Busan (S. Korea) ~12
- Guangzhou (China) ~11
- Dubai ~11
- Ningbo (China) ~10.5
- Qingdao (China) ~10.5
- Rotterdam ~9.5

INTERNET AND TELECOMMUNICATIONS

Percentage of total population
using the Internet (2009)

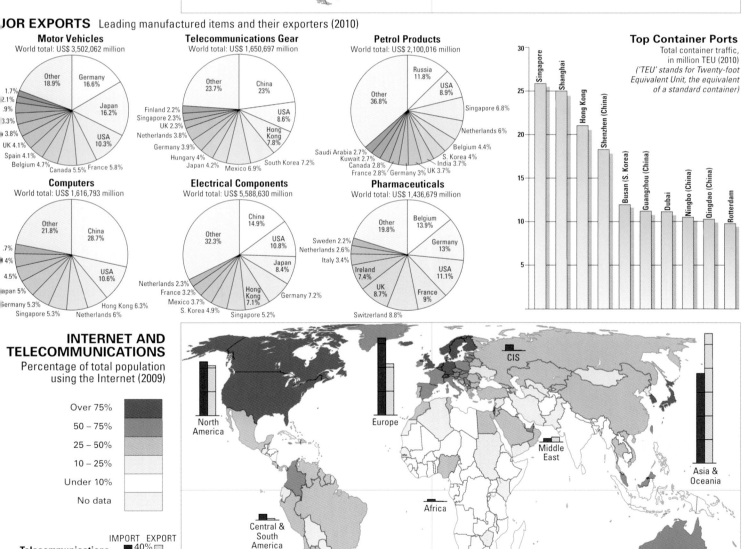

Over 75%

50 – 75%

25 – 50%

10 – 25%

Under 10%

No data

Telecommunications

Trade in office machines
and telecom equipment,
percentage of world total
(2009)

IMPORT   EXPORT

40%

30%

20%

10%

Map regions: North America, Central & South America, Europe, CIS, Middle East, Africa, Asia & Oceania

Projection: Eckert IV

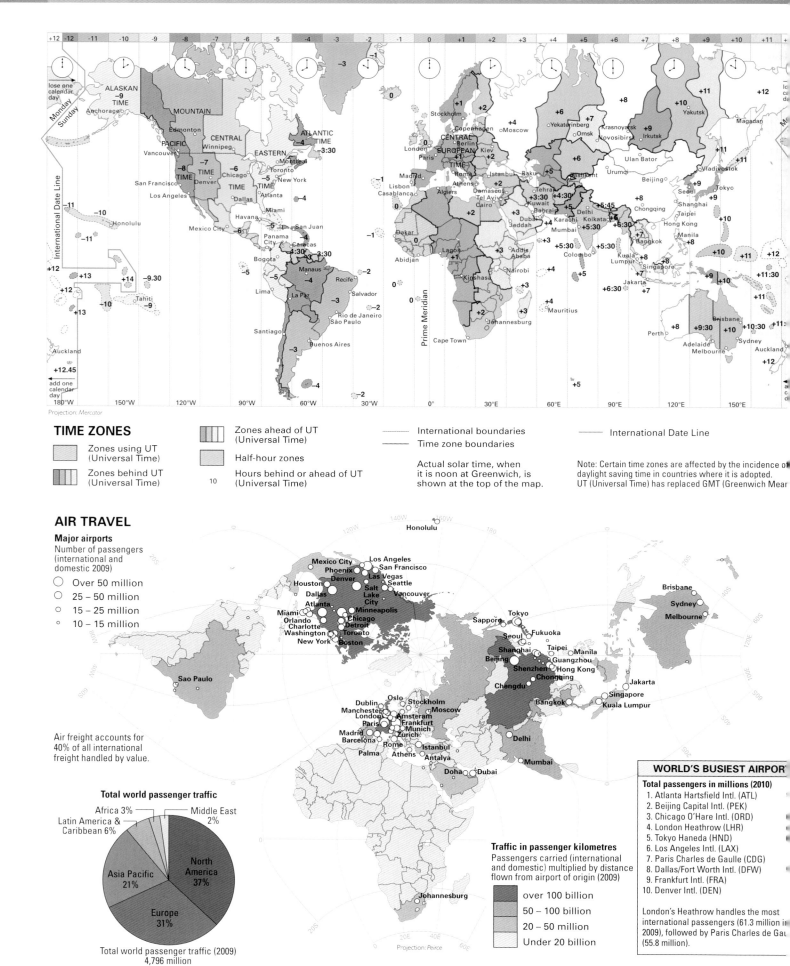

Projection: Mercator

TIME ZONES

	Zones using UT (Universal Time)
	Zones behind UT (Universal Time)
	Zones ahead of UT (Universal Time)
	Half-hour zones
10	Hours behind or ahead of UT (Universal Time)

-------- International boundaries
-------- Time zone boundaries

———— International Date Line

Actual solar time, when it is noon at Greenwich, is shown at the top of the map.

Note: Certain time zones are affected by the incidence of daylight saving time in countries where it is adopted.
UT (Universal Time) has replaced GMT (Greenwich Mean

AIR TRAVEL

Major airports
Number of passengers (international and domestic 2009)

- ○ Over 50 million
- ○ 25 – 50 million
- ○ 15 – 25 million
- ○ 10 – 15 million

Air freight accounts for 40% of all international freight handled by value.

Total world passenger traffic

- Africa 3%
- Latin America & Caribbean 6%
- Middle East 2%
- North America 37%
- Asia Pacific 21%
- Europe 31%

Total world passenger traffic (2009) 4,796 million

Traffic in passenger kilometres
Passengers carried (international and domestic) multiplied by distance flown from airport of origin (2009)

	over 100 billion
	50 – 100 billion
	20 – 50 million
	Under 20 billion

Projection: Peirce

WORLD'S BUSIEST AIRPOR

Total passengers in millions (2010)
1. Atlanta Hartsfield Intl. (ATL)
2. Beijing Capital Intl. (PEK)
3. Chicago O'Hare Intl. (ORD)
4. London Heathrow (LHR)
5. Tokyo Haneda (HND)
6. Los Angeles Intl. (LAX)
7. Paris Charles de Gaulle (CDG)
8. Dallas/Fort Worth Intl. (DFW)
9. Frankfurt Intl. (FRA)
10. Denver Intl. (DEN)

London's Heathrow handles the most international passengers (61.3 million in 2009), followed by Paris Charles de Gau (55.8 million).

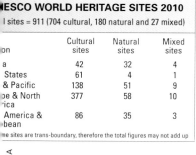

ESCO WORLD HERITAGE SITES 2010

l sites = 911 (704 cultural, 180 natural and 27 mixed)

on	Cultural sites	Natural sites	Mixed sites
a	42	32	4
States	61	4	1
& Pacific	138	51	9
e & North rica	377	58	10
America & bean	86	35	3

e sites are trans-boundary, therefore the total figures may not add up

Europe at larger scale

Destinations

- ■ Cultural & historical centres
- □ Coastal resorts
- □ Ski resorts
- ■ Centres of entertainment
- ■ Places of pilgrimage
- ■ Places of great natural beauty

Other tourist destinations

TOURIST DESTINATIONS
Projection: Peirce

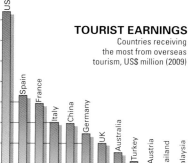

TOURIST EARNINGS
Countries receiving the most from overseas tourism, US$ million (2009)

Movement of tourists

More than 10 million

5 – 10 million

3 – 5 million

Less than 3 million

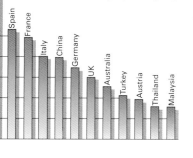

TOURIST SPENDING
Countries spending the most on overseas tourism, US$ million (2009)

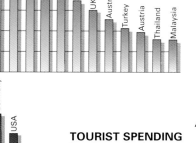

IMPORTANCE OF TOURISM
Tourism receipts as a percentage of Gross National Income (2009)

- ■ Over 10%
- ■ 5 – 10%
- ■ 2.5 – 5%
- ■ 1 – 2.5%
- □ Under 1%
- □ No data

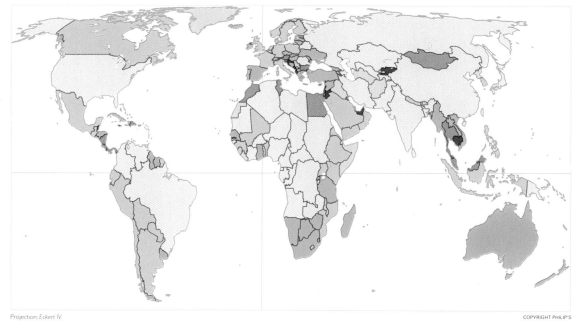

Tourist arrivals in millions (2010)

France	76.8
USA	59.7
China	55.7
Spain	52.7
Italy	43.6
UK	28.1

Projection: Eckert IV

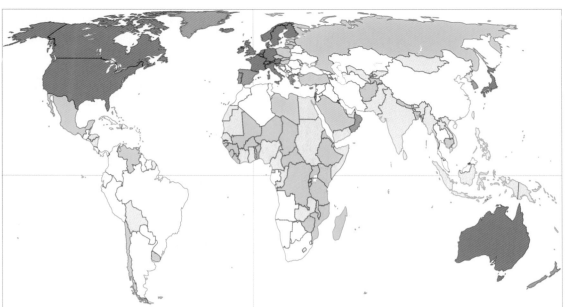

WEALTH

The value of total production divided by the population (the Gross National Income per capita, in 2009)

	Over 400% of world average
	200 – 400% of world average
	100 – 220% of world average

World average U$8,732

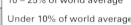

	50 – 100% of world average
	25 – 50% of world average
	10 – 25% of world average
	Under 10% of world average
	No data

Wealthiest countries		Poorest countries	
Norway	$86,640	Burundi	$150
Lux'bourg	$76,710	Liberia	$160
Switz.	$65,430	Congo (DR)	$160

UK $41,370

WATER SUPPLY

The percentage of total population with access to safe drinking water (latest available year)

Over 90%	
80 – 90%	
70 – 80%	
60 – 70%	
Under 60%	
No data	

Least well-provided countries

Afghanistan	22%
Western Sahara	26%
Somalia	29%
Papua New Guinea	40%
Ethiopia	42%

UK 100% with safe water

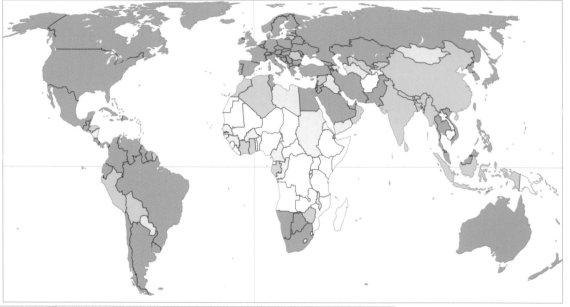

HUMAN DEVELOPMENT

The Human Development Index (HDI), calculated by the UN Development Programme (UNDP), gives a value to countries using indicators of life expectancy, education and standards of living in 2010 . Higher values show more developed countries.

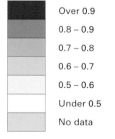

	Over 0.9
	0.8 – 0.9
	0.7 – 0.8
	0.6 – 0.7
	0.5 – 0.6
	Under 0.5
	No data

Highest values		Lowest values	
Norway	0.938	Zimbabwe	0.140
Australia	0.937	Congo (DR)	0.239
New Zealand	0.907	Niger	0.261

UK 0.849

Projection: *Eckert IV*

HEALTH CARE
Number of qualified doctors
per 100,000 people (2009)

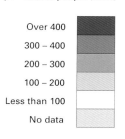

	Over 400
	300 – 400
	200 – 300
	100 – 200
	Less than 100
	No data

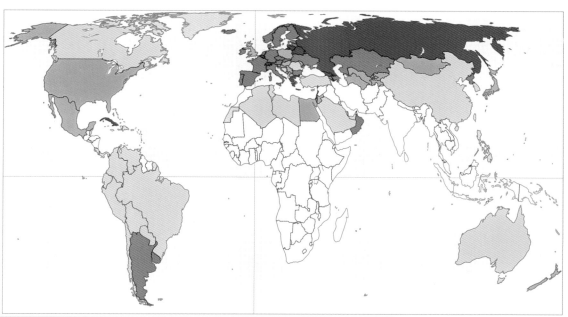

Countries with the most and least
doctors per 100,000 people

Most doctors		Least doctors	
Cuba	640	Tanzania	2
Greece	540	Sierra Leone	3
St Lucia	500	Niger	3
Belarus	490	Liberia	3
Georgia	450	Burundi	3

UK 210 doctors

ILLITERACY
Percentage of adult total
population unable to read or
write (2009)

	Over 50%
	25 – 50%
	10 – 25%
	5 – 10%
	Under 5%
	No data

Countries with the highest
and lowest illiteracy rates

Highest (%)		Lowest (%)	
Mali	74	Australia	0
South Sudan	73	Denmark	0
Burkina Faso	71	Finland	0
Niger	71	Luxembourg	0
Chad	67	Norway	0

UK 1% adults

GENDER INEQUALITY INDEX

The Gender Inequality Index (GII) is a
composite measure reflecting inequality in
achievements between women and men in
three categories: reproductive health,
empowerment and the labour market.
It varies between 0, when women and men
fare equally, and 1, when women or men
fare poorly compared to the other in all
categories (2009).

	Over 0.75
	0.5 – 0.75
	0.25 – 0.5
	Under 0.25
	No data

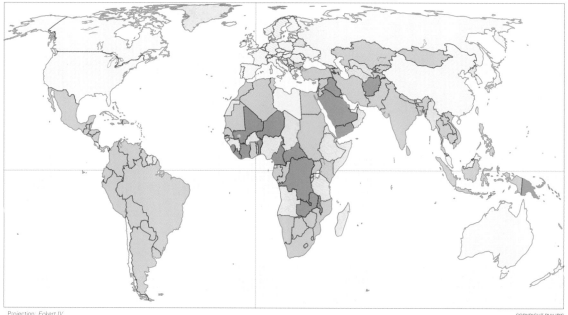

Highest values		Lowest values	
Netherlands	0.174	Yemen	0.853
Denmark	0.209	Congo (DR)	0.814
Sweden	0.212	Niger	0.807

UK 0.355

Projection: *Eckert IV*

AGE DISTRIBUTION PYRAMIDS

The bars represent the percentage of the total population (males plus females) in each age group. More Economically Developed Countries (MEDCs), such as New Zealand, have populations spread evenly across age groups and usually a growing percentage of elderly people. Less Economically Developed Countries (LEDCs), such as Kenya, have the great majority of their people in the younger age groups, about to enter their most fertile years.

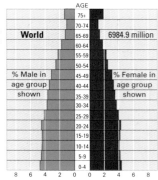

World — 6984.9 million

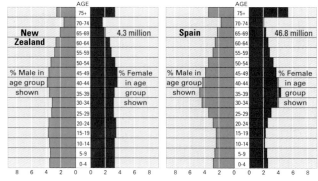

New Zealand — 4.3 million

Spain — 46.8 million

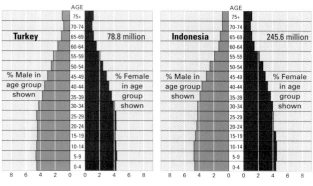

Turkey — 78.8 million

Indonesia — 245.6 million

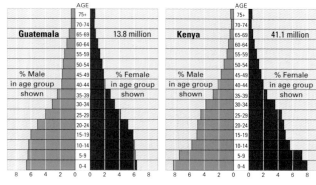

Guatemala — 13.8 million

Kenya — 41.1 million

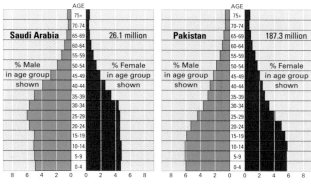

Saudi Arabia — 26.1 million

Pakistan — 187.3 million

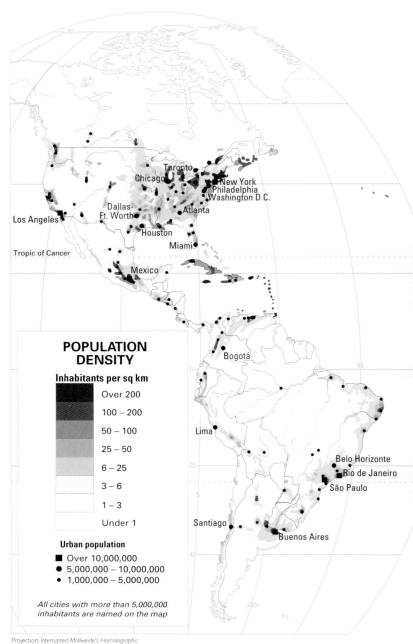

POPULATION DENSITY

Inhabitants per sq km

- Over 200
- 100 – 200
- 50 – 100
- 25 – 50
- 6 – 25
- 3 – 6
- 1 – 3
- Under 1

Urban population

- ■ Over 10,000,000
- ● 5,000,000 – 10,000,000
- • 1,000,000 – 5,000,000

All cities with more than 5,000,000 inhabitants are named on the map

Projection: Interrupted Mollweide's Homolographic

POPULATION CHANGE 1930–2020

Population totals are in millions

Figures in italics represent the percentage average annual increase for the period shown

	1930	1930–1960	1960	1960–1990	1990	1990–2020	2020
World	2,013	*1.4%*	3,019	*1.9%*	5,292	*1.4%*	8,062
Africa	155	*2.0%*	281	*2.9%*	648	*2.7%*	1,441
North America	135	*1.3%*	199	*1.1%*	276	*0.6%*	327
Latin America*	129	*1.8%*	218	*2.4%*	448	*1.6%*	719
Asia	1,073	*1.5%*	1,669	*2.1%*	3,108	*1.4%*	4,680
Europe	355	*0.6%*	425	*0.6%*	498	*0.1%*	514
Oceania	10	*1.4%*	16	*1.8%*	27	*1.1%*	37
CIS†	176	*0.7%*	214	*1.0%*	288	*0.6%*	343

* South America plus Central America, Mexico and the West Indies
† Commonwealth of Independent States, formerly the USSR

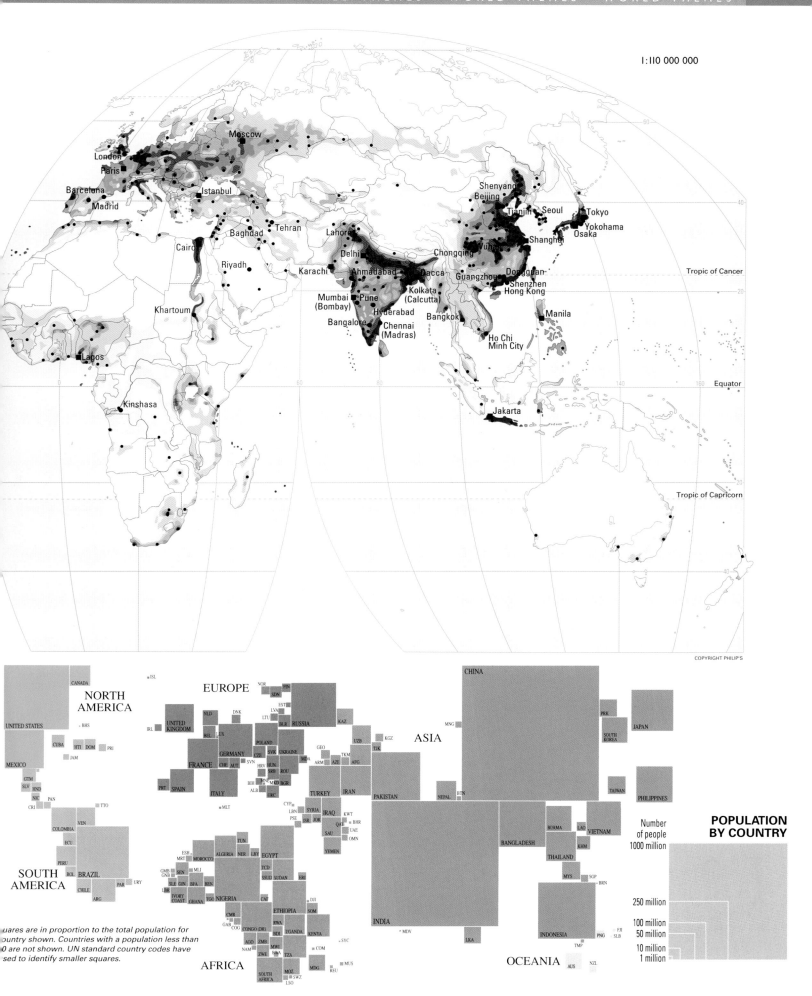

1:110 000 000

Tropic of Cancer

Equator

Tropic of Capricorn

COPYRIGHT PHILIP'S

NORTH AMERICA

EUROPE

ASIA

SOUTH AMERICA

AFRICA

OCEANIA

POPULATION BY COUNTRY

Number of people
1000 million

250 million

100 million
50 million

10 million
1 million

...quares are in proportion to the total population for
...ountry shown. Countries with a population less than
...0 are not shown. UN standard country codes have
...sed to identify smaller squares.

MATERNAL MORTALITY

The number of mothers who died per 100,000 live births (2008)

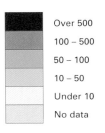

- Over 500
- 100 – 500
- 50 – 100
- 10 – 50
- Under 10
- No data

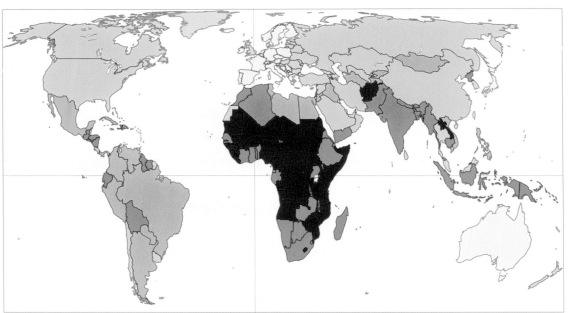

Countries with the highest and lowest maternal mortality

Highest		Lowest	
Afghanistan	1,400	Greece	2
Chad	1,200	Ireland	3
Somalia	1,200	Sweden	5
Guinea-Bissau	1,000	Italy	5
Liberia	990	Iceland	5

UK 12 mothers

POPULATION CHANGE

The projected population change for the years 2004–2050

- Over 125% gain
- 100 – 125% gain
- 50 – 100% gain
- 25 – 50% gain
- 0 – 25% gain
- No change or loss

Based on estimates for the year 2050, the ten most populous nations in the world will be, in millions:

India	1,628	Pakistan	295
China	1,437	Bangladesh	280
USA	420	Brazil	221
Indonesia	308	Congo (DR)	181
Nigeria	307	Ethiopia	171

UK (2050) 77 million

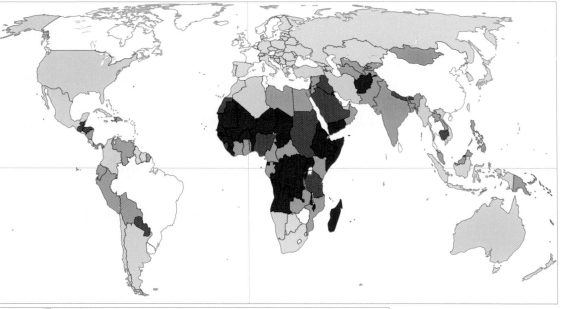

URBAN POPULATION

Percentage of total population living in towns and cities (2010)

- Over 80%
- 60 – 80%
- 40 – 60%
- 20 – 40%
- Under 20%
- No data

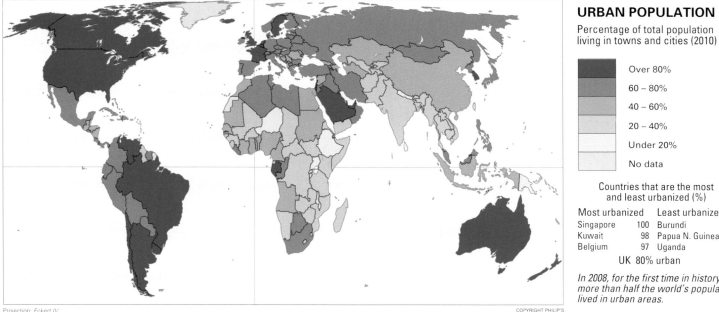

Countries that are the most and least urbanized (%)

Most urbanized		Least urbanized	
Singapore	100	Burundi	11
Kuwait	98	Papua N. Guinea	13
Belgium	97	Uganda	13

UK 80% urban

In 2008, for the first time in history, more than half the world's population lived in urban areas.

Projection: *Eckert IV*

COPYRIGHT PHILIP'S

INFANT MORTALITY

Number of babies who died under the age of one, per 1,000 live births (2010)

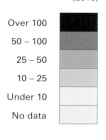

	Over 100
	50 – 100
	25 – 50
	10 – 25
	Under 10
	No data

Countries with the highest and lowest child mortality

Highest		Lowest	
Angola	176	Monaco	2
Afghanistan	149	Singapore	2
Niger	112	Sweden	3

UK 5 babies

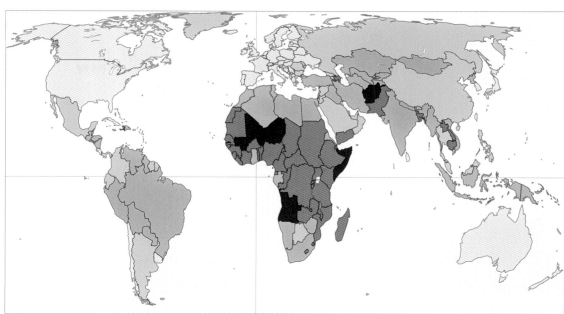

LIFE EXPECTANCY

The average expected lifespan of babies born in 2010

	Over 80
	70 – 80
	60 – 70
	50 – 60
	Under 50
	No data

Countries with the highest and lowest life expectancy at birth in years

Highest		Lowest	
Australia	82	Angola	39
Italy	82	Afghanistan	45
Japan	82	Nigeria	48
Singapore	82	Chad	48
Canada	81	South Africa	49

UK 80 years

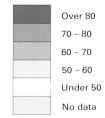

FAMILY SIZE

Children born per woman (2010)

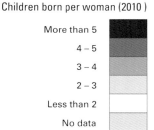

	More than 5
	4 – 5
	3 – 4
	2 – 3
	Less than 2
	No data

Countries with the largest and smallest family size

Largest		Smallest	
Niger	7.6	Singapore	1.1
Uganda	6.7	Japan	1.2
Mali	6.4	Taiwan	1.2
Somalia	6.4	South Korea	1.2
Burundi	6.2	Lithuania	1.3

UK 1.9 children

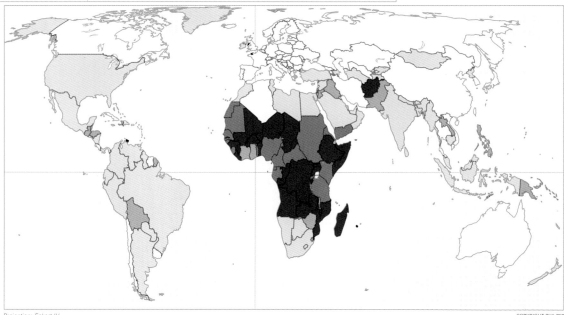

Projection: *Eckert IV*

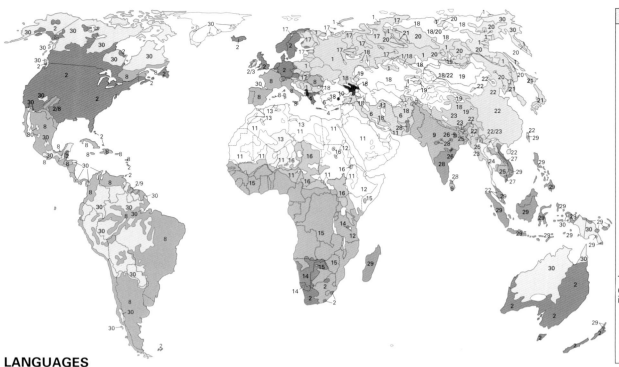

Languages of the World

Language can be classified by ancestry and structure. For example, the Romance and Germanic groups are both derived from an Indo-European language believed to have been spoken 5,000 years ago.

First-language speakers in millions (2009)

Chinese 1,213, Spanish 329, English 328, Arabic 221, Hindi 182, Bengali 181, Portuguese 178, Russian 144, Japanese 122, German 90, Javanese 85, Lahnda 78, Telugu 70, Vietnamese 69, French 68, Marathi 68, Korean 66, Tamil 66, Italian 62, Urdu 61.

Distribution of living languages

The figures refer to the number of languages currently in use in the regions shown

Asia 2,322
Africa 2,110
Pacific 1,250
The Americas 993
Europe 234

LANGUAGES

INDO-EUROPEAN FAMILY

1. Balto-Slavic group (incl. Russian, Ukrainian)
2. Germanic group (incl. English, German)
3. Celtic group
4. Greek
5. Albanian
6. Iranian group
7. Armenian
8. Romance group (incl. Spanish, Portuguese, French, Italian)
9. Indo-Aryan group (incl. Hindi, Bengali, Urdu, Punjabi, Marathi)

CAUCASIAN FAMILY

AFRO-ASIATIC FAMILY

11. Semitic group (incl. Arabic)
12. Kushitic group
13. Berber group

14. KHOISAN FAMILY

15. NIGER-CONGO FAMILY

16. NILO-SAHARAN FAMILY

17. URALIC FAMILY

ALTAIC FAMILY

18. Turkic group (incl. Turkish)
19. Mongolian group
20. Tungus-Manchu group
21. Japanese and Korean

SINO-TIBETAN FAMILY

22. Sinitic (Chinese) languages (incl. Mandarin, Wu, Yue)
23. Tibetic-Burmic languages

24. TAI FAMILY

AUSTRO-ASIATIC FAMILY

25. Mon-Khmer group
26. Munda group
27. Vietnamese

DRAVIDIAN FAMILY
28. (incl. Telugu, Tamil)

AUSTRONESIAN FAMILY
29. (incl. Malay-Indonesian, Javanese)

30. OTHER LANGUAGES

RELIGIONS

- ▲ Roman Catholicism
- Orthodox and other Eastern Churches
- • Protestantism
- Sunni Islam
- Shiite Islam
- Buddhism
- Hinduism
- Confucianism
- ✱ Judaism
- Shintoism
- Tribal Religions

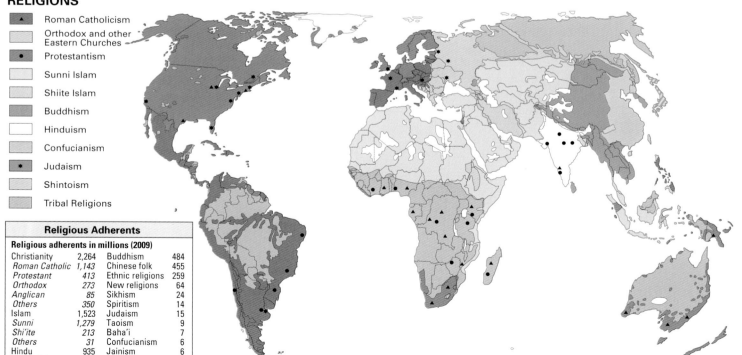

Religious Adherents

Religious adherents in millions (2009)

Christianity	2,264	Buddhism	484
Roman Catholic	*1,143*	Chinese folk	455
Protestant	*413*	Ethnic religions	259
Orthodox	*273*	New religions	64
Anglican	*85*	Sikhism	24
Others	*350*	Spiritism	14
Islam	1,523	Judaism	15
Sunni	*1,279*	Taoism	9
Shi'ite	*213*	Baha'i	7
Others	*31*	Confucianism	6
Hindu	935	Jainism	6
Non-religious/ Agnostic/Atheist	779		

United Nations

Created in 1945 to promote peace and co-operation, and based in New York, the United Nations is the world's largest international organization, with 192 members and an annual budget of US $5.16 billion (2010). Each member of the General Assembly has one vote, while the five permanent members of the 15-nation Security Council – China, France, Russia, the UK and the USA – hold a veto. The Secretariat is the UN's principal administrative arm. The 54 members of the Economic and Social Council are responsible for economic, social, cultural, educational, health and related matters. The UN has 16 specialized agencies – based in Canada, France, Switzerland and Italy, as well as the USA – which help members in fields such as education (UNESCO), agriculture (FAO), medicine (WHO) and finance (IFC). By the end of 1994, all the original 11 trust territories of the Trusteeship Council had become independent.

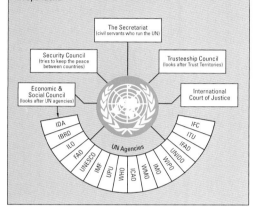

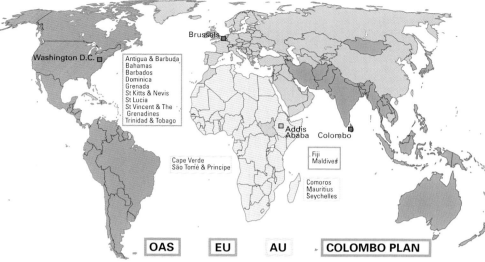

AU The African Union was set up in 2002, taking over from the Organization of African Unity (1963). It has 53 members. Working languages are Arabic, English, French and Portuguese.

COLOMBO PLAN (formed in 1951) Its 25 members aim to promote economic and social development in Asia and the Pacific.

OAS Organization of American States (formed in 1948). It aims to promote social and economic co-operation between countries in the developed North America and developing Latin America.

EU European Union (evolved from the European Community in 1993). Cyprus, the Czech Republic, Estonia, Hungary, Latvia, Lithuania, Malta, Poland, the Slovak Republic and Slovenia joined the EU in May 2004, Bulgaria and Romania joined in 2007. The other 15 members of the EU are Austria, Belgium, Denmark, Finland, France, Germany, Greece, Ireland, Italy, Luxembourg, Netherlands, Portugal, Spain, Sweden and the UK. Together, the 27 members aim to integrate economies, co-ordinate social developments and bring about political union. Its member states have set up common institutions to which they delegate some of their sovereignty so that decisions on specific matters of joint interest can be made democratically at European level.

ACP African-Caribbean-Pacific (formed in 1963). Members enjoy economic ties with the EU.

APEC Asia-Pacific Economic Co-operation (formed in 1989). It aims to enhance economic growth and prosperity for the region and to strengthen the Asia-Pacific community. APEC is the only intergovernmental grouping in the world operating on the basis of non-binding commitments, open dialogue, and equal respect for the views of all participants. There are 21 member economies.

G8 Group of eight leading industrialized nations, comprising Canada, France, Germany, Italy, Japan, Russia, the UK and the USA. Periodic meetings are held to discuss major world issues, such as world recessions.

OECD Organization for Economic Co-operation and Development (formed in 1961). It comprises 30 major free-market economies. The 'G8' is its 'inner group' of leading industrial nations, comprising Canada, France, Germany, Italy, Japan, Russia, the UK and the USA.

OPEC Organization of Petroleum Exporting Countries (formed in 1960). It controls about three-quarters of the world's oil supply. Gabon formally withdrew from OPEC in August 1996.

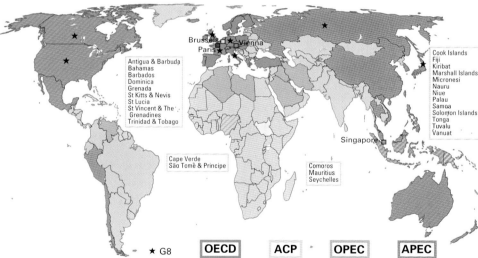

ARAB LEAGUE (1945) Aims to promote economic, social, political and military co-operation. There are 22 member nations.

ASEAN Association of South-east Asian Nations (formed in 1967). Cambodia joined in 1999.

BRIC This acronym refers to the four largest and fastest growing developing economies, Brazil, Russia, India and China.

COMMONWEALTH The Commonwealth of Nations evolved from the British Empire. Pakistan was suspended in 1999, but reinstated in 2004. Zimbabwe was suspended in 2002 and, in response to its continued suspension, left the Commonwealth in 2003. Fiji Islands was suspended in 2006 following a military coup. Rwanda joined the Commonwealth in 2009, as the 54th member state, becoming only the second country which was not formerly a British colony to be admitted to the group.

LAIA The Latin American Integration Association (formed in 1980) superceded the Latin American Free Trade Association formed in 1961. Its aim is to promote freer regional trade.

NATO North Atlantic Treaty Organization (formed in 1949). It continues despite the winding-up of the Warsaw Pact in 1991. Bulgaria, Estonia, Latvia, Lithuania, Romania, the Slovak Republic and Slovenia became members in 2004.

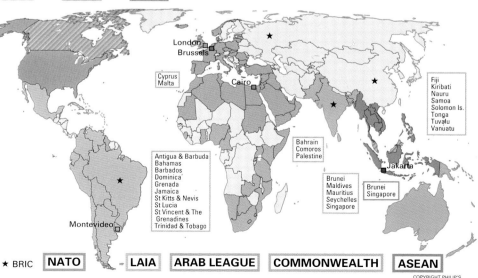

COPYRIGHT PHILIP'S

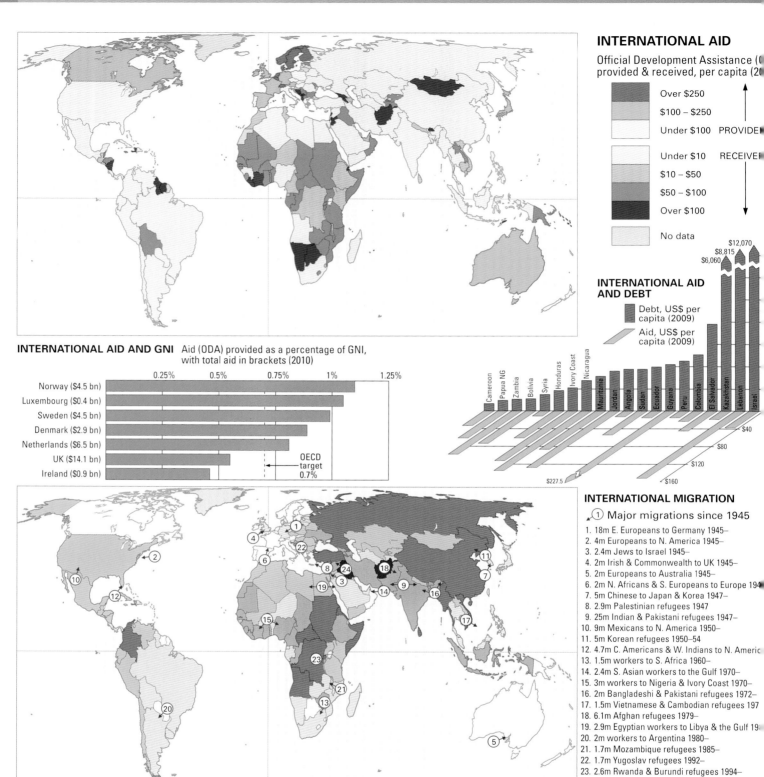

INTERNATIONAL AID

Official Development Assistance (
provided & received, per capita (2

	Over $250
	$100 – $250
	Under $100 PROVIDE
	Under $10 RECEIVE
	$10 – $50
	$50 – $100
	Over $100
	No data

INTERNATIONAL AID AND GNI

Aid (ODA) provided as a percentage of GNI, with total aid in brackets (2010)

	0.25%	0.5%	0.75%	1%	1.25%
Norway ($4.5 bn)					
Luxembourg ($0.4 bn)					
Sweden ($4.5 bn)					
Denmark ($2.9 bn)					
Netherlands ($6.5 bn)					
UK ($14.1 bn)					
Ireland ($0.9 bn)					

OECD target 0.7%

INTERNATIONAL AID AND DEBT

$12,070
$8,815
$6,060

- Debt, US$ per capita (2009)
- Aid, US$ per capita (2009)

Cameroon, Papua NG, Zambia, Bolivia, Syria, Honduras, Ivory Coast, Nicaragua, Mauritania, Jordan, Angola, Sudan, Ecuador, Guyana, Peru, Colombia, El Salvador, Kazakhstan, Lebanon, Israel

$40
$80
$120
$160
$227.5

INTERNATIONAL MIGRATION

① Major migrations since 1945

1. 18m E. Europeans to Germany 1945–
2. 4m Europeans to N. America 1945–
3. 2.4m Jews to Israel 1945–
4. 2m Irish & Commonwealth to UK 1945–
5. 2m Europeans to Australia 1945–
6. 2m N. Africans & S. Europeans to Europe 194
7. 5m Chinese to Japan & Korea 1947–
8. 2.9m Palestinian refugees 1947
9. 25m Indian & Pakistani refugees 1947–
10. 9m Mexicans to N. America 1950–
11. 5m Korean refugees 1950–54
12. 4.7m C. Americans & W. Indians to N. Americ
13. 1.5m workers to S. Africa 1960–
14. 2.4m S. Asian workers to the Gulf 1970–
15. 3m workers to Nigeria & Ivory Coast 1970–
16. 2m Bangladeshi & Pakistani refugees 1972–
17. 1.5m Vietnamese & Cambodian refugees 197
18. 6.1m Afghan refugees 1979–
19. 2.9m Egyptian workers to Libya & the Gulf 19
20. 2m workers to Argentina 1980–
21. 1.7m Mozambique refugees 1985–
22. 1.7m Yugoslav refugees 1992–
23. 2.6m Rwanda & Burundi refugees 1994–
24. 1.8m Iraqi refugees 2003–

REFUGEES

By country of origin (2009)

	Over 1 million
	100,000 – 1 million
	10,000 – 100,000
	1,000 – 10,000
	100 – 1,000
	Under 100
	No data

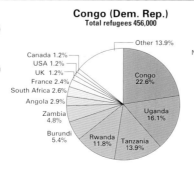

Congo (Dem. Rep.)
Total refugees 456,000

Other 13.9%
Congo 22.6%
Uganda 16.1%
Tanzania 13.9%
Rwanda 11.8%
Burundi 5.4%
Zambia 4.8%
Angola 2.9%
South Africa 2.6%
France 2.4%
UK 1.2%
USA 1.2%
Canada 1.2%

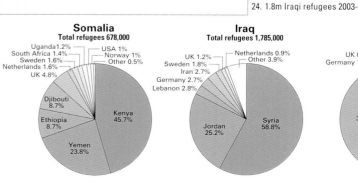

Somalia
Total refugees 678,000

Uganda 1.2%
South Africa 1.4%
Sweden 1.6%
Netherlands 1.6%
UK 4.8%
USA 1%
Norway 1%
Other 0.5%
Kenya 45.7%
Yemen 23.8%
Ethiopia 8.7%
Djibouti 8.7%

Iraq
Total refugees 1,785,000

UK 1.2%
Sweden 1.8%
Netherlands 0.9%
Other 3.9%
Iran 2.7%
Germany 2.7%
Lebanon 2.8%
Syria 58.8%
Jordan 25.2%

Afghanistan
Total refugees 2,887,00

UK 0.8%
Germany 1.1%
Other 2.4
Iran 35.4%
Pakista 60.3%

COPYRIGH

ARMED CONFLICTS

Current military and civilian death
Ills in countries with conflict (2010)

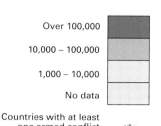

Over 100,000

10,000 – 100,000

1,000 – 10,000

No data

Countries with at least
one armed conflict
between 1994 and 2010

ding arms orting countries $ million)	Leading recipients of arms deliveries (US $ million)	
$14,000	Saudi Arabia	$4,100
sia $5,800	China	$2,900
$3,300	Israel	$1,500

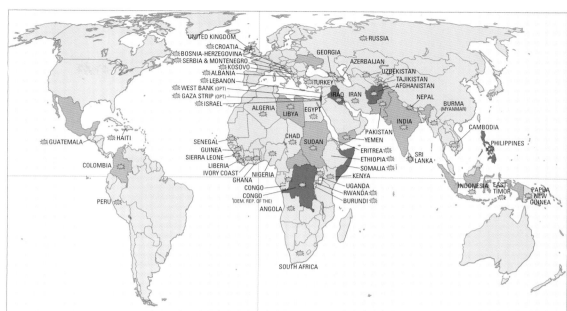

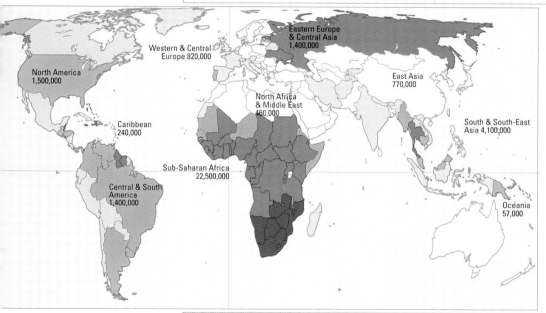

SPREAD OF HIV/AIDS

Percentage of the population
living with HIV/AIDS (2009)

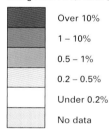

Over 10%

1 – 10%

0.5 – 1%

0.2 – 0.5%

Under 0.2%

No data

Caribbean 240,000	Total number of adults and children living with HIV/AIDS by region (2009)

Human Immunodeficiency Virus (HIV) is passed
from one person to another and attacks the
body's defence against illness. It develops into
the Acquired Immunodeficiency Syndrome
(AIDS) when a particularly severe illness, such as
cancer, takes hold. The pandemic started just
over 20 years ago and by 2009 33 millon people
were living with HIV or AIDS.

TRAFFIC IN DRUGS

Countries producing illegal drugs

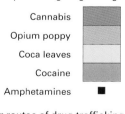

Cannabis

Opium poppy

Coca leaves

Cocaine

Amphetamines ■

Major routes of drug trafficking

Opium

Coca leaves

Cocaine

Heroin

Cannabis

Amphetamines
(usually used within
producing countries)

Conflicts relating to
drug trafficking

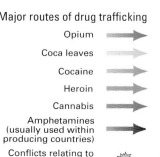

Projection: *Eckert IV*

COPYRIGHT PHILIP'S

	POPULATION						WEALTH						TRADE		
	Total population (millions 2010)	Population density (persons per km² 2010)	Population change (average annual percentage 2010)	Birth rate (births per thousand people 2010)	Death rate (deaths per thousand people 2010)	Urban population (percentage of total 2010)	Gross National income (million US$ 2009)	Gross National Income per capita (PPP US$ 2009)	GDP growth rate (percentage 2010)	GDP from agriculture (percentage of GDP 2010)	GDP from industry (percentage of GDP 2010)	GDP from services (percentage of GDP 2010)	Imports (US$ per capita 2010)	Exports (US$ per capita 2010)	Tourism receipts (US$ per capita 2009)
Afghanistan	29.1	45	2.4	38	17	22	9,053	310	8.2	31.0	26.0	43.0	182	19	
Albania	3.0	104	0.3	12	6	52	12,634	4,000	3.5	18.9	23.5	57.6	1,537	519	
Algeria	34.6	15	1.2	17	5	67	154,202	4,420	3.3	8.3	61.5	30.2	1,072	1,523	
Angola	13.1	10	2.0	43	23	59	69,373	3,750	1.6	9.6	65.8	24.6	1,385	3,952	
Argentina	41.3	15	1.0	18	7	92	304,070	7,550	7.5	8.5	31.6	59.9	1,273	1,645	
Armenia	3.0	100	0.1	13	8	64	9,544	3,100	2.6	22.0	46.6	31.4	1,007	285	
Australia	21.5	3	1.1	12	7	89	957,519	43,770	2.7	4.0	24.8	71.2	9,314	9,793	
Austria	8.2	98	0.0	9	10	68	388,529	46,450	2.0	1.5	29.4	69.1	18,992	19,162	
Azerbaijan	8.3	96	0.8	18	8	52	42,529	4,840	5.0	5.5	61.4	33.1	847	3,380	
Bahamas	0.3	22	0.9	16	7	84	9,117	14,920	0.5	1.2	14.7	84.1	7,735	2,171	
Bahrain	0.7	1,110	2.8	15	3	89	19,712	25,420	4.1	0.5	56.6	42.9	16,450	20,501	
Bangladesh	156.1	1,084	1.6	23	6	28	93,470	580	6.0	18.4	28.7	52.9	137	104	
Barbados	0.3	663	0.4	12	8	44	3,551	16,140	-0.5	6.0	16.0	78.0	5,552	1,348	
Belarus	9.6	46	-0.4	10	14	75	53,707	5,560	7.6	9.0	42.9	48.1	3,099	2,548	
Belgium	10.4	341	0.1	10	11	97	488,429	45,270	2.0	0.7	22.1	77.2	27,025	26,786	
Belize	0.3	14	2.1	26	6	52	1,205	3,740	2.0	29.0	16.9	54.1	2,353	1,284	
Benin	9.1	80	2.9	38	9	42	6,715	750	2.5	33.2	14.5	52.3	200	124	
Bhutan	0.7	15	1.2	19	7	35	1,416	2,020	2.5	17.6	45.0	37.4	762	733	
Bolivia	9.9	9	1.7	25	7	67	16,061	1,630	4.2	11.0	38.0	51.0	539	699	
Bosnia-Herzegovina	4.6	90	0.0	9	9	49	17,704	4,700	0.8	6.5	28.4	65.1	1,995	1,039	
Botswana	2.0	3	1.7	22	11	61	12,211	6,260	8.6	2.3	45.8	51.9	2,226	2,178	
Brazil	201.1	24	1.1	18	6	87	1,557,007	8,070	7.5	6.1	26.4	67.5	933	993	
Brunei	0.4	68	1.7	18	3	76	10,211	49,900	4.1	0.7	74.1	25.2	6,607	27,011	
Bulgaria	7.1	64	-0.8	9	14	71	45,961	6,060	0.2	6.0	30.3	63.7	3,187	2,704	
Burkina Faso	16.2	59	3.1	44	13	26	8,036	510	5.8	30.1	20.7	49.2	91	61	
Burma (Myanmar)	53.4	79	1.1	19	8	34	17,766	150	5.3	43.2	20.0	36.8	85	147	
Burundi	9.9	354	3.5	41	10	11	1,232	1,290	3.9	31.6	21.4	47.0	34	7	
Cambodia	14.5	80	1.7	25	8	20	9,099	650	6.0	33.4	21.4	45.2	415	324	
Cameroon	19.3	41	2.1	33	12	58	23,189	1,190	3.0	20.0	30.9	49.1	252	227	
Canada	33.8	3	0.8	10	8	81	1,416,347	41,980	3.1	2.0	20.0	78.0	12,038	12,050	
Cape Verde Is.	0.5	126	1.4	21	6	61	1,520	3,010	5.4	9.0	16.2	74.8	1,687	224	
Central African Rep.	4.8	8	2.1	36	15	39	1,975	450	3.3	55.0	20.0	25.0	49	30	
Chad	10.5	8	2.0	39	15	28	5,845	600	5.1	50.5	7.0	42.5	250	288	
Chile	16.7	22	0.8	14	6	89	160,655	9,470	5.3	5.6	40.5	53.9	3,238	3,838	
China	1,330.1	139	0.5	14	7	47	4,856,148	3,650	10.3	9.6	46.8	43.6	983	1,132	
Colombia	44.2	39	1.2	17	5	75	227,814	4,990	4.3	9.3	38.0	52.7	820	910	
Comoros	0.8	356	2.7	34	7	28	571	810	2.1	40.0	4.0	56.0	185	41	
Congo	4.1	12	2.8	41	11	62	7,671	2,080	9.1	4.4	63.6	32.0	874	2,230	
Congo (Dem. Rep.)	70.9	30	2.6	38	11	35	10,609	160	7.2	37.4	26.0	36.6	73	54	
Costa Rica	4.5	88	1.3	17	4	64	28,664	6,260	4.2	6.3	22.9	70.8	2,949	2,216	
Croatia	4.5	79	-0.1	17	12	58	60,797	13,770	-1.4	6.8	27.2	66.0	4,665	2,565	
Cuba	11.5	104	-0.1	10	7	75	62,196	5,550	1.5	4.4	22.7	72.9	893	288	
Cyprus	1.1	119	1.6	11	6	70	21,366	30,480	1.0	2.1	18.6	79.3	7,221	2,024	
Czech Republic	10.2	129	-0.1	8	11	74	181,547	17,310	2.3	2.2	38.3	59.5	10,704	11,420	
Denmark	5.5	128	0.3	10	10	87	326,535	59,060	2.1	1.1	22.8	76.1	16,468	18,016	
Djibouti	0.7	32	2.2	25	8	76	1,106	1,280	4.5	3.2	14.9	81.9	870	135	
Dominican Republic	9.8	202	1.3	20	4	69	45,937	4,550	7.8	11.5	21.0	67.5	1,479	627	
East Timor	1.2	77	2.0	26	6	28	2,706	2,460	6.1	32.2	12.8	55.0	168	9	
Ecuador	14.8	52	1.4	20	5	67	54,130	3,970	3.2	6.4	35.9	57.7	1,193	1,174	
Egypt	80.5	80	2.0	25	5	43	172,048	2,070	5.1	13.5	37.9	48.6	578	315	
El Salvador	6.1	288	0.3	18	6	64	20,785	3,370	0.7	11.0	29.1	59.9	1,319	723	
Equatorial Guinea	0.7	23	2.6	35	9	40	8,398	12,420	-0.8	2.2	93.9	3.9	8,826	15,737	
Eritrea	5.8	48	2.5	33	8	22	1,351	320	2.2	11.8	20.4	67.8	127	4	
Estonia	1.3	29	-0.6	10	14	69	18,846	14,060	3.1	2.5	28.7	68.8	9,426	8,907	
Ethiopia	88.0	78	3.2	43	11	17	27,149	330	8.0	42.9	13.7	43.4	85	20	
Fiji	0.9	48	0.8	21	6	52	3,259	3,840	0.1	8.9	13.5	77.6	3,562	1,372	
Finland	5.3	16	0.1	10	10	85	245,256	45,940	3.1	2.6	29.1	68.3	13,151	13,992	
France	64.8	118	0.5	12	9	85	2,750,916	42,620	1.5	1.8	19.2	79.0	8,919	7,854	
Gabon	1.5	6	2.0	35	13	86	10,869	7,370	5.7	4.5	62.7	32.8	1,574	4,403	
Gambia, The	1.8	161	2.4	34	8	58	743	440	5.7	30.1	16.3	53.6	168	59	
Gaza Strip (OPT)*	1.6	4,456	3.2	35	3	74	2,843	2,968	7.0	5.0	14.0	81.0	2,351	330	
Georgia	4.6	66	-0.3	11	10	53	11,096	2,530	6.4	11.0	27.0	62.0	1,049	498	
Germany	82.3	230	-0.2	8	11	74	3,476,100	42,450	3.5	0.8	27.9	71.3	13,612	16,249	
Ghana	24.3	102	1.8	28	9	51	28,383	1,190	5.7	33.7	24.7	41.6	418	301	
Greece	10.7	81	0.1	9	11	61	327,703	29,040	-4.5	4.0	17.6	78.4	4,177	1,967	

	ENERGY			LAND & AGRICULTURE				SOCIAL INDICATORS							
	Energy produced (tonnes of oil equivalent per capita 2008)	Energy consumed (tonnes of oil equivalent per capita 2008)	CO_2 emissions (tonnes per capita 2009)	Land area (thousand km²)	Arable and Permanent crops (% of land area 2008)	Permanent pasture (% of land area 2008)	Forest (% of land area 2009)	Human Development Index (HDI) value 2009	Life expectancy (years 2010)	Food intake (calories per capita per day 2007)	Adults living with HIV/AIDS (percentage 2009)	Gender Inequality Index (GII value 2009)	Adult illiteracy rate (percentage 2008)	Motor vehicles (per thousand people 2009)	Internet usage (per thousand people 2009)
nistan	0.01	0.01	0.03	652	12	46	2	0.349	45	–	–	0.797	72	27	3.5
ia	0.36	0.77	1.52	28.7	25	18	28	0.719	77	2,880	0.1	0.545	1	114	35.7
ia	5.79	1.27	3.32	2,382	4	14	1	0.677	75	3,153	0.1	0.594	25	112	13.8
a	8.66	0.40	1.86	1,247	3	43	47	0.403	39	1,973	2.0	–	33	40	4.7
ntina	2.21	2.03	4.06	2,780	12	36	11	0.775	77	2,941	0.5	0.534	2	314	33.5
nia	0.38	1.82	3.83	29.8	18	44	9	0.695	73	2,280	0.1	0.570	1	105	7.0
alia	14.26	6.85	19.64	7,741	6	49	20	0.937	82	3,227	0.1	0.296	1	687	74.4
ia	1.63	4.63	8.43	83.9	17	21	47	0.851	80	3,819	0.3	0.300	1	562	74.8
aijan	7.68	2.08	4.24	86.6	25	32	11	0.713	67	2,961	0.1	0.553	1	89	29.4
nas	0.00	5.56	17.02	13.9	1	0	51	0.784	71	2,713	3.1	–	–	82	37.7
in	19.19	19.08	42.55	0.69	6	5	1	0.801	78	–	0.1	0.512	11	509	57.6
adesh	0.11	0.14	0.36	144	67	5	11	0.469	70	2,281	0.1	0.734	47	2	0.4
dos	0.30	1.79	5.02	0.43	40	5	19	0.788	74	3,056	1.4	0.448	–	406	66.1
s	0.21	2.99	6.28	208	27	16	45	0.732	71	3,146	0.3	–	1	282	27.4
m	1.20	7.00	13.19	30.5	26	16	22	0.867	79	3,694	0.2	0.236	1	543	77.9
	0.78	1.39	3.19	23	4	2	62	0.694	68	2,718	2.3	0.600	25	178	11.7
	0.00	0.14	0.40	113	26	5	22	0.435	60	2,533	1.2	0.759	60	21	2.3
n	2.64	2.01	0.48	47	4	11	54	0.619	67	–	0.2	–	47	47	7.2
a	1.78	0.68	1.39	1,099	4	30	53	0.643	68	2,064	0.2	0.672	9	68	11.3
a-Herzegovina	1.27	1.62	3.98	51.2	21	20	43	0.710	79	3,078	0.1	–	3	135	30.8
vana	0.30	0.84	2.28	582	0	45	20	0.633	58	2,264	24.8	0.663	17	113	6.0
	1.09	1.35	2.14	8,514	8	23	62	0.699	73	3,113	0.6	0.631	10	198	38.2
i	53.86	12.20	19.52	5.8	2	1	73	0.805	76	2,968	–	0.399	5	696	81.1
ia	1.36	2.87	6.18	111	30	18	35	0.743	74	2,766	0.1	0.627	2	353	47.1
na Faso	0.00	0.03	0.09	274	23	22	21	0.305	54	2,677	1.2	–	71	11	1.1
a (Myanmar)	0.30	0.14	0.24	677	18	0	50	0.451	65	2,465	0.6	–	10	7	0.2
di	0.01	0.02	0.04	27.8	50	35	7	0.282	59	1,685	3.3	–	41	6	1.7
odia	0.00	0.12	0.28	181	37	9	51	0.494	63	2,268	0.5	0.672	24	1	0.5
roon	0.30	0.13	0.40	475	15	4	51	0.460	54	2,269	5.3	0.763	32	4	4.0
da	14.39	10.56	16.15	9,971	6	2	34	0.888	81	3,532	0.2	0.289	1	605	80.5
Verde Is.	0.00	0.27	0.68	4	17	6	21	0.534	71	2,572	–	–	16	94	34.9
al African Rep.	0.01	0.03	0.06	623	3	5	36	0.315	50	1,986	4.7	0.768	51	1	0.5
	0.72	0.01	0.03	1,284	3	36	9	0.295	48	2,056	3.4	–	68	6	1.6
	0.55	1.85	3.77	757	2	19	22	0.783	78	2,920	0.4	0.505	4	172	42.2
	1.49	1.60	5.82	9,597	13	43	22	0.663	75	2,981	0.1	0.405	7	37	29.1
nbia	2.23	0.76	1.61	1,139	3	35	55	0.689	75	2,685	0.5	0.658	7	58	51.6
ros	0.00	0.06	0.20	2.2	73	8	2	0.428	64	1,884	0.1	–	25	33	3.2
o	3.34	0.24	1.57	342	2	29	66	0.489	55	2,512	3.4	0.744	19	26	6.1
o (Dem. Rep.)	0.04	0.04	0.04	2,345	3	7	68	0.239	55	1,605	3.2	0.814	33	5	0.4
Rica	0.58	1.18	1.53	51.1	10	25	50	0.725	78	2,840	0.3	0.501	4	163	34.9
ia	0.90	2.27	4.74	56.5	17	6	34	0.767	76	2,990	0.1	0.345	1	388	49.8
	0.37	0.91	2.66	111	37	25	26	0.760	78	3,274	0.1	0.473	1	38	14.0
s	0.00	4.19	8.72	9.3	12	0	19	0.810	78	3,181	0.1	0.284	2	659	40.0
Republic	2.54	3.95	9.33	78.9	42	13	34	0.841	77	3,260	0.1	0.330	1	513	65.4
ark	4.99	3.81	9.01	43.1	57	6	13	0.866	79	3,416	0.2	0.209	1	477	86.4
uti	0.00	1.19	2.43	23.2	0	73	0	0.402	61	2,291	2.5	–	–	4	3.6
nican Republic	0.05	0.78	2.04	48.5	27	25	41	0.663	77	2,295	0.9	0.646	11	123	28.0
imor	4.40	0.11	0.34	14.9	15	10	51	0.502	68	2,066	–	–	50	–	0.2
or	2.22	0.89	1.89	284	10	20	41	0.695	76	2,301	0.4	0.645	9	63	23.0
	1.18	0.97	2.40	1,001	4	0	0	0.620	73	3,195	0.1	0.714	34	43	25.5
ador	0.18	0.48	0.98	21	44	31	14	0.659	73	2,590	0.8	0.653	18	84	10.4
rial Guinea	37.59	2.43	7.27	28.1	7	4	59	0.538	62	–	5.0	–	13	2	2.3
a	0.00	0.05	0.14	118	7	68	15	–	63	1,605	0.8	–	3	11	3.5
a	2.60	4.67	13.51	45.1	14	5	53	0.812	73	3,154	1.2	0.409	1	477	74.8
ia	0.01	0.04	0.08	1,104	15	20	13	0.328	56	1,980	2.1	–	64	3	0.5
	0.17	1.07	2.56	18.3	14	10	55	0.669	71	3,041	0.1	–	–	175	12.1
d	2.35	6.16	9.93	338	7	0	73	0.871	79	3,221	0.1	0.248	1	534	83.7
e	2.00	4.40	6.30	552	35	18	29	0.872	81	3,532	0.4	0.260	1	598	0.1
a	9.20	0.80	3.03	268	2	18	85	0.648	52	2,755	5.2	0.678	14	7	6.5
ia,The	0.00	0.08	0.25	11.3	40	26	48	0.390	64	2,385	2.0	0.742	–	7	7.3
Strip (OPT)*	0.00	0.94	0.78	0.4	36	25	2	–	74	2,020	–	–	8	39	88.9
ia	0.39	0.90	1.14	69.7	8	28	40	0.698	77	2,859	0.1	0.597	1	116	28.2
any	1.52	4.36	9.30	357	35	14	32	0.885	80	3,547	0.1	0.240	1	554	79.1
	0.08	0.18	0.34	239	32	37	23	0.467	61	2,907	1.8	0.729	35	33	5.4
e	0.90	3.43	9.35	132	25	11	30	0.855	80	3,725	0.1	0.317	3	560	46.3

	POPULATION						WEALTH						TRADE		
	Total population (millions 2010)	Population density (persons per km² 2010)	Population change (percentage average annual 2010)	Birth rate (births per thousand people 2010)	Death rate (deaths per thousand people 2010)	Urban population (percentage of total 2010)	Gross National Income (million US$ 2009)	Gross National Income per capita (PPP US$ 2009)	GDP growth rate (percentage 2010)	GDP from agriculture (percentage of GDP 2010)	GDP from industry (percentage of GDP 2010)	GDP from services (percentage of GDP 2010)	Imports (US$ per capita 2010)	Exports (US$ per capita 2010)	Tourism receipts (US$ per capita 2009)
Guatemala	13.6	124	2.0	27	5	49	37,189	2,650	2.6	13.3	24.4	62.3	934	625	
Guinea	10.3	42	2.6	37	10	35	3,771	370	1.9	25.8	45.7	28.5	150	142	
Guinea-Bissau	1.6	43	2.0	35	15	30	826	510	3.5	62.0	12.0	26.0	128	85	
Guyana	0.7	3	-0.4	17	7	29	1,109	2,660	3.6	24.3	24.7	51.0	1,825	1,088	
Haiti	9.6	348	0.8	24	8	52	10,000	1,180	-5.1	23.0	20.0	57.0	253	58	
Honduras	8.0	71	1.9	25	5	52	13,452	1,800	2.8	12.4	26.9	60.7	1,111	736	
Hungary	10.0	107	-0.2	10	13	68	130,114	12,980	1.2	3.3	30.8	65.9	8,751	9,381	
Iceland	0.3	3	0.7	13	7	93	13,858	43,430	-3.5	5.5	24.7	69.8	11,903	14,953	
India	1,173.1	357	1.3	21	7	30	1,367,105	1,220	10.4	16.1	28.6	55.3	279	171	
Indonesia	243.0	127	1.1	18	6	44	470,980	2,050	6.1	16.5	46.4	37.1	457	602	
Iran	76.9	47	1.2	19	6	71	330,619	4,530	1.0	11.0	45.9	43.1	767	1,023	
Iraq	29.7	68	2.4	29	5	66	69,653	2,210	0.8	9.7	63.0	27.3	1,434	1,655	
Ireland	4.6	66	1.1	16	6	62	197,065	44,280	-1.0	2.0	29.0	69.0	15,220	25,027	
Israel	7.4	354	1.6	19	5	92	191,956	25,790	4.6	2.4	32.6	65.0	7,561	7,385	
Italy	58.1	193	0.4	9	10	68	2,114,481	35,110	1.3	1.8	24.9	73.3	7,913	7,891	
Ivory Coast	21.1	65	2.1	31	10	51	22,545	1,070	2.6	28.2	21.3	50.5	333	487	
Jamaica	2.8	259	0.7	19	7	52	12,402	4,590	-1.1	5.7	29.7	64.6	1,889	522	
Japan	126.8	336	-0.3	7	10	67	4,857,203	38,080	3.9	1.1	23.0	75.9	5,022	6,034	
Jordan	6.4	69	1.0	27	3	79	23,662	3,980	3.1	3.4	30.3	66.3	2,024	1,145	
Kazakhstan	15.5	6	0.4	17	9	59	109,977	6,920	7.0	5.4	42.8	51.8	1,948	3,832	
Kenya	40.0	69	2.5	34	9	22	30,269	760	5.0	22.0	16.0	62.0	260	128	
Korea, North	22.8	189	0.5	15	9	60	205,000	8,991	-0.9	21.0	46.9	32.1	136	88	
Korea, South	48.6	494	0.2	9	6	83	966,600	19,830	6.1	3.0	39.4	57.6	8,592	9,588	
Kosovo	1.8	220	–	–	–	–	5,855	3,240	4.0	12.9	22.6	64.5	1,432	290	
Kuwait	2.8	157	2.0	21	2	98	116,984	49,970	2.0	0.3	48.1	51.6	7,300	23,315	
Kyrgyzstan	5.5	28	1.4	24	7	35	4,613	870	-1.4	24.6	25.0	50.4	558	305	
Laos	6.4	27	1.6	26	8	33	5,550	880	7.7	29.8	31.7	38.5	236	306	
Latvia	2.2	34	-0.6	10	14	68	27,936	12,390	-0.3	4.2	20.6	75.2	4,127	3,556	
Lebanon	4.1	397	0.2	15	7	87	34,052	8,060	7.5	5.1	15.9	79.0	4,356	1,257	
Lesotho	1.9	63	0.3	27	15	27	2,036	980	2.4	7.1	34.6	58.3	920	513	
Liberia	3.7	33	2.7	37	11	48	651	160	5.1	76.9	5.4	17.7	1,938	325	
Libya	6.5	4	2.1	24	3	78	77,185	12,020	4.2	2.6	63.8	33.6	3,787	6,947	
Lithuania	3.5	54	-0.3	9	11	67	38,095	11,410	1.3	4.3	27.6	68.1	5,737	5,441	
Luxembourg	0.5	192	1.1	12	8	85	38,188	76,710	3.4	0.4	13.6	86.0	47,574	35,816	
Macedonia (FYROM)	2.1	82	0.2	12	9	59	8,983	4,400	0.7	8.7	22.1	69.2	2,468	1,530	
Madagascar	21.3	36	3.0	38	8	30	7,932	430	-2.0	26.5	16.7	56.8	92	66	
Malawi	15.4	130	2.8	41	13	20	4,198	290	6.6	33.4	21.7	44.9	108	77	
Malaysia	28.3	86	1.6	21	5	72	201,839	7,350	7.2	9.1	41.6	49.3	6,165	7,438	
Mali	13.8	11	2.6	46	14	36	8,862	680	4.5	45.0	17.0	38.0	171	21	
Malta	0.4	1,287	0.4	10	9	95	7,621	18,360	3.7	1.7	17.4	80.9	10,015	7,262	
Mauritania	3.2	3	2.3	33	9	41	3,159	990	4.7	12.5	46.7	40.8	460	435	
Mauritius	1.3	634	0.7	14	7	42	9,243	7,250	4.0	4.8	24.6	70.6	3,041	1,577	
Mexico	112.5	57	1.1	19	5	78	962,076	8,960	5.5	4.2	33.3	62.5	2,721	2,694	
Micronesia, Fed. States	0.1	153	-0.3	22	4	23	277	2,500	0.3	28.9	15.2	55.9	1,238	131	
Moldova	4.3	128	-0.1	11	11	47	5,568	1,560	6.9	16.3	20.1	63.6	848	336	
Mongolia	3.1	2	1.5	21	6	62	4,361	1,630	6.1	21.2	29.5	49.3	690	616	
Montenegro	0.7	48	-0.7	11	9	61	4,149	6,650	1.1	10.0	20.0	70.0	902	257	
Morocco	31.6	71	1.1	19	5	58	89,933	2,770	3.2	17.1	31.6	51.3	1,081	458	
Mozambique	22.1	28	2.4	40	13	38	9,964	440	7.0	28.8	26.0	45.2	160	114	
Namibia	2.1	3	0.9	21	13	38	9,264	4,270	4.4	9.0	32.7	58.3	2,421	2,009	
Nepal	29.0	206	1.6	22	7	19	12,985	440	4.0	33.0	15.0	52.0	182	29	
Netherlands	16.8	404	0.4	10	9	83	801,120	48,460	1.7	2.6	24.9	72.5	24,334	26,890	
New Zealand	4.3	16	0.9	14	7	86	116,389	28,810	1.5	4.6	24.0	71.4	7,111	7,817	
Nicaragua	6.0	46	1.1	19	5	57	5,726	1,000	4.5	17.6	26.4	56.0	784	531	
Niger	15.9	13	3.6	51	14	17	5,197	340	7.5	39.0	17.0	44.0	50	27	
Nigeria	152.2	165	1.9	36	16	50	184,656	1,190	8.4	31.9	32.9	35.2	225	501	
Norway	4.7	14	0.3	11	9	79	408,542	84,640	0.4	2.1	40.1	57.8	15,829	29,297	
Oman	3.0	14	2.0	24	3	73	49,833	17,890	4.2	1.4	48.2	50.4	6,503	12,171	
Pakistan	184.4	229	1.6	25	7	36	169,778	1,000	4.8	21.8	23.6	54.6	177	110	
Panama	3.4	44	1.4	19	5	75	22,683	6,570	7.5	5.8	16.6	77.6	4,706	3,671	
Papua New Guinea	6.1	13	2.0	26	7	13	7,911	1,180	7.0	32.2	35.7	32.1	585	985	
Paraguay	6.4	16	1.3	17	5	62	14,279	2,250	15.3	21.7	18.2	60.1	1,501	1,250	
Peru	29.9	23	1.0	19	6	77	122,355	4,200	8.8	15.4	32.0	52.6	861	1,128	
Philippines	99.9	333	1.9	25	5	49	188,941	1,790	7.3	13.9	31.3	54.8	600	508	
Poland	38.5	123	-0.1	10	10	61	467,545	12,260	3.8	3.9	31.8	64.3	4,352	4,181	

	ENERGY			LAND & AGRICULTURE				SOCIAL INDICATORS							
	Energy produced (tonnes of oil equivalent per capita 2008)	Energy consumed (tonnes of oil equivalent per capita 2008)	CO₂ emissions (tonnes per capita 2009)	Land area (thousand km²)	Arable and permanent crops (% of land area 2008)	Permanent pasture (% of land area 2008)	Forest (% of land area 2008)	Human Development Index (HDI) value 2009	Life expectancy (years 2010)	Food intake (calories per capita per day 2007)	Adults living with HIV/AIDS (percentage 2009)	Gender Inequality Index (GII value 2009)	Adult illiteracy rate (percentage 2008)	Motor vehicles (per thousand people 2009)	Internet usage (per thousand people 2009)
emala	0.16	0.40	0.86	109	21	18	35	0.560	71	2,159	0.8	0.713	27	117	17.2
a	0.01	0.06	0.13	246	13	44	27	0.340	58	2,568	1.3	–	71	1	0.9
a-Bissau	0.00	0.10	0.30	36.1	19	39	78	0.289	49	2,306	2.5	–	35	33	2.4
a	0.00	0.68	2.02	215	2	6	77	0.611	67	2,759	1.2	0.667	–	95	25.2
	0.00	0.08	0.21	27.8	47	18	4	0.404	62	1,870	1.9	0.739	38	11	11.1
uras	0.08	0.44	1.02	112	13	16	49	0.604	71	2,623	0.8	0.680	16	97	9.3
ary	0.98	2.79	5.00	93	53	11	22	0.805	75	3,465	0.1	0.382	1	384	62.3
d	16.58	20.52	11.12	103	0	23	0	0.869	81	3,362	0.3	0.279	1	767	98.3
	0.30	0.43	1.38	3,287	57	3	23	0.519	67	2,352	0.3	0.748	34	15	5.3
esia	1.26	0.61	1.73	1,905	20	6	53	0.600	71	2,538	0.2	0.680	8	77	8.3
	5.07	3.08	6.96	1,648	12	18	7	0.702	70	3,044	0.2	0.674	18	128	12.4
	4.57	1.20	3.75	438	12	9	2	–	71	–	0.1	0.751	26	–	1.1
d	0.30	4.15	8.79	70.3	16	45	10	0.895	80	3,612	0.2	0.344	1	534	72.4
	0.19	3.02	9.69	20.6	18	6	7	0.872	81	3,527	0.2	0.332	3	313	62.6
	0.52	3.40	7.01	301	33	12	31	0.854	82	3,646	0.3	0.251	1	673	50.3
Coast	0.26	0.15	0.32	322	22	42	33	0.397	57	2,528	3.4	0.765	51	20	4.7
a	0.03	1.53	4.26	11	22	21	31	0.688	73	2,852	1.7	0.638	14	188	55.9
	0.74	4.38	8.64	378	13	0	68	0.884	82	2,812	0.1	0.273	1	593	78.0
	0.03	1.23	3.15	89.3	3	8	1	0.681	80	3,015	0.1	0.616	9	146	26.2
hstan	9.03	3.54	11.96	2,725	8	69	1	0.714	69	3,490	0.1	0.575	1	197	34.4
	0.04	0.14	0.29	580	10	37	6	0.470	59	2,089	6.3	0.738	26	21	10.2
, North	0.97	0.94	3.51	121	24	0	49	–	69	2,087	–	–	–	–	–
, South	0.79	5.11	10.89	99.3	18	1	64	0.877	79	3,074	0.1	0.310	1	346	81.2
o	–	–	–	10.9	–	–	–	–	74	–	0.1	–	8	–	–
t	60.68	11.48	31.08	17.8	1	8	0	0.771	77	3,064	0.1	0.451	6	507	40.9
zstan	0.54	0.86	1.04	200	7	49	5	0.598	70	2,644	0.3	0.560	1	59	40.4
	0.17	0.16	0.20	237	6	4	69	0.497	62	2,240	0.2	0.650	27	21	4.4
	0.35	1.81	3.90	64.6	19	10	54	0.769	73	2,962	0.7	0.316	1	474	67.4
on	0.02	1.29	3.70	10.4	28	39	13	0.803	75	3,107	0.1	–	10	–	24.9
no	0.02	0.07	0.13	30.4	12	66	1	0.427	52	2,476	23.6	0.685	18	–	3.6
a	0.00	0.07	0.20	111	6	21	46	0.300	57	2,204	1.5	0.766	45	3	0.6
	18.14	3.17	8.70	1,760	1	8	0	0.755	78	3,143	0.1	0.504	13	291	5.6
nia	0.73	2.76	4.48	65.2	30	12	34	0.783	75	3,436	0.1	0.359	1	546	55.2
bourg	0.16	10.05	21.51	2.6	24	26	33	0.852	80	3,681	0.3	0.318	1	747	86.3
donia (FYROM)	0.75	1.51	3.57	25.7	19	24	39	0.701	75	3,105	0.1	–	3	144	51.1
gascar	0.01	0.06	0.15	587	6	64	22	0.435	63	2,160	0.2	–	29	27	1.5
wi	0.03	0.06	0.09	118	38	20	35	0.385	52	2,172	11.0	0.758	28	9	4.8
sia	3.75	2.43	5.38	330	23	1	63	0.744	74	2,923	0.5	0.493	8	334	59.7
	0.01	0.03	0.06	1,240	4	28	10	0.309	53	2,614	1.0	0.799	74	9	1.9
	0.00	2.62	7.64	0.3	31	0	1	0.815	80	3,611	0.1	0.395	8	674	59.4
tania	0.21	0.29	0.93	1,026	0	38	0	0.433	61	2,841	0.7	0.738	44	–	2.4
tius	0.02	1.22	3.54	2	45	3	17	0.701	74	2,965	1.0	0.466	13	159	22.6
o	2.09	1.66	3.99	1,958	14	39	33	0.750	76	3,266	0.3	0.576	7	264	27.9
nesia, Fed. States	–	–	–	0.7	28	4	0	0.614	72	–	–	–	–	36	15.8
ova	0.00	0.80	1.63	33.9	65	11	11	0.623	71	2,771	0.4	0.429	1	139	30.9
olia	0.76	0.74	2.43	1,567	1	74	7	0.622	68	2,285	0.1	0.523	3	72	10.9
enegro	1.04	1.32	2.89	14	14	24	40	0.769	75	2,447	0.1	–	4	–	41.7
cco	0.01	0.41	1.16	447	20	47	11	0.567	76	3,236	0.1	0.693	44	71	42.2
mbique	0.32	0.20	0.11	802	6	56	39	0.284	52	2,067	11.5	0.718	56	13	2.8
ia	0.18	0.89	1.93	824	1	46	9	0.606	52	2,383	13.1	0.615	12	109	6.0
	0.03	0.06	0.12	147	17	12	25	0.428	66	2,360	0.5	0.716	44	5	2.0
erlands	4.33	6.50	14.89	41.5	33	25	11	0.890	80	3,278	0.2	0.174	1	515	89.0
Zealand	4.37	5.28	9.28	271	12	41	31	0.907	81	3,159	0.1	0.320	1	733	80.7
agua	0.06	0.33	0.74	130	18	25	27	0.565	72	2,403	0.2	0.674	22	57	3.4
	0.01	0.03	0.09	1,267	11	23	1	0.261	53	2,376	0.8	0.807	71	–	0.8
ia	1.01	0.19	0.52	924	44	42	11	0.423	48	2,741	3.6	–	28	31	29.5
ay	54.51	10.46	8.49	324	3	1	32	0.938	80	3,464	0.1	0.234	1	575	95.1
an	19.06	5.38	16.80	310	0	5	0	0.846	74	–	0.1	–	16	225	42.9
an	0.24	0.36	0.77	796	28	5	2	0.490	66	2,293	0.1	0.721	46	11	11.7
na	0.29	1.80	4.54	75.5	9	21	44	0.755	78	2,484	0.9	0.634	7	120	42.9
New Guinea	0.39	0.31	0.82	463	2	0	64	0.431	66	2,175	0.9	0.784	42	9	11.7
uay	1.98	1.60	0.63	407	11	41	45	0.640	76	2,634	0.3	0.643	5	82	15.8
	0.47	0.59	1.21	1,285	3	13	53	0.723	72	2,457	0.4	0.614	10	55	31.0
pines	0.14	0.34	0.74	300	35	5	25	0.638	72	2,565	0.1	0.623	7	33	8.4
d	1.72	2.52	7.43	323	43	10	31	0.795	76	3,421	0.1	0.325	1	495	59.3

	POPULATION						WEALTH						TRADE		
	Total population (millions 2010)	Population density (persons per km² 2010)	Population change (percentage average annual 2010)	Birth rate (births per thousand people 2010)	Death rate (deaths per thousand people 2010)	Urban population (percentage of total 2010)	Gross National Income (million US$ 2009)	Gross National Income per capita (PPP US$ 2009)	GDP growth rate (percentage 2010)	GDP from agriculture (percentage of GDP 2010)	GDP from industry (percentage of GDP 2010)	GDP from services (percentage of GDP 2010)	Imports (US$ per capita 2010)	Exports (US$ per capita 2010)	Tourism receipts (US$ per capita 2009)
Portugal	10.7	116	0.2	10	11	61	232,937	21,910	1.4	2.6	23.0	74.4	6,354	4,310	
Qatar	0.8	74	0.8	15	2	96	17,688	22,110	16.3	0.1	78.8	21.1	27,803	68,758	
Romania	22.0	92	–0.3	10	12	57	178,900	8,330	–1.3	12.8	36.0	51.2	2,725	2,364	
Russia	139.4	8	–0.5	11	16	73	1,324,416	9,340	4.0	4.2	33.8	62.0	1,702	2,702	
Rwanda	11.1	420	2.8	37	10	19	4,628	490	6.5	42.1	14.3	43.6	95	20	
Saudi Arabia	25.7	13	1.5	19	3	82	439,021	17,210	3.7	2.7	61.9	35.4	3,854	9,844	
Senegal	12.3	63	2.6	37	9	42	13,062	1,040	4.2	14.9	21.4	63.7	363	171	
Serbia†	7.3	83	–0.5	9	14	56	43,939	6,000	1.8	12.6	21.9	65.5	2,148	1,321	
Sierra Leone	5.2	73	2.3	38	12	38	1,938	340	5.0	49.0	31.0	20.0	107	41	
Singapore	4.7	6,784	0.8	9	5	100	185,655	37,220	14.5	0.0	27.2	72.8	66,028	74,706	
Slovak Republic	5.5	112	0.1	10	10	55	87,402	16,130	4.0	2.7	35.6	61.7	11,413	11,732	
Slovenia	2.0	99	–0.2	9	11	50	48,063	23,520	1.2	2.4	31.0	66.6	12,960	12,465	
Solomon Is.	0.6	20	2.2	28	4	19	477	910	5.6	42.0	11.0	47.0	458	424	
Somalia	10.1	16	1.6	43	15	37	959	130	2.6	65.0	10.0	25.0	79	30	
South Africa	49.1	40	–0.4	19	17	62	284,270	5,760	2.8	3.0	31.2	65.8	1,569	1,565	
South Sudan††	8.3	14	–	–	–	22.0	–	–	–	–	–	–	–	–	†
Spain	46.5	92	0.6	11	9	77	1,476,169	32,120	–0.1	2.9	25.5	71.6	6,980	5,769	
Sri Lanka	21.5	328	0.9	17	6	14	40,385	1,990	9.1	12.6	29.8	57.6	539	368	
Sudan	35.7	19	2.5	36	11	40	51,524	1,220	5.1	32.1	29.0	38.9	193	223	
Suriname	0.5	3	1.1	16	6	69	2,454	4,760	4.4	10.8	24.4	64.8	2,665	2,859	
Swaziland	1.4	78	1.2	17	15	21	2,932	2,470	2.0	8.6	42.0	49.4	1,213	1,046	
Sweden	9.1	20	0.2	10	10	85	454,355	48,840	5.5	1.7	26.1	72.2	17,478	17,919	
Switzerland	7.6	185	0.2	10	9	74	505,827	65,430	2.6	1.3	27.5	71.2	29,685	30,511	
Syria	22.2	120	0.9	24	4	56	50,869	2,410	3.2	17.6	26.8	55.6	611	578	
Taiwan	23.0	640	0.2	9	7	78	1,016,390	44,190	10.8	1.4	31.1	67.5	10,919	11,926	
Tajikistan	7.5	52	1.8	26	7	26	4,841	700	6.5	19.2	22.6	58.2	441	176	
Tanzania	41.9	44	2.0	33	12	26	21,337	500	6.5	41.9	18.7	39.4	151	91	
Thailand	67.1	131	0.6	13	7	34	254,743	3,760	7.8	10.4	45.6	44.0	2,339	2,851	
Togo	6.6	116	2.8	36	8	43	2,883	440	3.4	47.4	25.4	27.2	203	130	
Trinidad & Tobago	1.2	240	–0.1	14	8	14	22,356	16,700	0.0	0.5	59.4	40.1	6,701	9,815	
Tunisia	10.6	65	1.0	17	6	67	38,845	3,720	3.7	10.6	34.6	54.8	1,891	1,521	
Turkey	77.8	100	1.2	18	6	70	652,358	8,720	8.2	8.8	25.7	65.5	2,137	1,509	
Turkmenistan	4.9	10	1.1	20	6	50	17,498	3,420	9.2	10.2	30.0	59.8	989	1,958	
Uganda	33.4	141	3.6	47	12	13	15,200	460	5.2	23.6	24.5	51.9	134	88	
Ukraine	45.4	75	–0.6	10	16	69	128,920	2,800	4.2	9.8	32.3	57.9	1,179	1,095	
United Arab Emirates	5.0	60	3.3	16	2	84	74,075	14,815	3.2	0.9	51.5	47.6	31,956	39,352	
United Kingdom	62.3	255	0.6	12	9	80	2,558,048	41,370	1.3	0.9	22.1	77.0	8,765	6,505	
USA	310.2	32	1.0	14	8	82	14,233,516	46,360	2.8	1.2	22.2	76.6	6,134	4,094	
Uruguay	3.5	20	0.2	14	10	92	30,154	9,010	8.5	9.3	22.8	67.9	2,364	1,909	
Uzbekistan	27.9	62	0.9	17	5	36	30,643	1,100	8.5	21.2	32.4	46.4	339	471	
Venezuela	27.2	30	1.5	20	5	93	286,354	10,090	–1.9	4.1	34.8	61.1	1,152	2,383	
Vietnam	89.6	272	1.1	17	6	30	81,591	1,000	6.8	20.6	41.1	38.3	941	804	
West Bank (OPT)*	2.5	429	2.1	25	4	74	2,843	1,855	7.0	5.0	14.0	81.0	1,500	210	
Western Sahara	0.5	2	3.1	32	9	94	–	–	–	30.0	30.0	40.0	–	–	
Yemen	23.5	45	2.6	33	7	32	25,026	1,060	8.0	8.2	38.8	53.0	355	318	
Zambia	13.5	18	3.1	44	13	36	12,560	960	7.6	19.7	33.7	46.6	368	480	
Zimbabwe	11.7	30	4.3	32	14	38	10,500	360	9.0	19.5	24.0	56.5	246	160	

NOTES

SERBIA†
Kosovo separated from Serbia in February 2008.

SOUTH SUDAN††
South Sudan separated from Sudan in May 2011.

OPT*
Occupied Palestinian Territory.

POPULATION TOTAL
These are estimates of the mid-year total in 2010.

POPULATION DENSITY
The total population divided by the land area (both are recorded in the table above).

BIRTH/DEATH RATES
These are 2010 estimates from the CIA World Factbook.

URBAN POPULATION
The urban population shows the percentage of the total population living in towns and cities (each country will differ with regard to the size or type of town that is defined as an urban area).

GNI
Gross National Income: this used to be referred to as GNP (Gross National Product) and is a good indication of a country's wealth. It is the income in US dollars from goods and services in a country for one year, including income from overseas.

GNI PER CAPITA
The GNI (see note) divided by the total population by using the PPP method (see note).

PER CAPITA
An amount divided by the total population of a country or the amount per person.

PPP
Purchasing Power Parity (PPP) is a method used to enable real comparisons to be made between countries when measuring wealth. The UN International Comparison Programme gives estimates of the PPP for each country, so it can be used as an indicator of real price levels for goods and services rather than using currency exchange rates (see GNI and GNI per capita).

AGRICULTURE, INDUSTRY AND SERVICES
The percentage contributions that each of these three sectors makes to a country's Gross Domestic Pro (GDP).

IMPORTS AND EXPORTS
The total value of goods imported into a country and exported to oth countries, given in US dollars ($) per capita.

TOURISM RECEIPTS
The amount of income generated f tourism in US dollars per capita.

ENERGY				LAND & AGRICULTURE				SOCIAL INDICATORS								
	Energy produced (tonnes of oil equivalent per capita 2008)	Energy consumed (tonnes of oil equivalent per capita 2008)	CO₂ emissions (tonnes per capita 2009)	Land area (thousand km²)	Permanent crops (% of land area 2008)	Arable and Permanent crops (% of land area 2008)	Permanent pasture (% of land area 2008)	Forest (% of land area 2008)	Human Development Index (HDI value 2009)	Life expectancy (years 2010)	Food intake (calories per capita per day 2007)	Adults living with HIV/AIDS (percentage 2009)	Gender Inequality Index (GII value 2009)	Adult illiteracy rate (percentage 2008)	Motor vehicles (per thousand people 2009)	Internet usage (per thousand people 2009)
gal	0.34	2.48	5.28	88.8	18	20	38	0.795	79	3,584	0.6	0.310	5	509	48.3
r	156.24	30.38	76.38	11	1	4	0	0.803	76	–	0.1	0.671	7	724	67.7
nia	1.34	1.88	3.63	238	40	19	28	0.767	74	3,455	0.1	0.478	2	219	35.1
a	9.61	5.41	11.12	17,075	8	6	49	0.719	66	3,376	1.0	0.442	1	245	29.2
da	0.00	0.03	0.07	26.3	64	18	17	0.385	58	2,085	2.9	0.638	35	4	4.2
Arabia	22.42	5.98	17.30	2,150	2	79	0	0.752	74	3,144	0.1	0.760	17	340	34.1
al	0.01	0.17	0.52	197	18	29	44	0.411	60	2,348	0.9	0.727	58	23	13.3
at†	1.13	1.79	5.45	77.5	41	16	30	0.735	74	2,710	0.1	–	4	227	55.7
Leone	0.00	0.07	0.26	71.7	27	31	39	0.317	56	2,170	1.6	0.756	62	5	0.3
ore	0.00	12.89	33.57	0.7	1	0	3	0.846	82	–	0.1	0.255	6	150	69.5
k Republic	1.22	3.68	6.54	49	29	11	40	0.818	76	2,893	0.1	0.352	1	319	74.4
nia	1.92	4.08	8.67	20.3	10	15	62	0.828	77	3,223	0.1	0.293	1	565	64.7
on Is.	0.00	0.14	0.53	28.9	3	0	79	0.494	74	2,422	–	–	23	–	1.7
lia	0.00	0.03	0.09	638	2	69	11	–	50	–	0.7	–	–	–	1.1
Africa	3.16	2.93	9.20	1,221	13	69	8	0.597	49	2,999	17.8	0.635	12	159	9.0
Sudan††	–	–	–	620	–	–	–	–	–	–	3.1	–	73	–	–
nka	0.84	4.02	7.13	498	37	21	29	0.863	81	3,272	0.4	0.280	2	606	69.4
	0.00	0.25	0.59	65.6	35	7	30	0.658	75	2,361	0.1	0.599	9	61	8.3
	0.56	0.12	0.30	1,886	9	49	29	0.379	55	2,282	1.1	0.708	39	28	10.2
ame	2.38	1.85	4.22	163	0	49	95	0.646	74	2,492	1.0	–	10	–	33.9
land	0.22	0.43	1.03	17.4	11	60	32	0.498	49	2,292	25.9	0.668	20	89	6.7
en	3.90	6.13	5.58	450	6	1	69	0.885	81	3,110	0.1	0.212	1	521	92.7
erland	2.13	4.35	6.00	41.3	11	28	31	0.874	81	3,465	0.4	0.228	1	89	80.9
	1.44	1.06	2.67	185	31	45	3	0.589	75	3,034	0.1	0.687	17	62	20.5
n	0.52	4.97	12.15	36	23	–	58	–	78	–	–	–	–	–	70.3
stan	0.55	0.89	0.84	143	6	28	3	0.580	66	2,118	0.2	0.568	1	38	9.5
nia	0.03	0.07	0.16	945	12	27	39	0.398	53	2,032	5.6	–	28	73	1.7
nd	0.76	1.51	3.82	513	37	2	37	0.654	74	2,539	1.3	0.586	6	287	26.5
	0.00	0.17	0.45	56.8	48	18	6	0.428	63	2,161	3.2	0.731	47	2	5.9
ad & Tobago	35.79	18.01	38.60	5.1	14	1	44	0.736	71	2,725	1.5	0.473	1	351	48.2
a	0.73	0.84	2.19	164	32	31	6	0.683	75	3,326	0.1	0.515	22	114	33.4
y	0.42	1.50	3.29	775	32	19	14	0.679	73	3,517	0.1	0.621	11	138	35.5
enistan	14.48	4.80	11.60	488	4	65	9	0.669	69	2,731	0.1	–	1	106	16.5
da	0.01	0.00	0.06	241	40	26	16	0.422	53	2,211	6.5	0.715	26	7	9.9
ne	1.67	3.43	5.52	604	58	14	17	0.710	68	3,224	1.1	0.463	1	152	17.0
d Arab Emirates	43.97	17.62	40.30	83.6	3	4	4	0.815	77	3,171	0.1	0.464	10	313	71.9
d Kingdom	2.88	3.83	8.35	242	25	48	12	0.849	80	3,458	0.2	0.355	1	526	84.2
	6.04	8.19	17.67	9,629	19	26	33	0.902	78	3,748	0.6	0.400	1	809	79.7
uay	0.37	1.20	2.06	175	10	75	9	0.765	76	2,829	0.5	0.508	2	–	40.2
kistan	2.51	2.15	4.17	447	11	52	8	0.617	73	2,581	0.1	–	3	–	17.0
uela	7.27	3.02	5.93	912	4	20	53	0.696	74	2,632	0.7	0.561	5	147	33.3
am	0.42	0.47	1.11	332	30	2	44	0.572	72	2,816	0.4	0.530	10	13	26.4
Bank (OPT)*	0.00	0.58	0.78	5.9	36	25	2	–	75	2,020	–	–	–	39	57.1
ern Sahara	0.00	0.27	0.66	266	0	19	3	–	61	–	–	–	–	–	–
n	0.68	0.34	1.13	528	3	42	1	0.439	64	2,068	0.1	0.853	41	35	10.3
ia	0.20	0.27	0.20	753	3	27	57	0.395	52	1,873	13.5	0.752	29	18	6.9
abwe	0.27	0.36	0.93	391	10	31	42	0.140	50	2,238	14.3	0.705	9	106	12.5

UCTION AND CONSUMPTION
ERGY
tal amount of commercial energy
ed or consumed in a country per
(see note). It is expressed in metric
of oil equivalent (an energy unit
he heating value derived from one
of oil).

ON DIOXIDE EMISSIONS
nount of carbon dioxide that each
y produces per capita.

AREA
the total land area of a country,
e area of major lakes and rivers,
re kilometres.

LE AND PERMANENT CROPS
figures give a percentage of the

total land area that is used for crops and
fruit (including temporary fallow land or
meadows).

PERMANENT PASTURE
This is the percentage of land area that
has permanent forage crops for cattle or
horses, cultivated or wild. Some land may
be classified both as permanent pasture
or as forest.

FOREST
Natural/planted trees including cleared
land that will be reforested in the near
future as a percentage of the land area.

HUMAN DEVELOPMENT INDEX (HDI)
Produced by the UN Development
Programme using indicators of life
expectancy, knowledge and standards

of living to give a value between 0 and 1
for each country. A high value shows a
higher human development.

LIFE EXPECTANCY
The average age that a child born today
is expected to live to, if mortality levels
of today last throughout its lifetime.

FOOD INTAKE
The amount of food (measured in
calories) supplied, divided by the total
population to show the amount each
person consumes.

ADULTS LIVING WITH HIV/AIDS
The percentage of all adults (aged
15–49) who have the Human Immunodeficiency Virus or the Acquired
Immunodeficiency Syndrome.

The total number of adults and children
with HIV/AIDS in 2009 was 33 million.

GENDER INEQUALITY INDEX
Like the HDI (see note), the GII uses the
same UNDP indicators but gives a value
between 0 and 1 to measure the social and
economic differences between men and
women. The higher the value, the more
equality exists between men and women.

ILLITERACY
The percentage of all adult men and
women (over 15 years) who cannot
read or write simple sentences.

MOTOR VEHICLES AND
INTERNET USAGE
These are good indicators of a country's
development wealth.

Each topic list is divided into continents and within a continent the items are listed in order of size. The bottom part of many of the lists is selective in order to give examples from as many different countries as possible. The figures are rounded as appropriate.

WORLD, CONTINENTS, OCEANS

	km²	miles²	%
The World	509,450,000	196,672,000	–
Land	149,450,000	57,688,000	29.3
Water	360,000,000	138,984,000	70.7
Asia	44,500,000	17,177,000	29.8
Africa	30,302,000	11,697,000	20.3
North America	24,241,000	9,357,000	16.2
South America	17,793,000	6,868,000	11.9
Antarctica	14,100,000	5,443,000	9.4
Europe	9,957,000	3,843,000	6.7
Australia & Oceania	8,557,000	3,303,000	5.7
Pacific Ocean	155,557,000	60,061,000	46.4
Atlantic Ocean	76,762,000	29,638,000	22.9
Indian Ocean	68,556,000	26,470,000	20.4
Southern Ocean	20,327,000	7,848,000	6.1
Arctic Ocean	14,056,000	5,427,000	4.2

OCEAN DEPTHS

Atlantic Ocean		m	ft
Puerto Rico (Milwaukee) Deep		8,605	28,232
Cayman Trench		7,680	25,197
Gulf of Mexico		5,203	17,070
Mediterranean Sea		5,121	16,801
Black Sea		2,211	7,254
North Sea		660	2,165
Indian Ocean		m	ft
Java Trench		7,450	24,442
Red Sea		2,635	8,454
Pacific Ocean		m	ft
Mariana Trench		11,022	36,161
Tonga Trench		10,882	35,702
Japan Trench		10,554	34,626
Kuril Trench		10,542	34,587
Arctic Ocean		m	ft
Molloy Deep		5,608	18,399
Southern Ocean		m	ft
South Sandwich Trench		7,235	23,737

MOUNTAINS

Europe		m	ft
Elbrus	Russia	5,642	18,510
Dykh-Tau	Russia	5,205	17,076
Shkhara	Russia/Georgia	5,201	17,064
Koshtan-Tau	Russia	5,152	16,903
Kazbek	Russia/Georgia	5,047	16,558
Pushkin	Russia/Georgia	5,033	16,512
Katyn-Tau	Russia/Georgia	4,979	16,335
Shota Rustaveli	Russia/Georgia	4,860	15,945
Mont Blanc	France/Italy	4,808	15,774
Monte Rosa	Italy/Switzerland	4,634	15,203
Dom	Switzerland	4,545	14,911
Liskamm	Switzerland	4,527	14,852
Weisshorn	Switzerland	4,505	14,780
Taschorn	Switzerland	4,490	14,730
Matterhorn/Cervino	Italy/Switzerland	4,478	14,691
Grossglockner	Austria	3,797	12,457
Mulhacén	Spain	3,478	11,411
Zugspitze	Germany	2,962	9,718
Olympus	Greece	2,917	9,570
Galdhøpiggen	Norway	2,469	8,100
Kebnekaise	Sweden	2,117	6,946
Ben Nevis	UK	1,344	4,409
Asia		m	ft
Everest	China/Nepal	8,850	29,035
K2 (Godwin Austen)	China/Kashmir	8,611	28,251
Kanchenjunga	India/Nepal	8,598	28,208
Lhotse	China/Nepal	8,516	27,939
Makalu	China/Nepal	8,481	27,824
Cho Oyu	China/Nepal	8,201	26,906
Dhaulagiri	Nepal	8,167	26,795
Manaslu	Nepal	8,156	26,758
Nanga Parbat	Kashmir	8,126	26,660
Annapurna	Nepal	8,078	26,502
Gasherbrum	China/Kashmir	8,068	26,469
Broad Peak	China/Kashmir	8,051	26,414
Xixabangma	China	8,012	26,286
Kangbachen	Nepal	7,858	25,781
Trivor	Pakistan	7,720	25,328
Pik Imeni Ismail Samani	Tajikistan	7,495	24,590
Demavend	Iran	5,604	18,386
Ararat	Turkey	5,165	16,945
Gunong Kinabalu	Malaysia (Borneo)	4,101	13,455
Fuji-San	Japan	3,776	12,388
Africa		m	ft
Kilimanjaro	Tanzania	5,895	19,340
Mt Kenya	Kenya	5,199	17,057
Ruwenzori	Uganda/Congo (D.R.)	5,109	16,762
Meru	Tanzania	4,565	14,977
Ras Dashen	Ethiopia	4,553	14,937
Karisimbi	Rwanda/Congo (D.R.)	4,507	14,787
Mt Elgon	Kenya/Uganda	4,321	14,176
Batu	Ethiopia	4,307	14,130
Toubkal	Morocco	4,165	13,665
Mt Cameroun	Cameroon	4,070	13,353

Oceania		m	ft
Puncak Jaya	Indonesia	4,884	16,024
Puncak Trikora	Indonesia	4,730	15,518
Puncak Mandala	Indonesia	4,702	15,427
Mt Wilhelm	Papua New Guinea	4,508	14,790
Mauna Kea	USA (Hawaii)	4,205	13,796
Mauna Loa	USA (Hawaii)	4,169	13,678
Aoraki Mt Cook	New Zealand	3,753	12,313
Mt Kosciuszko	Australia	2,228	7,310
North America		m	ft
Mt McKinley (Denali)	USA (Alaska)	6,194	20,321
Mt Logan	Canada	5,959	19,551
Pico de Orizaba	Mexico	5,610	18,405
Mt St Elias	USA/Canada	5,489	18,008
Popocatépetl	Mexico	5,452	17,887
Mt Foraker	USA (Alaska)	5,304	17,401
Iztaccihuatl	Mexico	5,286	17,342
Lucania	Canada	5,226	17,146
Mt Steele	Canada	5,073	16,644
Mt Bona	USA (Alaska)	5,005	16,420
Mt Whitney	USA	4,418	14,495
Tajumulco	Guatemala	4,220	13,845
Chirripó Grande	Costa Rica	3,837	12,589
Pico Duarte	Dominican Rep.	3,175	10,417
South America		m	ft
Aconcagua	Argentina	6,962	22,841
Bonete	Argentina	6,872	22,546
Ojos del Salado	Argentina/Chile	6,863	22,516
Pissis	Argentina	6,779	22,241
Mercedario	Argentina/Chile	6,770	22,211
Huascarán	Peru	6,768	22,204
Llullaillaco	Argentina/Chile	6,723	22,057
Nevado de Cachi	Argentina	6,720	22,047
Yerupaja	Peru	6,632	21,758
Sajama	Bolivia	6,520	21,391
Chimborazo	Ecuador	6,267	20,561
Pico Cristóbal Colón	Colombia	5,800	19,029
Pico Bolivar	Venezuela	5,007	16,427
Antarctica		m	ft
Vinson Massif		4,897	16,066
Mt Kirkpatrick		4,528	14,855

RIVERS

Europe		km	miles
Volga	Caspian Sea	3,700	2,300
Danube	Black Sea	2,850	1,770
Ural	Caspian Sea	2,535	1,575
Dnieper	Black Sea	2,285	1,420
Kama	Volga	2,030	1,260
Don (Dnieper)	Volga	1,990	1,240
Petchora	Arctic Ocean	1,790	1,110
Oka	Volga	1,480	920
Dniester	Black Sea	1,400	870
Vyatka	Kama	1,370	850
Rhine	North Sea	1,320	820
North Dvina	Arctic Ocean	1,290	800
Elbe	North Sea	1,145	710
Asia		km	miles
Yangtse	Pacific Ocean	6,380	3,960
Yenisey–Angara	Arctic Ocean	5,550	3,445
Huang He	Pacific Ocean	5,464	3,395
Ob–Irtysh	Arctic Ocean	5,410	3,360
Mekong	Pacific Ocean	4,500	2,795
Amur	Pacific Ocean	4,442	2,760
Lena	Arctic Ocean	4,402	2,735
Irtysh	Ob	4,250	2,640
Yenisey	Arctic Ocean	4,090	2,540
Ob	Arctic Ocean	3,680	2,285
Indus	Indian Ocean	3,100	1,925
Brahmaputra	Indian Ocean	2,900	1,800
Syrdarya	Aralkum Desert	2,860	1,775
Salween	Indian Ocean	2,800	1,740
Euphrates	Indian Ocean	2,700	1,675
Amudarya	Aralkum Desert	2,540	1,575
Africa		km	miles
Nile	Mediterranean	6,695	4,160
Congo	Atlantic Ocean	4,670	2,900
Niger	Atlantic Ocean	4,180	2,595
Zambezi	Indian Ocean	3,540	2,200
Oubangi/Uele	Congo (Dem. Rep.)	2,250	1,400
Kasai	Congo (Dem. Rep.)	1,950	1,210
Shaballe	Indian Ocean	1,930	1,200
Orange	Atlantic Ocean	1,860	1,155
Cubango	Okavango Delta	1,800	1,120
Limpopo	Indian Ocean	1,770	1,100
Senegal	Atlantic Ocean	1,640	1,020
Australia		km	miles
Murray–Darling	Southern Ocean	3,750	2,330
Darling	Murray	3,070	1,905
Murray	Southern Ocean	2,575	1,600
Murrumbidgee	Murray	1,690	1,050
North America		km	miles
Mississippi–Missouri	Gulf of Mexico	5,971	3,710
Mackenzie	Arctic Ocean	4,240	2,630
Missouri	Mississippi	4,088	2,540
Mississippi	Gulf of Mexico	3,782	2,350
Yukon	Pacific Ocean	3,185	1,980
Rio Grande	Gulf of Mexico	3,030	1,880
Arkansas	Mississippi	2,340	1,450

Colorado	Pacific Ocean	2,330	1,445
Red	Mississippi	2,040	1,270
Columbia	Pacific Ocean	1,950	1,210
Saskatchewan	Lake Winnipeg	1,940	1,205
South America		km	miles
Amazon	Atlantic Ocean	6,450	4,010
Paraná–Plate	Atlantic Ocean	4,500	2,800
Purus	Amazon	3,350	2,080
Madeira	Amazon	3,200	1,990
São Francisco	Atlantic Ocean	2,900	1,800
Paraná	Plate	2,800	1,740
Tocantins	Atlantic Ocean	2,750	1,710
Orinoco	Atlantic Ocean	2,740	1,700
Paraguay	Paraná	2,550	1,580
Pilcomayo	Paraná	2,500	1,550
Araguaia	Tocantins	2,250	1,400

LAKES

Europe		km²	miles²
Lake Ladoga	Russia	17,700	6,800
Lake Onega	Russia	9,700	3,700
Saimaa system	Finland	8,000	3,100
Vänern	Sweden	5,500	2,100
Asia		km²	miles²
Caspian Sea	Asia	371,000	143,000
Lake Baikal	Russia	30,500	11,780
Tonlé Sap	Cambodia	20,000	7,700
Lake Balqash	Kazakhstan	18,500	7,100
Aral Sea	Kazakhstan/Uzbekistan	17,160	6,625
Africa		km²	miles²
Lake Victoria	East Africa	68,000	26,000
Lake Tanganyika	Central Africa	33,000	13,000
Lake Malawi/Nyasa	East Africa	29,600	11,430
Lake Chad	Central Africa	25,000	9,700
Lake Turkana	Ethiopia/Kenya	8,500	3,290
Lake Volta	Ghana	8,480	3,270
Australia		km²	miles²
Lake Eyre	Australia	8,900	3,400
Lake Torrens	Australia	5,800	2,200
Lake Gairdner	Australia	4,800	1,900
North America		km²	miles²
Lake Superior	Canada/USA	82,350	31,800
Lake Huron	Canada/USA	59,600	23,010
Lake Michigan	USA	58,000	22,400
Great Bear Lake	Canada	31,800	12,280
Great Slave Lake	Canada	28,500	11,000
Lake Erie	Canada/USA	25,700	9,900
Lake Winnipeg	Canada	24,400	9,400
Lake Ontario	Canada/USA	19,500	7,500
Lake Nicaragua	Nicaragua	8,200	3,200
South America		km²	miles²
Lake Titicaca	Bolivia/Peru	8,300	3,200
Lake Poopo	Bolivia	2,800	1,100

ISLANDS

Europe		km²	miles²
Great Britain	UK	229,880	88,700
Iceland	Atlantic Ocean	103,000	39,800
Ireland	Ireland/UK	84,400	32,600
Novaya Zemlya (N.)	Russia	48,200	18,600
Sicily	Italy	25,500	9,800
Asia		km²	miles²
Borneo	South-east Asia	744,360	287,400
Sumatra	Indonesia	473,600	182,860
Honshu	Japan	230,500	88,980
Celebes	Indonesia	189,000	73,000
Java	Indonesia	126,700	48,900
Luzon	Philippines	104,700	40,400
Hokkaido	Japan	78,400	30,300
Africa		km²	miles²
Madagascar	Indian Ocean	587,040	226,660
Socotra	Indian Ocean	3,600	1,400
Réunion	Indian Ocean	2,500	965
Oceania		km²	miles²
New Guinea	Indonesia/Papua NG	821,030	317,000
New Zealand (S.)	Pacific Ocean	150,500	58,100
New Zealand (N.)	Pacific Ocean	114,700	44,300
Tasmania	Australia	67,800	26,200
New Caledonia	Pacific Ocean	16,650	6,470
North America		km²	miles²
Greenland	Atlantic Ocean	2,175,600	839,800
Baffin I.	Canada	508,000	196,100
Victoria I.	Canada	212,200	81,900
Ellesmere I.	Canada	212,000	81,800
Cuba	Caribbean Sea	110,860	42,800
Hispaniola	Dominican Rep./Haiti	76,200	29,400
Jamaica	Caribbean Sea	11,400	4,400
Puerto Rico	Atlantic Ocean	8,900	3,400
South America		km²	miles²
Tierra del Fuego	Argentina/Chile	47,000	18,100
Chiloé	Chile	8,480	3,275
Falkland I. (E.)	Atlantic Ocean	6,800	2,600

How to use the Index

The index contains the names of all the principal places and features shown on the maps. Each name is followed by an additional entry in italics giving the country or region within which it is located. The alphabetical order of names composed of two or more words is governed primarily by the first word and then by the second. This is an example of the rule:

Albert, L. *Africa* 1°30N 31°0E **96** D6
Albert Lea *U.S.A.* 43°39N 93°22W **111** B8
Albert Nile → *Uganda* 3°36N 32°2E **96** D6
Alberta □ *Canada* 54°40N 115°0W **108** D8
Albertville *France* 45°40N 6°22E **66** D7

Physical features composed of a proper name (Erie) and a description (Lake) are positioned alphabetically by the proper name. The description is positioned after the proper name and is usually abbreviated:

Erie, L. *N. Amer.* 42°15N 81°0W **112** D7

Where a description forms part of a settlement or administrative name, however, it is always written in full and put in its true alphabetical position:

Mount Isa *Australia* 20°42S 139°26E **98** E6

Names beginning with M' and Mc are indexed as if they were spelled Mac. Names beginning St. are alphabetized under Saint, but Santa and San are spelled in full and are alphabetized accordingly. If the same place name occurs two or more times in the index and all are in the same country, each is followed by the name of the administrative subdivision in which it is located.

The geographical co-ordinates that follow each name in the index give the latitude and longitude of each place. The first co-ordinate indicates latitude – the distance north or south of the Equator. The second co-ordinate indicates longitude – the distance east or west of the Greenwich Meridian. Both latitude and longitude are measured in degrees and minutes (there are 60 minutes in a degree).

The latitude is followed by N(orth) or S(outh) and the longitude by E(ast) or W(est).

The number in bold type that follows the geographical co-ordinates refers to the number of the map page where that feature or place will be found. This is usually the largest scale at which the place or feature appears.

The letter and figure that are immediately after the page number give the grid square on the map page, within which the feature is situated. The letter represents the latitude and the figure the longitude. A lower-case letter immediately after the page number refers to an inset map on that page.

In some cases the feature itself may fall within the specified square, while the name is outside. This is usually the case only with features that are larger than a grid square.

Rivers are indexed to their mouths or confluences, and carry the symbol → after their names. The following symbols are also used in the index: ■ country, ⧄ overseas territory or dependency, □ first-order administrative area, △ national park, ✈ (LHR) principal airport (and location identifier).

Abbreviations used in the Index

Afghan. – Afghanistan
Ala. – Alabama
Alta. – Alberta
Amer. – America(n)
Arch. – Archipelago
Ariz. – Arizona
Ark. – Arkansas
Atl. Oc. – Atlantic Ocean
B. – Baie, Bahía, Bay, Bucht, Bugt
B.C. – British Columbia
Bangla. – Bangladesh
C. – Cabo, Cap, Cape, Coast
C.A.R. – Central African Republic
Calif. – California
Cent. – Central
Chan. – Channel
Colo. – Colorado
Conn. – Connecticut
Cord. – Cordillera
Cr. – Creek
D.C. – District of Columbia
Del. – Delaware
Dom. Rep. – Dominican Republic
E. – East
El Salv. – El Salvador
Eq. Guin. – Equatorial Guinea
Fla. – Florida
Falk. Is. – Falkland Is.
G. – Golfe, Golfo, Gulf
Ga. – Georgia
Hd. – Head
Hts. – Heights
I.(s). – Île, Ilha, Insel, Isla, Island, Isle(s)
Ill. – Illinois
Ind. – Indiana
Ind. Oc. – Indian Ocean
Ivory C. – Ivory Coast
Kans. – Kansas
Ky. – Kentucky
L. – Lac, Lacul, Lago, Lagoa, Lake, Limni, Loch, Lough
La. – Louisiana
Lux. – Luxembourg
Madag. – Madagascar
Man. – Manitoba
Mass. – Massachusetts
Md. – Maryland
Me. – Maine
Mich. – Michigan
Minn. – Minnesota
Miss. – Mississippi
Mo. – Missouri
Mont. – Montana
Mozam. – Mozambique
Mt.(s) – Mont, Monte, Monti, Montaña, Mountain
N. – Nord, Norte, North, Northern,
N.B. – New Brunswick
N.C. – North Carolina
N. Cal. – New Caledonia
N. Dak. – North Dakota
N.H. – New Hampshire
N.J. – New Jersey
N. Mex. – New Mexico
N.S. – Nova Scotia
N.S.W. – New South Wales
N.W.T. – North West Territory
N.Y. – New York
N.Z. – New Zealand
Nat. Park – National Park
Nebr. – Nebraska
Neths. – Netherlands
Nev. – Nevada
Nfld. – Newfoundland and Labrador
Nic. – Nicaragua
Okla. – Oklahoma
Ont. – Ontario
Oreg. – Oregon
P.E.I. – Prince Edward Island
Pa. – Pennsylvania
Pac. Oc. – Pacific Ocean
Papua N.G. – Papua New Guinea
Pen. – Peninsula, Péninsule
Phil. – Philippines
Pk. – Peak
Plat. – Plateau
Prov. – Province, Provincial
Pt. – Point
Pta. – Ponta, Punta
Pte. – Pointe
Qué. – Québec
Queens. – Queensland
R. – Rio, River
R.I. – Rhode Island
Ra.(s) – Range(s)
Reg. – Region
Rep. – Republic
Res. – Reserve, Reservoir
S. – San, South
Si. Arabia – Saudi Arabia
S.C. – South Carolina
S. Dak. – South Dakota
Sa. – Serra, Sierra
Sask. – Saskatchewan
Scot. – Scotland
Sd. – Sound
Sib. – Siberia
St. – Saint, Sankt, Sint
Str. – Strait, Stretto
Switz. – Switzerland
Tas. – Tasmania
Tenn. – Tennessee
Tex. – Texas
Trin. & Tob.. – Trinidad & Tobago
U.A.E. – United Arab Emirates
U.K. – United Kingdom
U.S.A. – United States of America
Va. – Virginia
Vic. – Victoria
Vol. – Volcano
Vt. – Vermont
W. – West
W. Va. – West Virginia
Wash. – Washington
Wis. – Wisconsin

A

Aachen *Germany* 50°45N 6°6E **64** C4
Aalborg *Denmark* 57°2N 9°54E **63** F5
Aarau *Switz.* 47°23N 8°4E **64** E5
Aare → *Switz.* 47°33N 8°14E **64** E5
Aarhus *Denmark* 56°8N 10°11E **63** F6
Aba *Nigeria* 5°10N 7°19E **94** G7
Abaco I. *Bahamas* 26°25N 77°10W **115** B9
Ābādān *Iran* 30°22N 48°20E **86** D7
Abaetetuba *Brazil* 1°40S 48°50W **120** C5
Abakan *Russia* 53°40N 91°10E **77** D10
Abancay *Peru* 13°35S 72°55W **120** D2
Abariringa *Kiribati* 2°50S 171°40W **99** A16
Abaya, L. *Ethiopia* 6°30N 37°50E **89** F2
Abbé, L. *Ethiopia* 11°8N 41°47E **89** E3
Abbeville *France* 50°6N 1°49E **66** A4
Abbey Town *U.K.* 54°51N 3°17W **26** C2
Abbot Ice Shelf *Antarctica* 73°0S 92°0W **55** D16
Abbots Bromley *U.K.* 52°50N 1°52W **27** G5
Abbotsbury *U.K.* 50°40N 2°37W **30** E3
ABC Islands *W. Indies* 12°15N 69°0W **115** E11
Abéché *Chad* 13°50N 20°35E **95** F10
Abeokuta *Nigeria* 7°3N 3°19E **94** G6
Aberaeron *U.K.* 52°15N 4°15W **28** C5
Aberchirder *U.K.* 57°34N 2°37W **23** G12
Aberdare *U.K.* 51°43N 3°27W **28** D7
Aberdaugleddau = Milford Haven *U.K.* 51°42N 5°7W **28** D3
Aberdeen *China* 22°14N 114°8E **79** a
Aberdeen *U.K.* 57°9N 2°5W **23** H13
Aberdeen *S. Dak., U.S.A.* 45°28N 98°29W **110** A7
Aberdeen *Wash., U.S.A.* 46°59N 123°50W **110** A2
Aberdeenshire □ *U.K.* 57°17N 2°36W **23** H12
Aberdovey = Aberdyfi *U.K.* 52°33N 4°3W **28** B5
Aberdyfi *U.K.* 52°33N 4°3W **28** B5
Aberfeldy *U.K.* 56°37N 3°51W **25** A8
Aberfoyle *U.K.* 56°11N 4°23W **24** B7
Abergavenny *U.K.* 51°49N 3°1W **28** D7
Abergele *U.K.* 53°17N 3°35W **28** A6
Abergwaun = Fishguard *U.K.* 52°0N 4°58W **28** D4
Aberhonddu = Brecon *U.K.* 51°57N 3°23W **28** D7
Abermaw = Barmouth *U.K.* 52°44N 4°4W **28** B5
Aberpennar = Mountain Ash *U.K.* 51°40N 3°23W **28** D7
Aberporth *U.K.* 52°8N 4°33W **28** C4
Abersoch *U.K.* 52°49N 4°30W **28** B5
Abersychan *U.K.* 51°44N 3°3W **28** D7
Abert, L. *U.S.A.* 42°38N 120°14W **110** B2
Abertawe = Swansea *U.K.* 51°37N 3°57W **29** D6
Aberteifi = Cardigan *U.K.* 52°5N 4°40W **28** C4
Abertillery *U.K.* 51°44N 3°8W **28** D7
Aberystwyth *U.K.* 52°25N 4°5W **28** C5
Abhā *Si. Arabia* 18°0N 42°34E **89** D3
Abidjan *Ivory C.* 5°26N 3°58W **94** G5
Abilene *U.S.A.* 32°28N 99°43W **110** D7
Abingdon *U.K.* 51°40N 1°17W **30** C6
Abitibi, L. *Canada* 48°40N 79°40W **109** E12
Abkhazia □ *Georgia* 43°12N 41°5E **71** F7
Abomey *Benin* 7°10N 2°5E **94** G6
Aboyne *U.K.* 57°4N 2°47W **23** H12
Abrolhos, Banco dos *Brazil* 18°0S 38°0W **122** C3
Absaroka Range *U.S.A.* 44°45N 109°50W **110** B5
Abu Dhabi *U.A.E.* 24°28N 54°22E **87** E8
Abu Hamed *Sudan* 19°32N 33°13E **95** E12
Abuja *Nigeria* 9°5N 7°32E **94** G7
Abunã *Brazil* 9°40S 65°20W **120** C3
Abunã → *Brazil* 9°41S 65°20W **120** C3
Abyei ⧄ *Sudan* 9°30N 28°30E **95** G11
Acaponeta *Mexico* 22°30N 105°22W **114** C3
Acapulco *Mexico* 16°51N 99°55W **114** D5
Acaraí, Serra *Brazil* 1°50N 57°50W **120** B4
Acarigua *Venezuela* 9°33N 69°12W **120** B3
Accomac *U.S.A.* 37°43N 75°40W **113** G10
Accra *Ghana* 5°35N 0°6W **94** G5
Accrington *U.K.* 53°45N 2°22W **27** E4
Aceh □ *Indonesia* 4°15N 97°30E **82** D1
Acharnes *Greece* 38°5N 23°44E **69** E10
Acheloos → *Greece* 38°19N 21°7E **69** E9
Achill Hd. *Ireland* 53°58N 10°15W **18** D1
Achill I. *Ireland* 53°58N 10°1W **18** D1
Acklins I. *Bahamas* 22°30N 74°0W **115** C10
Acle *U.K.* 52°39N 1°33E **31** A12
Aconcagua, Cerro *Argentina* 32°39S 70°0W **121** F3
Acre □ *Brazil* 9°1S 71°0W **120** C2
Acre → *Brazil* 8°45S 67°22W **120** C3
Acton Burnell *U.K.* 52°37N 2°41W **27** G3
Ad Dammām *Si. Arabia* 26°20N 50°5E **86** E7
Ad Dīwānīyah *Iraq* 32°0N 45°0E **86** D6
Adair, C. *Canada* 71°30N 71°34W **109** B12
Adak I. *U.S.A.* 51°45N 176°45W **108** D2
Adamaoua, Massif de l' *Cameroon* 7°20N 12°20E **95** G8
Adam's Bridge *Sri Lanka* 9°15N 79°40E **84** Q11
Adana *Turkey* 37°0N 35°16E **71** G6
Adare, C. *Antarctica* 71°0S 171°0E **55** D11
Addis Ababa *Ethiopia* 9°2N 38°42E **89** F2
Adelaide *Australia* 34°52S 138°30E **98** G6
Adelaide I. *Antarctica* 67°15S 68°30W **55** C17
Adelaide Pen. *Canada* 68°15N 97°30W **108** C10
Adélie, Terre *Antarctica* 68°0S 140°0E **55** C10
Aden *Yemen* 12°45N 45°0E **89** E4
Aden, G. of *Ind. Oc.* 12°30N 47°30E **89** E4
Adige → *Italy* 45°9N 12°20E **68** B5
Adigrat *Ethiopia* 14°20N 39°26E **89** E2
Adirondack Mts. *U.S.A.* 44°0N 74°0W **113** D10
Admiralty Is. *Papua N. G.* 2°0S 147°0E **102** H6
Adour → *France* 43°32N 1°32W **66** E3
Adrar *Mauritania* 20°30N 7°30W **94** D3
Adrian *U.S.A.* 41°54N 84°2W **112** E5
Adriatic Sea *Medit. S.* 43°0N 16°0E **68** C6
Adwa *Ethiopia* 14°15N 38°52E **89** E2
Adwick le Street *U.K.* 53°34N 1°10W **27** E6
Adygea □ *Russia* 45°0N 40°0E **71** F7
Ægean Sea *Medit. S.* 38°30N 25°0E **69** E11
Afghanistan ■ *Asia* 33°0N 65°0E **87** C11
Africa 10°0N 20°0E **90** E6
Afyon *Turkey* 38°45N 30°33E **71** G5
Agadez *Niger* 16°58N 7°59E **94** E7
Agadir *Morocco* 30°28N 9°55W **94** B4
Agartala *India* 23°50N 91°23E **85** H17
Agen *France* 44°12N 0°38E **66** D4
Agra *India* 27°17N 77°58E **84** F10
Ağri *Turkey* 39°44N 43°3E **71** G7
Agrigento *Italy* 37°19N 13°34E **68** F5
Agua Prieta *Mexico* 31°18N 109°34W **114** A3
Aguascalientes *Mexico* 21°53N 102°18W **114** C4
Aguja, C. de la *Colombia* 11°18N 74°12W **117** B3
Agulhas, C. *S. Africa* 34°52S 20°0E **97** L4
Ahaggar *Algeria* 23°0N 6°30E **94** D7
Ahmadabad *India* 23°0N 72°40E **84** H8
Ahmadnagar *India* 19°7N 74°46E **84** K9
Ahmadpur East *Pakistan* 29°12N 71°10E **84** E7
Ahvāz *Iran* 31°20N 48°40E **86** D7
Ahvenanmaa *Finland* 60°15N 20°0E **63** E8
Aḩwar *Yemen* 13°30N 46°40E **89** E4
Ailsa Craig *U.K.* 55°15N 5°6W **24** D5
Aimorés *Brazil* 19°30S 41°4W **122** C2
Aïn Témouchent *Algeria* 35°16N 1°8W **94** A5
Ainsdale *U.K.* 53°37N 3°2W **27** E2
Aïr *Niger* 18°30N 8°0E **94** E7
Air Force I. *Canada* 67°58N 74°5W **109** C12
Aird, The *U.K.* 57°25N 4°33W **23** H8
Airdrie *Canada* 51°18N 114°2W **108** D8
Airdrie *U.K.* 55°52N 3°57W **25** C8
Aire → *U.K.* 53°43N 0°55W **27** E7
Aisgill *U.K.* 54°23N 2°21W **26** D4
Aisne → *France* 49°26N 2°50E **66** B5
Aix-en-Provence *France* 43°32N 5°27E **66** E6
Aix-les-Bains *France* 45°41N 5°53E **66** D6
Aizawl *India* 23°40N 92°44E **85** H18
Aizuwakamatsu *Japan* 37°30N 139°56E **81** E6
Ajaccio *France* 41°55N 8°40E **66** F8
Ajanta Ra. *India* 20°28N 75°50E **84** J9
Ajaria □ *Georgia* 41°30N 42°0E **71** F7
Ajdābiyā *Libya* 30°54N 20°4E **95** B10
'Ajmān *U.A.E.* 25°25N 55°30E **87** E8
Ajmer *India* 26°28N 74°37E **84** F9
Aketi *Dem. Rep. of the Congo* 2°38N 23°47E **96** D4
Akhisar *Turkey* 38°56N 27°48E **71** G4
Akimiski I. *Canada* 52°50N 81°30W **109** D11
Akita *Japan* 39°45N 140°7E **81** D7
'Akko *Israel* 32°55N 35°4E **86** C3
Aklavik *Canada* 68°12N 135°0W **108** C6
Akola *India* 20°42N 77°2E **84** J10
Akpatok I. *Canada* 60°25N 68°8W **109** C13
Akranes *Iceland* 64°19N 22°5W **63** B1
Akron *U.S.A.* 41°5N 81°31W **112** E7
Aksai Chin *China* 35°15N 79°55E **84** B11
Aksaray *Turkey* 38°25N 34°2E **71** G5
Akşehir Gölü *Turkey* 38°30N 31°25E **71** G5
Aksu *China* 41°5N 80°10E **78** C5
Aksum *Ethiopia* 14°5N 38°40E **89** E2
Akure *Nigeria* 7°15N 5°5E **94** G7
Akureyri *Iceland* 65°40N 18°6W **63** A2
Al 'Amārah *Iraq* 31°55N 47°15E **86** D6
Al 'Aqabah *Jordan* 29°31N 35°0E **86** D3
Al 'Aramah *Si. Arabia* 25°30N 46°0E **86** E6
Al 'Ayn *U.A.E.* 24°15N 55°45E **87** E8
Al Bayḑā *Libya* 32°50N 21°44E **95** B10
Al Fallūjah *Iraq* 33°20N 43°55E **86** C5
Al Fāw *Iraq* 30°0N 48°30E **86** D7
Al Ḩadīthah *Iraq* 34°0N 41°13E **86** C5
Al Ḩasakah *Syria* 36°35N 40°45E **86** B5
Al Ḩillah *Iraq* 32°30N 44°25E **86** C6
Al Hoceïma *Morocco* 35°8N 3°58W **94** A5
Al Ḩudaydah *Yemen* 14°50N 43°0E **89** E3
Al Hufūf *Si. Arabia* 25°25N 49°45E **86** E7
Al Jahrah *Kuwait* 29°25N 47°40E **86** D6
Al Jawf *Libya* 24°10N 23°24E **95** D10
Al Jawf *Si. Arabia* 29°55N 39°40E **86** D4
Al Jubayl *Si. Arabia* 27°0N 49°50E **86** E7
Al Khalīl *West Bank* 31°32N 35°6E **86** D3
Al Khums *Libya* 32°40N 14°17E **95** B8
Al Kufrah *Libya* 24°17N 23°15E **95** D10
Al Kūt *Iraq* 32°30N 46°0E **86** C6
Al Manāmah *Bahrain* 26°10N 50°30E **87** E7
Al Mubarraz *Si. Arabia* 25°30N 49°40E **86** E7
Al Mukallā *Yemen* 14°33N 49°2E **89** E4
Al Musayyib *Iraq* 32°49N 44°20E **86** C6
Al Qāmishlī *Syria* 37°2N 41°14E **86** B5
Al Qaţīf *Si. Arabia* 26°35N 50°0E **86** E7
Al Qunfudhah *Si. Arabia* 19°3N 41°4E **89** D3
Al Qurayyāt *Si. Arabia* 31°20N 37°20E **86** D4
Ala Tau *Asia* 45°30N 80°40E **78** B5
Alabama □ *U.S.A.* 33°0N 87°0W **111** D9
Alabama → *U.S.A.* 31°8N 87°57W **111** D9
Alagoas □ *Brazil* 9°0S 36°0W **122** A3
Alagoinhas *Brazil* 12°7S 38°20W **122** B3
Alai Range *Asia* 39°45N 72°0E **87** B13
Alamogordo *U.S.A.* 32°54N 105°57W **110** D5
Alamosa *U.S.A.* 37°28N 105°52W **110** C5
Åland = Ahvenanmaa *Finland* 60°15N 20°0E **63** E8
Alanya *Turkey* 36°38N 32°0E **71** G5
Alaşehir *Turkey* 38°23N 28°30E **71** G4
Alaska □ *U.S.A.* 64°0N 154°0W **108** C5
Alaska, G. of *Pac. Oc.* 58°0N 145°0W **108** D5
Alaska Peninsula *U.S.A.* 56°0N 159°0W **108** D4
Alaska Range *U.S.A.* 62°50N 151°0W **108** C4
Alba-Iulia *Romania* 46°8N 23°39E **65** E12
Albacete *Spain* 39°0N 1°50W **67** C5
Albanel, L. *Canada* 50°55N 73°12W **109** D12
Albania ■ *Europe* 41°0N 20°0E **69** D9
Albany *Australia* 35°1S 117°58E **98** H2
Albany *Ga., U.S.A.* 31°35N 84°10W **111** D10
Albany *N.Y., U.S.A.* 42°39N 73°45W **113** D11
Albany *Oreg., U.S.A.* 44°38N 123°6W **110** B2
Albany → *Canada* 52°17N 81°31W **109** D11
Albemarle Sd. *U.S.A.* 36°5N 76°0W **111** C11
Albert, L. *Africa* 1°30N 31°0E **96** D6
Albert Lea *U.S.A.* 43°39N 93°22W **111** B8
Albert Nile → *Uganda* 3°36N 32°2E **96** D6
Alberta □ *Canada* 54°40N 115°0W **108** D8
Albertville *France* 45°40N 6°22E **66** D7
Albi *France* 43°56N 2°9E **66** E5
Albion *U.S.A.* 42°15N 84°45W **112** D5
Albrighton *U.K.* 52°38N 2°16W **27** G4
Albuquerque *U.S.A.* 35°5N 106°39W **110** C5
Albury *Australia* 36°3S 146°56E **98** H8

Alcalá de Henares Spain 40°28N 3°22W 67 B4
Alcester U.K. 52°14N 1°52W 30 B5
Alchevsk Ukraine 48°30N 38°45E 71 E6
Alcoy Spain 38°43N 0°30W 67 C5
Aldabra Is. Seychelles 9°22S 46°28E 91 G8
Aldan Russia 58°40N 125°30E 77 D13
Aldan → Russia 63°28N 129°35E 77 C13
Aldborough U.K. 54°5N 1°22W 26 D6
Aldbourne U.K. 51°29N 1°37W 30 D5
Aldbrough U.K. 53°49N 0°6W 27 E8
Aldeburgh U.K. 52°10N 1°37E 31 B12
Alderbury U.K. 51°3N 1°44W 30 D5
Alderley Edge U.K. 53°18N 2°13W 27 F4
Alderney U.K. 49°42N 2°11W 29 H9
Aldershot U.K. 51°15N 0°44W 31 D7
Aledo U.S.A. 41°12N 90°45W 112 E2
Alegrete Brazil 29°40S 56°0W 121 E4
Além Paraíba Brazil 21°52S 42°41W 122 D2
Alençon France 48°27N 0°4E 66 B4
Alenquer Brazil 1°56S 54°46W 120 C4
'Alenuihähä Channel
    U.S.A. 20°30N 156°0W 110 H17
Aleppo Syria 36°10N 37°15E 86 B4
Alert Canada 83°2N 60°0W 109 A13
Alès France 44°9N 4°5E 66 D6
Alessándria Italy 44°54N 8°37E 68 B3
Ålesund Norway 62°28N 6°12E 63 E5
Aleutian Is. Pac. Oc. 52°0N 175°0W 102 B10
Aleutian Trench Pac. Oc. 48°0N 180°0E 102 C10
Alexander Arch. 56°0N 136°0W 108 D6
Alexander I. Antarctica 69°0S 70°0W 55 C17
Alexandria Egypt 31°13N 29°58E 95 B11
Alexandria U.K. 55°59N 4°35W 24 C6
Alexandria La., U.S.A. 31°18N 92°27W 111 D8
Alexandria Va., U.S.A. 38°49N 77°5W 112 F9
Alford Aberds., U.K. 57°14N 2°41W 23 H12
Alford Lincs., U.K. 53°15N 0°10E 27 F9
Alfreton U.K. 53°6N 1°24W 27 F6
Alfriston U.K. 50°48N 0°10E 31 E9
Algarve Portugal 36°58N 8°20W 67 D1
Algeciras Spain 36°9N 5°28W 67 D3
Algeria ■ Africa 28°30N 2°0E 94 C6
Algiers Algeria 36°42N 3°8E 94 A6
Algoa B. S. Africa 33°50S 25°45E 90 K6
Alicante Spain 38°23N 0°30W 67 C5
Alice Springs Australia 23°40S 133°50E 98 E5
Aligarh India 27°55N 78°10E 84 F11
Alipur Duar India 26°30N 89°35E 85 F16
Aliquippa U.S.A. 40°37N 80°15W 112 E7
Aliwal North S. Africa 30°45S 26°45E 97 L5
Alkmaar Neths. 52°37N 4°45E 64 B3
Allahabad India 25°25N 81°58E 85 G12
Allegan U.S.A. 42°32N 85°51W 112 D5
Allegheny → U.S.A. 40°27N 80°1W 112 E8
Allegheny Mts. U.S.A. 38°15N 80°10W 111 C11
Allen → U.K. 54°58N 2°18W 26 C4
Allen, Bog of Ireland 53°15N 7°0W 21 B9
Allen, L. Ireland 54°8N 8°4W 18 C5
Allendale Town U.K. 54°53N 2°14W 26 C4
Allenheads U.K. 54°49N 2°12W 26 C4
Allentown U.S.A. 40°37N 75°29W 113 E10
Alleppey India 9°30N 76°28E 84 Q10
Alleynes B. Barbados 13°13N 59°39W 114 c
Alliance U.S.A. 42°6N 102°52W 110 B6
Allier → France 46°57N 3°4E 66 C5
Alligator Pond Jamaica 17°52N 77°34W 114 a
Alloa U.K. 56°7N 3°47W 25 B8
Allonby U.K. 54°46N 3°26W 26 C3
Alma U.S.A. 43°23N 84°39W 112 D5
Alma Ata Kazakhstan 43°15N 76°57E 76 E8
Almada Portugal 38°41N 9°9W 67 C1
Almelo Neths. 52°22N 6°42E 64 B4
Almería Spain 36°52N 2°27W 67 D4
Almondsbury U.K. 51°32N 2°34W 30 C3
Aln → U.K. 55°24N 1°37W 26 B5
Alness U.K. 57°41N 4°16W 23 G9
Alnmouth U.K. 55°24N 1°37W 26 B5
Alnwick U.K. 55°24N 1°42W 26 B5
Alor Indonesia 8°15S 124°30E 83 F6
Alor Setar Malaysia 6°7N 100°22E 82 C2
Alpena U.S.A. 45°4N 83°27W 112 C6
Alpes Maritimes Europe 44°10N 7°10E 66 D7
Alphington U.K. 50°42N 3°31W 29 F6
Alpine U.S.A. 30°22N 103°40W 110 D6
Alps Europe 46°30N 9°30E 64 E5
Alrewas U.K. 52°44N 1°44W 27 G5
Alsace □ France 48°15N 7°25E 66 B7
Alsager U.K. 53°6N 2°18W 27 F4
Alston U.K. 54°49N 2°25W 26 C4
Altai Mongolia 46°40N 92°45E 78 B7
Altamira Brazil 3°12S 52°10W 120 C4
Altamura Italy 40°49N 16°33E 68 D7
Altarnun U.K. 50°35N 4°32W 29 F4
Altay China 47°48N 88°10E 78 B6
Altay Mongolia 46°22N 96°15E 78 B8
Altiplano Bolivia 17°0S 68°0W 120 D3
Alton U.K. 51°9N 0°59W 31 D7
Alton U.S.A. 38°53N 90°11W 112 F2
Alton Towers U.K. 52°59N 1°53W 27 G5
Altoona U.S.A. 40°31N 78°24W 112 E8
Altrincham U.K. 53°24N 2°21W 27 F4
Altun Shan China 38°30N 88°0E 78 D6
Altus U.S.A. 34°38N 99°20W 110 D7
Alucra Turkey 40°22N 38°47E 71 F6
Alvechurch U.K. 52°21N 1°57W 30 B5
Alwar India 27°38N 76°34E 84 F10
Alwinton U.K. 55°21N 2°7W 26 B4
Alxa Zuoqi China 38°50N 105°40E 78 D10
Alyth U.K. 56°38N 3°13W 23 J11
Amadjuak L. Canada 65°0N 71°8W 109 C12
Amagasaki Japan 34°42N 135°23E 81 F4
Amapá Brazil 2°5N 50°50W 120 B4
Amapá □ Brazil 1°40N 52°0W 120 B4
Amarillo U.S.A. 35°13N 101°50W 110 C6
Amasya Turkey 40°40N 35°50E 71 F6
Amazon = Amazonas →
    S. Amer. 0°5S 50°0W 120 C4
Amazonas □ Brazil 5°0S 65°0W 120 C3
Amazonas → S. Amer. 0°5S 50°0W 120 C4
Ambala India 30°23N 76°56E 84 D10

Ambato Ecuador 1°5S 78°42W 120 C2
Ambergris Cay Belize 18°0N 87°55W 114 D7
Ambikapur India 23°15N 83°15E 85 H13
Ambilobé Madag. 13°10S 49°3E 97 G9
Amble U.K. 55°20N 1°36W 26 B5
Ambleside U.K. 54°26N 2°58W 26 D3
Ambon Indonesia 3°43S 128°12E 83 E7
Amchitka I. U.S.A. 51°32N 179°0E 108 D1
Amderma Russia 69°45N 61°30E 76 C7
Amdo China 32°20N 91°40E 78 E7
Ameca Mexico 20°33N 104°2W 114 C4
Ameland Neths. 53°27N 5°45E 64 B3
American Highland Antarctica 73°0S 75°0E 55 D6
American Samoa ☑ Pac. Oc. 14°20S 170°0W 99 C16
Americana Brazil 22°45S 47°20W 122 D1
Amersham U.K. 51°40N 0°36W 31 C7
Ames U.S.A. 42°2N 93°37W 111 B8
Amesbury U.K. 51°10N 1°46W 30 D5
Amherst Canada 45°48N 64°8W 109 E13
Amiens France 49°54N 2°16E 66 B5
Amirante Is. Seychelles 6°0S 53°0E 72 J7
Amlia I. U.S.A. 52°4N 173°30W 108 D2
Amlwch U.K. 53°24N 4°20W 28 A5
'Ammän Jordan 31°57N 35°52E 86 D3
Ammanford U.K. 51°48N 3°59W 28 D6
Amos Canada 48°35N 78°5W 109 E12
Ampleforth U.K. 54°13N 1°6W 26 D6
Ampthill U.K. 52°2N 0°30W 31 B8
Amravati India 20°55N 77°45E 84 J10
Amreli India 21°35N 71°17E 84 J7
Amritsar India 31°35N 74°57E 84 D9
Amroha India 28°53N 78°30E 84 E11
Amsterdam Neths. 52°23N 4°54E 64 B3
Amsterdam U.S.A. 42°56N 74°11W 113 D10
Amsterdam I. Ind. Oc. 38°30S 77°30E 53 F13
Amudarya → Uzbekistan 43°58N 59°34E 87 A9
Amund Ringnes I. Canada 78°20N 96°25W 109 B10
Amundsen Gulf Canada 71°0N 124°0W 108 B7
Amundsen Sea Antarctica 72°0S 115°0W 55 D15
Amuntai Indonesia 2°28S 115°25E 82 E5
Amur → Russia 52°56N 141°10E 77 D15
An Najaf Iraq 32°3N 44°15E 86 C6
Anaconda U.S.A. 46°8N 112°57W 110 A4
Anadyr Russia 64°35N 177°20E 77 C18
Anadyr, G. of Russia 64°0N 180°0E 77 C19
Anaheim U.S.A. 33°50N 117°55W 110 D3
Anambas, Kepulauan
    Indonesia 3°20N 106°30E 82 D3
Anamur Turkey 36°8N 32°58E 71 G5
Anantapur India 14°39N 77°42E 84 M10
Anápolis Brazil 16°15S 48°50W 122 C1
Anär Iran 30°55N 55°13E 87 D8
Anatolia Turkey 39°0N 30°0E 71 G5
Añatuya Argentina 28°20S 62°50W 121 E3
Ancaster U.K. 52°59N 0°32W 27 F7
Ancholme → U.K. 53°40N 0°32W 27 E7
Anchorage U.S.A. 61°13N 149°54W 108 C5
Anci China 39°20N 116°40E 79 D12
Ancohuma Bolivia 16°0S 68°50W 120 D3
Ancona Italy 43°38N 13°30E 68 C5
Ancrum U.K. 55°31N 2°35W 25 C10
Ancud Chile 42°0S 73°50W 121 G2
Ancud, G. de Chile 42°0S 73°0W 121 G2
Anda China 46°24N 125°19E 79 B14
Andalgalá Argentina 27°40S 66°30W 121 E3
Andalucia □ Spain 37°35N 5°0W 67 D3
Andalusia U.S.A. 31°18N 86°29W 111 D9
Andaman Is. Ind. Oc. 12°30N 92°45E 53 D14
Anderson Alaska, U.S.A. 64°25N 149°15W 108 C5
Anderson Ind., U.S.A. 40°10N 85°41W 112 E5
Anderson S.C., U.S.A. 34°31N 82°39W 111 D10
Anderson → Canada 69°42N 129°0W 108 C7
Andes, Cord. de los S. Amer. 20°0S 68°0W 121 E3
Andhra Pradesh □ India 18°0N 79°0E 84 L11
Andijon Uzbekistan 41°10N 72°15E 87 A13
Andorra ■ Europe 42°30N 1°30E 66 E4
Andorra La Vella Andorra 42°31N 1°32E 66 E4
Andover U.K. 51°12N 1°29W 30 D6
Andradina Brazil 20°54S 51°23W 120 E4
Andreanof Is. U.S.A. 51°30N 176°0W 108 D2
Ándria Italy 41°13N 16°17E 68 D7
Andros Greece 37°50N 24°57E 69 F11
Andros I. Bahamas 24°30N 78°0W 115 C9
Aneityum Vanuatu 20°12S 169°45E 99 E12
Ängara → Russia 58°5N 94°20E 77 D10
Angarsk Russia 52°30N 104°0E 77 D11
Ånge Sweden 62°31N 15°35E 63 E7
Angel Falls Venezuela 5°57N 62°30W 120 B3
Angeles Phil. 15°9N 120°33E 83 A6
Ångermanälven → Sweden 64°0N 17°20E 63 E7
Angers France 47°30N 0°35W 66 C3
Anglesey □ U.K. 53°16N 4°18W 28 A5
Angoche Mozam. 16°8S 39°55E 97 H7
Angola ■ Africa 12°0S 18°0E 97 G3
Angoulême France 45°39N 0°10E 66 D4
Angoumois France 45°50N 0°25E 66 D3
Angra dos Reis Brazil 23°0S 44°10W 122 D2
Angren Uzbekistan 41°1N 70°12E 87 A12
Anguilla ☑ W. Indies 18°14N 63°5W 115 D12
Angus □ U.K. 56°46N 2°56W 23 J11
Angus, Braes of U.K. 56°51N 3°10W 23 J11
Anhui □ China 32°0N 117°0E 79 E12
Anjou France 47°20N 0°15W 66 C3
Ankang China 32°40N 109°1E 79 E10
Ankara Turkey 39°57N 32°54E 71 G5
Ann, C. U.S.A. 42°38N 70°35W 113 D12
Ann Arbor U.S.A. 42°17N 83°45W 112 D6
Annaba Algeria 36°50N 7°46E 94 A7
Annalee → Ireland 54°2N 7°24W 18 C7
Annan U.K. 54°58N 3°16W 25 D9
Annandale U.K. 55°10N 3°25W 25 D9
Annapolis U.S.A. 38°59N 76°30W 112 F9
Annapurna Nepal 28°34N 83°50E 85 E14
Annecy France 45°55N 6°8E 66 D7
Annfield Plain U.K. 54°52N 1°44W 26 C5
Anniston U.S.A. 33°39N 85°50W 111 D9
Annobón Atl. Oc. 1°25S 5°36E 90 G4
Annotto B. Jamaica 18°17N 76°45W 114 a
Anqing China 30°23N 117°3E 79 E12

Anse la Raye St. Lucia 13°55N 61°3W 114 b
Anshan China 41°5N 122°58E 79 C13
Anshun China 26°18N 105°57E 78 F10
Anstey U.K. 52°41N 1°12W 27 G6
Anstruther U.K. 56°14N 2°41W 25 B10
Antalaha Madag. 14°57S 50°20E 97 G10
Antalya Turkey 36°52N 30°45E 71 G5
Antalya Körfezi Turkey 36°15N 31°30E 71 G5
Antananarivo Madag. 18°55S 47°31E 97 H9
Antarctic Pen. Antarctica 67°0S 60°0W 55 C18
Antarctica 90°0S 0°0 55 E3
Anti Atlas Morocco 30°0N 8°30W 94 C4
Antibes France 43°34N 7°6E 66 E7
Anticosti, Î. d' Canada 49°30N 63°0W 109 E13
Antigo U.S.A. 45°9N 89°9W 112 C3
Antigonish Canada 45°38N 61°58W 109 E13
Antigua & Barbuda ■
    W. Indies 17°20N 61°48W 115 D12
Antilles Cent. Amer. 15°0N 65°0W 115 E12
Antioch = Hatay Turkey 36°14N 36°10E 71 G6
Antioquia Colombia 6°40N 75°55W 120 B2
Antipodes Is. Pac. Oc. 49°45S 178°40E 102 M9
Antofagasta Chile 23°50S 70°30W 121 E2
Antrim U.K. 54°43N 6°14W 19 B9
Antrim □ U.K. 54°56N 6°25W 19 B9
Antrim, Mts. of U.K. 55°3N 6°14W 19 A9
Antsirabe Madag. 19°55S 47°2E 97 H9
Antsiranana Madag. 12°25S 49°20E 97 G9
Antwerp Belgium 51°13N 4°25E 64 C3
Anuradhapura Sri Lanka 8°22N 80°28E 84 Q12
Anxi China 40°30N 95°43E 78 C8
Anyang China 36°5N 114°21E 79 D11
Anzhero-Sudzhensk Russia 56°10N 86°0E 76 D9
Ánzio Italy 41°27N 12°37E 68 D5
Aomori Japan 40°45N 140°45E 81 C7
Aoraki Mount Cook N.Z. 43°36S 170°9E 99 J13
Aosta Italy 45°45N 7°20E 68 B2
Aozou Strip Chad 22°0N 19°0E 95 D9
Apalachee B. U.S.A. 30°0N 84°0W 111 E10
Apaporis → Colombia 1°23S 69°25W 120 C3
Aparecida de Goiânia Brazil 16°49S 49°14W 122 C1
Apatity Russia 67°34N 33°22E 70 A5
Apeldoorn Neths. 52°13N 5°57E 64 B3
Apennines Italy 44°0N 10°0E 68 B4
Apia Samoa 13°50S 171°50W 99 C16
Apostle Is. U.S.A. 47°0N 90°40W 112 B2
Appalachian Mts. U.S.A. 38°0N 80°0W 112 G7
Appennini Italy 44°0N 10°0E 68 B4
Appleby-in-Westmorland
    U.K. 54°35N 2°29W 26 C4
Applecross Forest U.K. 57°27N 5°40W 22 H6
Appledore Devon, U.K. 51°3N 4°13W 29 E5
Appledore Kent, U.K. 51°1N 0°47E 31 D10
Appleton U.S.A. 44°16N 88°25W 112 C3
Apure → Venezuela 7°37N 66°25W 120 B3
Apurímac → Peru 12°17S 73°56W 120 D2
Aqaba, G. of Red Sea 29°0N 34°40E 86 D3
Aqtaü Kazakhstan 43°39N 51°12E 71 F9
Aqtöbe Kazakhstan 50°17N 57°10E 71 D10
Aquitain, Bassin France 44°0N 0°30E 66 D3
Ar Ramädi Iraq 33°25N 43°20E 86 C5
Ar Raqqah Syria 35°59N 39°8E 86 C4
Ara India 25°35N 84°32E 85 G14
Arab, Bahr el → South Sudan 9°0N 29°30E 95 G11
'Arab, Shatt al → Asia 29°57N 48°34E 86 D7
Arabia Asia 25°0N 45°0E 72 E6
Arabian Sea Ind. Oc. 16°0N 65°0E 72 G8
Aracaju Brazil 10°55S 37°4W 122 B3
Aracati Brazil 4°30S 37°44W 120 C6
Araçatuba Brazil 21°10S 50°30W 120 E4
Araçuaí Brazil 16°52S 42°4W 122 C2
Arad Romania 46°10N 21°20E 65 E11
Arafura Sea E. Indies 9°0S 135°0E 98 B5
Aragón □ Spain 41°25N 0°40W 67 B5
Araguacema Brazil 8°50S 49°20W 120 C5
Araguaia → Brazil 5°21S 48°41W 120 C5
Araguari Brazil 18°38S 48°11W 122 C1
Arāk Iran 34°0N 49°40E 86 C7
Arakan Coast Burma 19°0N 94°0E 85 K19
Arakan Yoma Burma 20°0N 94°40E 85 K19
Aral Kazakhstan 46°41N 61°45E 76 E7
Aral Sea Asia 45°0N 58°20E 76 E6
Aran I. = Arranmore Ireland 55°0N 8°30W 18 B4
Aran Is. Ireland 53°6N 9°38W 20 B3
Aransas Pass U.S.A. 27°55N 97°9W 111 E7
Arapiraca Brazil 9°45S 36°39W 122 B3
Ar'ar Si. Arabia 30°59N 41°2E 86 D5
Araraquara Brazil 21°50S 48°0W 122 D1
Ararás Brazil 22°22S 47°23W 122 D1
Ararat Turkey 39°50N 44°15E 71 G7
Ararat, Chapada do Brazil 7°20S 40°0W 120 C5
Aras, Rüd-e → Asia 40°5N 48°29E 86 A7
Arauca → Venezuela 7°24N 66°35W 120 B3
Araxá Brazil 19°35S 46°55W 122 C1
Arbil Iraq 36°15N 44°5E 86 B6
Arbroath U.K. 56°34N 2°35W 25 A10
Arcachon France 44°40N 1°10W 66 D3
Arctic Bay Canada 73°1N 85°7W 109 B11
Arctic Ocean Arctic 78°0N 160°0W 54 B18
Ardabil Iran 38°15N 48°18E 86 B7
Ardee Ireland 53°52N 6°33W 19 D8
Ardennes Belgium 49°50N 5°5E 64 D3
Arderin Ireland 53°2N 7°39W 21 B7
Ardgour U.K. 56°45N 5°25W 22 J7
Ardingly U.K. 51°3N 0°4W 31 D8
Ardivachar Pt. U.K. 57°23N 7°26W 22 H3
Ardmore U.S.A. 34°10N 97°8W 111 D7
Ardnamurchan, Pt. of U.K. 56°43N 6°14W 22 J5
Ardnave Pt. U.K. 55°53N 6°20W 24 C3
Ardrossan U.K. 55°39N 4°49W 24 D6
Ards Pen. U.K. 54°33N 5°34W 19 B10
Arecibo Puerto Rico 18°29N 66°43W 115 D11
Arena, Pt. U.S.A. 38°57N 123°44W 110 C2
Arendal Norway 58°28N 8°46E 63 F5
Arequipa Peru 16°20S 71°30W 120 D2
Arezzo Italy 43°25N 11°53E 68 C4
Argentan France 48°45N 0°1W 66 B3
Argentina ■ S. Amer. 35°0S 66°0W 121 F3
Argentino, L. Argentina 50°10S 73°0W 121 H2
Argostoli Greece 38°11N 20°29E 69 E9

Argun → Russia 53°20N 121°28E 79 A13
Argyle, L. Australia 16°20S 128°40E 98 D4
Argyll □ U.K. 56°10N 5°20W 24 B5
Argyll & Bute □ U.K. 56°13N 5°28W 24 B4
Ariana Tunisia 36°52N 10°12E 95 A8
Arica Chile 18°32S 70°20W 120 D2
Arinos → Brazil 10°25S 58°20W 120 D4
Aripuanã → Brazil 5°7S 60°25W 120 C3
Arisaig U.K. 56°55N 5°51W 22 J6
Arizona □ U.S.A. 34°0N 112°0W 110 D4
Arkaig, L. U.K. 56°59N 5°10W 22 J7
Arkansas □ U.S.A. 35°0N 92°30W 111 D8
Arkansas → U.S.A. 33°47N 91°4W 111 D8
Arkansas City U.S.A. 37°4N 97°2W 111 C7
Arkhangelsk Russia 64°38N 40°36E 70 B7
Arkle → U.K. 54°24N 1°56W 26 D5
Arklow Ireland 52°48N 6°10W 21 C10
Arles France 43°41N 4°40E 66 E6
Arlington U.S.A. 38°53N 77°7W 112 F9
Arlon Belgium 49°42N 5°49E 64 D3
Armagh U.K. 54°21N 6°39W 19 C8
Armagh □ U.K. 54°18N 6°37W 19 C8
Armavir Russia 45°2N 41°7E 71 E7
Armenia Colombia 4°35N 75°45W 120 B2
Armenia ■ Asia 40°20N 45°0E 71 F7
Arnaud → Canada 59°59N 69°46W 109 D13
Arnhem Neths. 51°58N 5°55E 64 C3
Arnhem, C. Australia 12°20S 137°30E 98 C6
Arnhem Land Australia 13°10S 134°30E 98 C5
Arno → Italy 43°41N 10°17E 68 C4
Arnold U.K. 53°1N 1°7W 27 F6
Arnprior Canada 45°26N 76°21W 112 C9
Arnside U.K. 54°12N 2°49W 26 D3
Arra Mts. Ireland 52°50N 8°22W 20 C6
Arran U.K. 55°34N 5°12W 24 C5
Arranmore Ireland 55°0N 8°30W 18 B4
Arras France 50°17N 2°46E 66 A5
Arrecife Canary Is. 28°57N 13°37W 94 C3
Arrow, L. Ireland 54°3N 8°19W 18 C5
Artemovsk Ukraine 48°35N 38°0E 71 E6
Artigas Uruguay 30°20S 56°30W 121 F4
Artois France 50°20N 2°30E 66 A5
Artux China 39°40N 76°10E 78 D4
Artvin Turkey 41°14N 41°44E 71 F7
Aru, Kepulauan Indonesia 6°0S 134°30E 83 F8
Arua Uganda 3°1N 30°58E 96 D6
Aruanã Brazil 14°54S 51°10W 120 D4
Aruba ☑ W. Indies 12°30N 70°0W 115 E11
Arunachal Pradesh □ India 28°0N 95°0E 85 F19
Arundel U.K. 50°51N 0°33W 31 E7
Arusha Tanzania 3°20S 36°40E 96 E7
Aruwimi →
    Dem. Rep. of the Congo 1°13N 23°36E 96 D4
Arvayheer Mongolia 46°15N 102°48E 78 B9
Arviat Canada 61°6N 93°59W 108 C10
Arxan China 47°11N 119°57E 79 B12
Arzamas Russia 55°27N 43°55E 70 C7
As Sulaymänïyah Iraq 35°35N 45°29E 86 C6
As Sulaymänïyah Si. Arabia 24°9N 47°18E 86 E6
As Suwayq Oman 23°51N 57°26E 89 C6
Aş Şuwayrah Iraq 32°55N 45°0E 86 C6
Asahikawa Japan 43°46N 142°22E 81 B8
Asama-Yama Japan 36°24N 138°31E 81 E6
Asamankese Ghana 5°50N 0°40W 94 G5
Asansol India 23°40N 87°1E 85 H15
Asbestos Canada 45°47N 71°58W 113 C12
Asbury Park U.S.A. 40°13N 74°1W 113 E10
Ascension I. Atl. Oc. 7°57S 14°23W 52 E9
Áscoli Piceno Italy 42°51N 13°34E 68 C5
Ascot U.K. 51°25N 0°40W 31 D7
Aseb Eritrea 13°0N 42°40E 89 E3
Asenovgrad Bulgaria 42°1N 24°51E 69 C11
Asfordby U.K. 52°47N 0°57W 27 G7
Ash Kent, U.K. 51°16N 1°17E 31 D11
Ash Surrey, U.K. 51°15N 0°43W 31 D7
Ashbourne U.K. 53°2N 1°43W 27 F5
Ashburton N.Z. 43°53S 171°48E 99 J13
Ashburton → Australia 21°40S 114°56E 98 E1
Ashby de la Zouch U.K. 52°46N 1°29W 27 G6
Ashchurch U.K. 52°0N 2°5W 30 C4
Ashdown Forest U.K. 51°3N 0°5E 31 D9
Asheville U.S.A. 35°36N 82°33W 111 C10
Ashford Derby, U.K. 53°13N 1°42W 27 F5
Ashford Kent, U.K. 51°8N 0°53E 31 D10
Ashington U.K. 55°11N 1°33W 26 B5
Ashkhabad Turkmenistan 38°0N 57°50E 87 B9
Ashland Ky., U.S.A. 38°28N 82°38W 112 F6
Ashland Ohio, U.S.A. 40°52N 82°19W 112 E6
Ashland Wis., U.S.A. 46°35N 90°53W 111 A8
Ashqelon Israel 31°42N 34°35E 86 D3
Ashtabula U.S.A. 41°52N 80°47W 112 E7
Ashton-in-Makerfield U.K. 53°30N 2°40W 27 F3
Ashton under Lyne U.K. 53°29N 2°6W 27 F4
Ashuanipi, L. Canada 52°45N 66°15W 109 D13
Ashwater U.K. 50°43N 4°19W 29 F5
Ashwick U.K. 51°13N 2°31W 30 D3
Asia 45°0N 75°0E 72 E9
Asinara Italy 41°4N 8°16E 68 D3
'Asir Si. Arabia 18°40N 42°30E 89 D3
Asir, Ras Somalia 11°55N 51°10E 89 E5
Askrigg U.K. 54°19N 2°6W 26 D4
Aslackby U.K. 52°53N 0°24W 27 G8
Asmera Eritrea 15°19N 38°55E 89 D2
Aspatria U.K. 54°47N 3°19W 26 C2
Aspen U.S.A. 39°11N 106°49W 110 C5
Assal, L. Djibouti 11°40N 42°26E 89 E3
Assam □ India 26°0N 93°0E 85 G18
Assen Neths. 53°0N 6°35E 64 B4
Assiniboia Canada 49°40N 105°59W 108 E9
Assiniboine → Canada 49°53N 97°8W 108 E10
Assisi Italy 43°4N 12°37E 68 C5
Assynt U.K. 58°12N 5°12W 22 F7
Assynt, L. U.K. 58°10N 5°3W 22 F7
Astana Kazakhstan 51°10N 71°30E 76 D8
Asti Italy 44°54N 8°12E 68 B3
Astipálea Greece 36°32N 26°22E 69 F12
Astoria U.S.A. 46°11N 123°50W 110 A2
Astrakhan Russia 46°25N 48°5E 71 E8
Asturias □ Spain 43°15N 6°0W 67 A3
Asunción Paraguay 25°10S 57°30W 121 E4
Aswân Egypt 24°4N 32°57E 95 D12
Aswan High Dam Egypt 23°54N 32°54E 95 D12
Asyût Egypt 27°11N 31°4E 95 C12
At Tä'if Si. Arabia 21°5N 40°27E 89 C3
Atacama, Desierto de Chile 24°0S 69°20W 121 E3
Atatürk Barajı Turkey 37°28N 38°30E 71 G6
Atbara Sudan 17°42N 33°59E 95 E12
Atbara → Sudan 17°40N 33°56E 95 E12
Atchafalaya B. U.S.A. 29°25N 91°25W 111 E8
Athabasca Canada 54°45N 113°20W 108 D8
Athabasca → Canada 58°40N 110°50W 108 D8
Athabasca, L. Canada 59°15N 109°15W 108 D9
Athboy Ireland 53°36N 6°56W 19 D8
Athenry Ireland 53°18N 8°44W 20 B5
Athens Greece 37°58N 23°43E 69 F10
Athens Ga., U.S.A. 33°57N 83°23W 111 D10
Athens Ohio, U.S.A. 39°20N 82°6W 112 F6
Atherstone U.K. 52°35N 1°33W 27 G5
Atherton U.K. 53°32N 2°30W 27 F4
Athlone Ireland 53°25N 7°56W 20 B7
Atholl, Forest of U.K. 56°51N 3°50W 23 J10
Athos Greece 40°9N 24°22E 69 D11
Athy Ireland 53°0N 7°0W 21 B8
Atikokan Canada 48°45N 91°37W 112 A2
Atka I. U.S.A. 52°7N 174°30W 108 D2
Atlanta U.S.A. 33°45N 84°23W 111 D10
Atlantic City U.S.A. 39°21N 74°27W 113 F10
Atlantic Ocean 0°0 20°0W 50 D8
Atlas Saharien Algeria 33°30N 1°0E 94 B6
Atlin Canada 59°31N 133°41W 108 D6
Attawapiskat Canada 52°56N 82°24W 109 D11
Attawapiskat → Canada 52°57N 82°18W 109 D11
Attleborough U.K. 52°32N 1°1E 31 A11
Attu I. U.S.A. 52°55N 172°55E 108 D1
Atyraü Kazakhstan 47°5N 52°0E 71 E9
Au Sable → U.S.A. 44°25N 83°20W 112 C6
Aube → France 48°34N 3°43E 66 B5
Auburn Ind., U.S.A. 41°22N 85°4W 112 E5
Auburn N.Y., U.S.A. 42°56N 76°34W 112 D9
Aubusson France 45°57N 2°11E 66 D5
Auch France 43°39N 0°36E 66 E4
Auchterarder U.K. 56°18N 3°41W 25 B8
Auchtermuchty U.K. 56°18N 3°13W 25 B9
Auckland N.Z. 36°52S 174°46E 99 H13
Auckland Is. Pac. Oc. 50°40S 166°5E 102 N8
Aude → France 43°13N 3°14E 66 E5
Audlem U.K. 52°59N 2°30W 27 G3
Aughnacloy U.K. 54°25N 6°59W 19 C8
Augsburg Germany 48°25N 10°52E 64 D6
Augusta Australia 34°19S 115°9E 98 G2
Augusta U.S.A. 33°28N 81°58W 111 D10
Aunis France 46°5N 0°50W 66 C3
Aurangabad Bihar, India 24°45N 84°18E 85 G14
Aurangabad Maharashtra,
    India 19°50N 75°23E 84 K9
Aurillac France 44°55N 2°26E 66 D5
Aurora Colo., U.S.A. 39°43N 104°49W 110 C6
Aurora Ill., U.S.A. 41°45N 88°19W 112 E3
Austin U.S.A. 30°17N 97°45W 110 D7
Australia ■ Oceania 23°0S 135°0E 98 E3
Australian Capital Territory □
    Australia 35°30S 149°0E 98 H8
Austria ■ Europe 47°0N 14°0E 64 E8
Autun France 46°58N 4°17E 66 C6
Auvergne □ France 45°20N 3°15E 66 D5
Auvergne, Mts. d' France 45°20N 2°55E 66 D5
Auxerre France 47°48N 3°32E 66 C5
Availon France 47°30N 3°53E 66 C5
Avaré Brazil 23°4S 48°58W 122 D1
Avebury U.K. 51°26N 1°50W 30 D5
Avellaneda Argentina 34°40S 58°22W 121 F4
Avellino Italy 40°54N 14°47E 68 D6
Aversa Italy 40°58N 14°12E 68 D6
Aveton Gifford U.K. 50°18N 3°50W 29 G6
Aveyron → France 44°5N 1°16E 66 D4
Aviemore U.K. 57°12N 3°50W 23 H10
Avignon France 43°57N 4°50E 66 E6
Ávila Spain 40°39N 4°43W 67 B3
Avilés Spain 43°35N 5°57W 67 A3
Avoca → Ireland 52°48N 6°10W 21 C10
Avon → Bristol, U.K. 51°29N 2°41W 30 D3
Avon → Dorset, U.K. 50°44N 1°46W 30 E5
Avon → Warks., U.K. 52°0N 2°8W 30 B5
Avonmouth U.K. 51°30N 2°42W 30 D3
Avranches France 48°40N 1°20W 66 B3
Awasa Ethiopia 7°2N 38°28E 89 F2
Awash Ethiopia 9°1N 40°10E 89 F3
Awbäri, Idehan Libya 27°10N 11°30E 95 C8
Awe, L. U.K. 56°17N 5°16W 24 B5
Axbridge U.K. 51°17N 2°49W 30 D3
Axe → U.K. 50°42N 3°4W 29 F8
Axe Edge U.K. 53°14N 1°57W 27 F5
Axel Heiberg I. Canada 80°0N 90°0W 109 B11
Axholme, Isle of U.K. 53°32N 0°50W 27 E7
Axios → Greece 40°57N 22°35E 69 D10
Axminster U.K. 50°46N 3°0W 29 F7
Axmouth U.K. 50°42N 3°3W 29 F7
Ayacucho Argentina 37°5S 58°20W 121 F4
Ayacucho Peru 13°0S 74°0W 120 D2
Ayakkum Hu China 37°30N 89°20E 78 D6
Aydin Turkey 37°51N 27°51E 71 G4
Aydingkol Hu China 42°40N 89°15E 78 C6
Ayers Rock = Uluru Australia 25°23S 131°5E 98 F5
Aylesbury U.K. 51°49N 0°49W 31 C7
Aylesford U.K. 51°18N 0°30E 31 D10
Aylmer, L. Canada 64°5N 108°30W 108 C8
Aylsham U.K. 52°48N 1°15E 31 A11
Aynho U.K. 52°0N 1°15W 30 C6
Ayr U.K. 55°28N 4°38W 24 D6
Ayr → U.K. 55°28N 4°38W 24 D6
Aysgarth U.K. 54°18N 2°1W 26 D4
Ayton Borders, U.K. 55°51N 2°6W 25 C11
Ayton N. Yorks., U.K. 54°15N 0°28W 26 D6
Ayutthaya Thailand 14°25N 100°30E 82 B2
Ayvalik Turkey 39°20N 26°46E 71 G4
Az Zarqä Jordan 32°5N 36°4E 86 C4
Az Zäwiyah Libya 32°52N 12°56E 95 B8
Azad Kashmir □ Pakistan 33°50N 73°50E 84 B8
Azamgarh India 26°5N 83°13E 85 F13
Äzarbäyjän □ Iran 37°0N 44°30E 86 B6

Azare   Białystok

Azare *Nigeria* 11°55N 10°10E **94** F8
Azerbaijan ■ *Asia* 40°20N 48°0E **71** F8
Azores *Atl. Oc.* 38°0N 27°0W **91** C1
Azov *Russia* 47°3N 39°25E **71** E6
Azov, Sea of *Europe* 46°0N 36°30E **71** E6
Azuero, Pen. de *Panama* 7°30N 80°30W **115** F8
Azul *Argentina* 36°42S 59°43W **121** F4

B

Bab el Mandeb *Red Sea* 12°35N 43°25E **89** E3
Bābā, Koh-i- *Afghan.* 34°30N 67°0E **84** B5
Babine L. *Canada* 54°48N 126°0W **108** D7
Bābol *Iran* 36°40N 52°50E **87** B8
Babruysk *Belarus* 53°10N 29°15E **65** B15
Babuyan Chan. *Phil.* 18°40N 121°30E **83** A6
Babylon *Iraq* 32°34N 44°22E **86** C6
Bac Lieu *Vietnam* 9°17N 105°43E **82** C3
Bacabal *Brazil* 4°15S 44°45W **120** C5
Bacău *Romania* 46°35N 26°55E **65** E14
Back → *Canada* 65°10N 104°0W **108** C9
Bacolod *Phil.* 10°40N 122°57E **83** B6
Bacton *U.K.* 52°52N 1°27E **31** A11
Bacup *U.K.* 53°42N 2°11W **27** E4
Bad Axe *U.S.A.* 43°48N 83°0W **112** D6
Badagara *India* 11°35N 75°40E **84** P9
Badain Jaran Desert *China* 40°23N 102°0E **78** C9
Badajoz *Spain* 38°50N 6°59W **67** C2
Badakhshān □ *Afghan.* 36°30N 71°0E **87** B12
Badalona *Spain* 41°26N 2°15E **67** B7
Baden-Württemberg □ *Germany* 48°20N 8°40E **64** D5
Badenoch *U.K.* 56°59N 4°15W **23** J9
Badlands *U.S.A.* 43°55N 102°30W **110** B6
Baffin B. *N. Amer.* 72°0N 64°0W **109** B13
Baffin I. *Canada* 68°0N 75°0W **109** C12
Bafoulabé *Mali* 13°50N 10°55W **94** F3
Bafoussam *Cameroon* 5°28N 10°25E **96** C6
Bafra *Turkey* 41°34N 35°54E **71** F6
Bagamoyo *Tanzania* 6°28S 38°55E **96** F7
Bagé *Brazil* 31°20S 54°15W **121** F4
Bagenalstown *Ireland* 52°42N 6°58W **21** C9
Baggy Pt. *U.K.* 51°8N 4°16W **29** E5
Baghdād *Iraq* 33°20N 44°23E **86** C6
Baghlān *Afghan.* 32°12N 68°46E **87** B12
Bagshot *U.K.* 51°22N 0°41W **31** D7
Baguio *Phil.* 16°26N 120°34E **83** A6
Bahamas ■ *N. Amer.* 24°0N 75°0W **115** C10
Baharampur *India* 24°2N 88°27E **85** G16
Bahawalpur *Pakistan* 29°24N 71°40E **84** E7
Bahia = Salvador *Brazil* 13°0S 38°30W **122** D6
Bahía □ *Brazil* 12°0S 42°0W **122** B2
Bahía, Is. de la *Honduras* 16°45N 86°15W **114** D7
Bahía Blanca *Argentina* 38°35S 62°13W **121** F3
Bahir Dar *Ethiopia* 11°37N 37°10E **89** E2
Bahr el Ghazal □ *South Sudan* 7°30N 25°30E **95** G11
Bahraich *India* 27°38N 81°37E **85** F12
Bahrain ■ *Asia* 26°0N 50°35E **87** E7
Baia Mare *Romania* 47°40N 23°35E **65** E12
Baicheng *China* 45°38N 122°42E **79** B13
Baie-Comeau *Canada* 49°12N 68°10W **109** E13
Baie-St-Paul *Canada* 47°28N 70°32W **113** B12
Baie Verte *Canada* 49°55N 56°12W **109** E14
Ba'iji *Iraq* 35°0N 43°30E **86** C5
Baikal, L. *Russia* 53°0N 108°0E **77** D11
Baildon *U.K.* 53°51N 1°46W **27** E5
Baile Sear = Baleshare *U.K.* 57°31N 7°22W **22** G3
Bain → *U.K.* 53°6N 0°12W **27** F8
Bainbridge *U.K.* 54°18N 2°6W **26** D4
Baja, Pta. *Mexico* 29°58N 115°49W **114** B1
Baja California *Mexico* 31°10N 115°12W **114** A1
Baker, L. *Canada* 64°0N 96°0W **108** C10
Baker City *U.S.A.* 44°47N 117°50W **110** B3
Baker I. *Pac. Oc.* 0°10N 176°35W **99** A15
Baker Lake *Canada* 64°20N 96°3W **108** C10
Bakers Dozen Is. *Canada* 56°45N 78°45W **109** D12
Bakersfield *U.S.A.* 35°23N 119°1W **110** C3
Bakewell *U.K.* 53°13N 1°40W **27** F6
Baku *Azerbaijan* 40°29N 49°56E **71** F8
Bala *U.K.* 52°54N 3°36W **28** B6
Bala, L. *U.K.* 52°53N 3°37W **28** B6
Balabac Str. *E. Indies* 7°53N 117°5E **82** C5
Balaghat Ra. *India* 18°50N 76°30E **84** K10
Balaklava *Ukraine* 44°30N 33°30E **71** F5
Balakovo *Russia* 52°4N 47°55E **70** D8
Balashov *Russia* 51°30N 43°10E **71** D7
Balaton *Hungary* 46°50N 17°40E **65** E9
Balbi, Mt. *Papua N. G.* 5°55S 154°58E **99** H10
Balbina, Represa de *Brazil* 2°0S 59°30W **120** C4
Balbriggan *Ireland* 53°37N 6°11W **19** D9
Balcarce *Argentina* 38°0S 58°10W **121** F4
Balderton *U.K.* 53°3N 0°47W **27** F7
Baldock *U.K.* 52°0N 0°11W **31** C8
Baldoyle *Ireland* 53°24N 6°8W **19** D10
Baldwin *U.S.A.* 43°54N 85°51W **112** D5
Baldy Peak *U.S.A.* 33°54N 109°34W **110** D5
Balearic Is. *Spain* 39°30N 3°0E **67** C7
Baleine → *Canada* 58°15N 67°40W **109** D13
Baleshare *U.K.* 57°31N 7°22W **22** G3
Baleshwar *India* 21°35N 87°3E **85** J15
Bali *Indonesia* 8°20S 115°0E **82** F4
Balıkesir *Turkey* 39°39N 27°53E **71** G4
Balikpapan *Indonesia* 1°10S 116°55E **82** E5
Balkan Mts. *Bulgaria* 43°15N 23°0E **69** C10
Balkanabat *Turkmenistan* 39°30N 54°22E **87** B7
Balkhash, L. *Kazakhstan* 46°0N 74°50E **76** E8
Ballachulish *U.K.* 56°41N 5°8W **22** J7
Ballaghaderreen *Ireland* 53°55N 8°34W **18** D4
Ballantrae *U.K.* 55°6N 4°59W **24** D6
Ballarat *Australia* 37°33S 143°50E **98** H7
Ballater *U.K.* 57°3N 3°3W **23** H11
Ballenas, B. de *Mexico* 26°45N 113°26W **114** B2
Balleny Is. *Antarctica* 66°30S 163°0E **55** C11
Ballina *Ireland* 54°7N 9°9W **18** C3
Ballinasloe *Ireland* 53°20N 8°13W **20** B6
Ballinrobe *Ireland* 53°38N 9°13W **18** D3
Ballinskelligs B. *Ireland* 51°48N 10°13W **20** D2
Ballybunion *Ireland* 52°31N 9°40W **20** C3
Ballycastle *U.K.* 55°12N 6°15W **19** A9
Ballyclare *U.K.* 54°46N 6°0W **19** B10

Ballycroy △ *Ireland* 54°5N 9°50W **18** C2
Ballycummin *Ireland* 52°38N 8°38W **20** C5
Ballyhaunis *Ireland* 53°46N 8°46W **18** D4
Ballyhoura Mts. *Ireland* 52°18N 8°33W **20** D5
Ballymena *U.K.* 54°52N 6°17W **19** B9
Ballymoney *U.K.* 55°5N 6°31W **19** A8
Ballymote *Ireland* 54°5N 8°31W **18** C4
Ballynahinch *U.K.* 54°24N 5°54W **19** C10
Ballyquintin Pt. *U.K.* 54°20N 5°30W **19** C11
Ballyshannon *Ireland* 54°30N 8°11W **18** B5
Balmoral Forest *U.K.* 57°0N 3°15W **23** J11
Balrampur *India* 27°30N 82°20E **85** F13
Balsas → *Mexico* 17°55N 102°10W **114** D4
Baltic Sea *Europe* 57°0N 19°0E **63** F7
Baltimore *Ireland* 51°29N 9°22W **20** F4
Baltimore *U.S.A.* 39°17N 76°36W **112** F9
Baluchistan □ *Pakistan* 27°30N 65°0E **84** F4
Bam *Iran* 29°7N 58°14E **87** D9
Bamako *Mali* 12°34N 7°55W **94** F4
Bambari *C.A.R.* 5°40N 20°35E **96** C4
Bamberg *Germany* 49°54N 10°54E **64** D6
Bamburgh *U.K.* 55°37N 1°43W **26** A5
Bamenda *Cameroon* 5°57N 10°11E **96** C2
Bamford *U.K.* 53°22N 1°41W **27** F5
Bampton *Devon, U.K.* 50°59N 3°29W **27** F5
Bampton *Oxon., U.K.* 51°44N 1°32W **30** C5
Banaba *Kiribati* 0°45S 169°50E **102** H8
Bananal, I. do *Brazil* 11°30S 50°30W **120** D4
Banbridge *U.K.* 54°22N 6°16W **19** C9
Banbury *U.K.* 52°4N 1°20W **30** B6
Banchory *U.K.* 57°3N 2°29W **23** H13
Bancroft *Canada* 45°3N 77°51W **112** C9
Banda *India* 25°30N 80°26E **84** G12
Banda, Kepulauan *Indonesia* 4°37S 129°50E **83** E7
Banda Aceh *Indonesia* 5°35N 95°20E **82** C1
Banda Sea *Indonesia* 6°0S 130°0E **83** F7
Bandar-e Abbās *Iran* 27°15N 56°15E **87** E9
Bandar-e Anzalī *Iran* 37°30N 49°30E **86** B7
Bandar-e Ma'shur *Iran* 30°35N 49°10E **86** D7
Bandar-e Torkeman *Iran* 37°0N 54°10E **87** B8
Bandar Lampung *Indonesia* 5°20S 105°10E **82** F3
Bandar Seri Begawan *Brunei* 4°52N 115°0E **82** C4
Bandeira, Pico da *Brazil* 20°26S 41°47W **122** D2
Banderas, B. de *Mexico* 20°40N 105°25W **114** C3
Bandırma *Turkey* 40°20N 28°0E **71** F4
Bandon *Ireland* 51°44N 8°44W **20** E5
Bandon → *Ireland* 51°43N 8°37W **20** E5
Bandundu *Dem. Rep. of the Congo* 3°15S 17°22E **96** E3
Bandung *Indonesia* 6°54S 107°36E **82** F3
Banes *Cuba* 21°0N 75°42W **115** C9
Banff *Canada* 51°10N 115°34W **108** D8
Banff *U.K.* 57°40N 2°33W **23** G12
Bangalore *India* 12°59N 77°40E **84** N10
Bangassou *C.A.R.* 4°55N 23°7E **96** D4
Banggai, Kepulauan *Indonesia* 1°40S 123°30E **83** E6
Bangka *Indonesia* 2°0S 105°50E **82** E3
Bangkok *Thailand* 13°45N 100°35E **82** B2
Bangladesh ■ *Asia* 24°0N 90°0E **85** H17
Bangor *Down, U.K.* 54°40N 5°40W **19** B10
Bangor *Gwynedd, U.K.* 53°14N 4°8W **28** A5
Bangor *U.S.A.* 44°48N 68°46W **113** C13
Bangui *C.A.R.* 4°23N 18°35E **96** D3
Bangweulu, L. *Zambia* 11°0S 30°0E **96** G6
Banham *U.K.* 52°27N 1°2E **31** B11
Bani *Dom. Rep.* 18°16N 70°22W **115** D10
Banja Luka *Bos.-H.* 44°49N 17°11E **68** B7
Banjarmasin *Indonesia* 3°20S 114°35E **82** E4
Banjul *Gambia* 13°28N 16°40W **94** F2
Bankend *U.K.* 55°1N 3°33W **25** D8
Banks I. *Canada* 73°15N 121°30W **108** B7
Banks Is. *Vanuatu* 13°50S 167°30E **99** C12
Bann → *U.K.* 55°8N 6°41W **19** A8
Bannockburn *U.K.* 56°5N 3°55W **25** B8
Bannu *Pakistan* 33°0N 70°18E **84** C7
Banská Bystrica *Slovak Rep.* 48°46N 19°14E **65** D10
Bantry *Ireland* 51°41N 9°27W **20** E4
Bantry B. *Ireland* 51°37N 9°44W **20** E3
Banwell *U.K.* 51°19N 2°52W **30** D3
Banyak, Kepulauan *Indonesia* 2°10N 97°10E **82** D1
Banyuwangi *Indonesia* 8°13S 114°21E **82** F4
Bao'an *China* 22°34N 113°52E **79** a
Baoding *China* 38°50N 115°28E **79** D12
Baoji *China* 34°20N 107°5E **78** E10
Baoshan *China* 25°10N 99°5E **78** F8
Baotou *China* 40°32N 110°2E **79** C11
Ba'qūbah *Iraq* 33°45N 44°50E **86** C6
Bar Harbor *U.S.A.* 44°23N 68°13W **113** C13
Bar-le-Duc *France* 48°47N 5°10E **66** B6
Baraboo *U.S.A.* 43°28N 89°45W **112** D3
Baracoa *Cuba* 20°20N 74°30W **115** C10
Barahona *Dom. Rep.* 18°13N 71°7W **115** D10
Barail Range *India* 25°15N 93°20E **85** G18
Barakaldo *Spain* 43°18N 2°59W **67** A4
Baranavichy *Belarus* 53°10N 26°0E **65** B14
Baranof I. *U.S.A.* 57°0N 135°0W **108** D6
Barbacena *Brazil* 21°15S 43°56W **122** D2
Barbados ■ *W. Indies* 13°10N 59°30W **114** c
Barberton *U.S.A.* 41°1N 81°39W **112** E7
Barcelona *Spain* 41°22N 2°10E **67** B7
Barcelona *Venezuela* 10°10N 64°40W **120** A3
Barddhaman *India* 23°14N 87°39E **85** H15
Bardiyah *Libya* 31°45N 25°5E **95** B10
Bardney *U.K.* 53°13N 0°19W **27** F8
Bardsey I. *U.K.* 52°45N 4°47W **28** B4
Bardstown *U.S.A.* 37°49N 85°28W **112** G5
Bareilly *India* 28°22N 79°27E **84** E11
Barents Sea *Arctic* 73°0N 39°0E **54** B9
Barford *U.K.* 52°16N 1°35W **30** B5
Bargoed *U.K.* 51°42N 3°15W **28** D7
Barham *U.K.* 51°12N 1°11E **31** D11
Bari *India* 24°15N 85°25E **85** G14
Bari *Italy* 41°8N 16°51E **68** D7
Bari Doab *Pakistan* 30°20N 73°0E **84** D8
Barim *Yemen* 12°39N 43°25E **90** E8
Barinas *Venezuela* 8°36N 70°15W **120** B2
Baring, C. *Canada* 70°0N 117°30W **108** B8
Barisal *Bangla.* 22°45N 90°20E **85** H17
Barking and Dagenham □ *U.K.* 51°32N 0°10E **31** C9
Barkly Tableland *Australia* 17°50S 136°40E **98** D6
Barlborough *U.K.* 53°17N 1°17W **27** F6

Barlby *U.K.* 53°48N 1°2W **27** E6
Barlee, L. *Australia* 29°15S 119°30E **98** F2
Barletta *Italy* 41°19N 16°17E **68** D7
Barmby Moor *U.K.* 53°56N 0°49W **27** E7
Barmer *India* 25°45N 71°20E **84** G7
Barmoor Castle *U.K.* 55°39N 1°59W **26** A5
Barmouth *U.K.* 52°44N 4°4W **28** B5
Barnard Castle *U.K.* 54°33N 1°55W **26** C5
Barnaul *Russia* 53°20N 83°40E **76** D9
Barnet □ *U.K.* 51°38N 0°9W **31** C8
Barnetby le Wold *U.K.* 53°34N 0°24W **27** E8
Barnoldswick *U.K.* 53°55N 2°11W **27** E4
Barnsley *U.K.* 53°34N 1°27W **27** E6
Barnstaple *U.K.* 51°5N 4°4W **29** E5
Barnstaple Bay = Bideford Bay *U.K.* 51°5N 4°20W **29** E5
Barotseland *Zambia* 15°0S 24°0E **97** H4
Barques, Pt. Aux *U.S.A.* 44°4N 82°58W **112** C6
Barquisimeto *Venezuela* 10°4N 69°19W **120** A3
Barra *Brazil* 11°5S 43°10W **122** B2
Barra *U.K.* 57°0N 7°29W **22** J2
Barra, Sd. of *U.K.* 57°4N 7°25W **22** H3
Barra do Corda *Brazil* 5°30S 45°10W **120** C5
Barra do Pirai *Brazil* 22°30S 43°50W **122** D2
Barra Hd. *U.K.* 56°47N 7°40W **22** J2
Barra Mansa *Brazil* 22°35S 44°12W **122** D2
Barrancabermeja *Colombia* 7°0N 73°50W **120** B2
Barranquilla *Colombia* 11°0N 74°50W **120** A2
Barre *U.S.A.* 44°12N 72°30W **113** C11
Barreiras *Brazil* 12°8S 45°0W **122** B2
Barreiro *Portugal* 38°39N 9°5W **67** C1
Barreiros *Brazil* 8°49S 35°12W **122** A3
Barretos *Brazil* 20°30S 48°35W **122** D1
Barrhead *U.K.* 55°48N 4°23W **24** C7
Barrie *Canada* 44°24N 79°40W **109** E12
Barrow *U.S.A.* 71°18N 156°47W **108** B4
Barrow → *Ireland* 52°25N 6°58W **21** D9
Barrow, Pt. *U.S.A.* 71°23N 156°29W **104** B4
Barrow-in-Furness *U.K.* 54°7N 3°14W **26** D2
Barrow upon Humber *U.K.* 53°41N 0°23W **27** E8
Barrowford *U.K.* 53°51N 2°14W **27** E4
Barry *U.K.* 51°24N 3°16W **29** E7
Barry I. *U.K.* 51°23N 3°16W **29** E7
Barry's Bay *Canada* 45°29N 77°41W **112** C9
Barstow *U.S.A.* 34°54N 117°1W **110** D3
Bartlesville *U.S.A.* 36°45N 95°59W **111** C7
Barton *U.K.* 54°29N 1°38W **26** D5
Barton upon Humber *U.K.* 53°41N 0°25W **27** E8
Barú, Volcan *Panama* 8°55N 82°35W **115** F8
Baruun-Urt *Mongolia* 46°46N 113°15E **79** B11
Barwell *U.K.* 52°35N 1°21W **27** G6
Barysaw *Belarus* 54°17N 28°28E **65** A15
Bashkortostan □ *Russia* 54°0N 57°0E **70** D10
Basilan I. *Phil.* 6°35N 122°0E **83** C6
Basildon *U.K.* 51°34N 0°28E **31** C9
Basingstoke *U.K.* 51°15N 1°5W **30** D6
Baskatong, Rés. *Canada* 46°46N 75°50W **113** B10
Basle *Switz.* 47°35N 7°35E **64** E4
Basque Provinces = País Vasco □ *Spain* 42°50N 2°45W **67** A4
Basra *Iraq* 30°30N 47°50E **86** D6
Bass Rock *U.K.* 56°5N 2°38W **25** B10
Bass Str. *Australia* 39°15S 146°30E **98** H8
Bassas da India *Ind. Oc.* 22°0S 39°0E **97** J7
Basse-Terre *Guadeloupe* 16°0N 61°44W **115** D12
Bassein *Burma* 16°45N 94°30E **85** L19
Bassenthwaite L. *U.K.* 54°40N 3°14W **26** C2
Basseterre *St. Kitts & Nevis* 17°17N 62°43W **115** D12
Basti *India* 26°52N 82°55E **85** F13
Bastia *France* 42°40N 9°30E **66** E8
Baston *U.K.* 52°43N 0°21W **27** G8
Bata *Eq. Guin.* 1°57N 9°50W **96** D1
Batabanó, G. de *Cuba* 22°30N 82°30W **115** C8
Batangas *Phil.* 13°35N 121°10E **83** B6
Batatais *Brazil* 20°54S 47°37W **122** D1
Bataysk *Russia* 47°3N 39°45E **71** E6
Batdambang *Cambodia* 13°7N 103°12E **82** B2
Bath *Maine, U.S.A.* 43°55N 69°49W **113** D13
Bath *N.Y., U.S.A.* 42°20N 77°19W **112** D9
Bath *U.K.* 51°23N 2°22W **30** D4
Bathford *U.K.* 51°24N 2°18W **30** D4
Bathgate *U.K.* 55°54N 3°39W **25** C8
Bathsheba *Barbados* 13°13N 59°32W **114** c
Bathurst *Australia* 33°25S 149°31E **98** G8
Bathurst *Canada* 47°37N 65°43W **109** E13
Bathurst, C. *Canada* 70°34N 128°0W **104** B7
Bathurst I. *Canada* 76°0N 100°30W **104** B9
Bathurst Inlet *Canada* 66°50N 108°1W **108** C9
Batley *U.K.* 53°43N 1°38W **27** E5
Batman *Turkey* 37°55N 41°5E **71** G7
Batna *Algeria* 35°34N 6°15E **94** A7
Baton Rouge *U.S.A.* 30°27N 91°11W **111** D8
Batticaloa *Sri Lanka* 7°43N 81°45E **84** R12
Battle *U.K.* 50°55N 0°30E **31** E9
Battle Creek *U.S.A.* 42°19N 85°11W **112** D5
Batu, Kepulauan *Indonesia* 0°30S 98°25E **82** E1
Batu Pahat *Malaysia* 1°50N 102°56E **82** D2
Batumi *Georgia* 41°39N 41°44E **71** F7
Bauld, C. *Canada* 51°38N 55°26W **109** D14
Bauru *Brazil* 22°10S 49°0W **122** D1
Bavaria = Bayern □ *Germany* 48°50N 12°0E **64** D6
Bawdsey *U.K.* 52°1N 1°27E **31** B11
Bawtry *U.K.* 53°26N 1°2W **27** F6
Bay City *U.S.A.* 43°36N 83°54W **112** D6
Bayamo *Cuba* 20°20N 76°40W **115** C9
Bayan Har Shan *China* 34°0N 98°0E **78** E8
Bayan Obo *China* 41°52N 109°59E **79** C10
Baydhabo *Somalia* 3°8N 43°30E **89** G3
Bayern □ *Germany* 48°50N 12°0E **64** D6
Bayeux *France* 49°17N 0°42W **66** B3
Bayonne *France* 43°30N 1°28W **66** E3
Beachley *U.K.* 51°37N 2°39W **30** C4
Beachy Hd. *U.K.* 50°44N 0°15E **31** E9
Beacon *U.S.A.* 41°30N 73°58W **113** E11
Beaconsfield *U.K.* 51°36N 0°38W **31** C7
Beadnell *U.K.* 55°33N 1°38W **26** A5
Beagle, Canal *S. Amer.* 55°0S 68°30W **121** H3
Beaminster *U.K.* 50°48N 2°44W **30** E5
Bear I. *Arctic* 74°30N 19°0E **54** B8

Bear I. *Ireland* 51°38N 9°50W **20** E3
Bear L. *U.S.A.* 41°59N 111°21W **110** B4
Beardmore Glacier *Antarctica* 84°30S 170°0E **55** E11
Beardstown *U.S.A.* 40°1N 90°26W **112** E2
Béarn *France* 43°20N 0°30W **66** E3
Bearsden *U.K.* 55°55N 4°21W **24** C7
Bearsted *U.K.* 51°16N 0°35E **31** D10
Beatrice *U.S.A.* 40°16N 96°45W **111** B7
Beattock *U.K.* 55°20N 3°28W **25** D8
Beattock Summit *U.K.* 52°25N 3°32W **25** D8
Beauce, Plaine de la *France* 48°10N 1°45E **66** B4
Beaufort Sea *Arctic* 72°0N 140°0W **104** B5
Beaufort West *S. Africa* 32°18S 22°36E **97** L4
Beauharnois *Canada* 45°20N 73°52W **113** C11
Beaulieu *U.K.* 50°48N 1°27W **30** E6
Beauly *U.K.* 57°30N 4°28W **23** H9
Beauly → *U.K.* 57°29N 4°27W **23** H9
Beauly Firth *U.K.* 57°30N 4°20W **23** H9
Beaumaris *U.K.* 53°16N 4°6W **28** A5
Beaumont *U.S.A.* 30°5N 94°6W **111** D8
Beaune *France* 47°2N 4°50E **66** C6
Beauvais *France* 49°25N 2°8E **66** B5
Beaver → *Canada* 55°26N 107°45W **108** D9
Beaver Creek *Canada* 63°0N 141°0W **108** C5
Beaver Dam *U.S.A.* 43°28N 88°50W **112** D3
Beaver Falls *U.S.A.* 40°46N 80°20W **112** E7
Beaver I. *U.S.A.* 45°40N 85°33W **112** C5
Beawar *India* 26°3N 74°18E **84** F9
Bebedouro *Brazil* 21°0S 48°25W **122** D1
Bebington *U.K.* 53°22N 3°0W **27** F3
Beccles *U.K.* 52°27N 1°35E **31** B12
Béchar *Algeria* 31°38N 2°18W **94** B5
Beckermet *U.K.* 54°27N 3°30W **26** D1
Beckfoot *U.K.* 54°50N 3°24W **26** C2
Beckingham *U.K.* 53°24N 0°50W **27** F7
Beckley *U.S.A.* 37°47N 81°11W **112** G7
Bedale *U.K.* 54°18N 1°36W **26** D5
Beddgelert *U.K.* 53°1N 4°6W **28** A5
Bedford *U.K.* 52°8N 0°28W **31** B8
Bedford *Ind., U.S.A.* 38°52N 86°29W **112** F4
Bedford *Va., U.S.A.* 37°20N 79°31W **112** G8
Bedford □ *U.K.* 52°4N 0°28W **31** B8
Bedford Level *U.K.* 52°32N 0°7W **31** A8
Bedlington *U.K.* 55°8N 1°35W **26** B5
Bedworth *U.K.* 52°29N 1°28W **30** B6
Beeford *U.K.* 53°58N 0°17W **27** E8
Beer *U.K.* 50°41N 3°6W **29** F7
Be'er Sheva *Israel* 31°15N 34°48E **86** D3
Beeston *U.K.* 52°56N 1°14W **27** G6
Bei Jiang → *China* 23°2N 112°58E **79** a
Bei Shan *China* 41°30N 96°0E **78** C8
Bei'an *China* 48°10N 126°20E **79** B14
Beighton *U.K.* 53°21N 1°20W **27** F6
Beihai *China* 21°28N 109°6E **79** G10
Beijing *China* 39°53N 116°21E **79** D12
Beinn na Faoghla = Benbecula *U.K.* 57°26N 7°21W **22** H3
Beira *Mozam.* 19°50S 34°52E **97** H6
Beirut *Lebanon* 33°53N 35°31E **86** C3
Beitbridge *Zimbabwe* 22°12S 30°0E **97** J6
Beith *U.K.* 55°45N 4°38W **24** C6
Béja *Tunisia* 36°43N 9°12E **95** A7
Bejaïa *Algeria* 36°42N 5°2E **94** A7
Békéscsaba *Hungary* 46°40N 21°5E **65** E11
Bela *Pakistan* 26°12N 66°20E **84** F5
Belarus ■ *Europe* 53°30N 27°0E **70** D4
Belau = Palau ■ *Palau* 7°30N 134°30E **102** G5
Belbroughton *U.K.* 52°24N 2°7W **30** B4
Belcher Chan. *Canada* 77°15N 95°0W **109** B10
Belcher Is. *Canada* 56°15N 78°45W **109** D12
Beledweyne *Somalia* 4°30N 45°5E **89** G4
Belém *Brazil* 1°20S 48°30W **120** C5
Belep, Îs. *N. Cal.* 19°45S 163°40E **99** D11
Belfast *U.K.* 54°37N 5°56W **19** B10
Belfast L. *U.K.* 54°40N 5°50W **19** B10
Belford *U.K.* 55°36N 1°49W **26** A5
Belfort *France* 47°38N 6°50E **66** C7
Belgaum *India* 15°55N 74°35E **84** M9
Belgium ■ *Europe* 50°30N 5°0E **64** C3
Belgorod *Russia* 50°35N 36°35E **71** D6
Belgrade *Serbia* 44°50N 20°37E **69** B9
Belitung *Indonesia* 3°10S 107°50E **82** E3
Belize ■ *Cent. Amer.* 17°0N 88°30W **114** D7
Belize City *Belize* 17°25N 88°10W **114** D7
Bell Peninsula *Canada* 63°50N 82°0W **109** C11
Bell Ville *Argentina* 32°40S 62°40W **121** F3
Bella Coola *Canada* 52°25N 126°40W **108** D7
Bellaire *U.S.A.* 40°1N 80°45W **112** E7
Bellary *India* 15°10N 76°56E **84** M10
Belle Fourche → *U.S.A.* 44°26N 102°18W **110** B6
Belle-Île *France* 47°20N 3°10W **66** C2
Belle Isle *Canada* 51°57N 55°25W **109** D14
Belle Isle, Str. of *Canada* 51°30N 56°30W **109** D14
Bellefontaine *U.S.A.* 40°22N 83°46W **112** E6
Belleplaine *Barbados* 13°15N 59°34W **114** c
Belleville *Canada* 44°10N 77°23W **109** E12
Belleville *U.S.A.* 38°31N 89°59W **112** F3
Bellingham *U.K.* 55°9N 2°16W **26** B4
Bellingham *U.S.A.* 48°46N 122°29W **110** A2
Bellinghausen Sea *Antarctica* 66°0S 80°0W **55** C17
Bellinzona *Switz.* 46°11N 9°1E **64** E5
Belmonte *Brazil* 16°0S 39°0W **122** C3
Belmopan *Belize* 17°18N 88°30W **114** D7
Belmullet *Ireland* 54°14N 9°58W **18** B2
Belo Horizonte *Brazil* 19°55S 43°56W **122** C2
Belo Jardim *Brazil* 8°20S 36°26W **122** A3
Belogorsk *Russia* 51°0N 128°20E **77** D13
Beloit *U.S.A.* 42°31N 89°2W **112** D3
Belomorsk *Russia* 64°35N 34°54E **70** B5
Beloretsk *Russia* 53°58N 58°24E **70** D10
Beloye, L. *Russia* 60°10N 37°35E **70** B6
Belper *U.K.* 53°2N 1°29W **27** F6
Belsay *U.K.* 55°6N 1°51W **26** B5
Belton *N. Lincs., U.K.* 53°33N 0°48W **27** E7
Belton *Norfolk, U.K.* 52°35N 1°40E **31** A12
Belturbet *Ireland* 54°6N 7°26E **18** B7
Belukha *Russia* 49°50N 86°50E **76** E9
Belvidere *U.S.A.* 42°15N 88°50W **112** D3
Bembridge *U.K.* 50°41N 1°5W **30** E6
Bemidji *U.S.A.* 47°28N 94°53W **111** A8

Ben Cruachan *U.K.* 56°26N 5°8W **24** B5
Ben Dearg *U.K.* 57°47N 4°56W **23** G8
Ben Hope *U.K.* 58°25N 4°36W **23** F8
Ben Lawers *U.K.* 56°32N 4°14W **24** A7
Ben Lomond *U.K.* 56°11N 4°38W **24** B6
Ben Macdhui *U.K.* 57°4N 3°40W **23** H10
Ben Mhor *U.K.* 57°15N 7°18W **22** H3
Ben More *Argyll & Bute, U.K.* 56°26N 6°1W **24** B3
Ben More *Stirling, U.K.* 56°23N 4°32W **24** B6
Ben More Assynt *U.K.* 58°8N 4°52W **23** F8
Ben Nevis *U.K.* 56°48N 5°1W **22** J7
Ben Vorlich *U.K.* 56°21N 4°14W **24** B7
Ben Wyvis *U.K.* 57°40N 4°35W **23** G8
Benares = Varanasi *India* 25°22N 83°0E **85** G13
Benbecula *U.K.* 57°26N 7°21W **22** H3
Bend *U.S.A.* 44°4N 121°19W **110** B2
Benderloch *U.K.* 56°30N 5°22W **24** A5
Bendigo *Australia* 36°40S 144°15E **98** H7
Benevento *Italy* 41°8N 14°45E **68** D6
Bengal, Bay of *Ind. Oc.* 15°0N 90°0E **85** M17
Bengbu *China* 32°58N 117°20E **79** E12
Benghazi *Libya* 32°11N 20°3E **95** B10
Bengkulu *Indonesia* 3°50S 102°12E **82** E2
Benguela *Angola* 12°37S 13°25E **97** G2
Beni → *Bolivia* 10°23S 65°24W **120** D3
Beni Mellal *Morocco* 32°21N 6°21W **94** B4
Beni Suef *Egypt* 29°5N 31°6E **95** C12
Benidorm *Spain* 38°33N 0°9W **67** C5
Benin ■ *Africa* 10°0N 2°0E **94** G6
Benin, Bight of *W. Afr.* 5°0N 3°0E **94** H6
Benin City *Nigeria* 6°20N 5°31E **94** G7
Benington *U.K.* 53°0N 0°5E **27** F9
Benjamin Constant *Brazil* 4°40S 70°15W **120** C2
Benoni *S. Africa* 26°11S 28°18E **97** K5
Benson *U.K.* 51°37N 1°6W **30** C6
Bentley *Hants., U.K.* 51°12N 0°52W **31** D7
Bentley *S. Yorks., U.K.* 53°33N 1°8W **27** E6
Bentley Subglacial Trench *Antarctica* 80°0S 115°0W **55** E14
Benton *U.S.A.* 38°0N 88°55W **112** G3
Benton Harbor *U.S.A.* 42°6N 86°27W **112** D4
Benue → *Nigeria* 7°48N 6°46E **94** G7
Benxi *China* 41°20N 123°48E **79** C13
Beppu *Japan* 33°15N 131°30E **81** G2
Berber *Sudan* 18°0N 34°0E **95** E12
Berbera *Somalia* 10°30N 45°2E **89** E4
Berbérati *C.A.R.* 4°15N 15°40E **96** D3
Berbice → *Guyana* 6°20N 57°32W **120** B4
Berdyansk *Ukraine* 46°45N 36°50E **71** E6
Berdychiv *Ukraine* 49°57N 28°30E **71** E4
Bere Alston *U.K.* 50°29N 4°13W **29** G5
Bere Regis *U.K.* 50°45N 2°14W **30** E4
Berea *U.S.A.* 37°34N 84°17W **112** G5
Berens → *Canada* 52°25N 97°2W **108** D10
Berezina = Belarus 52°33N 30°14E **70** D5
Bereznik *Russia* 62°51N 42°40E **70** B7
Berezniki *Russia* 59°24N 56°46E **70** C10
Bérgamo *Italy* 45°41N 9°43E **68** B3
Bergen *Norway* 60°20N 5°20E **63** E5
Bergerac *France* 44°51N 0°30E **66** D4
Bering Sea *Pac. Oc.* 58°0N 171°0W **104** D2
Bering Strait *Pac. Oc.* 65°30N 169°0W **108** C3
Berkeley *U.K.* 51°41N 2°27W **30** C4
Berkhamsted *U.K.* 51°45N 0°33W **31** C7
Berkner I. *Antarctica* 79°30S 50°0W **55** D18
Berkshire Downs *U.K.* 51°33N 1°29W **30** C6
Berlin *Germany* 52°31N 13°23E **64** B7
Berlin *U.S.A.* 44°28N 71°11W **113** C12
Bermejo → *Argentina* 26°51S 58°23W **121** E4
Bermuda ☑ *Atl. Oc.* 32°18N 64°45W **52** C6
Bern *Switz.* 46°57N 7°28E **64** E4
Berneray *U.K.* 57°43N 7°11W **22** G3
Berry *France* 46°50N 2°0E **66** C5
Berry Hd. *U.K.* 50°24N 3°29W **29** G7
Berrybridge By. *Ireland* 53°22N 9°54W **20** B3
Berwick *U.S.A.* 41°3N 76°14W **112** E9
Berwick-upon-Tweed *U.K.* 55°46N 2°0W **26** A5
Berwyn Mts. *U.K.* 52°54N 3°26W **28** B7
Besançon *France* 47°15N 6°2E **66** C7
Bessarabiya *Moldova* 47°0N 28°10E **65** E15
Bessemer *U.S.A.* 46°29N 90°3W **112** B2
Bethel *U.S.A.* 60°48N 161°45W **108** C3
Bethesda *U.K.* 53°10N 4°3W **28** A5
Bethlehem *S. Africa* 28°14S 28°18E **97** K5
Bethlehem *U.S.A.* 40°37N 75°23W **113** E10
Béthune *France* 50°30N 2°38E **66** A5
Betim *Brazil* 19°58S 44°7W **122** C2
Bettiah *India* 26°48N 84°33E **85** F14
Betul *India* 21°58N 77°59E **84** J10
Betws-y-Coed *U.K.* 53°5N 3°48W **28** A6
Beverley *U.K.* 53°51N 0°26W **27** E8
Bewdley *U.K.* 52°23N 2°19W **30** B4
Bexhill *U.K.* 50°51N 0°29E **31** E9
Bexley □ *U.K.* 51°27N 0°9E **31** C9
Beyneu *Kazakhstan* 45°18N 55°9E **71** E10
Beypazarı *Turkey* 40°10N 31°56E **71** F5
Beyşehir Gölü *Turkey* 37°41N 31°33E **71** G5
Béziers *France* 43°20N 3°12E **66** E5
Bhagalpur *India* 25°10N 87°0E **85** G15
Bhaktapur *Nepal* 27°38N 85°24E **85** F14
Bhanrer Ra. *India* 23°40N 79°45E **84** H11
Bharatpur *India* 27°15N 77°30E **84** F10
Bharrraig = Barra *U.K.* 57°0N 7°29W **22** J2
Bharuch *India* 21°47N 73°0E **84** J8
Bhatpara *India* 22°50N 88°25E **85** H16
Bhavnagar *India* 21°45N 72°10E **84** J8
Bhearnaraigh = Berneray *U.K.* 57°43N 7°11W **22** G3
Bhilainagar-Durg *India* 21°13N 81°26E **85** J12
Bhilwara *India* 25°25N 74°38E **84** G9
Bhima → *India* 16°25N 77°17E **84** L10
Bhiwandi *India* 19°20N 73°0E **84** K8
Bhiwani *India* 28°50N 76°9E **84** E10
Bhopal *India* 23°20N 77°30E **84** H10
Bhubaneshwar *India* 20°15N 85°50E **85** J14
Bhuj *India* 23°15N 69°49E **84** H6
Bhusawal *India* 21°3N 75°46E **84** J9
Bhutan ■ *Asia* 27°25N 90°30E **85** F17
Biała Podlaska *Poland* 52°4N 23°6E **65** B12
Białystok *Poland* 53°10N 23°10E **65** B12

Biarritz France 43°29N 1°33W 66 E3
Bibury U.K. 51°45N 1°49W 30 C5
Bicester U.K. 51°54N 1°9W 30 C6
Bicton U.K. 52°44N 2°48W 27 G3
Bida Nigeria 9°3N 5°58E 94 G7
Biddeford U.S.A. 43°30N 70°28W 113 D12
Biddenden U.K. 51°7N 0°40E 31 D10
Biddulph U.K. 53°7N 2°10W 27 F4
Bideford U.K. 51°1N 4°13W 29 E5
Bideford Bay U.K. 51°5N 4°20W 29 E5
Bidford-on-Avon U.K. 52°11N 1°50W 30 B5
Bié Plateau Angola 12°0S 16°0E 97 G3
Biel Switz. 47°8N 7°14E 64 E4
Bielefeld Germany 52°1N 8°33E 64 B5
Biella Italy 45°34N 8°3E 68 B3
Bielsko-Biała Poland 49°50N 19°2E 65 D10
Bien Hoa Vietnam 10°57N 106°49E 82 B3
Bienville, L. Canada 55°5N 72°40W 109 D12
Big Belt Mts. U.S.A. 46°30N 111°25W 110 A4
Big Rapids U.S.A. 43°42N 85°29W 112 D5
Big Sioux ➔ U.S.A. 42°29N 96°27W 111 B7
Big Spring U.S.A. 32°15N 101°28W 110 D6
Big Trout L. Canada 53°40N 90°0W 109 D11
Bigbury U.K. 50°18N 3°53W 29 G6
Bigbury B. U.K. 50°16N 3°54W 29 G6
Biggar Canada 52°4N 108°0W 108 D9
Biggar U.K. 55°38N 3°32W 25 C8
Biggleswade U.K. 52°5N 0°14W 31 B8
Bighorn ➔ U.S.A. 46°10N 107°28W 110 A5
Bighorn Mts. U.S.A. 44°25N 107°0W 110 B5
Bihar India 25°5N 85°40E 85 G14
Bihar □ India 25°0N 86°0E 85 G15
Bijagós, Arquipélago dos Guinea-Biss. 11°15N 16°10W 94 F2
Bijapur India 16°50N 75°55E 84 L9
Bikaner India 28°2N 73°18E 84 E8
Bikini Atoll Marshall Is. 12°0N 167°30E 102 F8
Bila Tserkva Ukraine 49°45N 30°10E 65 D16
Bilaspur India 22°2N 82°15E 85 H13
Bilbao Spain 43°16N 2°56W 67 A4
Bilecik Turkey 40°5N 30°5E 71 F5
Bilhorod-Dnistrovskyy Ukraine 46°11N 30°23E 71 E5
Billericay U.K. 51°38N 0°26E 31 C9
Billesdon U.K. 52°38N 0°54W 27 G7
Billingham U.K. 54°36N 1°17W 26 C6
Billinghay U.K. 53°5N 0°15W 27 F8
Billings U.S.A. 45°47N 108°30W 110 A5
Billingshurst U.K. 51°2N 0°27W 31 D8
Bilma Niger 18°50N 13°30E 95 E8
Bilma, Grand Erg de Niger 18°30N 14°0E 95 E8
Biloxi U.S.A. 30°24N 88°53W 111 D9
Bilston U.K. 52°34N 2°4W 27 G4
Bimini Is. Bahamas 25°42N 79°25W 115 B9
Binbrook U.K. 53°26N 0°10W 27 F8
Bingham U.K. 52°57N 0°58W 27 G7
Binghamton U.S.A. 42°6N 75°55W 113 D10
Bingley U.K. 53°51N 1°50W 27 E5
Bioko Eq. Guin. 3°30N 8°40E 96 D1
Biratnagar Nepal 26°27N 87°17E 85 F15
Birchington U.K. 51°22N 1°19E 31 D11
Birdlip U.K. 51°50N 2°5W 30 C4
Birkdale U.K. 53°38N 3°1W 27 E2
Birkenhead U.K. 53°23N 3°2W 27 F2
Birmingham U.K. 52°29N 1°52W 27 H5
Birmingham U.S.A. 33°31N 86°48W 111 D9
Birmingham Int. ✕ (BHX) U.K. 52°26N 1°45W 27 H5
Birnin Kebbi Nigeria 12°32N 4°12E 94 F6
Birobidzhan Russia 48°50N 132°50E 77 E14
Birr Ireland 53°6N 7°54W 20 B7
Birtley Northumberland, U.K. 55°6N 2°12W 26 B4
Birtley Tyne & W., U.K. 54°54N 1°34W 26 C5
Biscay, B. of Atl. Oc. 45°0N 2°0W 66 D1
Bishkek Kyrgyzstan 42°54N 74°46E 76 E8
Bishop Auckland U.K. 54°39N 1°40W 26 C5
Bishop's Castle U.K. 52°30N 2°59W 27 H3
Bishop's Cleeve U.K. 51°57N 2°3W 30 C4
Bishop's Frome U.K. 52°8N 2°29W 30 B4
Bishop's Nympton U.K. 51°0N 3°47W 29 F6
Bishop's Stortford U.K. 51°52N 0°10E 31 C9
Bishop's Waltham U.K. 50°57N 1°11W 30 E6
Bishopsteignton U.K. 50°33N 3°33W 29 F6
Bishopstoke U.K. 50°58N 1°19W 30 E6
Biskra Algeria 34°50N 5°44E 94 B7
Bismarck U.S.A. 46°48N 100°47W 110 A6
Bismarck Arch. Papua N. G. 2°30S 150°0E 98 A9
Bissau Guinea-Biss. 11°45N 15°45W 94 F2
Bitolj Macedonia 41°1N 21°20E 69 D9
Bitterfontein S. Africa 31°1S 18°32E 97 L3
Bitterroot Range U.S.A. 46°0N 114°20W 110 A4
Bitton U.K. 51°25N 2°27W 30 D4
Biu Nigeria 10°40N 12°3E 95 F8
Biwa-Ko Japan 35°15N 136°10E 81 F5
Biysk Russia 52°40N 85°0E 76 D9
Bizerte Tunisia 37°15N 9°50E 95 A7
Blaby U.K. 52°35N 1°10W 27 G6
Black Combe U.K. 54°16N 3°20W 26 D2
Black Esk ➔ U.K. 55°12N 3°11W 25 D9
Black Forest = Schwarzwald Germany 48°30N 8°20E 64 D5
Black Hd. Ireland 53°9N 9°16W 20 B4
Black Hd. U.K. 50°0N 5°7W 29 H3
Black Hills U.S.A. 44°0N 103°45W 110 B6
Black Isle U.K. 57°35N 4°16W 23 G9
Black Mt. = Mynydd Du U.K. 51°52N 3°50W 28 D6
Black Mts. U.K. 51°55N 3°7W 28 D7
Black Range U.S.A. 33°15N 107°50W 110 D5
Black River Jamaica 18°0N 77°50W 114 a
Black River Falls U.S.A. 44°18N 90°51W 112 C2
Black Rock Barbados 13°7N 59°37W 114 c
Black Sea Eurasia 43°30N 35°0E 71 F6
Blackburn U.K. 53°45N 2°29W 27 E4
Blackdown Hills U.K. 50°57N 3°15W 30 E2
Blackmoor Vale U.K. 50°54N 2°28W 30 E4
Blackpool U.K. 53°49N 3°3W 27 E2
Blackrock Ireland 53°18N 6°11W 21 B10
Blacksburg U.S.A. 37°14N 80°25W 112 G7
Blacksod B. Ireland 54°6N 10°0W 18 C1
Blackwater ➔ Meath, Ireland 53°39N 6°41W 19 D8
Blackwater ➔ Waterford, Ireland 52°4N 7°52W 20 D7
Blackwater ➔ Armagh, U.K. 54°31N 6°35W 19 B8
Blackwater ➔ Essex, U.K. 51°44N 0°53E 31 C10
Blaenau Ffestiniog U.K. 53°0N 3°56W 28 B6
Blaenavon U.K. 51°46N 3°5W 28 D7
Blagdon U.K. 51°20N 2°43W 30 D3
Blagoevgrad Bulgaria 42°2N 23°5E 69 C10
Blagoveshchensk Russia 50°20N 127°30E 77 D13
Blair Atholl U.K. 56°46N 3°50W 23 J10
Blairgowrie U.K. 56°35N 3°21W 25 A9
Blakeney Gloucs., U.K. 51°46N 2°28W 30 C4
Blakeney Norfolk, U.K. 52°58N 1°1E 31 A11
Blanc, Mont Europe 45°48N 6°50E 66 D7
Blanca, B. Argentina 39°10S 61°30W 121 F3
Blanca Peak U.S.A. 37°35N 105°29W 110 C5
Blanchardstown Ireland 53°23N 6°23W 21 B10
Blanco, C. Costa Rica 9°34N 85°8W 104 J11
Blanco, C. U.S.A. 42°51N 124°34W 110 B2
Blandford Forum U.K. 50°51N 2°9W 30 E4
Blanquilla, I. Venezuela 11°51N 64°37W 115 E12
Blantyre Malawi 15°45S 35°0E 97 H6
Blarney Ireland 51°56N 8°33W 20 E5
Blaydon U.K. 54°58N 1°42W 26 C5
Blean U.K. 51°18N 1°3E 31 D11
Bleasdale Moors U.K. 53°55N 2°35W 27 E3
Blenheim N.Z. 41°38S 173°57E 99 J13
Bletchingdon U.K. 51°51N 1°15W 30 C6
Bletchley U.K. 51°59N 0°44W 31 C7
Blida Algeria 36°30N 2°49E 94 A6
Blisworth U.K. 52°10N 0°56W 31 B7
Blitar Indonesia 8°5S 112°11E 82 F4
Blockley U.K. 52°1N 1°44W 30 B5
Bloemfontein S. Africa 29°6S 26°7E 97 K5
Blofield U.K. 52°38N 1°26E 31 A11
Blois France 47°35N 1°20E 66 C4
Bloody Foreland Ireland 55°10N 8°17W 18 A5
Bloomington Ill., U.S.A. 40°28N 89°0W 112 E3
Bloomington Ind., U.S.A. 39°10N 86°32W 112 F4
Bloomsburg U.S.A. 41°0N 76°27W 112 E9
Bloxham U.K. 52°1N 1°21W 30 B6
Blue Mountain Pk. Jamaica 18°3N 76°36W 114 a
Blue Mt. U.S.A. 40°30N 76°30W 112 E9
Blue Mts. Jamaica 18°3N 76°36W 114 a
Blue Mts. U.S.A. 45°0N 118°20W 110 A3
Blue Nile ➔ Sudan 15°38N 32°31E 95 E12
Blue Ridge U.S.A. 36°40N 80°50W 111 C10
Blue Stack Mts. Ireland 54°42N 8°12W 18 B5
Bluefield U.S.A. 37°15N 81°17W 112 G7
Bluefields Nic. 12°20N 83°50W 115 E8
Blumenau Brazil 27°0S 49°0W 121 E5
Blundeston U.K. 52°31N 1°42E 31 A12
Blyth Northumberland, U.K. 55°8N 1°31W 26 B5
Blyth Notts., U.K. 53°22N 1°3W 27 F6
Blyth ➔ U.K. 55°8N 1°33W 26 B5
Blyth Bridge U.K. 55°42N 3°22W 25 C9
Blyton U.K. 53°27N 0°42W 27 F7
Bo S. Leone 7°55N 11°50W 94 G3
Bo Hai China 39°0N 119°0E 79 D12
Boa Vista Brazil 2°48N 60°30W 120 B3
Bobcaygeon Canada 44°33N 78°33W 112 C8
Bobo-Dioulasso Burkina Faso 11°8N 4°13W 94 F5
Bóbr ➔ Poland 52°4N 15°4E 64 B8
Bochum Germany 51°28N 7°13E 64 C4
Boddam U.K. 59°56N 1°17W 22 C15
Boden Sweden 65°50N 21°42E 63 D8
Bodiam U.K. 51°0N 0°34E 31 D10
Bodinnick U.K. 50°20N 4°38W 29 G4
Bodmin U.K. 50°28N 4°43W 29 G4
Bodmin Moor U.K. 50°33N 4°36W 29 F4
Bodø Norway 67°17N 14°24E 63 D6
Bodrog ➔ Hungary 48°11N 21°22E 65 D11
Bodrum Turkey 37°3N 27°30E 71 G4
Bogalusa U.S.A. 30°47N 89°52W 111 D9
Bogda Shan China 43°35N 89°40E 78 C6
Boggeragh Mts. Ireland 52°2N 8°55W 20 D5
Bognor Regis U.K. 50°47N 0°40W 31 E7
Bogor Indonesia 6°36S 106°48E 82 F3
Bogotá Colombia 4°34N 74°0W 120 B2
Bogra Bangla. 24°51N 89°22E 85 G16
Böhmerwald Germany 49°8N 13°14E 64 D7
Bohol Sea Phil. 9°0N 124°0E 83 C6
Boise U.S.A. 43°37N 116°13W 110 B3
Bole China 44°55N 81°37E 78 C5
Bolivar, Pico Venezuela 8°32N 71°2W 115 F10
Bolivia ■ S. Amer. 17°6S 64°0W 120 D3
Bollington U.K. 53°18N 2°6W 27 F4
Bolney U.K. 50°59N 0°12W 31 E8
Bologna Italy 44°29N 11°20E 68 B4
Bologoye Russia 57°55N 34°5E 70 C5
Bolsena, L. di Italy 42°36N 11°56E 68 C4
Bolsover U.K. 53°14N 1°16W 27 F6
Bolt Head U.K. 50°12N 3°48W 29 G6
Bolt Tail U.K. 50°14N 3°52W 29 G6
Bolton U.K. 53°35N 2°26W 27 E4
Bolton Abbey U.K. 53°59N 1°53W 27 E5
Bolton by Bowland U.K. 53°56N 2°20W 27 E4
Bolton le Sands U.K. 54°6N 2°48W 26 D3
Bolu Turkey 40°45N 31°35E 71 F5
Bolvadin Turkey 38°45N 31°4E 71 G5
Bolzano Italy 46°31N 11°22E 68 A4
Bom Despacho Brazil 19°43S 45°15W 122 C1
Bom Jesus da Lapa Brazil 13°15S 43°25W 122 B2
Boma Dem. Rep. of the Congo 5°50S 13°4E 96 F2
Bombala Australia 36°56S 149°15E 98 H8
Bombay = Mumbai India 18°56N 72°50E 84 K8
Bomi China 29°50N 95°45E 78 F8
Bomu ➔ C.A.R. 4°40N 22°30E 96 D4
Bon, C. Tunisia 37°1N 11°2E 90 C5
Bonaire W. Indies 12°10N 68°15W 115 E11
Bonar Bridge U.K. 57°54N 4°20W 23 G9
Bonavista Canada 48°40N 53°5W 109 E14
Bonchester Bridge U.K. 55°24N 2°39W 25 D10
Bonchurch U.K. 50°37N 1°11W 30 E6
Bo'ness U.K. 56°1N 3°37W 25 B8
Bongor Chad 10°35N 15°20E 95 F9
Bongos, Massif des C.A.R. 8°40N 22°25E 96 C4
Bonifacio France 41°24N 9°10E 66 F8
Bonn Germany 50°46N 7°6E 64 C4
Bonny, Bight of Africa 3°30N 9°20E 96 D1
Bonnyrigg U.K. 55°53N 3°6W 25 C9
Bööн Tsagaan Nuur Mongolia 45°35N 99°9E 78 B8
Boonville U.S.A. 38°3N 87°16W 112 F4
Boosaaso Somalia 11°12N 49°18E 89 E4
Boot U.K. 54°24N 3°13W 26 D2
Boothia, Gulf of Canada 71°0N 90°0W 109 B11
Boothia Pen. Canada 71°0N 94°0W 108 B10
Bootle Cumb., U.K. 54°18N 3°22W 26 D2
Bootle Mersey., U.K. 53°28N 3°1W 27 F2
Borås Sweden 57°43N 12°56E 63 F6
Borborema, Planalto da Brazil 7°0S 37°0W 117 D7
Bordeaux France 44°50N 0°36W 66 D3
Borden I. Canada 78°30N 111°30W 109 B8
Borden Pen. Canada 73°0N 83°0W 109 B11
Borders = Scottish Borders □ U.K. 55°35N 2°50W 25 C10
Bordon U.K. 51°8N 0°52W 31 D7
Borehamwood U.K. 51°40N 0°15W 31 C8
Boreland U.K. 55°13N 3°17W 25 D9
Borger U.S.A. 35°39N 101°24W 110 C6
Borhoyn Tal Mongolia 43°50N 111°58E 79 C11
Borisoglebsk Russia 51°27N 42°5E 71 D7
Borkou Chad 18°15N 18°50E 95 E9
Borneo E. Indies 1°0N 115°0E 82 D5
Bornholm Denmark 55°10N 15°0E 63 F7
Borohoro Shan China 44°6N 83°10E 78 C5
Boroughbridge U.K. 54°6N 1°24W 26 D6
Borovichi Russia 58°25N 33°55E 70 C5
Borrowdale U.K. 54°31N 3°10W 26 C2
Borth U.K. 52°29N 4°2W 28 C5
Borūjerd Iran 33°55N 48°50E 86 C7
Bosbury U.K. 52°5N 2°26W 30 B4
Boscastle U.K. 50°41N 4°42W 29 F4
Boscobelle Barbados 13°17N 59°35W 114 c
Bose China 23°53N 106°35E 78 G10
Bosham U.K. 50°49N 0°51W 31 E7
Bosnia-Herzegovina ■ Europe 44°0N 18°0E 69 B7
Bosporus Turkey 41°5N 29°3E 71 F4
Bossangoa C.A.R. 6°35N 17°30E 96 C3
Bosten Hu China 41°55N 87°40E 78 C6
Boston U.K. 52°59N 0°2W 27 G8
Boston U.S.A. 42°22N 71°3W 113 D12
Bothel U.K. 54°45N 3°15W 26 C2
Bothnia, G. of Europe 62°0N 20°0E 63 E8
Botletle ➔ Botswana 20°10S 23°15E 97 J4
Botoşani Romania 47°42N 26°41E 65 E14
Botswana ■ Africa 22°0S 24°0E 97 J4
Bottesford U.K. 52°57N 0°47W 27 G7
Botucatu Brazil 22°55S 48°30W 122 D1
Bou Saâda Algeria 35°11N 4°9E 94 A6
Bouaké Ivory C. 7°40N 5°2W 94 G4
Bouar C.A.R. 6°0N 15°40E 96 C3
Bouârfa Morocco 32°32N 1°58W 94 B5
Bougainville I. Papua N. G. 6°0S 155°0E 99 B10
Boulder U.S.A. 40°1N 105°17W 110 B5
Boulogne-sur-Mer France 50°42N 1°36E 66 A4
Bounty Is. Pac. Oc. 48°0S 178°30E 102 M9
Bourbonnais France 46°28N 3°0E 66 C5
Bourg-en-Bresse France 46°13N 5°12E 66 C6
Bourges France 47°9N 2°25E 66 C5
Bourgogne □ France 47°0N 4°50E 66 C6
Bourke Australia 30°8S 145°55E 98 G8
Bourne U.K. 52°47N 0°22W 27 G8
Bournemouth U.K. 50°43N 1°52W 30 E5
Bourton-on-the-Water U.K. 51°52N 1°45W 30 C5
Bouvet I. Antarctica 54°26S 3°24E 52 G10
Bovey Tracey U.K. 50°36N 3°41W 29 F6
Bow ➔ Canada 49°57N 111°41W 108 D8
Bowes U.K. 54°32N 1°59W 26 C5
Bowland, Forest of U.K. 54°0N 2°30W 27 E3
Bowling Green Ky., U.S.A. 36°59N 86°27W 112 G4
Bowling Green Ohio, U.S.A. 41°23N 83°39W 112 E6
Bowmore U.K. 55°45N 6°17W 24 C3
Bowness-on-Solway U.K. 54°57N 3°12W 26 C2
Bowness-on-Windermere U.K. 54°22N 2°55W 26 D3
Box U.K. 51°25N 2°15W 30 D4
Box Hill U.K. 51°15N 0°16W 31 D8
Boyle Ireland 53°59N 8°18W 18 D5
Boyne ➔ Ireland 53°43N 6°15W 19 D9
Boyoma, Chutes Dem. Rep. of the Congo 0°35N 25°23E 90 F6
Bozeat U.K. 52°14N 0°40W 31 B7
Bozeman U.S.A. 45°41N 111°2W 110 A4
Bozoum C.A.R. 6°25N 16°35E 96 C3
Brač Croatia 43°20N 16°40E 68 C7
Bracadale, L. U.K. 57°20N 6°30W 22 H4
Bracebridge Canada 45°2N 79°19W 112 C8
Bracebridge Heath U.K. 53°12N 0°32W 27 F7
Bräcke Sweden 62°45N 15°26E 63 E7
Brackley U.K. 52°2N 1°8W 30 B6
Bracknell U.K. 51°25N 0°43W 31 D7
Bradford U.K. 53°47N 1°45W 27 E5
Bradford U.S.A. 41°58N 78°38W 112 E8
Bradford on Avon U.K. 51°21N 2°14W 30 D4
Brading U.K. 50°41N 1°8W 30 E6
Bradwell-on-Sea U.K. 51°43N 0°56E 31 C10
Bradworthy U.K. 50°53N 4°24W 29 F5
Braemar U.K. 57°2N 3°26W 23 H11
Braga Portugal 41°35N 8°25W 67 B1
Bragança Brazil 1°0S 47°2W 120 C5
Bragança Paulista Brazil 22°55S 46°32W 122 D1
Brahmanbaria Bangla. 23°58N 91°15E 85 H17
Brahmani ➔ India 20°39N 86°46E 85 J15
Brahmapur India 19°15N 84°54E 85 K14
Brahmaputra ➔ Asia 23°40N 90°35E 85 H16
Braich-y-pwll U.K. 52°47N 4°46W 28 B4
Brăila Romania 45°19N 27°59E 65 F14
Brailsford U.K. 52°58N 1°35W 27 G5
Brainerd U.S.A. 46°22N 94°12W 111 A8
Braintree U.K. 51°53N 0°34E 31 C10
Bramford U.K. 52°4N 1°7E 31 B11
Brampton Canada 43°45N 79°45W 112 D8
Brampton Cambs., U.K. 52°20N 0°14W 31 B8
Brampton Cumb., U.K. 54°57N 2°44W 26 C3
Brancaster U.K. 52°58N 0°38E 31 A10
Branco ➔ Brazil 1°20S 61°50W 120 C3
Brandenburg Germany 52°25N 12°33E 64 B7
Brandenburg □ Germany 52°50N 13°0E 64 B7
Branderburgh U.K. 57°43N 3°17W 23 G11
Brandon Canada 49°50N 99°57W 108 E10
Brandon Durham, U.K. 54°46N 1°37W 26 C5
Brandon Suffolk, U.K. 52°27N 0°38E 31 B10
Brandon B. Ireland 52°17N 10°8W 20 D2
Brandon Mt. Ireland 52°15N 10°15W 20 D2
Branston U.K. 53°12N 0°27W 27 F8
Brantford Canada 43°10N 80°15W 112 D7
Bras d'Or L. Canada 45°50N 60°50W 113 C17
Brasília Brazil 15°47S 47°55W 122 C1
Braşov Romania 45°38N 25°35E 65 F13
Bratislava Slovak Rep. 48°10N 17°7E 65 D9
Bratsk Russia 56°10N 101°30E 77 D11
Bratsk Res. Russia 56°15N 101°45E 77 D11
Brattleboro U.S.A. 42°51N 72°34W 113 D11
Braunschweig Germany 52°15N 10°31E 64 B6
Braunton U.K. 51°7N 4°10W 29 E5
Bray Ireland 53°13N 6°7W 21 B10
Bray U.K. 51°30N 0°41W 31 D7
Brazil U.S.A. 39°32N 87°8W 112 F4
Brazil ■ S. Amer. 12°0S 50°0W 120 D4
Brazilian Highlands Brazil 18°0S 46°30W 117 E6
Brazos ➔ U.S.A. 28°53N 95°23W 111 E7
Brazzaville Congo 4°9S 15°12E 96 E3
Breadalbane U.K. 56°30N 4°15W 24 A7
Breage U.K. 50°6N 5°20W 29 G3
Breamish ➔ U.K. 55°35N 2°2W 26 A4
Brechin U.K. 56°44N 2°39W 23 J12
Breckland U.K. 52°30N 0°40E 31 B10
Brecon U.K. 51°57N 3°23W 28 D7
Brecon Beacons △ U.K. 51°50N 3°30W 28 D6
Breda Neths. 51°35N 4°45E 64 C3
Brede U.K. 50°56N 0°36E 31 E10
Bredon Hill U.K. 52°3N 2°2W 30 B4
Bregenz Austria 47°30N 9°45E 64 E5
Breiðafjörður Iceland 65°15N 23°15W 63 A1
Bremen Germany 53°4N 8°47E 64 B5
Bremerhaven Germany 53°33N 8°36E 64 B5
Bremerton U.S.A. 47°34N 122°37W 110 A2
Brendon Hills U.K. 51°6N 3°25W 30 D2
Brennerpass Austria 47°2N 11°30E 64 E6
Brent □ U.K. 51°33N 0°16W 31 C8
Brentwood U.K. 51°37N 0°19E 31 C9
Bréscia Italy 45°33N 10°15E 68 B4
Bressay U.K. 60°9N 1°6W 22 B15
Brest Belarus 52°10N 23°40E 65 B12
Brest France 48°24N 4°31W 66 B1
Bretagne □ France 48°10N 3°0W 66 B2
Breton Sd. U.S.A. 29°35N 89°15W 111 E9
Brewer U.S.A. 44°48N 68°46W 113 C13
Brewood U.K. 52°41N 2°9W 27 G4
Briançon France 44°54N 6°39E 66 D7
Bridestowe U.K. 50°41N 4°7W 29 F5
Bridge U.K. 51°15N 1°8E 31 D11
Bridgefield Barbados 13°9N 59°36W 114 c
Bridgend U.K. 51°30N 3°34W 29 D6
Bridgeport U.S.A. 41°11N 73°12W 113 E11
Bridgeton U.S.A. 39°26N 75°14W 113 F10
Bridgetown Barbados 13°6N 59°37W 114 c
Bridgewater Canada 44°25N 64°31W 109 E13
Bridgnorth U.K. 52°32N 2°25W 27 G4
Bridgwater U.K. 51°8N 2°59W 30 D3
Bridgwater B. U.K. 51°15N 3°15W 30 D2
Bridlington U.K. 54°5N 0°12W 26 D8
Bridlington B. U.K. 54°4N 0°10W 27 D8
Bridport U.K. 50°44N 2°45W 30 E3
Brierfield U.K. 53°49N 2°14W 27 E4
Brierley Hill U.K. 52°29N 2°6W 27 H4
Brigg U.K. 53°34N 0°28W 27 E8
Brigham City U.S.A. 41°31N 112°1W 110 B4
Brighouse U.K. 53°42N 1°46W 27 E5
Brighstone U.K. 50°38N 1°23W 30 E6
Brightlingsea U.K. 51°49N 1°2E 31 C11
Brighton U.K. 50°49N 0°7W 31 E8
Brigstock U.K. 52°27N 0°36W 31 B7
Brill U.K. 51°49N 1°1W 30 C6
Brimfield U.K. 52°18N 2°41W 30 B3
Brindisi Italy 40°39N 17°55E 69 D7
Brinklow U.K. 52°25N 1°22W 30 B6
Brinkworth U.K. 51°33N 1°59W 30 C5
Brisbane Australia 27°25S 153°2E 98 F9
Bristol U.K. 51°26N 2°35W 30 D3
Bristol B. U.S.A. 58°0N 160°0W 108 D4
Bristol Channel U.K. 51°18N 4°30W 29 E5
Briston U.K. 52°51N 1°4E 31 A11
British Columbia □ Canada 55°0N 125°15W 108 D7
British Isles Europe 54°0N 4°0W 62 D5
British Virgin Is. ☑ W. Indies 18°30N 64°30W 115 D12
Brittany = Bretagne □ France 48°10N 3°0W 66 B2
Brive-la-Gaillarde France 45°10N 1°32E 66 D4
Brixham U.K. 50°23N 3°31W 29 G6
Brixworth U.K. 52°20N 0°54W 31 B7
Brize Norton U.K. 51°46N 1°34W 30 C5
Brno Czech Rep. 49°10N 16°35E 65 D9
Broad B. U.K. 58°14N 6°18W 22 F5
Broad Chalke U.K. 51°2N 1°56W 30 D5
Broad Haven Ireland 54°20N 9°55W 18 C2
Broad Law U.K. 55°30N 3°21W 25 C9
Broad Sd. U.K. 49°55N 6°21W 29 H1
Broadclyst U.K. 50°46N 3°27W 29 F7
Broadhembury U.K. 50°49N 3°18W 29 F7
Broadstairs U.K. 51°21N 1°27E 31 D11
Broadway U.K. 52°2N 1°50W 30 B5
Broadwindsor U.K. 50°48N 2°47W 30 E3
Brochet Canada 57°53N 101°40W 108 D9
Brock I. Canada 77°52N 114°19W 109 B8
Brocken Germany 51°47N 10°37E 64 C6
Brockenhurst U.K. 50°49N 1°34W 30 E5
Brockville Canada 44°35N 75°41W 113 C10
Brockworth U.K. 51°51N 2°9W 30 C4
Brodeur Pen. Canada 72°30N 88°10W 109 B11
Brodick U.K. 55°35N 5°9W 24 C5
Broken Hill Australia 31°58S 141°29E 98 G7
Bromfield U.K. 52°24N 2°45W 27 H3
Bromham U.K. 51°23N 2°1W 30 D4
Bromley □ U.K. 51°24N 0°2E 31 D9
Brompton U.K. 54°21N 1°25W 26 D6
Bromsgrove U.K. 52°21N 2°2W 30 B4
Bromyard U.K. 52°11N 2°30W 30 B4
Brookings U.S.A. 44°19N 96°48W 111 B7
Brooks Canada 50°35N 111°55W 108 D8
Brooks Range U.S.A. 68°0N 152°0W 108 C5
Broom, L. U.K. 57°55N 5°15W 22 G7
Broome Australia 18°0S 122°15E 98 D3
Broomhill U.K. 55°18N 1°36W 26 B5
Brora U.K. 58°0N 3°52W 23 F10
Brora ➔ U.K. 58°0N 3°51W 23 F10
Broseley U.K. 52°37N 2°29W 27 G4
Brosna ➔ Ireland 53°14N 7°58W 20 B7
Brotherton U.K. 53°0N 0°7W 27 F8
Brotton U.K. 54°35N 0°56W 26 C7
Brough Cumb., U.K. 54°32N 2°18W 26 C4
Brough E. Riding, U.K. 53°44N 0°36W 27 E7
Brough Hd. U.K. 59°8N 3°20W 23 D11
Broughton Borders, U.K. 55°37N 3°24W 25 C9
Broughton N. Lincs., U.K. 53°34N 0°34W 27 E7
Broughton Northants., U.K. 52°22N 0°46W 31 B7
Broughton-in-Furness U.K. 54°17N 3°13W 26 D2
Broughty Ferry U.K. 56°29N 2°51W 25 B10
Brown Willy U.K. 50°35N 4°37W 29 F4
Brownhills U.K. 52°39N 1°54W 27 G5
Brownsville U.S.A. 25°54N 97°30W 111 E7
Brownwood U.S.A. 31°43N 98°59W 110 D7
Broxburn U.K. 55°56N 3°28W 25 C9
Bruay-la-Buissière France 50°29N 2°33E 66 A5
Bruce, Mt. Australia 22°37S 118°8E 98 E2
Brue ➔ U.K. 51°13N 2°59W 30 D3
Brugge Belgium 51°13N 3°13E 64 C2
Brumado Brazil 14°14S 41°40W 122 B2
Brunei ■ Asia 4°50N 115°0E 82 D4
Brunswick Ga., U.S.A. 31°10N 81°30W 111 D10
Brunswick Maine, U.S.A. 43°55N 69°58W 113 D13
Brunton U.K. 55°2N 2°6W 26 B4
Brussels Belgium 50°51N 4°21E 64 C3
Bruton U.K. 51°7N 2°27W 30 D4
Bryan Ohio, U.S.A. 41°28N 84°33W 112 E5
Bryan Tex., U.S.A. 30°40N 96°22W 111 D7
Bryansk Russia 53°13N 34°25E 70 D5
Bryher U.K. 49°57N 6°22W 29 H1
Brynamman U.K. 51°49N 3°51W 28 D6
Brynmawr U.K. 51°48N 3°10W 28 D7
Bucaramanga Colombia 7°0N 73°0W 120 B2
Buchan U.K. 57°32N 2°21W 23 G13
Buchan Ness U.K. 57°29N 1°46W 23 H14
Buchanan Liberia 5°57N 10°2W 94 G3
Bucharest Romania 44°27N 26°10E 65 F14
Buckden U.K. 52°18N 0°14W 31 B8
Buckfastleigh U.K. 50°28N 3°48W 29 G6
Buckhannon U.S.A. 39°0N 80°8W 112 F7
Buckhaven U.K. 56°11N 3°3W 25 B9
Buckie U.K. 57°41N 2°58W 23 G12
Buckingham Canada 45°37N 75°24W 113 C10
Buckingham U.K. 51°59N 0°57W 31 C7
Buckinghamshire □ U.K. 51°53N 0°55W 31 C7
Buckland Brewer U.K. 50°58N 4°15W 29 F5
Buckland Newton U.K. 50°50N 2°26W 30 E4
Buckley U.K. 53°10N 3°5W 28 A7
Budapest Hungary 47°29N 19°3E 65 E10
Bude U.K. 50°49N 4°34W 29 F4
Bude B. U.K. 50°49N 4°35W 29 F4
Budle B. U.K. 55°37N 1°45W 26 A5
Budleigh Salterton U.K. 50°37N 3°19W 29 F7
Buena Vista U.S.A. 37°44N 79°21W 112 G8
Buenaventura Colombia 3°53N 77°4W 120 B2
Buenos Aires Argentina 34°36S 58°22W 121 F4
Buffalo N.Y., U.S.A. 42°53N 78°53W 112 D8
Buffalo Wyo., U.S.A. 44°21N 106°42W 110 B5
Bug ➔ Poland 52°31N 21°5E 65 B11
Bug ➔ Ukraine 46°59N 31°58E 71 E5
Bugle U.K. 50°24N 4°47W 29 G4
Bugulma Russia 54°33N 52°48E 70 D9
Buguruslan Russia 53°39N 52°26E 70 D9
Builth Wells U.K. 52°9N 3°25W 28 C7
Buir Nur Mongolia 47°50N 117°42E 79 B12
Buji China 22°37N 114°5E 79 a
Bujumbura Burundi 3°16S 29°18E 96 E5
Bukavu Dem. Rep. of the Congo 2°20S 28°52E 96 E5
Bukhara Uzbekistan 39°48N 64°25E 87 B11
Bukittinggi Indonesia 0°20S 100°20E 82 E2
Bulawayo Zimbabwe 20°7S 28°32E 97 J5
Bulford U.K. 51°11N 1°45W 30 D5
Bulgaria ■ Europe 42°35N 25°30E 69 C11
Bullhead City U.S.A. 35°8N 114°32W 110 C4
Bunbury Australia 33°20S 115°35E 98 G2
Bunclody Ireland 52°39N 6°40W 21 C9
Buncrana Ireland 55°8N 7°27W 18 A7
Bundaberg Australia 24°54S 152°22E 98 E9
Bundi India 25°30N 75°35E 84 G9
Bundoran Ireland 54°28N 8°18W 18 C5
Bungay U.K. 52°27N 1°28E 31 B11
Buntingford U.K. 51°56N 0°0 31 C9
Bunwell U.K. 52°30N 1°9E 31 A11
Buon Ma Thuot Vietnam 12°40N 108°3E 82 B3
Bûr Safâga Egypt 26°43N 33°57E 95 C12
Buraydah Si. Arabia 26°20N 43°59E 86 E5
Burbage Derby, U.K. 53°15N 1°55W 27 F5
Burbage Leics., U.K. 52°32N 1°21W 27 G6
Burbage Wilts., U.K. 51°21N 1°39W 30 D5
Burco Somalia 9°32N 45°32E 89 F4
Burdur Turkey 37°45N 30°17E 71 G5
Bure ➔ U.K. 52°38N 1°43E 31 A12
Burford U.K. 51°49N 1°38W 30 C5
Burgas Bulgaria 42°33N 27°29E 69 C12
Burgess Hill U.K. 50°58N 0°6W 31 E8
Burgh le Marsh U.K. 53°9N 0°15E 27 F9
Burghead U.K. 57°43N 3°30W 23 G11
Burgos Spain 42°21N 3°41W 67 A4
Burgundy = Bourgogne □ France 47°0N 4°50E 66 C6
Burhanpur India 21°18N 76°14E 84 J10
Burica, Pta. Costa Rica 8°3N 82°51W 104 J11
Burkina Faso ■ Africa 12°0N 1°0W 94 F5
Burley Hants., U.K. 50°49N 1°43W 30 E5
Burley W. Yorks., U.K. 53°54N 1°45W 27 E5
Burley U.S.A. 42°32N 113°48W 110 B4
Burlington Colo., U.S.A. 39°18N 102°16W 110 C6
Burlington Iowa, U.S.A. 40°49N 91°14W 111 B8
Burlington Vt., U.S.A. 44°29N 73°12W 113 C11
Burlington Wis., U.S.A. 42°41N 88°17W 112 D3
Burma ■ Asia 21°0N 96°30E 85 J20
Burnham Market U.K. 52°57N 0°44E 31 A10
Burnham-on-Crouch U.K. 51°38N 0°49E 31 C10
Burnham-on-Sea U.K. 51°14N 3°0W 30 D2
Burnie Australia 41°4S 145°56E 98 J8

Burnley   Cheshire East

Burnley *U.K.* 53°47N 2°14W **27** E4
Burnmouth *U.K.* 55°50N 2°4W **25** C11
Burns *U.S.A.* 43°35N 119°3W **110** B3
Burnside → *Canada* 66°51N 108°4W **108** C9
Burntisland *U.K.* 56°4N 3°13W **25** B9
Burqin *China* 47°43N 87°0E **78** B6
Burray *U.K.* 58°51N 2°54W **23** E12
Burren △ *Ireland* 53°1N 8°58W **20** B4
Burrow Hd. *U.K.* 54°41N 4°24W **24** E7
Burry Port *U.K.* 51°41N 4°15W **28** D5
Bursa *Turkey* 40°15N 29°5E **71** F4
Burstwick *U.K.* 53°44N 0°8W **27** E8
Burton *U.K.* 54°11N 2°43W **26** D3
Burton Agnes *U.K.* 54°4N 0°18W **26** D8
Burton Bradstock *U.K.* 50°42N 2°43W **30** E3
Burton Fleming *U.K.* 54°8N 0°20W **26** D8
Burton Latimer *U.K.* 52°22N 0°41W **31** B7
Burton upon Stather *U.K.* 53°39N 0°41W **27** E7
Burton upon Trent *U.K.* 52°48N 1°38W **27** G5
Buru *Indonesia* 3°30S 126°30E **83** E7
Burundi ■ *Africa* 3°15S 30°0E **96** E5
Burwash *U.K.* 50°59N 0°23E **31** E9
Burwell *U.K.* 52°17N 0°20E **31** B9
Burwick *U.K.* 58°45N 2°58W **23** E12
Bury *U.K.* 53°35N 2°17W **27** E4
Bury St. Edmunds *U.K.* 52°15N 0°43E **31** B10
Buryatia □ *Russia* 53°0N 110°0E **77** D11
Busan *S. Korea* 35°5N 129°0E **79** D14
Büshehr *Iran* 28°55N 50°55E **87** D7
Bushey *U.K.* 51°38N 0°22W **31** C8
Busto Arsízio *Italy* 45°37N 8°51E **68** B3
Buta *Dem. Rep. of the Congo* 2°50N 24°53E **96** D4
Butare *Rwanda* 2°31S 29°52E **96** E5
Butaritari *Kiribati* 3°30N 174°0E **102** G9
Bute *U.K.* 55°48N 5°2W **24** C5
Bute, Kyles of *U.K.* 55°55N 5°10W **24** C5
Butembo *Dem. Rep. of the Congo* 0°9N 29°18E **96** D5
Butler *U.S.A.* 40°52N 79°54W **112** E8
Buton *Indonesia* 5°0S 122°45E **83** E6
Butte *U.S.A.* 46°0N 112°32W **110** A4
Buttermere *U.K.* 54°32N 3°16W **26** C2
Butterworth *Malaysia* 5°24N 100°23E **82** C2
Buttevant *Ireland* 52°14N 8°40W **20** D5
Butuan *Phil.* 8°57N 125°33E **83** C7
Buurhakaba *Somalia* 3°12N 44°20E **89** G3
Buxton *U.K.* 53°16N 1°54W **27** F5
Buyant-Uhaa *Mongolia* 44°55N 110°11E **79** C11
Buzău *Romania* 45°10N 26°50E **65** F14
Buzuluk *Russia* 52°48N 52°12E **70** D9
Bydgoszcz *Poland* 53°10N 18°0E **65** B9
Byfield *U.K.* 52°10N 1°14W **30** B6
Bylot I. *Canada* 73°13N 78°34W **109** B12
Byrranga Ra. *Russia* 75°0N 100°0E **77** B11
Bytom *Poland* 50°25N 18°54E **65** C10

C

Ca Mau *Vietnam* 9°7N 105°8E **82** C3
Cabanatuan *Phil.* 15°30N 120°58E **83** A6
Cabedelo *Brazil* 7°0S 34°50W **120** C6
Cabimas *Venezuela* 10°23N 71°25W **120** A2
Cabinda *Angola* 5°33S 12°11E **96** F2
Cabinda □ *Angola* 5°0S 12°30E **96** F2
Cabo Frio *Brazil* 22°51S 42°3W **122** D2
Cabo San Lucas *Mexico* 22°53N 109°54W **114** C3
Cabonga, Réservoir *Canada* 47°20N 76°40W **109** E12
Cabora Bassa Dam *Mozam.* 15°20S 32°50E **97** H6
Cabot Str. *Canada* 47°15N 59°40W **109** E14
Čačak *Serbia* 43°54N 20°20E **69** C9
Cáceres *Brazil* 16°5S 57°40W **120** D4
Cáceres *Spain* 39°26N 6°23W **67** C2
Cachimbo, Serra do *Brazil* 9°30S 55°30W **120** C4
Cachoeira *Brazil* 12°30S 39°0W **122** B3
Cachoeira do Sul *Brazil* 30°3S 52°53W **121** F4
Cachoeiro de Itapemirim
   Brazil 20°51S 41°7W **122** D2
Cader Idris *U.K.* 52°42N 3°53W **28** B6
Cadillac *U.S.A.* 44°15N 85°24W **112** C5
Cádiz *Spain* 36°30N 6°20W **67** D2
Cádiz, G. de *Spain* 36°40N 7°0W **67** D2
Caen *France* 49°10N 0°22W **66** B3
Caenby Corner *U.K.* 53°24N 0°33W **27** F7
Caerdydd = Cardiff *U.K.* 51°29N 3°10W **29** F7
Caerfyrddin = Carmarthen
   U.K. 51°52N 4°19W **28** D5
Caergybi = Holyhead *U.K.* 53°18N 4°38W **28** A4
Caernarfon *U.K.* 53°8N 4°16W **28** A5
Caernarfon B. *U.K.* 53°4N 4°40W **28** A4
Caerphilly *U.K.* 51°35N 3°13W **29** D7
Caersws *U.K.* 52°31N 3°26W **28** B7
Caeté *Brazil* 19°55S 43°40W **122** C2
Caetité *Brazil* 13°50S 42°32W **122** D2
Cagayan de Oro *Phil.* 8°30N 124°40E **83** C6
Cágliari *Italy* 39°13N 9°7E **68** E3
Caguas *Puerto Rico* 18°14N 66°2W **115** D11
Caha Mts. *Ireland* 51°45N 9°40W **20** E3
Cahir *Ireland* 52°22N 7°56W **20** D7
Cahirciveen *Ireland* 51°56N 10°14W **20** E2
Cahore Pt. *Ireland* 52°33N 6°12W **21** C10
Cahors *France* 44°27N 1°27E **66** D4
Cairn Gorm *U.K.* 57°7N 3°39W **23** H10
Cairngorm Mts. *U.K.* 57°6N 3°42W **23** H10
Cairngorms △ *U.K.* 57°10N 3°50W **23** H11
Cairnryan *U.K.* 54°59N 5°1W **24** E5
Cairns *Australia* 16°57S 145°45E **98** D8
Cairnsmore of Fleet *U.K.* 54°59N 4°20W **24** E7
Cairo *Egypt* 30°2N 31°13E **95** B12
Cairo *U.S.A.* 37°0N 89°11W **112** G3
Caister-on-Sea *U.K.* 52°40N 1°43E **31** A12
Caistor *U.K.* 53°30N 0°18W **27** E8
Caithness *U.K.* 58°25N 3°35W **23** F10
Caithness, Ord of *U.K.* 58°8N 3°36W **23** F10
Cajamarca *Peru* 7°5S 78°28W **120** C2
Calabar *Nigeria* 4°57N 8°20E **94** H7
Calábria □ *Italy* 39°0N 16°30E **68** E7
Calais *France* 50°57N 1°56E **66** A4
Calais *U.S.A.* 45°11N 67°17W **113** C14
Calama *Chile* 22°30S 68°55W **121** E3
Calamian Group *Phil.* 11°50N 119°55E **83** B5
Calanscio, Sarir *Libya* 27°30N 22°30E **95** C10
Calapan *Phil.* 13°25N 121°7E **83** B6

Calbayog *Phil.* 12°4N 124°38E **83** B6
Calcutta = Kolkata *India* 22°34N 88°21E **85** H16
Caldbeck *U.K.* 54°45N 3°3W **26** C2
Calder → *U.K.* 53°44N 1°22W **27** E6
Calder Bridge *U.K.* 54°27N 3°29W **26** D2
Caldera *Chile* 27°5S 70°55W **121** E2
Caldew → *U.K.* 54°54N 2°56W **26** C3
Caldwell *U.S.A.* 43°40N 116°41W **110** B3
Caledonian Canal *U.K.* 57°29N 4°15W **23** H9
Calgary *Canada* 51°0N 114°10W **108** D8
Cali *Colombia* 3°25N 76°35W **120** B2
Calicut *India* 11°15N 75°43E **84** P9
California □ *U.S.A.* 37°30N 119°30W **110** C2
California, G. de *Mexico* 27°0N 111°0W **114** B2
Callan *Ireland* 52°32N 7°24W **21** C8
Callander *U.K.* 56°15N 4°13W **24** B7
Callao *Peru* 12°3S 77°8W **120** D2
Calne *U.K.* 51°26N 2°0W **30** D5
Calshot *U.K.* 50°48N 1°19W **30** E6
Calstock *U.K.* 50°30N 4°13W **29** F5
Caltanissetta *Italy* 37°29N 14°4E **68** F6
Calvi *France* 42°34N 8°45E **66** E8
Calvinia *S. Africa* 31°28S 19°45E **97** L3
Cam → *U.K.* 52°21N 0°16E **31** B9
Cam Ranh *Vietnam* 11°54N 109°12E **82** B3
Camagüey *Cuba* 21°20N 77°55W **115** C9
Camargue *France* 43°34N 4°34E **66** E6
Camberley *U.K.* 51°20N 0°44W **31** D7
Cambo *U.K.* 55°10N 1°57W **26** B5
Cambodia ■ *Asia* 12°15N 105°0E **82** B3
Camborne *U.K.* 50°12N 5°19W **29** G3
Cambrai *France* 50°11N 3°14E **66** A5
Cambrian Mts. *U.K.* 52°3N 3°57W **28** C6
Cambridge *Jamaica* 18°18N 77°54W **114** a
Cambridge *U.K.* 52°12N 0°8E **31** B9
Cambridge *Mass., U.S.A.* 42°23N 71°7W **113** D12
Cambridge *Md., U.S.A.* 38°34N 76°5W **113** F9
Cambridge *Ohio, U.S.A.* 40°2N 81°35W **112** E7
Cambridge Bay *Canada* 69°10N 105°0W **108** C9
Cambridgeshire □ *U.K.* 52°25N 0°7W **31** B8
Camden *Ark., U.S.A.* 33°35N 92°50W **111** D8
Camden *N.J., U.S.A.* 39°55N 75°7W **113** F10
Camden □ *U.K.* 51°32N 0°8W **31** C8
Camel → *U.K.* 50°31N 4°51W **29** F4
Camelford *U.K.* 50°37N 4°42W **29** F4
Cameroon ■ *Africa* 6°0N 12°30E **96** C2
Cameroun, Mt. *Cameroon* 4°13N 9°10E **96** D1
Cametá *Brazil* 2°12S 49°30W **120** C5
Camocim *Brazil* 2°55S 40°50W **120** C5
Campana, I. *Chile* 48°20S 75°20W **121** G2
Campánia □ *Italy* 41°0N 14°30E **68** D6
Campbell I. *Pac. Oc.* 52°30S 169°0E **102** N8
Campbell River *Canada* 50°5N 125°20W **108** D7
Campbellton *Canada* 47°57N 66°43W **109** E13
Campbelltown *U.K.* 55°26N 5°36W **24** D4
Campeche *Mexico* 19°51N 90°32W **114** D6
Campeche, Golfo de *Mexico* 19°30N 93°0W **114** D6
Campina Grande *Brazil* 7°20S 35°47W **120** C6
Campinas *Brazil* 22°50S 47°0W **122** D1
Campo Belo *Brazil* 20°52S 45°16W **122** D1
Campo Grande *Brazil* 20°25S 54°40W **120** E4
Campobasso *Italy* 41°34N 14°39E **68** D6
Campos *Brazil* 21°50S 41°20W **122** D2
Campos Belos *Brazil* 13°10S 47°3W **122** B1
Camrose *Canada* 53°0N 112°50W **108** D8
Can Tho *Vietnam* 10°2N 105°46E **82** B3
Canada ■ *N. Amer.* 60°0N 100°0W **108** C10
Canadian → *U.S.A.* 35°28N 95°3W **111** C7
Canadian Shield *Canada* 53°0N 75°0W **104** D12
Çanakkale *Turkey* 40°8N 26°24E **71** F4
Canandaigua *U.S.A.* 42°54N 77°17W **112** D9
Cananea *Mexico* 31°0N 110°18W **114** A2
Canaries *St. Lucia* 13°55N 61°4W **114** b
Canary Is. *Atl. Oc.* 28°30N 16°0W **94** C2
Canaveral, C. *U.S.A.* 28°27N 80°32W **111** E10
Canavieiras *Brazil* 15°39S 39°0W **122** C3
Canberra *Australia* 35°15S 149°8E **98** H8
Cancún *Mexico* 21°8N 86°44W **114** C7
Cangzhou *China* 38°19N 116°52E **79** D12
Caniapiscau → *Canada* 56°40N 69°30W **109** D13
Caniapiscau, L. *Canada* 54°10N 69°55W **109** D13
Çankırı *Turkey* 40°40N 33°37E **71** F5
Canna *U.K.* 57°3N 6°33W **22** H4
Canna, Sd. of *U.K.* 57°1N 6°30W **22** H5
Cannanore *India* 11°53N 75°27E **84** P9
Cannes *France* 43°32N 7°1E **66** E7
Cannington *U.K.* 51°9N 3°4W **30** D2
Cannock *U.K.* 52°41N 2°1W **27** G4
Cannock Chase *U.K.* 52°44N 2°4W **27** G4
Canoas *Brazil* 29°56S 51°11W **121** E4
Cañon City *U.S.A.* 38°27N 105°14W **110** C5
Canonbie *U.K.* 55°5N 2°58W **25** D10
Canora *Canada* 51°40N 102°30W **108** D9
Canso *Canada* 45°20N 61°0W **113** C17
Cantabria □ *Spain* 43°10N 4°0W **67** A4
Cantábrica, Cordillera *Spain* 43°0N 5°10W **67** A3
Canterbury *U.K.* 51°16N 1°6E **31** D11
Canton = Guangzhou *China* 23°6N 113°13E **79** G11
Canton *Ill., U.S.A.* 40°33N 90°2W **112** E2
Canton *N.Y., U.S.A.* 44°36N 75°10W **113** C10
Canton *Ohio, U.S.A.* 40°48N 81°23W **112** E7
Canvey *U.K.* 51°31N 0°37E **31** C10
Cap-de-la-Madeleine
   Canada 46°22N 72°31W **113** B11
Cap-Haïtien *Haiti* 19°40N 72°20W **115** D10
Cap Pt. *St. Lucia* 14°7N 60°57W **114** b
Cape Breton I. *Canada* 46°0N 60°30W **113** C17
Cape Charles *U.S.A.* 37°16N 76°1W **113** G10
Cape Coast *Ghana* 5°5N 1°15W **94** G5
Cape Coral *U.S.A.* 26°33N 81°57W **111** E10
Cape Fear → *U.S.A.* 33°53N 78°1W **111** D11
Cape Girardeau *U.S.A.* 37°19N 89°32W **112** G3
Cape May *U.S.A.* 38°56N 74°56W **113** F10
Cape Town *S. Africa* 33°55S 18°22E **97** L3
Cape Verde Is. ■ *Atl. Oc.* 16°0N 24°0W **91** E1
Cape York Peninsula
   Australia 12°0S 142°30E **98** C7
Capela *Brazil* 10°30S 37°0W **122** B3
Capreol *Canada* 46°43N 80°56W **112** B7
Capri *Italy* 40°33N 14°14E **68** D6

Caprivi Strip *Namibia* 18°0S 23°0E **97** H4
Caquetá → *Colombia* 1°15S 69°15W **120** C3
Caracas *Venezuela* 10°30N 66°55W **120** A3
Caracol *Brazil* 9°15S 43°22W **122** A2
Carangola *Brazil* 20°44S 42°5W **122** D2
Caratasca, L. de *Honduras* 15°20N 83°40W **115** D8
Caratinga *Brazil* 19°50S 42°10W **122** C2
Caravelas *Brazil* 17°45S 39°15W **122** C3
Carbón, L. del *Argentina* 49°35S 68°21W **121** G3
Carbondale *Ill., U.S.A.* 37°44N 89°13W **112** G3
Carbondale *Pa., U.S.A.* 41°35N 75°30W **113** E10
Carbonear *Canada* 47°42N 53°13W **109** E14
Carcassonne *France* 43°13N 2°20E **66** E5
Carcross *Canada* 60°13N 134°45W **108** C6
Cardamon Hills *India* 9°30N 77°15E **84** Q10
Cárdenas *Cuba* 23°0N 81°30W **115** C8
Cardiff *U.K.* 51°29N 3°10W **29** E7
Cardigan *U.K.* 52°5N 4°40W **28** C4
Cardigan B. *U.K.* 52°30N 4°30W **28** B4
Cardington *U.K.* 52°6N 0°25W **31** B8
Cardston *Canada* 49°15N 113°20W **108** E8
Cariacica *Brazil* 20°16S 40°25W **122** D2
Caribbean Sea *W. Indies* 15°0N 75°0W **115** E10
Cariboo Mts. *Canada* 53°0N 121°0W **108** D7
Caribou *U.S.A.* 46°52N 68°1W **113** B13
Caribou Mts. *Canada* 59°12N 115°40W **108** D8
Carinhanha *Brazil* 14°15S 44°46W **122** B2
Carinhanha → *Brazil* 14°20S 43°47W **122** B2
Carinthia = Kärnten □
   Austria 46°52N 13°30E **64** E8
Carisbrooke *U.K.* 50°41N 1°19W **30** E6
Cark *U.K.* 54°11N 2°58W **26** D3
Carleton Place *Canada* 45°8N 76°9W **113** C10
Carleton Rode *U.K.* 52°30N 1°7E **31** A11
Carlingford L. *U.K.* 54°3N 6°9W **19** B9
Carlinville *U.S.A.* 39°17N 89°53W **112** F3
Carlisle *U.K.* 54°54N 2°56W **26** C3
Carlisle *U.S.A.* 40°12N 77°12W **112** E9
Carlisle B. *Barbados* 13°5N 59°37W **114** c
Carlops *U.K.* 55°47N 3°20W **25** D9
Carlow *Ireland* 52°50N 6°56W **21** C9
Carlow □ *Ireland* 52°43N 6°50W **21** C9
Carlsbad *U.S.A.* 32°25N 104°14W **110** D6
Carlton *U.K.* 52°59N 1°5W **27** G6
Carlton Colville *U.K.* 52°27N 1°43E **31** B12
Carlton Miniott *U.K.* 54°12N 1°22W **26** D5
Carluke *U.K.* 55°45N 3°50W **25** C8
Carmacks *Canada* 62°5N 136°16W **108** C6
Carman *Canada* 49°30N 98°0W **108** D10
Carmarthen *U.K.* 51°52N 4°19W **28** D5
Carmarthen B. *U.K.* 51°40N 4°30W **28** D5
Carmarthenshire □ *U.K.* 51°55N 4°13W **28** D5
Carmaux *France* 44°3N 2°10E **66** D5
Carmi *U.S.A.* 38°5N 88°10W **112** F3
Carn Ban *U.K.* 57°7N 4°15W **23** H9
Carn Eige *U.K.* 57°17N 5°8W **22** H7
Carnarvon *Australia* 24°51S 113°42E **98** E1
Carnarvon *S. Africa* 30°56S 22°8E **97** L4
Carndonagh *Ireland* 55°16N 7°15W **19** A7
Carnegie, L. *Australia* 26°5S 122°30E **98** F3
Carnforth *U.K.* 54°7N 2°45W **26** D3
Carno *U.K.* 52°34N 3°30W **28** B6
Carnoustie *U.K.* 56°30N 2°42W **25** B10
Carnsore Pt. *Ireland* 52°10N 6°22W **21** D10
Caro *U.S.A.* 43°29N 83°24W **112** D6
Caroline I. *Kiribati* 9°58S 150°13W **103** H12
Caroline Is. *Micronesia* 8°0N 150°0E **102** G6
Carondelet Reef *Kiribati* 5°33S 173°50E **99** B16
Caroní → *Venezuela* 8°21N 62°43W **120** B3
Carpathians *Europe* 49°30N 21°0E **65** D11
Carpentaria, G. of *Australia* 14°0S 139°0E **98** C6
Carpentras *France* 44°3N 5°2E **66** D6
Carpi *Italy* 44°47N 10°53E **68** B4
Carraúntoohill *Ireland* 52°0N 9°45W **20** E3
Carrick-on-Shannon *Ireland* 53°57N 8°7W **18** D5
Carrick-on-Suir *Ireland* 52°21N 7°24W **21** D8
Carrickfergus *U.K.* 54°43N 5°49W **19** B10
Carrickmacross *Ireland* 53°59N 6°43W **19** D8
Carrigaline *Ireland* 51°48N 8°23W **20** E6
Carrollton *U.S.A.* 39°18N 90°24W **112** F2
Carron → *U.K.* 57°53N 4°22W **23** H9
Carron, L. *U.K.* 57°22N 5°35W **22** H6
Carson City *U.S.A.* 39°10N 119°46W **110** C3
Carson Sink *U.S.A.* 39°50N 118°25W **110** C3
Cartagena *Colombia* 10°25N 75°33W **120** A2
Cartagena *Spain* 37°38N 0°59W **67** D5
Cartago *Colombia* 4°45N 75°55W **120** B2
Carthage *Tunisia* 36°52N 10°20E **95** A8
Cartmel *U.K.* 54°12N 2°57W **26** D2
Cartwright *Canada* 53°41N 56°58W **109** D14
Caruaru *Brazil* 8°15S 35°55W **122** A3
Carúpano *Venezuela* 10°39N 63°15W **120** A3
Cas-gwent = Chepstow *U.K.* 51°38N 2°41W **28** D8
Casa Grande *U.S.A.* 32°53N 111°45W **110** D4
Casa Nova *Brazil* 9°25S 41°5W **122** A2
Casablanca *Morocco* 33°36N 7°36W **94** B4
Cascade Ra. *U.S.A.* 47°0N 121°30W **110** A2
Cascavel *Ceará, Brazil* 4°7S 38°14W **120** C6
Cascavel *Paraná, Brazil* 24°57S 53°28W **121** E4
Caserta *Italy* 41°4N 14°20E **68** D6
Cashel *Ireland* 52°30N 7°53W **20** D7
Casiquiare → *Venezuela* 2°1N 67°7W **120** B3
Casnewydd = Newport *U.K.* 51°35N 3°0W **29** D8
Casper *U.S.A.* 42°51N 106°19W **110** B5
Caspian Depression *Eurasia* 47°0N 48°0E **71** E8
Caspian Sea *Eurasia* 43°0N 50°0E **71** F9
Cassiar Mts. *Canada* 59°30N 130°30W **108** D6
Castell-Nedd = Neath *U.K.* 51°39N 3°48W **28** D6
Castellammare di Stábia *Italy* 40°42N 14°29E **68** D6
Castelló de la Plana *Spain* 39°58N 0°3W **67** C5
Castelsarrasin *France* 44°2N 1°7E **66** E4
Castilla-La Mancha □ *Spain* 39°30N 3°30W **67** C4
Castilla y Leon □ *Spain* 42°0N 5°0W **67** B3
Castle Acre *U.K.* 52°42N 0°42E **31** A10
Castle Cary *U.K.* 51°6N 2°31W **30** D3
Castle Donington *U.K.* 52°51N 1°20W **27** G6
Castle Douglas *U.K.* 54°56N 3°56W **25** E8
Castlebar *Ireland* 53°52N 9°18W **18** D2
Castlebay *U.K.* 56°57N 7°31W **22** J2
Castleblayney *Ireland* 54°7N 6°44W **19** C8
Castlederg *U.K.* 54°42N 7°36W **18** B6

Castleford *U.K.* 53°43N 1°21W **27** E6
Castlemaine Harbour *Ireland* 52°8N 9°50W **20** D3
Castlepollard *Ireland* 53°41N 7°19W **18** D7
Castlerea *Ireland* 53°46N 8°29W **18** D5
Castleside *U.K.* 54°50N 1°52W **26** C5
Castleton *Derby., U.K.* 53°22N 1°46W **27** F5
Castleton *N. Yorks., U.K.* 54°28N 0°57W **26** D7
Castletown *I. of Man* 54°5N 4°38W **19** C12
Castletown Bearhaven *Ireland* 51°39N 9°55W **20** E3
Castries *St. Lucia* 14°2N 60°58W **114** b
Castro *Chile* 42°30S 73°50W **121** G2
Castro Alves *Brazil* 12°46S 39°33W **122** B3
Cat I. *Bahamas* 24°30N 75°30W **115** C9
Cataguases *Brazil* 21°23S 42°39W **122** D2
Catalão *Brazil* 18°10S 47°57W **122** C1
Cataluña □ *Spain* 41°40N 1°15E **67** B6
Catamarca *Argentina* 28°30S 65°50W **121** E3
Catanduanes *Phil.* 13°50N 124°20E **83** B6
Catanduva *Brazil* 21°5S 48°58W **122** D1
Catánia *Italy* 37°30N 15°6E **68** F6
Catanzaro *Italy* 38°54N 16°35E **68** E7
Catcleugh *U.K.* 55°20N 2°24W **26** B4
Caterham *U.K.* 51°15N 0°4W **31** D8
Catoche, C. *Mexico* 21°35N 87°5W **114** C7
Caton *U.K.* 54°5N 2°42W **26** D3
Catsfield *U.K.* 50°54N 0°28E **31** E9
Catskill *U.S.A.* 42°14N 73°52W **113** D11
Catskill Mts. *U.S.A.* 42°10N 74°25W **113** D10
Catterick *U.K.* 54°23N 1°37W **26** D5
Catterick Camp *U.K.* 54°22N 1°42W **26** D5
Catton *U.K.* 54°55N 2°15W **26** C4
Cauca → *Colombia* 8°54N 74°28W **120** B2
Caucaia *Brazil* 3°40S 38°35W **120** C6
Caucasus Mountains *Eurasia* 42°50N 44°0E **71** F7
Caulkerbush *U.K.* 54°54N 3°41W **25** E9
Caura → *Venezuela* 7°38N 64°53W **120** B3
Causeway *India* 11°9N 78°52E **84** P11
Cauvery → *India* 11°9N 78°52E **84** P11
Cavan *Ireland* 54°0N 7°22W **18** D7
Cavan □ *Ireland* 54°1N 7°16W **19** C7
Caviana, I. *Brazil* 0°10N 50°10W **120** B4
Cawood *U.K.* 53°50N 1°8W **27** E6
Cawston *U.K.* 52°47N 1°9E **31** A11
Caxias *Brazil* 4°55S 43°20W **120** C5
Caxias do Sul *Brazil* 29°10S 51°10W **121** E4
Cayenne *Fr. Guiana* 5°5N 52°18W **120** B4
Cayman Brac *W. Indies* 19°40N 80°30W **115** D8
Cayman Trench *Caribbean* 17°0N 83°0W **115** D8
Cayuga L. *U.S.A.* 42°41N 76°41W **112** D9
Ceará □ *Brazil* 5°0S 40°0W **120** C6
Cebu *Phil.* 10°18N 123°54E **83** B6
Cedar City *U.S.A.* 37°41N 113°4W **110** C4
Cedar L. *Canada* 53°10N 100°0W **108** D10
Cedar Rapids *U.S.A.* 41°59N 91°40W **111** B8
Cefalù *Italy* 38°2N 14°1E **68** E6
Cegléd *Hungary* 47°11N 19°47E **65** E10
Celaya *Mexico* 20°31N 100°37W **114** C4
Celebes Sea *Indonesia* 3°0N 123°0E **83** D6
Celina *U.S.A.* 40°33N 84°35W **112** E5
Cellar Hd. *U.K.* 58°25N 6°11W **22** F5
Celtic Sea *Atl. Oc.* 50°9N 9°34W **62** F2
Cemaes *U.K.* 53°24N 4°27W **28** A5
Central, Cordillera *Colombia* 5°0N 75°0W **117** C3
Central African Rep. ■ *Africa* 7°0N 20°0E **96** C4
Central America *America* 12°0N 85°0W **104** H11
Central Bedfordshire □ *U.K.* 52°5N 0°20W **31** B8
Central Makran Range
   Pakistan 26°30N 64°15E **84** F4
Central Russian Uplands
   Europe 54°0N 36°0E **56** E13
Central Siberian Plateau
   Russia 65°0N 105°0E **72** B12
Centralia *Ill., U.S.A.* 38°32N 89°8W **112** F3
Centralia *Wash., U.S.A.* 46°43N 122°58W **110** A2
Cephalonia = Kefalonia
   Greece 38°15N 20°30E **69** E9
Ceredigion □ *U.K.* 52°16N 4°15W **28** C5
Cerignola *Italy* 41°17N 15°53E **68** D6
Cerne Abbas *U.K.* 50°49N 2°29W **30** E4
Cerrigydrudion *U.K.* 53°1N 3°35W **28** A6
Cerro de Pasco *Peru* 10°45S 76°10W **120** D2
Cesena *Italy* 44°8N 12°15E **68** B5
České Budějovice *Czech Rep.* 48°55N 14°25E **64** D8
Çeşme *Turkey* 38°20N 26°23E **71** G4
Ceuta *N. Afr.* 35°52N 5°18W **67** E3
Ceve-i-Ra *Fiji* 21°46S 174°31E **99** E13
Cévennes *France* 44°10N 3°50E **66** D5
Chacewater *U.K.* 50°15N 5°11W **29** G3
Chachapoyas *Peru* 6°15S 77°50W **120** C2
Chaco Austral *S. Amer.* 27°0S 61°30W **121** E3
Chaco Boreal *S. Amer.* 22°0S 60°0W **121** E4
Chaco Central *S. Amer.* 24°0S 61°0W **121** E3
Chad ■ *Africa* 15°0N 17°15E **95** F8
Chad, L. *Chad* 13°30N 14°30E **95** F8
Chadron *U.S.A.* 42°50N 103°0W **110** B6
Chagford *U.K.* 50°40N 3°50W **29** F6
Chaghcharān *Afghan.* 34°31N 65°15E **87** C11
Chagos Arch. ☑ *Ind. Oc.* 6°0S 72°0E **53** E13
Chäh Bahār *India* 29°30N 64°0E **87** D10
Chakradharpur *India* 22°45N 85°40E **85** H14
Chaleur B. *Canada* 47°55N 65°30W **113** B15
Chalisgaon *India* 20°30N 75°10E **84** J9
Challenger Deep *Pac. Oc.* 11°30N 142°0E **102** F6
Chalon-sur-Saône *France* 46°48N 4°50E **66** C6
Châlons-en-Champagne
   France 48°58N 4°20E **66** B6
Chambal → *India* 26°29N 79°15E **84** F11
Chambersburg *U.S.A.* 39°56N 77°40W **112** F9
Chambéry *France* 45°34N 5°55E **66** D6
Chamonix-Mont Blanc *France* 45°55N 6°51E **66** D7
Champagne *France* 48°40N 4°20E **66** B6
Champaign *U.S.A.* 40°7N 88°15W **112** E3
Champlain, L. *U.S.A.* 44°40N 73°20W **113** C11
Chañaral *Chile* 26°23S 70°40W **121** E2
Chancery Lane *Barbados* 13°3N 59°30W **114** c
Chandigarh *India* 30°43N 76°47E **84** D10
Chandler's Ford *U.K.* 50°59N 1°22W **30** E6
Chandpur *Bangla.* 23°8N 90°45E **85** H17
Chandrapur *India* 19°57N 79°25E **84** K11
Changbai Shan *China* 42°20N 129°0E **79** C14
Changchun *China* 43°57N 125°17E **79** C14

Changde *China* 29°4N 111°35E **79** F11
Changhua *Taiwan* 24°2N 120°30E **79** G13
Changji *China* 44°1N 87°19E **78** C6
Changsha *China* 28°12N 113°0E **79** F11
Changzhi *China* 36°10N 113°6E **79** D11
Changzhou *China* 31°47N 119°58E **79** E12
Chania *Greece* 35°30N 24°4E **69** G11
Channel Is. □ *U.K.* 49°19N 2°24W **29** J9
Channel Is. *U.S.A.* 33°40N 119°15W **110** D2
Channel-Port aux Basques
   Canada 47°30N 59°9W **109** E14
Chantrey Inlet *Canada* 67°48N 96°20W **108** C10
Chaoyang *China* 41°35N 120°22E **79** C13
Chaozhou *China* 23°42N 116°32E **79** G12
Chapala, L. de *Mexico* 20°15N 103°0W **114** C4
Chapayevsk *Russia* 53°0N 49°40E **70** D8
Chapel en le Frith *U.K.* 53°20N 1°54W **27** F5
Chapel St. Leonards *U.K.* 53°13N 0°20E **27** F9
Chapleau *Canada* 47°50N 83°24W **109** E11
Charaña *Bolivia* 17°30S 69°25W **120** D3
Chard *U.K.* 50°52N 2°58W **30** E3
Chari → *Chad* 12°58N 14°31E **95** F8
Chārīkār *Afghan.* 35°0N 69°10E **87** C12
Charing *U.K.* 51°12N 0°49E **31** D10
Charlbury *U.K.* 51°53N 1°28W **30** C6
Charleroi *Belgium* 50°24N 4°27E **64** C3
Charles, C. *U.S.A.* 37°7N 75°58W **113** G10
Charles City *U.S.A.* 43°4N 92°41W **111** B8
Charleston *Ill., U.S.A.* 39°30N 88°10W **112** F3
Charleston *Mo., U.S.A.* 36°55N 89°21W **112** G3
Charleston *S.C., U.S.A.* 32°46N 79°56W **111** D11
Charleston *W. Va., U.S.A.* 38°21N 81°38W **112** F7
Charlestown *Ireland* 53°58N 8°48W **18** D4
Charlestown of Aberlour
   U.K. 57°28N 3°14W **23** H11
Charleville *Australia* 26°24S 146°15E **98** F8
Charleville *Ireland* 52°21N 8°40W **20** D5
Charleville-Mézières *France* 49°44N 4°40E **66** B6
Charlevoix *U.S.A.* 45°19N 85°16W **112** C5
Charlotte *Mich., U.S.A.* 42°34N 84°50W **112** D5
Charlotte *N.C., U.S.A.* 35°13N 80°50W **111** C10
Charlotte Amalie
   U.S. Virgin Is. 18°21N 64°56W **115** D12
Charlotte Harbor *U.S.A.* 26°57N 82°4W **111** E10
Charlottesville *U.S.A.* 38°2N 78°30W **112** F8
Charlottetown *Canada* 46°14N 63°8W **113** B16
Charlton I. *Canada* 52°0N 79°20W **109** D12
Charlton Kings *U.K.* 51°53N 2°3W **30** C4
Charlwood *U.K.* 51°9N 0°13W **31** D8
Charminster *U.K.* 50°44N 2°28W **30** E4
Charmouth *U.K.* 50°44N 2°54W **30** E3
Charnwood Forest *U.K.* 52°44N 1°17W **27** G6
Charolles *France* 46°27N 4°16E **66** C6
Charters Towers *Australia* 20°5S 146°13E **98** E8
Chartham *U.K.* 51°14N 1°1E **31** D11
Chartres *France* 48°29N 1°30E **66** B4
Chascomús *Argentina* 35°30S 58°0W **121** F4
Châteaubriant *France* 47°43N 1°23W **66** C3
Châteaulin *France* 48°11N 4°8W **66** B1
Châteauroux *France* 46°50N 1°40E **66** C4
Châtellerault *France* 46°50N 0°30E **66** C4
Chatham *N.B., Canada* 47°2N 65°28W **109** E13
Chatham *Ont., Canada* 42°24N 82°11W **112** D6
Chatham *U.K.* 51°22N 0°32E **31** D10
Chatham Is. *Pac. Oc.* 44°0S 176°40W **99** J15
Chatsworth *U.K.* 53°13N 1°36W **27** F5
Chattahoochee → *U.S.A.* 30°54N 84°57W **104** F11
Chattanooga *U.S.A.* 35°3N 85°19W **111** C9
Chatteris *U.K.* 52°28N 0°2E **31** B9
Chatton *U.K.* 55°35N 2°0W **26** A5
Chaumont *France* 48°7N 5°8E **66** B6
Chaykovskiy *Russia* 56°47N 54°9E **70** C9
Cheadle *Gt. Man., U.K.* 53°23N 2°12W **27** F4
Cheadle *Staffs., U.K.* 52°59N 1°58W **27** G5
Cheb *Czech Rep.* 50°9N 12°28E **64** C7
Cheboksary *Russia* 56°8N 47°12E **70** C8
Cheboygan *U.S.A.* 45°39N 84°29W **112** C5
Chech, Erg *Africa* 25°0N 2°15W **94** D5
Chechnia □ *Russia* 43°30N 45°29E **71** F8
Chedabucto B. *Canada* 45°25N 61°8W **113** C17
Cheddar *U.K.* 51°17N 2°46W **30** D3
Cheddleton *U.K.* 53°4N 2°2W **27** F4
Cheduba I. *Burma* 18°45N 93°40E **85** K18
Chegutu *Zimbabwe* 18°10S 30°14E **97** H6
Chek Lap Kok *China* 22°18N 113°56E **79** a
Chełm *Poland* 51°8N 23°30E **65** C12
Chelmer → *U.K.* 51°44N 0°30E **31** C10
Chelmsford *U.K.* 51°44N 0°29E **31** C9
Cheltenham *U.K.* 51°54N 2°4W **30** C4
Chelyabinsk *Russia* 55°10N 61°24E **76** D7
Chelyuskin, C. *Russia* 77°30N 103°0E **77** B11
Chemnitz *Germany* 50°51N 12°54E **64** C7
Chenab → *Pakistan* 30°23N 71°2E **84** D7
Chengde *China* 40°59N 117°58E **79** C12
Chengdu *China* 30°38N 104°2E **78** E9
Chennai *India* 13°8N 80°19E **84** N12
Cheò, Eilean a' = Skye *U.K.* 57°15N 6°10W **22** H5
Chepstow *U.K.* 51°38N 2°41W **28** D8
Cher → *France* 47°21N 0°29E **66** C4
Cherbourg *France* 49°39N 1°40W **66** B3
Cheremkhovo *Russia* 53°8N 103°1E **78** a
Cherepovets *Russia* 59°5N 37°55E **70** C6
Chergui, Chott ech *Algeria* 34°21N 0°25E **94** B6
Cheriton *U.K.* 51°3N 1°8W **30** D6
Cheriton Fitzpaine *U.K.* 50°51N 3°35W **29** F6
Cherkasy *Ukraine* 49°27N 32°4E **71** E5
Cherkessk *Russia* 44°15N 42°5E **71** F7
Chernihiv *Ukraine* 51°28N 31°20E **71** D5
Chernivtsi *Ukraine* 48°15N 25°52E **65** D13
Chernobyl *Ukraine* 51°20N 30°15E **71** D6
Cherokee *U.S.A.* 42°45N 95°33W **111** B7
Cherrapunji *India* 25°17N 91°47E **85** G17
Cherski Ra. *Russia* 65°0N 143°0E **77** C15
Chertsey *U.K.* 51°23N 0°30W **31** D7
Cherwell → *U.K.* 51°44N 1°14W **30** C6
Chesapeake B. *U.S.A.* 38°0N 76°10W **112** F9
Chesham *U.K.* 51°43N 0°36W **31** C7
Cheshire East □ *U.K.* 53°15N 2°15W **27** F4

Cheshire West and Chester   Cuenca

Cheshire West and Chester □
  U.K.   53°15N 2°40W 27 F3
Cheshunt U.K.   51°43N 0°1W 31 C8
Chesil Beach U.K.   50°37N 2°33W 30 E3
Chester U.K.   53°12N 2°53W 27 F3
Chester U.S.A.   39°51N 75°22W 113 F10
Chester-le-Street U.K.   54°51N 1°34W 26 C5
Chesterfield U.K.   53°15N 1°25W 27 F6
Chesterfield, Îs. N. Cal.   19°52S 158°15E 99 D10
Chesterfield Inlet Canada   63°30N 90°45W 108 C10
Chesuncook L. U.S.A.   46°0N 69°21W 113 B13
Chetumal Mexico   18°30N 88°20W 114 D7
Chetwynd Canada   55°45N 121°36W 108 D7
Cheviot, The U.K.   55°29N 2°9W 26 B4
Cheviot Hills U.K.   55°20N 2°30W 26 B3
Chew Bahir Ethiopia   4°40N 36°50E 89 G2
Chew Magna U.K.   51°22N 2°37W 30 D3
Cheyenne U.S.A.   41°8N 104°49W 110 B6
Cheyenne → U.S.A.   44°41N 101°18W 110 B6
Chhapra India   25°48N 84°44E 85 G14
Chhattisgarh □ India   22°0N 82°0E 85 J12
Chi → Thailand   15°11N 104°43E 82 A3
Chiai Taiwan   23°29N 120°25E 79 G13
Chiávari Italy   44°19N 9°19E 68 B3
Chiba Japan   35°30N 140°7E 81 F7
Chibougamau Canada   49°56N 74°24W 109 E12
Chibougamau, L. Canada   49°50N 74°20W 113 A10
Chic-Chocs, Mts. Canada   48°55N 66°0W 113 A14
Chicago U.S.A.   41°52N 87°38W 112 E4
Chichagof I. U.S.A.   57°30N 135°30W 108 D6
Chichester U.K.   50°50N 0°47W 31 E7
Chickasha U.S.A.   35°3N 97°58W 110 C7
Chiclayo Peru   6°42S 79°50W 120 C2
Chico U.S.A.   39°44N 121°50W 110 C2
Chico → Chubut, Argentina   44°0S 67°0W 121 G3
Chico → Santa Cruz, Argentina   50°0S 68°30W 121 G3
Chicopee U.S.A.   42°9N 72°37W 113 D11
Chicoutimi Canada   48°28N 71°5W 113 A12
Chiddingfold U.K.   51°7N 0°37W 31 D7
Chidley, C. Canada   60°23N 64°26W 109 C13
Chieti Italy   42°21N 14°10E 68 C6
Chifeng China   42°18N 118°58E 79 C12
Chihuahua Mexico   28°38N 106°5W 114 B3
Chilapa Mexico   17°36N 99°10W 114 D5
Chilaw Sri Lanka   7°30N 79°50E 84 R11
Childress U.S.A.   34°25N 100°13W 110 D6
Chile ■ S. Amer.   35°0S 72°0W 121 F2
Chilham U.K.   51°15N 0°59E 31 D9
Chililabombwe Zambia   12°18S 27°43E 97 G5
Chilka L. India   40°40N 85°25E 85 K14
Chillán Chile   36°40S 72°10W 121 F2
Chillicothe Ill., U.S.A.   40°55N 89°29W 112 E3
Chillicothe Ohio, U.S.A.   39°20N 82°59W 112 F6
Chilliwack Canada   49°10N 121°54W 108 E7
Chiloé, I. de Chile   42°30S 73°50W 121 G2
Chilpancingo Mexico   17°33N 99°30W 114 D5
Chiltern Hills U.K.   51°40N 0°53W 31 C7
Chilton U.S.A.   44°2N 88°10W 112 C3
Chilung Taiwan   25°3N 121°45E 79 F13
Chilwa, L. Malawi   15°15S 35°40E 97 H7
Chimborazo Ecuador   1°29S 78°55W 120 C2
Chimbote Peru   9°0S 78°35W 120 C2
Chimoio Mozam.   19°4S 33°30E 97 H6
Chin □ Burma   22°0N 93°0E 85 J18
Chin Hills Burma   22°30N 93°30E 85 H18
China ■ Asia   30°0N 110°0E 78 E11
China, Great Plain of Asia   35°0N 115°0E 72 E13
Chinandega Nic.   12°35N 87°12W 114 E7
Chincha Alta Peru   13°25S 76°7W 120 D2
Chindwin → Burma   21°26N 95°15E 85 J19
Chingola Zambia   12°31S 27°53E 97 G5
Chinhoyi Zimbabwe   17°20S 30°8E 97 H6
Chiniot Pakistan   31°45N 73°0E 84 D8
Chinmen Tao Taiwan   24°26N 118°22E 79 G12
Chinon France   47°10N 0°15E 66 C4
Chióggia Italy   45°13N 12°17E 68 B5
Chipata Zambia   13°38S 32°28E 97 G6
Chipman Canada   46°6N 65°53W 113 B15
Chippenham U.K.   51°27N 2°6W 30 D4
Chippewa Falls U.S.A.   44°56N 91°24W 112 C2
Chipping Campden U.K.   52°3N 1°45W 30 B5
Chipping Norton U.K.   51°56N 1°32W 30 C5
Chipping Ongar U.K.   51°42N 0°15E 31 C9
Chipping Sodbury U.K.   51°33N 2°23W 30 C4
Chiquinquira Colombia   5°37N 73°50W 120 B3
Chirbury U.K.   52°35N 3°4W 27 G2
Chirchiq Uzbekistan   41°29N 69°35E 87 A12
Chiredzi Zimbabwe   21°0S 31°38E 97 J6
Chirnside U.K.   55°48N 2°12W 25 C11
Chiseldon U.K.   51°31N 1°44W 30 C5
Chistopol Russia   55°25N 50°38E 70 C9
Chita Russia   52°0N 113°35E 77 D12
Chitral Pakistan   35°50N 71°56E 84 B7
Chittagong Bangla.   22°19N 91°48E 85 H17
Chitungwiza Zimbabwe   18°0S 31°6E 97 H6
Choiseul St. Lucia   13°47N 61°3W 114 b
Choiseul Solomon Is.   7°0S 156°40E 99 B10
Chōkai-San Japan   39°6N 140°3E 81 D7
Cholet France   47°4N 0°52W 66 C3
Chollerton U.K.   55°4N 2°7W 26 B4
Cholsey U.K.   51°35N 1°8W 30 C6
Choluteca Honduras   13°20N 87°14W 114 E7
Choluteca → Honduras   13°21N 101°1E 82 B2
Ch'ongjin N. Korea   41°47N 129°50E 79 C14
Chongqing China   29°35N 106°25E 78 F10
Chongqing Shi □ China   30°0N 108°0E 78 F10
Chonos, Arch. de los Chile   45°0S 75°0W 121 G2
Chorley U.K.   53°39N 2°38W 27 E3
Chorzów Poland   50°18N 18°57E 65 C10
Choybalsan Mongolia   48°4N 114°30E 79 B11
Choyr Mongolia   46°24N 108°30E 79 B10
Christchurch N.Z.   43°33S 172°47E 99 K4
Christchurch U.K.   50°44N 1°47W 30 E5
Christmas I. Ind. Oc.   10°30S 105°40E 102 J2
Chubut → Argentina   43°20S 65°5W 121 G3
Chudleigh U.K.   50°36N 3°36W 29 F6
Chudskoye, L. Russia   58°13N 27°30E 70 C4
Chukchi Sea Russia   68°0N 175°0W 77 C19
Chukot Ra. Russia   68°0N 175°0E 77 C18
Chulmleigh U.K.   50°54N 3°51W 29 F6

Chuncheon S. Korea   37°58N 127°44E 79 D14
Chuquicamata Chile   22°15S 69°0W 121 E3
Chur Switz.   46°52N 9°32E 64 E5
Church Stretton U.K.   52°32N 2°48W 27 G3
Churchdown U.K.   51°52N 2°10W 30 C4
Churchill Canada   58°47N 94°11W 108 D10
Churchill → Man., Canada   58°47N 94°12W 108 D10
Churchill → Nfld. & L.,
  Canada   53°19N 60°10W 109 D13
Churchill, C. Canada   58°46N 93°12W 108 D10
Churchill Falls Canada   53°36N 64°19W 109 D13
Churchill L. Canada   55°55N 108°20W 108 D9
Churchill Pk. Canada   58°10N 125°10W 108 D7
Churu India   28°20N 74°50E 84 E9
Chuska Mts. U.S.A.   36°15N 108°50W 110 C5
Chusovoy Russia   58°22N 57°50E 70 C10
Chuxiong China   25°2N 101°28E 78 F9
Cicero U.S.A.   41°51N 87°44W 112 E4
Ciechanów Poland   52°52N 20°38E 65 B11
Ciego de Ávila Cuba   21°50N 78°50W 115 C9
Cienfuegos Cuba   22°10N 80°30W 115 C8
Cíjo Perak *Indonesia*   7°45S 108°32E 82 F3
Cimarron → U.S.A.   36°10N 96°16W 111 C7
Cincinnati U.S.A.   39°9N 84°27W 112 F5
Cinderford U.K.   51°49N 2°30W 30 C3
Cinto, Mte. France   42°24N 8°54E 66 E8
Circle U.S.A.   65°50N 144°4W 108 C5
Circleville U.S.A.   39°36N 82°57W 112 F6
Cirebon Indonesia   6°45S 108°32E 82 F3
Cirencester U.K.   51°43N 1°57W 30 C5
Ciudad Acuña Mexico   29°18N 100°55W 114 B4
Ciudad Bolívar Venezuela   8°5N 63°36W 120 B3
Ciudad del Carmen Mexico   18°38N 91°50W 114 D6
Ciudad del Este Paraguay   25°30S 54°50W 121 E4
Ciudad Guayana Venezuela   8°0N 62°30W 120 B3
Ciudad Guzmán Mexico   19°41N 103°29W 114 D4
Ciudad Juárez Mexico   31°44N 106°29W 114 A3
Ciudad Madero Mexico   22°19N 97°50W 114 C5
Ciudad Mante Mexico   22°44N 98°59W 114 C5
Ciudad Obregón Mexico   27°29N 109°56W 114 B3
Ciudad Real Spain   38°59N 3°55W 67 C4
Ciudad Valles Mexico   21°59N 99°1W 114 C5
Ciudad Victoria Mexico   23°44N 99°8W 114 C5
Civitavécchia Italy   42°6N 11°48E 68 C4
Cizre Turkey   37°19N 42°10E 71 G7
Clackmannan U.K.   56°7N 3°45W 25 B8
Clacton-on-Sea U.K.   51°47N 1°11E 31 C11
Claire, L. Canada   58°35N 112°5W 108 D8
Clara Ireland   53°21N 7°37W 18 E6
Clare U.K.   52°4N 0°34E 31 B10
Clare □ Ireland   52°45N 9°0W 20 D3
Clare → Ireland   53°20N 9°2W 18 E3
Clare I. Ireland   53°47N 10°0W 18 D1
Claremont U.S.A.   43°23N 72°20W 113 D11
Clarion Fracture Zone
  Pac. Oc.   20°0N 120°0W 104 H7
Clark Fork → U.S.A.   48°9N 116°15W 110 A3
Clarksburg U.S.A.   39°17N 80°30W 112 F7
Clarksdale U.S.A.   34°12N 90°35W 111 D8
Clarksville U.S.A.   36°32N 87°21W 111 C9
Claverley U.K.   52°32N 2°18W 27 G4
Clay Cross U.K.   53°10N 1°25W 27 F6
Claydon U.K.   52°7N 1°8E 31 B11
Clear, C. Ireland   51°25N 9°32W 20 F3
Clear I. Ireland   51°26N 9°30W 20 F3
Clearfield U.S.A.   41°2N 78°27W 112 E8
Clearwater U.S.A.   27°59N 82°48W 111 E10
Cleator Moor U.K.   54°32N 3°30W 26 C2
Clee Hills U.K.   52°26N 2°35W 27 H3
Cleethorpes U.K.   53°33N 0°3W 27 E8
Cleeve Cloud U.K.   51°56N 2°0W 30 C5
Clent Hills U.K.   52°25N 2°4W 30 B4
Cleobury Mortimer U.K.   52°22N 2°28W 27 H4
Clermont-Ferrand France   45°46N 3°4E 66 D5
Clevedon U.K.   51°26N 2°52W 30 D3
Cleveland Miss., U.S.A.   33°45N 90°43W 111 D8
Cleveland Ohio, U.S.A.   41°29N 81°41W 112 E7
Cleveland Hills U.K.   54°25N 1°11W 26 D6
Clew B. Ireland   53°50N 9°49W 18 D2
Cley U.K.   52°57N 1°2E 31 A11
Clifden Ireland   53°29N 10°1W 18 E1
Cliffe U.K.   51°28N 0°31E 31 D10
Clifford U.K.   52°7N 3°6W 30 B2
Clinton Iowa, U.S.A.   41°51N 90°12W 112 E3
Clinton Okla., U.S.A.   35°31N 98°58W 110 C7
Clinton Colden L. Canada   63°58N 107°27W 108 C9
Clipperton, Î. Pac. Oc.   10°18N 109°13W 103 F17
Clipston U.K.   52°27N 0°58W 31 B7
Clitheroe U.K.   53°53N 2°22W 27 E4
Cloghaneely Ireland   55°8N 8°5W 18 A5
Clogher Hd. Ireland   53°48N 6°14W 19 D9
Cloghran Ireland   53°27N 6°14W 21 B10
Clonakilty Ireland   51°37N 8°53W 20 E5
Clonakilty B. Ireland   51°35N 8°51W 20 E5
Cloncurry → Australia   18°37S 140°40E 98 E7
Clondalkin Ireland   53°19N 6°25W 21 B10
Clones Ireland   54°11N 7°15W 18 C7
Clonmel Ireland   52°21N 7°42W 21 D7
Clontarf Ireland   53°22N 6°11W 21 B10
Cloughton U.K.   54°20N 0°26W 26 D8
Clovelly U.K.   51°0N 4°25W 29 E5
Clovis U.S.A.   34°24N 103°12W 110 D6
Clowne U.K.   53°16N 1°17W 27 F6
Cluj-Napoca Romania   46°47N 23°38E 65 E12
Clun Forest U.K.   52°27N 3°7W 27 H2
Clunbury U.K.   52°25N 2°55W 27 H3
Clwyd → U.K.   53°19N 3°31W 28 A6
Clyde → U.K.   55°55N 4°30W 24 C6
Clyde River Canada   70°30N 68°30W 109 B13
Clydebank U.K.   55°54N 4°23W 24 C7
Clydesdale U.K.   55°42N 3°50W 25 C8
Coalbrookdale U.K.   52°38N 2°30W 27 G3
Coalisland U.K.   54°33N 6°42W 19 B8
Coalville U.K.   52°44N 1°23W 27 G6
Coast Mts. Canada   55°0N 129°20W 108 D7
Coast Ranges U.S.A.   39°0N 123°0W 110 B2
Coatbridge U.K.   55°52N 4°6W 24 C7
Coaticook Canada   45°10N 71°46W 113 C12
Coats I. Canada   62°30N 83°0W 109 C11

Coats Land Antarctica   77°0S 25°0W 55 D1
Coatzacoalcos Mexico   18°7N 94°25W 114 D6
Cobán Guatemala   15°30N 90°21W 114 D6
Cobar Australia   31°27S 145°48E 98 G8
Cobh Ireland   51°51N 8°17W 20 E6
Cobija Bolivia   11°0S 68°50W 120 D3
Cobourg Canada   43°58N 78°10W 112 D8
Cochabamba Bolivia   17°26S 66°10W 120 D3
Cochin India   9°58N 76°20E 84 Q10
Cochrane Canada   49°0N 81°0W 109 E11
Cockburn, Canal Chile   54°30S 72°0W 121 H2
Cockburn I. Canada   45°55N 83°22W 112 C6
Cockburn Town Bahamas   24°2N 74°31W 115 C10
Cockerham U.K.   53°58N 2°49W 27 E3
Cockermouth U.K.   54°40N 3°22W 26 C2
Cockfield U.K.   52°10N 0°48E 31 B10
Cockpit Country, The Jamaica   18°15N 77°45W 114 a
Coco → Cent. Amer.   15°0N 83°8W 115 E8
Cocos I. Pac. Oc.   5°25N 87°55W 114 F7
Cocos Is. Ind. Oc.   12°10S 96°55E 102 J1
Cod, C. U.S.A.   42°5N 70°10W 113 D12
Coddenham U.K.   52°9N 1°8E 31 B11
Codó Brazil   4°30S 43°55W 120 C5
Cody U.S.A.   44°32N 109°3W 110 B5
Coeur d'Alene U.S.A.   47°41N 116°46W 110 A3
Coggeshall U.K.   51°52N 0°42E 31 C10
Cognac France   45°41N 0°20W 66 D3
Coigach Scotland U.K.   57°59N 5°14W 22 G7
Coigeach, Rubha U.K.   58°6N 5°26W 22 F7
Coimbatore India   11°2N 76°59E 84 P10
Coimbra Portugal   40°15N 8°27W 67 B1
Colatina Brazil   19°32S 40°37W 122 C2
Colchester U.K.   51°54N 0°55E 31 C10
Cold Fell U.K.   54°53N 2°36W 26 C3
Coldstream U.K.   55°39N 2°15W 25 C11
Colebrook U.S.A.   44°54N 71°30W 113 C12
Colebrooke U.K.   50°47N 3°44W 29 F6
Coleford U.K.   51°47N 2°36W 30 C3
Colerain U.K.   55°8N 6°41W 19 A8
Coleshill U.K.   52°30N 1°41W 27 G6
Colgrave Sd. U.K.   60°36N 0°58W 22 A16
Colima Mexico   19°14N 103°43W 114 D4
Colima, Nevado de Mexico   19°33N 103°38W 114 D4
Coll U.K.   56°39N 6°34W 24 J4
Collier Law U.K.   54°47N 1°59W 26 C5
Collingbourne Kingston U.K.   51°18N 1°40W 30 D5
Collingham U.K.   53°8N 0°46W 27 F7
Collingwood Canada   44°29N 80°13W 112 C7
Collooney Ireland   54°11N 8°29W 18 C5
Colmar France   48°5N 7°20E 66 B7
Colne U.K.   53°51N 2°9W 27 E4
Colne → Bucks., U.K.   51°27N 0°32W 31 D7
Colne → Essex, U.K.   51°51N 0°58E 31 C10
Cologne Germany   50°56N 6°57E 64 C4
Colombia ■ S. Amer.   3°45N 73°0W 120 B2
Colombian Basin Caribbean   14°0N 76°0W 104 H12
Colombo Sri Lanka   6°56N 79°58E 84 R11
Colonsay U.K.   56°5N 6°12W 24 B3
Colorado □ U.S.A.   39°30N 105°30W 110 C5
Colorado → Argentina   39°50S 62°8W 121 F3
Colorado → N. Amer.   31°45N 114°40W 110 D4
Colorado → U.S.A.   28°36N 95°59W 111 E7
Colorado Plateau U.S.A.   37°0N 110°0W 110 C4
Colorado Springs U.S.A.   38°50N 104°49W 110 C6
Colsterworth U.K.   52°49N 0°37W 27 G7
Coltishall U.K.   52°44N 1°21E 31 A11
Columbia Mo., U.S.A.   38°57N 92°20W 111 C8
Columbia S.C., U.S.A.   34°0N 81°2W 111 D10
Columbia Tenn., U.S.A.   35°37N 87°2W 111 C9
Columbia → N. Amer.   46°15N 124°5W 110 A2
Columbia, District of □
  U.S.A.   38°55N 77°0W 112 F9
Columbia Plateau U.S.A.   44°0N 117°30W 110 B3
Columbus Ga., U.S.A.   32°28N 84°59W 111 D10
Columbus Ind., U.S.A.   39°13N 85°55W 112 F5
Columbus Miss., U.S.A.   33°30N 88°25W 111 D9
Columbus Nebr., U.S.A.   41°26N 97°22W 111 E7
Columbus Ohio, U.S.A.   39°58N 83°0W 112 F6
Colville → U.S.A.   70°25N 150°30W 108 B4
Colwell U.K.   55°5N 2°4W 26 B4
Colwich U.K.   52°48N 1°58W 27 G5
Colwyn Bay U.K.   53°18N 3°44W 28 A6
Colyton U.K.   50°44N 3°5W 29 F7
Comayagua Honduras   14°25N 87°37W 114 E7
Combe Martin U.K.   51°12N 4°3W 29 E5
Comber U.K.   54°33N 5°45W 19 B10
Comeragh Mts. Ireland   52°18N 7°34W 21 D7
Comilla Bangla.   23°28N 91°10E 85 H17
Comitán Mexico   16°15N 92°8W 114 D6
Committee B. Canada   68°30N 86°30W 109 C11
Como Italy   45°47N 9°5E 68 B3
Como, Lago di Italy   46°0N 9°11E 68 B3
Comodoro Rivadavia
  Argentina   45°50S 67°40W 121 G3
Comoros ■ Ind. Oc.   12°10S 44°15E 91 H8
Compass Mt. S. Africa   31°45S 24°32E 90 K6
Compiègne France   49°24N 2°50E 66 B5
Conakry Guinea   9°29N 13°49W 94 G3
Conceição da Barra Brazil   18°35S 39°45W 122 C3
Concepción Chile   36°50S 73°0W 121 F2
Concepción Paraguay   23°22S 57°26W 121 E4
Concepción, Est. de Chile   50°30S 74°55W 121 H2
Concepción del Oro Mexico   24°38N 101°25W 114 C4
Concepción del Uruguay
  Argentina   32°35S 58°20W 121 F4
Conception, Pt. U.S.A.   34°27N 120°28W 110 D2
Conchos → Mexico   29°35N 104°25W 114 B4
Concord Calif., U.S.A.   37°59N 122°2W 110 C2
Concord N.H., U.S.A.   43°12N 71°32W 113 D12
Concordia Argentina   31°20S 58°2W 121 F4
Condeúba Brazil   14°52S 42°0W 122 B2
Condover U.K.   52°39N 2°44W 27 G3
Congleton U.K.   53°10N 2°13W 27 F4
Congo → Africa   1°0S 16°10E 96 E3
Congo ■ Africa   1°0S 16°0E 96 E3
Congo, Dem. Rep. of the ■ Africa 3°0S 23°0E 96 E4
Congo Basin Africa   0°10S 24°30E 96 E4
Congresbury U.K.   51°22N 2°48W 30 D3

Coningsby U.K.   53°7N 0°10W 27 F8
Conisbrough U.K.   53°29N 1°14W 27 F6
Coniston Canada   46°29N 80°51W 112 B7
Coniston U.K.   54°22N 3°5W 26 D2
Coniston Water U.K.   54°20N 3°5W 26 D2
Conn, L. Ireland   54°3N 9°15W 18 C3
Connah's Quay U.K.   53°13N 3°4W 28 A7
Connaught □ Ireland   53°43N 9°12W 18 D3
Conneaut U.S.A.   41°57N 80°34W 112 E7
Connecticut □ U.S.A.   41°30N 72°45W 113 E11
Connecticut → U.S.A.   41°16N 72°20W 113 E11
Connellsville U.S.A.   40°1N 79°35W 112 E8
Connemara Ireland   53°29N 9°45W 18 E2
Connemara △ Ireland   53°32N 9°52W 18 E2
Connersville U.S.A.   39°39N 85°8W 112 F5
Conselheiro Lafaiete Brazil   20°40S 43°48W 122 D2
Consett U.K.   54°51N 1°50W 26 C5
Constance, L. Europe   47°35N 9°25E 64 E5
Constanța Romania   44°14N 28°38E 65 F15
Constantine Algeria   36°25N 6°42E 94 A7
Constitución Chile   35°20S 72°30W 121 F2
Contagem Brazil   19°56S 44°3W 122 C2
Contas → Brazil   14°17S 39°1W 122 B3
Contwoyto L. Canada   65°42N 110°50W 108 C8
Conway Ark., U.S.A.   35°5N 92°26W 111 C8
Conway N.H., U.S.A.   43°59N 71°7W 113 D12
Conwy □ U.K.   53°10N 3°44W 28 A6
Conwy → U.K.   53°17N 3°50W 28 A6
Coober Pedy Australia   29°1S 134°43E 98 F6
Cook Inlet U.S.A.   60°0N 152°0W 108 D4
Cook Is. ☑ Pac. Oc.   17°0S 160°0W 103 J12
Cook Strait N.Z.   41°15S 174°29E 99 J5
Cookstown U.K.   54°38N 6°45W 19 B8
Cookstown Australia   15°30S 145°16E 98 D8
Coondapoor India   13°42N 74°40E 84 N9
Coos Bay U.S.A.   43°22N 124°13W 110 B2
Cootehill Ireland   54°4N 7°5W 18 C7
Copenhagen Denmark   55°40N 12°26E 63 F6
Copiapó Chile   27°30S 70°20W 121 E2
Copper Harbor U.S.A.   47°28N 87°53W 112 B4
Coppermine → Canada   67°49N 116°4W 108 C8
Coquet → U.K.   55°20N 1°32W 26 B5
Coquet I. U.K.   55°20N 1°32W 26 B5
Coquimbo Chile   30°0S 71°20W 121 E2
Coracora Peru   15°5S 73°45W 120 D2
Coral Harbour Canada   64°8N 83°10W 109 C11
Coral Sea Pac. Oc.   15°0S 150°0E 98 C9
Corbin U.S.A.   36°57N 84°6W 112 G5
Corbridge U.K.   54°58N 2°0W 26 C5
Corby U.K.   52°30N 0°41W 31 A7
Corby Glen U.K.   52°49N 0°30W 27 G7
Cordele U.S.A.   31°58N 83°47W 111 D10
Córdoba Argentina   31°20S 64°10W 121 F3
Córdoba Mexico   18°53N 96°56W 114 D5
Córdoba Spain   37°50N 4°50W 67 D3
Córdoba, Sierra de Argentina   31°10S 64°25W 121 F3
Cordova U.S.A.   60°33N 145°45W 108 C5
Corfe Castle U.K.   50°38N 2°3W 30 E4
Corfe Mullen U.K.   50°46N 2°1W 30 E4
Corfu Greece   39°38N 19°50E 69 E8
Corinth Greece   37°56N 22°55E 69 F10
Corinth U.S.A.   34°56N 88°31W 111 D9
Corinto Brazil   18°20S 44°30W 122 C2
Cork Ireland   51°54N 8°29W 20 E6
Cork □ Ireland   51°57N 8°40W 20 E5
Cork Harbour Ireland   51°47N 8°16W 20 E6
Corner Brook Canada   48°57N 57°58W 109 E14
Corning U.S.A.   42°9N 77°3W 112 D9
Cornwall Canada   45°2N 74°44W 113 C10
Cornwall □ U.K.   50°26N 4°40W 29 G4
Cornwall, C. U.K.   50°8N 5°43W 29 G2
Cornwall I. Canada   77°37N 94°38W 109 B10
Cornwallis I. Canada   75°8N 95°0W 109 B10
Coro Venezuela   11°25N 69°41W 120 A3
Corocoro Bolivia   17°15S 68°28W 120 D3
Coromandel Coast India   12°30N 81°0E 84 N12
Coronation Gulf Canada   68°25N 110°0W 108 B8
Coronel Chile   37°0S 73°10W 121 F2
Coronel Fabriciano Brazil   19°31S 42°38W 122 C2
Coronel Pringles Argentina   38°0S 61°30W 121 F3
Coronel Suárez Argentina   37°30S 61°52W 121 F3
Coropuna, Nevado Peru   15°30S 72°41W 120 D2
Corpus Christi U.S.A.   27°47N 97°24W 110 E7
Corran Pen. Ireland   53°54N 9°54W 18 D2
Corrib, L. Ireland   53°27N 9°16W 20 B4
Corrientes Argentina   27°30S 58°45W 121 E4
Corrientes, C. Colombia   5°30N 77°34W 120 B2
Corrientes, C. Mexico   20°25N 105°42W 114 C3
Corringham U.K.   53°25N 0°41W 27 F7
Corry U.S.A.   41°55N 79°39W 112 E8
Corse, C. France   43°1N 9°25E 66 E8
Corsham U.K.   51°27N 2°10W 30 D4
Corsica □ France   42°0N 9°0E 66 F8
Corsicana U.S.A.   32°6N 96°28W 111 D7
Corsley U.K.   51°13N 2°14W 30 D4
Corte France   42°19N 9°11E 66 E8
Cortez U.S.A.   37°21N 108°35W 110 C5
Cortland U.S.A.   42°36N 76°11W 113 D9
Corton U.K.   52°31N 1°45E 31 A12
Çorum Turkey   40°30N 34°57E 71 F5
Corumbá Brazil   19°0S 57°30W 120 D4
Corunna = La Coruña Spain   43°20N 8°25W 67 A1
Corvallis U.S.A.   44°34N 123°16W 110 B2
Corve → U.K.   52°22N 2°43W 27 H3
Coseley U.K.   52°33N 2°5W 27 G4
Cosenza Italy   39°18N 16°15E 68 E7
Cosham U.K.   50°51N 1°2W 30 E6
Coshocton U.S.A.   40°16N 81°51W 112 E7
Costa Blanca Spain   38°25N 0°10W 67 C5
Costa Brava Spain   41°30N 3°0E 67 B7
Costa Cálida Spain   37°30N 1°30W 67 D5
Costa Daurada Spain   41°12N 1°15E 67 B6
Costa de la Luz Spain   36°15N 5°58W 67 D2
Costa del Azahar Spain   39°30N 0°13W 67 C6
Costa del Sol Spain   36°30N 4°30W 67 D4
Costa Rica ■ Cent. Amer.   10°0N 84°0W 115 F8
Costa Verde Spain   43°20N 5°30W 67 A3
Costessey U.K.   52°40N 1°13E 31 A11
Cotabato Phil.   7°14N 124°15E 83 C6
Côte d'Azur France   43°25N 7°10E 66 E7

Côte-d'Ivoire = Ivory Coast ■
  Africa   7°30N 5°0W 94 G4
Coteau du Missouri U.S.A.   47°0N 100°0W 110 A6
Cotentin France   49°15N 1°30W 66 B3
Cotherstone U.K.   54°35N 1°59W 26 C5
Cotonou Benin   6°20N 2°25E 94 G6
Cotopaxi Ecuador   0°40S 78°30W 120 C2
Cotswold Hills U.K.   51°42N 2°10W 30 C4
Cottbus Germany   51°45N 14°20E 64 C8
Cottenham U.K.   52°18N 0°9E 31 B9
Coudersport U.S.A.   41°46N 78°1W 112 E8
Council Bluffs U.S.A.   41°16N 95°52W 111 B7
Courantyne → S. Amer.   5°55N 57°5W 120 B4
Courtenay Canada   49°45N 125°0W 108 E7
Cove U.K.   56°0N 4°51W 24 B6
Coventry U.K.   52°25N 1°28W 30 B6
Cover → U.K.   54°17N 1°47W 26 D5
Coverack U.K.   50°1N 5°7W 29 G3
Covington U.S.A.   39°5N 84°30W 112 F5
Cowal U.K.   56°5N 5°8W 24 B5
Cowbridge U.K.   51°27N 3°27W 29 E7
Cowdenbeath U.K.   56°7N 3°21W 25 B9
Cowes U.K.   50°45N 1°18W 30 E6
Cowfold U.K.   50°59N 0°16W 31 E8
Cowpen U.K.   55°8N 1°32W 26 B5
Cox's Bazar Bangla.   21°26N 91°59E 85 J17
Cozumel, Isla Mexico   20°30N 86°40W 114 C7
Crab Hill Barbados   13°19N 59°38W 114 c
Cradock S. Africa   32°8S 25°36E 97 L5
Craig U.S.A.   40°31N 107°33W 110 B5
Craigavon U.K.   54°27N 6°23W 19 C9
Crail U.K.   56°16N 2°37W 25 B10
Craiova Romania   44°21N 23°48E 65 F12
Cramlington U.K.   55°6N 1°34W 26 B5
Cranborne U.K.   50°55N 1°54W 30 E5
Cranborne Chase U.K.   50°56N 2°6W 30 E4
Cranbrook Canada   49°30N 115°46W 108 E8
Cranbrook U.K.   51°6N 0°34E 31 D10
Crandon U.S.A.   45°34N 88°54W 112 C3
Crane, The Barbados   13°6N 59°27W 114 c
Cranleigh U.K.   51°8N 0°28W 31 D8
Cranwell U.K.   53°3N 0°27W 27 F7
Crateús Brazil   5°10S 40°39W 120 C5
Crato Brazil   7°10S 39°25W 120 C6
Craven Arms U.K.   52°26N 2°50W 27 H3
Crawfordsville U.S.A.   40°2N 86°54W 112 E4
Crawley U.K.   51°7N 0°11W 31 D8
Credenhill U.K.   52°5N 2°48W 30 B3
Crediton U.K.   50°47N 3°40W 29 F6
Cree → Canada   58°57N 105°47W 108 D9
Cree → U.K.   54°55N 4°25W 24 E7
Cree L. Canada   57°30N 106°30W 108 D9
Cremona Italy   45°7N 10°2E 68 B4
Cres Croatia   44°58N 14°25E 68 B6
Crete Greece   35°15N 25°0E 69 G11
Créteil France   48°47N 2°27E 66 B5
Creuse → France   47°0N 0°34E 66 C4
Crewe U.K.   53°6N 2°26W 27 F4
Crewkerne U.K.   50°53N 2°48W 30 E3
Crianlarich U.K.   56°24N 4°37W 24 B6
Criccieth U.K.   52°55N 4°13W 28 B5
Crick U.K.   52°22N 1°8W 30 B6
Crickhowell U.K.   51°52N 3°8W 28 D7
Cricklade U.K.   51°38N 1°50W 30 C5
Crieff U.K.   56°22N 3°50W 25 B8
Criffell U.K.   54°56N 3°39W 25 E8
Crimea □ Ukraine   45°30N 33°10E 71 E5
Crimean Pen. Ukraine   45°0N 34°0E 71 F5
Crișul Alb → Romania   46°42N 21°17E 65 E11
Crișul Negru → Romania   46°42N 21°16E 65 E11
Croagh Patrick Ireland   53°46N 9°40W 18 D2
Croaghan Ireland   53°59N 10°10W 18 D1
Croatia ■ Europe   45°20N 16°0E 68 B7
Croglin U.K.   54°50N 2°39W 26 C3
Crohy Hd. Ireland   54°55N 8°26W 18 B5
Croker, C. Australia   10°58S 132°35E 98 C5
Cromarty U.K.   57°40N 4°2W 23 G9
Cromarty Firth U.K.   57°40N 4°15W 23 G9
Cromdale, Hills of U.K.   57°20N 3°28E 23 H11
Cromer U.K.   52°56N 1°17E 31 A11
Crondall U.K.   51°14N 0°51W 31 D7
Crook U.K.   54°43N 1°45W 26 C5
Crooked I. Bahamas   22°50N 74°10W 115 C10
Crooklands U.K.   54°16N 2°42W 26 D3
Crosby Cumb., U.K.   54°45N 3°25W 26 C2
Crosby Mersey., U.K.   53°30N 3°3W 27 F2
Crosby Ravensworth U.K.   54°33N 2°35W 26 C4
Cross Fell U.K.   54°43N 2°28W 26 C4
Cross Sound U.S.A.   58°0N 135°0W 108 D6
Crosshaven Ireland   51°47N 8°17W 20 E6
Crossmaglen U.K.   54°5N 6°36W 19 C8
Crossmichael U.K.   54°58N 3°59W 25 E8
Crotone Italy   39°5N 17°8E 68 E7
Crouch → U.K.   51°37N 0°53E 31 C10
Crow Hd. Ireland   51°35N 10°9W 20 F2
Crow Sound U.K.   49°56N 6°16W 29 H1
Crowborough U.K.   51°3N 0°11E 31 D9
Crowland U.K.   52°41N 0°10W 27 G8
Crowle U.K.   53°36N 0°49W 27 E7
Crowsnest Pass Canada   49°40N 114°40W 108 E8
Croyde U.K.   51°7N 4°14W 29 E5
Croydon □ U.K.   51°22N 0°5W 31 D8
Crozet, Îs. Ind. Oc.   46°27S 52°0E 53 G12
Cruden Bay U.K.   57°25N 1°52W 23 H14
Crudgington U.K.   52°46N 2°32W 27 G3
Crummock Water U.K.   54°33N 3°18W 26 C2
Cruz das Almas Brazil   12°0S 39°6W 122 B3
Cruzeiro Brazil   22°33S 45°0W 122 D1
Cruzeiro do Sul Brazil   7°35S 72°35W 120 C2
Crystal Falls U.S.A.   46°5N 88°20W 112 B3
Cuando → Angola   17°30S 23°15E 97 H4
Cuango = Kwango →
  Dem. Rep. of the Congo   3°14S 17°22E 96 E3
Cuanza → Angola   9°21S 13°9E 96 F2
Cuauhtémoc Mexico   28°25N 106°52W 114 B3
Cuba ■ W. Indies   22°0N 79°0W 115 C9
Cubango → Africa   18°50S 22°25E 97 H4
Cuckfield U.K.   51°1N 0°8W 31 D8
Cúcuta Colombia   7°54N 72°31W 120 B2
Cuddalore India   11°46N 79°45E 84 P11
Cuenca Ecuador   2°50S 79°9W 120 C2
Cuenca Spain   40°5N 2°10W 67 B4

Cuernavaca

East Sea

Cuernavaca *Mexico* 18°55N 99°15W **114** D5
Cuiabá *Brazil* 15°30S 56°0W **120** D4
Cuihangcun *China* 22°27N 113°32E **79** a
Cuillin Hills *U.K.* 57°13N 6°15W **22** H5
Cuillin Sd. *U.K.* 57°4N 6°20W **22** H5
Cuito → *Angola* 18°1S 20°48E **97** H4
Culiacán *Mexico* 24°50N 107°23W **114** C3
Cullen *U.K.* 57°42N 2°49W **23** G12
Cullompton *U.K.* 50°51N 3°24W **29** F7
Culm → *U.K.* 50°46N 3°31W **29** F6
Culpeper *U.S.A.* 38°30N 78°0W **112** F9
Cumaná *Venezuela* 10°30N 64°5W **120** A3
Cumberland *U.S.A.* 39°39N 78°46W **112** F8
Cumberland → *U.S.A.* 37°9N 88°25W **111** C9
Cumberland Pen. *Canada* 67°0N 64°0W **109** C13
Cumberland Plateau *U.S.A.* 36°0N 85°0W **111** C10
Cumberland Sd. *Canada* 65°30N 66°0W **109** C13
Cumbernauld *U.K.* 55°57N 3°58W **25** C8
Cumbrae Is. *U.K.* 55°46N 4°54W **24** C6
Cumbria □ *U.K.* 54°42N 2°52W **26** D5
Cumbrian Mts. *U.K.* 54°30N 3°0W **26** D2
Cummertrees *U.K.* 54°59N 3°20W **25** E9
Cumnock *U.K.* 55°28N 4°17W **24** D7
Cumnor *U.K.* 51°44N 1°19W **30** C6
Cumwhinton *U.K.* 54°52N 2°50W **26** D5
Cunene → *Angola* 17°20S 11°50E **97** H2
Cúneo *Italy* 44°23N 7°32E **68** D7
Cunnamulla *Australia* 28°2S 145°38E **98** F8
Cunninghame *U.K.* 55°38N 4°35W **24** C6
Cupar *U.K.* 56°19N 3°1W **25** B9
Curaçao *W. Indies* 12°10N 69°0W **115** E11
Curicó *Chile* 34°55S 71°20W **121** F2
Curitiba *Brazil* 25°20S 49°10W **122** E1
Curlew Mts. *Ireland* 54°0N 8°20W **18** D5
Curry Rivel *U.K.* 51°1N 2°52W **30** D3
Curvelo *Brazil* 18°45S 44°27W **122** C2
Cusco *Peru* 13°32S 72°0W **120** D2
Cuttack *India* 20°25N 85°57E **85** J14
Cuxhaven *Germany* 53°51N 8°41E **64** B5
Cuyahoga Falls *U.S.A.* 41°8N 81°29W **112** E7
Cuyuni → *Guyana* 6°23N 58°41W **120** B4
Cwmbran *U.K.* 51°39N 3°2W **28** D7
Cyclades *Greece* 37°0N 24°30E **69** F11
Cynthiana *U.S.A.* 38°23N 84°18W **112** F5
Cyprus ■ *Asia* 35°0N 33°0E **86** C3
Cyrenaica *Libya* 27°0N 23°0E **95** C10
Czech Rep. ■ *Europe* 50°0N 15°0E **64** D8
Częstochowa *Poland* 50°49N 19°7E **65** C10

D

Da Lat *Vietnam* 11°56N 108°25E **82** B3
Da Nang *Vietnam* 16°4N 108°13E **82** A3
Da Yunhe → *China* 34°25N 120°5E **79** E13
Daba Shan *China* 32°0N 109°0E **79** C10
Dabie Shan *China* 31°20N 115°20E **79** C12
Dadra & Nagar Haveli □ *India* 20°5N 73°0E **84** J8
Dadu *Pakistan* 26°45N 67°45E **84** F5
Daegu *S. Korea* 35°50N 128°37E **79** D14
Daejeon *S. Korea* 36°20N 127°28E **79** D14
Dagestan □ *Russia* 42°30N 47°0E **71** F8
Dagupan *Phil.* 16°3N 120°20E **83** A6
Dahod *India* 22°50N 74°15E **84** H9
Dahongliutan *China* 35°45N 79°20E **78** D4
Daingean *Ireland* 53°18N 7°17W **21** B8
Dajarra *Australia* 21°42S 139°30E **98** E6
Dakar *Senegal* 14°34N 17°29W **94** F2
Dakhla *W. Sahara* 23°50N 15°53W **94** D2
Dakhla, El Wâhât el *Egypt* 25°30N 28°50E **95** C11
Dalandzadgad *Mongolia* 43°27N 104°30E **78** C9
Dalbeattie *U.K.* 54°56N 3°50W **25** E8
Dalhart *U.S.A.* 36°4N 102°31W **110** C6
Dalhousie *Canada* 48°5N 66°26W **113** A14
Dali *China* 25°40N 100°10E **78** D9
Dalian *China* 38°50N 121°40E **79** D13
Daliang Shan *China* 28°0N 102°45E **78** F9
Dalkeith *U.K.* 55°54N 3°4W **25** C9
Dalkey *Ireland* 53°16N 6°6W **21** B10
Dallas *U.S.A.* 32°47N 96°48W **111** D7
Dalles, The *U.S.A.* 45°36N 121°10W **110** A2
Dalmatia *Croatia* 43°20N 17°0E **68** C7
Dalmellington *U.K.* 55°19N 4°23W **24** D7
Daloa *Ivory C.* 7°0N 6°30W **94** G4
Dalry *U.K.* 55°42N 4°43W **24** C6
Dalrymple, L. *Australia* 20°40S 147°0E **98** E8
Dalton *Dumf. & Gall., U.K.* 55°4N 3°24W **25** D9
Dalton *N. Yorks., U.K.* 54°28N 1°32W **26** D5
Dalton-in-Furness *U.K.* 54°10N 3°11W **26** D2
Daly Waters *Australia* 16°15S 133°24E **98** D5
Daman *India* 20°25N 72°57E **84** J8
Damanhûr *Egypt* 31°0N 30°30E **95** B12
Damaraland *Namibia* 20°0S 15°0E **97** H2
Damascus *Syria* 33°30N 36°18E **86** C4
Damerham *U.K.* 50°56N 1°51W **30** E5
Dampier *Australia* 20°41S 116°42E **98** E2
Danakil Desert *Ethiopia* 12°45N 41°0E **89** E3
Danbury *U.S.A.* 41°24N 73°28W **113** E11
Dandong *China* 40°10N 124°20E **79** C13
Danube → *Europe* 45°20N 29°40E **65** F15
Danville *Ill., U.S.A.* 40°8N 87°37W **112** E4
Danville *Ky., U.S.A.* 37°39N 84°46W **112** G5
Danville *Va., U.S.A.* 36°36N 79°23W **111** C11
Daqing *China* 46°35N 125°0E **79** B13
Dar Banda *Africa* 8°0N 23°0E **90** F6
Dar es Salaam *Tanzania* 6°50S 39°12E **96** F7
Darbhanga *India* 26°15N 85°55E **85** F14
Dardanelles *Turkey* 40°17N 26°32E **69** D12
Darent → *U.K.* 51°28N 0°14E **31** D9
Dârfûr *Sudan* 13°40N 24°0E **95** F10
Darhan *Mongolia* 49°37N 106°21E **78** B10
Darién, G. del *Colombia* 9°0N 77°0W **120** B2
Darjiling *India* 27°3N 88°18E **85** F16
Darling → *Australia* 34°4S 141°54E **98** G7
Darling Ra. *Australia* 32°30S 116°0E **98** G2
Darlington *U.K.* 54°32N 1°33W **26** C5
Darmstadt *Germany* 49°51N 8°39E **64** D5
Darnah *Libya* 32°45N 22°45E **95** B10
Darnley, C. *Antarctica* 68°0S 69°0E **55** C6
Darnley B. *Canada* 69°30N 123°30W **108** C7
Dart → *U.K.* 50°24N 3°39W **29** G6
Dartford *U.K.* 51°26N 0°13E **31** D9

Dartington *U.K.* 50°27N 3°43W **29** G6
Dartmoor △ *U.K.* 50°37N 3°59W **29** F6
Dartmouth *Canada* 44°40N 63°30W **113** C16
Dartmouth *U.K.* 50°21N 3°36W **29** G6
Darton *U.K.* 53°35N 1°31W **27** E5
Darwen *U.K.* 53°42N 2°29W **27** E4
Darwin *Australia* 12°25S 130°51E **98** C5
Dashen, Ras *Ethiopia* 13°8N 38°26E **89** E2
Dasht → *Pakistan* 25°10N 61°40E **84** G2
Daşoguz *Turkmenistan* 41°49N 59°58E **87** A9
Datong *China* 40°6N 113°18E **79** C11
Daugava → *Latvia* 57°4N 24°3E **63** F9
Daugavpils *Latvia* 55°53N 26°32E **63** F9
Dauphin *Canada* 51°9N 100°5W **108** D9
Dauphiné *France* 45°15N 5°25E **66** D6
Davangere *India* 14°25N 75°55E **84** M9
Davao *Phil.* 7°0N 125°40E **83** C7
Davenport *U.S.A.* 41°32N 90°35W **112** E2
Daventry *U.K.* 52°16N 1°10W **30** B6
David *Panama* 8°30N 82°30W **115** F8
Davis Str. *N. Amer.* 65°0N 58°0W **104** C14
Dawlish *U.K.* 50°35N 3°28W **29** F7
Dawna Ra. *Burma* 16°30N 98°30E **85** L21
Dawros Hd. *Ireland* 54°50N 8°33W **18** B4
Dawson City *Canada* 64°10N 139°30W **108** C6
Dawson Creek *Canada* 55°45N 120°15W **108** D7
Dax *France* 43°44N 1°3W **66** E3
Daxian *China* 31°15N 107°23E **78** E10
Daxue Shan *China* 30°30N 101°30E **78** E9
Dayr az Zawr *Syria* 35°20N 40°5E **86** C5
Dayton *U.S.A.* 39°45N 84°12W **112** F5
Daytona Beach *U.S.A.* 29°13N 81°1W **111** E10
De Aar *S. Africa* 30°39S 24°0E **97** L4
De Pere *U.S.A.* 44°27N 88°4W **112** C3
Dead Sea *Asia* 31°30N 35°30E **86** D3
Deal *U.K.* 51°13N 1°25E **31** D11
Dean, Forest of *U.K.* 51°45N 2°33W **30** C3
Dearham *U.K.* 54°44N 3°25W **26** C2
Dease → *Canada* 59°56N 128°32W **108** D7
Dease Lake *Canada* 58°25N 130°6W **108** D6
Death Valley *U.S.A.* 36°15N 116°50W **110** C3
Deben → *U.K.* 52°0N 1°25E **31** B11
Debenham *U.K.* 52°14N 1°12E **31** B11
Debre Markos *Ethiopia* 10°20N 37°40E **89** E2
Debre Tabor *Ethiopia* 11°50N 38°26E **89** E2
Debrecen *Hungary* 47°33N 21°42E **65** E11
Decatur *Ala., U.S.A.* 34°36N 86°59W **111** D9
Decatur *Ill., U.S.A.* 39°51N 88°57W **112** F3
Decatur *Ind., U.S.A.* 40°50N 84°56W **112** E5
Deccan *India* 18°0N 79°0E **84** L11
Deddington *U.K.* 51°59N 1°18W **30** C6
Dee → *Aberds., U.K.* 57°9N 2°5W **23** H13
Dee → *Dumf. & Gall., U.K.* 54°51N 4°3W **24** E7
Dee → *Wales, U.K.* 53°22N 3°17W **28** A7
Deeping Fen *U.K.* 52°45N 0°15W **27** G8
Deeping St. Nicholas *U.K.* 52°44N 0°12W **27** G8
Deer Lake *Canada* 49°11N 57°27W **109** E14
Defiance *U.S.A.* 41°17N 84°22W **112** E5
Dehra Dun *India* 30°20N 78°4E **84** D11
DeKalb *U.S.A.* 41°56N 88°46W **112** E3
Del Rio *U.S.A.* 29°22N 100°54W **110** E6
Delabole *U.K.* 50°37N 4°46W **29** F4
Delaware *U.S.A.* 40°18N 83°4W **112** E6
Delaware □ *U.S.A.* 39°0N 75°20W **113** F10
Delaware → *U.S.A.* 39°15N 75°20W **113** F10
Delaware B. *U.S.A.* 39°0N 75°10W **111** C12
Delgado, C. *Mozam.* 10°45S 40°40E **96** G8
Delhi *India* 28°39N 77°13E **84** E10
Delice *Turkey* 39°54N 34°2E **71** G5
Delicias *Mexico* 28°13N 105°28W **114** B3
Déline *Canada* 65°11N 123°25W **108** C7
Delphos *U.S.A.* 40°51N 84°21W **112** E5
Delta Junction *U.S.A.* 64°2N 145°44W **108** C5
Demanda, Sierra de la *Spain* 42°15N 3°0W **67** A4
Demavend *Iran* 35°56N 52°10E **87** C8
Deming *U.S.A.* 32°16N 107°46W **110** D5
Demopolis *U.S.A.* 32°31N 87°50W **111** D9
Den Helder *Neths.* 52°57N 4°45E **64** B3
Denbigh *U.K.* 53°12N 3°25W **28** A7
Denbighshire □ *U.K.* 53°8N 3°22W **28** A7
Denby Dale *U.K.* 53°34N 1°40W **27** E5
Denham, Mt. *Jamaica* 18°13N 77°32W **114** a
Denia *Spain* 38°49N 0°8E **67** C6
Denizli *Turkey* 37°42N 29°2E **71** G4
Denmark ■ *Europe* 55°45N 10°0E **63** F6
Denmark Str. *Atl. Oc.* 66°0N 30°0W **104** C17
Dennery *St. Lucia* 13°55N 60°54W **114** b
Denny *U.K.* 56°1N 3°55W **25** B8
Denpasar *Indonesia* 8°39S 115°13E **82** F5
Dent *U.K.* 54°17N 2°27W **26** D4
Denton *Gt. Man., U.K.* 53°27N 2°9W **27** F4
Denton *Lincs., U.K.* 52°53N 0°43W **27** G7
Denton *U.S.A.* 33°13N 97°8W **111** D7
D'Entrecasteaux Is. *Papua N. G.* 9°0S 151°0E **98** B9
Denver *U.S.A.* 39°42N 104°59W **110** C5
Deoghar *India* 24°30N 86°42E **85** G15
Deolali *India* 19°58N 73°50E **84** K8
Deosai Mts. *Pakistan* 35°40N 75°0E **84** B9
Dera Ghazi Khan *Pakistan* 30°5N 70°43E **84** D7
Dera Ismail Khan *Pakistan* 31°50N 70°50E **84** D7
Derbent *Russia* 42°5N 48°15E **71** F8
Derby *Australia* 17°18S 123°38E **98** D3
Derby *U.K.* 52°56N 1°28W **27** G6
Derby □ *U.K.* 53°11N 1°38W **27** F5
Dereham *U.K.* 52°41N 0°57E **31** A10
Derg → *U.K.* 54°44N 7°26W **18** B7
Derg, L. *Ireland* 53°0N 8°20W **20** C6
Deridder *U.S.A.* 30°51N 93°17W **111** D8
Derry = Londonderry *U.K.* 55°0N 7°20W **18** A7
Derrynasaggart Mts. *Ireland* 51°58N 9°15W **20** E4
Derryveagh Mts. *Ireland* 54°56N 8°11W **18** B5
Derwent → *Derby, U.K.* 52°57N 1°28W **27** G6
Derwent → *N. Yorks., U.K.* 53°45N 0°58W **27** E7
Derwent → *Tyne & W., U.K.* 54°58N 1°41W **26** C5
Derwent Water *U.K.* 54°35N 3°9W **26** C2
Des Moines *U.S.A.* 41°35N 93°37W **111** B8
Des Moines → *U.S.A.* 40°23N 91°25W **111** B8
Desborough *U.K.* 52°27N 0°49W **31** B7
Deschutes → *U.S.A.* 45°38N 120°55W **110** A2
Dese *Ethiopia* 11°5N 39°40E **89** E2
Deseado → *Argentina* 47°45S 65°54W **121** G3

Desford *U.K.* 52°37N 1°17W **27** G6
Desolación, I. *Chile* 53°0S 74°0W **121** H2
Dessau *Germany* 51°51N 12°14E **64** C7
Detour, Pt. *U.S.A.* 45°40N 86°40W **112** C4
Detroit *U.S.A.* 42°19N 83°12W **112** D6
Deutsche Bucht *Germany* 54°15N 8°0E **64** A5
Deventer *Neths.* 52°15N 6°10E **64** B4
Deveron → *U.K.* 57°41N 2°32W **23** G12
Devils Lake *U.S.A.* 48°7N 98°52W **110** A7
Devizes *U.K.* 51°22N 1°58W **30** D5
Devon □ *U.K.* 50°50N 3°40W **29** F6
Devon I. *Canada* 75°10N 85°0W **109** B11
Devonport *U.K.* 50°22N 4°11W **29** G5
Dewsbury *U.K.* 53°42N 1°37W **27** E5
Dexter *U.S.A.* 36°48N 89°57W **112** G3
Deyang *China* 31°3N 104°27E **78** E9
Dezfūl *Iran* 32°20N 48°30E **86** C7
Dezhneva, C. *Russia* 66°5N 169°40W **77** C20
Dezhou *China* 37°26N 116°18E **79** D12
Dhahran *Si. Arabia* 26°10N 50°7E **86** E7
Dhaka *Bangla.* 23°43N 90°26E **85** H17
Dhaka □ *Bangla.* 24°25N 90°25E **85** G17
Dhamār *Yemen* 14°30N 44°20E **89** E3
Dhamtari *India* 20°42N 81°35E **85** J12
Dhanbad *India* 23°50N 86°30E **85** H15
Dharwad *India* 15°30N 75°4E **84** M9
Dhaulagiri *Nepal* 28°39N 83°28E **85** E13
Dhenkanal *India* 20°45N 85°35E **85** J14
Dhuburi *India* 26°2N 89°59E **85** F16
Dhule *India* 20°58N 74°50E **84** J9
Diamantina *Brazil* 18°17S 43°40W **122** C2
Diamantina → *Australia* 26°45S 139°10E **98** F6
Diamantino *Brazil* 14°30S 56°30W **120** D4
Dibrugarh *India* 27°29N 94°55E **85** F19
Dickinson *U.S.A.* 46°53N 102°47W **110** A6
Didcot *U.K.* 51°36N 1°14W **30** C6
Diefenbaker, L. *Canada* 51°0N 106°55W **108** D9
Dieppe *France* 49°54N 1°4E **66** B4
Digby *Canada* 44°38N 65°50W **109** E13
Digne-les-Bains *France* 44°5N 6°12E **66** D7
Dijon *France* 47°20N 5°3E **66** C6
Dikson *Russia* 73°40N 80°5E **76** B9
Dili *E. Timor* 8°39S 125°34E **83** F7
Dillingham *U.S.A.* 59°3N 158°28W **108** D4
Dimitrovgrad *Bulgaria* 42°5N 25°35E **69** C11
Dimitrovgrad *Russia* 54°14N 49°39E **70** D8
Dinajpur *Bangla.* 25°33N 88°43E **85** G16
Dinan *France* 48°28N 2°2W **66** B2
Dinant *Belgium* 50°16N 4°55E **64** C3
Dinaric Alps *Croatia* 44°0N 16°30E **68** C7
Dinbych-y-Pysgod = Tenby *U.K.* 51°40N 4°42W **28** D4
Dingle *Ireland* 52°9N 10°17W **20** D2
Dingle B. *Ireland* 52°3N 10°20W **20** D2
Dingle Pen. *Ireland* 52°12N 10°5W **20** D2
Dingwall *U.K.* 57°36N 4°26W **23** G9
Dipolog *Phil.* 8°36N 123°20E **83** C6
Dire Dawa *Ethiopia* 9°35N 41°45E **89** F3
Dirranbandi *Australia* 28°33S 148°17E **98** F8
Disappointment, C. *U.S.A.* 46°18N 124°5W **110** A2
Disappointment, L. *Australia* 23°20S 122°40E **98** E3
Diss *U.K.* 52°23N 1°7E **31** B11
Distington *U.K.* 54°36N 3°32W **26** C1
Distrito Federal □ *Brazil* 15°45S 47°45W **122** C1
Ditchingham *U.K.* 52°28N 1°28E **31** B11
Ditchling Beacon *U.K.* 50°54N 0°6W **31** E8
Dittisham *U.K.* 50°22N 3°37W **29** G6
Ditton Priors *U.K.* 52°30N 2°34W **27** H4
Diu *India* 20°45N 70°58E **84** J7
Divinópolis *Brazil* 20°10S 44°54W **122** D2
Dixon *U.S.A.* 41°50N 89°29W **112** E3
Dixon Entrance *U.S.A.* 54°30N 132°0W **108** D6
Diyarbakır *Turkey* 37°55N 40°18E **71** G7
Dizzard Pt. *U.K.* 50°44N 4°40W **29** F4
Djerba, Î. de *Tunisia* 33°50N 10°48E **95** B8
Djerid, Chott *Tunisia* 33°42N 8°30E **94** B7
Djibouti *Djibouti* 11°30N 43°5E **89** E3
Djibouti ■ *Africa* 12°0N 43°0E **89** E3
Djourab, Erg du *Chad* 16°40N 18°50E **95** E9
Dmitri Laptev Str. *Russia* 73°0N 140°0E **77** B15
Dnepropetrovsk *Ukraine* 48°30N 35°0E **71** E6
Dnieper → *Ukraine* 46°30N 32°18E **71** E5
Dniester → *Europe* 46°18N 30°17E **65** E16
Dniprodzerzhynsk *Ukraine* 48°32N 34°37E **71** E5
Doba *Chad* 8°40N 16°50E **95** G9
Doberai, Jazirah *Indonesia* 1°25S 133°0E **83** E8
Dobrich *Bulgaria* 43°37N 27°49E **69** C12
Dobruja *Europe* 44°30N 28°15E **65** F15
Docking *U.K.* 52°54N 0°38E **31** A10
Doddington *Cambs., U.K.* 52°30N 0°3E **31** B9
Doddington *Northumberland, U.K.* 55°33N 1°54W **26** A5
Dodecanese *Greece* 36°35N 27°0E **69** F12
Dodge City *U.S.A.* 37°45N 100°1W **110** C6
Dodman Pt. *U.K.* 50°13N 4°48W **29** G4
Dodoma *Tanzania* 6°8S 35°45E **96** F7
Doha *Qatar* 25°15N 51°35E **87** E7
Dokdo *S. Korea* 37°15N 131°52E **79** D15
Dolbeau-Mistassini *Canada* 48°53N 72°14W **109** E12
Dole *France* 47°7N 5°31E **66** C6
Dolgarrog *U.K.* 53°11N 3°50W **28** A6
Dolgellau *U.K.* 52°45N 3°53W **28** B6
Dolo *Ethiopia* 4°11N 42°3E **89** G3
Dolomites *Italy* 46°23N 11°51E **68** A4
Dolores *U.S.A.* 36°20S 57°40W **121** F4
Dolphin and Union Str. *Canada* 69°5N 114°45W **108** C8
Dolphinton *U.K.* 55°42N 3°25W **25** C9
Dolton *U.K.* 50°53N 4°1W **29** F5
Dominica ■ *W. Indies* 15°20N 61°20W **115** D12
Dominican Rep. ■ *W. Indies* 19°0N 70°30W **115** D10
Don → *Russia* 47°4N 39°18E **71** E6
Don → *Aberds., U.K.* 57°11N 2°5W **23** H13
Don → *S. Yorks., U.K.* 53°41N 0°52W **27** E7
Don Figueroa Mts. *Jamaica* 18°5N 77°36W **114** a
Donaghadee *U.K.* 54°39N 5°33W **19** B10
Doncaster *U.K.* 53°32N 1°6W **27** E6
Dondra Head *Sri Lanka* 5°55N 80°40E **84** S12
Donegal *Ireland* 54°39N 8°5W **18** B5
Donegal □ *Ireland* 54°53N 8°0W **18** B5
Donegal B. *Ireland* 54°31N 8°49W **18** B4

Donets → *Russia* 47°33N 40°55E **71** E7
Donetsk *Ukraine* 48°0N 37°45E **71** E6
Dong Hoi *Vietnam* 17°29N 106°36E **82** A3
Dongchuan *China* 26°8N 103°1E **78** F9
Dongguan *China* 22°58N 113°44E **79** G11
Dongola *Sudan* 19°9N 30°22E **95** E12
Dongsha Dao *S. China Sea* 20°45N 116°43E **79** G12
Dongsheng *China* 39°50N 110°0E **79** D10
Dongting Hu *China* 29°18N 112°45E **79** F11
Donhead *U.K.* 51°1N 2°7W **30** D4
Donington *U.K.* 52°54N 0°12W **27** G8
Donna Nook *U.K.* 53°29N 0°8E **27** F9
Donostia-San Sebastián *Spain* 43°17N 1°58W **67** A5
Doon → *U.K.* 55°27N 4°39W **24** D6
Dorchester *Dorset, U.K.* 50°42N 2°27W **30** E4
Dorchester *Oxon., U.K.* 51°39N 1°10W **30** C6
Dorchester, C. *Canada* 65°27N 77°27W **109** C12
Dordogne → *France* 45°2N 0°36W **66** D3
Dordrecht *Neths.* 51°48N 4°39E **64** C3
Dores do Indaiá *Brazil* 19°27S 45°36W **122** C1
Dorking *U.K.* 51°14N 0°19W **31** D8
Dornie *U.K.* 57°17N 5°31W **22** H6
Dornoch *U.K.* 57°53N 4°2W **23** G9
Dornoch Firth *U.K.* 57°51N 4°4W **23** G9
Döröö Nuur *Mongolia* 48°0N 93°0E **78** B7
Dorset □ *U.K.* 50°45N 2°26W **30** E4
Dorstone *U.K.* 52°3N 2°59W **30** B3
Dortmund *Germany* 51°30N 7°28E **64** C4
Dos Bahías, C. *Argentina* 44°58S 65°32W **121** G3
Dos Hermanas *Spain* 37°16N 5°55W **67** D3
Dothan *U.S.A.* 31°13N 85°24W **111** D9
Douai *France* 50°21N 3°4E **66** A5
Douala *Cameroon* 4°0N 9°45E **96** D1
Doubs → *France* 46°53N 5°1E **66** C6
Douglas *I. of Man* 54°10N 4°28W **19** C13
Douglas *U.S.A.* 31°21N 109°33W **110** D5
Dounreay *U.K.* 58°35N 3°44W **23** E10
Dourados *Brazil* 22°9S 54°50W **120** E4
Douro → *Europe* 41°8N 8°40W **67** B1
Dove → *Derby, U.K.* 52°51N 1°36W **27** G5
Dove → *N. Yorks., U.K.* 54°15N 0°55W **26** D7
Dove Dale *U.K.* 53°7N 1°46W **27** F5
Dover *U.K.* 51°7N 1°19E **31** D11
Dover, Str. of *Europe* 51°0N 1°30E **62** F7
Dover-Foxcroft *U.S.A.* 45°11N 69°13W **113** C13
Doveridge *U.K.* 52°54N 1°49W **27** G5
Dovey = Dyfi → *U.K.* 52°32N 4°3W **28** B5
Down □ *U.K.* 54°23N 6°2W **19** C9
Downham *U.K.* 52°26N 0°14E **31** B9
Downham Market *U.K.* 52°37N 0°23E **31** A9
Downpatrick *U.K.* 54°20N 5°43W **19** C10
Downpatrick Hd. *Ireland* 54°20N 9°21W **18** C2
Downton *U.K.* 50°59N 1°44W **30** E5
Drãa, Oued → *Morocco* 28°40N 11°10W **94** C3
Draguignan *France* 43°32N 6°27E **66** E7
Drake Passage *S. Ocean* 58°0S 68°0W **55** B17
Drakensberg *S. Africa* 31°0S 28°0E **97** L5
Drammen *Norway* 59°42N 10°12E **63** F6
Drava → *Croatia* 45°33N 18°55E **69** B8
Dresden *Germany* 51°3N 13°44E **64** C7
Dreux *France* 48°44N 1°23E **66** B4
Driffield *U.K.* 54°0N 0°26W **27** D8
Drina → *Bos.-H.* 44°53N 19°21E **69** B8
Drobeta-Turnu Severin *Romania* 44°39N 22°41E **65** F12
Drogheda *Ireland* 53°43N 6°22W **19** D9
Drohobych *Ukraine* 49°20N 23°30E **71** E3
Droitwich *U.K.* 52°16N 2°8W **30** B4
Dromore *U.K.* 54°31N 7°28W **18** B7
Dromore West *U.K.* 54°15N 8°52W **18** C4
Dronfield *U.K.* 53°19N 1°27W **27** F6
Dronning Maud Land *Antarctica* 72°30S 12°0E **55** D3
Drum Hills *Ireland* 52°1N 7°45W **20** D2
Drumheller *Canada* 51°25N 112°40W **108** D8
Drummond I. *U.S.A.* 46°1N 83°39W **112** C6
Drummondville *Canada* 45°55N 72°25W **113** C12
Drumochter, Pass of *U.K.* 56°50N 4°15W **23** J9
Druridge B. *U.K.* 55°17N 1°32W **26** B5
Dry Harbour Mts. *Jamaica* 18°19N 77°24W **114** a
Dryden *Canada* 49°47N 92°50W **108** E10
Drygalski I. *Antarctica* 66°0S 92°0E **55** C7
Du Quoin *U.S.A.* 38°1N 89°14W **112** F3
Duarte, Pico *Dom. Rep.* 19°2N 70°59W **115** D10
Dubai *U.A.E.* 25°18N 55°20E **87** E8
Dubawnt → *Canada* 64°33N 100°6W **108** C9
Dubawnt L. *Canada* 63°8N 101°28W **108** C9
Dubbo *Australia* 32°11S 148°35E **98** G8
Dublin *Ireland* 53°21N 6°15W **21** B10
Dublin *U.S.A.* 32°32N 82°54W **111** D10
Dublin □ *Ireland* 53°24N 6°20W **21** B10
Dublin ✈ (DUB) *Ireland* 53°26N 6°15W **21** B10
DuBois *U.S.A.* 41°7N 78°46W **112** E8
Dubrovnik *Croatia* 42°39N 18°6E **69** C8
Dubuque *U.S.A.* 42°30N 90°41W **112** D2
Duddington *U.K.* 52°36N 0°32W **31** A7
Duddon → *U.K.* 54°12N 3°15W **26** D2
Dudinka *Russia* 69°30N 86°13E **77** C9
Dudley *U.K.* 52°31N 2°5W **27** G4
Duffield *U.K.* 52°59N 1°29W **27** G6
Dufftown *U.K.* 57°27N 3°8W **23** H11
Dugi Otok *Croatia* 44°0N 15°3E **68** C6
Duisburg *Germany* 51°32N 6°45E **64** C4
Dukinfield *U.K.* 53°28N 2°6W **27** F4
Dulce → *Argentina* 30°32S 62°33W **121** F3
Duluth *U.S.A.* 46°47N 92°6W **112** B1
Dulverton *U.K.* 51°2N 3°33W **29** E6
Dumaguete *Phil.* 9°17N 123°15E **83** C6
Dumbarton *U.K.* 55°57N 4°33W **24** C6
Dumfries *U.K.* 55°4N 3°37W **25** D8
Dumfries & Galloway □ *U.K.* 55°9N 3°58W **25** D8
Dumyât *Egypt* 31°24N 31°48E **95** B12
Dún Laoghaire *Ireland* 53°17N 6°8W **21** B10
Dunbar *U.K.* 56°0N 2°31W **25** B10
Dunblane *U.K.* 56°11N 3°58W **25** B8
Duncan *U.S.A.* 34°30N 97°57W **110** D7
Duncansby Head *U.K.* 58°38N 3°1W **23** E11

Dunchurch *U.K.* 52°21N 1°17W **30** B6
Dund-Us *Mongolia* 48°1N 91°38E **78** B7
Dundalk *Ireland* 54°1N 6°24W **19** C9
Dundalk Bay *Ireland* 53°55N 6°15W **19** D9
Dundee *U.K.* 56°28N 2°59W **25** B10
Dundrum *Ireland* 53°18N 6°14W **21** B10
Dundrum *U.K.* 54°16N 5°52W **19** C10
Dundrum B. *U.K.* 54°13N 5°47W **19** C10
Dunedin *N.Z.* 45°50S 170°33E **99** K13
Dunfermline *U.K.* 56°5N 3°27W **25** B9
Dungannon *U.K.* 54°31N 6°46W **19** B8
Dungarvan *Ireland* 52°5N 7°37W **21** D7
Dungarvan Harbour *Ireland* 52°4N 7°35W **21** D7
Dungeness *U.K.* 50°54N 0°59E **31** E10
Dunhua *China* 43°20N 128°14E **79** C14
Dunhuang *China* 40°8N 94°36E **78** C7
Dunkeld *U.K.* 56°34N 3°35W **25** A8
Dunkerque *France* 51°2N 2°20E **66** A5
Dunkery Beacon *U.K.* 51°9N 3°36W **29** E6
Dunkirk *U.S.A.* 42°29N 79°20W **112** D8
Dunleer *Ireland* 53°50N 6°24W **19** D9
Dunmanway *Ireland* 51°43N 9°6W **20** E4
Dunmore *U.S.A.* 41°25N 75°38W **113** E10
Dunnet Hd. *U.K.* 58°40N 3°21W **23** E11
Dunoon *U.K.* 55°57N 4°56W **24** C6
Duns *U.K.* 55°47N 2°20W **25** C11
Dunsford *U.K.* 50°41N 3°42W **29** F6
Dunstable *U.K.* 51°53N 0°32W **31** C7
Dunster *U.K.* 51°11N 3°27W **30** D2
Dunston *U.K.* 52°46N 2°7W **27** G4
Dunvegan *U.K.* 57°27N 6°35W **22** H4
Duolun *China* 42°12N 116°28E **79** C12
Duque de Caxias *Brazil* 22°46S 43°18W **122** D2
Durance → *France* 43°55N 4°45E **66** E6
Durango *Mexico* 24°3N 104°39W **114** C4
Durango *U.S.A.* 37°16N 107°53W **110** C5
Durant *U.S.A.* 33°59N 96°25W **111** D7
Durazno *Uruguay* 33°25S 56°31W **121** F4
Durban *S. Africa* 29°49S 31°1E **97** K6
Düren *Germany* 50°48N 6°29E **64** C4
Durgapur *India* 23°30N 87°20E **85** H15
Durham *U.K.* 54°47N 1°34W **26** C6
Durham *U.S.A.* 35°59N 78°54W **111** C11
Durham □ *U.K.* 54°42N 1°45W **26** C5
Durlston Hd. *U.K.* 50°36N 1°57W **30** E5
Durness *U.K.* 58°34N 4°45W **23** E8
Durrës *Albania* 41°19N 19°28E **69** D8
Durrington *U.K.* 51°12N 1°47W **30** D5
Durrow *Ireland* 52°51N 7°24W **21** C8
Dursey I. *Ireland* 51°36N 10°12W **20** E2
Dursley *U.K.* 51°40N 2°21W **30** C4
Dushanbe *Tajikistan* 38°33N 68°48E **87** B12
Düsseldorf *Germany* 51°14N 6°47E **64** C4
Dutch Harbor *U.S.A.* 53°53N 166°32W **108** D3
Duyun *China* 26°18N 107°29E **78** F10
Dvina, N. → *Russia* 64°32N 40°30E **70** B7
Dvina B. *Russia* 65°0N 39°0E **70** B6
Dwarka *India* 22°18N 69°8E **84** H6
Dyce *U.K.* 57°13N 2°12W **23** H13
Dyer, C. *Canada* 66°37N 61°16W **109** C13
Dyersburg *U.S.A.* 36°3N 89°23W **111** C9
Dyfi → *U.K.* 52°32N 4°3W **28** B5
Dymchurch *U.K.* 51°1N 1°0E **31** D11
Dymock *U.K.* 51°59N 2°26W **30** C4
Dzavhan Gol → *Mongolia* 48°54N 93°23E **78** B7
Dzerzhinsk *Russia* 56°14N 43°30E **70** C7
Dzhankoy *Ukraine* 45°40N 34°20E **71** E5
Dzhugdzhur Ra. *Russia* 57°30N 138°0E **77** D14
Dzungarian Basin *China* 44°30N 86°0E **78** B6
Dzungarian Gate *Asia* 45°10N 82°0E **78** B5
Dzüünmod *Mongolia* 47°45N 106°58E **78** B10

E

Eagle *U.S.A.* 64°47N 141°12W **108** C5
Eagle L. *U.S.A.* 46°20N 69°22W **113** B13
Eagle Pass *U.S.A.* 28°43N 100°30W **110** E6
Eagle River *U.S.A.* 47°25N 88°18W **112** B3
Eaglesfield *U.K.* 55°4N 3°12W **25** D9
Eakring *U.K.* 53°9N 0°58W **27** F7
Ealing □ *U.K.* 51°31N 0°20W **31** D8
Earby *U.K.* 53°55N 2°7W **27** E4
Eardisley *U.K.* 52°8N 3°1W **30** B2
Earl Shilton *U.K.* 52°35N 1°18W **27** G6
Earl Soham *U.K.* 52°14N 1°18E **31** B11
Earls Barton *U.K.* 52°16N 0°45W **31** B7
Earl's Colne *U.K.* 51°56N 0°43E **31** C10
Earlston *U.K.* 55°39N 2°40W **25** C10
Earn → *U.K.* 56°21N 3°18W **25** B9
Earn, L. *U.K.* 56°23N 4°13W **24** B7
Earsdon *U.K.* 55°3N 1°29W **26** B6
Easebourne *U.K.* 51°0N 0°43W **31** E7
Easington *Durham, U.K.* 54°47N 1°21W **26** C6
Easington *E. Riding, U.K.* 53°39N 0°6E **27** E9
Easington Colliery *U.K.* 54°48N 1°19W **26** C6
Easingwold *U.K.* 54°8N 1°11W **26** D6
East Ayrshire □ *U.K.* 55°26N 4°11W **24** D7
East Bengal *Bangla.* 24°0N 90°0E **85** H17
East Bergholt *U.K.* 51°59N 1°3E **31** C11
East Beskids *Europe* 49°20N 22°0E **65** D11
East Brent *U.K.* 51°15N 2°56W **30** D3
East China Sea *Asia* 30°0N 126°0E **79** F14
East Cowes *U.K.* 50°45N 1°16W **30** E6
East Falkland *Falk. Is.* 51°30S 58°30W **121** H4
East Fen *U.K.* 53°4N 0°5E **27** F9
East Grinstead *U.K.* 51°7N 0°0 **31** D9
East Harling *U.K.* 52°26N 0°56E **31** B10
East Ilsley *U.K.* 51°33N 1°15W **30** C6
East Indies *Asia* 0°0 120°0E **72** J14
East Kilbride *U.K.* 55°47N 4°11W **24** C7
East Lansing *U.S.A.* 42°44N 84°29W **112** D5
East London *S. Africa* 33°0S 27°55E **97** L5
East Lothian □ *U.K.* 55°58N 2°44W **25** C10
East Markham *U.K.* 53°16N 0°53W **27** F7
East Moor *U.K.* 53°15N 1°31W **27** F6
East Pt. *Canada* 46°27N 61°58W **113** B17
East St. Louis *U.S.A.* 38°37N 90°9W **112** F2
East Sea = Dezhneva, C. *Russia* 66°5N 169°40W **77** C20
East Sea = Japan, Sea of *Asia* 40°0N 135°0E **81** D4

East Siberian Sea   Frederick

East Siberian Sea Russia 73°0N 160°0E 77 B17
East Sussex □ U.K. 50°56N 0°19E 31 E9
East Timor ■ Asia 8°50S 126°0E 83 F7
East Wittering U.K. 50°46N 0°52W 31 E7
East Woodhay U.K. 51°21N 1°25W 30 D6
Eastbourne U.K. 50°46N 0°18E 31 E9
Eastchurch U.K. 51°24N 0°53E 31 D10
Eastern Desert Egypt 27°30N 32°30E 95 C12
Eastern Ghats India 14°0N 78°50E 84 N11
Eastern Group Fiji 17°0S 178°30W 99 D15
Eastleigh U.K. 50°58N 1°21W 30 E6
Eastmain Canada 52°10N 78°30W 109 D12
Eastmain → Canada 52°27N 78°26W 109 D12
Eastnor U.K. 52°2N 2°23W 30 B4
Easton Dorset, U.K. 50°33N 2°26W 30 E4
Easton Northants., U.K. 52°37N 0°31W 31 A7
Easton Md., U.S.A. 38°47N 76°5W 113 F9
Easton Pa., U.S.A. 40°41N 75°13W 113 E10
Easton-in-Gordano U.K. 51°28N 2°42W 30 D3
Eastport U.S.A. 44°56N 67°0W 113 C14
Eastry U.K. 51°14N 1°19E 31 D11
Eastwood U.K. 53°1N 1°18W 27 F6
Eaton U.K. 52°51N 0°49W 27 G7
Eaton Socon U.K. 52°13N 0°17W 31 B8
Eau Claire U.S.A. 44°49N 91°30W 112 C2
Eau Claire, L. à l' Canada 56°10N 74°25W 109 D12
Ebberston U.K. 54°14N 0°37W 26 D7
Ebbw Vale U.K. 51°46N 3°12W 28 D7
Eberswalde-Finow Germany 52°50N 13°49E 64 B7
Ebetsu Japan 43°7N 141°34E 81 B7
Ebinur Hu China 44°55N 82°55E 78 C5
Ebolowa Cameroon 2°55N 11°10E 96 D2
Ebro → Spain 40°43N 0°54E 67 B6
Ecclefechan U.K. 55°4N 3°16W 25 D9
Eccleshall U.K. 52°52N 2°15W 27 G4
Ech Chéliff Algeria 36°10N 1°20E 94 A6
Echo Bay Canada 66°5N 117°55W 108 C8
Eckington U.K. 53°18N 1°22W 27 F6
Eclipse Sd. Canada 72°38N 79°0W 109 B12
Ecuador ■ S. Amer. 2°0S 78°0W 120 C2
Ed Damazin Sudan 11°46N 34°21E 95 F12
Eday U.K. 59°11N 2°47W 23 D12
Eddrachillis B. U.K. 58°17N 5°14W 22 F7
Eddystone U.K. 50°11N 4°16W 29 G5
Eden → U.K. 54°57N 3°1W 26 C2
Edenbridge U.K. 51°12N 0°5E 31 D9
Edenderry Ireland 53°21N 7°4W 21 B8
Edfu Egypt 24°55N 32°49E 95 D12
Edge Hill U.K. 52°8N 1°26W 30 B6
Edinburgh U.K. 55°57N 3°13W 25 C9
Edinburgh ✈ (EDI) U.K. 55°54N 3°22W 25 C9
Edington U.K. 51°17N 2°5W 30 D4
Edirne Turkey 41°40N 26°34E 71 F4
Edmonton Canada 53°30N 113°30W 108 D8
Edmundbyers U.K. 54°50N 1°58W 26 C5
Edmundston Canada 47°23N 68°20W 109 E13
Edremit Turkey 39°34N 27°0E 86 B1
Edson Canada 53°35N 116°28W 108 D8
Edward, L. Africa 0°25S 29°40E 96 E5
Edward VII Land Antarctica 80°0S 150°0W 55 E13
Edwards Plateau U.S.A. 30°45N 101°20W 110 D6
Effingham U.S.A. 39°7N 88°33W 112 F3
Égadi, Ísole Italy 37°55N 12°16E 68 F5
Eganville Canada 45°32N 77°5W 112 C9
Eger Hungary 47°53N 20°27E 65 E11
Egham U.K. 51°25N 0°32W 31 D7
Eglinton I. Canada 75°48N 118°30W 109 B7
Egremont U.K. 54°29N 3°32W 26 D1
Eğridir Turkey 37°52N 30°51E 71 G5
Eğridir Gölü Turkey 37°53N 30°50E 71 G5
Egton U.K. 54°28N 0°44W 26 D7
Egypt ■ Africa 28°0N 31°0E 95 C12
Eifel Germany 50°15N 6°50E 64 C4
Eigg U.K. 56°54N 6°10W 22 J5
Eil, L. U.K. 56°51N 5°16W 22 J7
Eilean Siar = Western Isles □
U.K. 57°30N 7°10W 22 G3
Eindhoven Neths. 51°26N 5°28E 64 C3
Eire = Ireland ■ Europe 53°50N 7°52W 62 E2
Eiriosgaigh = Eriskay U.K. 57°4N 7°18W 22 H3
Eivissa Spain 38°54N 1°26E 67 C6
Ekaterinburg Russia 56°50N 60°30E 76 D7
Ekibastuz Kazakhstan 51°50N 75°10E 76 D8
El Aaiún W. Sahara 27°9N 13°12W 94 C3
El Alamein Egypt 30°48N 28°58E 95 B11
El Centro U.S.A. 32°48N 115°34W 110 D3
El Djouf Mauritania 20°0N 9°0W 94 D4
El Dorado U.S.A. 33°12N 92°40W 111 D8
El Faiyûm Egypt 29°19N 30°50E 95 C12
El Fâsher Sudan 13°33N 25°26E 95 F11
El Fuerte Mexico 26°25N 108°39W 114 B3
El Geneina Sudan 13°27N 22°45E 95 F10
El Gezira □ Sudan 15°0N 33°0E 95 F12
El Gîza Egypt 30°0N 31°12E 95 C12
El Istiwa'iya Sudan 5°0N 28°0E 95 G11
El Jadida Morocco 33°11N 8°17W 94 B4
El Khârga Egypt 25°30N 30°33E 95 C12
El Mahalla el Kubra Egypt 31°0N 31°0E 95 B12
El Mansûra Egypt 31°0N 31°19E 95 B12
El Minyâ Egypt 28°7N 30°33E 95 C12
El Obeid Sudan 13°8N 30°10E 95 F12
El Oued Algeria 33°20N 6°58E 94 B7
El Paso U.S.A. 31°45N 106°29W 110 D5
El Puerto de Santa María
Spain 36°36N 6°13W 67 D2
El Reno U.S.A. 35°32N 97°57W 110 C7
El Salvador ■ Cent. Amer. 13°50N 89°0W 114 E7
El Tigre Venezuela 8°44N 64°15W 120 B3
El Uqsur Egypt 25°41N 32°38E 95 C12
Elat Israel 29°30N 34°56E 86 D3
Elâzığ Turkey 38°37N 39°14E 71 G6
Elba Italy 42°46N 10°17E 68 C4
Elbasan Albania 41°9N 20°9E 69 D9
Elbe → Europe 53°50N 9°0E 64 B5
Elbert, Mt. U.S.A. 39°7N 106°27W 110 C5
Elbeuf France 49°17N 1°2E 66 B4
Elbląg Poland 54°10N 19°25E 65 A10
Elbrus Russia 43°21N 42°30E 71 F7
Elburz Mts. Iran 36°0N 52°0E 87 B8
Elche Spain 38°15N 0°42W 67 C5
Elda Spain 38°29N 0°47W 67 C5

Eldoret Kenya 0°30N 35°17E 96 D7
Elektrostal Russia 55°41N 38°32E 70 C6
Elemi Triangle Africa 5°0N 35°20E 96 C7
Elephant Butte Res. U.S.A. 33°9N 107°11W 110 D5
Elephant I. Antarctica 61°0S 55°0W 55 C18
Eleuthera I. Bahamas 25°0N 76°20W 115 C9
Elgin U.K. 57°39N 3°19W 23 G11
Elgin U.S.A. 42°2N 88°17W 112 D3
Elgon, Mt. Africa 1°10N 34°30E 96 D6
Elham U.K. 51°9N 1°8E 31 D11
Elishaw U.K. 55°15N 2°14W 26 B4
Elista Russia 46°16N 44°14E 71 E7
Elizabeth U.S.A. 40°39N 74°12W 113 E10
Elizabeth City U.S.A. 36°18N 76°14W 111 C11
Elizabethtown U.S.A. 37°42N 85°52W 112 G5
Elkhart U.S.A. 41°41N 85°58W 112 E5
Elkins U.S.A. 38°55N 79°51W 112 F8
Elko U.S.A. 40°50N 115°46W 110 B3
Elland U.K. 53°41N 1°50W 27 E5
Ellef Ringnes I. Canada 78°30N 102°2W 109 B9
Ellen → U.K. 54°44N 3°30W 26 C2
Ellensburg U.S.A. 46°59N 120°34W 110 A2
Ellerton Barbados 13°7N 59°33W 114 c
Ellesmere U.K. 52°55N 2°53W 27 G3
Ellesmere I. Canada 79°30N 80°0W 109 B12
Ellesmere Port U.K. 53°17N 2°54W 27 F3
Ellington U.K. 55°14N 1°33W 26 B5
Elliot Lake Canada 46°25N 82°35W 109 E11
Ellon U.K. 57°22N 2°4W 23 H13
Ellsworth Land Antarctica 76°0S 89°0W 55 D16
Elmalı Turkey 36°44N 29°56E 71 G4
Elmira U.S.A. 42°6N 76°48W 112 D9
Elmswell U.K. 52°15N 0°55E 31 B10
Eluru India 16°48N 81°8E 85 L12
Ely U.K. 52°24N 0°16E 31 B9
Ely U.S.A. 39°15N 114°54W 110 C4
Elyria U.S.A. 41°22N 82°7W 112 E6
eMalahleni S. Africa 25°51S 29°14E 97 K5
Emämrüd Iran 36°30N 55°0E 87 B8
Embarcación Argentina 23°10S 64°0W 121 E3
Embleton U.K. 55°29N 1°38W 26 B5
Emden Germany 53°21N 7°12E 64 B4
Emerald Australia 37°56S 145°29E 98 E8
Emmen Neths. 52°48N 6°57E 64 B4
Emmonak U.S.A. 62°47N 164°31W 108 C3
Empalme Mexico 27°58N 110°51W 114 B2
Empangeni S. Africa 28°50S 31°52E 97 K6
Empedrado Argentina 28°0S 58°46W 121 E4
Emporia U.S.A. 38°25N 96°11W 111 C7
Emporium U.S.A. 41°31N 78°14W 112 E8
Empty Quarter = Rub' al Khālī
Si. Arabia 19°0N 48°0E 89 D4
Ems → Germany 53°20N 7°12E 64 B4
En Nahud Sudan 12°45N 28°25E 95 F11
Enard B. U.K. 58°5N 5°20W 22 F7
Encarnación Paraguay 27°15S 55°50W 121 E4
Encounter B. Australia 35°45S 138°45E 98 H6
Ende Indonesia 8°45S 121°40E 83 F6
Enderbury Kiribati 3°8S 171°5W 102 H10
Enderby U.K. 52°36N 1°13W 27 G6
Enderby Land Antarctica 66°0S 53°0E 55 C5
Endicott U.S.A. 42°6N 76°4W 113 D9
Enewetak Atoll Marshall Is. 11°30N 162°15E 102 F8
Enez Turkey 40°45N 26°5E 71 F4
Enfield □ U.K. 51°38N 0°5W 31 C8
Engadin Switz. 46°45N 10°10E 64 E6
Engels Russia 51°28N 46°6E 71 D8
Enggano Indonesia 5°20S 102°40E 82 F2
England □ U.K. 53°0N 2°0W 62 E6
English → Canada 49°12N 91°5W 108 D10
English Channel Europe 50°0N 2°0W 62 F6
Enid U.S.A. 36°24N 97°53W 110 C7
Ennadai L. Canada 60°58N 101°20W 108 C9
Ennedi Chad 17°15N 22°0E 95 E10
Ennerdale Water U.K. 54°32N 3°24W 26 C2
Ennis Ireland 52°51N 8°59W 20 C5
Enniscorthy Ireland 52°30N 6°34W 21 D9
Enniskillen U.K. 54°21N 7°39W 18 C6
Ennistimon Ireland 52°57N 9°17W 20 C4
Enns → Austria 48°14N 14°32E 64 D8
Enschede Neths. 52°13N 6°53E 64 B4
Ensenada Mexico 31°52N 116°37W 114 A1
Enshi China 30°18N 109°29E 79 E10
Enstone U.K. 51°55N 1°27W 30 C6
Entebbe Uganda 0°4N 32°28E 96 D6
Entre Ríos □ Argentina 30°30S 58°30W 121 F4
Enugu Nigeria 6°20N 7°30E 94 G7
Eólie, Ís. Italy 38°30N 14°57E 68 E6
Épernay France 49°3N 3°56E 66 B5
Épinal France 48°10N 6°27E 66 B7
Epping U.K. 51°41N 0°7E 31 C9
Epping Forest U.K. 51°40N 0°5E 31 C9
Epsom U.K. 51°19N 0°16W 31 D8
Epworth U.K. 53°32N 0°48W 27 E7
Equatorial Guinea ■ Africa 2°0N 8°0E 96 D1
Er Rachidia Morocco 31°58N 4°20W 94 B4
Erciyeş Dağı Turkey 38°30N 35°30E 86 B3
Erebus, Mt. Antarctica 77°35S 167°0E 55 D11
Ereğli Konya, Turkey 37°31N 34°4E 71 G5
Ereğli Zonguldak, Turkey 41°15N 31°24E 71 F5
Erenhot China 43°48N 112°2E 79 C11
Erfurt Germany 50°58N 11°2E 64 C6
Ergeni Lowlands Russia 47°0N 44°0E 71 E7
Eriboll, L. U.K. 58°30N 4°42W 23 E8
Erie U.S.A. 42°8N 80°5W 112 D7
Erie, L. N. Amer. 42°15N 81°0W 112 D7
Eriskay U.K. 57°4N 7°18W 22 H3
Eritrea ■ Africa 14°0N 38°30E 89 E2
Erlangen Germany 49°36N 11°0E 64 D6
Ermoupoli Greece 37°28N 24°57E 69 F11
Ernakulam India 9°58N 76°22E 84 Q10
Erne → Ireland 54°30N 8°16W 18 C5
Erne, Lower L. U.K. 54°28N 7°47W 18 C6
Erne, Upper L. U.K. 54°14N 7°32W 18 C6
Erode India 11°24N 77°45E 84 P10
Erramala Hills India 15°30N 78°15E 84 M11
Errigal Ireland 55°2N 8°6W 18 A5
Erris Hd. Ireland 54°17N 10°0W 18 B1
Erromango Vanuatu 18°45S 169°5E 99 D12
Erzgebirge Germany 50°27N 12°55E 64 C7
Erzincan Turkey 39°46N 39°30E 71 G6

Erzurum Turkey 39°57N 41°15E 71 G7
Esbjerg Denmark 55°29N 8°29E 63 F5
Escada Brazil 8°22S 35°8W 122 A3
Escanaba U.S.A. 45°45N 87°4W 112 C4
Esch-sur-Alzette Lux. 49°32N 6°0E 64 D3
Escrick U.K. 53°53N 1°2W 27 E6
Escuinapa de Hidalgo
Mexico 22°50N 105°50W 114 C3
Escuintla Guatemala 14°20N 90°48W 114 E6
Esfahān Iran 32°39N 51°43E 87 C7
Esha Ness U.K. 60°29N 1°38W 22 B14
Esk → Cumb., U.K. 54°20N 3°24W 26 D2
Esk → Dumf. & Gall., U.K. 54°58N 3°2W 25 E9
Esk → N. Yorks., U.K. 54°30N 0°37W 26 D7
Eskdale U.K. 55°12N 3°4W 25 D9
Esker Siding Canada 53°53N 66°25W 109 D13
Eskilstuna Sweden 59°22N 16°32E 63 F7
Eskişehir Turkey 39°50N 30°30E 71 G5
Eslāmābād-e Gharb Iran 34°10N 46°30E 86 C6
Esna Egypt 25°17N 32°30E 95 C12
Esperance Australia 33°45S 121°55E 98 G3
Espinhaço, Serra do Brazil 17°30S 43°30W 122 C2
Espírito Santo □ Brazil 20°0S 40°45W 122 C2
Espiritu Santo Vanuatu 15°15S 166°50E 99 D12
Espoo Finland 60°12N 24°40E 63 E8
Essaouira Morocco 31°32N 9°42W 94 B4
Essen Germany 51°28N 7°2E 64 C4
Essequibo → Guyana 6°50N 58°30W 120 B4
Essex □ U.K. 51°54N 0°27E 31 C9
Esslingen Germany 48°44N 9°18E 64 D5
Estados, I. de Los Argentina 54°40S 64°30W 121 H3
Estância Brazil 11°16S 37°26W 122 B3
Estevan Canada 49°10N 102°59W 108 E9
Estonia ■ Europe 58°30N 25°30E 63 F8
Estrela, Serra da Portugal 40°10N 7°45W 67 B2
Estrondo, Serra do Brazil 7°20S 48°0W 120 C5
Etawah India 26°48N 79°6E 84 F11
Etchingham U.K. 51°0N 0°26E 31 D9
Ethiopia ■ Africa 8°0N 40°0E 89 F3
Ethiopian Highlands Ethiopia 10°0N 37°0E 89 F2
Etive, L. U.K. 56°29N 5°10W 24 B5
Etna Italy 37°50N 14°55E 68 F6
Eton U.K. 51°30N 0°36W 31 C7
Etosha Pan Namibia 18°40S 16°30E 97 H3
Ettington U.K. 52°8N 1°35W 30 B6
Ettrick Forest U.K. 55°30N 3°0W 25 D9
Ettrick Water → U.K. 55°31N 2°55W 25 C10
Euclid U.S.A. 41°34N 81°32W 112 E7
Eugene U.S.A. 44°5N 123°4W 110 B2
Euphrates → Asia 31°0N 47°25E 86 D6
Eureka Canada 80°0N 85°56W 109 B11
Eureka U.S.A. 40°47N 124°9W 110 B1
Europa, Île Ind. Oc. 22°20S 40°22E 97 J8
Europa, Picos de Spain 43°10N 4°49W 67 A3
Europe 50°0N 20°0E 56 E10
Eurotunnel Terminal U.K. 51°6N 1°10E 31 D11
Euxton U.K. 53°41N 2°41W 27 E3
Evanston Ill., U.S.A. 42°3N 87°40W 112 D4
Evanston Wyo., U.S.A. 41°16N 110°58W 110 B4
Evansville U.S.A. 37°58N 87°35W 112 G4
Evercreech U.K. 51°9N 2°30W 30 D4
Everest, Mt. Nepal 28°5N 86°58E 85 E15
Everett U.S.A. 47°59N 122°12W 110 A2
Everglades, The U.S.A. 25°50N 81°0W 111 E10
Evesham U.K. 52°6N 1°56W 30 B5
Évora Portugal 38°33N 7°57W 67 C2
Évreux France 49°3N 1°8E 66 B4
Evros → Greece 41°40N 26°34E 69 D12
Ewe, L. U.K. 57°49N 5°38W 22 G6
Ewell U.K. 51°20N 0°14W 31 D8
Ewhurst U.K. 51°9N 0°25W 31 D8
Exe → U.K. 50°41N 3°29W 29 F7
Exeter U.K. 50°43N 3°31W 29 F6
Exminster U.K. 50°40N 3°29W 29 F7
Exmoor △ U.K. 51°8N 3°42W 29 E6
Exmouth U.K. 50°37N 3°25W 29 F7
Exton U.K. 52°42N 0°38W 27 G7
Extremadura □ Spain 39°30N 6°5W 67 C2
Eyam U.K. 53°17N 1°40W 27 F5
Eyasi, L. Tanzania 3°30S 35°0E 96 E6
Eye Cambs., U.K. 52°37N 0°11W 31 A8
Eye Suffolk, U.K. 52°19N 1°9E 31 B11
Eye Pen. U.K. 58°13N 6°10W 22 F5
Eyemouth U.K. 55°52N 2°5W 25 C11
Eyjafjallajökull Iceland 63°38N 19°36W 63 B2
Eynsham U.K. 51°47N 1°22W 30 C6
Eyre, L. Australia 29°30S 137°26E 98 F6
Eyre Pen. Australia 33°30S 136°17E 98 G6

F

F.Y.R.O.M. = Macedonia ■
Europe 41°53N 21°40E 69 D9
Faenza Italy 44°17N 11°53E 68 B4
Fair Hd. U.K. 55°14N 6°9W 19 A9
Fair Isle U.K. 59°32N 1°38W 22 C14
Fairbanks U.S.A. 64°51N 147°43W 108 C5
Fairfield U.S.A. 38°23N 88°22W 112 F3
Fairford U.K. 51°43N 1°46W 30 C5
Fairlight U.K. 50°52N 0°40E 31 E10
Fairmont U.S.A. 39°29N 80°9W 112 F7
Fairweather, Mt. U.S.A. 58°55N 137°32W 108 D6
Faisalabad Pakistan 31°30N 73°5E 84 D8
Faizabad India 26°45N 82°10E 85 F13
Fakenham U.K. 52°51N 0°51E 31 A10
Falcon Res. U.S.A. 26°34N 99°10W 110 E7
Faldingworth U.K. 53°21N 0°24W 27 F8
Falkirk U.K. 56°0N 3°47W 25 C8
Falkland U.K. 56°16N 3°12W 25 B9
Falkland Is. ☑ Atl. Oc. 51°30S 59°0W 121 H4
Fall River U.S.A. 41°43N 71°10W 113 E12
Falmouth Jamaica 18°30N 77°40W 114 a
Falmouth U.K. 50°9N 5°5W 29 G3
Falmouth B. U.K. 50°6N 5°5W 29 G3
Falsa, Pta. Mexico 27°51N 115°3W 104 G8
False B. S. Africa 34°15S 18°40E 97 L3
Falstone U.K. 55°11N 2°26W 26 B4
Falun Sweden 60°37N 15°37E 63 E7
Famagusta Cyprus 35°8N 33°55E 86 C3
Fanad Hd. Ireland 55°17N 7°38W 18 A6

Fannich, L. U.K. 57°38N 4°59W 23 G8
Fano Italy 43°50N 13°1E 68 C5
Far East Asia 40°0N 130°0E 72 E14
Farāh Afghan. 32°20N 62°7E 87 C10
Farasān, Si. Arabia 16°45N 41°55E 89 D3
Fareham U.K. 50°51N 1°11W 30 E6
Farewell C. Greenland 59°48N 43°55W 104 D15
Farghona Uzbekistan 40°23N 71°19E 76 E7
Fargo U.S.A. 46°53N 96°48W 111 A7
Faridabad India 28°26N 77°19E 84 E10
Faringdon U.K. 51°39N 1°34W 30 C5
Farmington U.S.A. 36°44N 108°12W 110 C5
Farmville U.S.A. 37°18N 78°24W 112 G8
Farnborough U.K. 51°16N 0°45W 31 D7
Farne Is. U.K. 55°38N 1°37W 26 A5
Farnham U.K. 51°13N 0°47W 31 D7
Farnworth U.K. 53°34N 2°25W 27 E4
Faro Canada 62°11N 133°22W 108 C6
Faro Portugal 37°2N 7°55W 67 D2
Faroe Is. ☑ Atl. Oc. 62°0N 7°0W 57 C4
Fārs □ Iran 29°30N 55°0E 87 D8
Faslane U.K. 56°5N 4°49W 24 B6
Fataka Solomon Is. 11°55S 170°12E 99 C12
Fatehgarh India 27°25N 79°35E 84 F11
Fatehpur Raj., India 28°0N 74°40E 84 F9
Fatehpur Ut. P., India 25°56N 81°13E 85 G12
Fauldhouse U.K. 55°50N 3°43W 25 C8
Faversham U.K. 51°19N 0°56E 31 D10
Fawley U.K. 50°50N 1°20W 30 E6
Fayetteville Ark., U.S.A. 36°4N 94°10W 111 C8
Fayetteville N.C., U.S.A. 35°3N 78°53W 111 D11
Fazeley U.K. 52°37N 1°40W 27 G5
Fazilka India 30°27N 74°2E 84 D9
Fdérik Mauritania 22°40N 12°45W 94 D3
Feale → Ireland 52°27N 9°37W 20 D3
Fear, C. U.S.A. 33°50N 77°58W 111 D11
Fécamp France 49°45N 0°22E 66 B4
Fehmarn Germany 54°27N 11°7E 64 A6
Feira de Santana Brazil 12°15S 38°57W 122 B3
Felipe Carrillo Puerto Mexico 19°38N 88°3W 114 D7
Felixstowe U.K. 51°58N 1°23E 31 C11
Felton U.K. 55°18N 1°42W 26 B5
Feltwell U.K. 52°30N 0°32E 31 B10
Fenny Bentley U.K. 53°3N 1°45W 27 F5
Fenny Compton U.K. 52°10N 1°23W 30 B6
Fenny Stratford U.K. 52°0N 0°44W 31 C7
Fens, The U.K. 52°38N 0°2W 31 A8
Fenyang China 37°18N 111°48E 79 D11
Feodosiya Ukraine 45°2N 35°16E 71 E6
Fergus Falls U.S.A. 46°17N 96°4W 111 A7
Ferkéssédougou Ivory C. 9°35N 5°6W 94 G4
Fermanagh □ U.K. 54°21N 7°40W 18 C6
Fermont Canada 52°47N 67°5W 109 D13
Fermoy Ireland 52°9N 8°16W 20 D6
Fernhurst U.K. 51°3N 0°43W 31 D7
Ferrara Italy 44°50N 11°35E 68 B4
Ferret, C. France 44°38N 1°15W 66 D3
Ferrol Spain 43°29N 8°15W 67 A1
Ferryhill U.K. 54°41N 1°33W 26 C5
Fès Morocco 34°0N 5°0W 94 B5
Fethiye Turkey 36°36N 29°6E 71 G4
Fetlar U.K. 60°36N 0°52W 22 A16
Feuilles → Canada 58°47N 70°4W 109 D12
Feyzābād Afghan. 37°7N 70°33E 87 B12
Ffestiniog U.K. 52°57N 3°55W 28 B6
Fianarantsoa Madag. 21°26S 47°5E 97 J9
Fife □ U.K. 56°16N 3°1W 25 B9
Fife Ness U.K. 56°17N 2°35W 25 B10
Figeac France 44°37N 2°2E 66 D5
Figueres Spain 42°18N 2°58E 67 A7
Fiji ■ Pac. Oc. 17°20S 179°0E 99 D14
Filby U.K. 52°40N 1°39E 31 A12
Filey U.K. 54°12N 0°18W 26 D8
Filey B. U.K. 54°12N 0°15W 26 D8
Filton U.K. 51°30N 2°34W 30 C3
Fincham U.K. 52°38N 0°30E 31 A9
Findhorn → U.K. 57°38N 3°38W 23 G10
Findlay U.S.A. 41°2N 83°39W 112 E6
Finedon U.K. 52°21N 0°39W 31 B7
Fingal's Cave U.K. 56°26N 6°21W 24 B3
Finglas Ireland 53°23N 6°19W 21 B10
Finike Turkey 36°21N 30°10E 86 B2
Finland ■ Europe 63°0N 27°0E 63 E9
Finland, G. of Europe 60°0N 26°0E 63 F9
Finlay → Canada 57°0N 125°10W 108 D7
Finn → Ireland 54°51N 7°28W 18 B7
Firozabad India 27°10N 78°25E 84 F11
Firozpur India 30°55N 74°40E 84 D9
Fish → Namibia 28°7S 17°10E 97 K3
Fishguard U.K. 52°0N 4°58W 28 D3
Fishtoft U.K. 52°58N 0°1E 27 G9
Fisterra, C. Spain 42°50N 9°19W 67 A1
Fitchburg U.S.A. 42°35N 71°48W 113 D12
Flagstaff U.S.A. 35°12N 111°39W 110 C4
Flamborough U.K. 54°7N 0°7W 26 D8
Flamborough Hd. U.K. 54°7N 0°5W 26 D8
Flandre Europe 50°50N 2°30E 64 C2
Flathead L. U.S.A. 47°51N 114°8W 110 A4
Flattery, C. U.S.A. 48°23N 124°29W 110 A2
Fleet U.K. 51°17N 0°50W 31 D7
Fleetwood U.K. 53°55N 3°1W 27 E2
Flensburg Germany 54°47N 9°27E 64 A5
Flers France 48°47N 0°33W 66 B3
Flimby U.K. 54°42N 3°30W 26 C2
Flin Flon Canada 54°46N 101°53W 108 D9
Flinders → Australia 17°36S 140°36E 98 D7
Flinders I. Australia 40°0S 148°0E 98 H8
Flinders Ranges Australia 31°30S 138°30E 98 G6
Flint U.K. 53°15N 3°8W 28 A7
Flint U.S.A. 43°1N 83°41W 112 D6
Flint → U.S.A. 30°57N 84°34W 111 D10
Flint I. Kiribati 11°26S 151°48W 103 J12
Flintshire □ U.K. 53°17N 3°17W 28 A7
Flitwick U.K. 52°0N 0°30W 31 C8
Flodden U.K. 55°37N 2°8W 26 A4
Flora U.S.A. 38°40N 88°29W 112 F3
Florence Italy 43°46N 11°15E 68 C4
Florencia Colombia 1°36N 75°36W 120 B2
Flores Indonesia 8°35S 121°0E 83 F6

Flores Sea Indonesia 6°30S 120°0E 83 F6
Florianópolis Brazil 27°30S 48°30W 121 E5
Florida Uruguay 34°7S 56°10W 121 F4
Florida □ U.S.A. 28°0N 82°0W 111 E10
Florida, Straits of U.S.A. 25°0N 80°0W 115 C9
Florida Keys U.S.A. 24°40N 81°0W 111 F10
Florø Norway 61°35N 5°1E 63 E5
Fly → Papua N. G. 8°25S 143°0E 98 B7
Fochabers U.K. 57°37N 3°6W 23 G11
Focşani Romania 45°41N 27°15E 65 F14
Fóggia Italy 41°27N 15°34E 68 D6
Foix France 42°58N 1°38E 66 E4
Foligno Italy 42°57N 12°42E 68 C5
Folkestone U.K. 51°5N 1°12E 31 D11
Fond-du-Lac Canada 59°19N 107°12W 108 D9
Fond du Lac U.S.A. 43°47N 88°27W 112 D3
Fongafale Tuvalu 8°31S 179°13E 99 B14
Fonseca, G. de Cent. Amer. 13°10N 87°40W 104 H11
Fontainebleau France 48°24N 2°40E 66 B5
Fontenay-le-Comte France 46°28N 0°48W 66 C3
Fordham U.K. 52°19N 0°23E 31 B9
Fordingbridge U.K. 50°56N 1°47W 30 E5
Forel, Mt. Greenland 66°52N 36°55W 54 C6
Forest Row U.K. 51°5N 0°3E 31 D9
Forfar U.K. 56°39N 2°53W 23 J12
Forlì Italy 44°13N 12°3E 68 B5
Formartine U.K. 57°20N 2°15W 23 H13
Formby U.K. 53°34N 3°4W 27 E2
Formby Pt. U.K. 53°33N 3°6W 27 E2
Formentera Spain 38°43N 1°27E 67 C6
Formiga Brazil 20°27S 45°25W 122 D1
Formosa Argentina 26°15S 58°10W 121 E4
Formosa Brazil 15°32S 47°20W 122 C1
Forres U.K. 57°37N 3°37W 23 G10
Forsayth Australia 18°33S 143°34E 98 D7
Fort Albany Canada 52°15N 81°35W 109 D11
Fort Augustus U.K. 57°9N 4°42W 23 H8
Fort Chipewyan Canada 58°42N 111°8W 108 D8
Fort Collins U.S.A. 40°35N 105°5W 110 B5
Fort-Coulonge Canada 45°50N 76°45W 112 C9
Fort-de-France Martinique 14°36N 61°5W 115 E12
Fort Dodge U.S.A. 42°30N 94°11W 111 B8
Fort Good Hope Canada 66°14N 128°40W 108 C7
Fort Kent U.S.A. 47°15N 68°36W 113 B13
Fort Lauderdale U.S.A. 26°7N 80°8W 111 E10
Fort Liard Canada 60°14N 123°30W 108 C7
Fort MacKay Canada 57°12N 111°41W 108 D8
Fort Macleod Canada 49°45N 113°30W 108 E8
Fort McMurray Canada 56°44N 111°7W 108 D8
Fort McPherson Canada 67°30N 134°55W 108 C6
Fort Morgan U.S.A. 40°15N 103°48W 110 B6
Fort Myers U.S.A. 26°39N 81°52W 111 E10
Fort Nelson Canada 58°50N 122°44W 108 D7
Fort Nelson → Canada 59°32N 124°0W 108 D7
Fort Peck L. U.S.A. 48°0N 106°26W 110 A5
Fort Providence Canada 61°3N 117°40W 108 C8
Fort Resolution Canada 61°10N 113°40W 108 C8
Fort St. John Canada 56°15N 120°50W 108 D7
Fort Scott U.S.A. 37°50N 94°42W 111 C8
Fort Shevchenko Kazakhstan 44°35N 50°23E 71 F9
Fort Simpson Canada 61°45N 121°15W 108 C7
Fort Smith Canada 60°0N 111°51W 108 C8
Fort Smith U.S.A. 35°23N 94°25W 111 C8
Fort Stockton U.S.A. 30°53N 102°53W 110 D6
Fort Wayne U.S.A. 41°4N 85°9W 112 E5
Fort William U.K. 56°49N 5°7W 22 J7
Fort Worth U.S.A. 32°43N 97°19W 111 D7
Fort Yukon U.S.A. 66°34N 145°16W 108 C5
Fortaleza Brazil 3°45S 38°35W 120 C6
Forth → U.K. 56°9N 3°50W 25 B8
Forth, Firth of U.K. 56°5N 2°55W 25 B10
Fortrose U.K. 57°35N 4°9W 23 G9
Foshan China 23°3N 113°9E 79 G11
Fostoria U.S.A. 41°10N 83°25W 112 E6
Fothergill U.K. 54°43N 3°29W 26 C2
Fotheringhay U.K. 52°32N 0°27W 31 A8
Fougères France 48°21N 1°14W 66 B3
Foula U.K. 60°10N 2°5W 22 a
Foulness I. U.K. 51°36N 0°55E 31 C10
Foulness Pt. U.K. 51°37N 0°58E 31 C10
Foulsham U.K. 52°48N 0°59E 31 A10
Fountainhall U.K. 55°44N 2°53W 25 C10
Fouta Djallon Guinea 11°20N 12°10W 94 F3
Fovant U.K. 51°4N 2°0W 30 D5
Fowey U.K. 50°20N 4°39W 29 G4
Fownhope U.K. 52°0N 2°36W 30 B3
Foxe Basin Canada 66°0N 77°0W 109 C12
Foxe Chan. Canada 65°0N 80°0W 109 C11
Foxe Pen. Canada 65°0N 76°0W 109 C12
Foyle → U.K. 55°3N 7°15W 19 A7
Foyle, Lough U.K. 55°7N 7°4W 19 A7
Foynes Ireland 52°37N 9°7W 20 D4
Foz do Iguaçu Brazil 25°30S 54°30W 121 E4
Fraddon U.K. 50°23N 4°58W 29 G4
Framlingham U.K. 52°14N 1°21E 31 B11
Franca Brazil 20°33S 47°30W 122 D1
France ■ Europe 47°0N 3°0E 66 C5
Franceville Gabon 1°40S 13°32E 96 E2
Franche-Comté □ France 46°50N 5°55E 66 C6
Francis Case, L. U.S.A. 43°4N 98°34W 111 B7
Francistown Botswana 21°7S 27°33E 97 J5
François L. Canada 54°0N 125°30W 108 D7
Frankfort Ind., U.S.A. 40°17N 86°31W 112 E4
Frankfort Ky., U.S.A. 38°12N 84°52W 112 F5
Frankfurt Brandenburg,
Germany 52°20N 14°32E 64 B8
Frankfurt Hessen, Germany 50°7N 8°41E 64 C5
Fränkische Alb Germany 49°10N 11°23E 64 D6
Franklin N.H., U.S.A. 43°27N 71°39W 113 D12
Franklin Pa., U.S.A. 41°24N 79°50W 112 E8
Franklin D. Roosevelt L.
U.S.A. 48°18N 118°9W 110 A3
Franklin L. Canada 40°25N 115°22W 110 B3
Franklin Mts. Canada 65°0N 125°0W 108 C7
Franklin Str. Canada 72°0N 96°0W 108 B10
Frant U.K. 51°5N 0°16E 31 D9
Franz Josef Land Arctic 82°0N 55°0E 54 A10
Fraser → Canada 49°7N 123°11W 108 E7
Fraserburgh U.K. 57°42N 2°1W 23 G13
Frederick U.S.A. 39°25N 77°25W 112 F9

Fredericksburg   Guadix

Fredericksburg U.S.A. 38°18N 77°28W 112 F9
Fredericktown U.S.A. 37°34N 90°18W 112 G2
Fredericton Canada 45°57N 66°40W 113 C14
Frederikshavn Denmark 57°28N 10°31E 63 F6
Fredonia U.S.A. 42°26N 79°20W 112 D8
Fredrikstad Norway 59°13N 10°57E 63 F6
Free State □ S. Africa 28°30S 27°0E 97 K5
Freeport Bahamas 26°30N 78°47W 115 B9
Freeport Ill., U.S.A. 42°17N 89°36W 112 D3
Freeport Tex., U.S.A. 28°57N 95°21W 111 E7
Freetown S. Leone 8°30N 13°17W 94 G3
Freiburg Germany 47°59N 7°51E 64 E4
Fréjus France 43°25N 6°44E 66 E7
Fremont U.S.A. 41°21N 83°7W 112 E6
French Creek → U.S.A. 41°24N 79°50W 112 E8
French Guiana ☑ S. Amer. 4°0N 53°0W 120 B4
French Polynesia ☑ Pac. Oc. 20°0S 145°0W 103 J13
Frenchman Cr. →
  N. Amer. 48°31N 107°10W 110 A5
Freshwater U.K. 50°41N 1°31W 30 E5
Fresnillo Mexico 23°10N 102°53W 114 C4
Fresno U.S.A. 36°44N 119°47W 110 C3
Fria, C. Namibia 18°0S 12°0E 90 H5
Fridaythorpe U.K. 54°2N 0°39W 27 D7
Friedrichshafen Germany 47°39N 9°30E 64 E5
Frimley U.K. 51°19N 0°44W 31 D7
Frinton-on-Sea U.K. 51°49N 1°15E 31 C11
Frio, C. Brazil 22°50S 41°50W 117 F6
Frizington U.K. 54°33N 3°28W 26 C2
Frobisher B. Canada 62°30N 66°0W 109 C13
Frobisher L. Canada 56°20N 108°15W 108 D9
Frodsham U.K. 53°18N 2°43W 27 F3
Frome U.K. 51°14N 2°19W 30 D4
Frome → U.K. 50°41N 2°6W 30 E4
Front Range U.S.A. 40°25N 105°45W 110 B5
Front Royal U.S.A. 38°55N 78°12W 112 F8
Frutal Brazil 20°0S 49°0W 122 C1
Frýdek-Místek Czech Rep. 49°40N 18°20E 65 D10
Fuchū Japan 34°34N 133°14E 81 F3
Fuengirola Spain 36°32N 4°41W 67 D3
Fuerte → Mexico 25°54N 109°22W 114 B3
Fuerteventura Canary Is. 28°30N 14°0W 94 C3
Fuidhaigh = Wiay U.K. 57°24N 7°13W 22 H3
Fuji Japan 35°9N 138°39E 81 F6
Fuji-San Japan 35°22N 138°44E 81 F6
Fujian □ China 26°0N 118°0E 79 F12
Fujin China 47°16N 132°1E 79 B15
Fukui Japan 36°5N 136°10E 81 E5
Fukuoka Japan 33°39N 130°21E 81 G2
Fukushima Japan 37°44N 140°28E 81 F7
Fukuyama Japan 34°35N 133°20E 81 F3
Fulda Germany 50°32N 9°40E 64 C5
Fulda → Germany 51°25N 9°39E 64 C5
Fulton U.S.A. 43°19N 76°25W 112 D9
Fulwood U.K. 53°47N 2°40W 27 E3
Funabashi Japan 35°45N 140°0E 81 F7
Funchal Madeira 32°38N 16°54W 94 B2
Fundy, B. of Canada 45°0N 66°0W 113 C15
Furnas, Represa de Brazil 20°50S 45°30W 122 D1
Furneaux Group Australia 40°10S 147°50E 98 J8
Fürth Germany 49°28N 10°59E 64 D6
Fury and Hecla Str. Canada 69°56N 84°0W 109 C11
Fushun China 41°50N 123°56E 79 C13
Fustic Barbados 13°16N 59°38W 114 c
Fuxin China 42°5N 121°48E 79 C13
Fuyang China 33°0N 115°48E 79 E12
Fuyong China 22°40N 113°49E 79 a
Fuyu Heilongjiang, China 47°49N 124°27E 79 B13
Fuyu Jilin, China 45°12N 124°43E 79 B13
Fuyun China 47°0N 89°28E 78 B6
Fuzhou China 26°5N 119°16E 79 F12
Fylingdales Moor U.K. 54°25N 0°41W 26 D7
Fyn Denmark 55°20N 10°30E 63 F6
Fyne, L. U.K. 55°59N 5°23W 24 C5

G

Gaalkacyo Somalia 6°30N 47°30E 89 F4
Gabès Tunisia 33°53N 10°2E 95 B8
Gabès, G. de Tunisia 34°0N 10°30E 95 B8
Gabon ■ Africa 0°10S 10°0E 96 E2
Gaborone Botswana 24°45S 25°57E 97 J5
Gabrovo Bulgaria 42°52N 25°19E 69 C11
Gachsārān Iran 30°15N 50°45E 87 D7
Gadarwara India 22°50N 78°50E 84 H11
Gadsden U.S.A. 34°1N 86°1W 111 D9
Gafsa Tunisia 34°24N 8°43E 95 B7
Găgăuzia □ Moldova 46°10N 28°40E 65 E15
Gagnoa Ivory C. 6°56N 5°16W 94 G4
Gagnon Canada 51°50N 68°5W 109 D13
Gainesville Fla., U.S.A. 29°40N 82°20W 111 E10
Gainesville Ga., U.S.A. 34°18N 83°50W 111 D10
Gainford U.K. 54°34N 1°43W 26 C5
Gainsborough U.K. 53°24N 0°46W 27 F7
Gairdner, L. Australia 31°30S 136°0E 98 G6
Gairloch U.K. 57°43N 5°41W 22 G6
Gairloch, L. U.K. 57°43N 5°45W 22 G6
Galapagos Ecuador 0°0 91°0W 117 D1
Galashiels U.K. 55°37N 2°49W 25 C10
Galați Romania 45°27N 28°2E 65 F15
Galdhøpiggen Norway 61°38N 8°18E 63 E5
Galena U.S.A. 64°44N 156°56W 108 C4
Galesburg U.S.A. 40°57N 90°22W 112 E2
Galgate U.K. 53°59N 2°46W 27 E3
Galicia □ Spain 42°43N 7°45W 67 A2
Galilee, Sea of Israel 32°45N 35°35E 86 C3
Galina Pt. Jamaica 18°24N 76°58W 114 a
Gallan Hd. U.K. 58°15N 7°2W 22 F3
Galle Sri Lanka 6°5N 80°10E 84 R12
Galley Hd. Ireland 51°32N 8°55W 20 E5
Gallinas, Pta. Colombia 12°28N 71°40W 120 A2
Gallipoli Italy 40°3N 18°0E 69 D8
Gallipolis U.S.A. 38°49N 82°12W 112 F6
Gällivare Sweden 67°9N 20°40E 63 D7
Galloway U.K. 55°1N 4°29W 24 D7
Galloway, Mull of U.K. 54°39N 4°52W 24 E4
Gallup U.S.A. 35°32N 108°45W 110 C5
Galmpton U.K. 50°23N 3°59W 29 G6
Galmudug Somalia 6°30N 48°0E 89 F4
Galston U.K. 55°36N 4°24W 24 C7
Galty Mts. Ireland 52°22N 8°10W 20 D6
Galtymore Ireland 52°21N 8°11W 20 D6

Galveston U.S.A. 29°18N 94°48W 111 E8
Galway Ireland 53°17N 9°3W 20 B4
Galway □ Ireland 53°22N 9°1W 20 B4
Galway B. Ireland 53°13N 9°10W 20 B4
Gambia ■ W. Afr. 13°25N 16°0W 94 F2
Gambia → W. Afr. 13°28N 16°34W 94 F2
Gamlingay U.K. 52°10N 0°11W 31 B8
Gan Jiang → China 29°15N 116°0E 79 F12
Gananoque Canada 44°20N 76°10W 113 C9
Gäncä Azerbaijan 40°45N 46°20E 71 F8
Gand = Gent Belgium 51°2N 3°42E 64 C2
Gandak → India 25°39N 85°13E 85 G14
Gander Canada 48°58N 54°35W 109 E14
Gandhi Sagar India 24°40N 75°40E 84 G9
Gandia Spain 38°58N 0°9W 67 C5
Ganganagar India 29°56N 73°56E 84 E8
Ganges → India 23°20N 90°30E 85 H17
Gangneung S. Korea 37°45N 128°54E 79 D14
Gangtok India 27°20N 88°37E 85 F16
Gannett Peak U.S.A. 43°11N 109°39W 110 B5
Gansu □ China 36°0N 104°0E 78 D9
Ganzhou China 25°51N 114°56E 79 F11
Gao Mali 16°15N 0°5W 94 E5
Gap France 44°33N 6°5E 66 D7
Gar China 32°10N 79°58E 78 E4
Garanhuns Brazil 8°50S 36°30W 122 A3
Garboldisham U.K. 52°23N 0°57E 31 B10
Garda, L. di Italy 45°40N 10°41E 68 B4
Garden City U.S.A. 37°58N 100°53W 110 C6
Gardēz Afghan. 33°37N 69°9E 87 C12
Gare L. U.K. 56°1N 4°50W 24 B6
Garforth U.K. 53°47N 1°24W 27 E6
Gargrave U.K. 53°59N 2°7W 27 E4
Garioch U.K. 57°18N 2°40W 23 H12
Garissa Kenya 0°25S 39°40E 96 E7
Garonne → France 45°2N 0°36W 66 D3
Garoowe Somalia 8°25N 48°33E 89 F4
Garoua Cameroon 9°19N 13°21E 95 G8
Garron Pt. U.K. 55°3N 5°59W 19 A10
Garry → U.K. 56°44N 3°47W 23 J10
Garry, L. Canada 65°58N 100°18W 108 C9
Garsdale Head U.K. 54°20N 2°20W 26 D4
Garstang U.K. 53°55N 2°46W 27 E3
Gary U.S.A. 41°36N 87°20W 112 E4
Garzê China 31°38N 100°1E 78 E9
Gascogne France 43°45N 0°20E 66 E4
Gascogne, G. de Europe 44°0N 2°0W 66 E2
Gashua Nigeria 12°54N 11°0E 95 F8
Gaspé Canada 48°52N 64°30W 109 E13
Gaspé, C. de Canada 48°48N 64°7W 113 A15
Gaspésie, Pén. de la Canada 48°45N 65°40W 113 A15
Gata, Sierra de Spain 40°20N 6°45W 67 B2
Gatehouse of Fleet U.K. 54°53N 4°12W 24 E7
Gateshead U.K. 54°57N 1°35W 26 C5
Gatineau Canada 45°29N 75°39W 113 C10
Gatineau → Canada 45°27N 75°42W 113 C10
Gatley U.K. 53°24N 2°15W 27 F4
Gävle Sweden 60°40N 17°9E 63 E7
Gawilgarh Hills India 21°15N 76°45E 84 J10
Gawthwaite U.K. 54°16N 3°8W 26 D2
Gaxun Nur China 42°22N 100°30E 78 C9
Gaya India 24°47N 85°4E 85 G14
Gaylord U.S.A. 45°2N 84°41W 112 C5
Gayton U.K. 52°45N 0°36E 31 A10
Gaywood U.K. 52°46N 0°26E 31 A10
Gaza Gaza Strip 31°30N 34°28E 86 D3
Gaza Strip ■ Asia 31°29N 34°25E 86 D3
Gaziantep Turkey 37°6N 37°23E 71 G6
Gdańsk Poland 54°22N 18°40E 65 A10
Gdynia Poland 54°35N 18°33E 65 A10
Gebze Turkey 40°47N 29°25E 71 F4
Gedaref Sudan 14°2N 35°28E 95 F13
Gedney U.K. 52°48N 0°4E 27 G9
Gedser Denmark 54°35N 11°55E 63 G6
Geelong Australia 38°10S 144°22E 98 H7
Gejiu China 23°20N 103°10E 78 G9
Gela Italy 37°4N 14°15E 68 F6
Gelibolu Turkey 40°28N 26°43E 71 F4
Gelsenkirchen Germany 51°32N 7°6E 64 C4
General Acha Argentina 37°20S 64°38W 121 F3
General Alvear Argentina 35°0S 67°40W 121 F3
General Carrera, L. S. Amer. 46°35S 72°0W 121 G2
General Pico Argentina 35°45S 63°50W 121 F3
General Santos Phil. 6°5N 125°14E 83 C7
Geneva Switz. 46°12N 6°9E 64 E4
Geneva U.S.A. 42°52N 76°59W 112 D9
Geneva, L. = Léman, L. Europe 46°26N 6°30E 64 E4
Gennargentu, Mti. del Italy 40°19N 9°16E 68 D3
Genoa Italy 44°25N 8°57E 68 B3
Génova, G. di Italy 44°0N 9°0E 68 C3
Gent Belgium 51°2N 3°42E 64 C2
George S. Africa 33°58S 22°29E 97 L4
George → Canada 58°49N 66°10W 109 D13
George, L. U.S.A. 29°17N 81°36W 111 E10
George Town Cayman Is. 19°20N 81°24W 115 D8
George Town Malaysia 5°25N 100°20E 82 C2
George V Land Antarctica 69°0S 148°0E 55 C10
Georgetown Guyana 6°50N 58°12W 120 B4
Georgetown Ky., U.S.A. 38°13N 84°33W 112 F5
Georgetown S.C., U.S.A. 33°23N 79°17W 111 D11
Georgia □ U.S.A. 32°50N 83°15W 111 D10
Georgia ■ Asia 42°0N 43°0E 71 F7
Georgia, Str. of N. Amer. 49°25N 124°0W 104 E7
Georgian B. Canada 45°15N 81°0W 112 C7
Georgiyevsk Russia 44°12N 43°28E 71 F7
Gera Germany 50°53N 12°4E 64 C7
Geraldton Australia 28°48S 114°32E 98 F1
Germany ■ Europe 51°0N 10°0E 64 C6
Germiston S. Africa 26°13S 28°10E 97 K5
Gerrards Cross U.K. 51°35N 0°33W 31 C7
Getafe Spain 40°18N 3°43W 67 B4
Ghaghara → India 25°45N 84°40E 85 G14
Ghana ■ W. Afr. 8°0N 1°0W 94 G5
Ghardaïa Algeria 32°20N 3°37E 94 B6
Gharyān Libya 32°10N 13°0E 95 B8
Ghats, Eastern India 14°0N 78°50E 84 N11
Ghats, Western India 14°0N 75°0E 84 N9
Ghazal, Bahr el → Chad 13°0N 15°47E 95 F9

Ghazal, Bahr el →
  South Sudan 9°31N 30°25E 95 G12
Ghaziabad India 28°42N 77°26E 84 E10
Ghazipur India 25°38N 83°35E 85 G13
Ghazni Afghan. 33°30N 68°28E 87 C12
Ghent = Gent Belgium 51°2N 3°42E 64 C2
Giants Causeway U.K. 55°16N 6°29W 19 A9
Gibraltar ☑ Europe 36°7N 5°22W 67 D3
Gibraltar, Str. of Medit. S. 35°55N 5°40W 67 E3
Gibraltar Pt. U.K. 53°6N 0°19E 27 F9
Gibson Desert Australia 24°0S 126°0E 98 E4
Gifu Japan 35°30N 136°45E 81 F5
Giggleswick U.K. 54°5N 2°17W 26 D4
Gigha U.K. 55°42N 5°44W 24 C4
Gijón Spain 43°32N 5°42W 67 A3
Gila → U.S.A. 32°43N 114°33W 110 D4
Gīlān □ Iran 37°0N 50°0E 86 B7
Gilbert Is. Kiribati 1°0N 172°0E 102 G9
Gilgit India 35°50N 74°15E 84 B9
Gillam Canada 56°20N 94°40W 108 D10
Gillette U.S.A. 44°18N 105°30W 110 B5
Gillingham Dorset, U.K. 51°2N 2°18W 30 D4
Gillingham Medway, U.K. 51°23N 0°33E 31 D10
Gilsland U.K. 55°0N 2°34W 26 C3
Gimie, Mt. St. Lucia 13°54N 61°0W 114 b
Girdle Ness U.K. 57°9N 2°3W 23 H13
Giresun Turkey 40°55N 38°30E 71 F6
Girga Egypt 26°17N 31°55E 95 C12
Girona Spain 41°58N 2°46E 67 B7
Gironde → France 45°32N 1°7W 66 D3
Girvan U.K. 55°14N 4°51W 24 D6
Gisborne N.Z. 38°39S 178°5E 99 H14
Gisburn U.K. 53°56N 2°16W 27 E4
Gitega Burundi 3°26S 29°56E 96 E5
Gizhiga Russia 62°3N 160°30E 77 C17
Gjoa Haven Canada 68°38N 95°53W 108 C10
Glace Bay Canada 46°11N 59°58W 113 B18
Glacier Nat. Park △ U.S.A. 48°42N 113°48W 110 A4
Gladstone Australia 23°52S 151°16E 98 E9
Gladstone U.S.A. 45°51N 87°1W 112 C4
Gladwin U.S.A. 43°59N 84°29W 112 D5
Glamorgan, Vale of □ U.K. 51°28N 3°25W 29 E7
Glanaruddery Mts. Ireland 52°20N 9°27W 20 D4
Glanton U.K. 55°26N 1°54W 26 B5
Glasgow U.K. 55°51N 4°15W 24 C7
Glasgow Ky., U.S.A. 37°0N 85°55W 112 G5
Glasgow Mont., U.S.A. 48°12N 106°38W 110 A5
Glasgow Int. ✈ (GLA) U.K. 55°51N 4°21W 24 C7
Glasnevin U.K. 53°22N 6°15W 21 B10
Glastonbury U.K. 51°9N 2°43W 30 D5
Glazov Russia 58°9N 52°40E 70 C9
Glemsford U.K. 52°6N 0°40E 31 B10
Glen → U.K. 52°51N 0°7W 27 G8
Glen Affric U.K. 57°17N 5°1W 22 H7
Glen Almond U.K. 56°28N 3°50W 25 B8
Glen Coe U.K. 56°40N 5°0W 22 J7
Glen Etive U.K. 56°37N 5°0W 24 A5
Glen Garry Highl., U.K. 57°3N 5°7W 22 H7
Glen Garry Perth & Kinr., U.K. 56°47N 4°5W 23 J8
Glen Mor U.K. 57°9N 4°37W 23 H8
Glen Moriston U.K. 57°11N 4°52W 23 H8
Glen Orchy U.K. 56°27N 4°52W 24 B6
Glen Orrin U.K. 57°31N 4°45W 23 G8
Glen Oykel U.K. 58°5N 4°50W 23 F8
Glen Roy U.K. 56°56N 4°50W 23 J8
Glen Shee U.K. 56°50N 3°28W 23 J11
Glen Shiel U.K. 57°9N 5°18W 22 H6
Glen Spean U.K. 56°53N 4°40W 23 J8
Glendale Ariz., U.S.A. 33°32N 112°11W 110 D4
Glendale Calif., U.S.A. 34°9N 118°15W 110 D3
Glendive U.S.A. 47°7N 104°43W 110 A6
Gleneagles U.K. 56°17N 3°43W 25 B9
Glenfinnan U.K. 56°53N 5°27W 22 J7
Glengarriff Ireland 51°45N 9°34W 20 E3
Glenkens, The U.K. 55°12N 4°12W 24 D7
Glenluce U.K. 54°52N 4°48W 24 E6
Glennallen U.S.A. 62°7N 145°33W 108 C5
Glennamaddy Ireland 53°37N 8°33W 18 D4
Glenrothes U.K. 56°12N 3°10W 25 B9
Glens Falls U.S.A. 43°19N 73°39W 113 D11
Glenties Ireland 54°48N 8°17W 18 B5
Glenveagh △ Ireland 55°3N 8°1W 18 A5
Gliwice Poland 50°22N 18°41E 65 C10
Globe U.S.A. 33°24N 110°47W 110 D4
Głogów Poland 51°37N 16°5E 64 C9
Glomma → Norway 59°12N 10°57E 63 F6
Glossop U.K. 53°27N 1°56W 27 F5
Gloucester U.K. 51°53N 2°15W 30 C4
Gloucestershire □ U.K. 51°46N 2°15W 30 C4
Gloversville U.S.A. 43°3N 74°21W 113 D10
Glyn Ebwy = Ebbw Vale U.K. 51°46N 3°12W 28 D7
Gniezno Poland 52°30N 17°35E 65 B9
Gnosall U.K. 52°48N 2°14W 27 G4
Goa India 15°33N 73°59E 84 M8
Goa □ India 15°33N 73°59E 84 M8
Goat Fell U.K. 55°38N 5°11W 24 D5
Gobi Asia 44°0N 110°0E 79 C10
Godalming U.K. 51°11N 0°36W 31 D7
Godavari → India 16°25N 82°18E 85 L13
Goderich Canada 43°45N 81°41W 112 D7
Godhra India 22°49N 73°40E 84 H8
Godmanchester U.K. 52°20N 0°11W 31 B8
Godoy Cruz Argentina 32°56S 68°52W 121 F3
Gods → Canada 56°22N 92°51W 108 D10
Gods L. Canada 54°40N 94°15W 108 D10
Godshill U.K. 50°38N 1°15W 30 E6
Godstone U.K. 51°14N 0°3W 31 D8
Gogama Canada 47°35N 81°43W 112 B7
Goiânia Brazil 16°43S 49°20W 122 C1
Goiás Brazil 15°55S 50°10W 120 D4
Goiás □ Brazil 12°10S 48°0W 122 B1
Goio-Erê Brazil 24°12S 53°1W 121 E4
Gold Coast Australia 28°0S 153°25E 98 F9
Gold Coast W. Afr. 4°0N 1°40W 94 H5
Golden Vale Ireland 52°33N 8°17W 20 D6
Goldsboro U.S.A. 35°23N 77°59W 111 C11
Golästan □ Iran 37°20N 55°25E 87 B8
Golmud China 36°25N 94°53E 78 D7
Golspie U.K. 57°58N 3°59W 23 G10
Goma Dem. Rep. of the Congo 1°37S 29°10E 96 E5
Gomel Belarus 52°28N 31°0E 65 B16

Gomera Canary Is. 28°7N 17°14W 94 C2
Gómez Palacio Mexico 25°34N 103°30W 114 B4
Gonābād Iran 34°15N 58°45E 87 C9
Gonaïves Haiti 19°20N 72°42W 115 D10
Gonda India 27°9N 81°58E 85 F12
Gonder Ethiopia 12°39N 37°30E 89 E2
Gongbei China 22°12N 113°32E 79 a
Gongga Shan China 29°40N 101°55E 78 F9
Good Hope, C. of S. Africa 34°24S 18°30E 97 L3
Goodrich U.K. 51°52N 2°37W 30 C3
Goodwood U.K. 50°53N 0°44W 31 E7
Goole U.K. 53°42N 0°53W 27 E7
Goose L. U.S.A. 41°56N 120°26W 110 B2
Gorakhpur India 26°47N 83°23E 85 F13
Gordon U.K. 55°41N 2°34W 25 C10
Gore Ethiopia 8°12N 35°32E 89 F2
Gorebridge U.K. 55°50N 3°2W 25 C9
Gorey Ireland 52°41N 6°18W 21 C10
Gorgān Iran 36°55N 54°30E 87 B8
Goring U.K. 51°31N 1°7W 30 C6
Goring-by-Sea U.K. 50°49N 0°24W 31 E8
Gorleston U.K. 52°35N 1°44E 31 A12
Görlitz Germany 51°9N 14°58E 64 C8
Gorno-Altay □ Russia 51°0N 86°0E 76 D9
Gorontalo Indonesia 0°35N 123°5E 83 D6
Gort Ireland 53°3N 8°49W 20 B5
Gorzów Wielkopolski Poland 52°43N 15°15E 64 B8
Gosberton U.K. 52°53N 0°9W 27 G8
Gosforth U.K. 54°26N 3°27W 26 D2
Gosport U.K. 50°48N 1°9W 30 E6
Göta kanal Sweden 58°30N 15°58E 63 F7
Götaland Sweden 57°30N 14°30E 63 F6
Göteborg Sweden 57°43N 11°59E 63 F6
Gotha Germany 50°56N 10°42E 64 C6
Gothenburg = Göteborg Sweden 57°43N 11°59E 63 F6
Gotland Sweden 57°30N 18°33E 63 F7
Gotō-Rettō Japan 32°55N 129°5E 81 G1
Göttingen Germany 51°31N 9°55E 64 C5
Gouda Neths. 52°1N 4°42E 64 B3
Goudhurst U.K. 51°6N 0°29E 31 D9
Gouin, Rés. Canada 48°35N 74°40W 113 A10
Goulburn Australia 34°44S 149°44E 98 G8
Goulimine Morocco 28°56N 10°0W 94 C3
Goundam Mali 16°27N 3°40W 94 E5
Gourock U.K. 55°57N 4°49W 24 C6
Governador Valadares Brazil 18°15S 41°57W 122 C2
Gower U.K. 51°35N 4°10W 28 D5
Gowna, L. Ireland 53°51N 7°34W 18 D6
Goya Argentina 29°10S 59°10W 121 E4
Gozo Malta 36°3N 14°15E 68 a
Graaff-Reinet S. Africa 32°13S 24°32E 97 L4
Gracias a Dios, C. Honduras 15°0N 83°10W 115 E8
Grafham Water U.K. 52°19N 0°18W 31 B8
Grafton Australia 29°38S 152°58E 98 F9
Grafton U.S.A. 48°25N 97°25W 111 A7
Graham Land Antarctica 65°0S 64°0W 55 C17
Grahamstown S. Africa 33°19S 26°31E 97 L5
Grain Coast W. Afr. 4°20N 10°0W 94 H3
Grainthorpe U.K. 53°27N 0°5E 27 F9
Grampian Mts. U.K. 56°50N 4°0W 23 J9
Gran Canaria Canary Is. 27°55N 15°35W 94 C2
Gran Chaco S. Amer. 25°0S 61°0W 121 E3
Gran Sasso d'Itália Italy 42°27N 13°42E 68 C5
Granada Nic. 11°58N 86°0W 114 E7
Granada Spain 37°10N 3°35W 67 D4
Granard Ireland 53°47N 7°30W 18 D6
Granby Canada 45°25N 72°45W 109 E12
Grand → U.S.A. 45°40N 100°45W 110 A6
Grand Bahama I. Bahamas 26°40N 78°30W 115 B9
Grand Canal = China 39°10N 117°10E 79 D12
Grand Canyon U.S.A. 36°3N 112°9W 110 C4
Grand Canyon Nat. Park △ U.S.A. 36°15N 112°30W 110 C4
Grand Cayman Cayman Is. 19°20N 81°20W 115 D8
Grand Falls Canada 47°3N 67°44W 109 E13
Grand Falls-Windsor Canada 48°56N 55°40W 109 E14
Grand Forks U.S.A. 47°55N 97°3W 111 A7
Grand Haven U.S.A. 43°4N 86°13W 112 D4
Grand Island U.S.A. 40°55N 98°21W 110 B7
Grand Junction U.S.A. 39°4N 108°33W 110 C5
Grand L. Canada 45°57N 66°7W 113 C14
Grand Manan I. Canada 44°45N 66°52W 113 C14
Grand-Mère Canada 46°36N 72°40W 113 C11
Grand Rapids Canada 53°12N 99°19W 108 D10
Grand Rapids U.S.A. 42°58N 85°40W 112 D4
Grand St-Bernard, Col du Europe 45°50N 7°10E 64 F4
Grand Teton U.S.A. 43°54N 110°50W 110 B4
Grande → Bolivia 15°51S 64°39W 120 D3
Grande → Brazil 11°30S 44°30W 122 B2
Grande, B. Argentina 50°30S 68°20W 121 H3
Grande, Rio → N. Amer. 25°58N 97°9W 111 E7
Grande Baleine → Canada 55°16N 77°47W 109 D12
Grande Prairie Canada 55°10N 118°50W 108 D8
Grange-over-Sands U.K. 54°12N 2°54W 26 D3
Grangemouth U.K. 56°1N 3°42W 25 B8
Grangeville U.S.A. 45°56N 116°7W 110 A3
Grantham U.K. 52°55N 0°38W 27 G7
Grantown-on-Spey U.K. 57°20N 3°36W 23 H10
Grants Pass U.S.A. 42°26N 123°19W 110 B2
Granville U.S.A. 43°24N 73°16W 113 D11
Grasmere U.K. 54°28N 3°1W 26 D2
Grasse France 43°38N 6°56E 66 E7
Grassington U.K. 54°5N 1°59W 26 D5
Graulhet France 43°45N 1°59E 66 E4
Gravesend U.K. 51°26N 0°22E 31 D9
Grayling U.S.A. 44°40N 84°43W 112 C5
Grayrigg U.K. 54°23N 2°39W 26 D3
Grays U.K. 51°28N 0°21E 31 D9
Graz Austria 47°4N 15°27E 64 E8
Great Australian Bight Australia 33°30S 130°0E 98 G5
Great Ayton U.K. 54°30N 1°8W 26 D6
Great Baddow U.K. 51°43N 0°31E 31 C10
Great Barrier Reef Australia 18°0S 146°50E 98 D8
Great Basin U.S.A. 40°0N 117°0W 110 B3
Great Bear → Canada 65°0N 126°0W 108 C7

Great Bear L. Canada 65°30N 120°0W 108 B7
Great Bend U.S.A. 38°22N 98°46W 110 C7
Great Bentley U.K. 51°51N 1°4E 31 C11
Great Bernera U.K. 58°14N 6°50W 22 F4
Great Blasket I. Ireland 52°6N 10°32W 20 D1
Great Britain Europe 54°0N 2°15W 62 D5
Great Broughton U.K. 54°26N 1°9W 26 D6
Great Chesterford U.K. 52°4N 0°13E 31 B9
Great Clifton U.K. 54°39N 3°29W 26 D2
Great Dividing Ra. Australia 23°0S 146°0E 98 E8
Great Dunmow U.K. 51°52N 0°23E 31 C9
Great Exuma I. Bahamas 23°30N 75°50W 115 C9
Great Falls U.S.A. 47°30N 111°17W 110 A4
Great Glen = Glen Mor U.K. 57°9N 4°37W 23 H8
Great Harwood U.K. 53°47N 2°24W 27 E4
Great Inagua I. Bahamas 21°0N 73°20W 115 C10
Great Karoo S. Africa 31°55S 21°0E 97 L4
Great Khingan Mts. China 48°0N 121°0E 79 B13
Great Lakes N. Amer. 46°0N 84°0W 104 E11
Great Malvern U.K. 52°7N 2°18W 30 B4
Great Massingham U.K. 52°47N 0°40E 31 A10
Great Missenden U.K. 51°42N 0°41W 31 C7
Great Ormes Head U.K. 53°20N 3°52W 28 A6
Great Ouse → U.K. 52°48N 0°21E 31 A9
Great Pedro Bluff Jamaica 17°51N 77°44W 114 a
Great Plains N. Amer. 47°0N 105°0W 110 A6
Great Salt Desert Iran 34°30N 55°0E 87 C8
Great Salt L. U.S.A. 41°15N 112°40W 110 B4
Great Salt Lake Desert U.S.A. 40°50N 113°30W 110 B4
Great Sandy Desert Australia 21°0S 124°0E 98 E3
Great Sandy Desert U.S.A. 43°35N 120°15W 110 B2
Great Shefford U.K. 51°28N 1°28W 30 D6
Great Shelford U.K. 52°9N 0°8E 31 B9
Great Shunner Fell U.K. 54°22N 2°14W 26 D4
Great Skellig Ireland 51°47N 10°33W 20 E1
Great Slave L. Canada 61°23N 115°38W 108 C8
Great Snow Mt. Canada 57°26N 124°0W 108 D7
Great Torrington U.K. 50°57N 4°9W 29 F5
Great Victoria Desert Australia 29°30S 126°30E 98 F4
Great Wall of China China 38°30N 109°30E 79 D10
Great Waltham U.K. 51°47N 0°28E 31 C9
Great Whernside U.K. 54°10N 1°58W 26 D5
Great Yarmouth U.K. 52°37N 1°44E 31 A12
Greater Antilles W. Indies 17°40N 74°0W 115 D10
Greater London □ U.K. 51°31N 0°6W 31 C8
Greater Manchester □ U.K. 53°30N 2°15W 27 F4
Greater Sunda Is. Indonesia 7°0S 112°0E 82 F4
Greece ■ Europe 40°0N 23°0E 69 E9
Greeley U.S.A. 40°25N 104°42W 110 B6
Greely Fd. Canada 80°30N 85°0W 109 A11
Green → Ky., U.S.A. 37°54N 87°30W 112 G4
Green → Utah, U.S.A. 38°11N 109°53W 110 C5
Green B. U.S.A. 45°0N 87°30W 112 C4
Green Bay U.S.A. 44°31N 88°0W 112 C4
Green Hammerton U.K. 54°1N 1°18W 27 D6
Green River U.S.A. 41°32N 109°28W 110 B5
Greencastle U.S.A. 39°38N 86°52W 112 F4
Greenfield Ind., U.S.A. 39°47N 85°46W 112 F5
Greenfield Mass., U.S.A. 42°35N 72°36W 113 D11
Greenland ☑ N. Amer. 66°0N 45°0W 54 C5
Greenland Sea Arctic 73°0N 10°0W 54 B7
Greenlaw U.K. 55°43N 2°27W 25 C11
Greenock U.K. 55°57N 4°46W 24 C6
Greenodd U.K. 54°14N 3°4W 26 D2
Greenore Ireland 54°1N 6°9W 19 C9
Greenore Pt. Ireland 52°14N 6°19W 21 D10
Greensboro U.S.A. 36°4N 79°48W 111 C11
Greensburg Ind., U.S.A. 39°20N 85°29W 112 F5
Greensburg Pa., U.S.A. 40°18N 79°33W 112 E8
Greenstone Pt. U.K. 57°55N 5°37W 22 G6
Greenville Liberia 5°1N 9°6W 94 H4
Greenville Maine, U.S.A. 45°28N 69°35W 113 C13
Greenville Mich., U.S.A. 43°11N 85°15W 112 D5
Greenville Miss., U.S.A. 33°24N 91°4W 111 D8
Greenville Ohio, U.S.A. 40°6N 84°38W 112 E5
Greenville S.C., U.S.A. 34°51N 82°24W 111 D10
Greenwich □ U.K. 51°29N 0°1E 31 D9
Greenwood U.S.A. 33°31N 90°11W 111 D8
Gremikha Russia 67°59N 39°47E 70 A6
Grenada ■ W. Indies 12°10N 61°40W 115 E12
Grenoble France 45°12N 5°42E 66 D6
Greta → U.K. 54°9N 2°37W 26 D3
Gretna U.K. 55°0N 3°3W 25 D9
Gretna Green U.K. 55°1N 3°3W 25 D9
Gretton U.K. 52°33N 0°40W 31 A7
Grey Ra. Australia 27°0S 143°30E 98 F7
Greymouth N.Z. 42°29S 171°13E 99 J13
Greystoke U.K. 54°41N 2°51W 26 D3
Greystones Ireland 53°9N 6°5W 21 B10
Griffith Australia 34°18S 146°2E 98 G8
Grimsay U.K. 57°29N 7°14W 22 H3
Grimsby U.K. 53°34N 0°5W 27 E8
Griomasaigh = Grimsay U.K. 57°29N 7°14W 22 H3
Gris-Nez, C. France 50°52N 1°35E 66 A4
Grise Fiord Canada 76°25N 82°57W 109 B11
Grizebeck U.K. 54°16N 3°10W 26 D2
Groningen Neths. 53°15N 6°35E 64 B4
Groote Eylandt Australia 14°0S 136°40E 98 C6
Gros Islet St. Lucia 14°5N 60°58W 114 b
Gros Piton St. Lucia 13°49N 61°5W 114 b
Gros Piton Pt. St. Lucia 13°49N 61°5W 114 b
Grosseto Italy 42°46N 11°8E 68 C4
Grossglockner Austria 47°5N 12°40E 64 E7
Groundhog → Canada 48°45N 82°58W 112 A6
Grozny Russia 43°20N 45°45E 71 F8
Grudziądz Poland 53°30N 18°47E 65 B10
Gruinard B. U.K. 57°56N 5°35W 22 G6
Guadalajara Mexico 20°40N 103°20W 114 C4
Guadalajara Spain 40°37N 3°12W 67 B4
Guadalcanal Solomon Is. 9°32S 160°12E 99 B11
Guadalquivir → Spain 36°47N 6°22W 67 D2
Guadarrama, Sierra de Spain 41°0N 4°0W 67 B4
Guadeloupe ☑ W. Indies 16°15N 61°40W 115 D12
Guadiana → Portugal 37°14N 7°22W 67 D2
Guadix Spain 37°18N 3°11W 67 D4

Guafo, Boca del

Guafo, Boca del *Chile* 43°35S 74°0W 121 G2
Guajará-Mirim *Brazil* 10°50S 65°20W 120 D3
Guajira, Pen. de la *Colombia* 12°0N 72°0W 120 A2
Gualeguaychú *Argentina* 33°3S 59°31W 121 F4
Guam ☑ *Pac. Oc.* 13°27N 144°45E 102 F6
Guamúchil *Mexico* 25°28N 108°6W 114 B3
Guanajuato *Mexico* 21°1N 101°15W 114 C4
Guane *Cuba* 22°10N 84°7W 115 C8
Guangdong □ *China* 23°0N 113°0E 79 G11
Guangxi Zhuang □ *China* 24°0N 109°0E 79 G10
Guangyuan *China* 32°26N 105°51E 78 E10
Guangzhou *China* 23°6N 113°13E 79 G11
Guantánamo *Cuba* 20°10N 75°14W 115 C9
Guantánamo B. *Cuba* 19°59N 75°10W 115 D9
Guaporé → *Brazil* 11°55S 65°4W 120 D3
Guaqui *Bolivia* 16°41S 68°54W 120 D3
Guarapuava *Brazil* 25°20S 51°30W 121 E4
Guaratinguetá *Brazil* 22°49S 45°9W 122 D1
Guarulhos *Brazil* 23°29S 46°33W 122 D1
Guatemala ■ *Guatemala* 14°40N 90°22W 114 E6
Guatemala ■ *Cent. Amer.* 15°40N 90°30W 114 D6
Guatemala Trench *Pac. Oc.* 14°0N 95°0W 104 H10
Guaviare → *Colombia* 4°3N 67°44W 120 B3
Guaxupé *Brazil* 21°10S 47°5W 122 D1
Guayaquil *Ecuador* 2°15S 79°52W 120 C2
Guayaquil, G. de *Ecuador* 3°10S 81°0W 120 C1
Guaymas *Mexico* 27°56N 110°54W 114 B2
Gubkin *Russia* 51°17N 37°32E 71 D6
Guelph *Canada* 43°35N 80°20W 112 D7
Guéret *France* 46°11N 1°51E 66 C4
Guernsey *U.K.* 49°26N 2°35W 29 J8
Guestling Green *U.K.* 50°53N 0°39E 31 E10
Guiana Highlands *S. Amer.* 5°10N 60°40W 117 C5
Guidónia-Montecélio *Italy* 42°1N 12°45E 68 C5
Guildford *U.K.* 51°14N 0°34W 31 D7
Guilin *China* 25°18N 110°15E 79 F11
Guinea ■ *W. Afr.* 10°20N 11°30W 94 F3
Guinea, Gulf of *Atl. Oc.* 3°0N 2°30E 90 F4
Guinea-Bissau ■ *Africa* 12°0N 15°0W 94 F3
Güines *Cuba* 22°50N 82°0W 115 C8
Guingamp *France* 48°34N 3°10W 66 B2
Guisborough *U.K.* 54°33N 1°4W 26 C6
Guiyang *China* 26°32N 106°40E 78 F10
Guizhou □ *China* 27°0N 107°0E 78 F10
Gujarat □ *India* 23°20N 71°0E 84 H7
Gujranwala *Pakistan* 32°10N 74°12E 84 C9
Gujrat *Pakistan* 32°40N 74°2E 84 C9
Gulbarga *India* 17°20N 76°50E 84 L10
Gulf, The = Persian Gulf *Asia* 27°0N 50°0E 87 E7
Gulfport *U.S.A.* 30°22N 89°6W 111 D9
Gulian *China* 52°56N 122°21E 79 A13
Gulu *Uganda* 2°48N 32°17E 96 D6
Guna *India* 24°40N 77°19E 84 G10
Gunnison → *U.S.A.* 39°4N 108°35W 110 C5
Gunsan *S. Korea* 35°59N 126°45E 79 D14
Guntur *India* 16°23N 80°30E 85 L12
Gurbantüngüt Desert *China* 45°8N 87°20E 78 B6
Gurgueia → *Brazil* 6°50S 43°24W 120 C5
Guri, Embalse de *Venezuela* 7°50N 62°52W 120 B3
Gurkha *Nepal* 28°5N 84°40E 85 E14
Gurnard's Hd. *U.K.* 50°11N 5°37W 29 G2
Gürün *Turkey* 38°43N 37°15E 71 G6
Gurupi *Brazil* 11°43S 49°4W 122 B1
Gurupi → *Brazil* 1°13S 46°6W 120 C5
Gurvan Sayhan Uul *Mongolia* 43°50N 104°0E 78 C9
Gusau *Nigeria* 12°12N 6°40E 94 F7
Guwahati *India* 26°10N 91°45E 85 F17
Guyana ■ *S. Amer.* 5°0N 59°0W 120 B4
Guyenne *France* 44°30N 0°40E 66 D4
Gwãdar *Pakistan* 25°10N 62°18E 84 G3
Gwalchmai *U.K.* 53°16N 4°25W 28 A5
Gwalior *India* 26°12N 78°10E 84 F11
Gwanda *Zimbabwe* 20°55S 29°0E 97 J5
Gwangju *S. Korea* 35°9N 126°54E 79 D14
Gweebarra B. *Ireland* 54°51N 8°23W 18 B5
Gweedore *Ireland* 55°3N 8°14W 18 A5
Gweek *U.K.* 50°5N 5°13W 29 G3
Gwennap *U.K.* 50°12N 5°11W 29 G3
Gweru *Zimbabwe* 19°28S 29°45E 97 H5
Gwynedd □ *U.K.* 52°52N 4°10W 28 B6
Gyaring Hu *China* 34°50N 97°40E 78 E8
Gydan Peninsula *Russia* 70°0N 78°0E 76 B8
Gympie *Australia* 26°11S 152°38E 98 F9
Győr *Hungary* 47°41N 17°40E 65 E9
Gyumri *Armenia* 40°47N 43°50E 71 F7

H

Ha'apai Group *Tonga* 19°47S 174°27W 99 D16
Haarlem *Neths.* 52°23N 4°39E 64 B3
Hachinohe *Japan* 40°30N 141°29E 81 C7
Hackney □ *U.K.* 51°33N 0°3W 31 C8
Hackthorpe *U.K.* 54°34N 2°42W 26 C3
Ḥadd, Ra's al *Oman* 22°35N 59°50E 87 F9
Haddenham *U.K.* 51°46N 0°55W 31 D7
Haddington *U.K.* 55°57N 2°47W 25 C10
Hadejia *Nigeria* 12°30N 10°5E 94 F7
Hadleigh *U.K.* 52°3N 0°58E 31 B10
Hadlow *U.K.* 51°13N 0°20E 31 D9
Ḥaḍramawt □ *Yemen* 15°30N 49°30E 89 D4
Hadrian's Wall *U.K.* 55°0N 2°30W 26 B4
Haeju *N. Korea* 38°3N 125°45E 79 D14
Hafizabad *Pakistan* 32°5N 73°40E 84 C8
Hagen *Germany* 51°21N 7°27E 64 C4
Hagerstown *U.S.A.* 39°39N 77°43W 112 F9
Hags Hd. *Ireland* 52°57N 9°28W 20 C4
Hague, C. de la *France* 49°44N 1°56W 66 B3
Hague, The *Neths.* 52°7N 4°17E 64 B3
Haguenau *France* 48°49N 7°47E 66 B7
Haifa *Israel* 32°46N 35°0E 86 C3
Haikou *China* 20°1N 110°16E 79 G10
Ḥā'il *Si. Arabia* 27°28N 41°45E 86 E5
Hailar *China* 49°10N 119°38E 79 B12
Hailey *U.S.A.* 43°31N 114°19W 110 B4
Haileybury *Canada* 47°30N 79°38W 112 B8
Hailsham *U.K.* 50°52N 0°16E 31 E9
Hailun *China* 47°28N 126°50E 79 B14
Hainan □ *China* 19°0N 109°30E 79 H10
Hainan Dao *China* 19°0N 109°30E 79 H10
Hainan Str. *China* 20°10N 110°15E 79 G11
Haines Junction *Canada* 60°45N 137°30W 108 C6

Hainton *U.K.* 53°21N 0°14W 27 F8
Haiphong *Vietnam* 20°47N 106°41E 78 G10
Haiti ■ *W. Indies* 19°0N 72°30W 115 D10
Haji Ibrahim *Iraq* 36°40N 44°30E 86 B6
Ḥajjah *Yemen* 15°42N 43°36E 89 D3
Hakkoda-San *Japan* 40°39N 140°53E 81 C7
Hakodate *Japan* 41°45N 140°44E 81 C7
Haku-San *Japan* 36°9N 136°46E 81 E5
Halaib Triangle *Africa* 22°30N 35°20E 95 D12
Halberstadt *Germany* 51°54N 11°3E 64 C6
Halberton *U.K.* 50°54N 3°25W 29 F7
Halden *Norway* 59°9N 11°23E 63 F6
Haldia *India* 22°5N 88°3E 85 H16
Haldwani *India* 29°31N 79°30E 84 E11
Halesowen *U.K.* 52°27N 2°3W 27 H4
Halesworth *U.K.* 52°20N 1°31E 31 B12
Halifax *Canada* 44°38N 63°35W 113 C16
Halifax *U.K.* 53°43N 1°52W 27 E5
Halkirk *U.K.* 58°30N 3°29W 23 E11
Hall Beach *Canada* 68°46N 81°12W 109 C11
Hall Pen. *Canada* 63°30N 66°0W 109 C13
Halle *Germany* 51°30N 11°56E 64 C6
Hallow *U.K.* 52°14N 2°15W 30 B4
Halls Creek *Australia* 18°16S 127°38E 98 D4
Hallworthy *U.K.* 50°39N 4°35W 29 F4
Halmahera *Indonesia* 0°40N 128°0E 83 D7
Halmstad *Sweden* 56°41N 12°52E 63 F6
Halstead *U.K.* 51°57N 0°40E 31 C10
Haltwhistle *U.K.* 54°58N 2°26W 26 C4
Hamadān *Iran* 34°52N 48°32E 86 C7
Ḥamāh *Syria* 35°5N 36°40E 86 C4
Hamamatsu *Japan* 34°45N 137°45E 81 F5
Hamar *Norway* 60°48N 11°7E 63 E6
Hambantota *Sri Lanka* 6°10N 81°10E 84 R12
Hambledon *U.K.* 50°55N 1°5W 30 E6
Hambleton Hills *U.K.* 54°17N 1°12W 26 D6
Hamburg *Germany* 53°33N 9°59E 64 B5
Hämeenlinna *Finland* 61°0N 24°28E 63 E8
Hameln *Germany* 52°6N 9°21E 64 B5
Hamersley Ra. *Australia* 22°0S 117°45E 98 E2
Hamhŭng *N. Korea* 39°54N 127°30E 79 D14
Hami *China* 42°55N 93°25E 78 B6
Hamilton *Canada* 43°15N 79°50W 112 D8
Hamilton *N.Z.* 37°47S 175°19E 99 H14
Hamilton *U.K.* 55°46N 4°2W 24 C7
Hamilton *U.S.A.* 39°24N 84°34W 112 F5
Hamilton Inlet *Canada* 54°0N 57°30W 104 D14
Hamm *Germany* 51°40N 7°50E 64 C4
Hammerfest *Norway* 70°39N 23°41E 63 C8
Hammersmith and Fulham □
U.K. 51°30N 0°14W 31 D8
Hammond *U.S.A.* 41°38N 87°30W 112 E4
Hammonton *U.S.A.* 39°39N 74°48W 113 F10
Hampshire □ *U.K.* 51°7N 1°23W 30 D6
Hampshire Downs *U.K.* 51°15N 1°10W 30 D6
Hampton in Arden *U.K.* 52°26N 1°41W 27 H5
Han Shui → *China* 30°34N 114°17E 79 E11
Hancock *U.S.A.* 47°8N 88°35W 112 B3
Handan *China* 36°35N 114°28E 79 D11
Hanford *U.S.A.* 36°20N 119°39W 110 C3
Hangayn Nuruu *Mongolia* 47°30N 99°0E 78 B8
Hangzhou *China* 30°18N 120°11E 79 E13
Hangzhou Wan *China* 30°15N 120°45E 79 E13
Hankö *Finland* 59°50N 22°57E 63 F8
Hanna *Canada* 51°40N 111°54W 108 D8
Hannibal *U.S.A.* 39°42N 91°22W 111 C8
Hanningfield Res. *U.K.* 51°40N 0°31E 31 D10
Hannover *Germany* 52°22N 9°46E 64 B5
Hanoi *Vietnam* 21°5N 105°55E 78 G10
Hanover *U.S.A.* 39°48N 76°59W 112 F9
Hanover, I. *Chile* 51°0S 74°50W 121 H2
Hans I. *Arctic* 80°49N 66°38W 109 A13
Hanzhong *China* 33°10N 107°1E 78 E10
Haora *India* 22°34N 88°18E 85 H16
Haparanda *Sweden* 65°52N 24°8E 63 D8
Happy Valley-Goose Bay
Canada 53°15N 60°20W 109 D13
Har Hu *China* 38°20N 97°38E 78 D8
Har Us Nuur *Mongolia* 48°0N 92°0E 78 B7
Ḥaraḍ *Si. Arabia* 24°22N 49°0E 86 E7
Harare *Zimbabwe* 17°43S 31°2E 97 H6
Harbin *China* 45°48N 126°40E 79 B14
Harbor Beach *U.S.A.* 43°51N 82°39W 112 D6
Hardangerfjorden *Norway* 60°5N 6°0E 63 E5
Hardy, Pte. *St. Lucia* 14°6N 60°56W 114 b
Harer *Ethiopia* 9°20N 42°8E 89 F3
Harewood *U.K.* 53°54N 1°30W 27 E6
Hargeisa *Somalia* 9°30N 44°2E 89 F3
Haridwar *India* 29°58N 78°9E 84 E11
Haringey □ *U.K.* 51°34N 0°5W 31 C8
Haringhata → *Bangla.* 22°0N 89°58E 85 J16
Harirūd → *Asia* 37°24N 60°38E 87 B9
Harlech *U.K.* 52°52N 4°6W 28 B5
Harleston *U.K.* 52°24N 1°18E 31 B11
Harlingen *U.S.A.* 26°12N 97°42W 110 E7
Harlow *U.K.* 51°46N 0°8E 31 C9
Harney L. *U.S.A.* 43°14N 119°8W 110 B3
Härnösand *Sweden* 62°38N 17°55E 63 E7
Haroldswick *U.K.* 60°48N 0°50W 22 A16
Harpenden *U.K.* 51°49N 0°21W 31 C8
Harricana → *Canada* 50°56N 79°32W 109 D12
Harrietsham *U.K.* 51°14N 0°41E 31 D10
Harrington *U.K.* 54°37N 3°33W 26 C1
Harris *U.K.* 57°50N 6°55W 22 G4
Harris, Sd. of *U.K.* 57°44N 7°6E 22 G3
Harrisburg *U.S.A.* 40°16N 76°53W 112 E9
Harrison, C. *Canada* 54°55N 57°55W 109 D14
Harrisonburg *U.S.A.* 38°27N 78°52W 112 F8
Harrisville *U.S.A.* 44°39N 83°17W 112 C6
Harrogate *U.K.* 54°0N 1°33W 27 D5
Harrow □ *U.K.* 51°35N 0°21W 31 C8
Hart *U.S.A.* 43°42N 86°22W 112 D4
Hartford *Conn., U.S.A.* 41°46N 72°41W 113 E11
Hartford *Ky., U.S.A.* 37°27N 86°55W 112 G4
Hartford *Wis., U.S.A.* 43°19N 88°22W 112 D3
Hartland *U.K.* 50°59N 4°29W 29 F5
Hartland Pt. *U.K.* 51°1N 4°32W 29 F4
Hartlebury *U.K.* 52°20N 2°14W 30 B4
Hartlepool *U.K.* 54°42N 1°13W 26 C6
Hartley *U.K.* 55°5N 1°28W 26 B6

Hartpury *U.K.* 51°55N 2°17W 30 C4
Harvey *U.S.A.* 41°36N 87°50W 112 E4
Harwell *U.K.* 51°36N 1°17W 30 C6
Harwich *U.K.* 51°56N 1°17E 31 C11
Haryana □ *India* 29°0N 76°10E 84 E10
Hasa *Si. Arabia* 25°50N 49°0E 86 E7
Haslemere *U.K.* 51°5N 0°43W 31 D7
Haslingden *U.K.* 53°42N 2°19W 27 E4
Hastings *U.K.* 50°51N 0°35E 31 E10
Hastings *U.S.A.* 40°35N 98°23W 110 B7
Hat Yai *Thailand* 7°1N 100°27E 82 C2
Hatay *Turkey* 36°14N 36°10E 71 G6
Hatfield *U.K.* 51°46N 0°13W 31 C8
Hatgal *Mongolia* 50°26N 100°9E 78 A9
Hatherleigh *U.K.* 50°49N 4°5W 29 F5
Hathersage *U.K.* 53°20N 1°39W 27 F5
Hathras *India* 27°36N 78°6E 84 F11
Hatia *Bangla.* 22°30N 91°5E 85 H17
Hatteras, C. *U.S.A.* 35°14N 75°32W 111 C11
Hattiesburg *U.S.A.* 31°20N 89°17W 111 D9
Haugesund *Norway* 59°23N 5°13E 63 F5
Haughley *U.K.* 52°14N 0°57E 31 B10
Haut Atlas *Morocco* 32°30N 5°0W 94 B4
Hauts Plateaux *Algeria* 35°0N 1°0E 94 B6
Havana = La Habana *Cuba* 23°8N 82°22W 115 C8
Havant *U.K.* 50°51N 0°58W 31 E7
Havasu, L. *U.S.A.* 34°18N 114°28W 110 D4
Havel → *Germany* 52°50N 12°3E 64 B7
Haverfordwest *U.K.* 51°48N 4°58W 28 D4
Haverhill *U.K.* 52°5N 0°28E 31 B9
Haverhill *U.S.A.* 42°47N 71°5W 113 D12
Haverigg *U.K.* 54°13N 3°17W 26 D2
Havering □ *U.K.* 51°34N 0°13E 31 C9
Havre *U.S.A.* 48°33N 109°41W 110 A5
Havre-St.-Pierre *Canada* 50°18N 63°33W 109 D13
Hawai'i □ *U.S.A.* 19°30N 155°30W 110 J17
Hawai'i I. *U.S.A.* 19°30N 156°30W 110 H16
Hawaiian Is. *Pac. Oc.* 20°30N 156°0W 103 E12
Hawes *U.K.* 54°19N 2°12W 26 D4
Haweswater *U.K.* 54°31N 2°47W 26 C3
Hawick *U.K.* 55°26N 2°47W 25 D10
Hawkchurch *U.K.* 50°48N 2°56W 30 E3
Hawkesbury *Canada* 45°37N 74°37W 113 C10
Hawkesbury Upton *U.K.* 51°33N 2°18W 30 C4
Hawkhurst *U.K.* 51°2N 0°32E 31 D10
Hawkshead *U.K.* 54°23N 2°59W 26 D3
Haworth *U.K.* 53°50N 1°58W 27 E5
Hawsker *U.K.* 54°27N 0°34W 26 D7
Haxby *U.K.* 54°1N 1°4W 27 D6
Hay *Australia* 34°30S 144°51E 98 G8
Hay → *Canada* 60°50N 116°26W 108 C8
Hay-on-Wye *U.K.* 52°5N 3°8W 28 C7
Hay River *Canada* 60°51N 115°44W 108 C8
Haydon Bridge *U.K.* 54°58N 2°14W 26 C4
Hayes → *Canada* 57°3N 92°12W 108 D10
Hayle *U.K.* 50°11N 5°26W 29 G3
Hays *U.S.A.* 38°53N 99°20W 110 C7
Hayton *U.K.* 54°55N 2°45W 26 C3
Haywards Heath *U.K.* 51°0N 0°5W 31 E8
Hazar *Turkmenistan* 39°34N 53°16E 71 G9
Hazard *U.S.A.* 37°15N 83°12W 112 G6
Hazaribag *India* 23°58N 85°26E 85 H14
Heacham *U.K.* 52°54N 0°29E 31 A9
Headcorn *U.K.* 51°10N 0°38E 31 D10
Heanor *U.K.* 53°1N 1°21W 27 F6
Heard I. *Ind. Oc.* 53°6S 72°36E 53 G13
Hearst *Canada* 49°40N 83°41W 109 E11
Heathfield *U.K.* 50°58N 0°16E 31 E9
Hebburn *U.K.* 54°59N 1°32W 26 C6
Hebden Bridge *U.K.* 53°45N 2°0W 27 E5
Hebei □ *China* 39°0N 116°0E 79 D12
Hebrides *U.K.* 57°30N 7°0W 56 D4
Hebrides, Sea of the *U.K.* 57°5N 7°0W 22 H3
Hebron *Canada* 58°5N 62°30W 109 D13
Hecate Str. *Canada* 53°10N 130°30W 108 D6
Hechi *China* 24°40N 108°2E 78 G10
Hechuan *China* 30°2N 106°12E 78 E10
Heckington *U.K.* 52°59N 0°17W 27 F8
Hednesford *U.K.* 52°43N 1°59W 27 G5
Hedon *U.K.* 53°44N 0°12W 27 E8
Heerlen *Neths.* 50°55N 5°58E 64 C3
Hefei *China* 31°52N 117°18E 79 E12
Hegang *China* 47°20N 130°19E 79 B15
Heidelberg *Germany* 49°24N 8°42E 64 D5
Heihe *China* 50°10N 127°30E 79 A14
Heilbronn *Germany* 49°9N 9°13E 64 D5
Heilongjiang □ *China* 48°0N 126°0E 79 B14
Heimaey *Iceland* 63°26N 20°17W 63 B1
Hekla *Iceland* 63°56N 19°35W 63 B2
Helena *U.S.A.* 46°36N 112°2W 110 A4
Helensburgh *U.K.* 56°1N 4°43W 24 B6
Helgoland *Germany* 54°10N 7°53E 64 A4
Hellifield *U.K.* 54°1N 2°12W 27 D4
Helmand → *Afghan.* 31°12N 61°34E 87 D10
Helmsdale *U.K.* 58°7N 3°39W 23 F10
Helmsley *U.K.* 54°15N 1°3W 26 D6
Helperby *U.K.* 54°8N 1°19W 26 D6
Helsby *U.K.* 53°17N 2°46W 27 F3
Helsingborg *Sweden* 56°3N 12°42E 63 F6
Helsinki *Finland* 60°10N 24°55E 63 E9
Helston *U.K.* 50°6N 5°17W 29 G3
Helvellyn *U.K.* 54°32N 3°1W 26 D2
Helwân *Egypt* 29°50N 31°20E 95 C12
Hemel Hempstead *U.K.* 51°44N 0°28W 31 C8
Hempton *U.K.* 52°50N 0°50E 31 A10
Hemsworth *U.K.* 53°37N 1°21W 27 E6
Hemyock *U.K.* 50°54N 3°15W 29 F7
Henan □ *China* 34°0N 114°0E 79 E11
Henderson *Ky., U.S.A.* 37°50N 87°35W 112 G4
Henderson *Nev., U.S.A.* 36°2N 114°58W 110 D3
Henfield *U.K.* 50°56N 0°16W 31 E8
Hengduan Shan *China* 28°30N 98°50E 78 F8
Henganga *China* 22°39N 114°12E 79 a
Hengyang *China* 26°59N 112°22E 79 F11
Henley-in-Arden *U.K.* 52°18N 1°46W 30 B5
Henley-on-Thames *U.K.* 51°32N 0°54W 31 C7
Henlopen, C. *U.S.A.* 38°48N 75°6W 113 F10
Henlow *U.K.* 52°2N 0°17W 31 B8

Henrietta Maria, C. *Canada* 55°9N 82°20W 109 D11
Henstridge *U.K.* 50°58N 2°24W 30 E4
Hentiyn Nuruu *Mongolia* 48°30N 108°30E 79 B10
Herāt *Afghan.* 34°20N 62°7E 87 C10
Hereford *U.K.* 52°4N 2°43W 30 B3
Herefordshire □ *U.K.* 52°8N 2°40W 30 B3
Herford *Germany* 52°7N 8°39E 64 B5
Herlen → *Asia* 48°48N 117°0E 79 B12
Herm *U.K.* 49°30N 2°28W 29 J9
Herma Ness *U.K.* 60°50N 0°54W 22 A16
Hermosillo *Mexico* 29°10N 111°0W 114 B2
Hernád → *Hungary* 47°56N 21°8E 65 D11
Herne Bay *U.K.* 51°21N 1°8E 31 D11
Herstmonceux *U.K.* 50°53N 0°20E 31 E9
Hertford *U.K.* 51°48N 0°4W 31 C8
Hertfordshire □ *U.K.* 51°51N 0°5W 31 C8
's-Hertogenbosch *Neths.* 51°42N 5°17E 64 C3
Hessen □ *Germany* 50°30N 9°0E 64 C5
Hessle *U.K.* 53°44N 0°24W 27 E8
Hethersett *U.K.* 52°36N 1°10E 31 A11
Hetton-le-Hole *U.K.* 54°50N 1°26W 26 C6
Hexham *U.K.* 54°58N 2°4W 26 C4
Heybridge *U.K.* 51°45N 0°42E 31 C10
Heysham *U.K.* 54°3N 2°53W 26 D3
Heytesbury *U.K.* 51°11N 2°6W 30 D4
Heywood *U.K.* 53°35N 2°12W 27 E4
Heze *China* 35°14N 115°20E 79 D12
Hibbing *U.S.A.* 47°25N 92°56W 111 A8
Hickman *U.S.A.* 36°34N 89°11W 112 G3
Hidalgo del Parral *Mexico* 26°56N 105°40W 114 B3
Hierro *Canary Is.* 27°44N 18°0W 94 C2
Higashiōsaka *Japan* 34°39N 135°37E 81 F4
High Bentham *U.K.* 54°7N 2°28W 26 D4
High Ercall *U.K.* 52°45N 2°35W 27 G3
High Hesket *U.K.* 54°48N 2°49W 26 C3
High Level *Canada* 58°31N 117°8W 108 D8
High Pike *U.K.* 54°42N 3°4W 26 C2
High Prairie *Canada* 55°30N 116°30W 108 D8
High River *Canada* 50°30N 113°50W 108 D8
High Veld *Africa* 27°0S 27°0E 90 J6
High Willhays *U.K.* 50°40N 4°0W 29 F5
High Wycombe *U.K.* 51°37N 0°45W 31 C7
Higham Ferrers *U.K.* 52°19N 0°35W 31 B7
Highbridge *U.K.* 51°13N 2°58W 30 D3
Highclere *U.K.* 51°20N 1°21W 30 D6
Highland □ *U.K.* 57°17N 4°21W 22 H7
Highley *U.K.* 52°27N 2°23W 27 H4
Hightae *U.K.* 55°5N 3°26W 25 D9
Highworth *U.K.* 51°37N 1°43W 30 C5
Hiiumaa *Estonia* 58°50N 22°45E 63 F8
Ḥijāz *Si. Arabia* 24°0N 40°0E 86 E4
Hildesheim *Germany* 52°9N 9°56E 64 B5
Hilgay *U.K.* 52°34N 0°24E 31 A9
Hillaby, Mt. *Barbados* 13°12N 59°35W 114 c
Hillcrest *Barbados* 13°13N 59°31W 114 c
Hillingdon □ *U.K.* 51°32N 0°27W 31 C8
Hillsborough *U.K.* 54°28N 6°5W 19 C9
Hillsdale *U.S.A.* 41°56N 84°38W 112 E5
Hilo *U.S.A.* 19°44N 155°5W 110 J17
Hilpsford Pt. *U.K.* 54°3N 3°12W 26 D2
Hilversum *Neths.* 52°14N 5°10E 64 B3
Himachal Pradesh □ *India* 31°30N 77°0E 84 D10
Himalaya *Asia* 29°0N 84°0E 85 E14
Himeji *Japan* 34°50N 134°40E 81 F4
Hinckley *U.K.* 52°33N 1°22W 27 G6
Hinderwell *U.K.* 54°32N 0°45W 26 D7
Hindhead *U.K.* 51°7N 0°43W 31 D7
Hindley *U.K.* 53°33N 2°35W 27 E3
Hindu Kush *Asia* 36°0N 71°0E 87 C12
Hingham *U.K.* 52°35N 1°0E 31 A10
Hingoli *India* 19°41N 77°15E 84 K10
Hinkley Pt. *U.K.* 51°12N 3°8W 30 D2
Hinstock *U.K.* 52°50N 2°27W 27 G4
Hinton *U.S.A.* 37°40N 80°54W 112 G7
Hios *Greece* 38°27N 26°9E 73 E12
Hirosaki *Japan* 40°34N 140°28E 81 C7
Hiroshima *Japan* 34°24N 132°30E 81 F3
Hisar *India* 29°12N 75°45E 84 E9
Hispaniola *W. Indies* 19°0N 71°0W 115 D10
Histon *U.K.* 52°16N 0°7E 31 B9
Hitachi *Japan* 36°36N 140°39E 81 E7
Hitchin *U.K.* 51°58N 0°16W 31 C8
Hjälmaren *Sweden* 59°18N 15°40E 63 F7
Hkakabo Razi *Burma* 28°25N 97°23E 85 D20
Ho Chi Minh City *Vietnam* 10°58N 106°40E 82 B3
Hoare B. *Canada* 65°17N 62°30W 109 C13
Hobart *Australia* 42°50S 147°21E 98 J8
Hobbs *U.S.A.* 32°42N 103°8W 110 D6
Hodder → *U.K.* 53°57N 2°27W 27 E4
Hoddesdon *U.K.* 51°45N 0°1W 31 C8
Hodge → *U.K.* 54°16N 0°56W 26 D7
Hodgson *Canada* 51°13N 97°36W 108 D10
Hódmezővásárhely *Hungary* 46°28N 20°22E 65 E11
Hodna, Chott el *Algeria* 35°26N 4°43E 94 A6
Hoek van Holland *Neths.* 52°0N 4°7E 64 B3
Hoff *U.K.* 54°34N 2°31W 26 D3
Hōfu *Japan* 34°3N 131°34E 81 F2
Hog's Back *U.K.* 51°13N 0°38W 31 D7
Hoh Xil Shan *China* 36°30N 89°0E 78 D6
Hoher Rhön *Germany* 50°24N 9°58E 64 C5
Hohhot *China* 40°52N 111°40E 79 C11
Hokkaidō □ *Japan* 43°30N 143°0E 81 B8
Holbeach *U.K.* 52°48N 0°1E 27 G9
Holbeach Marsh *U.K.* 52°52N 0°5E 27 G9
Holderness *U.K.* 53°45N 0°5W 27 E8
Holetown *Barbados* 13°11N 59°38W 114 c
Holguín *Cuba* 20°50N 76°20W 115 C9
Holkham *U.K.* 52°57N 0°49E 31 A10
Holland *U.S.A.* 42°47N 86°7W 112 D4
Holland Fen *U.K.* 53°0N 0°8W 27 F8
Holland on Sea *U.K.* 51°48N 1°13E 31 C11
Holman *Canada* 70°44N 117°44W 108 A8
Holme *U.K.* 53°50N 0°46W 27 E7
Holmes Chapel *U.K.* 53°12N 2°21W 27 F4
Holmfirth *U.K.* 53°35N 1°46W 27 E5
Holstebro *Denmark* 56°22N 8°37E 63 F5
Holsworthy *U.K.* 50°48N 4°22W 29 F5
Holt *U.K.* 52°55N 1°6E 31 A11
Holy I. *Anglesey, U.K.* 53°17N 4°37W 28 A4
Holy I. *Northumberland, U.K.* 55°40N 1°47W 26 B6

Holyhead *U.K.* 53°18N 4°38W 28 A4
Holywell *U.K.* 53°16N 3°14W 28 A7
Home B. *Canada* 68°40N 67°10W 109 C13
Homer *U.S.A.* 59°39N 151°33W 108 D4
Homs *Syria* 34°40N 36°45E 86 C4
Honduras ■ *Cent. Amer.* 14°40N 86°30W 114 E7
Honduras, G. of *Caribbean* 16°50N 87°0W 114 D7
Hønefoss *Norway* 60°10N 10°18E 63 E6
Honey L. *U.S.A.* 40°15N 120°19W 110 B2
Hong Kong □ *China* 22°11N 114°14E 79 a
Hong Kong Int. ✈ (HKG)
China 22°19N 113°57E 79 a
Hongjiang *China* 27°7N 109°59E 79 F10
Hongshui He → *China* 23°48N 109°30E 79 F10
Hongze Hu *China* 33°15N 118°35E 79 E12
Honiara *Solomon Is.* 9°27S 159°57E 99 B10
Honington *U.K.* 52°59N 0°35W 27 G7
Honiton *U.K.* 50°47N 3°11W 29 F7
Honolulu *U.S.A.* 21°19N 157°52W 103 E12
Honshū *Japan* 36°0N 138°0E 81 F6
Hoo *U.K.* 51°25N 0°35E 31 D10
Hood, Mt. *U.S.A.* 45°23N 121°42W 110 A2
Hook *U.K.* 51°17N 0°57W 31 D7
Hook Hd. *Ireland* 52°7N 6°56W 21 D9
Hooper Bay *U.S.A.* 61°32N 166°6W 108 C3
Hoopeston *U.S.A.* 40°28N 87°40W 112 E4
Hoorn *Neths.* 52°38N 5°4E 64 B3
Hoover Dam *U.S.A.* 36°1N 114°44W 110 D4
Hope *U.S.A.* 33°40N 93°36W 111 D8
Hope, Pt. *U.S.A.* 68°21N 166°47W 104 C3
Hopedale *Canada* 55°28N 60°13W 109 D13
Horden *U.K.* 54°46N 1°19W 26 C6
Horley *U.K.* 51°10N 0°10W 31 D8
Horlivka *Ukraine* 48°19N 38°5E 71 E6
Hormuz, Str. of *The Gulf* 26°30N 56°30E 87 E9
Horn, C. = Hornos, C. de
Chile 55°50S 67°30W 121 H3
Horn, Is. *Wall. & F. Is.* 14°16S 178°6W 99 D15
Horn Head *Ireland* 55°14N 8°0W 18 A6
Hornavan *Sweden* 66°15N 17°30E 63 D7
Horncastle *U.K.* 53°13N 0°7W 27 F8
Horndean *U.K.* 50°55N 1°1W 30 E6
Hornell *U.S.A.* 42°20N 77°40W 112 D9
Hornepayne *Canada* 49°14N 84°48W 112 A5
Horningsham *U.K.* 51°11N 2°15W 30 D4
Hornos, C. de *Chile* 55°50S 67°30W 121 H3
Hornsea *U.K.* 53°55N 0°11W 27 E8
Horqin Youyi Qianqi *China* 46°5N 122°3E 79 B13
Horsforth *U.K.* 53°50N 1°39W 27 E5
Horsham *Australia* 36°44S 142°13E 98 H7
Horsham *U.K.* 51°4N 0°20W 31 D8
Horsham St. Faith *U.K.* 52°43N 1°14E 31 A11
Horsted Keynes *U.K.* 51°2N 0°1W 31 D8
Horton → *Canada* 69°56N 126°52W 108 C7
Horton in Ribblesdale *U.K.* 54°9N 2°17W 26 D4
Horwich *U.K.* 53°36N 2°33W 27 E3
Hoste, I. *Chile* 55°0S 69°0W 121 H3
Hot Springs *Ark., U.S.A.* 34°31N 93°3W 111 D8
Hot Springs *S. Dak., U.S.A.* 43°26N 103°29W 110 B6
Hotan *China* 37°25N 79°55E 78 D4
Hotan He → *China* 40°22N 80°56E 78 C5
Houghton *U.S.A.* 47°7N 88°34W 112 B3
Houghton L. *U.S.A.* 44°21N 84°44W 112 C5
Houghton-le-Spring *U.K.* 54°51N 1°28W 26 C6
Houghton Regis *U.K.* 51°54N 0°32W 31 C7
Houlton *U.S.A.* 46°8N 67°51W 113 C14
Houma *U.S.A.* 29°36N 90°43W 111 E8
Hounslow □ *U.K.* 51°28N 0°21W 31 D8
Hourn, L. *U.K.* 57°7N 5°35W 22 H6
Houston *U.S.A.* 29°45N 95°21W 111 E7
Hove *U.K.* 50°50N 0°10W 31 E8
Hoveton *U.K.* 52°43N 1°25E 31 A11
Hovingham *U.K.* 54°11N 0°58W 26 D7
Hövsgöl Nuur *Mongolia* 51°0N 100°30E 78 A8
Howden *U.K.* 53°45N 0°52W 27 E7
Howe, C. *Australia* 37°30S 150°0E 98 H9
Howell *U.S.A.* 42°36N 83°56W 112 D6
Howland I. *Pac. Oc.* 0°48N 176°38W 102 G10
Howth *Ireland* 53°23N 6°7W 21 B10
Howth Hd. *Ireland* 53°22N 6°4W 21 B10
Hoxne *U.K.* 52°21N 1°12E 31 B11
Hoy *U.K.* 58°50N 3°15W 23 C11
Høyanger *Norway* 61°13N 6°4E 63 E5
Hoylake *U.K.* 53°24N 3°10W 27 E2
Hradec Králové *Czech Rep.* 50°15N 15°50E 64 C8
Hrodna *Belarus* 53°42N 23°52E 65 B12
Hron → *Slovak Rep.* 47°49N 18°45E 65 E10
Hsinchu *Taiwan* 24°48N 120°58E 79 F13
Huacho *Peru* 11°10S 77°35W 120 D2
Huai He → *China* 33°0N 118°30E 79 E12
Huaibei *China* 34°0N 116°48E 79 E12
Huaihua *China* 27°32N 109°57E 79 F10
Huainan *China* 32°38N 116°58E 79 E12
Huallaga → *Peru* 5°15S 75°30W 120 C2
Huambo *Angola* 12°42S 15°54E 97 G3
Huancavelica *Peru* 12°50S 75°5W 120 D2
Huancayo *Peru* 12°5S 75°12W 120 D2
Huang He → *China* 37°55N 118°50E 79 D12
Huangshan *China* 29°42N 118°25E 79 F12
Huangshi *China* 30°10N 115°3E 79 E12
Huánuco *Peru* 9°55S 76°15W 120 C2
Huaraz *Peru* 9°30S 77°32W 120 C2
Huascarán, Nevado *Peru* 9°7S 77°37W 120 C2
Huasco *Chile* 28°30S 71°15W 121 E2
Huatabampo *Mexico* 26°50N 109°38W 114 B3
Hubei □ *China* 31°0N 112°0E 79 E11
Hubli *India* 15°22N 75°15E 84 M9
Hucknall *U.K.* 53°3N 1°13W 27 F6
Huddersfield *U.K.* 53°39N 1°47W 27 E5
Hudiksvall *Sweden* 61°43N 17°10E 63 E7
Hudson → *U.S.A.* 40°42N 74°2W 113 E10
Hudson Bay *Canada* 60°0N 86°0W 109 D11
Hudson Falls *U.S.A.* 43°18N 73°35W 113 D11
Hudson Str. *Canada* 62°0N 70°0W 109 C13
Hue *Vietnam* 16°30N 107°35E 82 A3
Huelva *Spain* 37°18N 6°57W 67 D2
Huesca *Spain* 42°8N 0°25W 67 A5
Hugh Town *U.K.* 49°55N 6°19W 29 H1
Hughenden *Australia* 20°52S 144°10E 98 E7
Hugli → *India* 21°56N 88°4E 85 J16

Hugli

Huila, Nevado del Colombia 3°0N 76°0W 120 B2
Hull = Kingston upon Hull U.K. 53°45N 0°21W 27 E8
Hull Canada 45°26N 75°43W 113 C10
Hull → U.K. 53°44N 0°20W 27 E8
Hullavington U.K. 51°32N 2°8W 30 C4
Hulme End U.K. 53°8N 1°50W 27 F5
Hulun Nur China 49°0N 117°30E 79 B12
Humaitá Brazil 7°35S 63°1W 120 C3
Humber → U.K. 53°42N 0°27W 27 E8
Humber, Mouth of the U.K. 53°32N 0°8E 27 E9
Humboldt Canada 52°15N 105°9W 108 D9
Humboldt → U.S.A. 39°59N 118°36W 110 B3
Humen China 22°50N 113°40E 79 a
Humphreys Peak U.S.A. 35°21N 111°41W 110 C4
Humshaugh U.K. 55°3N 2°8W 26 B4
Húnaflói Iceland 65°50N 20°50W 63 A1
Hunan ☐ China 27°30N 112°0E 79 F11
Hunchun China 42°52N 130°28E 79 C15
Hungary ■ Europe 47°20N 19°20E 65 E10
Hungary, Plain of Europe 47°0N 20°0E 56 F10
Hungerford U.K. 51°25N 1°31W 30 D5
Hŭngnam N. Korea 39°49N 127°45E 79 D14
Hunmanby U.K. 54°10N 0°20W 26 D8
Hunsrück Germany 49°56N 7°27E 64 D4
Hunstanton U.K. 52°56N 0°29E 31 A9
Huntingdon U.K. 52°20N 0°11W 31 B8
Huntington Ind., U.S.A. 40°53N 85°30W 112 E5
Huntington W. Va., U.S.A. 38°25N 82°27W 112 F6
Huntly U.K. 57°27N 2°47W 23 H12
Huntsville Canada 45°20N 79°14W 109 E12
Huntsville Ala., U.S.A. 34°44N 86°35W 111 D9
Huntsville Tex., U.S.A. 30°43N 95°33W 111 D7
Hurghada Egypt 27°15N 33°50E 95 C12
Hurley U.S.A. 46°27N 90°11W 112 B2
Huron U.S.A. 44°22N 98°13W 110 B7
Huron, L. U.S.A. 44°30N 82°40W 112 C6
Hursley U.K. 51°2N 1°23W 30 D6
Hurstbourne Tarrant U.K. 51°17N 1°26W 30 D6
Hurstpierpoint U.K. 50°56N 0°11W 31 E8
Húsavík Iceland 66°3N 17°21W 63 A2
Husband's Bosworth U.K. 52°28N 1°4W 27 H6
Hutchinson U.S.A. 38°5N 97°56W 110 C7
Huyton U.K. 53°25N 2°51W 27 F3
Huzhou China 30°51N 120°8E 79 E13
Hvar Croatia 43°11N 16°28E 68 C7
Hwang Ho = Huang He → China 37°55N 118°50E 79 D12
Hwange Zimbabwe 18°18S 26°30E 97 H5
Hwllfordd = Haverfordwest U.K. 51°48N 4°58W 28 D4
Hyargas Nuur Mongolia 49°0N 93°0E 78 B7
Hyde U.K. 53°27N 2°4W 27 F4
Hyderabad India 17°22N 78°29E 84 L11
Hyderabad Pakistan 25°23N 68°24E 84 G6
Hyères France 43°8N 6°9E 66 E7
Hyères, Îs. d' France 43°0N 6°20E 66 E7
Hyndman Peak U.S.A. 43°45N 114°8W 110 B4
Hythe U.K. 51°4N 1°5E 31 D11

I

Ialomiţa → Romania 44°42N 27°51E 65 F14
Iaşi Romania 47°10N 27°40E 65 E14
Ibadan Nigeria 7°22N 3°58E 94 G6
Ibagué Colombia 4°20N 75°20W 120 B2
Ibarra Ecuador 0°21N 78°7W 120 B2
Ibb Yemen 14°2N 44°10E 89 E3
Iberian Peninsula Europe 40°0N 5°0W 56 H5
Ibiá Brazil 19°30S 46°30W 122 C1
Ibiapaba, Sa. da Brazil 4°0S 41°30W 120 C5
Ibicaraí Brazil 14°51S 39°36W 122 B3
Ibiza = Eivissa Spain 38°54N 1°26E 67 C6
Ibotirama Brazil 12°13S 43°12W 122 B2
Ibstock U.K. 52°42N 1°24W 27 G6
Ica Peru 14°0S 75°48W 120 D2
Iça → Brazil 2°55S 67°58W 120 C3
İçel Turkey 36°51N 34°36E 71 G5
Iceland ■ Europe 64°45N 19°0W 63 B2
Ichihara Japan 35°28N 140°5E 81 F7
Ichinomiya Japan 35°18N 136°48E 81 F5
Icy C. U.S.A. 70°20N 161°52W 104 B3
Idaho ☐ U.S.A. 45°0N 115°0W 110 B4
Idaho Falls U.S.A. 43°30N 112°2W 110 B4
Idar-Oberstein Germany 49°43N 7°16E 64 D4
Idle → U.K. 53°27N 0°49W 27 F7
Idlib Syria 35°55N 36°36E 86 C4
Idmiston U.K. 51°9N 1°42W 30 D5
Ife Nigeria 7°30N 4°31E 94 G6
Iforas, Adrar des Africa 19°40N 1°40E 94 C5
Igarapava Brazil 20°3S 47°47W 122 D1
Igarka Russia 67°30N 86°33E 76 C9
Iglésias Italy 39°19N 8°32E 68 E3
Iglulik Canada 69°20N 81°49W 109 C11
Ignace Canada 49°30N 91°40W 112 A2
Igoumenitsa Greece 39°32N 20°18E 69 E9
Iguaçu → Brazil 25°36S 54°36W 121 E4
Iguaçu, Cat. del Brazil 25°41S 54°26W 121 E4
Iguala Mexico 18°21N 99°32W 114 D5
Iguatu Brazil 6°20S 39°18W 120 C6
Iguidi, Erg Africa 27°0N 7°0W 94 C4
Iisalmi Finland 63°32N 27°10E 63 E9
Ijebu-Ode Nigeria 6°47N 3°58E 94 G6
IJsselmeer Neths. 52°45N 5°20E 64 B3
Ikare Nigeria 7°32N 5°40E 94 G7
Ikaria Greece 37°35N 26°10E 69 F12
Ikeda Japan 34°1N 133°48E 81 F3
Ilagan Phil. 17°7N 121°53E 83 A6
Īlām Iran 33°36N 46°36E 86 C6
Ilchester U.K. 51°0N 2°41W 30 D3
Île-de-France ☐ France 49°0N 2°20E 66 B5
Ilebo Dem. Rep. of the Congo 4°17S 20°55E 96 E4
Ilesha Nigeria 7°37N 4°40E 94 G6
Ilfracombe U.K. 51°12N 4°8W 29 E5
Ilhéus Brazil 14°49S 39°2W 122 B3
Ili → Kazakhstan 45°53N 77°10E 76 E8
Iliamna L. U.S.A. 59°30N 155°0W 108 D4
Iligan Phil. 8°12N 124°13E 83 C6
Ilkeston U.K. 52°58N 1°19W 27 G6
Ilkley U.K. 53°56N 1°48W 27 E5
Illapel Chile 32°0S 71°10W 121 F2
Iller → Germany 48°23N 9°58E 64 D6
Illimani Bolivia 16°30S 67°50W 120 D3
Illinois ☐ U.S.A. 40°15N 89°30W 111 B9
Illinois → U.S.A. 38°58N 90°28W 111 C8
Ilmen, L. Russia 58°15N 31°10E 70 C5
Ilminster U.K. 50°55N 2°55W 30 E3
Iloilo Phil. 10°45N 122°33E 83 B6
Ilorin Nigeria 8°30N 4°35E 94 G6
Imabari Japan 34°4N 133°0E 81 F3
Imandra, L. Russia 67°30N 33°0E 70 A5
Imatra Finland 61°12N 28°48E 63 E9
imeni Ismail Samani, Pik Tajikistan 39°0N 72°2E 87 B13
Immingham U.K. 53°37N 0°13W 27 E8
Ímola Italy 44°20N 11°42E 68 B4
Imperatriz Brazil 5°30S 47°29W 120 C5
Impéria Italy 43°53N 8°3E 68 C3
Imphal India 24°48N 93°56E 85 G18
In Salah Algeria 27°10N 2°32E 94 C6
Inari Finland 68°54N 27°1E 63 D9
Inarijärvi Finland 69°0N 28°0E 63 D9
İnce Burun Turkey 42°7N 34°56E 71 F5
Incheon S. Korea 37°27N 126°40E 79 D14
Incomáti → Mozam. 25°46S 32°43E 97 K6
Indalsälven → Sweden 62°36N 17°30E 63 E7
India ■ Asia 20°0N 78°0E 84 K11
Indian Ocean 5°0S 75°0E 53 E13
Indiana U.S.A. 40°37N 79°9W 112 E8
Indiana ☐ U.S.A. 40°0N 86°0W 112 E4
Indianapolis U.S.A. 39°46N 86°9W 112 F4
Indigirka → Russia 70°48N 148°54E 77 B15
Indira Gandhi Canal India 28°0N 72°0E 84 F8
Indo-China Asia 15°0N 102°0E 72 G12
Indonesia ■ Asia 5°0S 115°0E 82 F5
Indore India 22°42N 75°53E 84 H9
Indre → France 47°16N 0°11E 66 C4
Indus → Pakistan 24°20N 67°47E 84 G5
İnebolu Turkey 41°55N 33°40E 71 F5
Inga, Barrage d' Dem. Rep. of the Congo 5°39S 13°39E 96 F2
Ingatestone U.K. 51°40N 0°24E 31 C9
Ingleborough U.K. 54°10N 2°22W 26 D4
Ingleton U.K. 54°10N 2°27W 26 D4
Ingolstadt Germany 48°46N 11°26E 64 D6
Ingraj Bazar India 24°58N 88°10E 85 G16
Ingushetia ☐ Russia 43°20N 44°50E 71 F8
Inishbofin Ireland 53°37N 10°13W 18 D1
Inisheer Ireland 53°3N 9°32W 20 B3
Inishfree B. Ireland 55°4N 8°23W 18 A5
Inishkea North Ireland 54°9N 10°11W 18 C1
Inishkea South Ireland 54°7N 10°12W 18 C1
Inishmaan Ireland 53°5N 9°35W 20 B3
Inishmore Ireland 53°8N 9°45W 20 B3
Inishowen Pen. Ireland 55°14N 7°15W 19 A7
Inishshark Ireland 53°37N 10°16W 18 D1
Inishtrahull Ireland 55°26N 7°13W 19 A7
Inishturk Ireland 53°42N 10°7W 18 D1
Inishvickillane Ireland 52°3N 10°37W 20 D1
Inkberrow U.K. 52°13N 1°58W 30 B5
Inland Sea Japan 34°20N 133°30E 81 F3
Inn → Austria 48°35N 13°28E 64 D7
Inner Hebrides U.K. 57°0N 6°30W 22 J4
Inner Mongolia = Nei Mongol Zizhiqu ☐ China 42°0N 112°0E 79 C11
Inner Sound U.K. 57°30N 5°55W 22 H6
Innerleithen U.K. 55°37N 3°4W 25 C9
Innsbruck Austria 47°16N 11°23E 64 E6
Inowrocław Poland 52°50N 18°12E 65 B10
Insein Burma 16°50N 96°5E 85 L20
Inta Russia 66°5N 60°8E 70 A11
Interlaken Switz. 46°41N 7°50E 64 E4
Inukjuak Canada 58°25N 78°15W 109 D12
Inuvik Canada 68°16N 133°40W 108 C6
Inveraray U.K. 56°14N 5°5W 24 B5
Inverbervie U.K. 56°51N 2°17W 23 J13
Invercargill N.Z. 46°24S 168°24E 99 K12
Invergordon U.K. 57°41N 4°10W 23 G9
Inverkeithing U.K. 56°2N 3°24W 25 B9
Inverness U.K. 57°29N 4°13W 23 H9
Inverurie U.K. 57°17N 2°23W 23 H13
Ioannina Greece 39°42N 20°47E 69 E9
Iona U.K. 56°20N 6°25W 24 B3
Ionia U.S.A. 42°59N 85°4W 112 D5
Ionian Is. Greece 38°40N 20°0E 69 E9
Ionian Sea Medit. S. 37°30N 17°30E 69 E7
Ios Greece 36°41N 25°20E 69 F11
Iowa ☐ U.S.A. 42°18N 93°30W 111 B8
Iowa City U.S.A. 41°40N 91°32W 111 B8
Ipameri Brazil 17°44S 48°9W 122 C1
Ipatinga Brazil 19°32S 42°30W 122 C2
Ipiales Colombia 0°50N 77°37W 120 B2
Ipoh Malaysia 4°35N 101°5E 82 D2
Ipswich Australia 27°35S 152°40E 98 F9
Ipswich U.K. 52°4N 1°10E 31 B11
Iqaluit Canada 63°44N 68°31W 109 C13
Iquique Chile 20°19S 70°5W 120 E2
Iquitos Peru 3°45S 73°10W 120 C2
Iraklio Greece 35°20N 25°12E 69 G11
Iran ■ Asia 33°0N 53°0E 87 C8
Īrānshahr Iran 27°15N 60°40E 87 E10
Irapuato Mexico 20°41N 101°28W 114 C4
Iraq ■ Asia 33°0N 44°0E 86 C5
Irazú, Volcan Costa Rica 10°28N 84°42W 115 E8
Irchester U.K. 52°18N 0°39W 31 B7
Ireland ■ Europe 53°50N 7°52W 62 E2
Ireland's Eye Ireland 53°24N 6°4W 21 B10
Iringa Tanzania 7°48S 35°43E 96 F7
Irish Sea Europe 53°38N 4°48W 62 E4
Irkutsk Russia 52°18N 104°20E 77 D11
Irlam U.K. 53°26N 2°26W 27 F4
Iron Gate Europe 44°44N 22°30E 65 F12
Iron Mountain U.S.A. 45°49N 88°4W 112 C3
Ironbridge U.K. 52°38N 2°30W 27 G3
Ironton U.S.A. 38°32N 82°41W 112 F6
Ironwood U.S.A. 46°27N 90°9W 112 B2
Irrawaddy → Burma 15°50N 95°6E 85 M19
Irt → U.K. 54°23N 3°26W 26 D2
Irthlingborough U.K. 52°20N 0°37W 31 B7
Irtysh → Russia 61°4N 68°52E 76 C7
Irún Spain 43°20N 1°52W 67 A5
Irvine U.K. 55°37N 4°41W 24 C6
Irvinestown U.K. 54°28N 7°39W 18 C6
Ísafjörður Iceland 66°5N 23°9W 63 A1
Isar → Germany 48°48N 12°57E 64 D7
Íschia Italy 40°44N 13°57E 68 D5
Isère → France 44°59N 4°51E 66 D6
Ishim → Russia 57°45N 71°10E 76 D8
Ishinomaki Japan 38°32N 141°20E 81 D7
Ishpeming U.S.A. 46°29N 87°40W 112 B4
Isiro Dem. Rep. of the Congo 2°53N 27°40E 96 D5
İskenderun Turkey 36°32N 36°10E 71 G6
Isla → U.K. 56°32N 3°20W 25 A9
Islamabad Pakistan 33°40N 73°10E 84 C8
Island L. Canada 53°47N 94°25W 108 D10
Island Pond U.S.A. 44°49N 71°53W 113 C12
Islay U.K. 55°46N 6°10W 24 C3
Isleham U.K. 52°21N 0°25E 31 B9
Islington ☐ U.K. 51°33N 0°5W 31 C8
Islip U.K. 51°50N 1°12W 30 C6
Ismâ'ilîya Egypt 30°37N 32°18E 95 B12
Isparta Turkey 37°47N 30°30E 71 G5
Israel ■ Asia 32°0N 34°50E 86 C3
Issoire France 45°32N 3°15E 66 D5
Issyk Kul Kyrgyzstan 42°25N 77°15E 72 D9
İstanbul Turkey 41°0N 28°58E 71 F4
Istres France 43°31N 4°59E 66 E6
Istria Croatia 45°10N 14°0E 68 B5
Itaberaba Brazil 12°32S 40°18W 122 B2
Itabira Brazil 19°37S 43°13W 122 C2
Itabuna Brazil 14°48S 39°16W 122 B3
Itacoatiara Brazil 3°8S 58°25W 120 C4
Itaipú, Represa de Brazil 25°30S 54°30W 117 F5
Itajaí Brazil 27°50S 48°39W 121 E5
Itajubá Brazil 22°24S 45°30W 122 D1
Italy ■ Europe 42°0N 13°0E 68 C5
Itaperuna Brazil 21°10S 41°54W 122 D2
Itapetinga Brazil 15°15S 40°15W 122 C2
Itapetininga Brazil 23°36S 48°7W 122 D1
Itapicuru → Brazil 11°47S 37°32W 122 B3
Itararé Brazil 24°6S 49°23W 122 D1
Itaúna Brazil 20°4S 44°34W 122 D2
Itchen → U.K. 50°55N 1°22W 30 E6
Ithaca U.S.A. 42°27N 76°30W 112 D9
Ittoqqortoormiit Greenland 70°20N 23°0W 54 B6
Itu Brazil 23°17S 47°15W 122 D1
Ivanava Belarus 52°7N 25°29E 65 B13
Ivano-Frankivsk Ukraine 48°40N 24°40E 65 D13
Ivanovo Russia 57°5N 41°0E 70 C7
Iveragh Pen. Ireland 51°52N 10°15W 20 D2
Ivinghoe U.K. 51°50N 0°37W 31 C7
Ivory Coast ■ Africa 7°30N 5°0W 94 G4
Ivujivik Canada 62°24N 77°55W 109 C12
Ivybridge U.K. 50°23N 3°56W 29 G6
Iwaki Japan 37°3N 140°55E 81 E7
Iwakuni Japan 34°15N 132°8E 81 F3
Iwo Nigeria 7°39N 4°9E 94 G6
Ixworth U.K. 52°18N 0°51E 31 B10
Izhevsk Russia 56°51N 53°14E 70 C9
Izmayil Ukraine 45°22N 28°46E 71 E4
İzmir Turkey 38°25N 27°8E 71 G4
İznik Gölü Turkey 40°27N 29°30E 71 F4
Izumi-Sano Japan 34°23N 135°18E 81 F4

J

Jabalpur India 23°9N 79°58E 84 H11
Jaboatão Brazil 8°7S 35°1W 120 C6
Jaboticabal Brazil 21°15S 48°17W 122 D1
Jacareí Brazil 23°20S 46°0W 122 D1
Jackson Barbados 13°7N 59°36W 114 c
Jackson Ky., U.S.A. 37°33N 83°23W 112 G6
Jackson Mich., U.S.A. 42°15N 84°24W 112 D5
Jackson Miss., U.S.A. 32°18N 90°12W 111 D8
Jackson Mo., U.S.A. 37°23N 89°40W 112 G3
Jackson Tenn., U.S.A. 35°37N 88°49W 111 C9
Jacksonville Fla., U.S.A. 30°20N 81°39W 111 D10
Jacksonville Ill., U.S.A. 39°44N 90°14W 112 F2
Jacmel Haiti 18°14N 72°32W 115 D10
Jacobabad Pakistan 28°20N 68°29E 84 E6
Jacobina Brazil 11°11S 40°30W 122 B2
Jade Mt. Taiwan 23°25N 120°52E 79 G13
Jaén Spain 37°44N 3°43W 67 D4
Jaffna Sri Lanka 9°45N 80°2E 84 Q12
Jahrom Iran 28°30N 53°31E 87 D8
Jaipur India 27°0N 75°50E 84 F9
Jakarta Indonesia 6°9S 106°52E 82 F3
Jalālābād Afghan. 34°30N 70°29E 87 C12
Jalgaon India 21°0N 75°42E 84 J9
Jalna India 19°48N 75°38E 84 K9
Jalpaiguri India 26°32N 88°46E 85 F16
Jaluit I. Marshall Is. 6°0N 169°30E 102 G8
Jamaame Somalia 0°4N 42°44E 89 G3
Jamaica ■ W. Indies 18°10N 77°30W 114 a
Jamalpur Bangla. 24°52N 89°56E 85 G16
Jamalpur India 25°18N 86°28E 85 G15
Jambi Indonesia 1°38S 103°30E 82 E2
James → U.S.A. 42°52N 97°18W 111 B7
James B. Canada 54°0N 80°0W 109 D12
Jamestown N. Dak., U.S.A. 46°54N 98°42W 110 A7
Jamestown N.Y., U.S.A. 42°6N 79°14W 112 D8
Jammu India 32°43N 74°54E 84 C9
Jammu & Kashmir ☐ India 34°25N 77°0E 84 B10
Jamnagar India 22°30N 70°6E 84 H7
Jamshedpur India 22°44N 86°12E 85 H15
Jan Mayen Arctic 71°0N 9°0W 54 B7
Janaúba Brazil 15°48S 43°19W 122 C2
Janesville U.S.A. 42°41N 89°1W 112 D3
Januária Brazil 15°25S 44°25W 122 C2
Jaora India 23°40N 75°10E 84 H9
Japan ■ Asia 36°0N 136°0E 81 F5
Japan, Sea of Asia 40°0N 135°0E 81 D4
Japan Trench Pac. Oc. 32°0N 142°0E 102 D6
Japurá → Brazil 3°8S 65°46W 120 C3
Jari → Brazil 1°9S 51°54W 120 C4
Jarrow U.K. 54°59N 1°28W 26 C6
Jarvis I. Pac. Oc. 0°15S 160°5W 103 H12
Jāsk Iran 25°38N 57°45E 87 E9
Jasper Canada 52°55N 118°5W 108 D8
Jaú Brazil 22°10S 48°30W 122 D1
Jauja Peru 11°45S 75°15W 120 D2
Jaunpur India 25°46N 82°44E 85 G13
Java Indonesia 7°0S 110°0E 82 F3
Java Sea Indonesia 4°35S 107°15E 82 E3
Java Trench Ind. Oc. 9°0S 105°0E 82 F3
Jawhar Somalia 2°48N 45°30E 89 G4
Jaya, Puncak Indonesia 3°57S 137°17E 83 E9
Jebel, Bahr el → South Sudan 9°30N 30°25E 95 G12
Jedburgh U.K. 55°29N 2°33W 25 D10
Jedda Si. Arabia 21°29N 39°10E 86 F4
Jeffersonville U.S.A. 38°17N 85°44W 112 F5
Jeju S. Korea 33°31N 126°32E 79 E14
Jeju-do S. Korea 33°29N 126°34E 79 E14
Jelenia Góra Poland 50°50N 15°45E 64 C8
Jelgava Latvia 56°41N 23°49E 63 F8
Jena Germany 50°54N 11°35E 64 C6
Jeonju S. Korea 35°50N 127°4E 79 D14
Jequié Brazil 13°51S 40°5W 122 B2
Jequitinhonha Brazil 16°30S 41°0W 122 C2
Jequitinhonha → Brazil 15°51S 38°53W 122 C3
Jérémie Haiti 18°40N 74°10W 115 D10
Jerez de la Frontera Spain 36°41N 6°7W 67 D2
Jersey U.K. 49°11N 2°7W 29 J9
Jersey City U.S.A. 40°42N 74°4W 113 E10
Jerseyville U.S.A. 39°7N 90°20W 112 F2
Jerusalem Israel/West Bank 31°47N 35°10E 86 D3
Jervaulx U.K. 54°16N 1°43W 26 D5
Jessore Bangla. 23°10N 89°10E 85 H16
Jhang Maghiana Pakistan 31°15N 72°22E 84 D8
Jhansi India 25°30N 78°36E 84 G11
Jharkhand ☐ India 24°0N 85°50E 85 H14
Jhelum Pakistan 33°0N 73°45E 84 C8
Jhelum → Pakistan 31°20N 72°10E 84 D8
Jiamusi China 46°40N 130°26E 79 B15
Ji'an Jiangxi, China 27°6N 114°59E 79 F11
Ji'an Jilin, China 41°5N 126°10E 79 C14
Jiangsu ☐ China 33°0N 120°0E 79 E12
Jiangxi ☐ China 27°30N 116°0E 79 F12
Jiaxing China 30°49N 120°45E 79 E13
Jiayuguan China 39°49N 98°18E 78 D8
Jihlava → Czech Rep. 48°55N 16°36E 65 D9
Jijiga Ethiopia 9°20N 42°50E 89 F3
Jilib Somalia 0°29N 42°46E 89 G3
Jilin China 43°44N 126°30E 79 C14
Jilin ☐ China 44°0N 127°0E 79 C14
Jima Ethiopia 7°40N 36°47E 89 F2
Jiménez Mexico 27°8N 104°54W 114 B4
Jinan China 36°38N 117°1E 79 D12
Jinchang China 38°30N 102°10E 78 D9
Jincheng China 35°29N 112°50E 79 D11
Jinding China 22°22N 113°33E 79 a
Jingdezhen China 29°20N 117°11E 79 F12
Jingmen China 31°0N 112°10E 79 E11
Jinhua China 29°8N 119°38E 79 F12
Jining Nei Monggol Zizhiqu, China 41°5N 113°0E 79 C11
Jining Shandong, China 35°22N 116°34E 79 D12
Jinja Uganda 0°25N 33°12E 96 D6
Jinsha Jiang → China 28°50N 104°36E 78 F9
Jinxi China 40°52N 120°50E 79 C13
Jinzhong China 37°42N 112°46E 79 D11
Jinzhou China 41°5N 121°3E 79 C13
Jipijapa Ecuador 1°0S 80°40W 120 C1
Jishou China 28°21N 109°43E 79 F10
Jiujiang China 29°42N 115°58E 79 F12
Jiwani Pakistan 25°1N 61°44E 87 E10
Jixi China 45°20N 130°50E 79 B15
Jīzān Si. Arabia 17°0N 42°20E 89 D3
Jizzax Uzbekistan 40°6N 67°50E 87 A11
João Pessoa Brazil 7°10S 34°52W 120 C6
Jodhpur India 26°23N 73°8E 84 F8
Joensuu Finland 62°37N 29°49E 63 E9
Jōetsu Japan 37°12N 138°10E 81 E6
Johannesburg S. Africa 26°11S 28°2E 97 K5
John Crow Mts. Jamaica 18°5N 76°25W 114 a
John Day → U.S.A. 45°44N 120°39W 110 A2
John o' Groats U.K. 58°38N 3°4W 23 E11
Johnson City U.S.A. 36°19N 82°21W 111 C10
Johnston I. Pac. Oc. 17°10N 169°8W 103 F11
Johnstone U.K. 55°49N 4°31W 24 C6
Johnstown U.S.A. 40°20N 78°55W 112 E8
Johor Bahru Malaysia 1°28N 103°46E 82 D2
Joinville Brazil 26°15S 48°55W 121 E5
Joliet U.S.A. 41°32N 88°5W 112 E3
Joliette Canada 46°3N 73°24W 109 E12
Jolo Phil. 6°0N 121°0E 83 C6
Jones Sound Canada 76°0N 85°0W 109 B11
Jonesboro U.S.A. 35°50N 90°42W 111 C8
Jönköping Sweden 57°45N 14°8E 63 F6
Jonquière Canada 48°27N 71°14W 113 A12
Joplin U.S.A. 37°6N 94°31W 111 C8
Jordan ■ Asia 31°0N 36°0E 86 D4
Jordan → Asia 31°48N 35°32E 86 D3
Jos Nigeria 9°53N 8°51E 94 G7
Joseph Bonaparte G. Australia 14°35S 128°50E 98 C4
Jotunheimen Norway 61°35N 8°25E 63 E5
Juan de Fuca, Str of. N. Amer. 48°15N 124°0W 110 A2
Juan Fernández, Arch. de Pac. Oc. 33°50S 80°0W 103 L20
Juàzeiro Brazil 9°30S 40°30W 122 A2
Juàzeiro do Norte Brazil 7°10S 39°18W 120 C6
Juba South Sudan 4°50N 31°35E 95 H12
Juba → Somalia 1°30N 42°35E 89 G3
Juchitán de Zaragoza Mexico 16°26N 95°1W 114 D5
Juiz de Fora Brazil 21°43S 43°19W 122 D2
Juliaca Peru 15°25S 70°10W 120 D2
Julianatop Suriname 3°40N 56°30W 120 B4
Jullundur India 31°20N 75°40E 84 D9
Junagadh India 21°30N 70°30E 84 J7
Jundiaí Brazil 24°30S 47°0W 122 D1
Juneau U.S.A. 58°18N 134°25W 108 D6
Junín Argentina 34°33S 60°57W 121 F3
Jur, Nahr el → South Sudan 8°45N 29°15E 95 G11
Jura Europe 46°40N 6°5E 66 C6
Jura U.K. 56°0N 5°50W 24 C4
Jura, Sd. of U.K. 55°57N 5°45W 24 C4
Juruá → Brazil 2°37S 65°44W 120 C3
Juruena → Brazil 7°20S 58°3W 120 C4
Juticalpa Honduras 14°40N 86°12W 114 E7
Jutland Denmark 56°25N 9°30E 63 F5
Juventud, I. de la Cuba 21°40N 82°40W 115 C8
Jyväskylä Finland 62°14N 25°50E 63 E9

K

K2 Pakistan 35°58N 76°32E 84 B10
Kabardino-Balkaria ☐ Russia 43°30N 43°30E 71 F7
Kābul Afghan. 34°28N 69°11E 87 C12
Kabwe Zambia 14°30S 28°29E 97 G5
Kachchh, Gulf of India 22°50N 69°15E 84 H6
Kachchh, Rann of India 24°0N 70°0E 84 H7
Kachin ☐ Burma 26°0N 97°30E 85 G20
Kaçkar Turkey 40°45N 41°10E 71 F7
Kadavu Fiji 19°0S 178°15E 99 E14
Kade Ghana 6°7N 0°56W 94 G5
Kadoma Zimbabwe 18°20S 29°52E 97 H5
Kaduna Nigeria 10°30N 7°21E 94 F7
Kaesŏng N. Korea 37°58N 126°35E 79 D14
Kafue → Zambia 15°30S 29°0E 97 H5
Kaga Bandoro C.A.R. 7°0N 19°10E 96 C3
Kagera → Uganda 0°57S 31°47E 96 E6
Kagoshima Japan 31°35N 130°33E 81 H2
Kaho'olawe U.S.A. 20°33N 156°37W 110 H16
Kahramanmaraş Turkey 37°37N 36°53E 71 G6
Kai, Kepulauan Indonesia 5°55S 132°45E 83 F8
Kaidu He → China 41°46N 86°31E 78 C6
Kaieteur Falls Guyana 5°1N 59°10W 120 B4
Kaifeng China 34°48N 114°21E 79 E11
Kailua Kona U.S.A. 19°39N 155°59W 110 J17
Kainji Res. Nigeria 10°1N 4°40E 94 F6
Kairouan Tunisia 35°45N 10°5E 95 A8
Kaiserslautern Germany 49°26N 7°45E 64 D4
Kaitaia N.Z. 35°8S 173°17E 99 H13
Kaiyuan China 23°40N 103°12E 78 G9
Kajaani Finland 64°17N 27°46E 63 E9
Kajabbi Australia 20°0S 140°1E 98 E7
Kakamega Kenya 0°20N 34°46E 96 D6
Kakhovka Res. Ukraine 47°5N 34°0E 71 E5
Kakinada India 16°57N 82°11E 85 L13
Kalaallit Nunaat = Greenland ☒ N. Amer. 66°0N 45°0W 54 C5
Kalahari Africa 24°0S 21°30E 97 J4
Kalamata Greece 37°3N 22°10E 69 F10
Kalamazoo U.S.A. 42°17N 85°35W 112 D5
Kalamazoo → U.S.A. 42°40N 86°10W 112 D4
Kalemie Dem. Rep. of the Congo 5°55S 29°9E 96 F5
Kalgoorlie-Boulder Australia 30°40S 121°22E 98 G3
Kalimantan Indonesia 0°0 114°0E 82 E4
Kálimnos Greece 37°0N 27°0E 69 F12
Kaliningrad Russia 54°42N 20°32E 63 G8
Kalispell U.S.A. 48°12N 114°19W 110 A4
Kalisz Poland 51°45N 18°8E 65 C10
Kalkaska U.S.A. 44°44N 85°11W 112 C5
Kallsjön Sweden 63°38N 13°0E 63 E6
Kalmar Sweden 56°40N 16°20E 63 F7
Kalmykia ☐ Russia 46°5N 46°1E 71 E8
Kaluga Russia 54°35N 36°10E 70 D6
Kalutara Sri Lanka 6°35N 80°0E 84 R12
Kalyan India 19°15N 73°9E 84 K8
Kama → Russia 55°45N 52°0E 70 C9
Kamchatka Pen. Russia 57°0N 160°0E 77 D16
Kamensk Uralskiy Russia 56°25N 62°2E 76 D7
Kamina Dem. Rep. of the Congo 8°45S 25°0E 96 F5
Kamloops Canada 50°40N 120°20W 108 D7
Kampala Uganda 0°20N 32°32E 96 D6
Kampong Cham Cambodia 12°0N 105°30E 82 B3
Kampong Saom Cambodia 10°38N 103°30E 82 B2
Kamyanets-Podilskyy Ukraine 48°45N 26°40E 65 D14
Kamyshin Russia 50°10N 45°24E 71 D8
Kananga Dem. Rep. of the Congo 5°55S 22°18E 96 F4
Kanash Russia 55°30N 47°32E 70 C8
Kanawha → U.S.A. 38°50N 82°9W 112 F6
Kanazawa Japan 36°30N 136°38E 81 E5
Kanchenjunga Nepal 27°50N 88°10E 85 F16
Kanchipuram India 12°52N 79°45E 84 N11
Kandahār Afghan. 31°32N 65°43E 87 D11
Kandalaksha Russia 67°9N 32°30E 70 A5
Kandalaksha, G. of Russia 66°0N 35°0E 70 A6
Kandi Benin 11°7N 2°55E 94 F6
Kandy Sri Lanka 7°18N 80°43E 84 R12
Kane U.S.A. 41°40N 78°49W 112 E8
Kane Basin Greenland 79°1N 70°0W 104 B12
Käne'ohe U.S.A. 21°25N 157°48W 110 H16
Kangaroo I. Australia 35°45S 137°0E 98 H6
Kangiqsualujjuaq Canada 58°30N 65°59W 109 D13
Kangiqsujuaq Canada 61°30N 72°0W 109 C12
Kangirsuk Canada 60°0N 70°0W 109 D13
Kanin Pen. Russia 68°0N 45°0E 70 A8
Kankakee U.S.A. 41°7N 87°52W 112 E4
Kankakee → U.S.A. 41°23N 88°15W 112 E3
Kankan Guinea 10°23N 9°15W 94 F4
Kannyakumari India 8°3N 77°40E 84 Q10
Kano Nigeria 12°2N 8°30E 94 F7
Kanpur India 26°28N 80°20E 84 F12
Kansas ☐ U.S.A. 38°30N 99°0W 110 C7
Kansas → U.S.A. 39°7N 94°37W 111 C8
Kansas City U.S.A. 39°6N 94°35W 111 C8
Kansk Russia 56°20N 95°37E 77 D10
Kanturk Ireland 52°11N 8°54W 20 D5
Kanye Botswana 24°55S 25°28E 97 J5
Kaohsiung Taiwan 22°35N 120°16E 79 G13
Kaolack Senegal 14°5N 16°8W 94 F2
Kapa'a U.S.A. 22°5N 159°19W 110 G15
Kapiri Mposhi Zambia 13°59S 28°43E 97 G5
Kaposvár Hungary 46°25N 17°47E 65 E9
Kaptai L. Bangla. 22°40N 92°20E 85 H18
Kapuas → Indonesia 0°25S 109°20E 82 E3
Kapuskasing Canada 49°25N 82°30W 112 A6
Kara Bogaz Gol Turkmenistan 41°0N 53°30E 87 A8
Kara Kum Turkmenistan 39°30N 60°0E 87 B9
Kara Sea Russia 75°0N 70°0E 76 B7
Karabük Turkey 41°12N 32°37E 71 F5
Karachey-Cherkessia ☐ Russia 43°40N 41°30E 71 F7
Karachi Pakistan 24°50N 67°0E 84 G5
Karaganda Kazakhstan 49°50N 73°10E 76 E8
Karagiye Depression Kazakhstan 43°27N 51°45E 71 F9
Karakalpakstan ☐ Uzbekistan 43°0N 58°0E 87 A9
Karakoram Pakistan 35°30N 77°0E 84 B10
Karaman Turkey 37°14N 33°13E 71 G5
Karamay China 45°30N 84°58E 78 B5

Karatax Shan   Lafayette

Karatax Shan *China* 35°57N 81°0E **78** D5
Karayazı *Turkey* 39°41N 42°9E **71** G7
Karbalā' *Iraq* 32°36N 44°3E **86** C6
Karelia □ *Russia* 65°30N 32°30E **70** A5
Kariba, L. *Zimbabwe* 16°40S 28°25E **97** H5
Kariba Dam *Zimbabwe* 16°30S 28°35E **97** H5
Karimata, Str. of *Indonesia* 2°0S 108°40E **82** E3
Karlovac *Croatia* 45°31N 15°36E **68** B6
Karlskrona *Sweden* 56°10N 15°35E **63** F7
Karlsruhe *Germany* 49°0N 8°23E **64** D5
Karlstad *Sweden* 59°23N 13°30E **63** F6
Karnak *Egypt* 25°43N 32°39E **95** C12
Karnal *India* 29°42N 77°2E **84** E10
Karnataka □ *India* 13°15N 77°0E **84** N10
Kärnten □ *Austria* 46°52N 13°30E **64** E8
Karpathos *Greece* 35°37N 27°10E **69** G12
Kars *Turkey* 40°40N 43°5E **71** F7
Karwar *India* 14°55N 74°13E **84** M9
Kasai → *Dem. Rep. of the Congo* 3°30S 16°10E **96** E3
Kasaragod *India* 12°30N 74°58E **84** N9
Kasba L. *Canada* 60°20N 102°10W **108** C9
Kāshān *Iran* 34°5N 51°30E **87** C7
Kashi *China* 39°30N 76°2E **78** D4
Kasongo *Dem. Rep. of the Congo* 4°30S 26°33E **96** E5
Kaspiysk *Russia* 42°52N 47°40E **71** F8
Kassalâ *Sudan* 15°30N 36°0E **95** E13
Kassel *Germany* 51°18N 9°26E **64** C5
Kastamonu *Turkey* 41°25N 33°43E **71** F5
Kasur *Pakistan* 31°5N 74°25E **84** D9
Katanga □ *Dem. Rep. of the Congo* 8°0S 25°0E **96** F4
Kathiawar *India* 22°20N 71°0E **84** H7
Kathmandu *Nepal* 27°45N 85°20E **85** F14
Katihar *India* 25°34N 87°36E **85** G15
Katima Mulilo *Namibia* 17°28S 24°13E **97** H4
Katiola *Ivory C.* 8°10N 5°10W **94** G4
Katowice *Poland* 50°17N 19°5E **65** C10
Katrine, L. *U.K.* 56°15N 4°30W **24** B7
Katsina *Nigeria* 13°0N 7°32E **94** F7
Kattegat *Denmark* 56°40N 11°20E **63** F6
Kaua'i *U.S.A.* 22°3N 159°30W **110** H15
Kauai Channel *U.S.A.* 21°45N 158°50W **110** H15
Kaukauna *U.S.A.* 44°17N 88°17W **112** C3
Kaunakakai *U.S.A.* 21°6N 157°1W **110** H16
Kaunas *Lithuania* 54°54N 23°54E **63** G8
Kavala *Greece* 40°57N 24°28E **69** D11
Kavieng *Papua N. G.* 2°36S 150°51E **98** A9
Kawagoe *Japan* 35°55N 139°29E **81** F6
Kawaguchi *Japan* 35°52N 139°45E **81** F6
Kawardha *India* 22°0N 81°17E **85** J12
Kawasaki *Japan* 35°31N 139°43E **81** F6
Kawawachikamach *Canada* 54°48N 66°50W **109** D13
Kayes *Mali* 14°25N 11°30W **94** F3
Kayseri *Turkey* 38°45N 35°30E **71** G6
Kazan *Russia* 55°50N 49°10E **70** C8
Kazan-Rettō *Pac. Oc.* 25°0N 141°0E **102** E6
Kazanlŭk *Bulgaria* 42°38N 25°20E **69** C11
Kea *Greece* 37°35N 24°22E **69** F11
Kea *U.K.* 50°14N 5°6W **29** G3
Keady *U.K.* 54°15N 6°42W **19** C8
Kearney *U.S.A.* 40°42N 99°5W **110** B7
Keban *Turkey* 38°50N 38°50E **71** G6
Keban Baraji *Turkey* 38°41N 38°33E **71** G6
Kebnekaise *Sweden* 67°53N 18°33E **63** D7
Kebri Dehar *Ethiopia* 6°45N 44°17E **89** F3
Kebumen *Indonesia* 7°42S 109°40E **82** F3
Kecskemét *Hungary* 46°57N 19°42E **65** E10
Kediri *Indonesia* 7°51S 112°1E **82** F4
Keelby *U.K.* 53°35N 0°16W **27** E8
Keele *U.K.* 53°0N 2°17W **27** F4
Keene *U.S.A.* 42°56N 72°17W **113** D11
Keeper Hill *Ireland* 52°45N 8°16W **20** C6
Keetmanshoop *Namibia* 26°35S 18°8E **97** K3
Kefalonia *Greece* 38°15N 20°30E **69** E9
Keflavík *Iceland* 64°2N 22°35W **63** B1
Kegworth *U.K.* 52°50N 1°17W **27** G6
Keighley *U.K.* 53°52N 1°54W **27** E5
Keith *U.K.* 57°32N 2°57W **23** G12
Keld *U.K.* 54°24N 2°10W **26** D4
Kelkit → *Turkey* 40°45N 36°32E **71** F6
Kellett, C. *Canada* 72°0N 126°0W **109** B7
Kellogg *U.S.A.* 47°32N 116°7W **110** A3
Kells *Ireland* 53°44N 6°53W **19** D8
Kelowna *Canada* 49°50N 119°25W **108** E8
Kelsale *U.K.* 52°14N 1°31E **31** B12
Kelsall *U.K.* 53°13N 2°43W **27** F3
Kelso *U.K.* 55°36N 2°26W **25** C11
Kelvedon *U.K.* 51°50N 0°43E **31** C10
Kemble *U.K.* 51°40N 1°59W **30** C5
Kem *Russia* 65°0N 34°38E **70** B5
Kemerovo *Russia* 55°20N 86°5E **76** D9
Kemi *Finland* 65°44N 24°34E **63** D8
Kemijoki → *Finland* 65°47N 24°32E **63** D8
Kemp Land *Antarctica* 69°0S 55°0E **55** C5
Kempsey *U.K.* 52°8N 2°12W **30** B4
Kempston *U.K.* 52°7N 0°30W **31** B7
Kempten *Germany* 47°45N 10°17E **64** E6
Kenai *U.S.A.* 60°33N 151°16W **108** C4
Kendal *U.K.* 54°20N 2°44W **26** D3
Kendari *Indonesia* 3°50S 122°30E **83** E6
Kenema *S. Leone* 7°50N 11°14W **94** G3
Kenitra *Morocco* 34°15N 6°40W **94** B4
Kenmare *Ireland* 51°53N 9°36W **20** E3
Kenmare River → *Ireland* 51°48N 9°51W **20** E3
Kennet → *U.K.* 51°27N 0°57W **31** D7
Kennewick *U.S.A.* 46°12N 119°7W **110** A3
Kenninghall *U.K.* 52°26N 1°0E **31** B11
Kenogami → *Canada* 51°6N 84°28W **109** D11
Kenora *Canada* 49°47N 94°29W **108** E10
Kenosha *U.S.A.* 42°35N 87°49W **112** D2
Kent □ *U.K.* 51°12N 0°40E **31** D10
Kent Pen. *Canada* 68°30N 107°0W **108** C9
Kentisbeare *U.K.* 50°51N 3°20W **29** F7
Kenton *U.S.A.* 40°39N 83°37W **112** E6
Kentucky □ *U.S.A.* 37°0N 84°0W **112** G5
Kentucky → *U.S.A.* 38°41N 85°11W **112** F5
Kentville *Canada* 45°6N 64°29W **109** E13
Kenya ■ *Africa* 1°0N 38°0E **96** D7
Kenya, Mt. *Kenya* 0°10S 37°18E **96** E7

Kerala □ *India* 11°0N 76°15E **84** P10
Kerch *Ukraine* 45°20N 36°20E **71** E6
Kerguelen *Ind. Oc.* 49°15S 69°10E **53** G13
Kericho *Kenya* 0°22S 35°15E **96** E7
Kerinci *Indonesia* 1°40S 101°15E **82** E2
Kermadec Is. *Pac. Oc.* 30°0S 178°15W **99** G15
Kermadec Trench *Pac. Oc.* 30°30S 176°0W **99** G15
Kermān *Iran* 30°15N 57°1E **87** D9
Kermānshāh *Iran* 34°23N 47°0E **86** C6
Kernow = Cornwall □ *U.K.* 50°26N 4°40W **29** G4
Kerrera *Canada* 56°24N 5°33W **24** B4
Kerrobert *Canada* 51°56N 109°8W **108** D9
Kerry □ *Ireland* 52°7N 9°35W **20** D3
Kerry Hd. *Ireland* 52°25N 9°56W **20** D3
Kessingland *U.K.* 52°26N 1°43E **31** B12
Keswick *U.K.* 54°36N 3°8E **26** C2
Ketchikan *U.S.A.* 55°21N 131°39W **108** D6
Kettering *U.K.* 52°24N 0°43W **31** B7
Kettle Ness *U.K.* 54°33N 0°42W **26** C7
Kettlewell *U.K.* 54°9N 2°3W **26** D4
Kewaunee *U.S.A.* 44°27N 87°31W **112** C2
Keweenaw B. *U.S.A.* 47°0N 88°15W **112** B3
Keweenaw Pen. *U.S.A.* 47°15N 88°15W **112** B3
Keweenaw Pt. *U.S.A.* 47°25N 87°43W **112** B4
Kexby *U.K.* 53°22N 0°42W **27** F7
Key West *U.S.A.* 24°33N 81°48W **111** F10
Keyingham *U.K.* 53°43N 0°7W **27** E8
Keymer *U.K.* 50°55N 0°7W **31** E8
Keynsham *U.K.* 51°24N 2°29W **30** D4
Keyser *U.S.A.* 39°26N 78°59W **112** F8
Keyworth *U.K.* 52°52N 1°5W **27** G6
Khabarovsk *Russia* 48°30N 135°5E **77** E14
Khairpur *Pakistan* 27°32N 68°49E **84** F6
Khambhat *India* 22°23N 72°33E **84** H8
Khambhat, G. of *India* 20°45N 72°30E **84** J8
Khamis Mushayt *Si. Arabia* 18°18N 42°44E **89** D3
Khan Tengri, Pik *Asia* 42°12N 80°10E **78** C5
Khandyga *Russia* 62°42N 135°35E **77** C14
Khanewal *Pakistan* 30°20N 71°55E **84** D7
Khanka, L. *Asia* 45°0N 132°24E **79** C15
Kharagpur *India* 22°20N 87°25E **85** H15
Kharg *Iran* 29°15N 50°28E **86** D7
Khârga, El Wâhât el *Egypt* 24°58N 30°49E **95** C12
Kharkov *Ukraine* 49°58N 36°20E **71** E6
Khartoum *Sudan* 15°31N 32°35E **95** E12
Khasavyurt *Russia* 43°16N 46°40E **71** F8
Khaskovo *Bulgaria* 41°56N 25°30E **69** D11
Khatanga *Russia* 72°0N 102°20E **77** B11
Khemisset *Morocco* 33°50N 6°1W **94** B4
Khenchela *Algeria* 35°28N 7°11E **94** A7
Kherson *Ukraine* 46°35N 32°35E **71** E5
Khmelnytskyy *Ukraine* 49°23N 27°0E **65** D14
Khojak Pass *Afghan.* 30°51N 66°34E **87** D11
Kholm *Afghan.* 36°45N 67°40E **87** B11
Khon Kaen *Thailand* 16°30N 102°47E **82** A2
Khorāsān *Iran* 34°0N 58°0E **87** C9
Khorramābād *Iran* 33°30N 48°25E **86** C7
Khorramshahr *Iran* 30°29N 48°15E **86** D7
Khouribga *Morocco* 32°58N 6°57W **94** B4
Khūjand *Tajikistan* 40°17N 69°37E **87** B12
Khulna *Bangla.* 22°45N 89°34E **85** H16
Khunjerab Pass *Asia* 36°40N 75°25E **84** A9
Khushab *Pakistan* 32°20N 72°20E **84** C8
Khuzdar *Pakistan* 27°52N 66°30E **84** F5
Khūzestān □ *Iran* 31°0N 49°0E **86** D7
Khvoy *Iran* 38°35N 45°0E **86** B6
Khyber Pass *Afghan.* 34°10N 71°8E **84** B7
Kibworth Beauchamp *U.K.* 52°33N 0°59W **31** B7
Kicking Horse Pass *Canada* 51°28N 116°16W **108** D8
Kidderminster *U.K.* 52°24N 2°15W **30** B4
Kidlington *U.K.* 51°50N 1°15W **30** C6
Kidsgrove *U.K.* 53°5N 2°14W **27** F4
Kidstones *U.K.* 54°13N 2°2W **26** D4
Kidwelly *U.K.* 51°44N 4°18W **28** D5
Kiel *Germany* 54°19N 10°8E **64** A6
Kiel Canal = Nord-Ostsee-Kanal *Germany* 54°12N 9°32E **64** A5
Kielce *Poland* 50°52N 20°42E **65** C11
Kielder *U.K.* 55°14N 2°35W **26** B3
Kieler Bucht *Germany* 54°35N 10°25E **64** A6
Kiev *Ukraine* 50°30N 30°28E **65** C16
Kigali *Rwanda* 1°59S 30°4E **96** E6
Kigoma-Ujiji *Tanzania* 4°55S 29°36E **96** E5
Kikwit *Dem. Rep. of the Congo* 5°0S 18°45E **96** E3
Kīlauea *U.S.A.* 19°25N 155°17W **110** J17
Kilbirnie *U.K.* 55°46N 4°41W **24** C6
Kilbrannan Sd. *U.K.* 55°37N 5°26W **24** C5
Kildare *Ireland* 53°9N 6°55W **21** B9
Kildare □ *Ireland* 53°10N 6°50W **21** B9
Kilfinnane *Ireland* 52°21N 8°28W **20** D6
Kilham *U.K.* 54°4N 0°23W **26** D7
Kilifi *Kenya* 3°40S 39°48E **96** E7
Kilimanjaro *Tanzania* 3°7S 37°20E **96** E7
Kilindini *Kenya* 4°4S 39°40E **96** E7
Kilkee *Ireland* 52°41N 9°39W **20** C3
Kilkeel *U.K.* 54°7N 5°55W **19** C10
Kilkenny *Ireland* 52°39N 7°15W **21** C8
Kilkenny □ *Ireland* 52°35N 7°15W **21** C8
Kilkhampton *U.K.* 50°52N 4°31W **29** F4
Kilkieran B. *Ireland* 53°20N 9°41W **20** B3
Killala *Ireland* 54°13N 9°13W **18** C3
Killala B. *Ireland* 54°16N 9°8W **18** C3
Killaloe *Ireland* 52°48N 8°28W **20** C6
Killarney *Ireland* 52°4N 9°30W **20** D3
Killarney □ *Ireland* 52°0N 9°33W **20** D3
Killary Harbour *Ireland* 53°38N 9°52W **18** D2
Killeen *U.S.A.* 31°7N 97°44W **110** D7
Killin *U.K.* 56°28N 4°19W **24** B7
Killiney *Ireland* 53°15N 6°7W **21** B10
Killinghall *U.K.* 54°2N 1°33W **26** D5
Killorglin *Ireland* 52°6N 9°47W **20** D3
Killybegs *Ireland* 54°38N 8°26W **18** B5
Kilmarnock *U.K.* 55°37N 4°29W **24** C7
Kilrush *Ireland* 52°38N 9°29W **20** D3
Kilsby *U.K.* 52°20N 1°10W **30** B6
Kilsyth *U.K.* 55°59N 4°3W **24** C7
Kilwa Kivinje *Tanzania* 8°45S 39°25E **96** F7
Kilwinning *U.K.* 55°39N 4°43W **24** C6
Kimberley *Australia* 16°20S 127°0E **98** D4
Kimberley *S. Africa* 28°43S 24°46E **97** K4
Kimbolton *U.K.* 52°18N 0°24W **31** B8

Kimch'aek *N. Korea* 40°40N 129°10E **79** C14
Kimmirut *Canada* 62°50N 69°50W **109** C13
Kimry *Russia* 56°55N 37°15E **70** C6
Kinabalu, Gunung *Malaysia* 6°3N 116°14E **82** C5
Kincardine *Canada* 44°10N 81°40W **112** C7
Kincardine Aberds., *U.K.* 56°57N 2°25W **23** J13
Kincardine Fife, *U.K.* 56°4N 3°43W **25** B8
Kinder Scout *U.K.* 53°24N 1°52W **27** F5
Kindersley *Canada* 51°30N 109°10W **108** D9
Kindia *Guinea* 10°0N 12°52W **94** F3
Kindu *Dem. Rep. of the Congo* 2°55S 25°50E **96** E5
Kineshma *Russia* 57°30N 42°5E **70** C7
Kineton *U.K.* 52°10N 1°31W **30** B5
King George I. *Antarctica* 60°0S 60°0W **55** C18
King George Is. *Canada* 57°20N 80°30W **109** D11
King I. *Australia* 39°50S 144°0E **98** H7
King William I. *Canada* 69°10N 97°25W **108** C10
Kingman *U.S.A.* 35°12N 114°4W **110** C4
King's Lynn *U.K.* 52°45N 0°24E **31** A9
King's Sutton *U.K.* 52°2N 1°15W **30** B6
King's Worthy *U.K.* 51°6N 1°17W **30** D6
Kingsbridge *U.K.* 50°17N 3°47W **29** G6
Kingsbury *U.K.* 52°34N 1°40W **27** G5
Kingscourt *Ireland* 53°54N 6°48W **19** D8
Kingskerswell *U.K.* 50°29N 3°35W **29** G6
Kingsland *U.K.* 52°15N 2°48W **30** B3
Kingsteignton *U.K.* 50°33N 3°36W **29** F6
Kingston *Canada* 44°14N 76°30W **109** E12
Kingston *Jamaica* 17°55N 76°50W **114** a
Kingston N.Y. *U.S.A.* 41°56N 73°59W **113** E10
Kingston upon Hull *U.K.* 53°45N 0°21W **27** E8
Kingston-upon-Thames □ *U.K.* 51°24N 0°17W **31** D8
Kingstown *St. Vincent* 13°10N 61°10W **115** E12
Kingsville *U.S.A.* 27°31N 97°52W **110** E7
Kingswear *U.K.* 50°21N 3°35W **29** G6
Kingswood *U.K.* 51°27N 2°31W **30** C3
Kington *U.K.* 52°13N 3°1W **30** B2
Kingussie *U.K.* 57°6N 4°2W **23** H8
Kinlochleven *U.K.* 56°43N 5°0W **22** J7
Kinnairds Hd. *U.K.* 57°43N 2°1W **23** G13
Kinngait *Canada* 64°14N 76°32W **109** C12
Kinross *U.K.* 56°13N 3°25W **25** B9
Kinsale *Ireland* 51°42N 8°31W **20** E5
Kinsale, Old Hd. of *Ireland* 51°37N 8°33W **20** E5
Kinshasa *Dem. Rep. of the Congo* 4°20S 15°15E **96** E3
Kintore *U.K.* 57°14N 2°20W **23** H13
Kintyre *U.K.* 55°30N 5°35W **24** D4
Kintyre, Mull of *U.K.* 55°17N 5°47W **24** D4
Kippure *Ireland* 53°11N 6°21W **21** B10
Kirensk *Russia* 57°50N 107°55E **77** D11
Kirgiz Steppe *Eurasia* 50°0N 55°0E **71** E10
Kiribati ■ *Pac. Oc.* 3°0S 180°0E **102** H10
Kirikkale *Turkey* 39°51N 33°32E **71** G5
Kiritimati *Kiribati* 1°58N 157°27W **103** G12
Kirkbean *U.K.* 54°55N 3°36W **25** E9
Kirkbride *U.K.* 54°54N 3°12W **26** C2
Kirkburton *U.K.* 53°37N 1°42W **27** E5
Kirkby *U.K.* 53°30N 2°54W **27** F3
Kirkby-in-Ashfield *U.K.* 53°6N 1°14W **27** F6
Kirkby Lonsdale *U.K.* 54°12N 2°36W **26** D3
Kirkby Malzeard *U.K.* 54°10N 1°37W **26** D5
Kirkby Stephen *U.K.* 54°29N 2°21W **26** D4
Kirkby Thore *U.K.* 54°37N 2°32W **26** C3
Kirkbymoorside *U.K.* 54°17N 0°56W **26** D7
Kirkcaldy *U.K.* 56°7N 3°9W **25** B9
Kirkcudbright *U.K.* 54°50N 4°2W **24** E7
Kirkintilloch *U.K.* 55°56N 4°8W **24** C7
Kirkland Lake *Canada* 48°9N 80°2W **109** E11
Kirklareli *Turkey* 41°44N 27°15E **86** A1
Kirkoswald *U.K.* 54°46N 2°41W **26** C3
Kirksville *U.S.A.* 40°12N 92°35W **111** B8
Kirkūk *Iraq* 35°30N 44°21E **86** C6
Kirkwall *U.K.* 58°59N 2°58W **23** E12
Kirkwhelpington *U.K.* 55°9N 1°59W **26** B5
Kirov *Russia* 58°35N 49°40E **70** C8
Kirovohrad *Ukraine* 48°35N 32°20E **71** E5
Kirriemuir *U.K.* 56°41N 3°1W **23** J11
Kırşehir *Turkey* 39°14N 34°5E **71** G5
Kirthar Range *Pakistan* 27°0N 67°0E **84** F5
Kirtling *U.K.* 52°12N 0°28E **31** B10
Kirtlington *U.K.* 51°53N 1°15W **30** C6
Kirton *U.K.* 52°56N 0°3W **27** G8
Kirton in Lindsey *U.K.* 53°29N 0°34W **27** F7
Kiruna *Sweden* 67°52N 20°15E **63** D8
Kiryū *Japan* 36°24N 139°20E **81** E6
Kisangani *Dem. Rep. of the Congo* 0°35N 25°15E **96** D5
Kiselevsk *Russia* 54°5N 86°39E **76** D9
Kishanganj *India* 26°3N 88°14E **85** F16
Kishinev *Moldova* 47°2N 28°50E **65** E15
Kisii *Kenya* 0°40S 34°45E **96** E6
Kislovodsk *Russia* 43°50N 42°45E **71** F7
Kismaayo *Somalia* 0°22S 42°32E **89** H3
Kisumu *Kenya* 0°3S 34°45E **96** E6
Kitakyūshū *Japan* 33°50N 130°50E **81** G2
Kitale *Kenya* 1°0N 35°0E **96** D7
Kitami *Japan* 43°48N 143°54E **81** B8
Kitchener *Canada* 43°27N 80°29W **112** D7
Kithnos *Greece* 37°26N 24°27E **69** F11
Kitimat *Canada* 54°3N 128°38W **108** D7
Kittanning *U.S.A.* 40°49N 79°31W **112** E8
Kitwe *Zambia* 12°54S 28°13E **97** G5
Kivu, L. *Dem. Rep. of the Congo* 1°48S 29°0E **96** E5
Kızıl Irmak → *Turkey* 41°44N 35°58E **71** F6
Kizlyar *Russia* 43°51N 46°40E **71** F8
Kladno *Czech Rep.* 50°10N 14°7E **64** C8
Klagenfurt *Austria* 46°38N 14°20E **64** E8
Klaipėda *Lithuania* 55°43N 21°10E **63** G8
Klamath → *U.S.A.* 41°33N 124°5W **110** B2
Klamath Falls *U.S.A.* 42°13N 121°46W **110** B2
Klang *Malaysia* 3°2N 101°26E **82** D2
Klarälven → *Sweden* 59°23N 13°32E **63** F6
Klerksdorp *S. Africa* 26°53S 26°38E **97** K5
Kluane L. *Canada* 61°15N 138°40W **108** C6
Klyuchevskaya, Gora *Russia* 55°50N 160°30E **77** D17
Knaresborough *U.K.* 54°1N 1°28W **27** D6

Knebworth *U.K.* 51°52N 0°11W **31** C8
Knighton *U.K.* 52°21N 3°3W **28** C7
Knock *Ireland* 53°48N 8°55W **18** D4
Knockmealdown Mts. *Ireland* 52°14N 7°56W **20** D7
Knossos *Greece* 35°16N 25°10E **69** G11
Knottingley *U.K.* 53°43N 1°16W **27** E6
Knowle *U.K.* 52°24N 1°44W **27** H5
Knoxville *U.S.A.* 35°58N 83°55W **111** C10
Knoydart *U.K.* 57°3N 5°33W **22** H6
Knutsford *U.K.* 53°18N 2°21W **27** F4
Kōbe *Japan* 34°41N 135°13E **81** F4
Koblenz *Germany* 50°21N 7°36E **64** C4
Kocaeli *Turkey* 40°45N 29°50E **71** F4
Koch Bihar *India* 26°22N 89°29E **85** F16
Kōchi *Japan* 33°30N 133°35E **81** G3
Kodiak *U.S.A.* 57°47N 152°24W **108** D4
Kodiak I. *U.S.A.* 57°30N 152°45W **108** D4
Koforidua *Ghana* 6°3N 0°17W **94** G5
Kōfu *Japan* 35°40N 138°30E **81** F6
Kogalym *Russia* 62°16N 74°29E **76** C8
Kohat *Pakistan* 33°40N 71°29E **84** C7
Kohima *India* 25°35N 94°10E **85** G19
Kohtla-Järve *Estonia* 59°20N 27°20E **63** F9
Kokkola *Finland* 63°50N 23°8E **63** E8
Koko Kyunzu *Burma* 14°7N 93°22E **85** M18
Kokomo *U.S.A.* 40°29N 86°8W **112** E4
Kokopo *Papua N. G.* 4°22S 152°19E **98** A9
Kökshetaü *Kazakhstan* 53°20N 69°25E **76** D7
Koksoak → *Canada* 58°30N 68°10W **109** D13
Kola Pen. *Russia* 67°30N 38°0E **70** A6
Kolar Gold Fields *India* 12°58N 78°16E **84** N11
Kolguyev, Ostrov *Russia* 69°20N 48°30E **70** A8
Kolhapur *India* 16°43N 74°15E **84** L9
Kolkata *India* 22°34N 88°21E **85** H16
Kolomna *Russia* 55°8N 38°45E **70** C6
Kolomyya *Ukraine* 48°31N 25°2E **71** E4
Kolpino *Russia* 59°44N 30°39E **70** C5
Kolwezi *Dem. Rep. of the Congo* 10°40S 25°25E **96** G5
Kolyma → *Russia* 69°30N 161°0E **77** C17
Kolyma Ra. *Russia* 63°0N 157°0E **77** C16
Komatsu *Japan* 36°25N 136°30E **81** E5
Komi □ *Russia* 64°0N 55°0E **70** B10
Komsomolsk-na-Amur *Russia* 50°30N 137°0E **77** D14
Kondoz *Afghan.* 36°50N 68°50E **87** B12
Kongur Shan *China* 38°34N 75°18E **78** D4
Konin *Poland* 52°12N 18°15E **65** B10
Konosha *Russia* 61°0N 40°5E **70** B7
Konotop *Ukraine* 51°12N 33°7E **71** D5
Konqi He → *China* 41°0N 86°0E **78** C6
Konya *Turkey* 37°52N 32°35E **71** G5
Kootenay L. *Canada* 49°45N 116°50W **108** E8
Kopet Dagh *Asia* 38°0N 58°0E **87** B9
Korçë *Albania* 40°37N 20°50E **69** D9
Korčula *Croatia* 42°56N 16°57E **68** C7
Kordofân *Sudan* 13°0N 29°0E **95** F11
Korea Bay *Korea* 39°0N 124°0E **79** D13
Korea Strait *Asia* 34°0N 129°30E **79** E14
Korhogo *Ivory C.* 9°29N 5°28W **94** G4
Kōriyama *Japan* 37°24N 140°23E **81** E7
Korla *China* 41°45N 86°4E **78** C6
Koror *Palau* 7°20N 134°28E **102** G5
Körös → *Hungary* 46°43N 20°12E **65** E11
Korosten *Ukraine* 50°54N 28°36E **71** D4
Kortrijk *Belgium* 50°50N 3°17E **64** C2
Koryak Ra. *Russia* 61°0N 171°0E **77** C18
Kos *Greece* 36°50N 27°15E **69** F12
Kosciuszko, Mt. *Australia* 36°27S 148°16E **98** H8
Košice *Slovak Rep.* 48°42N 21°15E **65** D11
Kosovo ■ *Europe* 42°30N 21°0E **69** C9
Kôsti *Sudan* 13°8N 32°43E **95** F12
Kostroma *Russia* 57°50N 40°58E **70** C7
Koszalin *Poland* 54°11N 16°8E **64** A9
Kota *India* 25°14N 75°49E **84** G9
Kota Bharu *Malaysia* 6°7N 102°14E **82** C2
Kota Kinabalu *Malaysia* 6°0N 116°4E **82** C5
Kotabumi *Indonesia* 4°49S 104°54E **82** E2
Kotelnich *Russia* 58°22N 48°24E **70** C8
Kotka *Finland* 60°28N 26°58E **63** E9
Kotlas *Russia* 61°17N 46°43E **70** B8
Kotor *Montenegro* 42°25N 18°47E **69** C8
Kotri *Pakistan* 25°22N 68°22E **84** G6
Kotuy → *Russia* 71°54N 102°6E **77** B11
Kotzebue *U.S.A.* 66°53N 162°39W **108** C3
Kotzebue Sound *U.S.A.* 66°20N 163°0W **108** C3
Koudougou *Burkina Faso* 12°10N 2°20W **94** F5
Koumra *Chad* 8°50N 17°35E **95** G9
Kovel *Ukraine* 51°11N 24°38E **70** D3
Kovrov *Russia* 56°25N 41°25E **70** C7
Kowloon *China* 22°19N 114°11E **79** G11
Koyukuk → *U.S.A.* 64°55N 157°32W **108** C4
Kpalimé *Togo* 6°57N 0°44E **94** G6
Kra, Isthmus of *Thailand* 10°15N 99°30E **82** B1
Kragujevac *Serbia* 44°2N 20°56E **69** B9
Krakatoa *Indonesia* 6°10S 105°20E **82** F3
Kraków *Poland* 50°4N 19°57E **65** C10
Kraljevo *Serbia* 43°44N 20°41E **69** C9
Kramatorsk *Ukraine* 48°50N 37°30E **71** E6
Krasnodar *Russia* 45°5N 39°0E **71** E6
Krasnokamensk *Russia* 50°3N 118°0E **77** D12
Krasnoturinsk *Russia* 59°46N 60°12E **70** C11
Krasnoyarsk *Russia* 56°8N 93°0E **77** D10
Krasnyy Luch *Ukraine* 48°13N 39°0E **71** E6
Krefeld *Germany* 51°20N 6°33E **64** C4
Kremenchuk *Ukraine* 49°5N 33°25E **71** E5
Kribi *Cameroon* 2°57N 9°56E **96** D1
Krishna → *India* 15°57N 80°59E **85** M12
Kristiansand *Norway* 58°8N 8°1E **63** F5
Kristiansund *Norway* 63°7N 7°45E **63** E5
Krivoy Rog *Ukraine* 47°51N 33°20E **71** E5
Krk *Croatia* 45°8N 14°40E **68** B6
Kronshtadt *Russia* 59°57N 29°51E **70** B4
Kroonstad *S. Africa* 27°43S 27°19E **97** K5
Kropotkin *Russia* 45°28N 40°28E **71** E7
Krosno *Poland* 49°42N 21°46E **65** D11
Krugersdorp *S. Africa* 26°5S 27°46E **97** K5
Kruševac *Serbia* 43°35N 21°28E **69** C9
Ksar el Kebir *Morocco* 35°0N 6°0W **94** B4
Kuala Belait *Malaysia* 4°35N 114°11E **82** D4
Kuala Lumpur *Malaysia* 3°9N 101°41E **82** D2

Kuala Terengganu *Malaysia* 5°20N 103°8E **82** C2
Kuantan *Malaysia* 3°49N 103°20E **82** D2
Kuching *Malaysia* 1°33N 110°25E **82** D4
Kudymkar *Russia* 59°1N 54°39E **70** C9
Kugluktuk *Canada* 67°50N 115°5W **108** C8
Kuito *Angola* 12°22S 16°55E **97** G3
Kūlob *Tajikistan* 37°55N 69°50E **87** B12
Kuma → *Russia* 44°55N 47°0E **71** F8
Kumagaya *Japan* 36°9N 139°22E **81** E6
Kumamoto *Japan* 32°45N 130°45E **81** G2
Kumanovo *Macedonia* 42°9N 21°42E **69** C9
Kumasi *Ghana* 6°41N 1°38W **94** G5
Kumba *Cameroon* 4°36N 9°24E **96** D1
Kumbakonam *India* 10°58N 79°25E **84** P11
Kumertau *Russia* 52°45N 55°57E **70** D10
Kumtag Desert *China* 39°40N 92°0E **78** D7
Kungur *Russia* 57°25N 56°57E **70** C10
Kunlun Shan *Asia* 36°0N 86°30E **78** D6
Kunming *China* 25°1N 102°41E **78** F9
Kuopio *Finland* 62°53N 27°35E **63** E9
Kupang *Indonesia* 10°19S 123°39E **83** F6
Kuqa *China* 41°35N 82°30E **78** C5
Kür → *Azerbaijan* 39°29N 49°15E **71** G8
Kurdistan *Asia* 37°20N 43°30E **86** B5
Kure *Japan* 34°14N 132°32E **81** F3
Kurgan *Russia* 55°26N 65°18E **76** D7
Kuril Is. *Russia* 45°0N 150°0E **77** E16
Kuril-Kamchatka Trench *Pac. Oc.* 44°0N 153°0E **102** C7
Kurnool *India* 15°45N 78°0E **84** M11
Kursk *Russia* 51°42N 36°11E **70** D6
Kuruktag *China* 41°0N 89°0E **78** C6
Kurume *Japan* 33°15N 130°30E **81** G2
Kushiro *Japan* 43°0N 144°25E **81** B9
Kushtia *Bangla.* 23°55N 89°5E **85** H16
Kuskokwim → *U.S.A.* 60°5N 162°25W **104** C3
Kuskokwim B. *U.S.A.* 59°45N 162°25W **108** D3
Kütahya *Turkey* 39°30N 30°2E **71** G5
Kutaisi *Georgia* 42°19N 42°40E **71** F7
Kuujjuaq *Canada* 58°6N 68°15W **109** D13
Kuujjuarapik *Canada* 55°20N 77°35W **109** D12
Kuwait *Kuwait* 29°30N 48°0E **86** D7
Kuwait ■ *Asia* 29°30N 47°30E **86** D6
Kuybyshev Res. *Russia* 55°2N 49°30E **70** C8
Kuznetsk *Russia* 53°12N 46°40E **70** D8
Kuzomen *Russia* 66°22N 36°50E **70** A6
KwaMashu *S. Africa* 29°45S 30°58E **97** K6
KwaZulu Natal □ *S. Africa* 29°0S 30°0E **97** K6
Kwekwe *Zimbabwe* 18°58S 29°48E **97** H5
Kwun Tong *China* 22°19N 114°13E **79** a
Kyle of Lochalsh *U.K.* 57°17N 5°44W **22** H6
Kyōga, L. *Uganda* 1°35N 33°0E **96** D6
Kyōto *Japan* 35°0N 135°45E **81** F4
Kyrenia *Cyprus* 35°20N 33°20E **86** C3
Kyrgyzstan ■ *Asia* 42°0N 75°0E **76** E8
Kythira *Greece* 36°8N 23°0E **69** F10
Kyūshū *Japan* 33°0N 131°0E **81** G2
Kyustendil *Bulgaria* 42°16N 22°41E **69** C10
Kyzyl *Russia* 51°50N 94°30E **77** D10
Kyzyl Kum *Uzbekistan* 42°30N 65°0E **87** A10
Kyzyl-Orda *Kazakhstan* 44°48N 65°28E **76** E7

L

La Alcarria *Spain* 40°31N 2°45W **67** B4
La Barra *Nic.* 12°54N 83°33W **115** E8
La Ceiba *Honduras* 15°40N 86°50W **114** D7
La Coruña *Spain* 43°20N 8°25W **67** A1
La Crosse *U.S.A.* 43°48N 91°15W **112** D2
La Grande *U.S.A.* 45°20N 118°5W **110** A3
La Grande → *Canada* 53°50N 79°0W **109** D12
La Grange *U.S.A.* 33°2N 85°2W **111** D10
La Habana *Cuba* 23°8N 82°22W **115** C8
La Junta *U.S.A.* 37°59N 103°33W **110** C6
La Línea de la Concepción *Spain* 36°15N 5°23W **67** D3
La Loche *Canada* 56°29N 109°26W **108** D9
La Mancha *Spain* 39°10N 2°54W **67** C4
La Oroya *Peru* 11°32S 75°54W **120** D2
La Palma *Canary Is.* 28°40N 17°50W **94** C2
La Paz *Bolivia* 16°20S 68°10W **120** D3
La Paz *Mexico* 24°10N 110°18W **114** C2
La Perouse Str. *Asia* 45°40N 142°0E **79** B17
La Plata *Argentina* 35°0S 57°55W **121** F4
La Quiaca *Argentina* 22°5S 65°35W **121** E3
La Rioja *Argentina* 29°20S 67°0W **121** E3
La Rioja □ *Spain* 42°20N 2°20W **67** A4
La Roche-sur-Yon *France* 46°40N 1°25W **66** C3
La Rochelle *France* 46°10N 1°9W **66** C3
La Romana *Dom. Rep.* 18°27N 68°57W **115** D11
La Ronge *Canada* 55°5N 105°20W **108** D9
La Sarre *Canada* 48°45N 79°15W **109** E12
La Serena *Chile* 29°55S 71°10W **121** E2
La Seyne-sur-Mer *France* 43°7N 5°52E **66** E6
La Spézia *Italy* 44°7N 9°50E **68** B3
La Tortuga *Venezuela* 11°0N 65°22W **120** A3
La Tuque *Canada* 47°30N 72°50W **109** E12
La Vega *Dom. Rep.* 19°20N 70°30W **115** D10
Labé *Guinea* 11°24N 12°16W **94** F3
Labinsk *Russia* 44°40N 40°48E **71** F7
Laborie *St. Lucia* 13°45N 61°2W **114** b
Labrador *Canada* 53°20N 61°0W **109** D13
Labrador City *Canada* 52°57N 66°55W **109** D13
Labrador Sea *Atl. Oc.* 57°0N 54°0W **109** D14
Lac La Biche *Canada* 54°45N 111°58W **108** D8
Lac-Mégantic *Canada* 45°35N 70°53W **113** C12
Laccadive Is. = Lakshadweep Is. *India* 10°0N 72°30E **72** G9
Laceby *U.K.* 53°33N 0°10W **27** E8
Lacock *U.K.* 51°24N 2°8W **30** D4
Lacombe *Canada* 52°30N 113°44W **108** D8
Laconia *U.S.A.* 43°32N 71°28W **113** D12
Ladakh Ra. *India* 34°0N 78°0E **84** B11
Ladder Hills *U.K.* 57°13N 3°16W **23** H11
Ladock *U.K.* 50°19N 4°58W **29** G4
Ladoga, L. *Russia* 61°15N 30°30E **70** B5
Ladysmith *S. Africa* 28°32S 29°46E **97** K5
Ladysmith *U.S.A.* 45°28N 91°12W **112** C2
Lae *Papua N. G.* 6°40S 147°2E **98** B8
Lafayette *Ind. U.S.A.* 40°25N 86°54W **112** E4

Lafayette   Lynmouth

Lafayette La., U.S.A. 30°14N 92°1W 111 D8
Lafia Nigeria 8°30N 8°34E 94 G7
Lagan → U.K. 54°36N 5°55W 19 B10
Lagarto Brazil 10°54S 37°41W 122 B3
Lagdo, L. de Cameroon 8°40N 14°0E 95 G8
Laghouat Algeria 33°50N 2°59E 94 B6
Lagos Nigeria 6°25N 3°27E 94 G6
Lagos Portugal 37°5N 8°41W 67 D1
Lahn → Germany 50°19N 7°37E 64 C4
Lahore Pakistan 31°32N 74°22E 84 D9
Lahti Finland 60°58N 25°40E 63 E9
Lairg U.K. 58°2N 4°24W 23 F9
Laizhou China 37°8N 119°57E 79 D12
Lake Charles U.S.A. 30°14N 93°13W 111 D8
Lake City U.S.A. 30°11N 82°38W 111 D10
Lake District △ U.K. 54°30N 3°21W 26 C2
Lake Havasu City U.S.A. 34°27N 114°22W 110 D4
Lakeland U.S.A. 28°3N 81°57W 111 E10
Lakenheath U.K. 52°25N 0°32E 31 B10
Lakewood U.S.A. 41°28N 81°47W 112 E7
Lakshadweep Is. India 10°0N 72°30E 72 G9
Lamar U.S.A. 38°5N 102°37W 110 C6
Lambaréné Gabon 0°41S 10°12E 96 E2
Lambay I. Ireland 53°29N 6°1W 21 B10
Lamberhurst U.K. 51°5N 0°24E 31 D9
Lambeth □ U.K. 51°28N 0°6W 31 D8
Lambley U.K. 54°56N 2°30W 26 C4
Lambourn U.K. 51°30N 1°32W 30 C5
Lamesa U.S.A. 32°44N 101°58W 110 D6
Lammermuir U.K. 55°50N 2°25W 25 C11
Lammermuir Hills U.K. 55°50N 2°40W 25 C10
Lamon B. Phil. 14°30N 122°20E 83 B6
Lampedusa Medit. S. 35°36N 12°40E 68 G5
Lampeter U.K. 52°7N 4°4W 28 C3
Lamu Kenya 2°16S 40°55E 96 E8
Lanark U.K. 55°40N 3°47W 25 C8
Lancang Jiang → China 21°40N 101°10E 78 G9
Lancashire □ U.K. 53°50N 2°48W 27 E3
Lancaster U.K. 54°3N 2°48W 26 D3
Lancaster N.H., U.S.A. 44°29N 71°34W 113 C12
Lancaster Pa., U.S.A. 40°2N 76°19W 112 E9
Lancaster Wis., U.S.A. 42°51N 90°43W 112 D2
Lancaster Sd. Canada 74°13N 84°0W 109 B11
Lanchester U.K. 54°50N 1°44W 26 C5
Lancing U.K. 50°49N 0°19W 31 E8
Landes France 44°0N 1°0W 66 D3
Landkey U.K. 51°3N 4°0W 29 E6
Land's End U.K. 50°4N 5°44W 29 G2
Langholm U.K. 55°9N 3°0W 25 D10
Langport U.K. 51°2N 2°50W 30 D3
Langreo Spain 43°18N 5°40W 67 A3
Langres France 47°52N 5°20E 66 C6
Langres, Plateau de France 47°45N 5°3E 66 C6
Langsa Indonesia 4°30N 97°57E 82 D1
Langstrothdale Chase U.K. 54°14N 2°13W 26 D4
Langtoft U.K. 52°42N 0°20W 27 G8
Langtree U.K. 50°55N 4°13W 29 F5
Languedoc France 43°58N 3°55E 66 E5
Lannion France 48°46N 3°29W 66 B2
L'Annonciation Canada 46°25N 74°55W 113 B10
L'Anse U.S.A. 46°45N 88°27W 112 B3
Lansing U.S.A. 42°44N 84°33W 112 D5
Lantau I. China 22°15N 113°56E 79 a
Lanzarote Canary Is. 29°0N 13°40W 94 C3
Lanzhou China 36°1N 103°52E 78 D9
Laoag Phil. 18°7N 120°34E 83 A6
Laois □ Ireland 52°57N 7°27W 21 C7
Laon France 49°33N 3°35E 66 B5
Laos ■ Asia 17°45N 105°0E 82 A3
Lapeer U.S.A. 43°3N 83°19W 112 D6
Lapford U.K. 50°51N 3°48W 29 F6
Lapland Europe 68°7N 24°0E 63 D8
LaPorte U.S.A. 41°36N 86°43W 112 E4
Laptev Sea Russia 76°0N 125°0E 77 B13
L'Áquila Italy 42°22N 13°22E 68 C5
Laramie U.S.A. 41°19N 105°35W 110 B5
Laramie Mts. U.S.A. 42°0N 105°30W 110 B5
Laredo U.S.A. 27°30N 99°30W 110 E7
Largs U.K. 55°47N 4°52W 24 C6
Larisa Greece 39°36N 22°27E 69 E10
Larnaca Cyprus 34°55N 33°38E 86 C3
Larne U.K. 54°51N 5°51W 19 B10
Larne L. U.K. 54°50N 5°48W 19 B10
Larrimah Australia 15°35S 133°12E 98 D5
Larsen Ice Shelf Antarctica 67°0S 62°0W 55 C17
Larvik Norway 59°4N 10°2E 63 F6
Las Cruces U.S.A. 32°19N 106°47W 110 D5
Las Palmas Canary Is. 28°7N 15°26W 94 C2
Las Tunas Cuba 20°58N 76°59W 115 C9
Las Vegas N. Mex., U.S.A. 35°36N 105°13W 110 C5
Las Vegas Nev., U.S.A. 36°10N 115°8W 110 C3
Lashio Burma 22°56N 97°45E 85 H20
Lassen Pk. U.S.A. 40°29N 121°30W 110 B2
Lastoursville Gabon 0°55S 12°38E 96 E2
Latacunga Ecuador 0°50S 78°35W 120 C2
Latakia Syria 35°30N 35°45E 86 C3
Latina Italy 41°28N 12°52E 68 D5
Latvia ■ Europe 56°50N 24°0E 63 F8
Lauder U.K. 55°43N 2°43W 25 C10
Lauderdale U.K. 55°44N 2°41W 25 C10
Launceston Australia 41°24S 147°8E 98 J8
Launceston U.K. 50°38N 4°22W 29 F5
Laune → Ireland 52°7N 9°47W 20 D3
Laurel U.S.A. 31°41N 89°8W 111 D9
Laurencekirk U.K. 56°50N 2°28W 23 J13
Laurentian Plateau Canada 52°0N 70°0W 104 E12
Lausanne Switz. 46°32N 6°38E 64 E4
Lavagh More Ireland 54°46N 8°6W 18 B5
Laval Canada 45°33N 73°42W 113 C11
Laval France 48°4N 0°48W 66 B3
Lavendon U.K. 52°11N 0°39W 31 B7
Lavenham U.K. 52°6N 0°48E 31 B10
Lavras Brazil 21°20S 45°0W 122 D2
Lawrence Kans., U.S.A. 38°58N 95°14W 111 C7
Lawrence Mass., U.S.A. 42°43N 71°10W 113 D12
Lawton U.S.A. 34°37N 98°25W 110 D7
Laxey U.K. 54°14N 4°23W 19 C13
Laxfield U.K. 52°18N 1°22E 31 B11
Laxford, L. U.K. 58°24N 5°6W 22 F7
Lazio □ Italy 42°10N 12°30E 68 C5

Lazonby U.K. 54°46N 2°42W 26 C3
Le Creusot France 46°48N 4°24E 66 C6
Le Havre France 49°30N 0°5E 66 B4
Le Mans France 48°0N 0°10E 66 C4
Le Puy-en-Velay France 45°3N 3°52E 66 D5
Lea U.K. 53°22N 0°45W 27 F7
Lea → U.K. 51°31N 0°1E 31 C9
Leadenham U.K. 53°3N 0°35W 27 F7
Leamington Canada 42°3N 82°36W 112 D6
Leane, L. Ireland 52°2N 9°32W 20 D3
Leatherhead U.K. 51°18N 0°20W 31 D8
Leavenworth U.S.A. 39°19N 94°55W 111 C8
Lebanon Ind., U.S.A. 40°3N 86°28W 112 E4
Lebanon Ky., U.S.A. 37°34N 85°15W 112 G5
Lebanon Mo., U.S.A. 37°41N 92°40W 111 C8
Lebanon Pa., U.S.A. 40°20N 76°26W 112 E9
Lebanon ■ Asia 34°0N 36°0E 86 C3
Lebu Chile 37°40S 73°47W 121 F2
Lecce Italy 40°23N 18°11E 69 D8
Lechlade U.K. 51°42N 1°41W 30 C5
Ledbury U.K. 52°2N 2°25W 30 B4
Lee → France 51°53N 8°56W 20 E5
Lee-on-the-Solent U.K. 50°48N 1°12W 30 E6
Leech L. U.S.A. 47°10N 94°24W 111 A8
Leeds U.K. 53°48N 1°33W 27 E5
Leek U.K. 53°7N 2°1W 27 F4
Leeuwarden Neths. 53°15N 5°48E 64 B3
Leeuwin, C. Australia 34°20S 115°9E 98 G2
Leeward Is. Atl. Oc. 16°30N 63°30W 115 D12
Lefkada Greece 38°40N 20°43E 69 E9
Leganés Spain 40°19N 3°45W 67 B4
Legazpi Phil. 13°10N 123°45E 83 B6
Legionowo Poland 52°25N 20°50E 65 B11
Legnica Poland 51°12N 16°10E 64 C9
Leicester U.K. 52°38N 1°8W 27 G6
Leicestershire □ U.K. 52°41N 1°17W 27 G6
Leiden Neths. 52°9N 4°30E 64 B3
Leigh Gt. Man., U.K. 53°30N 2°32W 27 E3
Leigh Hereford, U.K. 52°11N 2°20W 30 B4
Leighton Buzzard U.K. 51°54N 0°38W 31 C7
Leine → Germany 52°43N 9°36E 64 B5
Leinster □ Ireland 53°3N 7°8W 21 B8
Leinster, Mt. Ireland 52°37N 6°46W 21 D9
Leintwardine U.K. 52°22N 2°51W 30 B3
Leipzig Germany 51°18N 12°22E 64 C7
Leiston U.K. 52°12N 1°36E 31 B12
Leith U.K. 55°59N 3°11W 25 C9
Leith Hill U.K. 51°11N 0°22W 31 D8
Leitholm U.K. 55°41N 2°20W 25 C11
Leitrim Ireland 54°0N 8°5W 18 C5
Leitrim □ Ireland 54°8N 8°0W 18 C6
Leixlip Ireland 53°22N 6°30W 21 B10
Leizhou Pen. China 21°0N 110°0E 79 G11
Lelant U.K. 50°11N 5°28W 29 G3
Léman, L. Europe 46°26N 6°30E 64 E4
Lena → Russia 72°52N 126°40E 77 B13
Lenham U.K. 51°14N 0°44E 31 D10
Leninsk-Kuznetskiy Russia 54°44N 86°10E 76 D9
Lennox Hills U.K. 56°3N 4°12W 24 B7
Lens France 50°26N 2°50E 66 A5
Leodhais = Lewis U.K. 58°9N 6°40W 22 F4
Leominster U.K. 52°14N 2°43W 30 B3
Leominster U.S.A. 42°32N 71°46W 113 D12
León Mexico 21°6N 101°41W 114 C4
León Nic. 12°27N 86°51W 114 E7
León Spain 42°38N 5°34W 67 A3
Leonora Australia 28°49S 121°19E 98 F3
Leopoldina Brazil 21°28S 42°40W 122 D2
Lerwick U.K. 60°9N 1°9W 22 B15
Les Cayes Haiti 18°15N 73°46W 115 D10
Les Sables-d'Olonne France 46°30N 1°45W 66 C3
Lesbos Greece 39°10N 26°20E 69 E12
Lesbury U.K. 55°25N 1°36W 26 B5
Leshan China 29°33N 103°41E 78 F9
Leskovac Serbia 43°0N 21°58E 69 C9
Lesosibirsk Russia 58°14N 92°29E 77 D10
Lesotho ■ Africa 29°40S 28°0E 97 K5
Lesser Antilles W. Indies 15°0N 61°0W 115 E12
Lesser Slave L. Canada 55°30N 115°25W 108 D8
Lesser Sunda Is. Indonesia 8°0S 120°0E 83 F6
Leszno Poland 51°50N 16°30E 65 C9
Letchworth U.K. 51°59N 0°13W 31 C8
Lethbridge Canada 49°45N 112°45W 108 E8
Leti, Kepulauan Indonesia 8°10S 128°0E 83 F7
Leticia Colombia 4°9S 70°0W 120 C2
Letterkenny Ireland 54°57N 7°45W 18 B6
Leuchars U.K. 56°24N 2°53W 25 B10
Leuven Belgium 50°52N 4°42E 64 C3
Leven E. Riding, U.K. 53°53N 0°18W 27 E8
Leven Fife, U.K. 56°12N 3°0W 25 B10
Leven → U.K. 54°31N 1°19W 26 C6
Leven, L. Highl., U.K. 56°42N 5°6W 22 J7
Leven, L. Perth & Kinr., U.K. 56°12N 3°22W 25 B9
Lévis Canada 46°48N 71°9W 113 C12
Lewes U.K. 50°52N 0°1E 31 E9
Lewis U.K. 58°9N 6°40W 22 F4
Lewis, Butt of U.K. 58°31N 6°16W 22 E5
Lewisham □ U.K. 51°27N 0°1W 31 D8
Lewisporte Canada 49°15N 55°3W 109 E14
Lewiston Idaho, U.S.A. 46°25N 117°1W 110 A3
Lewiston Maine, U.S.A. 44°6N 70°13W 113 C12
Lewistown Mont., U.S.A. 47°4N 109°26W 110 A5
Lewistown Pa., U.S.A. 40°36N 77°34W 112 E9
Lexington U.S.A. 38°3N 84°30W 112 F5
Lexington Park U.S.A. 38°16N 76°27W 112 F9
Leyburn U.K. 54°19N 1°48W 26 D5
Leyland U.K. 53°42N 2°43W 27 E3
Leysdown on Sea U.K. 51°24N 0°56E 31 D10
Leyte Phil. 11°0N 125°0E 83 B6
Lhasa China 29°25N 90°58E 78 F7
Lhazê China 29°5N 87°38E 78 F6
L'Hospitalet de Llobregat Spain 41°21N 2°6E 67 B7
Lianyungang China 34°40N 119°11E 79 E12
Liaodong Pen. China 40°0N 122°30E 79 D13
Liaoning □ China 41°40N 122°30E 79 D13
Liaotung, G. of China 40°20N 121°10E 79 D13
Liaoyang China 41°15N 122°58E 79 D13
Liaoyuan China 42°58N 125°2E 79 C14
Liard → Canada 61°51N 121°18W 108 C7
Liberal U.S.A. 37°3N 100°55W 110 C6
Liberec Czech Rep. 50°47N 15°7E 64 C8

Liberia ■ W. Afr. 6°30N 9°30W 94 G4
Libourne France 44°55N 0°14W 66 D3
Libreville Gabon 0°25N 9°26E 96 D1
Libya ■ N. Afr. 27°0N 17°0E 95 C9
Libyan Desert Africa 25°0N 25°0E 95 C10
Libyan Plateau Egypt 30°40N 26°30E 95 B11
Lichfield U.K. 52°41N 1°49W 27 G5
Lichinga Mozam. 13°13S 35°11E 97 G7
Liddesdale U.K. 55°14N 2°50W 25 D10
Liechtenstein ■ Europe 47°8N 9°35E 64 E5
Liège Belgium 50°38N 5°35E 64 C3
Liepāja Latvia 56°30N 21°0E 63 F8
Liffey → Ireland 53°21N 6°13W 21 B10
Lifford Ireland 54°51N 7°29W 18 B7
Liguria □ Italy 44°30N 8°50E 68 B3
Ligurian Sea Medit. S. 43°20N 9°0E 68 C3
Lihu'e U.S.A. 21°59N 159°23W 110 H15
Lijiang China 26°55N 100°20E 78 F9
Likasi Dem. Rep. of the Congo 10°55S 26°48E 96 G5
Lille France 50°38N 3°3E 66 A5
Lillehammer Norway 61°8N 10°30E 63 E6
Lilleshall U.K. 52°44N 2°23W 27 G4
Lilongwe Malawi 14°0S 33°48E 97 G6
Lima Peru 12°3S 77°2W 120 D2
Lima U.S.A. 40°44N 84°6W 112 E5
Limassol Cyprus 34°42N 33°1E 86 C3
Limavady U.K. 55°3N 6°56W 19 A8
Limay → Argentina 39°0S 68°0W 121 F3
Limbe Cameroon 4°1N 9°10E 96 D1
Limeira Brazil 22°35S 47°28W 122 D1
Limerick Ireland 52°40N 8°37W 20 D6
Limerick □ Ireland 52°30N 8°50W 20 D5
Limfjorden Denmark 56°55N 9°0E 63 F5
Limnos Greece 39°50N 25°5E 69 E11
Limoges France 45°50N 1°15E 66 D4
Limón Costa Rica 10°0N 83°2W 115 F8
Limousin □ France 45°30N 1°30E 66 D4
Limoux France 43°4N 2°12E 66 E5
Limpopo → Africa 25°5S 33°30E 97 K6
Linares Chile 35°50S 71°40W 121 F2
Linares Mexico 24°52N 99°34W 114 C5
Linares Spain 38°10N 3°40W 67 C4
Linchuan China 27°57N 116°15E 79 F12
Lincoln U.K. 53°14N 0°32W 27 F7
Lincoln Ill., U.S.A. 40°9N 89°22W 112 E3
Lincoln Maine, U.S.A. 45°22N 68°30W 113 C13
Lincoln Nebr., U.S.A. 40°49N 96°41W 111 B7
Lincoln Sea Arctic 84°0N 55°0W 54 A5
Lincolnshire □ U.K. 53°14N 0°32W 27 F7
Lincolnshire Wolds U.K. 53°26N 0°13W 27 F8
Lindale U.K. 54°14N 2°53W 26 D3
Lindesnes Norway 57°58N 7°3E 63 F5
Lindsay Canada 44°22N 78°43W 112 C8
Linfen China 36°3N 111°30E 79 D11
Lingfield U.K. 51°11N 0°1W 31 D8
Lingga, Kepulauan Indonesia 0°10S 104°30E 82 E2
Linhares Brazil 19°25S 40°4W 122 C2
Linhe China 40°48N 107°20E 78 C10
Linkinhorne U.K. 50°32N 4°24W 29 F5
Linköping Sweden 58°28N 15°36E 63 F7
Linnhe, L. U.K. 56°36N 5°25W 24 A5
Linslade U.K. 51°54N 0°41W 31 C7
Linstead Jamaica 18°8N 77°2W 114 a
Linton U.K. 52°6N 0°17E 31 B9
Linton U.S.A. 39°2N 87°10W 112 F4
Linxi China 43°36N 118°2E 79 C12
Linxia China 35°36N 103°10E 78 D9
Linyi China 35°5N 118°21E 79 D12
Linz Austria 48°18N 14°18E 64 D8
Lion, G. du France 43°10N 4°0E 66 E6
Lipa Phil. 13°57N 121°10E 83 B6
Lipari Italy 38°26N 14°58E 68 E6
Lipetsk Russia 52°37N 39°35E 70 D6
Lippe → Germany 51°39N 6°36E 64 C4
Lisbon Portugal 38°42N 9°8W 67 C1
Lisburn U.K. 54°31N 6°3W 19 B9
Liscannor B. Ireland 52°55N 9°24W 20 D4
Lisianski I. U.S.A. 26°2N 174°0W 102 E10
Lisieux France 49°10N 0°12E 66 B4
Liskeard U.K. 50°27N 4°29W 29 G5
Liski Russia 51°3N 39°30E 71 D6
Lismore Australia 28°44S 153°21E 98 F9
Lismore Ireland 52°8N 7°55W 20 D7
Liss U.K. 51°3N 0°54W 31 D7
Listowel Canada 43°44N 80°58W 112 D7
Listowel Ireland 52°27N 9°29W 20 D4
Litani → Lebanon 33°20N 35°15E 86 C3
Litcham U.K. 52°44N 0°47E 31 A10
Litchfield U.S.A. 39°11N 89°39W 112 F3
Litherland U.K. 53°29N 2°59W 27 F3
Lithuania ■ Europe 55°30N 24°0E 63 F8
Little Current Canada 45°55N 82°0W 112 C7
Little Khingan Mts. China 49°0N 127°0E 79 B14
Little Minch U.K. 57°35N 6°45W 22 G4
Little Missouri → U.S.A. 47°36N 102°25W 110 A6
Little Ouse → U.K. 52°22N 1°12E 31 B9
Little Rock U.S.A. 34°45N 92°17W 111 D8
Little Walsingham U.K. 52°54N 0°52E 31 A10
Littlehampton U.K. 50°49N 0°32W 31 E7
Littleport U.K. 52°27N 0°19E 31 B9
Littlestone-on-Sea U.K. 50°58N 0°58E 31 E10
Liupanshui China 26°38N 104°48E 78 F9
Liuwa Plain Zambia 14°20S 22°30E 97 G4
Liuzhou China 24°22N 109°22E 79 G10
Liverpool Canada 44°5N 64°41W 109 E13
Liverpool U.K. 53°25N 3°0W 27 F3
Liverpool Bay U.K. 53°30N 3°20W 27 F2
Livingston U.K. 55°54N 3°30W 25 C9
Livingston U.S.A. 45°40N 110°34W 110 A4
Livingstone Zambia 17°46S 25°52E 97 H5
Livonia U.S.A. 42°23N 83°23W 112 D6
Livorno Italy 43°33N 10°19E 68 C4
Lizard U.K. 49°58N 5°13W 29 H3
Lizard Pt. U.K. 49°57N 5°13W 29 H3
Ljubljana Slovenia 46°4N 14°33E 64 E8
Llandeilo U.K. 51°53N 3°59W 28 D6
Llandovery U.K. 51°59N 3°48W 28 D6
Llandrindod Wells U.K. 52°14N 3°22W 28 C7
Llandudno U.K. 53°19N 3°50W 28 A5
Llanelli U.K. 51°41N 4°10W 28 D5
Llanerchymedd U.K. 53°20N 4°23W 28 A3
Llanfair Caereinion U.K. 52°39N 3°20W 28 B7

Llanfair Talhaiarn U.K. 53°13N 3°37W 28 A6
Llanfair-ym-Muallt = Builth Wells
   U.K. 52°9N 3°25W 28 C7
Llanfairfechan U.K. 53°15N 3°58W 28 A6
Llangefni U.K. 53°15N 4°18W 28 A5
Llangollen U.K. 52°58N 3°11W 28 B7
Llanidloes U.K. 52°27N 3°31W 28 C6
Llanllyfni U.K. 53°2N 4°17W 28 A5
Llano Estacado U.S.A. 33°30N 103°0W 110 D6
Llanos S. Amer. 5°0N 71°35W 120 B2
Llanquihue, L. Chile 41°10S 72°50W 121 G2
Llanrhystyd U.K. 52°19N 4°7W 28 C5
Llantrisant U.K. 51°32N 3°22W 29 D7
Llantwit-Major U.K. 51°24N 3°29W 29 E7
Llanwrtyd Wells U.K. 52°7N 3°38W 28 C6
Llanyblodwel U.K. 52°48N 3°8W 28 B7
Llanymynech U.K. 52°47N 3°5W 28 B7
Lleida Spain 41°37N 0°39E 67 B6
Lleyn Peninsula U.K. 52°51N 4°36W 28 B4
Llobregat → Spain 41°19N 2°5E 67 B7
Lloret de Mar Spain 41°41N 2°53E 67 B7
Lloydminster Canada 53°17N 110°0W 108 D9
Llullaillaco, Volcán S. Amer. 24°43S 68°30W 121 E3
Lobatse Botswana 25°12S 25°40E 97 K5
Lobito Angola 12°18S 13°35E 97 G2
Loch Lomond and the Trossachs △
   U.K. 56°10N 4°40W 24 B6
Lochaber U.K. 56°59N 5°1W 22 J7
Locharbriggs U.K. 55°7N 3°35W 25 D8
Lochboisdale U.K. 57°9N 7°20W 22 H3
Loches France 47°7N 1°0E 66 C4
Lochgelly U.K. 56°7N 3°19W 25 B9
Lochgilphead U.K. 56°2N 5°26W 24 B5
Lochinver U.K. 58°9N 5°14W 22 F7
Lochmaben U.K. 55°8N 3°27W 25 D9
Lochmaddy U.K. 57°36N 7°10W 22 G3
Lochnagar U.K. 56°57N 3°15W 23 J11
Lochy, L. U.K. 57°0N 4°53W 23 J8
Lock Haven U.S.A. 41°8N 77°28W 112 E9
Lockerbie U.K. 55°7N 3°21W 25 D9
Loddon U.K. 52°32N 1°31E 31 A12
Lodwar Kenya 3°7N 35°36E 96 D7
Łódź Poland 51°45N 19°27E 65 C10
Lofoten Norway 68°30N 13°59E 63 D6
Loftus U.K. 54°34N 0°53W 26 C7
Logan Ohio, U.S.A. 39°32N 82°25W 112 F6
Logan Utah, U.S.A. 41°44N 111°50W 110 B4
Logan W. Va., U.S.A. 37°51N 81°59W 112 G7
Logan, Mt. Canada 60°34N 140°23W 108 C5
Logansport U.S.A. 40°45N 86°22W 112 E4
Logroño Spain 42°28N 2°27W 67 A4
Lohardaga India 23°27N 84°45E 85 H14
Loir → France 47°33N 0°32W 66 C3
Loire → France 47°16N 2°10W 66 C2
Loja Ecuador 3°59S 79°16W 120 C2
Lomami →
   Dem. Rep. of the Congo 0°46N 24°16E 96 D4
Lombárdia □ Italy 45°40N 9°30E 68 B3
Lomblen Indonesia 8°30S 123°32E 83 F6
Lombok Indonesia 8°45S 116°30E 82 F5
Lomé Togo 6°9N 1°20E 94 G6
Lomela →
   Dem. Rep. of the Congo 0°15S 20°40E 96 E4
Lomond, L. U.K. 56°8N 4°38W 24 B6
Łomża Poland 53°10N 22°2E 65 B12
London Canada 42°59N 81°15W 112 D7
London U.K. 51°30N 0°3W 31 D8
London Gatwick ✈ (LGW)
   U.K. 51°10N 0°11W 31 D8
London Heathrow ✈ (LHR)
   U.K. 51°28N 0°27W 31 D8
London Stansted ✈ (STN) U.K. 51°54N 0°14E 31 C9
Londonderry U.K. 55°0N 7°20W 18 A7
Londonderry □ U.K. 55°0N 7°20W 18 A7
Londonderry, C. Australia 13°45S 126°55E 98 C4
Londrina Brazil 23°18S 51°10W 121 E4
Long, L. U.K. 56°4N 4°50W 24 B6
Long Beach U.S.A. 33°46N 118°11W 110 D3
Long Bennington U.K. 52°59N 0°44W 27 G7
Long Branch U.S.A. 40°18N 74°0W 113 E11
Long Clawson U.K. 52°50N 0°55W 27 G7
Long Crendon U.K. 51°46N 0°59W 31 C7
Long Eaton U.K. 52°53N 1°15W 27 G6
Long I. Bahamas 23°20N 75°10W 115 C9
Long I. Ireland 51°30N 9°34W 20 E3
Long I. U.S.A. 40°45N 73°30W 113 E11
Long Itchington U.K. 52°16N 1°22W 30 B6
Long Melford U.K. 52°4N 0°45E 31 B10
Long Mynd, The U.K. 52°35N 2°50W 27 G3
Long Preston U.K. 54°2N 2°14W 27 D4
Long Sutton U.K. 52°48N 0°7E 27 G9
Long Xuyen Vietnam 10°19N 105°28E 82 B3
Longford Ireland 53°43N 7°49W 18 D6
Longford □ Ireland 53°42N 7°45W 18 D6
Longframlington U.K. 55°18N 1°47W 26 B5
Longhoughton U.K. 55°26N 1°37W 26 B5
Longhua China 22°39N 114°0E 79 a
Longlac Canada 49°45N 86°25W 112 A4
Longreach Australia 23°28S 144°14E 98 E7
Longridge U.K. 53°50N 2°35W 27 E4
Longton U.K. 53°44N 2°48W 27 E3
Longtown Cumb., U.K. 55°1N 2°58W 26 B3
Longtown Hereford, U.K. 51°58N 2°59W 30 C3
Longueuil Canada 45°31N 73°29W 113 C11
Longview Tex., U.S.A. 32°30N 94°44W 111 D8
Longview Wash., U.S.A. 46°8N 122°57W 110 A2
Longyan China 25°10N 117°0E 79 F12
Lons-le-Saunier France 46°40N 5°31E 66 C6
Looe U.K. 50°22N 4°28W 29 G5
Loop Hd. Ireland 52°34N 9°56W 20 D3
Lop China 37°3N 80°11E 78 D5
Lop Nur China 40°20N 90°10E 78 C7
Lopez, C. Gabon 0°47S 8°40E 90 G4
Lorain U.S.A. 41°28N 82°11W 112 E6
Loralai Pakistan 30°20N 68°41E 84 D6
Lorca Spain 37°41N 1°42W 67 D5
Lord Howe I. Pac. Oc. 31°33S 159°6E 99 L7
Lord Howe Rise Pac. Oc. 30°0S 162°30E 99 H12
Lordsburg U.S.A. 32°21N 108°43W 110 D5
Lorestān □ Iran 33°30N 48°40E 86 C7

Lorient France 47°45N 3°23W 66 C2
Lorn U.K. 56°26N 5°10W 24 B5
Lorn, Firth of U.K. 56°20N 5°40W 24 B4
Lorraine □ France 48°53N 6°0E 66 B7
Los Andes Chile 32°50S 70°40W 121 F2
Los Angeles Chile 37°28S 72°23W 121 F2
Los Angeles U.S.A. 34°4N 118°15W 110 D3
Los Mochis Mexico 25°45N 108°57W 114 B3
Los Roques, Is. Venezuela 11°50N 66°45W 120 A3
Lošinj Croatia 44°30N 14°30E 68 B6
Lossiemouth U.K. 57°42N 3°17W 23 G11
Lostwithiel U.K. 50°24N 4°41W 29 G4
Lot → France 44°18N 0°20E 66 D4
Lota Chile 37°5S 73°10W 121 F2
Loubomo Congo 4°9S 12°47E 96 E2
Loughborough U.K. 52°47N 1°11W 27 G6
Loughrea Ireland 53°12N 8°33W 20 B5
Loughros More B. Ireland 54°48N 8°32W 18 B4
Louhans France 46°38N 5°12E 66 C6
Louis XIV, Pte. Canada 54°37N 79°45W 109 D12
Louisa U.S.A. 38°7N 82°36W 112 F6
Louisiade Arch. Papua N. G. 11°10S 153°0E 98 C9
Louisiana □ U.S.A. 30°50N 92°0W 111 D8
Louisville U.S.A. 38°15N 85°46W 112 F5
Lourdes France 43°6N 0°3W 66 E3
Louth Ireland 53°58N 6°32W 19 D8
Louth U.K. 53°22N 0°1W 27 F8
Louth □ Ireland 53°56N 6°34W 19 D8
Lovech Bulgaria 43°8N 24°42E 69 C11
Lowell U.S.A. 42°38N 71°19W 113 D12
Lower Beeding U.K. 51°2N 0°15W 31 D8
Lower Saxony = Niedersachsen □
   Germany 52°50N 9°0E 64 B5
Lower Tunguska → Russia 65°48N 88°4E 77 C9
Lowestoft U.K. 52°29N 1°45E 31 B12
Lowick U.K. 55°39N 1°57W 26 A5
Lowther Hills U.K. 55°20N 3°40W 25 D8
Lowville U.S.A. 43°47N 75°29W 113 D10
Loyauté, Îs. N. Cal. 20°50S 166°30E 99 E12
Lu Wo China 22°33N 114°6E 79 a
Lualaba →
   Dem. Rep. of the Congo 0°26N 25°20E 96 D5
Lu'an China 31°45N 116°29E 79 E12
Luanda Angola 8°50S 13°15E 96 F2
Luangwa → Zambia 14°25S 30°25E 97 G6
Luanshya Zambia 13°3S 28°28E 97 G5
Luapula → Africa 9°26S 28°33E 96 F5
Lubango Angola 14°55S 13°30E 97 G2
Lubbock U.S.A. 33°35N 101°51W 110 D6
Lübeck Germany 53°52N 10°40E 64 B6
Lublin Poland 51°12N 22°38E 65 C12
Lubumbashi
   Dem. Rep. of the Congo 11°40S 27°28E 97 G5
Lucania, Mt. Canada 61°1N 140°27W 108 C5
Lucca Italy 43°50N 10°29E 68 C4
Luce Bay U.K. 54°45N 4°48W 24 E6
Lucea Jamaica 18°27N 78°10W 114 a
Lucena Phil. 13°56N 121°37E 83 B6
Lucena Spain 37°27N 4°31W 67 D3
Lucerne Switz. 47°3N 8°18E 64 E5
Lucknow India 26°50N 81°0E 85 F12
Lüda = Dalian China 38°50N 121°40E 79 D13
Lüderitz Namibia 26°41S 15°8E 97 K3
Ludgershall U.K. 51°15N 1°37W 30 D5
Ludgvan U.K. 50°9N 5°30W 29 G2
Ludhiana India 30°57N 75°56E 84 D9
Ludington U.S.A. 43°57N 86°27W 112 D4
Ludlow U.K. 52°22N 2°42W 27 H3
Ludwigsburg Germany 48°53N 9°11E 64 D5
Ludwigshafen Germany 49°29N 8°26E 64 D5
Lufkin U.S.A. 31°21N 94°44W 111 D8
Luga Russia 58°40N 29°55E 70 C4
Lugano Switz. 46°1N 8°57E 64 E5
Lugansk Ukraine 48°38N 39°15E 71 E6
Lugnaquilla Ireland 52°58N 6°28W 21 C10
Lugo Spain 43°2N 7°35W 67 A2
Lugwardine U.K. 52°4N 2°39W 30 B3
Luing U.K. 56°14N 5°39W 24 B4
Luleå Sweden 65°35N 22°10E 63 D8
Luleälven → Sweden 65°35N 22°10E 63 D8
Lundy U.K. 51°10N 4°41W 29 E4
Lune → U.K. 54°0N 2°51W 27 D3
Lüneburger Heide Germany 53°10N 10°12E 64 B6
Lunéville France 48°36N 6°30E 66 B7
Luni → India 24°41N 71°14E 84 G7
Luofu Dem. Rep. of the Congo 0°10S 29°15E 96 E5
Luoyang China 34°40N 112°26E 79 E11
Luray U.S.A. 38°40N 78°28W 112 F8
Lurgan U.K. 54°27N 6°20W 19 C9
Lusaka Zambia 15°28S 28°16E 97 H5
Lushnjë Albania 40°55N 19°41E 69 D8
Lüt, Dasht-e Iran 31°30N 58°0E 87 D9
Lutherstadt Wittenberg
   Germany 51°53N 12°39E 64 C7
Luton U.K. 51°53N 0°24W 31 C7
Lutsel K'e Canada 62°24N 110°44W 108 C8
Lutsk Ukraine 50°50N 25°15E 65 C13
Lutterworth U.K. 52°28N 1°12W 27 H6
Luvua → Dem. Rep. of the Congo 6°50S 27°30E 96 F5
Luxembourg Lux. 49°37N 6°9E 64 D4
Luxembourg ■ Europe 49°45N 6°0E 64 D4
Luxor = El Uqsur Egypt 25°41N 32°38E 95 C12
Luzern Switz. 47°3N 8°18E 64 E5
Luzhou China 28°52N 105°20E 78 F10
Luziânia Brazil 16°20S 48°0W 122 C2
Luzon Phil. 16°0N 121°0E 83 A6
Lviv Ukraine 49°50N 24°0E 65 D13
Lyakhov Is. Russia 73°40N 141°0E 77 B15
Lybster U.K. 58°18N 3°15W 23 F11
Lydd U.K. 50°57N 0°55E 31 E10
Lydford U.K. 50°38N 4°8W 29 F5
Lyme B. U.K. 50°42N 2°53W 30 E3
Lyme Regis U.K. 50°43N 2°57W 30 E3
Lymington U.K. 50°45N 1°32W 30 E5
Lymm U.K. 53°23N 2°29W 27 F4
Lympne U.K. 51°4N 1°2E 31 D11
Lyna → Poland 54°37N 21°14E 65 A11
Lynchburg U.S.A. 37°25N 79°9W 112 G8
Lyndhurst U.K. 50°52N 1°35W 30 E5
Lyneham U.K. 51°31N 1°58W 30 C5
Lynmouth U.K. 51°13N 3°49W 29 E6

Lynn Lake

Meta

Lynn Lake *Canada* 56°51N 101°3W **108** D9
Lynton *U.K.* 51°13N 3°50W **29** E6
Lyonnais *France* 45°45N 4°15E **66** D6
Lyons *France* 45°46N 4°50E **66** D6
Lysva *Russia* 58°7N 57°49E **70** C10
Lysychansk *Ukraine* 48°55N 38°30E **71** E6
Lytchett Minster *U.K.* 50°44N 2°4W **30** E4
Lytham St. Anne's *U.K.* 53°45N 3°0W **27** E2
Lythe *U.K.* 54°31N 0°41W **26** C7
Lyubertsy *Russia* 55°40N 37°51E **70** C6

M

Ma'ān *Jordan* 30°12N 35°44E **86** D3
Maas → *Neths.* 51°45N 4°32E **64** C3
Maastricht *Neths.* 50°50N 5°40E **64** C3
Mablethorpe *U.K.* 53°20N 0°15E **27** F9
Macaé *Brazil* 22°20S 41°43W **122** D2
McAlester *U.S.A.* 34°56N 95°46W **111** D7
McAllen *U.S.A.* 26°12N 98°14W **110** E7
MacAlpine L. *Canada* 66°32N 102°45W **108** C9
Macapá *Brazil* 0°5N 51°4W **120** B4
Macau *Brazil* 5°15S 36°40W **120** C6
Macau *China* 22°12N 113°33E **79** a
Macclesfield *U.K.* 53°15N 2°8W **27** F4
M'Clintock Chan. *Canada* 72°0N 102°0W **108** B9
M'Clure Str. *Canada* 75°0N 119°0W **109** B8
McComb *U.S.A.* 31°15N 90°27W **111** D8
McCook *U.S.A.* 40°12N 100°38W **110** B6
McDonald Is. *Ind. Oc.* 53°0S 73°0E **53** G13
MacDonnell Ranges *Australia* 23°40S 133°0E **98** E5
Macduff *U.K.* 57°40N 2°31W **23** G12
Macedonia □ *Greece* 40°39N 22°0E **69** D10
Macedonia ■ *Europe* 41°53N 21°40E **69** D9
Maceió *Brazil* 9°40S 35°41W **122** A3
Macgillycuddy's Reeks *Ireland* 51°58N 9°45W **20** E3
Mach *Pakistan* 29°50N 67°20E **84** E5
Machakos *Kenya* 1°30S 37°15E **96** E7
Machala *Ecuador* 3°20S 79°57W **120** C2
Machars, The *U.K.* 54°46N 4°30W **24** E6
Machias *U.S.A.* 44°43N 67°28W **113** C14
Machilipatnam *India* 16°12N 81°8E **85** L12
Machrihanish *U.K.* 55°25N 5°43W **24** D4
Machu Picchu *Peru* 13°8S 72°30W **120** D2
Machynlleth *U.K.* 52°35N 3°50W **28** B6
Mackay *Australia* 21°8S 149°11E **98** E8
Mackay, L. *Australia* 22°30S 129°0E **98** E4
McKeesport *U.S.A.* 40°20N 79°51W **112** E8
Mackenzie *Canada* 55°20N 123°5W **108** C6
Mackenzie → *Canada* 69°10N 134°20W **108** C6
Mackenzie Bay *Canada* 69°0N 137°30W **104** C6
Mackenzie King I. *Canada* 77°45N 111°0W **109** B8
Mackenzie Mts. *Canada* 64°0N 130°0W **108** C6
Mackinaw City *U.S.A.* 45°47N 84°44W **112** C5
McKinley, Mt. *U.S.A.* 63°4N 151°0W **108** C4
McKinley Sea *Arctic* 82°0N 0°0 **54** A7
McMinnville *U.S.A.* 45°13N 123°12W **110** A2
McMurdo Sd. *Antarctica* 77°0S 170°0E **55** D11
Macomb *U.S.A.* 40°27N 90°40W **112** E2
Mâcon *France* 46°19N 4°50E **66** C6
Macon *U.S.A.* 32°51N 83°38W **111** D10
McPherson *U.S.A.* 38°22N 97°40W **110** C7
Macquarie I. *Pac. Oc.* 54°36S 158°55E **102** N7
Macroom *Ireland* 51°54N 8°57W **20** E5
Madagascar ■ *Africa* 20°0S 47°0E **97** J9
Madang *Papua N. G.* 5°12S 145°49E **98** B8
Madeira *Atl. Oc.* 32°50N 17°0W **94** B2
Madeira → *Brazil* 3°22S 58°45W **120** C4
Madeleine, Îs. de la *Canada* 47°30N 61°40W **113** B17
Madeley *U.K.* 53°0N 2°20W **27** F4
Madhya Pradesh □ *India* 22°50N 78°0E **84** H11
Madison *Ind.., U.S.A.* 38°44N 85°23W **112** F5
Madison *S. Dak., U.S.A.* 44°0N 97°7W **111** B7
Madison *Wis., U.S.A.* 43°4N 89°24W **112** D3
Madisonville *U.S.A.* 37°20N 87°30W **112** G4
Madiun *Indonesia* 7°38S 111°32E **82** F4
Madley *U.K.* 52°2N 2°51W **30** D3
Madras = Chennai *India* 13°8N 80°19E **84** N12
Madre, L. *U.S.A.* 25°15N 97°30W **104** G10
Madre de Dios → *Bolivia* 10°59S 66°8W **120** D3
Madre de Dios, I. *Chile* 50°20S 75°10W **121** H2
Madre del Sur, Sierra
  Mexico 17°30N 100°0W **104** H10
Madre Occidental, Sierra
  Mexico 27°0N 107°0W **114** B3
Madre Oriental, Sierra
  Mexico 25°0N 100°0W **114** C5
Madrid *Spain* 40°24N 3°42W **67** B4
Madura *Indonesia* 7°30S 114°0E **82** F4
Madurai *India* 9°55N 78°10E **84** Q11
Maebashi *Japan* 36°24N 139°4E **81** E6
Maesteg *U.K.* 51°36N 3°40W **29** D6
Mafeking *S. Africa* 25°50S 25°38E **97** K5
Mafia *I. Tanzania* 7°45S 39°50E **96** F7
Magadan *Russia* 59°38N 150°50E **77** D16
Magallanes, Estrecho de
  Chile 52°30S 75°0W **121** H2
Magangué *Colombia* 9°14N 74°45W **120** B2
Magdalena → *Colombia* 11°6N 74°51W **120** A2
Magdeburg *Germany* 52°7N 11°38E **64** B6
Magee Isle *U.K.* 54°48N 5°43W **19** B10
Magelang *Indonesia* 7°29S 110°13E **82** F4
Magellan's Str. = Magallanes,
  Estrecho de *Chile* 52°30S 75°0W **121** H2
Maggiore, Lago *Italy* 45°57N 8°39E **68** B3
Maggotty *Jamaica* 18°9N 77°46W **114** a
Maghâgha *Egypt* 28°38N 30°50E **95** C12
Magherafelt *U.K.* 54°45N 6°37W **19** B8
Maghreb *N. Afr.* 32°0N 4°0W **90** C3
Maghull *U.K.* 53°31N 2°57W **27** E3
Magnetic Pole (North)
  Arctic 82°42N 114°24W **54** A2
Magnetic Pole (South)
  Antarctica 64°8S 138°8E **55** C9
Magnitogorsk *Russia* 53°27N 59°4E **70** D10
Magog *Canada* 45°18N 72°9W **113** C11
Magwe *Burma* 20°10N 95°0E **85** J19
Mahābād *Iran* 36°50N 45°45E **86** B6
Mahajanga *Madag.* 15°40S 46°25E **97** H9
Mahakam → *Indonesia* 0°35S 117°17E **82** E5
Mahalapye *Botswana* 23°1S 26°51E **97** J5

Maḥallāt *Iran* 33°55N 50°30E **87** C7
Mahanadi → *India* 20°20N 86°25E **85** J15
Maharashtra □ *India* 20°30N 75°30E **84** J9
Mahdia *Tunisia* 35°28N 11°0E **95** A8
Mahesana *India* 23°39N 72°26E **84** H8
Mahilyow *Belarus* 53°55N 30°18E **65** B16
Mai-Ndombe, L.
  Dem. Rep. of the Congo 2°0S 18°20E **96** E3
Maiden Bradley *U.K.* 51°9N 2°17W **30** D4
Maiden Newton *U.K.* 50°46N 2°34W **30** E3
Maidenhead *U.K.* 51°31N 0°42W **31** C7
Maidstone *U.K.* 51°16N 0°32E **31** D10
Maiduguri *Nigeria* 12°0N 13°20E **95** F8
Main → *Germany* 50°0N 8°18E **64** C5
Main → *U.K.* 54°48N 6°18W **19** B9
Maine *France* 48°20N 0°15W **66** C3
Maine □ *U.S.A.* 45°20N 69°0W **113** C13
Maine → *Ireland* 52°9N 9°45W **20** D2
Mainland *Orkney, U.K.* 58°59N 3°8W **23** E11
Mainland *Shet., U.K.* 60°15N 1°22W **27** F6
Mainz *Germany* 50°1N 8°14E **64** C5
Maiquetía *Venezuela* 10°36N 66°57W **120** A3
Majorca = Mallorca *Spain* 39°30N 3°0E **67** C7
Majuro *Marshall Is.* 7°9N 171°12E **102** G9
Makale *Indonesia* 3°6S 119°51E **83** E5
Makalu *Asia* 27°55N 87°8E **78** F6
Makassar *Indonesia* 5°10S 119°20E **83** F5
Makassar, Str. of *Indonesia* 1°0S 118°20E **83** E5
Makgadikgadi Salt Pans
  Botswana 20°40S 25°45E **97** J5
Makhachkala *Russia* 43°0N 47°30E **71** F8
Makhado *S. Africa* 23°1S 29°43E **97** J5
Makran Coast Range *Pakistan* 25°40N 64°0E **84** G4
Makurdi *Nigeria* 7°43N 8°35E **94** G7
Mal B. *Ireland* 52°50N 9°30W **20** C4
Malabar Coast *India* 11°0N 75°0E **84** P9
Malacca, Straits of *Indonesia* 3°0N 101°0E **82** D2
Málaga *Spain* 36°43N 4°23W **67** D3
Malahide *Ireland* 53°26N 6°9W **21** B10
Malaita *Solomon Is.* 9°0S 161°0E **99** B11
Malakal *South Sudan* 9°33N 31°40E **95** G12
Malakula *Vanuatu* 16°15S 167°30E **99** D12
Malang *Indonesia* 7°59S 112°45E **82** F4
Malanje *Angola* 9°36S 16°17E **96** F3
Mälaren *Sweden* 59°30N 17°10E **63** F7
Malatya *Turkey* 38°25N 38°20E **71** G6
Malawi ■ *Africa* 11°55S 34°0E **97** G6
Malawi, L. *Africa* 12°30S 34°30E **97** G6
Malay Pen. *Asia* 7°25N 100°0E **72** H12
Maläyer *Iran* 34°19N 48°51E **86** C7
Malaysia ■ *Asia* 5°0N 110°0E **82** D4
Malden *U.S.A.* 36°34N 89°57W **112** G3
Malden I. *Kiribati* 4°3S 155°1W **103** H12
Maldives ■ *Ind. Oc.* 5°0N 73°0E **73** H9
Maldon *U.K.* 51°44N 0°42E **31** C10
Maldonado *Uruguay* 34°59S 55°0W **121** F4
Malegaon *India* 20°30N 74°38E **84** J9
Malham Tarn *U.K.* 54°6N 2°10W **26** D4
Malheur L. *U.S.A.* 43°20N 118°48W **110** B3
Mali ■ *Africa* 17°0N 3°0W **94** E5
Malin Hd. *Ireland* 55°23N 7°23W **18** A7
Malin Pen. *Ireland* 55°20N 7°17W **19** A7
Malindi *Kenya* 3°12S 40°5E **96** E8
Mallaig *U.K.* 57°0N 5°50W **22** H6
Mallawi *Egypt* 27°44N 30°44E **95** C12
Mallorca *Spain* 39°30N 3°0E **67** C7
Mallow *Ireland* 52°8N 8°39W **20** D5
Malmesbury *U.K.* 51°35N 2°5W **30** C4
Malmö *Sweden* 55°36N 12°59E **63** F6
Malone *U.S.A.* 44°51N 74°18W **113** C10
Malpas *U.K.* 53°1N 2°45W **27** F3
Malpelo, I. de *Colombia* 4°3N 81°35W **115** G8
Malta ■ *Europe* 35°55N 14°26E **68** a
Maltby *U.K.* 53°25N 1°12W **27** E6
Malton *U.K.* 54°8N 0°49W **26** D7
Malvinas, Is. = Falkland Is. ☑
  Atl. Oc. 51°30S 59°0W **121** H4
Mamoré → *Bolivia* 10°23S 65°53W **120** D3
Mamoudzou *Mayotte* 12°48S 45°14E **91** H8
Man *Ivory C.* 7°30N 7°40W **94** G4
Man, I. of *U.K.* 54°15N 4°30W **19** C12
Manacles, The *U.K.* 50°2N 5°4W **29** G3
Manado *Indonesia* 1°29N 124°51E **83** D6
Managua *Nic.* 12°6N 86°20W **114** E7
Manaus *Brazil* 3°0S 60°0W **120** C3
Manby *U.K.* 53°21N 0°6E **27** F9
Manchester *U.K.* 53°29N 2°12W **27** F4
Manchester *U.S.A.* 42°59N 71°28W **113** D12
Manchester Int. ✈ (MAN)
  U.K. 53°21N 2°17W **27** F4
Manchuria *China* 45°0N 125°0E **79** C14
Manchurian Plain *China* 47°0N 124°0E **72** D14
Mandal *Norway* 58°2N 7°25E **63** F5
Mandalay *Burma* 22°0N 96°4E **85** J20
Mandan *U.S.A.* 46°50N 100°54W **110** A6
Mandaue *Phil.* 10°20N 123°56E **83** B6
Mandeville *Jamaica* 18°2N 77°31W **114** a
Mandla *India* 22°39N 80°30E **85** H12
Mandsaur *India* 24°3N 75°8E **84** G9
Mandvi *India* 22°51N 69°22E **84** H6
Manea *U.K.* 52°29N 0°10E **31** B9
Manfalût *Egypt* 27°20N 30°52E **95** C12
Manfredónia *Italy* 41°38N 15°55E **68** D6
Mangabeiras, Chapada das
  Brazil 10°0S 46°30W **122** B1
Mangalore *India* 12°55N 74°47E **84** N9
Mangnai *China* 37°52N 91°43E **78** D7
Mangole *Indonesia* 1°50S 125°55E **83** E6
Mangotsfield *U.K.* 51°29N 2°30W **30** C4
Manhattan *U.S.A.* 39°11N 96°35W **111** C7
Manhuaçu *Brazil* 20°15S 42°2W **122** D2
Manica *Mozam.* 18°58S 32°59E **97** H6
Manicoré *Brazil* 5°48S 61°16W **120** C3
Manicouagan → *Canada* 49°30N 68°30W **109** E13
Manicouagan, Rés. *Canada* 51°5N 68°40W **109** E13
Manihiki *Cook Is.* 10°24S 161°1W **103** J11
Manila *Phil.* 14°35N 120°58E **83** B6
Manipur □ *India* 25°0N 94°0E **85** G19
Manisa *Turkey* 38°38N 27°30E **71** G4
Manistee *U.S.A.* 44°15N 86°19W **112** C4
Manistee → *U.S.A.* 44°15N 86°21W **112** C4

Manistique *U.S.A.* 45°57N 86°15W **112** C4
Manitoba □ *Canada* 53°30N 97°0W **108** D10
Manitoba, L. *Canada* 51°0N 98°45W **108** D10
Manitou Is. *U.S.A.* 45°8N 86°0W **112** C4
Manitoulin I. *Canada* 45°40N 82°30W **112** C6
Manitowoc *U.S.A.* 44°5N 87°40W **112** C4
Manizales *Colombia* 5°5N 75°32W **120** B2
Mankato *U.S.A.* 44°10N 94°0W **111** B8
Mannar *Sri Lanka* 9°1N 79°54E **84** Q11
Mannar, G. of *Asia* 8°30N 79°0E **84** Q11
Mannheim *Germany* 49°29N 8°29E **64** D5
Manning *Canada* 56°53N 117°39W **108** D8
Manningtree *U.K.* 51°56N 1°5E **31** C11
Manokwari *Indonesia* 0°54S 134°0E **83** E8
Manosque *France* 43°49N 5°47E **66** E6
Manresa *Spain* 41°48N 1°50E **67** B6
Mansel I. *Canada* 62°0N 80°0W **109** C12
Mansfield *U.K.* 53°9N 1°11W **27** F6
Mansfield *U.S.A.* 40°45N 82°31W **112** E6
Mansfield Woodhouse *U.K.* 53°11N 1°12W **27** F6
Manta *Ecuador* 1°0S 80°40W **120** C1
Mantes-la-Jolie *France* 48°58N 1°41E **66** B4
Mantiqueira, Serra da *Brazil* 22°0S 44°0W **117** F6
Manton *U.K.* 52°38N 0°41W **27** G7
Manton *U.S.A.* 44°25N 85°24W **112** C5
Mántova *Italy* 45°9N 10°48E **68** B4
Manuel Alves → *Brazil* 11°19S 48°28W **122** B1
Manzai *Pakistan* 32°12N 70°15E **84** C7
Manzanillo *Cuba* 20°20N 77°31W **115** C9
Manzanillo *Mexico* 19°3N 104°20W **114** D4
Manzouli *China* 49°35N 117°25E **79** B12
Maó *Spain* 39°53N 4°16E **67** C8
Maoming *China* 21°50N 110°54E **79** G11
Mapam Yumco *China* 30°45N 81°28E **78** E5
Maputo *Mozam.* 25°58S 32°32E **97** K6
Maputo B. *Mozam.* 25°50S 32°45E **90** J7
Maqên Gangri *China* 34°55N 99°18E **78** E8
Maquinchao *Argentina* 41°15S 68°50W **121** G3
Maquoketa *U.S.A.* 42°4N 90°40W **112** D2
Mar *U.K.* 57°11N 2°53W **23** H12
Mar, Serra do *Brazil* 25°30S 49°0W **117** F6
Mar Chiquita, L. *Argentina* 30°40S 62°50W **121** F3
Mar del Plata *Argentina* 38°0S 57°30W **121** F4
Mara Rosa *Brazil* 14°1S 49°11W **122** B1
Marabá *Brazil* 5°20S 49°5W **120** C5
Maracá, I. de *Brazil* 2°10N 50°30W **120** B4
Maracaibo *Venezuela* 10°40N 71°37W **120** A2
Maracaibo, L. de *Venezuela* 9°40N 71°30W **120** B2
Maracay *Venezuela* 10°15N 67°28W **120** A3
Maradi *Niger* 13°29N 7°20E **94** F7
Maragogipe *Brazil* 12°46S 38°55W **122** B3
Marajó, I. de *Brazil* 1°0S 49°30W **120** C5
Maranguape *Brazil* 3°55S 38°50W **120** C6
Maranhão □ *Brazil* 5°0S 46°0W **120** C5
Marañón → *Peru* 4°30S 73°35W **120** C2
Marazion *U.K.* 50°7N 5°29W **29** G3
Marbella *Spain* 36°30N 4°57W **67** D3
March *U.K.* 52°33N 0°5E **31** B9
Marche *France* 46°5N 1°20E **66** C4
Marcus I. *Pac. Oc.* 24°20N 153°58E **102** E7
Mardan *Pakistan* 34°20N 72°0E **84** B8
Marden *U.K.* 52°7N 2°42W **30** B3
Mardin *Turkey* 37°20N 40°43E **71** G7
Maree, L. *U.K.* 57°40N 5°26W **22** G7
Mareham le Fen *U.K.* 53°8N 0°4W **27** F8
Marfleet *U.K.* 53°45N 0°17W **27** E8
Margarita, I. de *Venezuela* 11°0N 64°0W **120** A3
Margate *U.K.* 51°23N 1°23E **31** D11
Marghilon *Uzbekistan* 40°27N 71°42E **87** A12
Märgow, Dasht-e *Afghan.* 30°40N 62°30E **87** D10
Mari El □ *Russia* 56°30N 48°0E **70** C8
Mariana Trench *Pac. Oc.* 13°0N 145°0E **102** F6
Marias, Is. *Mexico* 21°25N 106°28W **114** C3
Maribor *Slovenia* 46°36N 15°40E **64** E8
Marie Byrd Land *Antarctica* 79°30S 125°0W **55** D14
Mariental *Namibia* 24°36S 18°0E **97** J3
Marietta *U.S.A.* 39°25N 81°27W **112** F7
Marília *Brazil* 22°13S 50°0W **120** E5
Marinette *U.S.A.* 45°6N 87°38W **112** C4
Maringá *Brazil* 23°26S 52°2W **121** E4
Marion *Ill., U.S.A.* 37°44N 88°56W **112** G3
Marion *Ind., U.S.A.* 40°32N 85°40W **112** E5
Marion *Ohio, U.S.A.* 40°35N 83°8W **112** E6
Mariupol *Ukraine* 47°5N 37°31E **71** E6
Marka *Somalia* 1°48N 44°50E **89** G3
Markam *China* 29°42N 98°38E **78** F8
Market Bosworth *U.K.* 52°38N 1°24W **27** G6
Market Deeping *U.K.* 52°41N 0°19W **27** G8
Market Drayton *U.K.* 52°54N 2°29W **27** G4
Market Harborough *U.K.* 52°29N 0°55W **27** H7
Market Lavington *U.K.* 51°17N 1°58W **30** D5
Market Rasen *U.K.* 53°24N 0°20W **27** F8
Market Weighton *U.K.* 53°52N 0°40W **27** E8
Markfield *U.K.* 52°42N 1°17W **27** G6
Markham, Mt. *Antarctica* 83°0S 164°0E **55** E11
Marks Tey *U.K.* 51°52N 0°49E **31** C10
Marlborough *U.K.* 51°25N 1°43W **30** D5
Marlborough Downs *U.K.* 51°27N 1°53W **30** D5
Marlow *U.K.* 51°34N 0°46W **31** C7
Marmara, Sea of *Turkey* 40°45N 28°15E **71** F4
Marmaris *Turkey* 36°50N 28°14E **86** D2
Marmora *Canada* 44°28N 77°41W **112** C9
Marne → *France* 48°47N 2°29E **66** B5
Marnhull *U.K.* 50°57N 2°19W **30** E4
Maroua *Cameroon* 10°40N 14°20E **95** F8
Marple *U.K.* 53°24N 2°4W **27** F4
Marquette *U.S.A.* 46°33N 87°24W **112** B4
Marquis *St. Lucia* 14°2N 60°54W **114** b
Marquises, Îs.
  French Polynesia 9°30S 140°0W **103** H14
Marrakesh *Morocco* 31°9N 8°0W **94** B4
Marree *Australia* 29°39S 138°1E **98** F6
Marsá Matrûh *Egypt* 31°19N 27°9E **95** B11
Marsabit *Kenya* 2°18N 38°0E **96** D7
Marsala *Italy* 37°48N 12°26E **68** F5
Marseilles *France* 43°18N 5°23E **66** E6
Marshall *U.S.A.* 29°34N 91°53W **111** E8
Marshall Is. ■ *Pac. Oc.* 9°0N 171°0E **102** G9
Marshfield *U.K.* 51°28N 2°19W **30** D4

Marshfield *U.S.A.* 44°40N 90°10W **112** C2
Marske by the Sea *U.K.* 54°36N 1°0W **26** C7
Marston Moor *U.K.* 53°58N 1°17W **27** E6
Martaban *Burma* 16°30N 97°35E **85** L20
Martaban, G. of *Burma* 16°5N 96°30E **85** L20
Martapura *Indonesia* 3°22S 114°47E **82** E4
Martham *U.K.* 52°42N 1°37E **31** A12
Martha's Vineyard *U.S.A.* 41°25N 70°38W **113** E12
Martigues *France* 43°24N 5°4E **66** E6
Martinique ☑ *W. Indies* 14°40N 61°0W **115** E12
Martins Bay *Barbados* 13°12N 59°29W **114** c
Martinsville *U.S.A.* 39°27N 77°58W **112** F9
Martley *U.K.* 52°15N 2°21W **30** B4
Martock *U.K.* 50°58N 2°46W **30** E3
Marwar *India* 25°43N 73°45E **84** G8
Mary *Turkmenistan* 37°40N 61°50E **87** B10
Maryborough *Australia* 25°31S 152°37E **98** F9
Maryland □ *U.S.A.* 39°0N 76°30W **112** F9
Maryport *U.K.* 54°44N 3°28W **26** C2
Marystown *Canada* 47°10N 55°10W **109** E14
Marytavy *U.K.* 50°36N 4°7W **29** F5
Marzūq *Libya* 25°53N 13°57E **95** C8
Masai Steppe *Tanzania* 4°30S 36°30E **96** E7
Masan *S. Korea* 35°11N 128°32E **79** D14
Masandam, Ra's *Oman* 26°30N 56°30E **89** B6
Masaya *Nic.* 12°0N 86°7W **114** E7
Masbate *Phil.* 12°21N 123°36E **83** B6
Mascara *Algeria* 35°26N 0°6E **94** A6
Maseru *Lesotho* 29°18S 27°30E **97** K5
Masham *U.K.* 54°14N 1°39W **26** D5
Mashhad *Iran* 36°20N 59°35E **87** B9
Mashonaland *Zimbabwe* 16°30S 31°0E **97** H6
Maşīrah, Jazīrat *Oman* 21°0N 58°50E **89** C6
Masjed Soleyman *Iran* 31°55N 49°18E **86** D7
Mask, L. *Ireland* 53°36N 9°22W **18** D3
Mason City *U.S.A.* 43°9N 93°12W **111** B8
Massa *Italy* 44°1N 10°9E **68** B4
Massachusetts □ *U.S.A.* 42°30N 72°0W **113** D11
Massawa *Eritrea* 15°35N 39°25E **89** D2
Massena *U.S.A.* 44°56N 74°54W **113** C10
Massiah Street *Barbados* 13°9N 59°29W **114** c
Massif Central *France* 44°55N 3°0E **66** D5
Massillon *U.S.A.* 40°48N 81°32W **112** E7
Masurian Lakes *Poland* 53°50N 21°0E **65** B11
Masvingo *Zimbabwe* 20°8S 30°49E **97** J6
Mata-Utu *Wall. & F. Is.* 13°17S 176°8W **99** C15
Matabeleland *Zimbabwe* 18°0S 27°0E **97** H5
Matadi *Dem. Rep. of the Congo* 5°52S 13°31E **96** F2
Matagalpa *Nic.* 13°0N 85°58W **114** E7
Matagami *Canada* 49°45N 77°34W **109** E12
Matagami, L. *Canada* 49°50N 77°40W **109** E12
Matagorda B. *U.S.A.* 28°15N 96°30W **111** E7
Matamoros *Coahuila,
  Mexico* 25°32N 103°15W **114** B4
Matamoros *Tamaulipas,
  Mexico* 25°53N 97°30W **114** B5
Matane *Canada* 48°50N 67°33W **109** E13
Matanzas *Cuba* 23°0N 81°40W **115** C8
Matara *Sri Lanka* 5°58N 80°30E **84** S12
Mataró *Spain* 41°32N 2°29E **67** B7
Matehuala *Mexico* 23°39N 100°39W **114** C4
Mateke Hills *Zimbabwe* 21°48S 31°0E **97** J6
Matera *Italy* 40°40N 16°36E **68** D7
Mathura *India* 27°30N 77°40E **84** F10
Mati *Phil.* 6°55N 126°15E **83** C7
Matlock *U.K.* 53°9N 1°33W **27** F5
Mato Grosso □ *Brazil* 14°0S 55°0W **120** D4
Mato Grosso, Planalto do
  Brazil 15°0S 55°0W **120** D4
Mato Grosso do Sul □ *Brazil* 18°0S 55°0W **120** D4
Matola *Mozam.* 25°57S 32°27E **97** K6
Matopo Hills *Zimbabwe* 20°36S 28°20E **97** J5
Maţruḥ *Oman* 23°37N 58°30E **87** F9
Matsu Tao *Taiwan* 26°8N 119°56E **79** F12
Matsue *Japan* 35°25N 133°10E **81** F3
Matsumoto *Japan* 36°15N 138°0E **81** E6
Matsusaka *Japan* 34°34N 136°32E **81** F5
Matsuyama *Japan* 33°45N 132°45E **81** G3
Mattagami → *Canada* 50°43N 81°29W **109** E11
Mattancheri *India* 9°50N 76°15E **84** Q10
Mattawa *Canada* 46°20N 78°45W **112** B8
Matterhorn *Switz.* 45°58N 7°39E **64** F4
Matthew, Î. *N. Cal.* 22°29S 171°15E **99** E13
Mattoon *U.S.A.* 39°29N 88°23W **112** F3
Maturín *Venezuela* 9°45N 63°11W **120** B3
Maubeuge *France* 50°17N 3°57E **66** A6
Maubin *Burma* 16°44N 95°39E **85** L19
Maudin Sun *Burma* 16°0N 94°30E **85** M19
Maui *U.S.A.* 20°48N 156°20W **110** H16
Maumee *U.S.A.* 41°42N 83°28W **112** E6
Maumee → *U.S.A.* 41°42N 83°28W **112** E6
Maumturk Mts. *Ireland* 53°32N 9°42W **18** D2
Maun *Botswana* 20°0S 23°26E **97** H4
Mauna Kea *U.S.A.* 19°50N 155°28W **110** J17
Mauna Loa *U.S.A.* 19°30N 155°35W **110** J17
Mauritania ■ *Africa* 20°50N 10°0W **94** E3
Mauritius ■ *Ind. Oc.* 20°0S 57°0E **91** J9
Mawgan *U.K.* 50°4N 5°13W **29** G3
Maxixe *Mozam.* 23°54S 35°17E **97** J7
Maxwellheugh *U.K.* 55°35N 2°26W **25** C11
May, I. of *U.K.* 56°11N 2°32W **25** B10
May Pen *Jamaica* 17°58N 77°15E **114** a
Mayaguana *I. Bahamas* 22°30N 72°44W **115** C10
Mayagüez *Puerto Rico* 18°12N 67°9W **115** D11
Maybole *U.K.* 55°21N 4°42W **24** D6
Mayfield *E. Sussex, U.K.* 51°1N 0°17E **31** D9
Mayfield *Staffs., U.K.* 53°1N 1°47W **27** F5
Maykop *Russia* 44°35N 40°10E **71** F7
Maynooth *Ireland* 53°23N 6°34W **21** B9
Mayo *Canada* 63°38N 135°57W **108** C6
Mayo □ *Ireland* 53°53N 9°3W **18** D3
Mayon Volcano *Phil.* 13°15N 123°41E **83** B6
Mayotte ☑ *Ind. Oc.* 12°50S 45°10E **97** G9
Maysville *U.S.A.* 38°39N 83°46W **112** F6
Māzandarān □ *Iran* 36°30N 52°0E **87** B8
Mazar *China* 36°32N 77°1E **78** D4
Mazār-e Sharīf *Afghan.* 36°41N 67°0E **87** B11
Mazaruni → *Guyana* 6°25N 58°35W **120** B4
Mazatlán *Mexico* 23°13N 106°25W **114** C3
Mazyr *Belarus* 51°59N 29°15E **70** D4

Mbabane *Swaziland* 26°18S 31°6E **97** K6
Mbaïki *C.A.R.* 3°53N 18°1E **96** D3
Mbala *Zambia* 8°46S 31°24E **96** F6
Mbale *Uganda* 1°8N 34°12E **96** D6
Mbandaka *Dem. Rep. of the Congo* 0°1N 18°18E **96** D3
Mbanza Ngungu
  Dem. Rep. of the Congo 5°12S 14°53E **96** F2
Mbeya *Tanzania* 8°54S 33°29E **96** F6
Mbour *Senegal* 14°22N 16°54W **94** F2
Mbuji-Mayi
  Dem. Rep. of the Congo 6°9S 23°40E **96** F4
Mdantsane *S. Africa* 32°56S 27°46E **97** L5
Mead, L. *U.S.A.* 36°0N 114°44W **110** C4
Meadow Lake *Canada* 54°10N 108°26W **108** D9
Meadville *U.S.A.* 41°39N 80°9W **112** E7
Meaford *Canada* 44°36N 80°35W **112** C7
Mealsgate *U.K.* 54°47N 3°13W **26** C2
Mearns, Howe of the *U.K.* 56°52N 2°26W **23** J13
Measham *U.K.* 52°43N 1°31W **27** G5
Meath □ *Ireland* 53°40N 6°57W **19** D8
Meaux *France* 48°58N 2°50E **66** B5
Mecca *Si. Arabia* 21°30N 39°54E **86** F4
Mechelen *Belgium* 51°2N 4°29E **64** C4
Mecklenburg *Germany* 53°33N 11°40E **64** B7
Mecklenburger Bucht
  Germany 54°20N 11°40E **64** A6
Medan *Indonesia* 3°40N 98°38E **82** D1
Médéa *Algeria* 36°12N 2°50E **94** A6
Medellín *Colombia* 6°15N 75°35W **120** B2
Medford *Oreg., U.S.A.* 42°19N 122°52W **110** B2
Medford *Wis., U.S.A.* 45°9N 90°20W **112** C2
Medicine Hat *Canada* 50°0N 110°45W **108** D8
Medina *Si. Arabia* 24°35N 39°52E **86** E4
Mediterranean Sea *Europe* 35°0N 15°0E **90** C5
Médoc *France* 45°10N 0°50W **66** D3
Medstead *U.K.* 51°8N 1°3W **30** D6
Medvezhyegorsk *Russia* 63°0N 34°25E **70** B5
Medway □ *U.K.* 51°27N 0°46E **31** D10
Meekatharra *Australia* 26°32S 118°29E **98** F2
Meerut *India* 29°1N 77°42E **84** E10
Meghalaya □ *India* 25°50N 91°0E **85** G17
Meghna → *Bangla.* 22°50N 90°50E **85** H17
Megisti *Greece* 36°8N 29°34E **86** D2
Meharry, Mt. *Australia* 22°59S 118°35E **98** D2
Meighen I. *Canada* 80°0N 99°30W **109** B10
Meiktila *Burma* 20°53N 95°54E **85** J19
Meizhou *China* 24°16N 116°6E **79** G12
Mejillones *Chile* 23°10S 70°30W **121** E2
Mekele *Ethiopia* 13°33N 39°30E **89** E2
Mekhtar *Pakistan* 30°30N 69°15E **84** D6
Meknès *Morocco* 33°57N 5°33W **94** B4
Mekong → *Asia* 9°30N 106°15E **82** C3
Melaka *Malaysia* 2°15N 102°15E **82** D2
Melanesia *Pac. Oc.* 4°0S 155°0E **102** H7
Melbourn *U.K.* 52°4N 0°1E **31** C9
Melbourne *Australia* 37°48S 144°58E **98** H8
Melbourne *U.K.* 52°50N 1°25W **27** G6
Melekeok *Palau* 7°27N 134°38E **102** G5
Mélèzes → *Canada* 57°40N 69°29W **109** D13
Melfort *Canada* 52°50N 104°37W **108** D9
Melilla *N. Afr.* 35°21N 2°57W **67** E4
Melitopol *Ukraine* 46°50N 35°22E **71** E6
Melksham *U.K.* 51°23N 2°8W **30** D4
Melmerby *U.K.* 54°45N 2°35W **26** C4
Melrhir, Chott *Algeria* 34°13N 6°30E **94** B7
Melrose *U.K.* 55°36N 2°43W **25** C10
Melsonby *U.K.* 54°29N 1°42W **26** D5
Melton Constable *U.K.* 52°52N 1°2E **31** A11
Melton Mowbray *U.K.* 52°47N 0°54W **27** G7
Melun *France* 48°32N 2°39E **66** B5
Melville *Canada* 50°55N 102°50W **108** D9
Melville, L. *Canada* 53°30N 60°0W **109** D14
Melville I. *Australia* 11°30S 131°0E **98** C5
Melville I. *Canada* 75°30N 112°0W **109** B8
Melville Pen. *Canada* 68°0N 84°0W **109** C11
Memphis *U.S.A.* 35°8N 90°2W **111** C9
Menai Bridge *U.K.* 53°14N 4°10W **28** A5
Menai Strait *U.K.* 53°11N 4°13W **28** A5
Mende *France* 44°31N 3°30E **66** D5
Mendip Hills *U.K.* 51°17N 2°40W **30** D3
Mendlesham *U.K.* 52°16N 1°6E **31** B11
Mendocino, C. *U.S.A.* 40°26N 124°25W **110** B2
Mendota *U.S.A.* 41°33N 89°7W **112** E3
Mendoza *Argentina* 32°50S 68°52W **121** F3
Menominee *U.S.A.* 45°6N 87°37W **112** C4
Menominee → *U.S.A.* 45°6N 87°35W **112** C4
Menomonie *U.S.A.* 44°53N 91°55W **112** C2
Menorca *Spain* 40°0N 4°0E **67** C8
Mentawai, Kepulauan *Indonesia* 2°0S 99°0E **82** E1
Merced *U.S.A.* 37°18N 120°29W **110** C2
Mercedes *Corrientes, Argentina* 29°10S 58°5W **121** E4
Mercedes *San Luis, Argentina* 33°40S 65°21W **121** F3
Mercedes *Uruguay* 33°12S 58°0W **121** F4
Mercy, C. *Canada* 65°0N 63°30W **109** C13
Mere *U.K.* 51°6N 2°16W **30** D4
Mergui *Burma* 12°26N 98°34E **82** B1
Merseyside □ *U.K.* 53°31N 3°2W **27** E2
Mere *U.K.* 51°25N 3°1W **27** D7
Merthyr Tydfil *U.K.* 51°45N 3°22W **28** D7
Meru *Kenya* 0°3N 37°40E **96** D7
Meru *Tanzania* 3°15S 36°46E **96** E7
Mesa *U.S.A.* 33°25N 111°50W **110** D4
Mesopotamia *Iraq* 33°30N 44°0E **86** C5
Messina *Italy* 38°11N 15°34E **68** E6
Messina, Str. di *Italy* 38°15N 15°35E **68** F6
Mestre, Espigão *Brazil* 12°30S 46°10W **122** B1
Meta → *S. Amer.* 6°12N 67°28W **120** B3

Meta Incognita Pen. Canada 62°45N 68°30W 109 C13
Metheringham U.K. 53°9N 0°23W 27 F8
Methwold U.K. 52°32N 0°33E 31 A10
Metlakatla U.S.A. 55°8N 131°35W 108 D6
Metropolis U.S.A. 37°9N 88°44W 112 G3
Metz France 49°8N 6°10E 66 B7
Meuse → Europe 50°45N 5°41E 64 C3
Mevagissey U.K. 50°16N 4°48W 29 G4
Mevagissey B. U.K. 50°17N 4°47W 29 G4
Mexborough U.K. 53°30N 1°15W 27 E6
Mexiana, I. Brazil 0°0 49°30W 120 B5
Mexicali Mexico 32°40N 115°30W 114 A1
Mexican Plateau Mexico 25°0N 104°0W 104 G9
México Mexico 19°24N 99°9W 114 D5
Mexico ■ Cent. Amer. 25°0N 105°0W 114 C4
Mexico, G. of Cent. Amer. 25°0N 90°0W 114 C7
Meymaneh Afghan. 35°53N 64°38E 87 C11
Mezen → Russia 65°44N 44°22E 70 A7
Mezhdurechensk Russia 53°41N 88°3E 76 D9
Mhonadh, Na h-Eileanan = Monach Is. U.K. 57°32N 7°40W 22 G2
Miami U.S.A. 25°46N 80°11W 111 E10
Miāndowāb Iran 37°0N 46°5E 86 B6
Miāneh Iran 37°30N 47°40E 86 B6
Mianwali Pakistan 32°38N 71°28E 84 C7
Mianyang China 31°22N 104°47E 78 E9
Miass Russia 54°59N 60°6E 70 D11
Micheldever U.K. 51°9N 1°14W 30 D6
Michigan □ U.S.A. 44°0N 85°0W 112 B4
Michigan, L. U.S.A. 44°0N 87°0W 112 D4
Michipicoten I. Canada 47°40N 85°40W 112 B5
Michurinsk Russia 52°58N 40°27E 70 D7
Mickle Fell U.K. 54°37N 2°18W 26 C4
Mickleover U.K. 52°55N 1°33W 27 G5
Mickleton U.K. 54°36N 2°2W 26 C4
Micoud St. Lucia 13°49N 60°54W 114 b
Micronesia Pac. Oc. 11°0N 160°0E 102 G7
Micronesia, Federated States of ■ Pac. Oc. 9°0N 150°0E 102 G7
Middelburg S. Africa 31°30S 25°0E 97 L5
Middle East Asia 35°0N 40°0E 72 E5
Middleham U.K. 54°17N 1°48W 26 D5
Middlemarsh U.K. 50°51N 2°28W 30 E4
Middlesbrough U.K. 54°35N 1°13W 26 C6
Middleton Gt. Man., U.K. 53°33N 2°12W 27 E4
Middleton Norfolk, U.K. 52°43N 0°29E 31 A9
Middleton Cheney U.K. 52°5N 1°16W 30 B6
Middleton in Teesdale U.K. 54°38N 2°4W 26 C4
Middleton on the Wolds U.K. 53°56N 0°35W 27 E7
Middletown U.K. 54°17N 6°51W 19 C8
Middletown N.Y., U.S.A. 41°27N 74°25W 113 E10
Middletown Ohio, U.S.A. 39°31N 84°24W 112 F5
Middlewich U.K. 53°12N 2°28W 27 F4
Middlezoy U.K. 51°5N 2°54W 30 D3
Midhurst U.K. 50°59N 0°44W 31 E7
Midi, Canal du → France 43°45N 1°21E 66 E4
Midland Canada 44°45N 79°50W 112 C8
Midland Mich., U.S.A. 43°37N 84°14W 112 D5
Midland Tex., U.S.A. 32°0N 102°3W 110 D6
Midleton Ireland 51°55N 8°10W 20 E6
Midsomer Norton U.K. 51°17N 2°28W 30 D4
Midway Is. Pac. Oc. 28°13N 177°22W 102 E10
Midwest U.S.A. 42°0N 90°0W 111 C9
Mieres Spain 43°18N 5°48W 67 A3
Mikhaylovka Russia 50°3N 43°5E 71 D7
Milan Italy 45°28N 9°10E 68 B3
Milborne Port U.K. 50°58N 2°28W 30 E4
Mildenhall U.K. 52°21N 0°32E 31 B10
Mildura Australia 34°13S 142°9E 98 G7
Miles City U.S.A. 46°25N 105°51W 110 A5
Milford U.S.A. 38°55N 75°26W 113 F10
Milford Haven U.K. 51°42N 5°7W 28 D3
Milford on Sea U.K. 50°43N 1°35W 30 E5
Milḩ, Baḩr al Iraq 32°40N 43°35E 86 C5
Milk → U.S.A. 48°4N 106°19W 110 A5
Millau France 44°8N 3°4E 66 D5
Millbrook U.K. 50°20N 4°14W 29 G5
Millet St. Lucia 13°55N 60°59W 114 b
Millinocket U.S.A. 45°39N 68°43W 113 C13
Millom U.K. 54°13N 3°16W 26 D2
Milltown Malbay Ireland 52°52N 9°24W 20 C4
Millville U.S.A. 39°24N 75°2W 113 F10
Milngavie U.K. 55°56N 4°19W 24 C7
Milnthorpe U.K. 54°14N 2°45W 26 D3
Milos Greece 36°44N 24°25E 69 F11
Milton Abbot U.K. 50°35N 4°16W 29 F5
Milton Keynes U.K. 52°1N 0°44W 31 B7
Milverton U.K. 51°1N 3°16W 30 D2
Milwaukee U.S.A. 43°2N 87°54W 112 D4
Milwaukee Deep Atl. Oc. 19°50N 68°0W 115 D11
Min Jiang → Fujian, China 26°0N 119°35E 79 F12
Min Jiang → Sichuan, China 28°45N 104°40E 78 F9
Minas Uruguay 34°20S 55°10W 121 F4
Minas Gerais □ Brazil 18°50S 46°0W 122 C1
Minatitlán Mexico 17°59N 94°31W 114 D6
Minchinhampton U.K. 51°42N 2°11W 30 C4
Mindanao Phil. 8°0N 125°0E 83 C6
Mindoro Phil. 13°0N 121°0E 83 B6
Mindoro Str. Phil. 12°30N 120°30E 83 B6
Minehead U.K. 51°12N 3°29W 30 D2
Mineral Wells U.S.A. 32°48N 98°7W 110 D7
Minfeng China 37°4N 82°46E 78 D5
Minginish U.K. 57°14N 6°15W 22 H5
Mingulay U.K. 56°49N 7°39W 22 J2
Minna Nigeria 9°37N 6°30E 94 G7
Minneapolis U.S.A. 44°57N 93°16W 111 B8
Minnesota □ U.S.A. 46°0N 94°15W 111 A8
Minorca = Menorca Spain 40°0N 4°0E 67 C8
Minot U.S.A. 48°14N 101°18W 110 A6
Minsk Belarus 53°52N 27°30E 65 B14
Minster Kent, U.K. 51°20N 1°20E 31 D11
Minster Kent, U.K. 51°25N 0°50E 31 D10
Minsterley U.K. 52°39N 2°54W 27 G3
Minto, L. Canada 57°13N 75°0W 109 D12
Miramichi B. Canada 47°15N 65°0W 113 B15
Mirim, L. S. Amer. 32°45S 52°50W 121 F4
Mirnyy Russia 62°33N 113°53E 77 C12
Mirpur Khas Pakistan 25°30N 69°0E 84 G6
Mirs Bay China 22°33N 114°24E 79 a
Mirtoo Sea Greece 37°0N 23°20E 69 F10
Mirzapur India 25°10N 82°34E 85 G13
Mishawaka U.S.A. 41°40N 86°11W 112 E4
Miskolc Hungary 48°7N 20°50E 65 D11
Misool Indonesia 1°52S 130°10E 83 E8
Mişrātah Libya 32°24N 15°3E 95 B9
Missinaibi → Canada 50°43N 81°29W 109 D11
Mississippi □ U.S.A. 33°0N 90°0W 111 D9
Mississippi → U.S.A. 29°9N 89°15W 111 E9
Mississippi River Delta U.S.A. 29°10N 89°15W 111 E9
Missoula U.S.A. 46°52N 114°1W 110 A4
Missouri □ U.S.A. 38°25N 92°30W 111 C8
Missouri → U.S.A. 38°49N 90°7W 111 C8
Mistassini, L. Canada 51°0N 73°30W 109 D12
Misterton Notts., U.K. 53°27N 0°50W 27 F7
Misterton Somst., U.K. 50°52N 2°47W 30 E3
Mitcheldean U.K. 51°51N 2°28W 30 C4
Mitchell U.S.A. 43°43N 98°2W 110 B7
Mitchell → Australia 15°12S 141°35E 98 D7
Mitchell, Mt. U.S.A. 35°46N 82°16W 104 F11
Mitchelstown Ireland 52°15N 8°16W 20 D6
Mito Japan 36°20N 140°30E 81 E7
Mitrovica Kosovo 42°54N 20°52E 69 C9
Mitú Colombia 1°15N 70°13W 120 B2
Mitumba, Mts. Dem. Rep. of the Congo 7°0S 27°30E 96 F5
Miugh Laigh = Mingulay U.K. 56°49N 7°39W 22 J2
Miyakonojō Japan 31°40N 131°5E 81 H2
Miyazaki Japan 31°56N 131°30E 81 H2
Mizen Hd. Cork, Ireland 51°27N 9°50W 20 F3
Mizen Hd. Wicklow, Ireland 52°51N 6°4W 21 C10
Mizoram □ India 23°30N 92°40E 85 H18
Mjøsa Norway 60°40N 11°0E 63 E6
Mljet Croatia 42°43N 17°30E 68 C7
Mo i Rana Norway 66°20N 14°7E 63 D6
Moab U.S.A. 38°35N 109°33W 110 C5
Moate Ireland 53°24N 7°44W 18 E6
Mobaye C.A.R. 4°25N 21°5E 96 D4
Moberly U.S.A. 39°25N 92°26W 111 C8
Mobile U.S.A. 30°41N 88°3W 111 D9
Mobridge U.S.A. 45°32N 100°26W 110 A6
Moçambique Mozam. 15°3S 40°42E 97 H8
Mochudi Botswana 24°27S 26°7E 97 J5
Mocoa Colombia 1°7N 76°35W 120 B2
Mococa Brazil 21°28S 47°0W 122 D1
Mocuba Mozam. 16°54S 36°57E 97 H7
Modbury U.K. 50°21N 3°55W 29 G6
Módena Italy 44°40N 10°55E 68 B4
Modesto U.S.A. 37°39N 121°0W 110 C2
Moffat U.K. 55°21N 3°27W 25 D9
Mogadishu Somalia 2°2N 45°25E 89 G4
Mogi-Mirim Brazil 22°29S 47°0W 122 D1
Mohammedia Morocco 33°44N 7°21W 94 B4
Moher, Cliffs of Ireland 52°58N 9°27W 20 C4
Moidart U.K. 56°49N 5°41W 22 J6
Moidart, L. U.K. 56°47N 5°52W 22 J6
Moisie → Canada 50°14N 66°5W 109 D13
Mojave Desert U.S.A. 35°0N 116°30W 110 D3
Moji das Cruzes Brazil 23°31S 46°11W 122 D1
Mokpo S. Korea 34°50N 126°25E 79 E14
Mold U.K. 53°9N 3°8W 28 A7
Molde Norway 62°45N 7°9E 63 E5
Moldova ■ Europe 47°0N 28°0E 65 E15
Mole → U.K. 51°24N 0°21W 31 D8
Molepolole Botswana 24°28S 25°28E 97 J5
Mollendo Peru 17°0S 72°0W 120 D2
Moloka'i U.S.A. 21°8N 157°0W 110 H16
Molopo → Africa 28°30S 20°12E 97 K4
Molucca Sea Indonesia 0°0 125°0E 83 E6
Moluccas Indonesia 1°0S 127°0E 83 E7
Mombasa Kenya 4°3S 39°40E 96 E7
Mompós Colombia 9°14N 74°26W 120 B2
Mon □ Burma 16°0N 97°30E 85 L20
Mona Passage W. Indies 18°30N 67°45W 115 D11
Monach Is. U.K. 57°32N 7°40W 22 G2
Monaco ■ Europe 43°46N 7°23E 66 E7
Monadhliath Mts. U.K. 57°10N 4°4W 23 H9
Monaghan Ireland 54°15N 6°57W 19 C8
Monaghan □ Ireland 54°11N 6°56W 19 C8
Monar, L. U.K. 57°26N 5°8W 22 H7
Monar Forest U.K. 57°27N 5°10W 22 H7
Monasterevin Ireland 53°8N 7°4W 21 B8
Monavullagh Mts. Ireland 52°14N 7°35W 21 D7
Mönchengladbach Germany 51°11N 6°27E 64 C4
Monclova Mexico 26°54N 101°25W 114 B4
Moncton Canada 46°7N 64°51W 113 B15
Moneague Jamaica 18°16N 77°7W 114 a
Moneymore U.K. 54°41N 6°40W 19 B8
Mongolia ■ Asia 47°0N 103°0E 78 B9
Mongolia, Plateau of Asia 45°0N 105°0E 72 D12
Mongu Zambia 15°16S 23°12E 97 H4
Monifieth U.K. 56°30N 2°48W 25 B10
Monmouth U.K. 51°48N 2°42W 28 D8
Monmouth U.S.A. 40°55N 90°39W 112 E2
Monmouthshire □ U.K. 51°48N 2°54W 28 D8
Monnow → U.K. 51°49N 2°43W 30 C3
Monroe La., U.S.A. 32°30N 92°7W 111 D8
Monroe Mich., U.S.A. 41°55N 83°24W 112 E6
Monroe Wis., U.S.A. 42°36N 89°38W 112 D3
Monrovia Liberia 6°18N 10°47W 94 G3
Mons Belgium 50°27N 3°58E 64 C3
Mont-de-Marsan France 43°54N 0°31W 66 E3
Mont-Laurier Canada 46°35N 75°30W 109 E12
Montana Bulgaria 43°27N 23°16E 69 C10
Montaña Peru 6°0S 73°0W 120 C2
Montana □ U.S.A. 47°0N 110°0W 110 A5
Montargis France 47°59N 2°43E 66 C5
Montauban France 44°2N 1°21E 66 D4
Montbéliard France 47°31N 6°48E 66 C7
Montceau-les-Mines France 46°40N 4°23E 66 C6
Monte Azul Brazil 15°9S 42°53W 122 C2
Monte-Carlo Monaco 43°44N 7°25E 66 E7
Monte Caseros Argentina 30°10S 57°50W 121 F4
Monte Cristi Dom. Rep. 19°52N 71°39W 115 D10
Montego Bay Jamaica 18°28N 77°55W 114 a
Montélimar France 44°33N 4°45E 66 D6
Montello U.S.A. 43°48N 89°20W 112 D3
Montemorelos Mexico 25°12N 99°49W 114 B5
Montenegro ■ Europe 42°40N 19°20E 69 C8
Monterey U.S.A. 36°37N 121°55W 110 C2
Montería Colombia 8°46N 75°53W 120 B2
Monterrey Mexico 25°40N 100°19W 114 B4
Montes Claros Brazil 16°30S 43°50W 122 C2
Montevideo Uruguay 34°50S 56°11W 121 F4
Montgomery U.K. 52°34N 3°8W 28 B7
Montgomery U.S.A. 32°23N 86°19W 111 D9
Monticello U.S.A. 40°45N 86°46W 112 E4
Montluçon France 46°22N 2°36E 66 C5
Montmagny Canada 46°58N 70°34W 113 B12
Montpelier Idaho, U.S.A. 42°19N 111°18W 110 B4
Montpelier Vt., U.S.A. 44°16N 72°35W 113 C11
Montpellier France 43°37N 3°52E 66 E5
Montréal Canada 45°30N 73°33W 113 C11
Montreux Switz. 46°26N 6°55E 64 E4
Montrose U.K. 56°44N 2°27W 23 J13
Montrose U.S.A. 38°29N 107°53W 110 C5
Montserrat ☒ W. Indies 16°40N 62°10W 115 D12
Monywa Burma 22°7N 95°11E 85 H19
Monza Italy 45°35N 9°16E 68 B3
Monze, C. Pakistan 24°47N 66°37E 84 G5
Moorfoot Hills U.K. 55°44N 3°8W 25 C9
Moorhead U.S.A. 46°53N 96°45W 111 A7
Moose Jaw Canada 50°24N 105°30W 108 D9
Moosehead L. U.S.A. 45°38N 69°40W 113 C13
Moosomin Canada 50°9N 101°40W 108 D9
Moosonee Canada 51°17N 80°39W 109 D11
Mopti Mali 14°30N 4°0W 94 F5
Mora Sweden 61°2N 14°38E 63 E6
Mora, Na h-Eileanan = Shiant Is. U.K. 57°54N 6°22W 22 G5
Moradabad India 28°50N 78°50E 84 E11
Morant Bay Jamaica 17°53N 76°25W 114 a
Morant Pt. Jamaica 17°55N 76°12W 114 a
Morar, L. U.K. 56°57N 5°40W 22 J6
Moratuwa Sri Lanka 6°45N 79°55E 84 R11
Morava → Serbia 44°36N 21°4E 69 B9
Morava → Slovak Rep. 48°10N 16°59E 65 D9
Moravian Hts. Czech Rep. 49°30N 15°40E 56 F9
Moray □ U.K. 57°31N 3°18W 23 G11
Moray Firth U.K. 57°40N 3°52W 23 G10
Morden Canada 49°15N 98°10W 108 E10
Mordvinia □ Russia 54°20N 44°30E 70 D7
Moreau → U.S.A. 45°18N 100°43W 110 A6
Morebattle U.K. 55°31N 2°22W 25 C11
Morecambe U.K. 54°5N 2°52W 26 D3
Morecambe B. U.K. 54°7N 3°0W 26 D3
Moree Australia 29°28S 149°54E 98 F9
Morehead U.S.A. 38°11N 83°26W 112 F6
Morelia Mexico 19°42N 101°7W 114 D4
Morena, Sierra Spain 38°20N 4°0W 67 C3
Moresby I. Canada 52°30N 131°40W 108 D6
Moreton-in-Marsh U.K. 51°59N 1°41W 30 C5
Moretonhampstead U.K. 50°39N 3°46W 29 F6
Morgan City U.S.A. 29°42N 91°12W 111 E8
Morgantown U.S.A. 39°38N 79°57W 112 F8
Morioka Japan 39°45N 141°8E 81 D7
Morlaix France 48°36N 3°52W 66 B2
Morley U.K. 53°45N 1°36W 27 E5
Morocco ■ N. Afr. 32°0N 5°50W 94 B4
Morogoro Tanzania 6°50S 37°40E 96 F7
Morón Cuba 22°8N 78°39W 115 C9
Mörön Mongolia 49°38N 100°9E 78 B9
Morondava Madag. 20°17S 44°17E 97 J8
Moroni Comoros Is. 11°40S 43°16E 91 H8
Morotai Indonesia 2°10N 128°30E 83 D7
Morpeth U.K. 55°10N 1°41W 26 B5
Morphou Cyprus 35°12N 32°59E 86 C3
Morrinhos Brazil 17°45S 49°10W 122 C1
Morris U.S.A. 41°22N 88°26W 112 E3
Morris Jesup, Kap Greenland 83°40N 34°0W 104 A16
Morte Bay U.K. 51°9N 4°14W 29 E5
Morte Pt. U.K. 51°11N 4°14W 29 E5
Mortehoe U.K. 51°11N 4°12W 29 E5
Mortimer's Cross U.K. 52°16N 2°50W 30 B3
Morton Fen U.K. 52°49N 0°20W 27 G8
Morvan France 47°5N 4°3E 66 C6
Morwenstow U.K. 50°54N 4°33W 29 F4
Moscos Is. Burma 14°0N 97°30E 85 N20
Moscow Russia 55°45N 37°37E 70 C6
Moscow U.S.A. 46°44N 117°0W 110 A3
Mosel → Europe 50°22N 7°36E 64 C4
Moses Lake U.S.A. 47°8N 119°17W 110 A3
Moshi Tanzania 3°22S 37°18E 96 E7
Mosjøen Norway 65°51N 13°12E 63 D6
Mosselbaai S. Africa 34°11S 22°8E 97 L4
Mossley U.K. 53°33N 2°1W 27 E4
Mossoró Brazil 5°10S 37°15W 120 C6
Most Czech Rep. 50°31N 13°38E 64 C7
Mostaganem Algeria 35°54N 0°5E 94 A6
Mostar Bos.-H. 43°22N 17°50E 69 C7
Mosul Iraq 36°15N 43°5E 86 B5
Motcombe U.K. 51°1N 2°13W 30 D4
Motherwell U.K. 55°47N 3°58W 25 C8
Motihari India 26°30N 84°55E 85 F14
Motril Spain 36°31N 3°37W 67 D4
Mottisfont U.K. 51°2N 1°32W 30 D5
Mouila Gabon 1°50S 11°0E 96 E2
Moule à Chique, C. St. Lucia 13°43N 60°57W 114 b
Moulins France 46°35N 3°19E 66 C5
Moulmein Burma 16°30N 97°40E 85 L20
Moulouya, O. → Morocco 35°5N 2°25W 94 B5
Moulton U.K. 52°17N 0°52W 31 B7
Moundou Chad 8°40N 16°10E 95 G9
Moundsville U.S.A. 39°55N 80°44W 112 F7
Mount Carmel U.S.A. 38°25N 87°46W 112 F4
Mount Desert I. U.S.A. 44°21N 68°20W 113 C13
Mount Gambier Australia 37°50S 140°46E 98 H7
Mount Hagen Papua N. G. 5°52S 144°16E 98 B7
Mount Isa Australia 20°42S 139°26E 98 E6
Mount Magnet Australia 28°2S 117°47E 98 F2
Mount Pleasant U.S.A. 43°36N 84°46W 112 D5
Mount Sterling U.S.A. 38°4N 83°56W 112 F6
Mount Vernon Ind., U.S.A. 37°56N 87°54W 112 F3
Mount Vernon Ohio, U.S.A. 40°23N 82°29W 112 E6
Mountain Ash U.K. 51°40N 3°23W 28 D7
Mountain Home U.S.A. 43°8N 115°41W 110 B3
Mountain View U.S.A. 19°33N 155°7W 110 J17
Mountmellick Ireland 53°7N 7°20W 21 B8
Mountrath Ireland 53°0N 7°28W 21 C8
Mount's Bay U.K. 50°5N 5°31W 29 G2
Mountsorrel U.K. 52°44N 1°8W 27 G6
Mourne → U.K. 54°52N 7°26W 18 B7
Mourne Mts. U.K. 54°10N 6°0W 19 C9
Moville Ireland 55°11N 7°3W 19 A7
Moy → Ireland 54°8N 9°8W 18 C3
Moyen Atlas Morocco 33°0N 5°0W 94 B4
Mozambique ■ Africa 19°0S 35°0E 97 H7
Mozambique Chan. Africa 17°30S 42°30E 90 H8
Mozdok Russia 43°45N 44°48E 71 F7
Mpanda Tanzania 6°23S 31°1E 96 F6
Mpumalanga S. Africa 29°50S 30°33E 97 K6
Msaken Tunisia 35°49N 10°33E 95 A8
Mthatha S. Africa 31°36S 28°49E 97 L5
Mtwara-Mikindani Tanzania 10°20S 40°20E 96 G8
Muar Malaysia 2°3N 102°34E 82 D2
Mubi Nigeria 10°18N 13°16E 95 F8
Much Dewchurch U.K. 51°58N 2°45W 30 C3
Much Marcle U.K. 51°59N 2°29W 30 C4
Much Wenlock U.K. 52°35N 2°33W 27 G3
Muchinga Mts. Zambia 11°30S 31°30E 97 G6
Muck U.K. 56°50N 6°15W 22 J5
Muckle Flugga U.K. 60°51N 0°54W 22 A16
Muckle Roe U.K. 60°23N 1°27W 22 B15
Mucuri Brazil 18°0S 39°36W 122 C3
Mudanjiang China 44°38N 129°30E 79 C14
Mufulira Zambia 12°32S 28°15E 97 G5
Muğla Turkey 37°15N 28°22E 71 G4
Muir of Ord U.K. 57°32N 4°28W 23 G9
Muktsar India 30°30N 74°30E 84 D9
Mulanje, Mt. Malawi 16°2S 35°33E 97 H7
Mulde → Germany 51°53N 12°15E 64 C7
Mulhacén Spain 37°4N 3°20W 67 D4
Mulhouse France 47°40N 7°20E 66 C7
Mull U.K. 56°25N 5°56W 24 B4
Mull, Sound of U.K. 56°30N 5°50W 24 A4
Mullaghareirk Mts. Ireland 52°20N 9°10W 20 D4
Mullet Pen. Ireland 54°13N 10°2W 18 C1
Mullingar Ireland 53°31N 7°21W 18 D7
Mullion U.K. 50°1N 5°16W 29 G3
Mulroy B. Ireland 55°15N 7°46W 18 A6
Multan Pakistan 30°15N 71°36E 84 D7
Mumbai India 18°56N 72°50E 84 K8
Mumbles Hd. U.K. 51°34N 3°59W 29 D6
Muna Indonesia 5°0S 122°30E 83 F6
Muncie U.S.A. 40°12N 85°23W 112 E5
Mundesley U.K. 52°53N 1°25E 31 A11
Mundo Novo Brazil 11°50S 40°29W 122 B2
Munger India 25°23N 86°30E 85 G15
Munich Germany 48°8N 11°34E 64 D6
Munising U.S.A. 46°25N 86°40W 112 B4
Münster Germany 51°58N 7°37E 64 C4
Munster □ Ireland 52°18N 8°44W 20 D5
Murashi Russia 59°30N 49°0E 70 C8
Murat → Turkey 38°46N 40°0E 71 G7
Murchison → Australia 27°45S 114°0E 98 F1
Murcia Spain 38°5N 1°10W 67 D5
Murcia □ Spain 37°50N 1°30W 67 D5
Mureş → Romania 46°15N 20°13E 65 E11
Murfreesboro U.S.A. 35°51N 86°24W 111 C9
Muriaé Brazil 21°8S 42°23W 122 D2
Müritz Germany 53°25N 12°42E 64 B7
Murmansk Russia 68°57N 33°10E 70 A5
Murom Russia 55°35N 42°3E 70 C7
Muroran Japan 42°25N 141°0E 81 B7
Murray U.S.A. 36°37N 88°19W 112 G3
Murray → Australia 35°20S 139°22E 98 H6
Murton U.K. 54°50N 1°22W 26 C6
Mururoa French Polynesia 21°52S 138°55W 103 K14
Murwara India 23°46N 80°28E 85 H12
Muş Turkey 38°45N 41°30E 71 G7
Mûsa, Gebel Egypt 28°33N 33°59E 86 D3
Muscat Oman 23°37N 58°36E 87 F9
Musgrave Ranges Australia 26°0S 132°0E 98 F5
Musina S. Africa 22°20S 30°5E 97 J6
Muskegon U.S.A. 43°14N 86°16W 112 D4
Muskegon → U.S.A. 43°14N 86°21W 112 D4
Muskogee U.S.A. 35°45N 95°22W 111 C7
Musselburgh U.K. 55°57N 3°2W 25 C9
Musselshell → U.S.A. 47°21N 107°57W 110 A5
Mutare Zimbabwe 18°58S 32°38E 97 H6
Mutton I. Ireland 52°49N 9°32W 20 C3
Muynak Uzbekistan 43°44N 59°10E 87 A9
Muz Tag China 36°25N 87°25E 78 D6
Muzaffarabad Pakistan 34°25N 73°30E 84 B8
Muzaffarnagar India 29°26N 77°40E 84 E10
Muztagh-Ata China 38°17N 75°7E 78 D4
Mwanza Tanzania 2°30S 32°58E 96 E6
Mweelrea Ireland 53°39N 9°49W 18 D2
Mwene-Ditu Dem. Rep. of the Congo 6°35S 22°27E 96 F4
Mweru, L. Zambia 9°0S 28°40E 96 F5
My Tho Vietnam 10°29N 106°23E 82 B3
Myanmar = Burma ■ Asia 21°0N 96°30E 85 J20
Mycenæ Greece 37°43N 22°46E 69 F10
Myddle U.K. 52°49N 2°47W 27 G3
Myingyan Burma 21°30N 95°20E 85 J19
Myitkyina Burma 25°24N 97°26E 85 G20
Mymensingh Bangla. 24°45N 90°24E 85 G17
Mynydd Du U.K. 51°52N 3°50W 28 D6
Mynydd Preseli U.K. 51°57N 4°48W 28 D4
Mysore India 12°17N 76°41E 84 N10
Mytishchi Russia 55°50N 37°50E 70 C6

N

Na Hearadh = Harris U.K. 57°50N 6°55W 22 G4
Na Hearadh a Deas = South Harris U.K. 57°50N 7°0W 22 G4
Na Hearadh a Tuath = North Harris U.K. 58°0N 6°55W 22 F4
Naab → Germany 49°1N 12°2E 64 D6
Naas Ireland 53°12N 6°40W 21 B9
Naberezhnyye Chelny Russia 55°42N 52°19E 70 C9
Nabeul Tunisia 36°30N 10°44E 95 A8
Nābulus West Bank 32°14N 35°15E 86 C3
Nacala Mozam. 14°32S 40°34E 97 G8
Nacogdoches U.S.A. 31°36N 94°39W 111 D8
Nacozari de García Mexico 30°25N 109°38W 114 A3
Nadiad India 22°41N 72°56E 84 H8
Nador Morocco 35°14N 2°58W 94 B5
Nafferton U.K. 54°1N 0°23W 27 D8
Nafud Desert Si. Arabia 28°15N 41°0E 86 D5
Naga Phil. 13°38N 123°15E 83 B6
Nagaland □ India 26°0N 94°30E 85 G19
Nagano Japan 36°40N 138°10E 81 E6
Nagaoka Japan 37°27N 138°51E 81 E6
Nagappattinam India 10°46N 79°51E 84 P11
Nagasaki Japan 32°47N 129°50E 81 G1
Nagaur India 27°15N 73°45E 84 F8
Nagercoil India 8°12N 77°26E 84 Q10
Nagles Mts. Ireland 52°8N 8°30W 20 D6
Nagorno-Karabakh □ Azerbaijan 39°55N 46°45E 71 F8
Nagoya Japan 35°10N 136°50E 81 F5
Nagpur India 21°8N 79°10E 84 J11
Nagqu China 31°29N 92°3E 78 E7
Naha Japan 26°13N 127°42E 79 F14
Nailsea U.K. 51°26N 2°44W 30 D3
Nailsworth U.K. 51°41N 2°14W 30 C4
Nain Canada 56°34N 61°40W 109 D13
Nairn U.K. 57°35N 3°53W 23 G10
Nairobi Kenya 1°17S 36°48E 96 E7
Naivasha Kenya 0°40S 36°30E 96 E7
Najafābād Iran 32°40N 51°15E 87 C7
Najd Si. Arabia 26°30N 42°0E 86 E5
Najibabad India 29°40N 78°20E 84 E11
Najin N. Korea 42°12N 130°15E 79 C15
Najrān Si. Arabia 17°34N 44°18E 89 D3
Nakhodka Russia 42°53N 132°54E 77 E14
Nakhon Ratchasima Thailand 14°59N 102°12E 82 B2
Nakhon Sawan Thailand 15°35N 100°10E 82 A2
Nakhon Si Thammarat Thailand 8°29N 100°0E 82 C2
Nakina Canada 50°10N 86°40W 109 D11
Nakuru Kenya 0°15S 36°4E 96 E7
Nalchik Russia 43°30N 43°33E 71 F7
Nallamalai Hills India 15°30N 78°50E 84 M11
Nam Co China 30°30N 90°45E 78 E7
Namak, Daryācheh-ye Iran 34°30N 52°0E 87 C8
Namaland Namibia 26°0S 17°0E 97 K3
Namangan Uzbekistan 41°0N 71°40E 87 A12
Namcha Barwa China 29°40N 95°10E 78 F8
Namib Desert Namibia 22°30S 15°0E 97 J3
Namibe Angola 15°7S 12°11E 97 H2
Namibia ■ Africa 22°0S 18°9E 97 J3
Nampa U.S.A. 43°34N 116°34W 110 B3
Namp'o N. Korea 38°52N 125°10E 79 D14
Nampula Mozam. 15°6S 39°15E 97 H7
Namumea Tuvalu 5°41S 176°9E 99 B14
Namur Belgium 50°27N 4°52E 64 C3
Nan-ch'ang China 28°42N 115°55E 79 F12
Nan Ling China 25°0N 112°30E 79 F11
Nanaimo Canada 49°10N 124°0W 108 E7
Nanchong China 30°43N 106°2E 78 E10
Nancy France 48°42N 6°12E 66 B7
Nanda Devi India 30°23N 79°59E 84 D11
Nanded India 19°10N 77°20E 84 K10
Nandurbar India 21°20N 74°15E 84 J9
Nanga Parbat Pakistan 35°10N 74°35E 84 B9
Nanjing China 32°2N 118°47E 79 E12
Nanning China 22°48N 108°20E 78 G10
Nanping China 26°38N 118°10E 79 F12
Nansen Sd. Canada 81°0N 91°0W 109 A10
Nantes France 47°12N 1°33W 66 C3
Nantong China 32°1N 120°52E 79 E13
Nantou China 22°32N 113°55E 79 a
Nantucket I. U.S.A. 41°16N 70°5W 113 E12
Nantwich U.K. 53°4N 2°31W 27 F3
Nanuque Brazil 17°50S 40°21W 122 C2
Nanyang China 33°11N 112°30E 79 E11
Nanyuki Kenya 0°2N 37°4E 96 D7
Napa U.S.A. 38°18N 122°17W 110 C2
Napier N.Z. 39°30S 176°56E 99 H14
Naples Italy 40°50N 14°15E 68 D6
Napo → Peru 3°20S 72°40W 120 C2
Nappa U.K. 53°58N 2°13W 27 E4
Narayanganj Bangla. 23°40N 90°33E 85 H17
Narberth U.K. 51°47N 4°44W 28 D4
Narbonne France 43°11N 3°0E 66 E5
Narborough U.K. 52°34N 1°13W 27 G6
Nares Str. Arctic 80°0N 70°0W 109 A13
Narmada → India 21°38N 72°36E 84 J8
Narodnaya Russia 65°5N 59°58E 70 A10
Narva Estonia 59°23N 28°12E 63 F9
Narvik Norway 68°28N 17°26E 63 D7
Naryan-Mar Russia 67°42N 53°12E 70 A9
Nasca Peru 14°50S 74°57W 120 D2
Naseby U.K. 52°24N 0°59W 31 B7
Nashua U.S.A. 42°45N 71°28W 113 D12
Nashville U.S.A. 36°10N 86°47W 111 C9
Nasik India 19°58N 73°50E 84 K8
Nasirabad India 26°15N 74°45E 84 F9
Nasiriyah Iraq 31°0N 46°15E 86 D6
Nassau Bahamas 25°5N 77°20W 115 B9
Nasser, L. Egypt 23°0N 32°30E 95 D12
Natal Brazil 5°47S 35°13W 120 C6
Natashquan Canada 50°14N 61°46W 109 D13
Natashquan → Canada 50°7N 61°50W 109 D13
Natchez U.S.A. 31°34N 91°24W 111 D8
Natchitoches U.S.A. 31°46N 93°5W 111 D8
Nathdwara India 24°55N 73°50E 84 G8
Natitingou Benin 10°20N 1°26E 94 F6
Natron, L. Tanzania 2°20S 36°0E 96 E7
Natuna Besar, Kepulauan Indonesia 4°0N 108°15E 82 D3
Nauru ■ Pac. Oc. 1°0S 166°0E 102 H8
Navan Ireland 53°39N 6°41W 19 D8
Navarino, I. Chile 55°0S 67°40W 121 H3
Navarra □ Spain 42°40N 1°40W 67 A5
Navenby U.K. 53°6N 0°31W 27 F7
Naver → U.K. 58°32N 4°14W 23 E9
Navoiy Uzbekistan 40°9N 65°22E 76 E7
Navojoa Mexico 27°6N 109°26W 114 B3
Navsari India 20°57N 72°59E 84 J8
Nawabshah Pakistan 26°15N 68°25E 84 F6
Naxçıvan □ Azerbaijan 39°25N 45°26E 71 G8
Naxos Greece 37°8N 25°25E 69 F11
Naypyidaw Burma 19°44N 96°12E 85 K20
Nazaré Brazil 13°2S 39°0W 122 B3
Nazas → Mexico 25°12N 104°12W 114 B4
Naze, The U.K. 51°53N 1°18E 31 C11
Nazret Ethiopia 8°32N 39°22E 89 F2

Ndjamena
Orléans, Î. d'

Ndjamena Chad 12°10N 15°0E 95 F8
Ndola Zambia 13°0S 28°34E 97 G5
Neagh, Lough U.K. 54°37N 6°25W 19 B9
Near Is. U.S.A. 52°30N 174°0E 108 D1
Neath U.K. 51°39N 3°48W 28 D6
Neblina, Pico da Brazil 0°48N 66°2W 120 B3
Nebraska □ U.S.A. 41°30N 99°30W 110 B7
Nébrodi, Monti Italy 37°54N 14°35E 68 F6
Neckar → Germany 49°27N 8°29E 64 D5
Necochea Argentina 38°30S 58°50W 121 F4
Needham Market U.K. 52°9N 1°4E 31 B11
Needles, The U.K. 50°39N 1°35W 30 E5
Neenah U.S.A. 44°11N 88°28W 112 C3
Neepawa Canada 50°15N 99°30W 108 D10
Neftekumsk Russia 44°46N 44°50E 71 F7
Nefteyugansk Russia 61°5N 72°42E 76 C8
Negaunee U.S.A. 46°30N 87°36W 112 B4
Negele Ethiopia 5°20N 39°36E 89 F2
Negombo Sri Lanka 7°12N 79°50E 84 R11
Negra, Pta. Peru 6°6S 81°10W 117 D2
Negril Jamaica 18°22N 78°20W 114 a
Negro → Argentina 41°2S 62°47W 121 G3
Negro → Brazil 3°0S 60°0W 120 C3
Negros Phil. 9°30N 122°40E 83 C6
Nei Mongol Zizhiqu □ China 42°0N 112°0E 79 C11
Neijiang China 29°35N 104°55E 78 F9
Neisse → Europe 52°4N 14°46E 64 B8
Neiva Colombia 2°56N 75°18W 120 B2
Nellore India 14°27N 79°59E 84 M11
Nelson Canada 49°30N 117°20W 108 E8
Nelson N.Z. 41°18S 173°16E 99 J13
Nelson U.K. 53°50N 2°13W 27 E4
Nelson → Canada 54°33N 98°2W 108 D10
Neman → Lithuania 55°25N 21°10E 63 F8
Nen Jiang → China 45°28N 124°30E 79 B13
Nenagh Ireland 52°52N 8°11W 20 C6
Nene → U.K. 52°49N 0°11E 31 A9
Nenjiang China 49°10N 125°10E 79 B14
Neosho → U.S.A. 36°48N 95°18W 111 C7
Nepal ■ Asia 28°0N 84°30E 85 F14
Nephi U.S.A. 39°43N 111°50W 110 C4
Nephin Ireland 54°1N 9°22E 18 B2
Nephin Beg Range Ireland 54°0N 9°40W 18 C2
Nerastro, Sarīr Libya 24°20N 20°37E 95 D10
Neryungri Russia 57°38N 124°28E 77 D13
Ness, L. U.K. 57°15N 4°32W 23 H8
Neston U.K. 53°17N 3°4W 27 F2
Netherbury U.K. 50°46N 2°45W 30 E3
Netherlands ■ Europe 52°0N 5°30E 64 B3
Netherlands Antilles = ABC Islands
W. Indies 12°15N 69°0W 115 E11
Netley U.K. 50°52N 1°20W 30 D5
Nettilling L. Canada 66°30N 71°0W 109 C12
Nettlebed U.K. 51°34N 0°59W 31 C7
Nettleham U.K. 53°16N 0°29W 27 F8
Neuchâtel Switz. 47°0N 6°55E 64 E4
Neuchâtel, Lac de Switz. 46°53N 6°50E 64 E4
Neuquén Argentina 38°55S 68°0W 121 F3
Neusiedler See Austria 47°50N 16°47E 65 E9
Neva → Russia 59°56N 30°20E 70 C5
Nevada □ U.S.A. 39°0N 117°0W 110 C3
Nevers France 47°0N 3°9E 66 C5
Nevinnomyssk Russia 44°40N 42°0E 71 F7
New Abbey U.K. 54°59N 3°37S 25 E9
New Alresford U.K. 51°5N 1°8W 30 D6
New Amsterdam Guyana 6°15N 57°36W 120 B4
New Bedford U.S.A. 41°38N 70°56W 113 E12
New Britain Papua N. G. 5°50S 150°20E 98 B9
New Britain U.S.A. 41°40N 72°47W 113 E11
New Brunswick U.S.A. 40°30N 74°27W 113 E10
New Brunswick □ Canada 46°50N 66°30W 113 B14
New Caledonia ☑ Pac. Oc. 21°0S 165°0E 99 E12
New Castle Ind., U.S.A. 39°55N 85°22W 112 F5
New Castle Pa., U.S.A. 41°0N 80°21W 112 E7
New Delhi India 28°36N 77°11E 84 E10
New England U.S.A. 46°32N 102°52W 110 A6
New Forest △ U.K. 50°53N 1°34W 30 E5
New Galloway U.K. 55°5N 4°9W 24 D7
New Georgia Is. Solomon Is. 8°15S 157°30E 99 B10
New Glasgow Canada 45°35N 62°36W 109 E13
New Guinea Oceania 4°0S 136°0E 98 B7
New Hampshire □ U.S.A. 44°0N 71°30W 113 D12
New Haven U.S.A. 41°18N 72°55W 113 E11
New Hebrides = Vanuatu ■
Pac. Oc. 15°0S 168°0E 99 D12
New Holland U.K. 53°42N 0°21W 27 E8
New Iberia U.S.A. 30°1N 91°49W 111 D8
New Ireland Papua N. G. 3°20S 151°50E 98 A9
New Jersey □ U.S.A. 40°0N 74°30W 113 E10
New Lexington U.S.A. 39°43N 82°13W 112 F6
New Liskeard Canada 47°31N 79°41W 109 E12
New London U.S.A. 41°22N 72°6W 113 E11
New Madrid U.S.A. 36°36N 89°32W 112 G3
New Mexico □ U.S.A. 34°30N 106°0W 110 D5
New Mills U.K. 53°23N 2°0W 27 F5
New Milton U.K. 50°45N 1°40W 30 E5
New Orleans U.S.A. 29°57N 90°4W 111 E8
New Philadelphia U.S.A. 40°30N 81°27W 112 E7
New Plymouth N.Z. 39°4S 174°5E 99 H13
New Providence Bahamas 25°25N 77°35W 115 B9
New Quay U.K. 52°13N 4°21W 28 C5
New Radnor U.K. 52°15N 3°9W 28 C7
New Romney U.K. 50°59N 0°57E 31 E10
New Ross Ireland 52°23N 6°57W 21 D9
New Rossington U.K. 53°29N 1°4W 27 F6
New Siberian Is. Russia 75°0N 142°0E 77 B15
New South Wales □ Australia 33°0S 146°0E 98 G8
New York U.S.A. 40°43N 74°0W 113 E11
New York □ U.S.A. 43°0N 75°0W 113 D9
New Zealand ■ Oceania 40°0S 176°0E 99 J14
Newark Del., U.S.A. 39°41N 75°46W 113 F10
Newark N.J., U.S.A. 40°44N 74°10W 113 E10
Newark N.Y., U.S.A. 43°3N 77°6W 112 D9
Newark Ohio, U.S.A. 40°3N 82°24W 112 E6
Newark-on-Trent U.K. 53°5N 0°48W 27 F7
Newberry U.S.A. 46°21N 85°30W 112 B5
Newbiggin-by-the-Sea U.K. 55°11N 1°31W 26 B5
Newbigging U.K. 55°42N 3°34W 25 C8
Newbridge Ireland 53°11N 6°48W 21 B9
Newburgh U.S.A. 41°30N 74°1W 113 E10
Newburn U.K. 54°59N 1°43W 26 C5

Newbury U.K. 51°24N 1°20W 30 D6
Newburyport U.S.A. 42°49N 70°53W 113 D12
Newby Bridge U.K. 54°17N 2°57W 26 D3
Newcastle Australia 33°0S 151°46E 98 G9
Newcastle Canada 47°1N 65°38W 113 B15
Newcastle Ireland 52°27N 9°3W 20 D4
Newcastle S. Africa 27°45S 29°58E 97 K5
Newcastle Emlyn U.K. 52°2N 4°28W 28 C5
Newcastle-under-Lyme U.K. 53°1N 2°14W 27 F4
Newcastle-upon-Tyne U.K. 54°58N 1°36W 26 C5
Newcastleton U.K. 55°11N 2°49W 25 D10
Newent U.K. 51°56N 2°24W 30 C4
Newfoundland Canada 49°0N 55°0W 104 E14
Newfoundland & Labrador □
Canada 52°0N 58°0W 109 D14
Newham □ U.K. 51°31N 0°3E 31 D9
Newhaven U.K. 50°47N 0°3E 31 E9
Newington Kent, U.K. 51°6N 1°7E 31 D11
Newington Kent, U.K. 51°21N 0°41E 31 D10
Newlyn U.K. 50°6N 5°34W 29 G2
Newlyn East U.K. 50°22N 5°5W 29 G3
Newman Australia 23°18S 119°45E 98 E2
Newmarket Ireland 52°13N 9°0W 20 D5
Newmarket U.K. 52°15N 0°25E 31 B9
Newnham U.K. 51°48N 2°27W 30 C4
Newport Ireland 53°53N 9°33W 18 D2
Newport Essex, U.K. 51°59N 0°14E 31 C9
Newport I. of W., U.K. 50°42N 1°17W 30 E6
Newport Newport, U.K. 51°35N 3°0W 29 D8
Newport Pembs., U.K. 52°1N 4°51W 28 C3
Newport Telford & Wrekin, U.K. 52°46N 2°22W 27 G4
Newport Ark., U.S.A. 35°37N 91°16W 111 C8
Newport Ky., U.S.A. 39°5N 84°29W 112 F5
Newport R.I., U.S.A. 41°29N 71°19W 113 E12
Newport Vt., U.S.A. 44°56N 72°13W 113 C11
Newport News U.S.A. 36°58N 76°25W 111 C11
Newport Pagnell U.K. 52°5N 0°43W 31 B7
Newquay U.K. 50°25N 5°6W 29 G3
Newry U.K. 54°11N 6°21W 19 C9
Newton Abbot U.K. 50°32N 3°37W 29 F6
Newton Arlosh U.K. 54°53N 3°14W 26 C2
Newton Aycliffe U.K. 54°37N 1°34W 26 C6
Newton Ferrers U.K. 50°19N 4°3W 29 G5
Newton le Willows U.K. 53°28N 2°38W 27 F3
Newton St. Cyres U.K. 50°46N 3°36W 29 F6
Newton Stewart U.K. 54°57N 4°30W 24 E6
Newtonmore U.K. 57°4N 4°8W 23 H9
Newtown U.K. 52°31N 3°19W 28 B7
Newtown St. Boswells U.K. 55°34N 2°39W 25 C10
Newtownabbey U.K. 54°40N 5°56W 19 B10
Newtownards U.K. 54°36N 5°42W 19 B10
Newtownstewart U.K. 54°43N 7°23W 18 B7
Neyshābūr Iran 36°10N 58°50E 87 B9
Ngamring China 29°14N 87°10E 78 E6
Nganglong Kangri China 33°0N 81°0E 78 E5
Ngaoundéré Cameroon 7°15N 13°35E 96 C2
Ngoring Hu China 34°55N 97°5E 78 E8
Ngorongoro Tanzania 3°11S 35°32E 96 E7
Nguru Nigeria 12°56N 10°29E 95 F8
Nha Trang Vietnam 12°16N 109°10E 82 B3
Nhamundá → Brazil 2°12S 56°41W 120 C4
Niagara Falls Canada 43°7N 79°5W 109 E12
Niagara Falls U.S.A. 43°5N 79°4W 112 D8
Niamey Niger 13°27N 2°6E 94 F6
Nias Indonesia 1°0N 97°30E 82 D1
Nicaragua ■ Cent. Amer. 11°40N 85°30W 114 E7
Nicaragua, L. de Nic. 12°0N 85°30W 114 E7
Nice France 43°42N 7°14E 66 E7
Nicholasville U.S.A. 37°53N 84°34W 112 G5
Nicobar Is. Ind. Oc. 8°0N 93°30E 53 D14
Nicosia Cyprus 35°10N 33°25E 86 C3
Nicoya, Pen. de Costa Rica 9°45N 85°40W 114 F7
Nidd → U.K. 53°59N 1°23W 27 E6
Nidderdale U.K. 54°5N 1°46W 26 D5
Niedersachsen □ Germany 52°50N 9°0E 64 B5
Nieuw Nickerie Suriname 6°0N 56°59W 120 B4
Niğde Turkey 37°58N 34°40E 86 B3
Niger → W. Afr. 17°30N 10°0E 94 E7
Niger ■ W. Afr. 5°33N 6°33E 94 G7
Nigeria ■ W. Afr. 8°30N 8°0E 94 G7
Niigata Japan 37°58N 139°0E 81 E6
Ni'ihau U.S.A. 21°54N 160°9W 110 H14
Nijmegen Neths. 51°50N 5°52E 64 C3
Nikolayev Ukraine 46°58N 32°0E 71 E5
Nikolayevsk-na-Amur
Russia 53°8N 140°44E 77 D15
Nikopol Ukraine 47°35N 34°25E 71 E5
Nikšić Montenegro 42°50N 18°57E 69 C8
Nile → Africa 30°10N 31°6E 95 B12
Nimach India 24°30N 74°56E 84 G9
Nîmes France 43°50N 4°23E 66 E6
Nineveh Iraq 36°25N 43°10E 86 B5
Ninfield U.K. 50°53N 0°26E 31 E9
Ningbo China 29°51N 121°28E 79 F13
Ningjing Shan China 31°0N 98°20E 78 E8
Ningxia Hui □ China 38°0N 106°0E 78 D10
Niobrara → U.S.A. 42°46N 98°3W 110 B7
Niort France 46°19N 0°29W 66 C3
Nipawin Canada 53°20N 104°0W 108 D9
Nipigon Canada 49°0N 88°17W 112 A3
Nipigon, L. Canada 49°50N 88°30W 109 E11
Nipissing, L. Canada 46°20N 80°0W 109 E12
Niquelândia Brazil 14°33S 48°23W 122 B1
Niš Serbia 43°19N 21°58E 69 C10
Niterói Brazil 22°53S 43°7W 122 D2
Nith → U.K. 55°14N 3°33W 25 D8
Nith → U.K. 50°35N 1°17W 30 E6
Nitra Slovak Rep. 48°19N 18°4E 65 D10
Nitra → Slovak Rep. 47°46N 18°10E 65 E10
Niuafo'ou Tonga 15°30S 175°58W 99 D17
Niue ☑ Pac. Oc. 19°2S 169°54W 99 D17
Nivernais France 47°15N 3°30E 66 C5
Nizamabad India 18°45N 78°7E 84 K11
Nizhnekamsk Russia 55°38N 51°49E 70 C9
Nizhnevartovsk Russia 60°56N 76°38E 76 C8
Nizhniy Novgorod Russia 56°20N 44°0E 70 C7
Nizhniy Tagil Russia 57°55N 59°57E 70 C10
Nizhyn Ukraine 51°5N 31°55E 71 D5
Nizwá Oman 22°56N 57°32E 89 C6
Nkawkaw Ghana 6°36N 0°49W 94 G5

Nkongsamba Cameroon 4°55N 9°55E 96 D1
Noakhali Bangla. 22°48N 91°10E 85 H17
Nobeoka Japan 32°36N 131°41E 81 G2
Noblesville U.S.A. 40°3N 86°1W 112 E5
Nogales Mexico 31°19N 110°56W 114 A2
Nogales U.S.A. 31°21N 110°56W 110 D4
Noirmoutier, Î. de France 46°58N 2°10W 66 C2
Nola C.A.R. 3°35N 16°4E 96 D3
Nome U.S.A. 64°30N 165°25W 108 C3
Nord-Ostsee-Kanal Germany 54°12N 9°32E 64 A5
Nordelph U.K. 52°35N 0°17E 31 A9
Norderstedt Germany 53°42N 10°1E 64 B6
Nordfriesische Inseln Germany 54°40N 8°20E 64 A5
Nordkapp Norway 71°10N 25°50E 63 C9
Nordrhein-Westfalen □
Germany 51°45N 7°30E 64 C4
Nordvik Russia 74°2N 111°32E 77 B12
Nore → Ireland 52°25N 6°58W 21 D9
Norfolk Nebr., U.S.A. 42°2N 97°25W 111 B7
Norfolk Va., U.S.A. 36°50N 76°17W 111 C11
Norfolk □ U.K. 52°39N 0°54E 31 A10
Norfolk Broads △ U.K. 52°45N 1°30E 31 A11
Norfolk I. Pac. Oc. 28°58S 168°3E 99 F12
Norham U.K. 55°43N 2°9W 26 A4
Norilsk Russia 69°20N 88°6E 77 C9
Normal U.S.A. 40°31N 88°59W 112 E3
Norman U.S.A. 35°13N 97°26W 111 C7
Norman Wells Canada 65°17N 126°51W 108 C7
Normandie France 48°45N 0°10E 66 B4
Normanton Australia 17°40S 141°10E 98 D7
Normanton U.K. 53°42N 1°24W 27 E6
Norristown U.S.A. 40°7N 75°21W 113 E10
Norrköping Sweden 58°37N 16°11E 63 F7
Norrland Sweden 62°15N 15°45E 63 E7
Norseman Australia 32°8S 121°43E 98 G3
Norte, Serra do Brazil 11°20S 59°0W 120 D4
North, C. Canada 47°2N 60°20W 113 B17
North America 40°0N 100°0W 104 F10
North Ayrshire □ U.K. 55°45N 4°44W 24 C6
North Battleford Canada 52°50N 108°17W 108 D9
North Bay Canada 46°20N 79°30W 109 E12
North Berwick U.K. 56°4N 2°42W 25 B10
North C. Canada 47°5N 64°0W 113 B15
North C. N.Z. 34°23S 173°4E 99 F13
North Canadian → U.S.A. 35°22N 95°37W 110 C7
North Carolina □ U.S.A. 35°30N 80°0W 111 C11
North Cerney U.K. 51°45N 1°57W 30 C5
North Channel Canada 46°0N 83°0W 112 B6
North Channel U.K. 55°13N 5°52W 24 D4
North Dakota □ U.S.A. 47°30N 100°15W 110 A7
North Dorset Downs U.K. 50°51N 2°30W 30 E4
North Downs U.K. 51°19N 0°21E 31 D9
North Esk → U.K. 56°46N 2°24W 23 J13
North European Plain Europe 55°0N 25°0E 56 E10
North Foreland U.K. 51°22N 1°28E 31 D11
North Harris U.K. 58°0N 6°55W 22 F4
North Hill U.K. 50°33N 4°27W 29 F5
North Hykeham U.K. 53°11N 0°35W 27 F7
North I. N.Z. 38°0S 175°0E 99 H14
North Korea ■ Asia 40°0N 127°0E 79 D14
North Magnetic Pole Arctic 82°42N 114°24W 54 A2
North Minch U.K. 58°5N 5°55W 22 F6
North Molton U.K. 51°3N 3°49W 29 E6
North Ossetia □ Russia 43°30N 44°30E 71 F7
North Petherton U.K. 51°5N 3°1W 30 D2
North Platte U.S.A. 41°8N 100°46W 110 B6
North Platte → U.S.A. 41°7N 100°42W 110 B6
North Pole Arctic 90°0N 0°0 54 A
North Pt. Barbados 13°20N 59°37W 114 c
North Ronaldsay U.K. 59°22N 2°26W 23 D12
North Saskatchewan →
Canada 53°15N 105°5W 108 D9
North Sea Europe 56°0N 4°0E 56 D6
North Sea Canal = Nord-Ostsee-Kanal
Germany 54°12N 9°32E 64 A5
North Somercotes U.K. 53°27N 0°8E 27 F9
North Sunderland U.K. 55°34N 1°40W 26 A5
North Tawton U.K. 50°48N 3°54W 29 F6
North Thompson →
Canada 50°40N 120°20W 108 D7
North Thoresby U.K. 53°28N 0°4W 27 F8
North Tidworth U.K. 51°15N 1°40W 30 D5
North Tyne → U.K. 55°0N 2°8W 26 C4
North Uist U.K. 57°40N 7°15W 22 G3
North Vernon U.S.A. 39°0N 85°38W 112 F5
North Walsham U.K. 52°50N 1°22E 31 A11
North West C. Australia 21°45S 114°9E 98 E1
North West Frontier □ Pakistan 34°0N 72°0E 84 B8
North West Highlands U.K. 57°33N 4°58W 23 H8
North York Moors △ U.K. 54°27N 0°51W 26 D7
North Yorkshire □ U.K. 54°15N 1°25W 26 D6
Northallerton U.K. 54°20N 1°26W 26 D6
Northam Australia 31°35S 116°42E 98 G2
Northam U.K. 51°2N 4°13W 29 E5
Northampton U.K. 52°15N 0°53W 31 B7
Northamptonshire □ U.K. 52°16N 0°55W 31 B7
Northern Areas □ Pakistan 36°30N 73°0E 84 B9
Northern Circars India 17°30N 82°30E 85 L13
Northern Ireland □ U.K. 54°45N 7°0W 19 B8
Northern Marianas ☑ Pac. Oc. 17°0N 145°0E 102 F6
Northern Sporades Greece 39°15N 23°30E 69 E10
Northern Territory □ Australia 20°0S 133°0E 98 E5
Northfleet U.K. 51°26N 0°20E 31 D9
Northiam U.K. 50°59N 0°36E 31 E10
Northleach U.K. 51°49N 1°50W 30 C5
Northrepps U.K. 52°54N 1°21E 31 A11
Northumberland □ Northumberland,
U.K. 55°15N 2°20W 26 B4
Northumberland Str.
Canada 46°20N 64°0W 109 E13
Northwest Territories □
Canada 63°0N 118°0W 108 C9
Northwich U.K. 53°15N 2°31W 27 F3
Northwold U.K. 52°33N 0°36E 31 A10
Norton N. Yorks., U.K. 54°8N 0°47W 26 D7
Norton Suffolk, U.K. 52°16N 0°52E 31 B10
Norton Fitzwarren U.K. 51°1N 3°8W 30 D2
Norton Sd. U.S.A. 63°50N 164°0W 108 C3

Norwalk U.S.A. 41°15N 82°37W 112 E6
Norway ■ Europe 63°0N 11°0E 63 E6
Norway House Canada 53°59N 97°50W 108 D10
Norwegian B. Canada 77°30N 90°0W 109 B11
Norwegian Sea Atl. Oc. 66°0N 1°0E 56 B6
Norwich U.K. 52°38N 1°18E 31 A11
Norwich U.S.A. 42°32N 75°32W 113 D10
Noss Hd. U.K. 58°28N 3°3W 23 F11
Nossa Senhora do Socorro
Brazil 10°52S 37°7W 122 B3
Nossob → S. Africa 26°55S 20°45E 97 K4
Notre Dame B. Canada 49°45N 55°30W 109 E14
Nottaway → Canada 51°22N 78°55W 109 D12
Nottingham U.K. 52°58N 1°10W 27 G6
Nottingham I. Canada 63°20N 77°55W 109 C12
Nottinghamshire □ U.K. 53°10N 1°3W 27 F6
Nouâdhibou Mauritania 20°54N 17°0W 94 D2
Nouâdhibou, Râs Mauritania 20°50N 17°0W 94 D2
Nouakchott Mauritania 18°9N 15°58W 94 E2
Nouméa N. Cal. 22°17S 166°30E 99 E12
Nova Friburgo Brazil 22°16S 42°30W 122 D2
Nova Iguaçu Brazil 22°45S 43°28W 122 D2
Nova Scotia □ Canada 45°10N 63°0W 113 C16
Nova Venécia Brazil 18°45S 40°24W 122 C2
Novara Italy 45°28N 8°38E 68 B3
Novaya Zemlya Russia 75°0N 56°0E 76 B6
Novgorod Russia 58°30N 31°25E 70 C5
Novi Pazar Serbia 43°12N 20°28E 69 C9
Novi Sad Serbia 45°18N 19°52E 69 B8
Novocherkassk Russia 47°27N 40°15E 71 E7
Novokuybyshevsk Russia 53°7N 49°58E 70 D8
Novokuznetsk Russia 53°45N 87°10E 76 D9
Novomoskovsk Russia 54°5N 38°15E 70 D6
Novorossiysk Russia 44°43N 37°46E 71 F6
Novoshakhtinsk Russia 47°46N 39°58E 71 E6
Novosibirsk Russia 55°0N 83°5E 76 D9
Novotroitsk Russia 51°10N 58°15E 70 D10
Novyy Urengoy Russia 65°48N 76°52E 76 C8
Nowy Sącz Poland 49°40N 20°41E 65 D11
Noyabrsk Russia 64°34N 76°21E 76 C8
Nu Jiang → China 29°58N 97°25E 78 F8
Nu Shan China 26°0N 99°20E 78 F8
Nubia Africa 21°0N 32°0E 90 D7
Nubian Desert Sudan 21°30N 33°30E 90 D7
Nueces → U.S.A. 27°51N 97°30W 110 E7
Nueltin L. Canada 60°30N 99°30W 108 C10
Nueva Rosita Mexico 27°57N 101°13W 114 B4
Nuevitas Cuba 21°30N 77°20S 115 C9
Nuevo Laredo Mexico 27°30N 99°31W 114 B5
Nuku'alofa Tonga 21°10S 175°12W 99 E16
Nukulaelae Tuvalu 9°23S 179°52E 99 B14
Nukus Uzbekistan 42°27N 59°41E 87 A9
Nullarbor Plain Australia 31°10S 129°0E 98 G4
Numan Nigeria 9°29N 12°3E 95 G8
Numazu Japan 35°7N 138°51E 81 F6
Nunavut □ Canada 66°0N 85°0W 109 C11
Nuneaton U.K. 52°32N 1°27W 27 G6
Nunivak I. U.S.A. 60°10N 166°30W 108 B3
Nunney U.K. 51°12N 2°22W 30 D4
Nuoro Italy 40°20N 9°20E 68 D3
Nuremberg Germany 49°27N 11°3E 64 D6
Nusaybin Turkey 37°3N 41°10E 71 G7
Nuuk Greenland 64°10N 51°35W 54 C5
Nuweveldberge S. Africa 32°10S 21°45E 97 L4
Nyagan Russia 62°30N 65°38E 76 C7
Nyahururu Kenya 0°2N 36°27E 96 D7
Nyaingêntanglha Shan China 30°0N 90°0E 78 F7
Nyâlâ Sudan 12°2N 24°58E 95 F10
Nyalam China 28°32N 86°4E 78 F6
Nyíregyháza Hungary 47°58N 21°47E 65 E11
Nysa Poland 50°30N 17°22E 65 C9
Nzérékoré Guinea 7°49N 8°48W 94 G4

O

Oa, Mull of U.K. 55°35N 6°20W 24 C3
Oadby U.K. 52°36N 1°5W 27 G6
Oahe, L. U.S.A. 44°27N 100°24W 110 A6
O'ahu U.S.A. 21°28N 157°58W 110 H16
Oak Hill U.S.A. 37°59N 81°9W 112 G7
Oak Ridge U.S.A. 36°1N 84°16W 111 C10
Oakengates U.K. 52°41N 2°26W 27 G4
Oakham U.K. 52°40N 0°43W 27 G7
Oakland U.S.A. 37°48N 122°18W 110 C2
Oates Land Antarctica 69°0S 160°0E 55 C11
Oaxaca Mexico 17°3N 96°43W 114 D5
Ob → Russia 66°45N 69°30E 76 C7
Ob, G. of Russia 69°0N 73°0E 76 C8
Oba Canada 49°4N 84°7W 109 E11
Oban U.K. 56°25N 5°29W 24 B5
Oberhausen Germany 51°28N 6°51E 64 C4
Obi, Kepulauan Indonesia 1°23S 127°45E 83 E7
Óbidos Brazil 1°50S 55°30W 120 C4
Obihiro Japan 42°56N 143°12E 81 B8
Obozerskiy Russia 63°34N 40°21E 70 B7
Obshchi Syrt Russia 52°0N 53°0E 56 E16
Ocala U.S.A. 29°11N 82°8W 111 E10
Occidental, Cordillera Colombia 5°0N 76°0W 117 C3
Occidental, Grand Erg Algeria 30°20N 1°0E 94 B6
Ocean City U.S.A. 39°17N 74°35W 113 F10
Oceanside U.S.A. 33°12N 117°23W 110 D3
Ochil Hills U.K. 56°14N 3°40W 25 B8
Ocho Rios Jamaica 18°24N 77°6W 114 a
Oconto U.S.A. 44°53N 87°52W 112 C4
Odawara Japan 35°20N 139°6E 81 F6
Odense Denmark 55°22N 10°23E 63 F6
Oder → Europe 53°33N 14°38E 64 B8
Odessa Ukraine 46°30N 30°45E 71 E5
Odessa U.S.A. 31°52N 102°23W 110 D6
Odiham U.K. 51°15N 0°55W 31 D7
Odintsovo Russia 55°40N 37°16E 70 C6
Odzi Zimbabwe 19°0S 32°20E 97 H6
Offa Nigeria 8°13N 4°42E 94 G6
Offaly □ Ireland 53°15N 7°30W 21 B8
Offenbach Germany 50°6N 8°44E 64 C5
Ogaden Ethiopia 7°30N 45°30E 89 F3
Ōgaki Japan 35°21N 136°37E 81 F5
Ogasawara Gunto Pac. Oc. 27°0N 142°0E 102 E6
Ogbomosho Nigeria 8°1N 4°11E 94 G6
Ogden U.S.A. 41°13N 111°58W 110 B4
Ogdensburg U.S.A. 44°42N 75°30W 113 C10

Ogooué → Gabon 1°0S 9°0E 96 E1
Ohio □ U.S.A. 40°15N 82°45W 112 E5
Ohio → U.S.A. 36°59N 89°8W 111 C9
Ohře → Czech Rep. 50°30N 14°10E 64 C8
Ohrid, L. Macedonia 41°8N 20°52E 69 D9
Oil City U.S.A. 41°26N 79°42W 112 E8
Oise → France 49°0N 2°4E 66 B5
Oistins Barbados 13°4N 59°33W 114 c
Oistins B. Barbados 13°4N 59°33W 114 c
Ōita Japan 33°14N 131°36E 81 G2
Ojos del Salado, Cerro
Argentina 27°0S 68°40W 121 E3
Oka → Russia 56°20N 43°59E 70 C7
Okara Pakistan 30°50N 73°31E 84 D8
Okavango Delta Botswana 18°45S 22°45E 97 H4
Okayama Japan 34°40N 133°54E 81 F3
Okazaki Japan 34°57N 137°10E 81 F5
Okeechobee, L. U.S.A. 27°0N 80°50W 111 E10
Okehampton U.K. 50°44N 4°0W 29 F5
Okhotsk Russia 59°20N 143°10E 77 D15
Okhotsk, Sea of Asia 55°0N 145°0E 77 D15
Oki-Shotō Japan 36°5N 133°15E 81 E3
Okinawa-Jima Japan 26°32N 128°0E 79 F14
Oklahoma □ U.S.A. 35°20N 97°30W 110 C7
Oklahoma City U.S.A. 35°30N 97°30W 110 C7
Oktyabrskiy Russia 54°28N 53°28E 70 D9
Öland Sweden 56°45N 16°38E 63 F7
Olavarría Argentina 36°55S 60°20W 121 F3
Olbia Italy 40°55N 9°31E 68 D3
Old Basing U.K. 51°16N 1°3W 30 D6
Old Crow Canada 67°30N 139°55W 108 C6
Old Fletton U.K. 52°33N 0°14W 31 A8
Old Leake U.K. 53°2N 0°5E 27 F9
Old Town U.S.A. 44°56N 68°39W 113 C13
Oldbury U.K. 51°38N 2°33W 30 C3
Oldcastle Ireland 53°46N 7°10W 18 D7
Oldenburg Germany 53°9N 8°13E 64 B5
Oldham U.K. 53°33N 2°7W 27 F4
Oldmeldrum U.K. 57°20N 2°19W 23 H13
Olean U.S.A. 42°5N 78°26W 112 D8
Olekminsk Russia 60°25N 120°30E 77 C13
Olenek → Russia 73°0N 120°10E 77 B13
Oléron, Î. d' France 45°55N 1°15W 66 D3
Ölgiy Mongolia 48°56N 89°57E 78 B6
Olimpia Brazil 20°44S 48°54W 122 D1
Oliveira Brazil 20°39S 44°50W 122 D2
Ollagüe Chile 21°15S 68°10W 120 E3
Ollerton U.K. 53°12N 1°1W 27 F6
Olmaliq Uzbekistan 40°50N 69°35E 76 E7
Olney U.K. 52°10N 0°41W 31 B7
Olney U.S.A. 38°44N 88°5W 112 F3
Olomouc Czech Rep. 49°38N 17°12E 65 D9
Olsztyn Poland 53°48N 20°29E 65 B11
Olt → Romania 43°43N 24°51E 65 G13
Olympia Greece 37°39N 21°39E 69 F9
Olympia U.S.A. 47°3N 122°53W 110 A2
Olympus, Mt. Greece 40°6N 22°23E 69 D10
Olympus, Mt. U.S.A. 47°48N 123°43W 110 A2
Omagh U.K. 54°36N 7°19W 18 B7
Omaha U.S.A. 41°17N 95°58W 111 B7
Oman ■ Asia 23°0N 58°0E 89 C6
Oman, G. of Asia 24°30N 58°30E 87 E9
Ombersley U.K. 52°16N 2°13W 30 B4
Omdurmân Sudan 15°40N 32°28E 95 E12
Ometepec Mexico 16°41N 98°25W 114 D5
Omsk Russia 55°0N 73°12E 76 D8
Ōmuta Japan 33°5N 130°26E 81 G2
Ondangwa Namibia 17°57S 16°4E 97 H3
Öndörhaan Mongolia 47°19N 110°39E 79 B11
Onega → Russia 63°58N 38°2E 70 B6
Onega, L. Russia 61°44N 35°22E 70 B6
Onega B. Russia 64°24N 36°38E 70 B6
Oneida U.S.A. 43°6N 75°39W 113 D10
O'Neill U.S.A. 42°27N 98°39W 110 B7
Oneonta U.S.A. 42°27N 75°4W 113 D10
Onitsha Nigeria 6°6N 6°42E 94 G7
Onny → U.K. 52°24N 2°47W 27 H3
Onslow B. U.S.A. 34°20N 77°15W 111 D11
Onslow Australia 44°2N 116°58W 110 B3
Ontario □ Canada 48°0N 83°0W 109 E11
Ontario, L. N. Amer. 43°20N 78°0W 112 D8
Ontonagon U.S.A. 46°52N 89°19W 112 B3
Oostende Belgium 51°15N 2°54E 64 C2
Opava Czech Rep. 49°57N 17°58E 65 D9
Opole Poland 50°42N 17°58E 65 C9
Oradea Romania 47°2N 21°58E 65 E11
Órafajökull Iceland 64°2N 16°39W 63 B2
Oral Kazakhstan 51°20N 51°20E 71 D9
Oran Algeria 35°45N 0°39W 94 A5
Orange Australia 33°15S 149°7E 98 G8
Orange France 44°8N 4°47E 66 D6
Orange → S. Africa 28°41S 16°28E 97 K3
Orange, C. Brazil 4°20N 51°30W 120 B4
Orangeburg U.S.A. 33°30N 80°52W 111 D10
Orangeville Canada 43°55N 80°5W 112 D7
Ordos Desert China 39°0N 109°0E 79 D10
Ordu Turkey 40°55N 37°53E 71 F6
Örebro Sweden 59°20N 15°18E 63 F7
Oregon □ U.S.A. 44°0N 121°0W 110 B2
Orekhovo-Zuyevo Russia 55°50N 38°55E 70 C6
Orel Russia 52°57N 36°3E 70 D6
Orem U.S.A. 40°19N 111°42W 110 B4
Orenburg Russia 51°45N 55°6E 70 D10
Orford U.K. 52°5N 1°33E 31 B12
Orford Ness U.K. 52°5N 1°35E 31 B12
Oriental, Cordillera Colombia 6°0N 73°0W 117 C3
Oriental, Grand Erg Algeria 30°0N 6°30E 94 B7
Orihuela Spain 38°7N 0°55W 67 C5
Orinoco → Venezuela 9°15N 61°30W 120 B3
Orissa □ India 20°0N 84°0E 85 K14
Oristano Italy 39°54N 8°36E 68 E3
Orizaba Mexico 18°51N 97°6W 114 D5
Orizaba, Pico de Mexico 18°58N 97°15W 114 D5
Orkhon → Mongolia 50°21N 106°0E 78 A10
Orkney □ U.K. 59°2N 3°13W 23 D11
Orkney Is. U.K. 59°0N 3°0W 23 E12
Orléanais France 48°0N 2°0E 66 C5
Orléans France 47°54N 1°52E 66 C4
Orléans, Î. d' Canada 46°54N 70°58W 113 B12

Ormara

Pori

Ormara Pakistan 25°16N 64°33E 84 G4
Ormesby St. Margaret U.K. 52°41N 1°41E 31 A12
Ormoc Phil. 11°0N 124°37E 83 B6
Ormskirk U.K. 53°35N 2°54W 27 E3
Örnsköldsvik Sweden 63°17N 18°40E 63 E7
Oronsay U.K. 56°1N 6°15W 24 B3
Orsha Belarus 54°30N 30°25E 70 D5
Ortegal, C. Spain 43°43N 7°52W 67 A2
Oruro Bolivia 18°0S 67°9W 120 D3
Orwell → U.K. 51°59N 1°18E 31 C11
Ōsaka Japan 34°42N 135°30E 81 F4
Osh Kyrgyzstan 40°37N 72°49E 76 E8
Oshakati Namibia 17°45S 15°40E 97 H3
Oshawa Canada 43°50N 78°50W 109 E12
Oshkosh U.S.A. 44°1N 88°33W 112 D3
Oshogbo Nigeria 7°48N 4°37E 94 G6
Osijek Croatia 45°34N 18°41E 69 B8
Osizweni S. Africa 27°49S 30°7E 97 K6
Oskaloosa U.S.A. 41°18N 92°39W 111 B8
Oskarshamn Sweden 57°15N 16°27E 63 F7
Öskemen Kazakhstan 50°0N 82°36E 76 E9
Oslo Norway 59°54N 10°43E 63 F6
Oslofjorden Norway 59°20N 10°35E 63 F6
Osmaniye Turkey 37°5N 36°10E 71 G6
Osmotherley U.K. 54°22N 1°18W 26 D6
Osnabrück Germany 52°17N 8°3E 64 B5
Osorno Chile 40°25S 73°0W 121 G2
Ossa, Mt. Australia 41°52S 146°3E 98 J8
Ossett U.K. 53°41N 1°34W 27 E5
Ostend = Oostende Belgium 51°15N 2°54E 64 C2
Österdalälven → Sweden 60°30N 15°7E 63 E6
Östersund Sweden 63°10N 14°38E 63 E6
Ostfriesische Inseln Germany 53°42N 7°0E 64 B4
Ostrava Czech Rep. 49°51N 18°18E 65 D10
Ostrołęka Poland 53°4N 21°32E 65 B11
Ostrów Wielkopolski Poland 51°36N 17°44E 65 C9
Ostrowiec-Świętokrzyski Poland 50°55N 21°22E 65 C11
Oswaldtwistle U.K. 53°43N 2°26W 27 E4
Oswego U.S.A. 43°27N 76°31W 112 D9
Oswestry U.K. 52°52N 3°3W 27 G2
Otaru Japan 43°10N 141°0E 81 B7
Otjiwarongo Namibia 20°30S 16°33E 97 J3
Otley U.K. 53°54N 1°41W 27 E5
Otranto Italy 40°9N 18°28E 69 D8
Otranto, Str. of Italy 40°15N 18°40E 69 D8
Ōtsu Japan 35°0N 135°50E 81 F4
Ottawa Canada 45°26N 75°42W 113 C10
Ottawa U.S.A. 41°21N 88°51W 112 E3
Ottawa Is. Canada 59°35N 80°10W 109 D11
Otter → U.K. 50°38N 3°19W 29 F7
Otterburn U.K. 55°14N 2°11W 26 B4
Ottery St. Mary U.K. 50°44N 3°17W 29 F7
Ottumwa U.S.A. 41°1N 92°25W 111 B8
Ouachita → U.S.A. 31°38N 91°49W 111 D8
Ouachita Mts. U.S.A. 34°30N 94°30W 111 D8
Ouagadougou Burkina Faso 12°25N 1°30W 94 F5
Oubangi → Dem. Rep. of the Congo 0°30S 17°50E 96 E3
Oudtshoorn S. Africa 33°35S 22°14E 97 L4
Ouezzane Morocco 34°51N 5°35W 94 B4
Oughterard Ireland 53°26N 9°18W 20 B4
Oujda Morocco 34°41N 1°55W 94 B5
Oulton U.K. 52°30N 1°43E 31 B12
Oulton Broad U.K. 52°28N 1°42E 31 B12
Oulu Finland 65°1N 25°29E 63 D9
Oulujärvi Finland 64°25N 27°15E 63 E9
Oulujoki → Finland 65°1N 25°30E 63 D9
Oundle U.K. 52°29N 0°28W 31 B8
Ourense Spain 42°19N 7°55W 67 A2
Ouro Fino Brazil 22°16S 46°25W 122 D1
Ouro Prêto Brazil 20°20S 43°30W 122 D2
Ouse → E. Sussex, U.K. 50°47N 0°4E 31 E9
Ouse → N. Yorks., U.K. 53°44N 0°55W 27 E7
Outaouais → Canada 45°27N 74°8W 109 E12
Outer Hebrides U.K. 57°30N 7°15W 22 H2
Outjo Namibia 20°5S 16°7E 97 J3
Outwell U.K. 52°37N 0°14E 31 B9
Ovalle Chile 30°33S 71°18W 121 F2
Ovamboland Namibia 18°30S 16°0E 97 H3
Over Wallop U.K. 51°9N 1°36W 30 D5
Overton U.K. 51°15N 1°15W 30 D5
Oviedo Spain 43°25N 5°50W 67 A3
Owatonna U.S.A. 44°5N 93°14W 111 C8
Owen Sound Canada 44°35N 80°55W 109 E11
Owen Stanley Ra. Papua N. G. 8°30S 147°0E 98 B8
Owens → U.S.A. 36°26N 117°57W 110 C3
Owensboro U.S.A. 37°46N 87°7W 112 G4
Owo Nigeria 7°10N 5°39E 94 G7
Owosso U.S.A. 43°0N 84°10W 112 D5
Owston Ferry U.K. 53°29N 0°47W 27 F7
Owyhee → U.S.A. 43°49N 117°2W 110 B3
Oxford U.K. 51°46N 1°15W 30 C6
Oxfordshire □ U.K. 51°48N 1°16W 30 C6
Oxnard U.S.A. 34°12N 119°11W 110 D3
Oyama Japan 36°18N 139°48E 81 E6
Oyem Gabon 1°34N 11°31E 96 D2
Oykel → U.K. 57°56N 4°26W 23 G9
Oyo Nigeria 7°46N 3°56E 94 G6
Ozark Plateau U.S.A. 37°20N 91°40W 111 C8
Ozarks, L. of the U.S.A. 38°12N 92°38W 111 C8

P

Paarl S. Africa 33°45S 18°56E 97 L3
Pab Hills Pakistan 26°30N 66°45E 84 F5
Pabaidh = Pabbay U.K. 57°46N 7°14W 22 G3
Pabbay U.K. 57°46N 7°14W 22 G3
Pabna Bangla. 24°1N 89°18E 85 G16
Pacaraima, Sa. S. Amer. 4°0N 62°30W 120 B3
Pacasmayo Peru 7°20S 79°35W 120 C2
Pachuca Mexico 20°7N 98°44W 114 C5
Pacific Ocean 10°0N 140°0W 103 G14
Padang Indonesia 1°0S 100°20E 82 E2
Padangsidempuan Indonesia 1°30N 99°15E 82 D1
Paddock Wood U.K. 51°11N 0°24E 31 D9
Paderborn Germany 51°42N 8°45E 64 C5
Padiham U.K. 53°48N 2°18W 27 E4
Padre I. U.S.A. 27°10N 97°25W 111 E7
Padstow U.K. 50°33N 4°58W 29 F4
Padstow B. U.K. 50°34N 4°57W 29 F4

Padua Italy 45°25N 11°53E 68 B4
Paducah U.S.A. 37°5N 88°37W 112 G3
Pag Croatia 44°25N 15°3E 68 B6
Pagadian Phil. 7°55N 123°30E 83 C6
Page U.S.A. 36°57N 111°27W 110 C4
Pāhala U.S.A. 19°12N 155°29W 110 J17
Paignton U.K. 50°26N 3°35W 29 G6
Paine Grande, Cerro Chile 50°59S 73°4W 121 H2
Painesville U.S.A. 41°43N 81°15W 112 E7
Painswick U.K. 51°47N 2°10W 30 C4
Painted Desert U.S.A. 36°0N 111°0W 110 C4
Paintsville U.S.A. 37°49N 82°48W 112 G6
Pais Vasco □ Spain 42°50N 2°45W 67 A4
Paisley U.K. 55°50N 4°25W 24 C7
Paita Peru 5°11S 81°9W 120 C1
Pakistan ■ Asia 30°0N 70°0E 84 E7
Pakxe Laos 15°5N 105°52E 82 A3
Palani Hills India 10°14N 77°33E 84 P10
Palanpur India 24°10N 72°25E 84 G8
Palapye Botswana 22°30S 27°7E 97 J5
Palau ■ Palau 7°30N 134°30E 102 G5
Palawan Phil. 9°30N 118°30E 82 C5
Palembang indonesia 3°0S 104°50E 82 E2
Palencia Spain 42°1N 4°34W 67 A3
Palermo Italy 38°7N 13°22E 68 E5
Palestine U.S.A. 31°46N 95°38W 111 D7
Palghat India 10°46N 76°42E 84 P10
Palgrave U.K. 52°22N 1°6E 31 B11
Pali India 25°50N 73°20E 84 G8
Palikir Micronesia 6°55N 158°9E 102 G7
Palk Strait Asia 10°0N 79°45E 84 Q11
Palm Springs U.S.A. 33°50N 116°33W 110 D3
Palma de Mallorca Spain 39°35N 2°39E 67 C7
Palmares Brazil 8°41S 35°28W 122 A3
Palmas Brazil 10°12S 48°21W 122 B1
Palmas, C. Liberia 4°27N 7°46W 94 H4
Palmeira dos Índios Brazil 9°25S 36°37W 122 A3
Palmer U.S.A. 61°36N 149°7W 108 C5
Palmer Land Antarctica 73°0S 63°0W 55 D18
Palmerston North N.Z. 40°21S 175°39E 99 J14
Palmira Colombia 3°32N 76°16W 120 B2
Palmyra Syria 34°36N 38°15E 86 C4
Palmyra Is. Pac. Oc. 5°52N 162°5W 103 G11
Palopo Indonesia 3°0S 120°16E 83 E6
Palu Indonesia 1°0S 119°52E 83 E5
Palu Turkey 38°45N 40°0E 71 G7
Pamiers France 43°7N 1°39E 66 E4
Pamir Tajikistan 37°40N 73°0E 87 B13
Pamlico Sd. U.S.A. 35°20N 76°0W 111 C11
Pampa U.S.A. 35°32N 100°58W 110 C6
Pampas Argentina 35°0S 63°0W 121 F3
Pamplona-Iruña Spain 42°48N 1°38W 67 A5
Pana U.S.A. 39°23N 89°5W 112 F3
Panaji India 15°25N 73°50E 84 M8
Panamá Panama 9°0N 79°25W 115 F9
Panama ■ Cent. Amer. 8°48N 79°55W 115 F9
Panamá, G. de Panama 8°4N 79°20W 115 F9
Panama, Isthmus of Cent. Amer. 9°0N 79°0W 115 F9
Panama Canal Panama 9°10N 79°37W 115 F9
Panama City U.S.A. 30°10N 85°40W 111 D9
Panay Phil. 11°10N 122°30E 83 B6
Pančevo Serbia 44°52N 20°41E 69 B9
Panevėžys Lithuania 55°42N 24°25E 63 F8
Pangani Tanzania 5°25S 38°58E 96 F7
Pangbourne U.K. 51°29N 1°6W 30 D6
Pangkalpinang Indonesia 2°10S 106°10E 82 E3
Pangnirtung Canada 66°8N 65°43W 109 C13
Pantar Indonesia 8°28S 124°10E 83 F6
Pante Macassar E. Timor 9°30S 123°58E 83 F6
Pantelleria Italy 36°50N 11°57E 68 F4
Panzhihua China 26°33N 101°44E 78 F9
Papa Stour U.K. 60°20N 1°42W 22 A14
Papa Westray U.K. 59°20N 2°55W 23 D12
Papantla Mexico 20°27N 97°19W 114 C5
Papeete Tahiti 17°32S 149°34W 103 J13
Paphos Cyprus 34°46N 32°25E 86 C3
Papua □ Indonesia 4°0S 137°0E 83 E9
Papua, G. of Papua N. G. 9°0S 144°50E 98 B7
Papua New Guinea ■ Oceania 8°0S 145°0E 98 B8
Pará □ Brazil 3°20S 52°0W 120 C4
Paracatu Brazil 17°10S 46°50W 122 C1
Paracel Is. S. China Sea 15°50N 112°0E 82 A4
Paragould U.S.A. 36°3N 90°29W 111 C8
Paraguaçu → Brazil 12°45S 38°54W 122 B3
Paraguaná, Pen. de Venezuela 12°0N 70°0W 120 A3
Paraguarí Paraguay 25°36S 57°0W 121 E4
Paraguay ■ S. Amer. 23°0S 57°0W 121 E4
Paraguay → Paraguay 27°18S 58°38W 121 E4
Paraíba □ Brazil 7°0S 36°0W 120 C6
Parakou Benin 9°25N 2°40E 94 G6
Paramaribo Suriname 5°50N 55°10W 120 B4
Paraná Argentina 31°45S 60°30W 121 F3
Paraná Brazil 12°30S 47°48W 122 B1
Paraná □ Brazil 24°30S 51°0W 121 E4
Paraná → Argentina 33°43S 59°15W 121 F4
Paranaguá Brazil 25°30S 48°30W 122 E1
Paranaíba → Brazil 20°6S 51°4W 120 E4
Paranapanema → Brazil 22°40S 53°9W 121 E4
Parbhani India 19°8N 76°52E 84 K10
Pardo → Brazil 15°40S 39°0W 122 C3
Pardubice Czech Rep. 50°3N 15°45E 64 C8
Parecis, Serra dos Brazil 13°0S 60°0W 120 D4
Parepare Indonesia 4°0S 119°40E 83 E5
Parima, Serra Brazil 2°30N 64°0W 120 B3
Pariñas, Pta. Peru 4°30S 82°0W 117 D2
Parintins Brazil 2°40S 56°50W 120 C4
Pariparit Kyun Burma 14°52N 93°41E 85 M18
Paris France 48°53N 2°20E 66 B5
Paris U.S.A. 33°40N 95°33W 111 D7
Park Falls U.S.A. 45°56N 90°27W 112 C2
Parkersburg U.S.A. 39°16N 81°34W 112 F7
Parla Spain 40°14N 3°46W 67 B4
Parma Italy 44°48N 10°20E 68 B4
Parnaguá Brazil 10°10S 44°38W 122 B2
Parnaíba Brazil 2°54S 41°47W 120 C5
Parnaíba → Brazil 3°0S 41°50W 120 C5
Pärnu Estonia 58°28N 24°33E 63 F8
Paros Greece 37°5N 25°12E 69 F11
Parracombe U.K. 51°11N 3°56W 29 E6
Parrett → U.K. 51°12N 3°1W 30 D2

Parry Is. Canada 77°0N 110°0W 109 B9
Parry Sound Canada 45°20N 80°0W 109 E12
Parsons U.S.A. 37°20N 95°16W 111 C7
Partney U.K. 53°12N 0°7E 27 F9
Parton U.K. 54°35N 3°33W 26 C1
Partry Mts. Ireland 53°40N 9°28W 18 D3
Paru → Brazil 1°33S 52°38W 120 C4
Pasadena Calif., U.S.A. 34°9N 118°8W 110 D3
Pasadena Tex., U.S.A. 29°43N 95°13W 111 E7
Paschimbanga □ India 23°0N 88°0E 85 H16
Pascua, I. de Chile 27°7S 109°23W 103 K17
Paso Robles U.S.A. 35°38N 120°41W 110 C2
Passage West Ireland 51°52N 8°21W 20 E6
Passau Germany 48°34N 13°28E 64 D7
Passo Fundo Brazil 28°10S 52°20W 121 E4
Passos Brazil 20°45S 46°37W 122 D1
Pastaza → Peru 4°50S 76°52W 120 C2
Pasto Colombia 1°13N 77°17W 120 B2
Patagonia Argentina 45°0S 69°0W 121 G3
Patan India 23°54N 72°14E 84 H8
Pateley Bridge U.K. 54°5N 1°44W 26 D5
Paterson U.S.A. 40°54N 74°9W 113 E10
Pathankot India 32°18N 75°45E 84 C9
Pathfinder Res. U.S.A. 42°28N 106°51W 110 B5
Patiala India 30°23N 76°26E 84 D9
Patkai Bum India 27°0N 95°30E 85 F19
Patmos Greece 37°21N 26°36E 69 F12
Patna India 25°35N 85°12E 85 G14
Patos Brazil 6°55S 37°16W 120 C6
Patos, L. dos Brazil 31°20S 51°0W 121 F4
Patos de Minas Brazil 18°35S 46°32W 122 C1
Patra Greece 38°14N 21°47E 69 E9
Patrington U.K. 53°41N 0°1W 27 E8
Patrocínio Brazil 18°57S 47°0W 122 C1
Patten U.S.A. 46°0N 68°38W 113 C13
Patterdale U.K. 54°32N 2°56W 26 C3
Pau France 43°19N 0°25W 66 E3
Paulatuk Canada 69°25N 124°0W 108 C7
Paulistana Brazil 8°9S 41°9W 122 A2
Paull U.K. 53°44N 0°14W 27 E8
Paulo Afonso Brazil 9°21S 38°15W 122 A3
Pavia Italy 45°7N 9°8E 68 B3
Pavlodar Kazakhstan 52°33N 77°0E 76 D8
Pavlohrad Ukraine 48°30N 35°52E 71 E6
Pavlovo Russia 55°58N 43°5E 70 C7
Pawtucket U.S.A. 41°53N 71°23W 113 E12
Paxton U.S.A. 40°27N 88°6W 112 E3
Payakumbuh Indonesia 0°20S 100°35E 82 E2
Payette U.S.A. 44°5N 116°56W 110 B3
Payne L. Canada 59°30N 74°30W 109 D12
Paysandú Uruguay 32°19S 58°8W 121 F4
Payson U.S.A. 34°14N 111°20W 110 D4
Paz, B. de la Mexico 24°9N 110°25W 114 C2
Pazardzhik Bulgaria 42°12N 24°20E 69 C11
Peace → Canada 59°0N 111°25W 108 D8
Peace River Canada 56°15N 117°18W 108 D8
Peacehaven U.K. 50°48N 0°1E 31 E8
Peak District △ U.K. 53°24N 1°46W 27 F5
Pearl City U.S.A. 21°24N 157°59W 110 H16
Pearl Harbor U.S.A. 21°21N 157°57W 110 H16
Pearl River Bridge China 22°15N 113°48E 79 a
Peasenhall U.K. 52°16N 1°27E 31 B11
Peawanuck Canada 55°15N 85°12W 109 D11
Pechora Russia 65°10N 57°11E 70 A10
Pechora → Russia 68°13N 54°15E 70 A9
Pechora B. Russia 68°40N 54°0E 70 A9
Pecos U.S.A. 31°26N 103°30W 110 D6
Pecos → U.S.A. 29°42N 101°22W 110 E6
Pécs Hungary 46°5N 18°15E 65 E10
Pedra Azul Brazil 16°2S 41°17W 122 C2
Pedro Afonso Brazil 9°0S 48°10W 122 A1
Peebles U.K. 55°40N 3°11W 25 C9
Peel I. of Man 54°13N 4°40W 19 C12
Peel → Canada 67°0N 135°0W 108 C6
Peel Fell U.K. 55°18N 2°34W 26 B3
Peel Sd. Canada 73°0N 96°0W 108 B10
Pegswood U.K. 55°11N 1°39W 26 B5
Pegu Burma 17°20N 96°29E 85 L20
Pegu Yoma Burma 19°0N 96°0E 85 K20
Pegwell Bay U.K. 51°18N 1°24E 31 D11
Peixe Brazil 12°0S 48°40W 122 B1
Peje Kosovo 42°40N 20°17E 69 C9
Pekalongan Indonesia 6°53S 109°40E 82 F3
Pekanbaru Indonesia 0°30N 101°15E 82 D2
Pekin U.S.A. 40°35N 89°40W 112 E3
Peking = Beijing China 39°53N 116°21E 79 D12
Pelagie, Is. Italy 35°39N 12°33E 68 G5
Pelée, Mt. Martinique 14°48N 61°10W 115 D12
Peleng Indonesia 1°20S 123°30E 83 E6
Pelješac Croatia 42°55N 17°25E 68 C7
Pelly → Canada 62°47N 137°19W 108 C6
Pelly Bay Canada 68°38N 89°50W 109 C11
Peloponnesos □ Greece 37°10N 22°0E 69 F10
Pelotas Brazil 31°42S 52°23W 121 F4
Pelvoux, Massif du France 44°52N 6°20E 66 D7
Pematangsiantar Indonesia 2°57N 99°5E 82 D1
Pemba Mozam. 12°58S 40°30E 97 G8
Pemba I. Tanzania 5°0S 39°45E 96 F7
Pembridge U.K. 52°13N 2°52W 30 B3
Pembroke Canada 45°50N 77°7W 109 E12
Pembroke U.K. 51°41N 4°55W 28 D4
Pembrokeshire □ U.K. 51°52N 4°56W 28 D3
Pembrokeshire Coast △ U.K. 51°50N 5°2W 28 D3
Pembury U.K. 51°8N 0°20E 31 D9
Pen-y-bont ar Ogwr = Bridgend U.K. 51°30N 3°34W 29 D6
Pen-y-Ghent U.K. 54°10N 2°14W 26 D4
Penarth U.K. 51°26N 3°11W 29 E7
Peñas, G. de Chile 47°0S 75°0W 121 G1
Pend Oreille, L. U.S.A. 48°10N 116°21W 110 A3
Pendeen U.K. 50°9N 5°41W 29 G2
Pendle Hill U.K. 53°52N 2°19W 27 E4
Pendleton U.S.A. 45°40N 118°47W 110 A3
Penedo Brazil 10°15S 36°36W 122 B3
Penetanguishene Canada 44°50N 79°55W 112 D8
Penfro = Pembroke U.K. 51°41N 4°55W 28 D4
Penicuik U.K. 55°50N 3°13W 25 C9
Peninsular Malaysia □ Malaysia 4°0N 102°0E 82 D2
Penistone U.K. 53°31N 1°37W 27 E5
Penkridge U.K. 52°44N 2°6W 27 G4

Penmarch, Pte. de France 47°48N 4°22W 66 C1
Penn Yan U.S.A. 42°40N 77°3W 112 D9
Pennines U.K. 54°45N 2°27W 26 C4
Pennsylvania □ U.S.A. 40°45N 77°30W 112 E8
Penong Australia 31°56S 133°1E 98 G5
Penrith U.K. 54°40N 2°45W 26 C3
Penryn U.K. 50°9N 5°7W 29 G3
Pensacola U.S.A. 30°25N 87°13W 111 D9
Pensacola Mts. Antarctica 84°0S 40°0W 55 E1
Penshurst U.K. 51°10N 0°12E 31 D9
Penticton Canada 49°30N 119°38W 108 E8
Pentire Pt. U.K. 50°35N 4°56W 29 F4
Pentland Firth U.K. 58°43N 3°10W 23 E11
Pentland Hills U.K. 55°48N 3°25W 25 C9
Penwortham U.K. 53°45N 2°46W 27 E3
Penygroes U.K. 53°3N 4°17W 28 A5
Penza Russia 53°15N 45°5E 70 D8
Penzance U.K. 50°7N 5°33W 29 G2
Peoria U.S.A. 40°42N 89°36W 112 E3
Perabumulih Indonesia 3°27S 104°15E 82 E2
Perdido, Mte. Spain 42°40N 0°5E 67 A6
Pereira Colombia 4°49N 75°43W 120 B2
Pergamino Argentina 33°52S 60°30W 121 F3
Péribonka → Canada 48°45N 72°5W 109 E12
Périgueux France 45°10N 0°42E 66 D4
Perlas, Punta de Nic. 12°30N 83°30W 104 H11
Perm Russia 58°0N 56°10E 70 C10
Pernambuco □ Brazil 8°0S 37°0W 120 C6
Pernik Bulgaria 42°35N 23°2E 69 C10
Perpignan France 42°42N 2°53E 66 E5
Perranporth U.K. 50°20N 5°11W 29 G3
Perranzabuloe U.K. 50°19N 5°9W 29 G3
Perryton U.S.A. 36°24N 100°48W 110 C6
Perryville U.S.A. 37°43N 89°52W 112 G3
Persepolis Iran 29°55N 52°50E 87 D8
Pershore U.K. 52°7N 2°4W 30 B4
Persian Gulf Asia 27°0N 50°0E 87 E7
Perth Australia 31°57S 115°52E 98 G2
Perth Canada 44°55N 76°15W 112 C9
Perth U.K. 56°24N 3°26W 25 B9
Perth & Kinross □ U.K. 56°45N 3°55W 23 J9
Peru U.S.A. 40°45N 86°4W 112 E4
Peru ■ S. Amer. 4°0S 75°0W 120 C2
Peru-Chile Trench Pac. Oc. 20°0S 72°0W 103 K20
Perúgia Italy 43°7N 12°23E 68 C5
Pervomaysk Ukraine 48°10N 30°46E 71 E5
Pervouralsk Russia 56°59N 59°59E 70 C10
Pésaro Italy 43°54N 12°55E 68 C5
Pescara Italy 42°28N 14°13E 68 C6
Peshawar Pakistan 34°2N 71°37E 84 B7
Pesqueira Brazil 8°20S 36°42W 122 A3
Petah Tiqwa Israel 32°6N 34°53E 86 C3
Peterborough Canada 44°20N 78°20W 109 E12
Peterborough U.K. 52°35N 0°15W 31 A8
Peterchurch U.K. 52°2N 2°56W 30 B3
Peterculter U.K. 57°6N 2°16W 23 H13
Peterhead U.K. 57°31N 1°48W 23 G14
Peterlee U.K. 54°47N 1°20W 26 C6
Petersburg Alaska, U.S.A. 56°48N 132°58W 108 D6
Petersburg Va., U.S.A. 37°14N 77°24W 112 G9
Petersfield U.K. 51°1N 0°56W 31 D7
Petit Piton St. Lucia 13°51N 61°5W 114 b
Petitot → Canada 60°14N 123°29W 108 C7
Petitsikapau L. Canada 54°37N 66°25W 109 D13
Peto Mexico 20°8N 88°55W 114 C7
Petoskey U.S.A. 45°22N 84°57W 112 C5
Petra Jordan 30°20N 35°22E 86 D3
Petrolândia Brazil 9°5S 38°20W 122 A3
Petrolina Brazil 9°24S 40°30W 122 A2
Petropavl Kazakhstan 54°53N 69°13E 76 D7
Petropavlovsk-Kamchatskiy Russia 53°3N 158°43E 77 D16
Petrópolis Brazil 22°33S 43°9W 122 D2
Petrozavodsk Russia 61°41N 34°20E 70 B5
Petworth U.K. 51°0N 0°36W 31 E7
Pevensey U.K. 50°49N 0°23E 31 E9
Pevensey Levels U.K. 50°50N 0°20E 31 E9
Pewsey U.K. 51°20N 1°45W 30 D5
Pewsey, Vale of U.K. 51°22N 1°40W 30 D5
Pforzheim Germany 48°52N 8°41E 64 D5
Phalodi India 27°12N 72°24E 84 F8
Phan Rang-Thap Cham Vietnam 11°34N 109°0E 82 B3
Phan Thiet Vietnam 11°1N 108°9E 82 B3
Phi Phi, Ko Thailand 7°45N 98°46E 82 C1
Philadelphia U.S.A. 39°57N 75°9W 113 E10
Philippine Sea Pac. Oc. 18°0N 125°0E 72 G14
Philippine Trench Pac. Oc. 12°0N 126°6E 83 B7
Philippines ■ Asia 12°0N 123°0E 83 B6
Phillips U.S.A. 45°42N 90°24W 112 C2
Phitsanulok Thailand 16°50N 100°12E 82 A2
Phnom Penh Cambodia 11°33N 104°55E 82 B2
Phoenix U.S.A. 33°26N 112°4W 110 D4
Phoenix Is. Kiribati 3°30S 172°0W 99 A16
Phuket Thailand 7°53N 98°24E 82 C1
Piacenza Italy 45°1N 9°40E 68 B3
Piatra Neamț Romania 46°56N 26°21E 65 E14
Piauí □ Brazil 7°0S 43°0W 120 C5
Piauí → Brazil 6°38S 42°42W 120 C5
Piave → Italy 45°32N 12°44E 68 B5
Picardie France 49°50N 3°0E 66 B5
Pichilemu Chile 34°22S 72°0W 121 F2
Pickering U.K. 54°15N 0°46W 26 D7
Pickering, Vale of U.K. 54°14N 0°45W 26 D7
Picos Brazil 7°5S 41°28W 120 C5
Picton Canada 44°1N 77°9W 112 C9
Pidley U.K. 52°23N 0°2W 31 B8
Pidurutalagala Sri Lanka 7°10N 80°50E 84 R12
Piedmont U.S.A. 34°42N 82°28W 111 D10
Piedras Negras Mexico 28°42N 100°31W 114 B4
Piemonte □ Italy 45°0N 8°0E 68 B2
Pierre U.S.A. 44°22N 100°21W 110 B6
Pietermaritzburg S. Africa 29°35S 30°25E 97 K6
Pikes Peak U.S.A. 38°50N 105°3W 110 C5
Pilar Paraguay 26°50S 58°20W 121 E4
Pilcomayo → Paraguay 25°21S 57°42W 121 E4
Pilibhit India 28°40N 79°50E 84 E11
Pilica → Poland 51°52N 21°17E 65 C11
Pilling U.K. 53°56N 2°54W 27 E3
Pilton U.K. 51°10N 2°36W 30 D3

Pimentel Peru 6°45S 79°55W 120 C2
Pinar del Rio Cuba 22°26N 83°40W 115 C8
Pinatubo, Mt. Phil. 15°8N 120°21E 83 A6
Pinchbeck U.K. 52°50N 0°9W 27 G8
Pinckneyville U.S.A. 38°5N 89°23W 112 F3
Pindus Mts. Greece 40°0N 21°0E 69 E9
Pine Bluff U.S.A. 34°13N 92°1W 111 D8
Pine Point Canada 60°50N 114°28W 108 C8
Pinega → Russia 64°30N 44°19E 70 B8
Pingdingshan China 33°43N 113°27E 79 E11
P'ingtung Taiwan 22°38N 120°30E 79 G13
Pingxiang Guangxi Zhuangzu, China 22°6N 106°46E 78 G10
Pingxiang Jiangxi, China 27°43N 113°48E 79 F11
Pinheiro Brazil 2°31S 45°5W 120 C5
Pinhoe U.K. 50°44N 3°29W 29 F7
Pinsk Belarus 52°10N 26°1E 70 D4
Piombino Italy 42°55N 10°32E 68 C4
Piotrków Trybunalski Poland 51°23N 19°43E 65 C10
Pipmuacan, Rés. Canada 49°45N 70°30W 113 A12
Piracicaba Brazil 22°45S 47°40W 122 D1
Pirapora Brazil 17°20S 44°56W 122 C2
Pireas Greece 37°57N 23°42E 69 F10
Pirmasens Germany 49°12N 7°36E 64 D4
Pisa Italy 43°43N 10°23E 68 C4
Pisagua Chile 19°40S 70°15W 120 D2
Pishan China 37°30N 78°33E 78 D4
Pistóia Italy 43°55N 10°54E 68 C4
Pit → U.S.A. 40°47N 122°6W 110 B2
Pitcairn I. Pac. Oc. 25°5S 130°5W 103 K14
Piteå Sweden 65°20N 21°25E 63 D8
Pitești Romania 44°52N 24°54E 65 F13
Pitlochry U.K. 56°42N 3°44W 23 J10
Pittsburg U.S.A. 37°25N 94°42W 111 C8
Pittsburgh U.S.A. 40°26N 79°58W 112 E8
Pittsfield U.S.A. 42°27N 73°15W 113 D11
Piura Peru 5°15S 80°38W 120 C1
Placentia Canada 47°20N 54°0W 109 E14
Placentia B. Canada 47°0N 54°40W 109 E14
Placetas Cuba 22°15N 79°44W 115 C9
Plainview U.S.A. 34°11N 101°43W 110 D6
Plata, Río de la → S. Amer. 34°45S 57°30W 121 F4
Platte → Mo., U.S.A. 39°16N 94°50W 111 C8
Platte → Nebr., U.S.A. 41°4N 95°53W 104 E10
Plattsburgh U.S.A. 44°42N 73°28W 113 C11
Plauen Germany 50°30N 12°8E 64 C7
Plenty, B. of N.Z. 37°45S 177°0E 99 H14
Plessisville Canada 46°14N 71°47W 113 B12
Pleven Bulgaria 43°26N 24°37E 69 C11
Płock Poland 52°32N 19°40E 65 B10
Ploiești Romania 44°57N 26°5E 65 F14
Plovdiv Bulgaria 42°8N 24°44E 69 C11
Plymouth U.K. 50°22N 4°10W 29 G5
Plymouth Ind., U.S.A. 41°21N 86°19W 112 E4
Plymouth Wis., U.S.A. 43°45N 87°59W 112 D4
Plympton U.K. 50°23N 4°5W 29 G5
Plymstock U.K. 50°21N 4°7W 29 G5
Plynlimon = Pumlumon Fawr U.K. 52°28N 3°46W 28 C6
Plzeň Czech Rep. 49°45N 13°22E 64 D7
Po → Italy 44°57N 12°4E 68 B5
Pocatello U.S.A. 42°52N 112°27W 110 B4
Pocklington U.K. 53°56N 0°46W 27 E7
Poços de Caldas Brazil 21°50S 46°33W 122 D1
Podgorica Montenegro 42°30N 19°19E 69 C8
Podolsk Russia 55°25N 37°30E 70 C6
Pohang S. Korea 36°1N 129°23E 79 D14
Pohnpei Micronesia 6°55N 158°10E 102 G7
Point Hope U.S.A. 68°21N 166°47W 108 C3
Point L. Canada 65°15N 113°4W 108 C8
Point Pleasant U.S.A. 38°51N 82°8W 112 F6
Pointe-à-Pitre Guadeloupe 16°15N 61°32W 115 D12
Pointe-Noire Congo 4°48S 11°53E 96 E2
Poitiers France 46°35N 0°20E 66 C4
Poitou France 46°40N 0°10W 66 C3
Pokhara Nepal 28°14N 83°58E 85 E13
Poland ■ Europe 52°0N 20°0E 65 C10
Polatsk Belarus 55°30N 28°50E 70 C4
Polden Hills U.K. 51°7N 2°50W 30 D3
Polegate U.K. 50°49N 0°16E 31 E9
Polesworth U.K. 52°37N 1°36W 27 G5
Polevskoy Russia 56°26N 60°11E 70 C11
Polokwane S. Africa 23°54S 29°25E 97 J5
Polperro U.K. 50°20N 4°32W 29 G4
Polruan U.K. 50°19N 4°38W 29 G4
Poltava Ukraine 49°35N 34°35E 71 E5
Polynesia Pac. Oc. 10°0S 162°0W 103 F11
Pomeranian Lakes Poland 53°40N 16°37E 65 B9
Ponca City U.S.A. 36°42N 97°5W 111 C7
Ponce Puerto Rico 18°1N 66°37W 115 D11
Pond Inlet Canada 72°40N 77°0W 109 B12
Ponferrada Spain 42°32N 6°35W 67 A2
Ponta Grossa Brazil 25°7S 50°10W 121 E4
Pontardawe U.K. 51°43N 3°51W 28 D6
Pontardulais U.K. 51°43N 4°3W 28 D5
Pontarlier France 46°54N 6°20E 66 C7
Pontchartrain, L. U.S.A. 30°5N 90°5W 111 D8
Ponte Nova Brazil 20°25S 42°54W 122 D2
Pontefract U.K. 53°42N 1°18W 27 E6
Ponteland U.K. 55°3N 1°45W 26 B5
Pontevedra Spain 42°26N 8°40W 67 A1
Pontiac Ill., U.S.A. 40°53N 88°38W 112 E3
Pontiac Mich., U.S.A. 42°38N 83°18W 112 D6
Pontianak Indonesia 0°3S 109°15E 82 E3
Pontine Mts. Turkey 41°0N 36°45E 71 F6
Pontivy France 48°5N 2°58E 66 B2
Pontrilas U.K. 51°56N 2°52W 30 C3
Pontypool U.K. 51°42N 3°2W 28 D7
Pontypridd U.K. 51°36N 3°20W 28 D7
Ponziane, Ísole Italy 40°55N 12°57E 68 D5
Poole U.K. 50°43N 1°59W 30 E5
Poole Harbour U.K. 50°41N 2°0W 30 E5
Pooley Bridge U.K. 54°37N 2°48W 26 C3
Poopó, L. de Bolivia 18°30S 67°35W 120 D3
Popayán Colombia 2°27N 76°36W 120 B2
Poplar Bluff U.S.A. 36°46N 90°24W 111 C8
Popocatépetl, Volcán Mexico 19°2N 98°38W 114 D5
Porbandar India 21°44N 69°43E 84 J6
Porcupine → U.S.A. 66°34N 145°19W 108 C5
Pori Finland 61°29N 21°48E 63 E8

Porlock   Robson, Mt.

Porlock U.K. 51°13N 3°35W 29 E6
Port Alberni Canada 49°14N 124°50W 108 E7
Port Antonio Jamaica 18°10N 76°26W 114 a
Port Arthur U.S.A. 29°54N 93°56W 111 E8
Port-au-Prince Haiti 18°40N 72°20W 115 D10
Port Augusta Australia 32°30S 137°50E 98 G6
Port Carlisle U.K. 54°57N 3°11W 26 C2
Port-Cartier Canada 50°2N 66°50W 109 D13
Port-de-Paix Haiti 19°50N 72°50W 115 D10
Port Elgin Canada 44°25N 81°25W 112 C7
Port Elizabeth S. Africa 33°58S 25°40E 97 L5
Port Ellen U.K. 55°38N 6°11W 24 C3
Port-Gentil Gabon 0°40S 8°50E 96 E1
Port Glasgow U.K. 55°56N 4°41W 24 C6
Port Harcourt Nigeria 4°40N 7°10E 94 H7
Port Hawkesbury Canada 45°36N 61°22W 109 E13
Port Hedland Australia 20°25S 118°35E 98 E2
Port Hope Simpson Canada 52°33N 56°18W 109 D14
Port Huron U.S.A. 42°58N 82°26W 112 D6
Port Isaac U.K. 50°35N 4°50W 29 F4
Port Isaac B. U.K. 50°36N 4°50W 29 F4
Port Lincoln Australia 34°42S 135°52E 98 G6
Port Louis Mauritius 20°10S 57°30E 91 H9
Port McNeill Canada 50°35N 127°6W 108 D7
Port Macquarie Australia 31°25S 152°25E 98 G9
Port Maria Jamaica 18°22N 76°54W 114 a
Port Morant Jamaica 17°54N 76°19W 114 a
Port Moresby Papua N. G. 9°24S 147°8E 98 B8
Port Nolloth S. Africa 29°17S 16°52E 97 K3
Port of Spain Trin. & Tob. 10°40N 61°31W 120 A3
Port Pirie Australia 33°10S 138°1E 98 G6
Port Said Egypt 31°16N 32°18E 95 B12
Port St. Lucie U.S.A. 27°18N 80°21W 111 E10
Port St. Mary U.K. 54°5N 4°44W 19 C12
Port Shepstone S. Africa 30°44S 30°28E 97 L6
Port Sudan Sudan 19°32N 37°9E 95 E13
Port Talbot U.K. 51°35N 3°47W 29 D6
Port Vila Vanuatu 17°45S 168°18E 99 D12
Port Washington U.S.A. 43°23N 87°53W 112 D4
Port William U.K. 54°46N 4°35W 24 E6
Portadown U.K. 54°25N 6°27W 19 C9
Portadown I. U.K. 54°23N 5°33W 19 C10
Portage U.S.A. 43°33N 89°28W 112 D4
Portage la Prairie Canada 49°58N 98°18W 108 E10
Portarlington Ireland 53°9N 7°14W 21 B8
Porth Tywyn = Burry Port
   U.K. 51°41N 4°15W 28 D5
Porthcawl U.K. 51°29N 3°42W 29 D6
Porthleven U.K. 50°4N 5°19W 29 G3
Porthmadog U.K. 52°55N 4°8W 28 B5
Portishead U.K. 51°29N 2°46W 30 D3
Portknockie U.K. 57°42N 2°51W 23 G12
Portland Maine, U.S.A. 43°39N 70°16W 113 D12
Portland Oreg., U.S.A. 45°32N 122°37W 110 A2
Portland, I. of U.K. 50°33N 2°26W 30 E4
Portland Bight Jamaica 17°52N 77°5W 114 a
Portland Bill U.K. 50°31N 2°28W 29 F9
Portland Pt. Jamaica 17°42N 77°11W 114 a
Portlaoise Ireland 53°2N 7°18W 21 B8
Portmarnock Ireland 53°26N 6°8W 21 B10
Portmore Jamaica 17°53N 76°53W 114 a
Porto Portugal 41°8N 8°40W 67 B1
Pôrto Alegre Brazil 30°5S 51°10W 121 F4
Porto Esperança Brazil 19°37S 57°29W 120 D4
Porto Nacional Brazil 10°40S 48°30W 122 D1
Porto-Novo Benin 6°23N 2°42E 94 G6
Porto Seguro Brazil 16°26S 39°5W 122 C3
Porto Tórres Italy 40°50N 8°24E 68 D3
Porto-Vecchio France 41°35N 9°16E 66 F8
Porto Velho Brazil 8°46S 63°54W 120 C3
Porton U.K. 51°8N 1°43W 30 D5
Portpatrick U.K. 54°51N 5°7W 24 E5
Portree U.K. 57°25N 6°12W 22 H5
Portrush U.K. 55°12N 6°40W 19 A8
Portslade U.K. 50°50N 0°12W 31 E8
Portsmouth U.K. 50°48N 1°6W 30 E6
Portsmouth N.H., U.S.A. 43°5N 70°45W 113 D12
Portsmouth Ohio, U.S.A. 38°44N 82°57W 112 F6
Portsmouth Va., U.S.A. 36°58N 76°23W 111 C11
Portsoy U.K. 57°41N 2°41W 23 G12
Portstewart U.K. 55°11N 6°43W 19 A8
Porttipahdan tekojärvi Finland 68°5N 26°40E 63 D9
Portugal ■ Europe 40°0N 8°0W 67 C1
Portumna Ireland 53°6N 8°14W 20 B6
Posadas Argentina 27°30S 55°50W 121 E4
Posse Brazil 14°4S 46°18W 122 B1
Postmasburg S. Africa 28°18S 23°5E 97 K4
Potchefstroom S. Africa 26°41S 27°7E 97 K5
Potenza Italy 40°38N 15°48E 68 D6
Poti Georgia 42°10N 41°38E 71 F7
Potiskum Nigeria 11°39N 11°2E 95 F8
Potomac → U.S.A. 38°0N 76°23W 112 F9
Potosi Bolivia 19°38S 65°50W 120 D3
Potsdam Germany 52°23N 13°3E 64 B7
Potsdam U.S.A. 44°40N 74°59W 113 C10
Potter Heigham U.K. 52°42N 1°34E 31 A12
Potterne U.K. 51°20N 2°0W 30 D4
Potters Bar U.K. 51°42N 0°11W 31 C8
Potterspury U.K. 52°5N 0°52W 31 B7
Pottstown U.S.A. 40°15N 75°39W 113 E10
Pottsville U.S.A. 40°41N 76°12W 113 E9
Pottuvil Sri Lanka 6°55N 81°50E 84 R12
Poughkeepsie U.S.A. 41°42N 73°56W 113 E11
Poulaphouca Res. Ireland 53°8N 6°30W 21 B10
Poulton-le-Fylde U.K. 53°51N 2°58W 27 E3
Poundstock U.K. 50°44N 4°36W 29 F4
Pouso Alegre Brazil 22°14S 45°57W 122 D1
Powder → U.S.A. 46°45N 105°26W 110 A5
Powell, L. U.S.A. 36°57N 111°29W 110 C4
Powell River Canada 49°50N 124°35W 108 E7
Powick U.K. 52°10N 2°14W 30 B4
Powys □ U.K. 52°20N 3°20W 28 C7
Poyang Hu China 29°5N 116°20E 79 F12
Poza Rica Mexico 20°33N 97°27W 114 C5
Poznań Poland 52°25N 16°55E 65 B9
Pozzuoli Italy 40°49N 14°7E 68 D6
Prado Brazil 17°20S 39°13W 122 C3
Prague Czech Rep. 50°4N 14°25E 64 C8
Praia C. Verde Is. 15°2N 23°34W 91 E1

Praia Grande Brazil 24°0S 46°24W 122 D1
Prairie du Chien U.S.A. 43°3N 91°9W 112 D2
Prata Brazil 19°25S 48°54W 122 C1
Prato Italy 43°53N 11°6E 68 C4
Pratt U.S.A. 37°39N 98°44W 110 C7
Prawle Pt. U.K. 50°12N 3°44W 29 G6
Praya Indonesia 8°39S 116°17E 82 F5
Prees U.K. 52°54N 2°40W 27 G3
Preesall U.K. 53°55N 2°57W 27 E3
Prescott Canada 44°45N 75°30W 113 C10
Prescott U.S.A. 34°33N 112°28W 110 D4
Presidencia Roque Saenz Peña
   Argentina 26°45S 60°30W 121 E3
Presidente Prudente Brazil 22°5S 51°25W 120 E4
Presidio U.S.A. 29°34N 104°22W 110 E6
Prespa, L. Macedonia 40°55N 21°0E 69 D9
Presque Isle U.S.A. 46°41N 68°1W 113 B13
Prestatyn U.K. 53°20N 3°24W 28 A7
Prestbury U.K. 51°54N 2°2W 30 C4
Presteigne U.K. 52°17N 3°0W 28 C7
Preston Borders, U.K. 55°49N 2°19W 25 C11
Preston Dorset, U.K. 50°38N 2°26W 30 E4
Preston Lancs., U.K. 53°46N 2°42W 27 E3
Preston U.K. 42°6N 111°53W 110 B4
Prestonpans U.K. 55°58N 2°58W 25 C10
Prestwich U.K. 53°32N 2°17W 27 E4
Prestwick U.K. 55°29N 4°37W 24 D6
Pretoria S. Africa 25°44S 28°12E 97 K5
Pribilof Is. U.S.A. 57°0N 170°0W 108 D2
Price U.S.A. 39°36N 110°49W 110 C4
Prieska S. Africa 29°40S 22°42E 97 K4
Prilep Macedonia 41°21N 21°32E 69 D9
Prince Albert Canada 53°15N 105°50W 108 D9
Prince Albert Pen. Canada 72°30N 116°0W 108 B8
Prince Albert Sd. Canada 70°25N 115°0W 108 B8
Prince Alfred, C. Canada 74°20N 124°40W 109 B7
Prince Charles I. Canada 67°47N 76°12W 109 C12
Prince Charles Mts. Antarctica 72°0S 67°0E 55 D6
Prince Edward I. □ Canada 46°20N 63°20W 113 B16
Prince Edward Is. Ind. Oc. 46°35S 38°0E 53 G11
Prince George Canada 53°55N 122°50W 108 D7
Prince Gustaf Adolf Sea
   Canada 78°30N 107°0W 109 B9
Prince of Wales, C. U.S.A. 65°36N 168°5W 104 C3
Prince of Wales I. Canada 73°0N 99°0W 108 B10
Prince of Wales I. U.S.A. 55°47N 132°50W 108 D6
Prince Patrick I. Canada 77°0N 120°0W 109 B8
Prince Rupert Canada 54°20N 130°20W 108 D6
Princes Risborough U.K. 51°43N 0°49W 31 C7
Princeton Ill., U.S.A. 41°23N 89°28W 112 E3
Princeton Ind., U.S.A. 38°21N 87°34W 112 F4
Princeton Ky., U.S.A. 37°7N 87°53W 112 G4
Princeton W. Va., U.S.A. 37°22N 81°6W 112 G7
Princetown U.K. 50°33N 4°0W 29 F5
Principe São Tomé & Príncipe 1°37N 7°25E 90 F4
Pripet → Europe 51°20N 30°15E 65 C16
Pripet Marshes Europe 52°10N 27°10E 65 B15
Priština Kosovo 42°40N 21°13E 69 C9
Privas France 44°45N 4°37E 66 D6
Prizren Kosovo 42°13N 20°45E 69 C9
Probolinggo Indonesia 7°46S 113°13E 82 F4
Probus U.K. 50°17N 4°58W 29 G4
Progreso Mexico 21°20N 89°40W 114 C7
Prome Burma 18°49N 95°13E 85 K19
Propriá Brazil 10°13S 36°51W 122 B3
Provence France 43°40N 5°46E 66 E6
Providence U.S.A. 41°49N 71°24W 113 E12
Providencia, I. de Colombia 13°25N 81°26W 115 E8
Provins France 48°33N 3°15E 66 B5
Provo U.S.A. 40°14N 111°39W 110 B4
Prudhoe U.K. 54°57N 1°52W 26 C5
Prudhoe Bay U.S.A. 70°18N 148°22W 108 B5
Pruszków Poland 52°9N 20°49E 65 B11
Prut → Romania 45°28N 28°10E 65 F15
Pryluky Ukraine 50°30N 32°24E 71 D5
Przemyśl Poland 49°50N 22°45E 65 D12
Pskov Russia 57°50N 28°25E 70 C4
Puddletown U.K. 50°44N 2°20W 30 E4
Pudsey U.K. 53°47N 1°40W 27 E5
Puducherry India 11°59N 79°50E 84 P11
Puebla Mexico 19°3N 98°12W 114 D5
Pueblo U.S.A. 38°16N 104°37W 110 C6
Puerto Aisén Chile 45°27S 73°0W 121 G2
Puerto Barrios Guatemala 15°40N 88°32W 114 D7
Puerto Cabello Venezuela 10°28N 68°1W 120 A3
Puerto Cabezas Nic. 14°0N 83°30W 115 E8
Puerto Carreño Colombia 6°12N 67°22W 120 B3
Puerto Cortés Honduras 15°51N 88°0W 114 D7
Puerto Deseado Argentina 47°55S 66°0W 121 G3
Puerto La Cruz Venezuela 10°13N 64°38W 120 A3
Puerto Madryn Argentina 42°48S 65°4W 121 G3
Puerto Maldonado Peru 12°30S 69°10W 120 D3
Puerto Montt Chile 41°28S 73°0W 121 G2
Puerto Plata Dom. Rep. 19°48N 70°45W 115 D10
Puerto Princesa Phil. 9°46N 118°45E 83 C5
Puerto Rico ☑ W. Indies 18°15N 66°45W 115 D11
Puerto Rico Trench Atl. Oc. 19°50N 66°0W 115 D11
Puerto San Julián Argentina 49°18S 67°43W 121 G3
Puerto Suárez Bolivia 18°58S 57°52W 120 D4
Puerto Wilches Colombia 7°21N 73°54W 120 B2
Puertollano Spain 38°43N 4°7W 67 C3
Puffin I. Ireland 51°50N 10°24W 20 E2
Puget Sound U.S.A. 47°50N 122°30W 110 A2
Pukapuka Cook Is. 10°53S 165°49W 103 J11
Pula Croatia 44°54N 13°57E 68 B5
Pulacayo Bolivia 20°25S 66°41W 120 D3
Pulaski U.S.A. 37°3N 80°47W 112 G7
Pulborough U.K. 50°58N 0°30W 31 E8
Pulham Market U.K. 52°26N 1°13E 31 B11
Pulham St. Mary U.K. 52°26N 1°15E 31 A11
Pullman U.S.A. 46°44N 117°10W 110 A3
Pumlumon Fawr U.K. 52°28N 3°46E 28 C6
Pune India 18°29N 73°57E 84 K8
Punjab □ India 31°0N 76°0E 84 D10
Punjab □ Pakistan 32°0N 72°30E 84 D9
Puno Peru 15°55S 70°3W 120 D2
Punta Arenas Chile 53°10S 71°0W 121 H2
Puntland Somalia 8°0N 49°0E 89 F4
Punxsutawney U.S.A. 40°57N 78°59W 112 E8
Purbeck, Isle of U.K. 50°39N 1°59W 30 E5

Purfleet U.K. 51°29N 0°16E 31 D9
Puri India 19°50N 85°58E 85 K14
Purley on Thames U.K. 51°29N 1°3W 30 D6
Purnia India 25°45N 87°31E 85 G15
Puruliya India 23°17N 86°24E 85 H15
Purus → Brazil 3°42S 61°28W 120 C3
Putian China 25°23N 119°0E 79 F12
Putorana, Gory Russia 69°0N 95°0E 77 C10
Puttalam Sri Lanka 8°1N 79°55E 84 Q11
Putumayo → S. Amer. 3°7S 67°58W 120 C3
Puvirnituq Canada 60°2N 77°10W 109 C12
Puy-de-Dôme France 45°46N 2°57E 66 D5
Puyehue Chile 40°40S 72°37W 121 G2
Pwllheli U.K. 52°53N 4°25W 28 B5
Pyinmana Burma 19°45N 96°12E 85 K20
P'yŏngyang N. Korea 39°0N 125°30E 79 D14
Pyramid L. U.S.A. 40°1N 119°35W 110 C3
Pyrénées Europe 42°45N 0°18E 66 E4

Q

Qaanaaq Greenland 77°30N 69°10W 54 B4
Qā'emshahr Iran 36°30N 52°53E 87 B8
Qaidam Basin China 37°0N 95°0E 78 D8
Qamdo China 31°15N 97°6E 78 E8
Qandyaghash Kazakhstan 49°28N 57°25E 71 E10
Qaqortoq Greenland 60°43N 46°0W 54 C5
Qarqan He → China 39°30N 88°30E 78 D6
Qarshi Uzbekistan 38°53N 65°48E 87 B11
Qatar ■ Asia 25°30N 51°15E 87 E7
Qattâra Depression Egypt 29°30N 27°30E 95 C11
Qazvin Iran 36°15N 50°0E 86 B7
Qena Egypt 26°10N 32°43E 95 C12
Qeqertarsuaq Greenland 69°15N 53°38W 54 C5
Qeshm Iran 26°55N 56°10E 87 E9
Qianshan China 22°15N 113°31E 79 a
Qi'ao Dao China 22°25N 113°38E 79 a
Qiemo China 38°8N 85°32E 78 D6
Qijiaojing China 43°28N 91°36E 78 B7
Qikiqtarjuaq Canada 67°33N 63°0W 109 C13
Qingdao China 36°5N 120°20E 79 D13
Qinghai □ China 36°0N 98°0E 78 D8
Qinghai Hu China 36°40N 100°10E 78 D9
Qinhuangdao China 39°56N 119°30E 79 D12
Qinling Shandi China 33°50N 108°10E 79 E10
Qinzhou China 21°58N 108°38E 78 G10
Qiqihar China 47°26N 124°0E 79 B13
Qira China 37°0N 80°48E 78 D5
Qitai China 44°2N 89°35E 78 B6
Qitaihe China 45°48N 130°51E 79 B15
Qom Iran 34°40N 51°0E 87 C7
Qostanay Kazakhstan 53°10N 63°35E 76 D7
Quadring U.K. 52°54N 0°10W 27 G8
Quang Ngai Vietnam 15°13N 108°58E 82 A3
Quanzhou China 24°55N 118°34E 79 F12
Quaqtaq Canada 60°55N 69°40W 109 C13
Quartu Sant'Élena Italy 39°15N 9°10E 68 E3
Québec Canada 46°52N 71°13W 113 B12
Québec □ Canada 48°0N 74°0W 109 C12
Queen Charlotte Is. Canada 53°20N 132°10W 108 D6
Queen Charlotte Sd. Canada 51°0N 128°0W 108 D7
Queen Elizabeth Is. Canada 76°0N 95°0W 109 B10
Queen Maud G. Canada 68°15N 102°30W 108 C9
Queenborough U.K. 51°25N 0°46E 31 D10
Queensbury U.K. 53°46N 1°50W 27 E5
Queensland □ Australia 22°0S 142°0E 98 E7
Queenstown N.Z. 45°1S 168°40E 99 K12
Queenstown S. Africa 31°52S 26°52E 97 L5
Queimadas Brazil 11°0S 39°38W 122 B3
Quelimane Mozam. 17°53S 36°58E 97 H7
Quendale, B. of U.K. 59°53N 1°20W 22 C15
Querétaro Mexico 20°36N 100°23W 114 C4
Quesnel Canada 53°0N 122°30W 108 D7
Quesnel L. Canada 52°30N 121°20W 108 D7
Quetta Pakistan 30°15N 66°55E 84 D5
Quetzaltenango Guatemala 14°50N 91°30W 114 E6
Quezon City Phil. 14°37N 121°2E 83 B6
Qui Nhon Vietnam 13°40N 109°13E 82 B3
Quibdó Colombia 5°42N 76°40W 120 B2
Quilán, C. Chile 43°15S 74°30W 121 G2
Quilon India 8°50N 76°38E 84 Q10
Quilpie Australia 26°35S 144°11E 98 F7
Quimper France 48°0N 4°9W 66 B1
Quincy Ill., U.S.A. 39°56N 91°23W 111 C8
Quincy Mass., U.S.A. 42°14N 71°0W 113 D12
Quito Ecuador 0°15S 78°35W 120 C2
Qujing China 25°32N 103°41E 78 F9
Qulsary Kazakhstan 46°59N 54°1E 71 E9
Qŭnghirot Uzbekistan 43°2N 58°50E 87 A9
Quorndon U.K. 52°46N 1°10W 27 G6
Qŭqon Uzbekistan 40°31N 70°56E 87 A12
Quseir Egypt 26°7N 34°16E 95 C12
Quzhou China 28°57N 118°54E 79 F12

R

Raahe Finland 64°40N 24°28E 63 E8
Raasay U.K. 57°25N 6°4W 22 H5
Raasay, Sd. of U.K. 57°30N 6°8W 22 H5
Raba Indonesia 8°36S 118°55E 83 F5
Rabat Morocco 34°2N 6°48W 94 B4
Rabaul Papua N. G. 4°24S 152°18E 98 A9
Rābigh Si. Arabia 22°50N 39°5E 89 C2
Race, C. Canada 46°40N 53°5W 109 E14
Rach Gia Vietnam 10°5N 105°5E 82 B3
Racine U.S.A. 42°44N 87°47W 112 D4
Rackheath U.K. 52°44N 1°22E 31 A11
Radcliffe U.K. 53°34N 2°18W 27 E4
Radcliffe-on-Trent U.K. 52°57N 1°2W 27 G6
Radford U.S.A. 37°8N 80°34W 112 G7
Radley U.K. 51°41N 1°14W 30 C6
Radnor Forest U.K. 52°17N 3°10W 28 C7
Radom Poland 51°23N 21°12E 65 C11
Radstock U.K. 51°17N 2°25W 30 D4
Rae Canada 62°50N 116°3W 108 C8
Rae Bareli India 26°18N 81°20E 85 F12
Rae Isthmus Canada 66°40N 87°30W 109 C11

Rafaela Argentina 31°10S 61°30W 121 F3
Rafsanján Iran 30°30N 56°5E 87 D9
Ragusa Italy 36°55N 14°44E 68 F6
Rahimyar Khan Pakistan 28°30N 70°25E 84 E7
Raichur India 16°10N 77°20E 84 L10
Raigarh India 21°56N 83°25E 85 J13
Rainbow Lake Canada 58°30N 119°23W 108 D8
Rainham U.K. 51°22N 0°37E 31 D10
Rainier, Mt. U.S.A. 46°52N 121°46W 110 A2
Rainworth U.K. 53°7N 1°7W 27 F6
Rainy L. Canada 48°42N 93°10W 108 E10
Raipur India 21°17N 81°45E 85 J12
Raj Nandgaon India 21°5N 81°5E 85 J12
Rajahmundry India 17°1N 81°48E 85 L12
Rajapalaiyam India 9°25N 77°35E 84 Q10
Rajasthan □ India 26°45N 73°30E 84 F8
Rajkot India 22°15N 70°56E 84 H7
Rajshahi Bangla. 24°22N 88°39E 85 G16
Rakhine □ Burma 19°0N 94°15E 85 K18
Raleigh U.S.A. 35°47N 78°39W 111 C11
Rame Head U.K. 50°19N 4°13W 29 G5
Ramgarh India 23°40N 85°35E 85 H14
Ramna Stacks U.K. 60°35N 1°24W 22 A15
Rampside U.K. 54°6N 3°9W 26 D2
Rampur India 28°50N 79°5E 84 E11
Ramree I. Burma 19°0N 93°40E 85 K19
Ramsbottom U.K. 53°38N 2°19W 27 E4
Ramsbury U.K. 51°26N 1°36W 30 D5
Ramsey I. of Man 54°20N 4°22W 19 C13
Ramsey Cambs., U.K. 52°27N 0°7W 31 B8
Ramsey Essex, U.K. 51°55N 1°13E 31 C11
Ramsgate U.K. 51°20N 1°25E 31 D11
Rancagua Chile 34°10S 70°50W 121 F2
Ranchi India 23°19N 85°27E 85 H14
Randalstown U.K. 54°45N 6°19W 19 B9
Randers Denmark 56°29N 10°1E 63 F6
Rangoon Burma 16°45N 96°20E 85 L20
Rangpur Bangla. 25°42N 89°22E 85 G16
Rankin Inlet Canada 62°30N 93°0W 108 C10
Rannoch U.K. 56°40N 4°20W 23 J9
Rannoch, L. U.K. 56°41N 4°20W 23 J9
Rannoch Moor U.K. 56°38N 4°48W 23 J8
Rantoul U.S.A. 40°19N 88°9W 112 E3
Rapa French Polynesia 27°35S 144°20W 103 K13
Rapallo Italy 44°21N 9°14E 68 B3
Raper, C. Canada 69°44N 67°6W 109 C13
Rapid City U.S.A. 44°5N 103°14W 110 B6
Rarotonga Cook Is. 21°30S 160°0W 103 K12
Ra's al Khaymah U.A.E. 25°50N 55°59E 87 E9
Rasht Iran 37°20N 49°40E 86 B7
Rat Islands U.S.A. 52°0N 178°0E 108 D1
Ratangarh India 28°5N 74°35E 84 E9
Rathcoole Ireland 53°17N 6°29W 21 B10
Rathdrum Ireland 52°56N 6°14W 21 C10
Rathkeale Ireland 52°32N 8°56W 20 C5
Rathlin I. U.K. 55°18N 6°14W 19 A9
Rathmelton Ireland 55°2N 7°39W 18 A6
Ratlam India 23°20N 75°0E 84 H9
Ratnagiri India 16°57N 73°18E 84 L8
Raton U.S.A. 36°54N 104°24W 110 C6
Rauma Finland 61°10N 21°30E 63 E8
Raunds U.K. 52°21N 0°32W 31 B7
Raurkela India 22°14N 84°50E 85 H14
Ravenglass U.K. 54°22N 3°24W 26 D2
Ravenna Italy 44°25N 12°12E 68 B5
Ravenstonedale U.K. 54°26N 2°25W 26 D4
Ravi → Pakistan 30°35N 71°49E 84 D7
Rawalpindi Pakistan 33°38N 73°8E 84 C8
Rawlins U.S.A. 41°47N 107°14W 110 B5
Rawmarsh U.K. 53°27N 1°21W 27 F6
Rawson Argentina 43°15S 65°5W 121 G3
Rawtenstall U.K. 53°42N 2°17W 27 E4
Ray, C. Canada 47°33N 59°15W 109 E14
Rayleigh U.K. 51°36N 0°37E 31 C10
Rayong Thailand 12°40N 101°20E 82 B2
Raz, Pte. du France 48°2N 4°47W 66 C1
Ré, Î. de France 46°12N 1°30W 66 C3
Reading U.K. 51°27N 0°58W 31 D7
Reading U.S.A. 40°20N 75°56W 113 E10
Reay Forest U.K. 58°22N 4°55W 23 F8
Rebiana Desert Libya 24°30N 21°0E 95 D10
Recife Brazil 8°0S 35°0W 122 A3
Reconquista Argentina 29°10S 59°45W 121 E4
Red → U.S.A. 31°1N 91°45W 111 D8
Red Bluff U.S.A. 40°11N 122°15W 110 B2
Red Deer Canada 52°20N 113°50W 108 D8
Red Dial U.K. 54°48N 3°10W 26 C2
Red L. Canada 51°3N 93°49W 104 D10
Red L. Canada 48°8N 94°45W 111 A8
Red Lake Canada 51°3N 93°49W 108 D10
Red Oak U.S.A. 41°1N 95°14W 111 B7
Red River of the North →
   N. Amer. 49°0N 97°15W 108 D10
Red Sea Asia 25°0N 36°0E 89 C2
Red Wing U.S.A. 44°34N 92°31W 111 B8
Redbridge □ U.K. 51°35N 0°7E 31 C9
Redcar U.K. 54°37N 1°4W 26 C6
Redding U.S.A. 40°35N 122°24W 110 B2
Redditch U.K. 52°18N 1°55W 30 B5
Rede → U.K. 55°9N 2°13W 26 B4
Redesmouth U.K. 55°8N 2°13W 26 B4
Redhill U.K. 51°14N 0°9W 31 D8
Redlynch U.K. 50°59N 1°41W 30 E5
Redmire U.K. 54°19N 1°55W 26 D5
Redon France 47°40N 2°6W 66 C2
Redruth U.K. 50°14N 5°14W 29 G3
Ree, L. Ireland 53°35N 8°0W 18 D6
Reedham U.K. 52°34N 1°34E 31 A12
Reepham U.K. 52°46N 1°6E 31 A11
Reese → U.S.A. 40°48N 117°4W 110 B3
Reeth U.K. 54°23N 1°56W 26 D5
Regensburg Germany 49°1N 12°6E 64 D7
Réggio di Calábria Italy 38°6N 15°39E 68 E6
Réggio nell'Emília Italy 44°43N 10°36E 68 B4
Regina Canada 50°27N 104°35W 108 D9
Reichenbach Germany 50°37N 12°17E 64 C7
Reigate U.K. 51°14N 0°12W 31 D8
Reims France 49°15N 4°1E 66 B6

Reina Adelaida, Arch. Chile 52°20S 74°0W 121 H2
Reindeer L. Canada 57°15N 102°15W 108 D9
Remanso Brazil 9°41S 42°4W 122 A2
Renfrew Canada 45°30N 76°40W 112 C9
Renfrew U.K. 55°52N 4°24W 24 C7
Rennell Solomon Is. 11°40S 160°10E 99 C11
Rennes France 48°7N 1°41W 66 B3
Reno U.S.A. 39°31N 119°48W 110 C3
Repton U.K. 52°50N 1°33W 27 G5
Republican → U.S.A. 39°4N 96°48W 111 C7
Repulse Bay Canada 66°30N 86°30W 109 C11
Resistencia Argentina 27°30S 59°0W 121 E4
Resolute Canada 74°42N 94°54W 109 B10
Resolution I. Canada 61°30N 65°0W 109 C13
Reston U.K. 55°51N 2°10W 25 C11
Retford U.K. 53°19N 0°56W 27 F7
Rethimno Greece 35°18N 24°30E 69 G11
Réunion ☑ Ind. Oc. 21°0S 56°0E 91 J9
Reus Spain 41°10N 1°5E 67 B6
Reutlingen Germany 48°29N 9°12E 64 D5
Revda Russia 56°48N 59°57E 70 C10
Revelstoke Canada 51°0N 118°10W 108 D8
Revillagigedo, Is. de Pac. Oc. 18°40N 112°0W 114 D2
Rewa India 24°33N 81°25E 85 G12
Rexburg U.S.A. 43°49N 111°47W 110 B4
Rey Malabo Eq. Guin. 3°45N 8°50E 96 D1
Reykjavík Iceland 64°10N 21°57E 63 B3
Reynosa Mexico 26°7N 98°18W 114 B5
Rézekne Latvia 56°30N 27°17E 63 F9
Rhayader U.K. 52°18N 3°29W 28 C7
Rheidol → U.K. 52°25N 4°5W 28 C5
Rheine Germany 52°17N 7°26E 64 B4
Rheinland-Pfalz □ Germany 50°0N 7°0E 64 C4
Rhine → Europe 51°52N 6°2E 64 C4
Rhinelander U.S.A. 45°38N 89°25W 112 C3
Rhinns Pt. U.K. 55°40N 6°29W 24 C3
Rhins, The U.K. 54°52N 5°3W 24 E5
Rhode Island □ U.S.A. 41°40N 71°30W 113 E12
Rhodes Greece 36°15N 28°10E 69 F13
Rhodope Mts. Bulgaria 41°40N 24°20E 69 D11
Rhondda U.K. 51°39N 3°31W 28 D6
Rhône → France 43°28N 4°42E 66 E6
Rhosllanerchrugog U.K. 53°1N 3°3W 28 A7
Rhossili U.K. 51°34N 4°17W 29 D5
Rhossili B. U.K. 51°32N 4°14W 29 D5
Rhum = Rùm U.K. 57°0N 6°20W 22 J7
Rhydaman = Ammanford
   U.K. 51°48N 3°59W 28 D6
Rhyl U.K. 53°19N 3°29W 28 A7
Rhymney U.K. 51°46N 3°17W 28 D7
Riau, Kepulauan □ Indonesia 0°30N 104°20E 82 D2
Ribble → U.K. 53°52N 2°25W 27 E4
Ribeirão Prêto Brazil 21°10S 47°50W 122 D1
Riberalta Bolivia 11°0S 66°0W 120 D3
Riccall U.K. 53°50N 1°3W 27 E6
Rice Lake U.S.A. 45°30N 91°44W 112 C2
Richards Bay S. Africa 28°48S 32°6E 97 K6
Richfield U.S.A. 38°46N 112°5W 110 C4
Richland U.S.A. 46°17N 119°18W 110 A3
Richland Center U.S.A. 43°21N 90°23W 112 D2
Richlands U.S.A. 37°6N 81°48W 112 G7
Richmond U.K. 54°25N 1°43W 26 D5
Richmond Ind., U.S.A. 39°50N 84°53W 112 F5
Richmond Ky., U.S.A. 37°45N 84°18W 112 G5
Richmond Va., U.S.A. 37°33N 77°27W 112 G9
Richmond-upon-Thames □
   U.K. 51°27N 0°17W 31 D8
Rickmansworth U.K. 51°38N 0°29W 31 C8
Ridgecrest U.S.A. 35°38N 117°40W 110 C3
Ridgway U.S.A. 41°25N 78°44W 112 E8
Ridsdale U.K. 55°9N 2°9W 26 B4
Rievaulx U.K. 54°16N 1°7W 26 D6
Rift Valley Africa 7°0N 30°0E 90 G7
Riga Latvia 56°53N 24°8E 63 F8
Riga, G. of Latvia 57°40N 23°45E 63 F8
Rigestān Afghan. 30°15N 65°0E 87 D11
Rigolet Canada 54°10N 58°23W 109 D14
Rijeka Croatia 45°20N 14°21E 68 B6
Rillington U.K. 54°9N 0°42W 26 D7
Rímini Italy 44°3N 12°33E 68 B5
Rimouski Canada 48°27N 68°30W 109 E13
Ringmer U.K. 50°53N 0°5E 31 E9
Ringwood U.K. 50°50N 1°47W 30 E5
Rio Branco Brazil 9°58S 67°49W 120 C3
Rio Claro Brazil 22°19S 47°35W 122 D1
Rio Cuarto Argentina 33°10S 64°25W 121 F3
Rio de Janeiro Brazil 22°54S 43°12W 122 D2
Rio de Janeiro □ Brazil 22°50S 43°0W 122 D2
Rio Gallegos Argentina 51°35S 69°15W 121 H3
Rio Grande Brazil 32°0S 52°20W 121 F4
Rio Grande de Santiago →
   Mexico 21°36N 105°26W 114 C3
Rio Grande do Norte □ Brazil 5°40S 36°0W 120 C6
Rio Grande do Sul □ Brazil 30°0S 53°0W 121 E4
Rio Largo Brazil 9°28S 35°50W 122 A3
Rio Muni □ Eq. Guin. 1°30N 10°0E 96 D2
Riohacha Colombia 11°33N 72°55W 120 A2
Ripley Derby, U.K. 53°3N 1°24W 27 F6
Ripley N. Yorks., U.K. 54°3N 1°34W 26 D5
Ripon U.K. 54°9N 1°31W 26 D5
Ripon U.S.A. 43°51N 88°50W 112 D3
Risca U.K. 51°37N 3°5W 29 D7
Rishton U.K. 53°46N 2°26W 27 E4
Rivera Uruguay 31°0S 55°50W 121 F4
Riverhead U.S.A. 40°55N 72°40W 113 E11
Riverside U.S.A. 33°59N 117°22W 110 D3
Riverton U.S.A. 43°2N 108°23W 110 B5
Riviera = Côte d'Azur France 43°25N 7°10E 66 E7
Rivière-du-Loup Canada 47°50N 69°30W 113 B13
Rivne Ukraine 50°40N 26°10E 65 C14
Riyadh Si. Arabia 24°41N 46°42E 86 E6
Rize Turkey 41°0N 40°30E 71 F7
Rizhao China 35°25N 119°30E 79 D12
Roade U.K. 52°9N 0°53W 31 B7
Roanne France 46°3N 4°4E 66 C6
Roanoke U.S.A. 37°16N 79°56W 112 G8
Roanoke → U.S.A. 35°57N 76°42W 111 C11
Roberton U.K. 55°25N 2°54W 25 D10
Roberval Canada 48°32N 72°15W 109 E12
Robin Hood's Bay U.K. 54°27N 0°32W 26 D7
Robson, Mt. Canada 53°10N 119°10W 108 D8

Roca, C. da   Santorini

Roca, C. da *Portugal* 38°40N 9°31W 67 C1
Rocester *U.K.* 52°57N 1°50W 27 G5
Rocha *Uruguay* 34°30S 54°25W 121 F4
Rochdale *U.K.* 53°38N 2°9W 27 E4
Roche *U.K.* 50°24N 4°50W 29 G4
Rochefort *France* 45°56N 0°57W 66 D3
Rochester *Medway, U.K.* 51°23N 0°31E 31 D10
Rochester *Northumberland, U.K.* 55°17N 2°17W 26 B4
Rochester *Ind., U.S.A.* 41°4N 86°13W 112 E4
Rochester *Minn., U.S.A.* 44°1N 92°28W 111 B8
Rochester *N.H., U.S.A.* 43°18N 70°59W 113 D12
Rochester *N.Y., U.S.A.* 43°10N 77°37W 112 D9
Rochford *U.K.* 51°34N 0°43E 31 C10
Rock Hill *U.S.A.* 34°56N 81°1W 111 D10
Rock Island *U.S.A.* 41°30N 90°34W 112 E2
Rock Springs *U.S.A.* 41°35N 109°14W 110 B5
Rockall *Atl. Oc.* 57°37N 13°42W 56 D3
Rockcliffe *U.K.* 54°57N 3°0W 26 C3
Rockford *U.S.A.* 42°16N 89°6W 112 D3
Rockhampton *Australia* 23°22S 150°32E 98 F9
Rockingham *U.K.* 52°31N 0°43W 31 A7
Rockingham Forest *U.K.* 52°29N 0°42W 31 B7
Rockland *U.S.A.* 44°6N 69°7W 113 C13
Rocky Mount *U.S.A.* 35°57N 77°48W 111 C11
Rocky Mts. *N. Amer.* 49°0N 115°0W 108 D7
Rodez *France* 44°21N 2°33E 66 D5
Roding → *U.K.* 51°31N 0°6E 31 C9
Rodrigues *Ind. Oc.* 19°45S 63°20E 53 E13
Roe → *U.K.* 55°6N 6°59W 19 A8
Roes Welcome Sd. *Canada* 65°0N 87°0W 109 C11
Rogans Seat *U.K.* 54°26N 2°7W 26 D4
Rogate *U.K.* 51°0N 0°50W 31 D7
Rogers City *U.S.A.* 45°25N 83°49W 112 C6
Rohri *Pakistan* 27°45N 68°51E 84 F6
Rojo, C. *Mexico* 21°33N 97°20W 114 C5
Rolla *U.S.A.* 37°57N 91°46W 111 C8
Roma *Australia* 26°32S 148°49E 98 F8
Romaine → *Canada* 50°18N 63°47W 109 D13
Romania ■ *Europe* 46°0N 25°0E 65 F12
Romans-sur-Isère *France* 45°3N 5°3E 66 D6
Rome *Italy* 41°54N 12°28E 68 D5
Rome *Ga., U.S.A.* 34°15N 85°10W 111 D9
Rome *N.Y., U.S.A.* 43°13N 75°27W 113 D10
Romney *U.S.A.* 39°21N 78°45W 112 F8
Romney Marsh *U.K.* 51°2N 0°54E 31 D10
Romorantin-Lanthenay *France* 47°21N 1°45E 66 C4
Romsey *U.K.* 51°0N 1°29W 30 E6
Rona *U.K.* 57°34N 5°59W 22 G6
Roncador, Serra do *Brazil* 12°30S 52°30W 120 D4
Rondônia □ *Brazil* 11°0S 63°0W 120 D3
Rondonópolis *Brazil* 16°28S 54°38W 120 D4
Ronge, L. la *Canada* 55°6N 105°17W 108 D9
Ronne Ice Shelf *Antarctica* 77°30S 60°0W 55 D18
Roosevelt → *Brazil* 7°35S 60°20W 120 C3
Roosevelt I. *Antarctica* 79°30S 162°0W 55 D12
Ropsley *U.K.* 52°54N 0°30W 27 G8
Roquetas de Mar *Spain* 36°46N 2°36W 67 D4
Roraima □ *Brazil* 2°0N 61°30W 120 B3
Roraima, Mt. *Venezuela* 5°10N 60°40W 120 B3
Rosario *Argentina* 33°0S 60°40W 121 F3
Rosario *Mexico* 22°58N 105°53W 114 C3
Rosario de la Frontera *Argentina* 25°50S 65°0W 121 E3
Roscommon *Ireland* 53°38N 8°11W 18 D5
Roscommon □ *Ireland* 53°49N 8°23W 18 D5
Roscrea *Ireland* 52°57N 7°49W 20 C7
Roseau *Dominica* 15°17N 61°24W 115 D12
Roseburg *U.S.A.* 43°13N 123°20W 110 B2
Rosedale Abbey *U.K.* 54°21N 0°52W 26 D7
Rosehearty *U.K.* 57°42N 2°7W 23 G13
Rosenheim *Germany* 47°51N 12°7E 64 E7
Rosetown *Canada* 51°35N 107°59W 108 D9
Roseville *U.S.A.* 38°45N 121°17W 110 C2
Roslavl *Russia* 53°57N 32°55E 70 D5
Ross Ice Shelf *Antarctica* 80°0S 180°0E 55 E12
Ross-on-Wye *U.K.* 51°54N 2°34W 30 C5
Ross River *Canada* 62°30N 131°30W 108 C6
Ross Sea *Antarctica* 74°0S 178°0E 55 D11
Rossall Pt. *U.K.* 53°55N 3°3W 27 E2
Rossan Pt. *Ireland* 54°42N 8°47W 18 B4
Rosses, The *Ireland* 55°2N 8°20W 18 A5
Rossignol L. *Canada* 44°12N 65°10W 113 C15
Rosslare *Ireland* 52°17N 6°24W 21 D10
Rosslare Harbour *Ireland* 52°15N 6°20W 21 D10
Rossosh *Russia* 50°15N 39°28E 71 D6
Rostock *Germany* 54°5N 12°8E 64 A7
Rostov *Russia* 47°15N 39°45E 71 E6
Roswell *Ga., U.S.A.* 34°2N 84°22W 111 D10
Roswell *N. Mex., U.S.A.* 33°24N 104°32W 110 D6
Rote *Indonesia* 10°50S 123°0E 83 F6
Rothbury *U.K.* 55°19N 1°58W 26 B5
Rothbury Forest *U.K.* 55°19N 1°54W 26 B5
Rother → *U.K.* 50°59N 0°45E 31 E10
Rotherham *U.K.* 53°26N 1°20W 27 F6
Rothes *U.K.* 57°32N 3°13W 23 G11
Rothesay *U.K.* 55°50N 5°3W 24 D6
Rothwell *Northants., U.K.* 52°25N 0°48W 31 B7
Rothwell *W. Yorks., U.K.* 53°45N 1°28W 27 E6
Rotorua *N.Z.* 38°9S 176°16E 99 H14
Rotterdam *Neths.* 51°55N 4°30E 64 C3
Rottingdean *U.K.* 50°48N 0°4W 31 E8
Rotuma *Fiji* 12°25S 177°5E 99 C14
Roubaix *France* 50°40N 3°10E 66 A5
Rouen *France* 49°27N 1°4E 66 B4
Round Mt. *Australia* 30°26S 152°16E 98 G9
Rousay *U.K.* 59°10N 3°2W 23 D11
Roussillon *France* 42°30N 2°35E 66 E5
Rouyn-Noranda *Canada* 48°20N 79°0W 109 E12
Rovaniemi *Finland* 66°29N 25°41E 63 D9
Rovigo *Italy* 45°4N 11°47E 68 B4
Rowanburn *U.K.* 55°5N 2°55W 25 D10
Roxas *Phil.* 11°36N 122°49E 83 B6
Roxburgh *U.K.* 55°35N 2°28W 25 C11
Roxby *U.K.* 53°38N 0°38W 27 E7
Royal Canal *Ireland* 53°30N 7°13W 21 B8
Royal Leamington Spa *U.K.* 52°18N 1°31W 30 B5
Royal Tunbridge Wells *U.K.* 51°7N 0°16E 31 D9
Royal Wootton Bassett *U.K.* 51°32N 1°54W 30 C5
Royale, Isle *U.S.A.* 48°0N 88°54W 112 B3
Royan *France* 45°37N 1°2W 66 D3

Royston *U.K.* 52°3N 0°0 31 B8
Royton *U.K.* 53°34N 2°8W 27 E4
Rub' al Khālī *Si. Arabia* 19°0N 48°0E 89 D4
Rubery *U.K.* 52°24N 2°1W 30 B4
Rubh a' Mhail *U.K.* 55°56N 6°8W 24 C3
Rubha Hunish *U.K.* 57°42N 6°20W 22 G5
Rubtsovsk *Russia* 51°30N 81°10E 76 D9
Ruby L. *U.S.A.* 40°10N 115°28W 110 B3
Rudnyy *Kazakhstan* 52°57N 63°7E 76 D7
Rudston *U.K.* 54°6N 0°20W 26 D8
Rufford *U.K.* 53°38N 2°50W 27 E3
Rufiji → *Tanzania* 7°50S 39°15E 96 F7
Rugby *U.K.* 52°23N 1°16W 30 B6
Rugeley *U.K.* 52°46N 1°55W 27 G5
Rügen *Germany* 54°22N 13°24E 64 A7
Ruhr → *Germany* 51°27N 6°43E 64 C4
Ruki → *Dem. Rep. of the Congo* 0°5N 18°17E 96 E3
Rukwa, L. *Tanzania* 8°0S 32°20E 96 F6
Rùm *U.K.* 57°0N 6°20W 22 J5
Rùm, Sound of *U.K.* 56°55N 6°14W 22 J5
Rumania = Romania ■ *Europe* 46°0N 25°0E 65 F12
Rumford *U.S.A.* 44°33N 70°33W 113 C12
Runaway Bay *Jamaica* 18°27N 77°20W 114 a
Runcorn *U.K.* 53°21N 2°44W 27 F3
Rundu *Namibia* 17°52S 19°43E 97 H3
Rungwe *Tanzania* 9°11S 33°32E 96 F6
Ruo Shui → *China* 41°0N 100°16E 78 C9
Ruoqiang *China* 38°55N 88°10E 78 D6
Rupert → *China* 42°37N 113°41W 110 B4
Rupert → *Canada* 51°29N 78°45W 109 D12
Ruse *Bulgaria* 43°48N 25°59E 69 C12
Rush *Ireland* 53°31N 6°6W 21 A10
Rushden *U.K.* 52°18N 0°35W 31 B7
Rushville *Ill., U.S.A.* 40°7N 90°34W 112 E2
Rushville *Ind., U.S.A.* 39°37N 85°27W 112 F5
Ruskington *U.K.* 53°3N 0°22W 27 F8
Russellville *U.S.A.* 35°17N 93°8W 111 C8
Russia ■ *Eurasia* 62°0N 105°0E 77 C11
Rustavi *Georgia* 41°30N 45°0E 71 F8
Rustenburg *S. Africa* 25°41S 27°14E 97 K5
Rutherglen *U.K.* 55°49N 4°13W 24 C7
Ruthin *U.K.* 53°6N 3°19W 28 A7
Ruthwell *U.K.* 55°0N 3°25W 25 E9
Rutog *China* 33°27N 79°42E 78 E4
Ruvuma → *Tanzania* 10°29S 40°28E 96 G8
Ruwenzori *Africa* 0°30N 29°55E 96 D5
Rwanda ■ *Africa* 2°0S 30°0E 96 E5
Ryan, L. *U.K.* 55°0N 5°2W 24 E5
Ryazan *Russia* 54°40N 39°40E 70 D6
Rybachi Pen. *Russia* 69°43N 32°0E 70 A5
Rybinsk *Russia* 58°5N 38°50E 70 C6
Rybinsk Res. *Russia* 58°30N 38°25E 70 C6
Rydal *U.K.* 54°27N 2°59W 26 D3
Ryde *U.K.* 50°43N 1°9W 30 E6
Rye → *U.K.* 50°57N 0°45E 31 E10
Rye → *U.K.* 54°11N 0°44W 26 D7
Rye Bay *U.K.* 50°52N 0°49E 31 E10
Ryhope *U.K.* 54°53N 1°21W 26 C6
Ryton *U.K.* 52°22N 1°25W 30 B6
Ryukyu Is. *Japan* 26°0N 126°0E 79 F14
Rzeszów *Poland* 50°5N 21°58E 65 C11
Rzhev *Russia* 56°20N 34°20E 70 C5

S

Saale → *Germany* 51°56N 11°54E 64 C6
Saar → *Europe* 49°41N 6°32E 64 D4
Saarbrücken *Germany* 49°14N 6°59E 64 D4
Saaremaa *Estonia* 58°30N 22°30E 63 F8
Sabadell *Spain* 41°28N 2°7E 67 B7
Sabah □ *Malaysia* 6°0N 117°0E 82 C5
Sabhā *Libya* 27°9N 14°29E 95 C8
Sabinas *Mexico* 27°51N 101°7W 114 B4
Sabinas Hidalgo *Mexico* 26°30N 100°10W 114 B4
Sabine → *U.S.A.* 29°59N 93°47W 111 E8
Sable, C. *Canada* 43°29N 65°38W 113 D15
Sable, C. *U.S.A.* 25°9N 81°8W 111 E10
Sable I. *Canada* 44°0N 60°0W 109 E14
Sachsen □ *Germany* 50°55N 13°10E 64 C7
Sachsen-Anhalt □ *Germany* 52°0N 12°0E 64 C7
Saco *U.S.A.* 43°30N 70°27W 113 D12
Sacramento *U.S.A.* 38°35N 121°29W 110 C2
Sacramento → *U.S.A.* 38°3N 121°56W 110 C2
Sacramento Mts. *U.S.A.* 32°30N 105°30W 110 D5
Sado *Japan* 38°0N 138°25E 81 D6
Safford *U.S.A.* 32°50N 109°43W 110 D5
Saffron Walden *U.K.* 52°1N 0°16E 31 B9
Safi *Morocco* 32°18N 9°20W 94 B4
Saga *Japan* 33°15N 130°16E 81 G2
Sagaing *Burma* 21°52N 95°59E 85 J19
Sagar *India* 23°50N 78°44E 84 H11
Saginaw *U.S.A.* 43°26N 83°56W 112 D6
Saginaw B. *U.S.A.* 43°50N 83°40W 112 D6
Sagua la Grande *Cuba* 22°50N 80°10W 115 C8
Saguenay → *Canada* 48°22N 71°0W 113 A12
Sagunt *Spain* 39°42N 0°18W 67 C5
Sahara *Africa* 23°0N 5°0E 94 D6
Saharanpur *India* 29°58N 77°33E 84 E10
Sahel *Africa* 16°0N 5°0E 94 E5
Sahiwal *Pakistan* 30°45N 73°8E 84 D8
Saidpur *Bangla.* 25°48N 89°0E 85 G16
St. Abb's Head *U.K.* 55°55N 2°8W 25 C11
St. Agnes *Corn., U.K.* 50°19N 5°13W 29 G3
St. Agnes *Corn., U.K.* 49°54N 6°21W 29 H1
St. Agnes Hd. *U.K.* 50°19N 5°15W 29 G3
St. Albans *U.K.* 51°45N 0°19W 31 C8
St. Albans *Vt., U.S.A.* 44°49N 73°5W 113 C11
St. Albans *W. Va., U.S.A.* 38°23N 81°50W 112 F7
St. Alban's Head *U.K.* 50°34N 2°4W 30 E5
St. Andrews *U.K.* 56°20N 2°47W 25 B10
St. Ann's *U.K.* 55°14N 3°28W 25 D9
St. Ann's Bay *Jamaica* 18°26N 77°12W 114 a
St. Anthony *Canada* 51°22N 55°35W 109 D14
St. Asaph *U.K.* 53°15N 3°27W 28 A7
St. Augustin *Canada* 51°13N 58°38W 109 D14
St. Augustine *U.S.A.* 29°54N 81°19W 111 E10
St. Austell *U.K.* 50°20N 4°47W 29 G4
St. Bees *U.K.* 54°30N 3°36W 26 D1
St. Bees Hd. *U.K.* 54°31N 3°38W 26 C1
St. Blazey *U.K.* 50°22N 4°43W 29 G4
St. Brides B. *U.K.* 51°49N 5°9W 28 D3

St-Brieuc *France* 48°30N 2°46W 66 B2
St. Buryan *U.K.* 50°4N 5°37W 29 G2
St. Catharines *Canada* 43°10N 79°15W 112 D8
St. Catherine's Pt. *U.K.* 50°34N 1°18W 30 E6
St. Charles *U.S.A.* 38°47N 90°29W 112 F8
St. Clair, L. *N. Amer.* 42°27N 82°39W 112 D6
St. Clears *U.K.* 51°49N 4°31W 28 D3
St. Cloud *U.S.A.* 45°34N 94°10W 111 A8
St. Columb Major *U.K.* 50°26N 4°58W 29 G4
St. Croix *U.S. Virgin Is.* 17°45N 64°45W 115 D12
St. David's *U.K.* 51°53N 5°16W 28 D3
St. David's Head *U.K.* 51°54N 5°19W 28 D3
St-Denis *France* 48°56N 2°20E 66 B5
St. Dennis *U.K.* 50°23N 4°53W 29 G4
St-Dizier *France* 48°38N 4°56E 66 B6
St. Dominick *U.K.* 50°29N 4°16W 29 G3
St. Elias, Mt. *U.S.A.* 60°18N 140°56W 108 C5
St. Elias Mts. *N. Amer.* 60°33N 139°28W 108 D6
St. Enoder *U.K.* 50°22N 4°59W 29 G4
St. Erth *U.K.* 50°9N 5°26W 29 G3
St-Étienne *France* 45°27N 4°22E 66 D6
St-Félicien *Canada* 48°40N 72°25W 113 A11
St-Flour *France* 45°2N 3°6E 66 D5
St. Gallen *Switz.* 47°26N 9°22E 64 E5
St-Gaudens *France* 43°6N 0°44E 66 E4
St. George *U.S.A.* 37°6N 113°35W 110 C4
St-Georges *Canada* 46°8N 70°40W 113 B12
St. George's *Grenada* 12°5N 61°43W 115 E12
St. George's Channel *Europe* 52°0N 6°0W 21 E11
St. Germans *U.K.* 50°23N 4°19W 29 G3
St. Helena *Atl. Oc.* 15°58S 5°42W 52 E9
St. Helens *U.K.* 53°27N 2°44W 27 F3
St. Helens, Mt. *U.S.A.* 46°12N 122°12W 110 A2
St. Helier *U.K.* 49°10N 2°7W 29 J9
St-Hyacinthe *Canada* 45°40N 72°58W 109 E12
St. Ignace *U.S.A.* 45°52N 84°44W 112 C5
St. Issey *U.K.* 50°30N 4°57W 29 G4
St. Ives *Cambs., U.K.* 52°20N 0°4W 31 B8
St. Ives *Corn., U.K.* 50°12N 5°30W 29 G3
St. Ives B. *U.K.* 50°13N 5°27W 29 G3
St-Jean, L. *Canada* 48°40N 72°0W 113 A12
St-Jérôme *Canada* 45°47N 74°0W 113 C11
St. John *Canada* 45°20N 66°8W 109 E13
St. John → *N. Amer.* 45°12N 66°5W 104 E13
St. John's *Antigua & B.* 17°6N 61°51W 115 D12
St. John's *Canada* 47°35N 52°40W 109 E14
St. Johns *U.S.A.* 43°0N 84°33W 112 D5
St. Johns → *U.S.A.* 30°24N 81°24W 111 E10
St. Johns Chapel *U.K.* 54°44N 2°10W 26 C4
St. John's Pt. *Ireland* 54°34N 8°27W 18 B5
St. Johnsbury *U.S.A.* 44°25N 72°1W 113 C11
St. Joseph *Mich., U.S.A.* 42°6N 86°29W 112 D4
St. Joseph *Mo., U.S.A.* 39°46N 94°50W 111 F8
St. Joseph, L. *Canada* 51°10N 90°35W 109 D10
St. Just *U.K.* 50°7N 5°42W 29 G2
St. Keverne *U.K.* 50°3N 5°6W 29 G3
St. Kilda *U.K.* 57°49N 8°34W 22 b
St. Kitts & Nevis ■ *W. Indies* 17°20N 62°40W 115 D12
St. Lawrence → *Canada* 49°30N 66°0W 109 E13
St. Lawrence, Gulf of *Canada* 48°25N 62°0W 109 E13
St. Lawrence I. *U.S.A.* 63°30N 170°30W 108 C3
St. Levan *U.K.* 50°2N 5°41W 29 G2
St-Lô *France* 49°7N 1°5W 66 B3
St-Louis *Senegal* 16°8N 16°27W 94 E2
St. Louis *U.S.A.* 38°37N 90°11W 112 F8
St. Lucia ■ *W. Indies* 14°0N 60°57W 114 b
St. Mabyn *U.K.* 50°30N 4°47W 29 G3
St. Magnus B. *U.K.* 60°25N 1°35W 22 B14
St-Malo *France* 48°39N 2°1W 66 B2
St-Marc *Haiti* 19°10N 72°41W 115 D10
St. Margaret's-at-Cliffe *U.K.* 51°9N 1°23E 31 D11
St-Martin □ *W. Indies* 18°5N 63°5W 115 D12
St. Martins *Barbados* 13°5N 59°28W 114 c
St. Martin's *U.K.* 49°58N 6°17W 29 H1
St. Mary Bourne *U.K.* 51°15N 1°24W 30 D6
St. Mary, Corn., *U.K.* 49°55N 6°18W 29 H1
St. Mary's *Orkney, U.K.* 58°54N 2°54W 23 C12
St. Marys *U.S.A.* 41°26N 78°34W 112 E8
St. Mary's Sd. *U.K.* 49°54N 6°20W 29 H1
St. Matthew I. *U.S.A.* 60°24N 172°42W 108 C2
St. Mawes *U.K.* 50°10N 5°2W 29 G3
St. Merryn *U.K.* 50°32N 5°1W 29 F3
St. Michael's Mount *U.K.* 50°7N 5°29W 29 G3
St. Minver *U.K.* 50°33N 4°53W 29 F3
St. Moritz *Switz.* 46°30N 9°51E 64 E5
St-Nazaire *France* 47°17N 2°12W 66 C2
St. Neots *U.K.* 52°14N 0°15W 31 B8
St-Omer *France* 50°45N 2°15E 66 A5
St. Osyth *U.K.* 51°47N 1°5E 31 C11
St. Paul *U.S.A.* 44°56N 93°5W 111 B8
St. Paul, Î. *Ind. Oc.* 38°55S 77°34E 53 F13
St. Peter Port *U.K.* 49°26N 2°33W 29 J8
St. Petersburg *Russia* 59°55N 30°20E 70 C5
St. Petersburg *U.S.A.* 27°46N 82°40W 111 E10
St-Pierre-et-Miquelon ☑ *N. Amer.* 46°55N 56°10W 109 E14
St-Quentin *France* 49°50N 3°16E 66 B5
St. Stephen *Canada* 45°16N 67°17W 113 C14
St. Stephen *U.K.* 50°21N 4°53W 29 G4
St. Teath *U.K.* 50°35N 4°45W 29 F4
St. Thomas *Canada* 42°45N 81°10W 112 D7
St-Tropez *France* 43°17N 6°38E 66 E7
St. Tudy *U.K.* 50°33N 4°45W 29 F4
St. Vincent, G. *Australia* 35°0S 138°0E 98 G6
St. Vincent & the Grenadines ■ *W. Indies* 13°0N 61°10W 115 E12
Ste. Genevieve *U.S.A.* 37°59N 90°2W 112 G8
Ste-Marie *Canada* 46°26N 71°0W 113 B12
Saintes *France* 45°45N 0°37W 66 D3
Saintfield *U.K.* 54°28N 5°49W 19 C10
Saintonge *France* 45°40N 0°50W 66 D3
Saipan *N. Marianas* 15°12N 145°45E 102 F6
Saitama *Japan* 35°54N 139°38E 81 F7
Sajama *Bolivia* 18°7S 69°0W 120 D3
Sakākah *Si. Arabia* 30°0N 40°8E 86 D5
Sakakawea, L. *U.S.A.* 47°30N 101°25W 110 A6
Sakarya *Turkey* 40°48N 30°25E 71 F5
Sakata *Japan* 38°55N 139°50E 81 D6
Sakha □ *Russia* 66°0N 130°0E 77 C13
Sakhalin *Russia* 51°0N 143°0E 77 D15

Sakurajima *Japan* 31°35N 130°39E 81 H2
Sala *Sweden* 59°58N 16°35E 63 F7
Sala-y-Gómez *Pac. Oc.* 26°28S 105°28W 103 K17
Salado → *La Pampa, Argentina* 37°30S 67°0W 121 F3
Salado → *Santa Fe, Argentina* 31°40S 60°41W 121 F3
Salālah *Oman* 16°56N 53°59E 89 D5
Salamanca *Spain* 40°58N 5°39W 67 B3
Salamanca *U.S.A.* 42°10N 78°43W 112 D8
Salavat *Russia* 53°21N 55°55E 70 D10
Salaverry *Peru* 8°15S 79°0W 120 C2
Salayar *Indonesia* 6°7S 120°30E 83 F6
Salcombe *U.K.* 50°14N 3°47W 29 G6
Saldanha *S. Africa* 33°0S 17°58E 97 L3
Sale *Morocco* 34°3N 6°48W 94 B4
Sale *Australia* 38°6S 147°6E 98 H8
Salekhard *Russia* 66°30N 66°35E 76 C7
Salem *India* 11°40N 78°11E 84 P11
Salem *Ind., U.S.A.* 38°36N 86°6W 112 F4
Salem *Mass., U.S.A.* 42°31N 70°53W 113 D12
Salem *Ohio, U.S.A.* 40°54N 80°52W 112 E7
Salem *Oreg., U.S.A.* 44°56N 123°2W 110 B2
Salem *Va., U.S.A.* 37°18N 80°3W 112 G7
Salerno *Italy* 40°41N 14°47E 68 D6
Salford *U.K.* 53°30N 2°18W 27 F4
Salford Priors *U.K.* 52°10N 1°53W 30 B5
Salida *U.S.A.* 38°32N 106°0W 110 C5
Salina *U.S.A.* 38°50N 97°37W 110 C7
Salina Cruz *Mexico* 16°10N 95°12W 114 D5
Salinas *Ecuador* 2°10S 80°58W 120 C1
Salinas *U.S.A.* 36°40N 121°39W 110 C2
Salinas Grandes *Argentina* 30°0S 65°0W 121 E3
Salisbury *U.K.* 51°4N 1°47W 30 D5
Salisbury *U.S.A.* 38°22N 75°36W 113 F10
Salisbury I. *Canada* 63°30N 77°0W 109 C12
Salisbury Plain *U.K.* 51°14N 1°55W 30 D5
Salmon *U.S.A.* 45°11N 113°54W 110 A4
Salmon → *U.S.A.* 45°51N 116°47W 110 A3
Salmon Arm *Canada* 50°40N 119°15W 108 D8
Salmon River Mts. *U.S.A.* 44°50N 115°30W 110 B6
Salon-de-Provence *France* 43°39N 5°6E 66 E6
Salsk *Russia* 46°28N 41°30E 71 E7
Salt → *U.S.A.* 33°23N 112°19W 110 D4
Salt Lake City *U.S.A.* 40°45N 111°53W 110 B8
Salta *Argentina* 24°57S 65°25W 121 E3
Saltash *U.K.* 50°24N 4°14W 29 G5
Saltburn by the Sea *U.K.* 54°35N 0°58W 26 C7
Saltcoats *U.K.* 55°38N 4°47W 24 C6
Saltee Is. *Ireland* 52°7N 6°37W 21 D9
Saltfleet *U.K.* 53°25N 0°11E 27 F9
Saltfleetby *U.K.* 53°23N 0°10E 27 F9
Saltillo *Mexico* 25°25N 101°0W 114 B4
Salton Sea *U.S.A.* 33°15N 115°45W 110 D3
Saltwood *U.K.* 51°4N 1°2E 31 D11
Salvador *Brazil* 13°0S 38°30W 122 B3
Salween → *Burma* 16°31N 97°37E 85 L20
Salyan *Azerbaijan* 39°33N 48°59E 71 G8
Salzburg *Austria* 47°48N 13°2E 64 E7
Salzgitter *Germany* 52°9N 10°19E 64 B6
Samar *Phil.* 12°0N 125°0E 83 B7
Samara *Russia* 53°8N 50°6E 70 D9
Samarinda *Indonesia* 0°30S 117°9E 82 E5
Samarqand *Uzbekistan* 39°40N 66°55E 87 B11
Sambalpur *India* 21°28N 84°4E 85 J14
Sambhal *India* 28°35N 78°37E 84 E11
Sambhar *India* 26°52N 75°6E 84 F9
Samoa ■ *Pac. Oc.* 14°0S 172°0W 99 C16
Samos *Greece* 37°45N 26°50E 69 F12
Samothraki *Greece* 40°28N 25°28E 69 D11
Sampford Courtenay *U.K.* 50°47N 3°58W 29 F6
Samsun *Turkey* 41°15N 36°22E 71 F6
Samui, Ko *Thailand* 9°30N 100°0E 82 C2
San → *Poland* 50°45N 21°51E 65 C11
San Ambrosio *Pac. Oc.* 26°28S 79°53W 103 K20
San Andrés, I. de *Caribbean* 12°42N 81°46W 115 E8
San Andres Mts. *U.S.A.* 33°0N 106°30W 110 D5
San Andrés Tuxtla *Mexico* 18°27N 95°13W 114 D5
San Angelo *U.S.A.* 31°28N 100°26W 110 D6
San Antonio *Chile* 33°40S 71°40W 121 F2
San Antonio *U.S.A.* 29°25N 98°29W 110 E7
San Antonio → *U.S.A.* 28°30N 96°54W 111 E7
San Antonio Oeste *Argentina* 40°40S 65°0W 121 G3
San Bernardino *U.S.A.* 34°7N 117°19W 110 D3
San Bernardino Str. *Phil.* 12°30N 124°10E 83 B6
San Bernardo *Chile* 33°40S 70°50W 121 F2
San Blas, C. *U.S.A.* 29°40N 85°21W 111 E9
San Carlos *Phil.* 10°29N 123°25E 83 B6
San Carlos de Bariloche *Argentina* 41°10S 71°25W 121 G2
San Carlos de Bolívar *Argentina* 36°15S 61°6W 121 F3
San Cristóbal *Argentina* 30°20S 61°10W 121 F3
San Cristóbal *Solomon Is.* 10°30S 161°0E 99 C11
San Cristóbal *Venezuela* 7°46N 72°14W 120 B2
San Cristóbal de las Casas *Mexico* 16°45N 92°38W 114 D6
San Diego *U.S.A.* 32°42N 117°9W 110 D3
San Felipe *Venezuela* 10°20N 68°44W 120 A3
San Félix *Pac. Oc.* 26°23S 80°0W 103 K20
San Fernando *Chile* 34°30S 71°0W 121 F2
San Fernando *Spain* 36°28N 6°17W 67 D2
San Fernando de Apure *Venezuela* 7°54N 67°15W 120 B3
San Francisco *U.S.A.* 37°46N 122°23W 110 C2
San Francisco, C. de *Colombia* 6°18N 77°29W 117 C3
San Francisco de Macoris *Dom. Rep.* 19°19N 70°15W 115 D10
San Gottardo, P. del *Switz.* 46°33N 8°33E 64 E5
San Ignacio *Bolivia* 16°20S 60°55W 120 D3
San Joaquin → *U.S.A.* 38°4N 121°51W 110 C2
San Jorge, G. *Argentina* 46°0S 66°0W 121 G3
San José *Costa Rica* 9°55N 84°2W 115 F8
San Jose *Phil.* 12°27N 121°4E 83 B6
San Jose *U.S.A.* 37°20N 121°53W 110 C2
San José → *U.S.A.* 34°25N 106°45W 110 D5
San José de Chiquitos *Bolivia* 17°53S 60°50W 120 D3
San José de Jáchal *Argentina* 30°5S 68°46W 121 F3
San José de Mayo *Uruguay* 34°27S 56°40W 121 F4
San José del Cabo *Mexico* 23°3N 109°41W 114 C3

San Juan *Argentina* 31°30S 68°30W 121 F3
San Juan *Puerto Rico* 18°28N 66°7W 115 D11
San Juan → *Nic.* 10°56N 83°42W 115 E8
San Juan → *U.S.A.* 37°16N 110°26W 110 C4
San Juan de la Maguana *Dom. Rep.* 18°49N 71°12W 115 D10
San Juan de los Morros *Venezuela* 9°55N 67°21W 120 B3
San Juan Mts. *U.S.A.* 37°30N 107°0W 110 C5
San Lorenzo, Mte. *Argentina* 47°40S 72°20W 121 G2
San Lucas, C. *Mexico* 22°52N 109°53W 114 C3
San Luis *Argentina* 33°20S 66°20W 121 F3
San Luis Obispo *U.S.A.* 35°17N 120°40W 110 C2
San Luis Potosí *Mexico* 22°9N 100°59W 114 C4
San Marcos *U.S.A.* 29°53N 97°56W 110 E7
San Marino ■ *Europe* 43°56N 12°25E 68 C5
San Matías, G. *Argentina* 41°30S 64°0W 121 G3
San Miguel *El Salv.* 13°30N 88°12W 114 E7
San Miguel de Tucumán *Argentina* 26°50S 65°20W 121 E3
San Nicolás *Argentina* 33°25S 60°10W 121 F3
San Pedro *Ivory C.* 4°50N 6°33W 94 H4
San Pedro de las Colonias *Mexico* 25°45N 102°59W 114 B4
San Pedro de Macorís *Dom. Rep.* 18°30N 69°18W 115 D11
San Pedro Sula *Honduras* 15°30N 88°0W 114 D7
San Pietro *Italy* 39°8N 8°17E 68 E3
San Rafael *Argentina* 34°40S 68°21W 121 F3
San Remo *Italy* 43°49N 7°46E 68 C2
San Salvador *El Salv.* 13°40N 89°10W 114 E7
San Salvador de Jujuy *Argentina* 24°10S 64°48W 121 E3
San Salvador I. *Bahamas* 24°0N 74°30W 115 C10
San Severo *Italy* 41°41N 15°23E 68 D6
San Valentín, Mte. *Chile* 46°30S 73°30W 121 G2
Sana' = Sanaa *Yemen* 15°27N 44°12E 89 D3
Sanaa *Yemen* 15°27N 44°12E 89 D3
Sanaga → *Cameroon* 3°35N 9°38E 96 D1
Sanandaj *Iran* 35°18N 47°1E 86 C6
Sancti Spíritus *Cuba* 21°52N 79°33W 115 C9
Sancy, Puy de *France* 45°32N 2°50E 66 D5
Sandakan *Malaysia* 5°53N 118°4E 82 C5
Sanday *U.K.* 59°16N 2°31W 23 D12
Sandbach *U.K.* 53°9N 2°21W 27 F4
Sandgate *U.K.* 51°4N 1°10E 31 D11
Sandhurst *U.K.* 51°21N 0°48W 31 D7
Sandness *U.K.* 60°18N 1°38W 22 A15
Sandnes *Norway* 58°50N 5°45E 63 F5
Sandoa *Dem. Rep. of the Congo* 9°41S 23°0E 96 F4
Sandomierz *Poland* 50°40N 21°43E 65 C11
Sandown *U.K.* 50°39N 1°10W 30 E6
Sandpoint *U.S.A.* 48°17N 116°33W 110 A3
Sandray *U.K.* 56°53N 7°31W 22 J2
Sandringham *U.K.* 52°51N 0°31E 31 A10
Sandusky *U.S.A.* 41°27N 82°42W 112 E6
Sandwich *U.K.* 51°16N 1°21E 31 D11
Sandy *U.K.* 52°8N 0°17W 31 B8
Sandy L. *Canada* 53°2N 93°0W 108 D10
Sanford, Mt. *U.S.A.* 62°13N 144°8W 108 C5
Sangihe, Pulau *Indonesia* 3°35N 125°30E 83 D7
Sangli *India* 16°55N 74°33E 84 L9
Sangre de Cristo Mts. *U.S.A.* 37°30N 105°20W 110 C5
Sanikiluaq *Canada* 56°32N 79°14W 109 D12
Sankt Pölten *Austria* 48°12N 15°38E 64 D8
Sankuru → *Dem. Rep. of the Congo* 4°17S 20°25E 96 E4
Şanlıurfa *Turkey* 37°12N 38°50E 71 G6
Sanlúcar de Barrameda *Spain* 36°46N 6°21W 67 D2
Sanmenxia *China* 34°47N 111°12E 79 E11
Sanming *China* 26°15N 117°40E 79 F12
Sanndraigh = Sandray *U.K.* 56°53N 7°31W 22 J2
Sanquhar *U.K.* 55°22N 3°54W 25 D8
Sant Feliu de Guíxols *Spain* 41°45N 3°1E 67 B7
Sant' Antioco *Italy* 39°4N 8°27E 68 E3
Santa Barbara *U.S.A.* 34°25N 119°42W 110 D3
Santa Catarina □ *Brazil* 27°25S 48°30W 121 E5
Santa Clara *Cuba* 22°20N 80°0W 115 C9
Santa Clarita *U.S.A.* 34°24N 118°33W 110 D3
Santa Coloma de Gramenet *Spain* 41°27N 2°13E 67 B7
Santa Cruz *Bolivia* 17°43S 63°10W 120 D3
Santa Cruz → *Argentina* 50°10S 68°20W 121 H3
Santa Cruz de Tenerife *Canary Is.* 28°28N 16°15W 94 C2
Santa Cruz Is. *Solomon Is.* 10°30S 166°0E 99 C12
Santa Cruz Mts. *Jamaica* 17°58N 77°43W 114 a
Santa Fé *Argentina* 31°35S 60°41W 121 F3
Santa Fe *U.S.A.* 35°41N 105°57W 110 C5
Santa Inês, I. *Chile* 54°0S 73°0W 121 H2
Santa Isabel *Solomon Is.* 8°0S 159°0E 99 B10
Santa Maria *Brazil* 29°40S 53°48W 121 E4
Santa Maria *U.S.A.* 34°57N 120°26W 110 D2
Santa María → *Mexico* 31°0N 107°14W 114 A3
Santa Marta *Colombia* 11°15N 74°13W 120 A2
Santa Marta, Sierra Nevada de *Colombia* 10°55N 73°50W 120 A2
Santa Rosa *Argentina* 36°40S 64°17W 121 F3
Santa Rosa *U.S.A.* 38°26N 122°43W 110 C2
Santai *China* 31°5N 104°58E 78 E9
Santana do Livramento *Brazil* 30°55S 55°30W 121 F4
Santander *Spain* 43°27N 3°51W 67 A4
Santanilla, Is. *Honduras* 17°22N 83°57W 115 D8
Santarém *Brazil* 2°25S 54°42W 120 C4
Santarém *Portugal* 39°12N 8°42W 67 C1
Santiago *Chile* 33°26S 70°40W 121 F2
Santiago de Compostela *Spain* 42°52N 8°37W 67 A1
Santiago de Cuba *Cuba* 20°0N 75°49W 115 D9
Santiago de los Caballeros *Dom. Rep.* 19°30N 70°40W 115 D10
Santiago del Estero *Argentina* 27°50S 64°15W 121 E3
Santo Amaro *Brazil* 12°30S 38°43W 122 B3
Santo André *Brazil* 23°39S 46°29W 122 D1
Santo Antônio de Jesus *Brazil* 12°58S 39°16W 122 B3
Santo Domingo *Dom. Rep.* 18°30N 69°59W 115 D11
Santo Domingo de los Colorados *Ecuador* 0°15S 79°9W 120 C2
Santorini *Greece* 36°23N 25°27E 69 F11

Santos   Somerby

Santos *Brazil* 24°0S 46°20W **122 D1**
Santos Dumont *Brazil* 22°55S 43°10W **122 D2**
Sanxiang *China* 22°21N 113°25E **79 a**
Sanya *China* 18°14N 109°29E **79 H10**
São Bernardo do Campo *Brazil* 23°45S 46°34W **122 D1**
São Borja *Brazil* 28°39S 56°0W **121 E4**
São Caitano *Brazil* 8°21S 36°6W **122 A3**
São Carlos *Brazil* 22°0S 47°50W **122 D1**
São Francisco → *Brazil* 10°30S 36°24W **122 B3**
São Gonçalo *Brazil* 22°48S 43°5W **122 D2**
São João da Boa Vista *Brazil* 22°0S 46°52W **122 D1**
São João de Meriti *Brazil* 22°48S 43°22W **122 D2**
São João del Rei *Brazil* 21°8S 44°15W **122 D2**
São João do Piauí *Brazil* 8°21S 42°15W **122 A2**
São José do Rio Preto *Brazil* 20°50S 49°20W **122 D1**
São José dos Campos *Brazil* 23°7S 45°52W **122 D1**
São Lourenço *Brazil* 22°7S 45°3W **122 D1**
São Luis *Brazil* 2°39S 44°15W **120 C5**
São Marcos → *Brazil* 18°15S 47°37W **122 C1**
São Marcos, B. de *Brazil* 2°0S 44°0W **120 C5**
São Mateus *Brazil* 18°44S 39°50W **122 C3**
São Paulo *Brazil* 23°32S 46°38W **122 D1**
São Paulo □ *Brazil* 22°0S 49°0W **120 E5**
São Roque, C. de *Brazil* 5°30S 35°16W **120 C6**
São Sebastião do Paraíso *Brazil* 20°54S 46°59W **122 D1**
São Tomé *São Tomé & Príncipe* 0°10N 6°39E **90 F4**
São Tomé & Príncipe ■ *Africa* 0°12N 6°39E **91 F4**
São Vicente *Brazil* 23°57S 46°23W **122 D1**
São Vicente, C. de *Portugal* 37°0N 9°0W **67 D1**
Saône → *France* 45°44N 4°50E **66 D6**
Sapele *Nigeria* 5°50N 5°40E **94 G7**
Sapporo *Japan* 43°0N 141°21E **81 B7**
Saqqez *Iran* 36°15N 46°20E **86 B6**
Sar-e Pol *Afghan.* 36°10N 66°0E **87 B11**
Saraburi *Thailand* 14°30N 100°55E **82 B2**
Sarajevo *Bos.-H.* 43°52N 18°26E **69 C8**
Saranac Lakes *U.S.A.* 44°20N 74°28W **113 C10**
Saransk *Russia* 54°10N 45°10E **70 D8**
Sarapul *Russia* 56°28N 53°48E **70 C9**
Sarasota *U.S.A.* 27°20N 82°32W **111 E10**
Saratoga Springs *U.S.A.* 43°5N 73°47W **113 D11**
Saratov *Russia* 51°30N 46°2E **71 D8**
Sarawak □ *Malaysia* 2°0N 113°0E **82 D4**
Sarda → *India* 27°21N 81°23E **85 F12**
Sardinia □ *Italy* 40°0N 9°0E **68 D3**
Sargasso Sea *Atl. Oc.* 27°0N 72°0W **104 G13**
Sargodha *Pakistan* 32°10N 72°40E **84 C8**
Sarh *Chad* 9°5N 18°23E **95 G9**
Sārī *Iran* 36°30N 53°4E **87 B8**
Sariwon *N. Korea* 38°31N 125°46E **79 D14**
Sark *U.K.* 49°25N 2°22W **29 J9**
Sarlat-la-Canéda *France* 44°54N 1°13E **66 D4**
Sarmiento *Argentina* 45°35S 69°5W **121 G3**
Sarnia *Canada* 42°58N 82°23W **109 E11**
Sarqan *Kazakhstan* 45°24N 79°55E **78 B4**
Sarreguemines *France* 49°5N 7°4E **66 B7**
Sarthe → *France* 47°33N 0°31W **66 C3**
Sasebo *Japan* 33°10N 129°43E **81 G1**
Saskatchewan □ *Canada* 54°40N 106°0W **108 D9**
Saskatchewan → *Canada* 53°37N 100°40W **108 D9**
Saskatoon *Canada* 52°10N 106°38W **108 D9**
Sássari *Italy* 40°43N 8°34E **68 D3**
Sassnitz *Germany* 54°29N 13°39E **64 A7**
Satmala Hills *Andhra Pradesh, India* 19°45N 78°45E **84 K11**
Satmala Hills *Maharashtra, India* 20°15N 74°40E **84 J9**
Satna *India* 24°35N 80°50E **85 G12**
Satpura Ra. *India* 21°25N 76°10E **84 J10**
Satu Mare *Romania* 47°46N 22°55E **65 E12**
Saudi Arabia ■ *Asia* 26°0N 44°0E **89 B3**
Sault Ste. Marie *Canada* 46°30N 84°20W **112 B5**
Saumur *France* 47°15N 0°5W **66 C3**
Saundersfoot *U.K.* 51°43N 4°42W **28 D4**
Saurimo *Angola* 9°40S 20°12E **96 F4**
Sava → *Serbia* 44°50N 20°26E **69 B9**
Savai'i *Samoa* 13°28S 172°24W **99 C16**
Savanna-la-Mar *Jamaica* 18°10N 78°10W **114 a**
Savannah *U.S.A.* 32°5N 81°6W **111 D10**
Savannah → *U.S.A.* 32°2N 80°53W **111 D10**
Savannakhet *Laos* 16°30N 104°49E **82 A2**
Savoie □ *France* 45°26N 6°25E **66 D7**
Savona *Italy* 44°17N 8°30E **68 B3**
Sawatch Range *U.S.A.* 39°0N 106°30W **110 C5**
Sawbridgeworth *U.K.* 51°48N 0°9E **31 C9**
Sawel Mt. *U.K.* 54°50N 7°2W **19 B7**
Sawston *U.K.* 52°8N 0°10E **31 B9**
Sawtry *U.K.* 52°27N 0°17W **31 B8**
Sawu *Indonesia* 10°35S 121°50E **83 F6**
Sawu Sea *Indonesia* 9°30S 121°50E **83 F6**
Saxilby *U.K.* 53°16N 0°38W **27 F7**
Saxlingham Nethergate *U.K.* 52°32N 1°18E **31 A11**
Saxmundham *U.K.* 52°13N 1°30E **31 B12**
Saxony = Sachsen □ *Germany* 50°55N 13°10E **64 C7**
Sayan Mts. *Russia* 54°0N 96°0E **77 D10**
Saydā *Lebanon* 33°35N 35°25E **86 C3**
Sayre *U.S.A.* 41°59N 76°32W **112 E9**
Sázava → *Czech Rep.* 49°53N 14°24E **64 D8**
Scafell Pike *U.K.* 54°27N 3°14W **26 D2**
Scalby *U.K.* 54°18N 0°26W **26 D8**
Scalloway *U.K.* 60°9N 1°17W **22 B15**
Scalpay *Highl., U.K.* 57°18N 6°0W **22 H6**
Scalpay *W. Isles, U.K.* 57°52N 6°40W **22 G4**
Scamblesby *U.K.* 53°17N 0°5W **27 F8**
Scandicci *Italy* 43°45N 11°11E **68 C4**
Scandinavia *Europe* 64°0N 12°0E **56 C8**
Scapa Flow *U.K.* 58°53N 3°3W **23 C11**
Scarba *U.K.* 56°11N 5°43W **24 B4**
Scarborough *U.K.* 54°17N 0°24W **26 D8**
Scariff I. *Ireland* 51°44N 10°15W **20 E2**
Scarning *U.K.* 52°41N 0°54E **31 A10**
Scarp *U.K.* 58°1N 7°8W **22 F3**
Schaffhausen *Switz.* 47°42N 8°39E **64 E5**
Schelde → *Belgium* 51°15N 4°16E **64 C3**
Schenectady *U.S.A.* 42°49N 73°57W **113 D11**
Schiehallion *U.K.* 56°40N 4°6W **24 A7**
Schleswig *Germany* 54°31N 9°34E **64 A5**
Schleswig-Holstein □ *Germany* 54°30N 9°30E **64 A5**

Schreiber *Canada* 48°45N 87°20W **112 A4**
Schwäbische Alb *Germany* 48°20N 9°30E **64 D5**
Schwarzwald *Germany* 48°30N 8°20E **64 D5**
Schwerin *Germany* 53°36N 11°22E **64 B6**
Schwyz *Switz.* 47°2N 8°39E **64 E5**
Scilly Is. *U.K.* 49°56N 6°22W **29 H1**
Scioto → *U.S.A.* 38°44N 83°1W **112 F6**
Scole *U.K.* 52°22N 1°10E **31 B11**
Scone *U.K.* 56°25N 3°24W **25 B9**
Scopwick *U.K.* 53°8N 0°24W **27 F8**
Scotia Sea *Antarctica* 56°5S 56°0W **55 B18**
Scotland □ *U.K.* 57°0N 4°0W **62 C5**
Scott I. *Antarctica* 67°0S 179°0E **55 C11**
Scottish Borders □ *U.K.* 55°35N 2°50W **25 C10**
Scottsbluff *U.S.A.* 41°52N 103°40W **110 B6**
Scottsburg *U.S.A.* 38°41N 85°47W **112 F5**
Scrabster *U.K.* 58°36N 3°33W **23 E10**
Scranton *U.S.A.* 41°25N 75°40W **113 E10**
Scremerston *U.K.* 55°44N 2°0W **26 A5**
Scunthorpe *U.K.* 53°36N 0°39W **27 E7**
Scutari *Albania* 42°4N 19°32E **69 C8**
Scutari *Turkey* 41°1N 29°0E **86 A2**
Seaford *U.K.* 50°47N 0°7E **31 E9**
Seaford *U.S.A.* 38°39N 75°37W **113 F10**
Seaforth, L. *U.K.* 57°52N 6°36W **22 G4**
Seaham *U.K.* 54°50N 1°20W **26 C6**
Seahouses *U.K.* 55°34N 1°39W **26 A5**
Seal → *Canada* 59°4N 94°48W **108 D10**
Seamer *U.K.* 54°15N 0°26W **26 D8**
Seascale *U.K.* 54°24N 3°29W **26 D2**
Seaton *Cumb., U.K.* 54°40N 3°31W **26 C1**
Seaton *Devon, U.K.* 50°42N 3°5W **29 F7**
Seaton Delaval *U.K.* 55°5N 1°33W **26 B5**
Seattle *U.S.A.* 47°36N 122°19W **110 A2**
Sebastián Vizcaíno, B. *Mexico* 28°0N 114°30W **114 B2**
Şebinkarahisar *Turkey* 40°22N 38°28E **71 F6**
Sedalia *U.S.A.* 38°42N 93°14W **111 C8**
Sedan *France* 49°43N 4°57E **66 B6**
Sedbergh *U.K.* 54°20N 2°31W **26 D3**
Sedgefield *U.K.* 54°40N 1°26W **26 C6**
Seend *U.K.* 51°21N 2°4W **30 D4**
Segesta *Italy* 37°56N 12°50E **68 F5**
Ségou *Mali* 13°30N 6°16W **94 F4**
Segovia *Spain* 40°57N 4°10W **67 B3**
Séguéla *Ivory C.* 7°55N 6°40W **94 G4**
Sehore *India* 23°10N 77°5E **84 H10**
Seil *U.K.* 56°18N 5°38W **24 B4**
Seine → *France* 49°26N 0°26E **66 B4**
Sekondi-Takoradi *Ghana* 4°58N 1°45W **94 H5**
Selborne *U.K.* 51°6N 0°56W **31 D7**
Selby *U.K.* 53°47N 1°5W **27 E6**
Selebi-Phikwe *Botswana* 21°58S 27°48E **97 J5**
Selenge Mörön → *Asia* 52°16N 106°16E **78 A10**
Selkirk *Canada* 50°10N 96°55W **108 D10**
Selkirk *U.K.* 55°33N 2°50W **25 C10**
Selkirk Mts. *Canada* 51°15N 117°40W **108 D8**
Sellafield *U.K.* 54°25N 3°29W **26 D2**
Selma *U.S.A.* 32°25N 87°1W **111 D9**
Selsey *U.K.* 50°44N 0°47W **31 E7**
Selsey Bill *U.K.* 50°43N 0°47W **31 E7**
Selvas *Brazil* 6°30S 67°0W **120 C3**
Selwyn L. *Canada* 60°0N 104°30W **108 C9**
Selwyn Mts. *Canada* 63°0N 130°0W **108 C6**
Semarang *Indonesia* 7°0S 110°26E **82 F4**
Semey *Kazakhstan* 50°30N 80°10E **76 D9**
Semnān *Iran* 35°40N 53°23E **87 C8**
Sena Madureira *Brazil* 9°5S 68°45W **120 C3**
Sendai *Japan* 38°15N 140°53E **81 D7**
Seneca L. *U.S.A.* 42°40N 76°54W **112 D9**
Senegal ■ *W. Afr.* 14°30N 14°30W **94 F3**
Senégal → *W. Afr.* 15°48N 16°32W **94 E2**
Senegambia *Africa* 12°45N 12°0W **90 E2**
Senhor-do-Bonfim *Brazil* 10°30S 40°10W **122 B2**
Senja *Norway* 69°25N 17°30E **63 D7**
Senkaku-Shoto *E. China Sea* 25°45N 123°30E **79 E13**
Senlis *France* 49°13N 2°35E **66 B5**
Sennen *U.K.* 50°4N 5°42W **29 G2**
Sens *France* 48°11N 3°15E **66 B5**
Seoul *S. Korea* 37°31N 126°58E **79 D14**
Seph → *U.K.* 54°18N 1°9W **26 D6**
Sept-Îles *Canada* 50°13N 66°22W **109 D13**
Seram *Indonesia* 3°10S 129°0E **83 E7**
Seram Sea *Indonesia* 2°30S 128°30E **83 E7**
Serang *Indonesia* 6°8S 106°10E **82 F3**
Serbia ■ *Europe* 43°20N 20°0E **69 B9**
Serdar *Turkmenistan* 39°4N 56°23E **87 B9**
Seremban *Malaysia* 2°43N 101°53E **82 D2**
Serengeti Plain *Tanzania* 2°40S 35°0E **96 E7**
Sergipe □ *Brazil* 10°30S 37°30W **122 B3**
Sergiyev Posad *Russia* 56°20N 38°10E **70 C6**
Serhetabat *Turkmenistan* 35°20N 62°18E **87 C10**
Serifos *Greece* 37°9N 24°30E **69 F11**
Serov *Russia* 59°29N 60°35E **70 C11**
Serowe *Botswana* 22°25S 26°43E **97 J5**
Serpukhov *Russia* 54°55N 37°28E **70 D6**
Serra *Brazil* 20°7S 40°18W **122 D2**
Serra de Mesa, Barragem de *Brazil* 14°30S 49°10W **122 B1**
Serrinha *Brazil* 11°39S 39°0W **122 B3**
Sète *France* 43°25N 3°42E **66 E5**
Sete Lagoas *Brazil* 19°27S 44°16W **122 C2**
Sétif *Algeria* 36°9N 5°26E **94 A7**
Settat *Morocco* 33°0N 7°40W **94 B4**
Settle *U.K.* 54°5N 2°16W **26 D3**
Setúbal *Portugal* 38°30N 8°58W **67 C1**
Setúbal, B. de *Portugal* 38°40N 8°56W **67 C1**
Seul, Lac *Canada* 50°20N 92°30W **108 D10**
Sevan, L. *Armenia* 40°30N 45°20E **71 F8**
Sevastopol *Ukraine* 44°35N 33°30E **71 F5**
Seven → *U.K.* 54°12N 0°52W **26 D7**
Sevenoaks *U.K.* 51°16N 0°11E **31 D9**
Severn → *Canada* 56°2N 87°36W **109 D11**
Severn → *U.K.* 51°35N 2°40W **30 C3**
Severn Beach *U.K.* 51°33N 2°39W **30 C3**
Severn Stoke *U.K.* 52°6N 2°12W **30 B4**
Severnaya Zemlya *Russia* 79°0N 100°0E **77 B10**
Severodvinsk *Russia* 64°27N 39°58E **70 B6**
Severomorsk *Russia* 69°5N 33°27E **70 A5**
Sevier → *U.S.A.* 39°4N 113°6W **110 C4**
Sevier L. *U.S.A.* 38°54N 113°9W **110 C4**

Seville *Spain* 37°23N 5°58W **67 D2**
Seward *U.S.A.* 60°7N 149°27W **108 C5**
Seward Peninsula *U.S.A.* 65°30N 166°0W **108 C3**
Seychelles ■ *Ind. Oc.* 5°0S 56°0E **91 G9**
Seyðisfjörður *Iceland* 65°16N 13°57W **63 A3**
Seydişehir *Turkey* 37°25N 31°51E **71 G5**
Seymour *U.S.A.* 38°58N 85°53W **112 F5**
Sfântu Gheorghe *Romania* 45°52N 25°48E **65 F13**
Sfax *Tunisia* 34°49N 10°48E **95 B8**
Sha Tin *China* 22°23N 114°12E **79 a**
Shaanxi □ *China* 35°0N 109°0E **79 D10**
Shabeelle → *Somalia* 2°0N 44°0E **89 G3**
Shache *China* 38°20N 77°10E **78 D4**
Shaftesbury *U.K.* 51°0N 2°11W **30 D4**
Shahjahanpur *India* 27°54N 79°57E **84 F11**
Shajing *China* 22°44N 113°48E **79 a**
Shakhty *Russia* 47°40N 40°16E **71 E7**
Shaki *Nigeria* 8°41N 3°21E **94 G6**
Shaldon *U.K.* 50°32N 3°31W **29 F6**
Shaluli Shan *China* 30°40N 99°55E **78 E8**
Shamo, L. *Ethiopia* 5°45N 37°30E **89 F2**
Shan □ *Burma* 21°30N 98°30E **85 J21**
Shandong □ *China* 36°0N 118°0E **79 D12**
Shandong Pen. *China* 37°0N 121°0E **79 D13**
Shanghai *China* 31°15N 121°26E **79 E13**
Shangqiu *China* 34°26N 115°36E **79 E12**
Shangrao *China* 28°25N 117°59E **79 F12**
Shanklin *U.K.* 50°38N 1°11W **30 E6**
Shannon → *Ireland* 52°35N 9°30W **20 C4**
Shannon ✈ (SNN) *Ireland* 52°42N 8°57W **20 C5**
Shannon, Mouth of the *Ireland* 52°30N 9°55W **20 D3**
Shantou *China* 23°18N 116°40E **79 G12**
Shanxi □ *China* 37°0N 112°0E **79 D11**
Shaoguan *China* 24°48N 113°35E **79 G11**
Shaoxing *China* 30°0N 120°35E **79 F13**
Shaoyang *China* 27°14N 111°25E **79 F11**
Shap *U.K.* 54°32N 2°40W **26 D5**
Shapinsay *U.K.* 59°3N 2°51W **23 D12**
Shaqra' *Si. Arabia* 25°15N 45°16E **86 E6**
Sharjah *U.A.E.* 25°23N 55°26E **87 E8**
Shark B. *Australia* 25°30S 113°32E **98 F1**
Sharm el Sheikh *Egypt* 27°53N 34°18E **86 E3**
Sharon *U.S.A.* 41°14N 80°31W **112 E7**
Sharpness *U.K.* 51°43N 2°28W **30 C4**
Sharya *Russia* 58°22N 45°20E **70 C8**
Shasta, Mt. *U.S.A.* 41°25N 122°12W **110 B2**
Shawano *U.S.A.* 44°47N 88°36W **112 C3**
Shawbury *U.K.* 52°48N 2°39W **27 G3**
Shawinigan *Canada* 46°35N 72°50W **109 E12**
Shawnee *U.S.A.* 35°20N 96°55W **111 D7**
Shebbear *U.K.* 50°51N 4°15W **29 F5**
Sheboygan *U.S.A.* 43°46N 87°45W **112 D4**
Sheelin, L. *Ireland* 53°48N 7°20W **18 D7**
Sheep Haven *Ireland* 55°11N 7°52W **18 A6**
Sheerness *U.K.* 51°26N 0°47E **31 D10**
Sheffield *U.K.* 53°23N 1°28W **27 F6**
Shefford *U.K.* 52°2N 0°20W **31 B8**
Shehy Mts. *Ireland* 51°47N 9°15W **20 E4**
Shekou *China* 22°30N 113°55E **79 a**
Shelburne *Canada* 43°47N 65°20W **113 D15**
Shelby *U.S.A.* 48°30N 111°51W **110 A4**
Shelbyville *Ill., U.S.A.* 39°24N 88°48W **112 F3**
Shelbyville *Ind., U.S.A.* 39°31N 85°47W **112 F5**
Shelikhov G. *Russia* 59°30N 157°0E **77 D16**
Shenandoah *U.S.A.* 40°49N 76°12W **113 E9**
Shenandoah → *U.S.A.* 39°19N 77°44W **112 F9**
Shendi *Sudan* 16°46N 33°22E **95 E12**
Shenfield *U.K.* 51°38N 0°22E **31 C9**
Shenyang *China* 41°48N 123°27E **79 C13**
Shenzhen *China* 22°32N 114°5E **79 a**
Shenzhen ✈ (SZX) *China* 22°41N 113°49E **79 a**
Shenzhen Wan *China* 22°27N 113°55E **79 a**
Shepparton *Australia* 36°23S 145°26E **98 H8**
Sheppey, I. of *U.K.* 51°25N 0°48E **31 D10**
Shepshed *U.K.* 52°47N 1°18W **27 G6**
Shepton Mallet *U.K.* 51°11N 2°33W **30 D3**
Sherborne *U.K.* 50°57N 2°31W **30 E3**
Sherborne St. John *U.K.* 51°17N 1°7W **30 D6**
Sherbrooke *Canada* 45°28N 71°57W **113 C12**
Sherburn *N. Yorks., U.K.* 54°11N 0°32W **26 D7**
Sherburn *N. Yorks., U.K.* 53°48N 1°15W **27 E6**
Shere *U.K.* 51°13N 0°27W **31 D8**
Sherfield English *U.K.* 51°1N 1°34W **30 D5**
Sheridan *U.S.A.* 44°48N 106°58W **110 B5**
Sheriff Hutton *U.K.* 54°5N 1°0W **26 D7**
Sheringham *U.K.* 52°56N 1°13E **31 A11**
Sherkin I. *Ireland* 51°28N 9°26W **20 F4**
Sherman *U.S.A.* 33°38N 96°36W **111 D7**
Sherston *U.K.* 51°34N 2°14W **30 C4**
Sherwood Forest *U.K.* 53°6N 1°7W **27 F6**
Shetland □ *U.K.* 60°30N 1°30W **22 B15**
Shetland Is. *U.K.* 60°30N 1°30W **22 B15**
Sheung Shui *China* 22°31N 114°7E **79 a**
Sheyenne → *U.S.A.* 47°2N 96°50W **111 A7**
Shiant Is. *U.K.* 57°54N 6°22W **22 G4**
Shibām *Yemen* 15°59N 48°36E **89 D4**
Shiel, L. *U.K.* 56°48N 5°34W **22 J6**
Shifnal *U.K.* 52°39N 2°23W **27 G4**
Shihezi *China* 44°15N 86°2E **78 C6**
Shijiazhuang *China* 38°2N 114°28E **79 D11**
Shikarpur *Pakistan* 27°57N 68°39E **84 F6**
Shikoku □ *Japan* 33°30N 133°30E **81 G3**
Shilbottle *U.K.* 55°22N 1°40W **26 B5**
Shildon *U.K.* 54°38N 1°38W **26 C5**
Shiliguri *India* 26°45N 88°25E **85 F16**
Shillelagh *Ireland* 52°45N 6°32W **21 C9**
Shillingstone *U.K.* 50°53N 2°15W **30 E4**
Shillong *India* 25°35N 91°53E **85 G17**
Shimla *India* 31°2N 77°9E **84 D10**
Shimoga *India* 13°57N 75°32E **84 N9**
Shimonoseki *Japan* 33°58N 130°55E **81 G2**
Shin, L. *U.K.* 58°5N 4°30W **23 F8**
Shinyanga *Tanzania* 3°45S 33°27E **96 E6**
Shipdham *U.K.* 52°38N 0°54E **31 A10**
Shiphoirt, L. = Seaforth, L. *U.K.* 57°52N 6°36W **22 G4**
Shipley *U.K.* 53°50N 1°47W **27 E6**
Shipston-on-Stour *U.K.* 52°3N 1°37W **30 B5**
Shipton under Wychwood *U.K.* 51°51N 1°36W **30 C5**

Shīrāz *Iran* 29°42N 52°30E **87 D8**
Shire → *Africa* 17°42S 35°19E **97 H7**
Shirebrook *U.K.* 53°12N 1°13W **27 F6**
Shivpuri *India* 25°26N 77°42E **84 G10**
Shizuishan *China* 39°15N 106°50E **78 D10**
Shizuoka *Japan* 34°57N 138°24E **81 F6**
Shoeburyness *U.K.* 51°32N 0°49E **31 C10**
Shoreham by Sea *U.K.* 50°50N 0°16W **31 E8**
Shreveport *U.S.A.* 32°31N 93°45W **111 D8**
Shrewsbury *U.K.* 52°43N 2°45W **27 G3**
Shrewton *U.K.* 51°12N 1°54W **30 D5**
Shrirampur *India* 22°44N 88°21E **85 H16**
Shrivenham *U.K.* 51°36N 1°38W **30 C5**
Shropshire □ *U.K.* 52°36N 2°45W **27 G3**
Shuangliao *China* 43°29N 123°30E **79 C13**
Shuangyashan *China* 46°28N 131°5E **79 B15**
Shule *China* 39°25N 76°3E **78 D4**
Shule He → *China* 40°20N 92°50E **78 D7**
Shumagin Is. *U.S.A.* 55°7N 160°30W **108 D4**
Shumen *Bulgaria* 43°18N 26°55E **69 C12**
Shunan *Japan* 34°3N 131°50E **81 F2**
Shuqrā' *Yemen* 13°22N 45°44E **89 E4**
Shwebo *Burma* 22°30N 95°45E **85 H19**
Shymkent *Kazakhstan* 42°18N 69°36E **87 A12**
Si Kiang = Xi Jiang → *China* 22°5N 113°20E **79 G11**
Siahan Range *Pakistan* 27°30N 64°40E **84 F4**
Sialkot *Pakistan* 32°32N 74°30E **84 C9**
Šiauliai *Lithuania* 55°56N 23°15E **63 F8**
Šibenik *Croatia* 43°48N 15°54E **68 C6**
Siberia *Russia* 60°0N 100°0E **72 B11**
Siberut *Indonesia* 1°30S 99°0E **82 E1**
Sibi *Pakistan* 29°30N 67°54E **84 E5**
Sibiu *Romania* 45°45N 24°9E **65 F13**
Sible Hedingham *U.K.* 51°59N 0°37E **31 C10**
Sibolga *Indonesia* 1°42N 98°45E **82 D1**
Sibsey *U.K.* 53°2N 0°1E **27 F9**
Sibu *Malaysia* 2°18N 111°49E **82 D4**
Sibuyan Sea *Phil.* 12°30N 122°20E **83 B6**
Sichuan □ *China* 30°30N 103°0E **78 E9**
Sicily *Italy* 37°30N 14°30E **68 F6**
Sicily, Str. of *Medit. S.* 37°35N 11°56E **68 F4**
Sicuani *Peru* 14°21S 71°10W **120 D2**
Sidbury *U.K.* 50°42N 3°14W **29 F7**
Sidi-bel-Abbès *Algeria* 35°13N 0°39W **94 A5**
Sidlaw Hills *U.K.* 56°32N 3°2W **25 A9**
Sidlesham *U.K.* 50°47N 0°47W **31 E7**
Sidmouth *U.K.* 50°40N 3°15W **29 F7**
Sidney *Nebr., U.S.A.* 41°8N 102°59W **110 B6**
Sidney *Ohio, U.S.A.* 40°17N 84°9W **112 E5**
Sidra = Surt *Libya* 31°11N 16°39E **95 B9**
Siedlce *Poland* 52°10N 22°20E **65 B12**
Siegen *Germany* 50°51N 8°0E **64 C5**
Siena *Italy* 43°19N 11°21E **68 C4**
Sierra Blanca Peak *U.S.A.* 33°23N 105°49W **110 D5**
Sierra Leone ■ *W. Afr.* 9°0N 12°0W **94 G3**
Sierra Madre *Mexico* 16°0N 93°0W **104 H10**
Sierra Nevada *Spain* 37°3N 3°15W **67 D4**
Sierra Nevada *U.S.A.* 39°0N 120°30W **110 C2**
Sierra Vista *U.S.A.* 31°33N 110°18W **110 D4**
Sifnos *Greece* 37°0N 24°45E **69 F11**
Sighty Crag *U.K.* 55°7N 2°38W **26 B3**
Sikar *India* 27°33N 75°10E **84 F9**
Sikasso *Mali* 11°18N 5°35W **94 F4**
Sikeston *U.S.A.* 36°53N 89°35W **112 G3**
Sikhote Alin Ra. *Russia* 45°0N 136°0E **77 E14**
Sikkim □ *India* 27°50N 88°30E **85 F16**
Silesia *Poland* 51°0N 16°30E **64 C9**
Silifke *Turkey* 36°22N 33°58E **71 G5**
Siling Co *China* 31°50N 89°20E **78 E6**
Silloth *U.K.* 54°52N 3°23W **26 C2**
Silsden *U.K.* 53°55N 1°55W **27 E5**
Silver City *U.S.A.* 32°46N 108°17W **110 D5**
Silvermine Mts. *Ireland* 52°47N 8°15W **20 C6**
Silverstone *U.K.* 52°5N 1°2W **30 B6**
Silverton *U.S.A.* 50°49N 3°29W **29 F7**
Simao *China* 22°47N 101°5E **78 G9**
Simcoe, L. *Canada* 44°25N 79°20W **112 C8**
Simeulue *Indonesia* 2°45N 95°45E **82 D1**
Simferopol *Ukraine* 44°55N 34°3E **71 F5**
Simi *Greece* 36°35N 27°50E **69 F12**
Simonsbath *U.K.* 51°8N 3°46W **29 E6**
Simonside *U.K.* 55°17N 1°59W **26 B5**
Simplonpass *Switz.* 46°15N 8°3E **64 E5**
Simpson Desert *Australia* 25°0S 137°0E **98 F6**
Simpson Pen. *Canada* 68°34N 88°45W **109 C11**
Sinai *Egypt* 29°0N 34°0E **95 C12**
Sincelejo *Colombia* 9°18N 75°24W **120 B2**
Sinclair's B. *U.K.* 58°31N 3°5W **23 E11**
Sind Sagar Doab *Pakistan* 32°0N 71°30E **84 D7**
Sindh □ *Pakistan* 26°0N 69°0E **84 G6**
Sines *Portugal* 37°56N 8°51W **67 D1**
Singapore ■ *Asia* 1°17N 103°51E **82 D2**
Singaraja *Indonesia* 8°7S 115°6E **82 F5**
Singida *Tanzania* 4°49S 34°48E **96 E6**
Singkawang *Indonesia* 1°0N 108°57E **82 D3**
Singleton *U.K.* 50°55N 0°46W **31 E7**
Sinkiang □ *China* 42°0N 86°0E **78 C6**
Sinop *Turkey* 42°1N 35°11E **71 F6**
Sintra *Portugal* 38°47N 9°25W **67 C1**
Sion *Switz.* 46°14N 7°20E **64 E4**
Sion Mills *U.K.* 54°48N 7°29W **18 B7**
Sioux City *U.S.A.* 42°30N 96°24W **111 B7**
Sioux Falls *U.S.A.* 43°33N 96°44W **111 B7**
Sioux Lookout *Canada* 50°10N 91°50W **108 D10**
Siping *China* 43°8N 124°21E **79 C13**
Sir James MacBrien, Mt. *Canada* 62°7N 127°41W **108 C7**
Siracusa *Italy* 37°4N 15°17E **68 F6**
Sirajganj *Bangla.* 24°25N 89°47E **85 G16**
Sīrjān *Iran* 29°30N 55°45E **87 D8**
Sirsa *India* 29°33N 75°4E **84 E9**
Sirte = Surt *Libya* 31°11N 16°39E **95 B9**
Sīstān *Asia* 30°50N 61°0E **87 D10**
Sitapur *India* 27°38N 80°45E **85 F12**
Sitges *Spain* 41°17N 1°47E **67 B6**
Sitka *U.S.A.* 57°3N 135°20W **108 D6**
Sittingbourne *U.K.* 51°21N 0°45E **31 D10**
Sittwe *Burma* 20°18N 92°45E **85 J18**
Sivas *Turkey* 39°43N 36°58E **71 G6**
Sivrihisar *Turkey* 39°30N 31°35E **71 G5**
Siwa *Egypt* 29°11N 25°31E **95 C11**

Siwalik Range *Nepal* 28°0N 83°0E **85 F13**
Siwan *India* 26°13N 84°21E **85 F14**
Six Cross Roads *Barbados* 13°7N 59°28W **114 c**
Sixmilebridge *Ireland* 52°44N 8°46W **20 C5**
Sizewell *U.K.* 52°12N 1°37E **31 B12**
Sjælland *Denmark* 55°30N 11°30E **63 F6**
Skagafjörður *Iceland* 57°30N 9°0E **63 F5**
Skagerrak *Denmark* 57°30N 9°0E **63 F5**
Skagway *U.S.A.* 59°28N 135°19W **108 D6**
Skeena → *Canada* 54°9N 130°5W **108 D6**
Skegness *U.K.* 53°9N 0°20E **27 F9**
Skeleton Coast *Namibia* 20°0S 13°0E **97 J2**
Skellefteå *Sweden* 64°45N 20°50E **63 E8**
Skellefteälven → *Sweden* 64°45N 21°10E **63 E8**
Skellingthorpe *U.K.* 53°15N 0°37W **27 F7**
Skelmersdale *U.K.* 53°33N 2°48W **27 E3**
Skelmorlie *U.K.* 55°52N 4°53W **24 C6**
Skelton *Cleve., U.K.* 54°34N 0°58W **26 C7**
Skelton *Cumb., U.K.* 54°43N 2°51W **26 C3**
Skerries, The *U.K.* 53°25N 4°36W **28 A4**
Skiathos *Greece* 39°12N 23°30E **69 E10**
Skibbereen *Ireland* 51°33N 9°16W **20 E4**
Skiddaw *U.K.* 54°39N 3°9W **26 C2**
Skien *Norway* 59°12N 9°35E **63 F5**
Skikda *Algeria* 36°50N 6°58E **94 A7**
Skipsea *U.K.* 53°58N 0°13W **27 E8**
Skipton *U.K.* 53°58N 2°3W **27 E4**
Skopelos *Greece* 39°9N 23°47E **69 E10**
Skopje *Macedonia* 42°1N 21°26E **69 C9**
Skovorodino *Russia* 54°0N 124°0E **77 D13**
Skowhegan *U.S.A.* 44°46N 69°43W **113 C13**
Skull *Ireland* 51°32N 9°34W **20 E3**
Skye *U.K.* 57°15N 6°10W **22 H5**
Skyros *Greece* 38°55N 24°34E **69 E11**
Slaidburn *U.K.* 53°58N 2°26W **27 E4**
Slaney → *Ireland* 52°26N 6°33W **21 D9**
Slatina *Romania* 44°28N 24°22E **65 F13**
Slave → *N. Amer.* 61°18N 113°39W **108 C8**
Slave Coast *W. Afr.* 6°0N 2°30E **94 G6**
Slave Lake *Canada* 55°17N 114°43W **108 D8**
Sleaford *U.K.* 53°0N 0°24W **27 F8**
Sleat, Sd. of *U.K.* 57°5N 5°47W **22 H6**
Sledmere *U.K.* 54°4N 0°35W **26 D7**
Sleeper Is. *Canada* 58°30N 81°0W **109 D11**
Sleights *U.K.* 54°27N 0°40W **26 D8**
Slieve Aughty *Ireland* 53°4N 8°30W **20 B5**
Slieve Bloom *Ireland* 53°4N 7°40W **21 B7**
Slieve Donard *U.K.* 54°11N 5°55W **19 C10**
Slieve Gamph *Ireland* 54°6N 9°0W **18 C4**
Slieve Gullion *U.K.* 54°7N 6°26W **19 C9**
Slieve League *Ireland* 54°40N 8°42W **18 B4**
Slieve Mish *Ireland* 52°12N 9°50W **20 D3**
Slievenamon *Ireland* 52°25N 7°34W **21 D7**
Sligo *Ireland* 54°16N 8°28W **18 C5**
Sligo □ *Ireland* 54°8N 8°42W **18 C4**
Sligo B. *Ireland* 54°18N 8°40W **18 C4**
Sliven *Bulgaria* 42°42N 26°19E **69 C12**
Slough *U.K.* 51°30N 0°36W **31 C7**
Slovak Rep. ■ *Europe* 48°30N 20°0E **65 D10**
Slovenia ■ *Europe* 45°58N 14°30E **64 F8**
Slovyansk *Ukraine* 48°55N 37°36E **71 E6**
Słupsk *Poland* 54°30N 17°3E **65 A9**
Slutsk *Belarus* 53°2N 27°31E **70 D4**
Slyne Hd. *Ireland* 53°25N 10°10W **18 E1**
Smallwood Res. *Canada* 54°5N 64°30W **109 D13**
Smederevo *Serbia* 44°40N 20°57E **69 B9**
Smerwick Harbour *Ireland* 52°12N 10°23W **20 D2**
Smethwick *U.K.* 52°30N 1°57W **27 G5**
Smithfield *U.K.* 54°59N 2°51W **26 C3**
Smiths Falls *Canada* 44°55N 76°0W **113 C9**
Smoky → *Canada* 56°10N 117°21W **108 D8**
Smoky Hill → *U.S.A.* 39°4N 96°48W **111 C7**
Smolensk *Russia* 54°45N 32°5E **70 D5**
Snaefell *I. of Man* 54°16N 4°27W **19 C13**
Snainton *U.K.* 54°14N 0°35W **26 D7**
Snaith *U.K.* 53°42N 1°1W **27 E6**
Snake → *U.S.A.* 46°12N 119°2W **110 A3**
Snape *U.K.* 52°10N 1°30E **31 B12**
Snettisham *U.K.* 52°53N 0°31E **31 A10**
Snizort, L. *U.K.* 57°33N 6°28W **22 G5**
Snøhetta *Norway* 62°19N 9°16E **63 E5**
Snow Hill *U.S.A.* 38°11N 75°24W **113 F10**
Snowdon *U.K.* 53°4N 4°5W **28 A3**
Snowdonia △ *U.K.* 53°7N 3°59W **28 A4**
Snowy Mts. *Australia* 36°30S 148°20E **98 H8**
Sobat, Nahr → *South Sudan* 9°22N 31°33E **95 G12**
Sobradinho, Represa de *Brazil* 9°30S 42°0W **122 A2**
Sobral *Brazil* 3°50S 40°20W **120 C5**
Soc Trang *Vietnam* 9°37N 105°50E **82 C3**
Sochi *Russia* 43°35N 39°40E **71 F6**
Société, Îs. de la *French Polynesia* 17°0S 151°0W **103 J12**
Socorro *U.S.A.* 34°4N 106°54W **110 D5**
Socotra *Yemen* 12°30N 54°0E **89 E5**
Söderhamn *Sweden* 61°18N 17°10E **63 E7**
Sofia *Bulgaria* 42°45N 23°20E **69 C10**
Sognefjorden *Norway* 61°10N 5°50E **63 E5**
Sohâg *Egypt* 26°33N 31°43E **95 C12**
Soham *U.K.* 52°21N 0°21E **31 B9**
Soissons *France* 49°25N 3°19E **66 B5**
Sokhumi *Georgia* 43°0N 41°0E **71 F7**
Sokodé *Togo* 9°0N 1°11E **94 G6**
Sokoto *Nigeria* 13°2N 5°16E **94 F7**
Solapur *India* 17°43N 75°56E **84 L9**
Soldotna *U.S.A.* 60°29N 151°3W **108 C4**
Soledad *Colombia* 10°55N 74°46W **120 A2**
Solent, The *U.K.* 50°45N 1°25W **30 E6**
Solihull *U.K.* 52°26N 1°47W **27 H5**
Solikamsk *Russia* 59°38N 56°50E **70 C10**
Solingen *Germany* 51°10N 7°5E **64 C4**
Söller *Spain* 39°46N 2°43E **67 C7**
Sologne *France* 47°40N 1°45E **66 C4**
Solomon Is. ■ *Pac. Oc.* 6°0S 155°0E **99 B10**
Solomon Sea *Papua N. G.* 7°0S 150°0E **98 B9**
Solon *China* 46°32N 121°10E **79 B13**
Solothurn *Switz.* 47°13N 7°32E **64 E4**
Solway Firth *U.K.* 54°49N 3°35W **26 C1**
Somali Pen. *Africa* 7°0N 46°0E **90 F8**
Somalia ■ *Africa* 7°0N 47°0E **89 F4**
Somaliland □ *Somalia* 10°0N 46°0E **89 F4**
Sombrerete *Mexico* 23°38N 103°39W **114 C4**
Somerby *U.K.* 52°42N 0°50W **27 G7**

Somerset   Tebay

Somerset _U.S.A._ 37°5N 84°36W **112** G5
Somerset □ _U.K._ 51°9N 3°0W **30** D2
Somerset I. _Canada_ 73°30N 93°0W **108** B10
Somersham _U.K._ 52°24N 0°1W **31** B8
Somerton _U.K._ 51°2N 2°43W **30** D3
Somme → _France_ 50°11N 1°38E **66** A4
Songhua Hu _China_ 43°35N 126°50E **79** C14
Songhua Jiang → _China_ 47°45N 132°30E **79** B15
Songkhla _Thailand_ 7°13N 100°37E **82** C2
Sonid Youqi _China_ 42°45N 112°48E **79** C11
Sonning _U.K._ 51°28N 0°54W **31** D7
Sonora → _Mexico_ 29°5N 110°55W **114** B2
Sonoran Desert _U.S.A._ 33°40N 113°30W **110** D4
Sonoyta _Mexico_ 31°51N 112°50W **114** A2
Sopot _Poland_ 54°27N 18°31E **65** A10
Sorel-Tracy _Canada_ 46°0N 73°10W **113** C11
Soria _Spain_ 41°43N 2°32W **67** B4
Sorocaba _Brazil_ 23°31S 47°27W **122** D1
Søroya _Norway_ 70°40N 22°30E **63** C8
Sosnowiec _Poland_ 50°20N 19°10E **65** C10
Soufrière _St. Lucia_ 13°51N 61°3W **114** b
Soufrière Bay _St. Lucia_ 13°51N 61°4W **114** b
Sound, The _U.K._ 50°20N 4°10W **29** G5
Souris → _N. Amer._ 49°40N 99°34W **108** E9
Sousse _Tunisia_ 35°50N 10°38E **95** A8
South Africa ■ _Africa_ 32°0S 23°0E **97** L4
South America 10°0S 60°0W **117** E5
South Australia □ _Australia_ 32°0S 139°0E **98** G6
South Ayrshire □ _U.K._ 55°18N 4°41W **24** D6
South Bend _U.S.A._ 41°41N 86°15W **112** E4
South Benfleet _U.K._ 51°33N 0°36E **31** C10
South Brent _U.K._ 50°25N 3°51W **29** G6
South Carolina □ _U.S.A._ 34°0N 81°0W **111** D10
South Cave _U.K._ 53°47N 0°37W **27** E7
South Charleston _U.S.A._ 38°22N 81°44W **112** F7
South China Sea _Asia_ 10°0N 113°0E **82** C4
South Dakota □ _U.S.A._ 44°15N 100°0W **110** B7
South Dorset Downs _U.K._ 50°40N 2°26W **30** E4
South Downs △ _U.K._ 50°50N 0°50W **31** E7
South East C. _Australia_ 43°40S 146°50E **98** J8
South Elkington _U.K._ 53°23N 0°4W **27** F8
South Esk → _U.K._ 56°43N 2°31W **23** J12
South Foreland _U.K._ 51°8N 1°24E **31** D11
South Georgia _Antarctica_ 54°30S 37°0W **55** B1
South Harris _U.K._ 57°50N 7°0W **22** G4
South Hayling _U.K._ 50°47N 0°58W **31** E7
South I. _N.Z._ 44°0S 170°0E **99** J13
South Korea ■ _Asia_ 36°0N 128°0E **79** D14
South Lanarkshire □ _U.K._ 55°37N 3°53W **25** C8
South Magnetic Pole _Antarctica_ 64°8S 138°8E **55** C9
South Molton _U.K._ 51°1N 3°51W **29** E6
South Nahanni → _Canada_ 61°3N 123°21W **108** C7
South Negril Pt. _Jamaica_ 18°16N 78°22W **114** a
South Orkney Is. _Antarctica_ 63°0S 45°0W **55** C18
South Ossetia □ _Georgia_ 42°21N 44°2E **71** F7
South Petherton _U.K._ 50°57N 2°46W **30** E3
South Petherwin _U.K._ 50°36N 4°24W **29** F5
South Platte → _U.S.A._ 41°7N 100°42W **110** B6
South Pole _Antarctica_ 90°0S 0°0 **55** E
South Pt. _Barbados_ 13°2N 59°32W **114** c
South Queensferry _U.K._ 56°0N 3°23W **25** C9
South Ronaldsay _U.K._ 58°48N 2°58W **23** E12
South Sandwich Is. _Antarctica_ 57°0S 27°0W **55** B1
South Saskatchewan →
  Canada 53°15N 105°5W **108** D9
South Shetland Is. _Antarctica_ 62°0S 59°0W **55** C18
South Shields _U.K._ 55°0N 1°25W **26** C6
South Sudan ■ _Africa_ 8°0N 30°0E **95** G11
South Tawton _U.K._ 50°44N 3°55W **29** F6
South Tyne → _U.K._ 54°59N 2°8W **26** C4
South Uist _U.K._ 57°20N 7°15W **22** H3
South Woodham Ferrers _U.K._ 51°39N 0°37E **31** C10
South Yorkshire □ _U.K._ 53°27N 1°36W **27** F5
Southam _U.K._ 52°18N 1°23W **30** B6
Southampton _U.K._ 50°54N 1°23W **30** E6
Southampton I. _Canada_ 64°30N 84°0W **109** C11
Southborough _U.K._ 51°9N 0°16E **31** D9
Southend-on-Sea _U.K._ 51°32N 0°44E **31** C10
Southern Alps _N.Z._ 43°41S 170°11E **99** J13
Southern Indian L. _Canada_ 57°10N 98°30W **108** D10
Southern Ocean 62°0S 60°0E **53** H13
Southern Uplands _U.K._ 55°28N 3°52W **25** D9
Southery _U.K._ 52°31N 0°24E **31** A9
Southminster _U.K._ 51°40N 0°51E **31** C10
Southport _U.K._ 53°39N 3°0W **27** E2
Southwark □ _U.K._ 51°29N 0°6W **31** D8
Southwell _U.K._ 53°4N 0°57W **27** F7
Southwick _U.K._ 50°50N 0°13W **31** E8
Southwold _U.K._ 52°20N 1°41E **31** B12
Sovetsk _Russia_ 55°6N 21°50E **63** F8
Sowerby _U.K._ 54°14N 1°21W **26** D6
Soweto _S. Africa_ 26°14S 27°57W **97** K5
Spain ■ _Europe_ 39°0N 4°0W **67** B4
Spalding _U.K._ 52°48N 0°9W **27** G8
Spanish _Canada_ 46°12N 82°20W **112** B6
Spanish Town _Jamaica_ 18°0N 76°57W **114** a
Sparkford _U.K._ 51°2N 2°33W **30** D3
Sparks _U.S.A._ 39°32N 119°45W **110** C3
Sparta _Greece_ 37°5N 22°25E **69** F10
Sparta _U.S.A._ 43°56N 90°49W **112** D2
Spartanburg _U.S.A._ 34°56N 81°57W **111** D10
Spartivento, C. _Italy_ 37°55N 16°4E **68** F7
Speightstown _Barbados_ 13°15N 59°39W **114** c
Speke _U.K._ 53°21N 2°52W **27** F3
Spencer _U.S.A._ 43°9N 95°9W **111** B7
Spencer G. _Australia_ 34°0S 137°20E **98** G6
Spennymoor _U.K._ 54°42N 1°36W **26** C5
Sperrin Mts. _U.K._ 54°50N 7°0W **19** B7
Spey → _U.K._ 57°40N 3°6W **23** G11
Spilsby _U.K._ 53°10N 0°6E **27** F9
Spithead _U.K._ 50°45N 1°10W **30** E6
Split _Croatia_ 43°31N 16°26E **68** C7
Spofforth _U.K._ 53°57N 1°27W **27** E6
Spokane _U.S.A._ 47°40N 117°24W **110** A3
Spooner _U.S.A._ 45°50N 91°53W **112** C2
Spratly Is. _S. China Sea_ 8°20N 112°0E **82** C4
Spree → _Germany_ 52°32N 13°12E **64** B7
Spring Hall _Barbados_ 13°18N 59°36W **114** c
Springbok _S. Africa_ 29°42S 17°54E **97** K3
Springfield _Ill., U.S.A._ 39°48N 89°39W **112** F3
Springfield _Mass., U.S.A._ 42°6N 72°35W **113** D11

Springfield _Mo., U.S.A._ 37°13N 93°17W **111** C8
Springfield _Ohio, U.S.A._ 39°55N 83°49W **112** F6
Springfield _Oreg., U.S.A._ 44°3N 123°1W **110** B2
Springhill _Canada_ 45°40N 64°4W **113** C15
Springs _S. Africa_ 26°13S 28°25E **97** K5
Sproatley _U.K._ 53°47N 0°11W **27** E8
Spurn Hd. _U.K._ 53°35N 0°8E **27** E9
Srebrenica _Bos.-H._ 44°6N 19°18E **69** B8
Sredinnyy Ra. _Russia_ 57°0N 160°0E **77** D16
Sri Lanka ■ _Asia_ 7°30N 80°50E **84** R12
Srikakulam _India_ 18°14N 83°58E **85** K13
Srinagar _India_ 34°5N 74°50E **84** B9
Stacks Mts. _Ireland_ 52°20N 9°34W **20** D3
Staffa _U.K._ 56°27N 6°21W **24** B3
Stafford _U.K._ 52°49N 2°7W **27** G4
Staffordshire □ _U.K._ 52°53N 2°10W **27** G4
Staindrop _U.K._ 54°36N 1°47W **26** C5
Staines _U.K._ 51°26N 0°29W **31** D8
Stainforth _U.K._ 53°37N 1°0W **27** E7
Stainmore Forest _U.K._ 54°29N 2°5W **26** D4
Stainton _U.K._ 53°18N 0°24W **27** F8
Staithes _U.K._ 54°34N 0°46W **26** C7
Stakhanov _Ukraine_ 48°35N 38°40E **71** E6
Stalbridge _U.K._ 50°57N 2°23W **30** E4
Stalham _U.K._ 52°47N 1°31E **31** A12
Stallingborough _U.K._ 53°35N 0°12W **27** E8
Stalybridge _U.K._ 53°28N 2°3W **27** F4
Stamford _U.K._ 52°39N 0°29W **27** G8
Stamford _U.S.A._ 41°3N 73°32W **113** E11
Stamford Bridge _U.K._ 54°0N 0°54W **27** E7
Stamfordham _U.K._ 55°3N 1°53W **26** B5
Standish _U.K._ 53°35N 2°41W **27** E3
Standish _U.S.A._ 43°59N 83°57W **112** D6
Stanford on Teme _U.K._ 52°18N 2°26W **30** B4
Stanhope _U.K._ 54°45N 2°1W **26** C4
Stanley _Falk. Is._ 51°40S 59°51W **121** H4
Stanley _U.K._ 54°53N 1°41W **26** C5
Stannington _U.K._ 55°7N 1°40W **26** B5
Stanovoy Ra. _Russia_ 55°0N 130°0E **77** D13
Stansted Mountfitchet _U.K._ 51°52N 0°11E **31** C9
Stanwix _U.K._ 54°55N 2°56W **26** C4
Stapleford _U.K._ 52°57N 1°16W **27** G6
Staplehurst _U.K._ 51°9N 0°34E **31** D10
Stara Zagora _Bulgaria_ 42°26N 25°39E **69** C11
Staraya Russa _Russia_ 57°58N 31°23E **70** C5
Starbuck I. _Kiribati_ 5°37S 155°55W **103** H12
Start B. _U.K._ 50°13N 3°39W **29** G6
Start Pt. _U.K._ 50°13N 3°39W **29** G6
Staryy Oskol _Russia_ 51°19N 37°55E **71** D6
State College _U.S.A._ 40°48N 77°52W **112** E9
Staten, I. = Estados, I. de Los
  Argentina 54°40S 64°30W **121** H3
Staunton _U.K._ 51°57N 2°17W **30** C4
Staunton _U.S.A._ 38°9N 79°4W **112** F8
Stavanger _Norway_ 58°57N 5°40E **63** F5
Staveley _Cumb., U.K._ 54°23N 2°48W **26** D3
Staveley _Derby., U.K._ 53°16N 1°21W **27** F6
Stavropol _Russia_ 45°5N 42°0E **71** E7
Steiermark □ _Austria_ 47°26N 15°0E **64** E8
Steinkjer _Norway_ 64°1N 11°31E **63** E6
Stellaland _Canada_ 45°32N 62°30W **113** C16
Stellenbosch _S. Africa_ 33°58S 18°50E **97** L3
Stenhousemuir _U.K._ 56°2N 3°48W **25** B8
Steornabhaigh = Stornoway
  _U.K._ 58°13N 6°23W **22** F5
Stephenville _Canada_ 48°31N 58°35W **109** E14
Steppe _Asia_ 50°0N 50°0E **72** C7
Sterling _Colo., U.S.A._ 40°37N 103°13W **110** B6
Sterling _Ill., U.S.A._ 41°48N 89°42W **112** E3
Sterlitamak _Russia_ 53°40N 56°0E **70** D10
Stettiner Haff _Germany_ 53°47N 14°15E **64** B8
Stettler _Canada_ 52°19N 112°40W **108** D8
Steubenville _U.S.A._ 40°22N 80°37W **112** E7
Stevenage _U.K._ 51°55N 0°13W **31** C8
Stevens Point _U.S.A._ 44°31N 89°34W **112** C3
Stevenston _U.K._ 55°39N 4°45W **24** C6
Stewart _Canada_ 55°56N 129°57W **108** D7
Stewart → _Canada_ 63°19N 139°26W **108** C6
Stewart I. _N.Z._ 46°58S 167°54E **99** K12
Stewarton _U.K._ 55°40N 4°32W **24** C6
Steyning _U.K._ 50°53N 0°18W **31** E8
Steyr _Austria_ 48°3N 14°25E **64** D8
Stikine → _Canada_ 56°40N 132°30W **108** D6
Stillington _U.K._ 54°6N 1°6W **26** D6
Stillwater _U.S.A._ 36°7N 97°4W **111** A8
Stiperstones _U.K._ 52°36N 2°55W **27** G3
Stirling _U.K._ 56°8N 3°57W **25** B8
Stirling □ _U.K._ 56°12N 4°18W **24** B7
Stobo _U.K._ 55°38N 3°17W **25** C9
Stockbridge _U.K._ 51°7N 1°29W **30** D6
Stockholm _Sweden_ 59°19N 18°4E **63** F7
Stockport _U.K._ 53°25N 2°9W **27** F4
Stocksbridge _U.K._ 53°29N 1°35W **27** F5
Stockton _U.S.A._ 37°58N 121°17W **110** C2
Stockton-on-Tees _U.K._ 54°35N 1°19W **26** D6
Stoer, Pt. of _U.K._ 58°16N 5°23W **22** F7
Stoke _U.K._ 51°26N 0°41E **31** D10
Stoke Ferry _U.K._ 52°34N 0°31E **31** A10
Stoke Fleming _U.K._ 50°19N 3°37W **29** G6
Stoke Mandeville _U.K._ 51°47N 0°47W **31** C7
Stoke-on-Trent _U.K._ 53°1N 2°11W **27** F4
Stoke Prior _U.K._ 52°19N 2°4W **30** B4
Stokesley _U.K._ 54°28N 1°12W **26** D6
Stone _Bucks., U.K._ 51°48N 0°52W **31** C7
Stone _Staffs., U.K._ 52°55N 2°9W **27** G4
Stonehaven _U.K._ 56°59N 2°12W **23** J13
Stonehouse _U.K._ 51°45N 2°16W **30** C4
Stonham Aspal _U.K._ 52°12N 1°8E **31** B11
Stony Stratford _U.K._ 52°3N 0°50W **31** B7
Stony Tunguska → _Russia_ 61°50N 90°13E **77** C10
Stora Lulevatten _Sweden_ 67°10N 19°30E **63** D7
Storavan _Sweden_ 65°45N 18°10E **63** D7
Store Bælt _Denmark_ 55°20N 11°0E **63** F6
Stormberge _S. Africa_ 31°16S 26°17E **97** L5
Stornoway _U.K._ 58°13N 6°23W **22** F5
Storsjön _Sweden_ 63°9N 14°30E **63** E6
Stort → _U.K._ 51°46N 0°2E **31** C9
Storuman _Sweden_ 65°5N 17°10E **63** D7
Stotfold _U.K._ 52°1N 0°13W **31** B8
Stour → _Dorset, U.K._ 50°43N 1°47W **30** E5
Stour → _Kent, U.K._ 51°18N 1°22E **31** D11

Stour → _Suffolk, U.K._ 51°57N 1°4E **31** C11
Stour → _Worcs., U.K._ 52°21N 2°17W **30** B4
Stourbridge _U.K._ 52°28N 2°8W **27** H4
Stourport-on-Severn _U.K._ 52°21N 2°17W **30** B4
Stow _U.K._ 55°42N 2°50W **25** C10
Stow Bardolph _U.K._ 52°38N 0°24E **31** A9
Stow-on-the-Wold _U.K._ 51°56N 1°42W **30** C5
Stowmarket _U.K._ 52°12N 1°0E **31** B10
Strabane _U.K._ 54°50N 7°27W **18** B7
Stradbroke _U.K._ 52°19N 1°16E **31** B11
Stralsund _Germany_ 54°18N 13°4E **64** A7
Strangford L. _U.K._ 54°30N 5°37W **19** C10
Stranraer _U.K._ 54°54N 5°1W **24** E5
Strasbourg _France_ 48°35N 7°42E **66** B7
Stratford _Canada_ 43°23N 81°0W **112** D7
Stratford St. Mary _U.K._ 51°58N 1°0E **31** C10
Stratford-upon-Avon _U.K._ 52°12N 1°42W **30** B5
Strath Avon _U.K._ 57°18N 3°23W **23** H11
Strath Dearn _U.K._ 57°20N 4°0W **23** H9
Strath Glass _U.K._ 57°22N 4°42W **23** H8
Strath Halladale _U.K._ 58°30N 3°51W **23** F10
Strath Naver _U.K._ 58°24N 4°12W **23** F9
Strath of Kildonan _U.K._ 58°14N 3°56W **23** F10
Strath Spey _U.K._ 57°9N 3°49W **23** H10
Strath Tay _U.K._ 56°40N 3°48W **25** A8
Strathaven _U.K._ 55°40N 4°5W **24** C7
Strathbogie _U.K._ 57°25N 2°45W **23** H12
Strathmore _Angus., U.K._ 56°37N 3°7W **23** J11
Strathmore _Highl., U.K._ 58°22N 4°40W **23** F8
Strathpeffer _U.K._ 57°35N 4°32W **23** G8
Strathroy _Canada_ 42°58N 81°38W **112** D7
Strathy Pt. _U.K._ 58°36N 4°1W **23** E9
Stratton _U.K._ 50°49N 4°32W **29** F4
Stratton St. Margaret _U.K._ 51°35N 1°44W **30** C5
Streatley _U.K._ 51°31N 1°8W **30** C6
Street _U.K._ 51°8N 2°44W **30** D3
Strensall _U.K._ 54°3N 1°4W **26** D6
Stretford _U.K._ 53°28N 2°17W **27** F4
Stroma _U.K._ 58°41N 3°7W **23** E11
Strómboli _Italy_ 38°47N 15°13E **68** E6
Stromeferry _U.K._ 57°21N 5°33W **22** H6
Stromness _U.K._ 58°58N 3°17W **23** E11
Stronsay _U.K._ 59°7N 2°35W **23** D12
Stroud _U.K._ 51°45N 2°13W **30** C4
Stuart L. _Canada_ 54°30N 124°30W **108** D7
Studland _U.K._ 50°39N 1°58W **30** E5
Studley _U.K._ 52°16N 1°53W **30** B5
Sturgeon Bay _U.S.A._ 44°50N 87°23W **112** C4
Sturgeon Falls _Canada_ 46°25N 79°57W **112** B8
Sturminster Marshall _U.K._ 50°47N 2°5W **30** E4
Sturminster Newton _U.K._ 50°55N 2°18W **30** E4
Sturt Stony Desert _Australia_ 28°30S 141°0E **98** F6
Sturton _U.K._ 53°19N 0°39W **27** F7
Stuttgart _Germany_ 48°48N 9°11E **64** D5
Stuttgart _U.S.A._ 34°30N 91°33W **111** D8
Suakin _Sudan_ 19°8N 37°20E **95** E13
Şūḇā _Si. Arabia_ 27°10N 35°40E **86** E3
Subotica _Serbia_ 46°6N 19°39E **69** A8
Suceava _Romania_ 47°38N 26°16E **65** E14
Suck → _Ireland_ 53°17N 8°3W **20** B6
Sucre _Bolivia_ 19°0S 65°15W **120** D3
Sudan ■ _Africa_ 15°0N 30°0E **95** E11
Sudbury _Canada_ 46°30N 81°0W **112** B7
Sudbury _Derby., U.K._ 52°54N 1°45W **27** G5
Sudbury _Suffolk, U.K._ 52°2N 0°45E **31** B10
Sudd _South Sudan_ 8°20N 30°0E **95** G12
Sudeten _Europe_ 50°20N 16°45E **65** C9
Suez _Egypt_ 29°58N 32°31E **95** C12
Suez, G. of _Egypt_ 28°40N 33°0E **95** C12
Suez Canal _Egypt_ 31°0N 32°20E **95** B12
Suffolk □ _U.K._ 52°16N 1°0E **31** B11
Sugluk _Canada_ 62°14N 75°38W **109** C12
Şuḩār _Oman_ 24°20N 56°40E **87** E9
Suihua _China_ 46°32N 126°55E **79** B14
Suining _China_ 30°26N 105°35E **78** E10
Suir → _Ireland_ 52°16N 7°9W **21** D8
Sukabumi _Indonesia_ 6°56S 106°50E **83** F3
Sukhona → _Russia_ 61°15N 46°39E **70** C6
Sukkur _Pakistan_ 27°42N 68°54E **84** F6
Sulaiman Range _Pakistan_ 30°30N 69°50E **84** D6
Sulawesi _Indonesia_ 2°0S 120°0E **83** E6
Sullana _Peru_ 4°52S 80°39W **120** C1
Sullom Voe _U.K._ 60°27N 1°20W **22** B15
Sulu Arch. _Phil._ 6°0N 121°0E **83** C6
Sulu Sea _E. Indies_ 8°0N 120°0E **83** C6
Sumare _Brazil_ 22°49S 47°16W **122** D1
Sumatra _Indonesia_ 0°40N 100°20E **82** D2
Sumba _Indonesia_ 9°45S 119°35E **83** F5
Sumbawa _Indonesia_ 8°26S 117°30E **82** F5
Sumburgh Hd. _U.K._ 59°52N 1°17W **22** C15
Summer L. _U.S.A._ 42°50N 120°45W **110** B2
Summerside _Canada_ 46°24N 63°47W **109** E13
Sumqayit _Azerbaijan_ 40°34N 49°38E **71** F8
Sumter _U.S.A._ 33°55N 80°21W **111** D10
Sumy _Ukraine_ 50°57N 34°50E **71** D5
Sun Valley _U.S.A._ 43°42N 114°21W **110** B4
Sunart, L. _U.K._ 56°43N 5°42W **22** J6
Sunart, L. _U.K._ 56°42N 5°43W **22** J6
Sunbury _U.S.A._ 40°52N 76°48W **112** E9
Sunda, Selat _Indonesia_ 6°20S 105°30E **82** F3
Sunda Is. _Indonesia_ 5°0S 105°0E **102** H2
Sundarbans _Asia_ 22°0N 89°0E **85** J16
Sunderland _U.K._ 54°55N 1°23W **26** C6
Sundsvall _Sweden_ 62°23N 17°17E **63** E7
Sungaipenuh _Indonesia_ 2°1S 101°20E **82** E2
Sunk Island _U.K._ 53°39N 0°6W **27** E8
Sunninghill _U.K._ 51°24N 0°39W **31** D7
Sunshine Coast _Australia_ 26°30S 153°0E **98** F9
Superior _U.S.A._ 46°44N 92°6W **112** B1
Superior, L. _N. Amer._ 47°0N 87°0W **112** B4
Şūr _Lebanon_ 33°19N 35°16E **86** C3
Sura → _Russia_ 56°6N 46°0E **70** C8
Surabaya _Indonesia_ 7°17S 112°45E **82** F4
Surakarta _Indonesia_ 7°35S 110°48E **82** F4
Surat _India_ 21°12N 72°55E **84** J8
Surgut _Russia_ 61°14N 73°20E **76** C8
Surigao _Phil._ 9°47N 125°29E **83** C7
Suriname ■ _S. Amer._ 4°0N 56°0W **120** B4
Surrey □ _U.K._ 51°15N 0°31W **31** D7
Surt _Libya_ 31°11N 16°39E **95** B9
Surt, Khalīj _Libya_ 31°40N 18°30E **95** B9

Surtsey _Iceland_ 63°20N 20°30W **63** B1
Susquehanna → _U.S.A._ 39°33N 76°5W **113** F9
Sussex _Canada_ 45°45N 65°37W **113** C15
Sutherland _U.K._ 58°12N 4°50W **23** F8
Sutlej → _Pakistan_ 29°23N 71°3E **84** E7
Sutterton _U.K._ 52°55N 0°6W **27** G8
Sutton □ _U.K._ 51°21N 0°11W **31** D8
Sutton Bridge _U.K._ 52°47N 0°10E **27** G9
Sutton Coldfield _U.K._ 52°35N 1°49W **27** G5
Sutton Courtenay _U.K._ 51°39N 1°16W **30** C6
Sutton in Ashfield _U.K._ 53°8N 1°16W **27** F6
Sutton-on-Sea _U.K._ 53°18N 0°16E **27** F9
Sutton Scotney _U.K._ 51°9N 1°20W **30** D6
Suva _Fiji_ 18°6S 178°30E **99** D14
Suwałki _Poland_ 54°8N 22°59E **65** A12
Suwarrow Is. _Cook Is._ 13°15S 163°5W **103** J11
Suzhou _China_ 31°19N 120°38E **79** E13
Svalbard _Arctic_ 78°0N 17°0E **54** B8
Svealand _Sweden_ 60°20N 15°0E **63** E7
Sverdrup Chan. _Canada_ 79°56N 96°25W **109** B10
Sverdrup Is. _Canada_ 79°0N 97°0W **109** B10
Svir → _Russia_ 60°30N 32°48E **70** B5
Svyatoy Nos _Russia_ 72°0N 140°0E **77** B14
Swadlincote _U.K._ 52°47N 1°33W **27** G5
Swaffham _U.K._ 52°39N 0°42E **31** A10
Swakopmund _Namibia_ 22°37S 14°30E **97** J2
Swan Hill _Australia_ 35°20S 143°33E **98** H7
Swan River _Canada_ 52°10N 101°16W **108** D9
Swanage _U.K._ 50°36N 1°58W **30** E5
Swansea _U.K._ 51°37N 3°57W **29** D6
Swansea B. _U.K._ 51°32N 3°57W **29** D6
Swartberge _S. Africa_ 33°20S 22°0E **90** K6
Swaziland ■ _Africa_ 26°30S 31°30E **97** K6
Sweden ■ _Europe_ 57°0N 15°0E **63** F7
Sweetwater _U.S.A._ 32°28N 100°25W **110** D6
Swellendam _S. Africa_ 34°1S 20°26E **97** L4
Swift Current _Canada_ 50°20N 107°45W **108** D9
Swilly, L. _Ireland_ 55°12N 7°33W **18** A6
Swindon _U.K._ 51°34N 1°46W **30** C5
Swineshead _U.K._ 52°57N 0°10W **27** G8
Swinford _Ireland_ 53°57N 8°58W **18** C3
Swinton _Borders, U.K._ 55°43N 2°15W **25** C11
Swinton _Gt. Man., U.K._ 53°31N 2°20W **27** E4
Swinton _S. Yorks., U.K._ 53°29N 1°20W **27** F6
Switzerland ■ _Europe_ 46°30N 8°0E **64** E5
Swords _Ireland_ 53°28N 6°13W **21** B10
Sydney _Australia_ 33°52S 151°12E **98** G9
Sydney _Canada_ 46°7N 60°7W **113** C17
Syktyvkar _Russia_ 61°45N 50°40E **70** B9
Sylhet _Bangla._ 24°54N 91°52E **85** G17
Symington _U.K._ 55°36N 3°36W **25** C8
Symonds Yat _U.K._ 51°51N 2°38W **30** C3
Syracuse _U.S.A._ 43°3N 76°9W **113** D9
Syrdarya → _Kazakhstan_ 46°3N 61°0E **76** E7
Syria ■ _Asia_ 35°0N 38°0E **86** C4
Syrian Desert _Asia_ 32°0N 40°0E **86** C4
Syston _U.K._ 52°42N 1°3W **27** G6
Syzran _Russia_ 53°12N 48°30E **70** D8
Szczecin _Poland_ 53°27N 14°27E **64** B8
Szczytno = Sichuan □ _China_ 30°30N 103°0E **78** E9
Szeged _Hungary_ 46°16N 20°10E **65** E11
Székesfehérvár _Hungary_ 47°15N 18°25E **65** E10
Szekszárd _Hungary_ 46°22N 18°42E **65** E10
Szolnok _Hungary_ 47°10N 20°15E **65** E11
Szombathely _Hungary_ 47°14N 16°38E **65** E9

T

Tabas _Iran_ 33°35N 56°55E **87** C9
Tablas I. _Phil._ 12°25N 122°2E **83** B6
Table B. _S. Africa_ 33°35S 18°25E **97** L3
Table Mt. _S. Africa_ 33°58S 18°26E **97** L3
Tabora _Tanzania_ 5°2S 32°50E **96** F6
Tabrīz _Iran_ 38°7N 46°20E **86** B6
Tabuaeran _Kiribati_ 3°51N 159°22W **103** G12
Tabūk _Si. Arabia_ 28°23N 36°36E **86** D4
Tacheng _China_ 46°40N 82°58E **78** B5
Tacloban _Phil._ 11°15N 124°58E **83** B6
Tacna _Peru_ 18°0S 70°20W **120** D2
Tacoma _U.S.A._ 47°14N 122°26W **110** A2
Tacuarembó _Uruguay_ 31°45S 56°0W **121** F4
Tadcaster _U.K._ 53°53N 1°16W **27** E6
Tademaït, Plateau du _Algeria_ 28°30N 2°30E **94** C6
Tadley _U.K._ 51°21N 1°7W **30** D6
Taganrog _Russia_ 47°12N 38°50E **71** E6
Taguatinga _Brazil_ 12°27S 46°22W **122** B1
Tagus → _Europe_ 38°40N 9°24E **67** C1
Tahiti _French Polynesia_ 17°37S 149°27W **103** J13
Tahoe, L. _U.S.A._ 39°6N 120°2W **110** C2
Tahoua _Niger_ 14°57N 5°16E **94** F7
Tahta _Egypt_ 26°44N 31°32E **95** C12
Tai Hu _China_ 31°5N 120°10E **79** E13
Tai'an _China_ 22°27N 114°1E **79** a
Tai'an _China_ 36°12N 117°8E **79** D12
T'aichung _Taiwan_ 24°9N 120°37E **79** G13
Tain _U.K._ 57°49N 4°4W **23** G9
T'ainan _Taiwan_ 23°0N 120°10E **79** G13
T'aipei _Taiwan_ 25°4N 121°29E **79** F13
Taiping _Malaysia_ 4°51N 100°44E **82** D2
Taitao, Pen. de _Chile_ 46°30S 75°0W **121** G2
T'aitung _Taiwan_ 22°43N 121°4E **79** G13
Taiwan ■ _Asia_ 23°30N 121°0E **79** G13
Taiwan Str. _Asia_ 24°40N 120°0E **79** G12
Taiyuan _China_ 37°52N 112°33E **79** D11
Taizhou _China_ 32°28N 119°55E **79** E12
Ta'izz _Yemen_ 13°35N 44°2E **89** E3
Tajikistan ■ _Asia_ 38°30N 70°0E **87** B12
Tak _Thailand_ 16°52N 99°8E **82** A1
Takamatsu _Japan_ 34°20N 134°5E **81** F4
Takaoka _Japan_ 36°47N 137°0E **81** E5
Takasaki _Japan_ 36°20N 139°0E **81** E6
Takeshima = Dokdo _Asia_ 37°15N 131°52E **81** E2
Taklamakan Desert _China_ 38°0N 83°0E **78** D5
Talaud, Kepulauan _Indonesia_ 4°30N 126°50E **83** D7
Talavera de la Reina _Spain_ 39°55N 4°46W **67** C3
Talca _Chile_ 35°28S 71°40W **121** F2
Talcahuano _Chile_ 36°40S 73°10W **121** F2
Taldyqorghan _Kazakhstan_ 45°10N 78°45E **76** E8
Talgarth _U.K._ 52°0N 3°14W **28** D7
Taliabu _Indonesia_ 1°50S 125°0E **83** E6

Tallaght _Ireland_ 53°17N 6°22W **21** B10
Tallahassee _U.S.A._ 30°27N 84°17W **111** D10
Tallinn _Estonia_ 59°22N 24°48E **63** F8
Talnakh _Canada_ 69°32N 93°32W **108** C10
Taltal _Chile_ 25°23S 70°33W **121** E2
Tamale _Ghana_ 9°22N 0°50W **94** G5
Tamana _Kiribati_ 2°30S 175°59E **99** A13
Tamanrasset _Algeria_ 22°50N 5°30E **94** D7
Tamar → _U.K._ 50°27N 4°15W **29** G5
Tambov _Russia_ 52°45N 41°28E **70** D7
Tame → _U.K._ 52°44N 1°43W **27** G5
Tamerton Foliot _U.K._ 50°25N 4°11W **29** G5
Tamil Nadu □ _India_ 11°0N 77°0E **84** P10
Tampa _U.S.A._ 27°56N 82°27W **111** E10
Tampa B. _U.S.A._ 27°50N 82°30W **111** E10
Tampere _Finland_ 61°30N 23°50E **63** E8
Tampico _Mexico_ 22°13N 97°51W **114** C5
Tamworth _Australia_ 31°7S 150°58E **98** G9
Tamworth _U.K._ 52°39N 1°41W **27** G5
Tana → _Kenya_ 2°32S 40°31E **96** E8
Tana → _Norway_ 70°30N 28°14E **63** C9
Tana, L. _Ethiopia_ 13°5N 37°30E **89** E2
Tanami Desert _Australia_ 18°50S 132°0E **98** D5
Tanana → _U.S.A._ 65°10N 151°58W **108** C4
Tandil _Argentina_ 37°15S 59°6W **121** F4
Tandragee _U.K._ 54°21N 6°24W **19** C9
Tanezrouft _Algeria_ 23°9N 0°11E **94** D6
Tanga _Tanzania_ 5°5S 39°2E **96** F7
Tanganyika, L. _Africa_ 6°40S 30°0E **96** F6
Tanggula Shan _China_ 32°40N 92°10E **78** E7
Tanggula Shankou _China_ 32°42N 92°27E **78** E7
Tangier _Morocco_ 35°50N 5°49W **94** A4
Tangjia _China_ 22°22N 113°35E **79** a
Tangra Yumco _China_ 31°0N 86°38E **78** E6
Tangshan _China_ 39°38N 118°10E **79** D12
Tanimbar, Kepulauan
  Indonesia 7°30S 131°30E **83** F8
Tanjungbalai _Indonesia_ 2°55N 99°44E **82** D1
Tanjungpandan _Indonesia_ 2°43S 107°38E **82** E3
Tanjungredeb _Indonesia_ 2°9N 117°29E **82** D5
Tanna _Vanuatu_ 19°30S 169°20E **99** D12
Tannu Ola _Asia_ 51°0N 94°0E **77** D10
Tanta _Egypt_ 30°45N 30°57E **95** B12
Tanworth _U.K._ 52°20N 1°50W **30** B5
Tanzania ■ _Africa_ 6°0S 34°0E **96** F6
Tanzhou _China_ 22°16N 113°28E **79** a
Taolanaro _Madag._ 25°2S 47°0E **97** K9
Taonan _China_ 45°22N 122°40E **79** B13
Taos _U.S.A._ 36°24N 105°35W **110** C5
Tapachula _Mexico_ 14°54N 92°17W **114** E6
Tapajós → _Brazil_ 2°24S 54°41W **120** C4
Tapti → _India_ 21°8N 72°41E **84** J8
Taquaritinga _Brazil_ 21°24S 48°30W **122** D1
Tarakan _Indonesia_ 3°20N 117°35E **82** D5
Taransay _U.K._ 57°54N 7°0W **22** G3
Táranto _Italy_ 40°28N 17°14E **68** D7
Táranto, G. di _Italy_ 40°8N 17°20E **68** D7
Tarasaigh = Taransay _U.K._ 57°54N 7°0W **22** G3
Tarawa _Kiribati_ 1°30N 173°0E **102** G9
Taraz _Kazakhstan_ 42°54N 71°22E **87** A12
Tarbagatay, Khrebet _Kazakhstan_ 48°0N 83°0E **76** E9
Tarbat Ness _U.K._ 57°52N 3°47W **23** G10
Tarbela Dam _Pakistan_ 34°8N 72°52E **84** B8
Tarbert _Argyll & Bute, U.K._ 55°52N 5°25W **24** C5
Tarbert _W. Isles, U.K._ 57°54N 6°49W **22** G4
Tarbes _France_ 43°15N 0°3E **66** E4
Tarcoola _Australia_ 30°44S 134°36E **98** G5
Taree _Australia_ 31°50S 152°30E **98** G9
Tarfaya _Morocco_ 27°55N 12°55W **94** C3
Târgovişte _Romania_ 44°55N 25°27E **65** F13
Târgu Jiu _Romania_ 45°5N 23°19E **65** F12
Târgu Mureş _Romania_ 46°31N 24°38E **65** E13
Tarija _Bolivia_ 21°30S 64°40W **120** E3
Tarim Basin _China_ 40°0N 84°0E **78** C5
Tarim He → _China_ 39°30N 88°30E **78** C6
Tarleton _U.K._ 53°41N 2°50W **27** E3
Tarn → _France_ 44°5N 1°6E **66** E4
Tarnów _Poland_ 50°3N 21°0E **65** C11
Taroudannt _Morocco_ 30°30N 8°52W **94** B4
Tarporley _U.K._ 53°10N 2°40W **27** F3
Tarragona _Spain_ 41°5N 1°17E **67** B6
Tarsus _Turkey_ 36°58N 34°55E **71** G5
Tartu _Estonia_ 58°20N 26°44E **63** F9
Tarṭūs _Syria_ 34°55N 35°55E **86** C3
Tashkent _Uzbekistan_ 41°20N 69°10E **87** A12
Tasiilaq _Greenland_ 65°40N 37°20W **54** C6
Tasikmalaya _Indonesia_ 7°18S 108°12E **82** F3
Tasman Sea _Pac. Oc._ 36°0S 160°0E **99** H10
Tasmania □ _Australia_ 42°0S 146°30E **98** J8
Tassili n'Ajjer _Algeria_ 25°47N 8°1E **94** C7
Tatar Str. _Russia_ 50°0N 141°0E **77** E14
Tatarstan □ _Russia_ 55°30N 51°30E **70** C9
Tatnam, C. _Canada_ 57°16N 91°0W **109** D10
Tatra _Slovak Rep._ 49°20N 20°0E **65** D11
Tattenhall _U.K._ 53°7N 2°46W **27** F3
Tatui _Brazil_ 23°25S 47°53W **122** D1
Tatvan _Turkey_ 38°31N 42°15E **71** G7
Taubaté _Brazil_ 23°0S 45°36W **122** D1
Tauern _Austria_ 47°15N 12°40E **64** E7
Taunggyi _Burma_ 20°50N 97°0E **85** J20
Taunton _U.K._ 51°1N 3°5W **30** D2
Taunton _U.S.A._ 41°54N 71°6W **113** E12
Taunus _Germany_ 50°13N 8°34E **64** C5
Taurus Mts. _Turkey_ 37°0N 32°30E **71** G5
Tavan Bogd Uul _Mongolia_ 49°10N 87°49E **78** B6
Tavistock _U.K._ 50°33N 4°9W **29** F5
Taw → _U.K._ 51°4N 4°4W **29** E5
Tawas City _U.S.A._ 44°16N 83°31W **112** C6
Tawau _Malaysia_ 4°20N 117°55E **82** D5
Taxkorgan Tajik Zizhixian
  China 37°49N 75°14E **78** D4
Tay → _U.K._ 56°37N 3°38W **25** B9
Tay, Firth of _U.K._ 56°25N 3°8W **25** B9
Tay, L. → _U.K._ 56°32N 4°8W **24** A7
Taylor, Mt. _U.S.A._ 35°14N 107°37W **110** C5
Taylorville _U.S.A._ 39°33N 89°18W **112** F3
Tayport _U.K._ 56°27N 2°52W **25** B10
Taz → _Russia_ 67°32N 78°40E **76** C8
Taza _Morocco_ 34°16N 4°6W **94** B5
Tbilisi _Georgia_ 41°43N 44°50E **71** F7
Tebay _U.K._ 54°26N 2°35W **26** D3

Tébessa

Tébessa *Algeria* 35°22N 8°8E **94 A7**
Tees → *U.K.* 54°37N 1°10W **26 C6**
Teesdale *U.K.* 54°37N 2°10W **26 C6**
Teesside *U.K.* 54°36N 1°15W **26 C6**
Tegal *Indonesia* 6°52S 109°8E **82 F3**
Tegid, L. = Bala, L. *U.K.* 52°53N 3°37W **28 B6**
Tegucigalpa *Honduras* 14°5N 87°14W **114 E7**
Tehrān *Iran* 35°41N 51°25E **87 C7**
Tehuantepec *Mexico* 16°21N 95°13W **114 D5**
Tehuantepec, G. de *Mexico* 15°50N 95°12W **114 D5**
Tehuantepec, Istmo de *Mexico* 17°15N 94°30W **114 D6**
Teifi → *U.K.* 52°5N 4°41W **28 C4**
Teign → *U.K.* 50°32N 3°32W **29 F6**
Teignmouth *U.K.* 50°33N 3°31W **29 F6**
Tejen *Turkmenistan* 37°23N 60°31E **87 B10**
Tekirdağ *Turkey* 40°58N 27°30E **71 F4**
Tel Aviv-Jaffa *Israel* 32°4N 34°48E **86 C3**
Tela *Honduras* 15°40N 87°28W **114 D7**
Telegraph Creek *Canada* 58°0N 131°10W **108 D6**
Teles Pires → *Brazil* 7°21S 58°3W **120 C4**
Telford *U.K.* 52°40N 2°27W **27 G4**
Tell City *U.S.A.* 37°57N 86°46W **112 G4**
Tellicherry *India* 11°45N 75°30E **84 P9**
Telpos Iz *Russia* 63°16N 59°13E **70 B10**
Teluk Intan *Malaysia* 4°3N 101°0E **82 D2**
Tema *Ghana* 5°41N 0°0W **94 G5**
Teme → *U.K.* 52°11N 2°13W **30 B4**
Temirtau *Kazakhstan* 50°5N 72°56E **76 D8**
Témiscaming *Canada* 46°44N 79°5W **112 B8**
Temple *U.S.A.* 31°6N 97°21W **111 D7**
Temple Combe *U.K.* 51°0N 2°24W **30 D4**
Temple Ewell *U.K.* 51°8N 1°17E **31 D11**
Temple Sowerby *U.K.* 54°38N 2°36W **26 C4**
Templemore *Ireland* 52°47N 7°51W **20 C7**
Temuco *Chile* 38°45S 72°40W **121 F2**
Tenali *India* 16°15N 80°35E **85 L12**
Tenbury Wells *U.K.* 52°19N 2°35W **30 B3**
Tenby *U.K.* 51°40N 4°42W **28 D4**
Tenerife *Canary Is.* 28°15N 16°35W **94 C2**
Tengchong *China* 25°0N 98°28E **78 G8**
Tengger Desert *China* 38°0N 104°10E **78 D9**
Tennant Creek *Australia* 19°30S 134°15E **98 D5**
Tennessee □ *U.S.A.* 36°0N 86°30W **111 C9**
Tennessee → *U.S.A.* 37°4N 88°34W **111 C9**
Tenterden *U.K.* 51°4N 0°42E **31 D10**
Teófilo Otoni *Brazil* 17°50S 41°30W **122 C2**
Tepic *Mexico* 21°30N 104°54W **114 C4**
Teraina *Kiribati* 4°43N 160°25W **103 G12**
Téramo *Italy* 42°39N 13°42E **68 C5**
Teresina *Brazil* 5°9S 42°45W **120 C5**
Termiz *Uzbekistan* 37°15N 67°15E **87 B11**
Ternate *Indonesia* 0°45N 127°25E **83 D7**
Terni *Italy* 42°34N 12°37E **68 C5**
Ternopil *Ukraine* 49°30N 25°40E **65 D13**
Terrace *Canada* 54°30N 128°35W **108 D7**
Terrassa *Spain* 41°34N 2°1E **67 B7**
Terre Haute *U.S.A.* 39°28N 87°25W **112 F4**
Terschelling *Neths.* 53°25N 5°20E **64 B3**
Teruel *Spain* 40°22N 1°8W **67 B5**
Tesiyn Gol → *Mongolia* 50°40N 93°20E **78 A7**
Teslin *Canada* 60°10N 132°43W **108 C6**
Teslin → *Canada* 61°34N 134°35W **104 C6**
Test → *U.K.* 50°56N 1°29W **30 E6**
Tetbury *U.K.* 51°38N 2°10W **30 C4**
Tete *Mozam.* 16°13S 33°33E **97 H6**
Tetney *U.K.* 53°29N 0°1W **27 E8**
Tétouan *Morocco* 35°35N 5°21W **94 A4**
Tetovo *Macedonia* 42°1N 20°59E **69 C9**
Teuco → *Argentina* 25°35S 60°11W **121 E3**
Teutoburger Wald *Germany* 52°5N 8°22E **64 B5**
Teviot → *U.K.* 55°29N 2°38W **25 D10**
Teviotdale *U.K.* 55°25N 2°50W **25 D10**
Teviothead *U.K.* 55°20N 2°56W **25 D10**
Tewkesbury *U.K.* 51°59N 2°9W **30 C4**
Texarkana *U.S.A.* 33°26N 94°3W **111 D8**
Texas □ *U.S.A.* 31°40N 98°30W **110 D7**
Texel *Neths.* 53°5N 4°50E **64 B3**
Teynham *U.K.* 51°20N 0°50E **31 D10**
Tezpur *India* 26°40N 92°45E **85 F18**
Thabana Ntlenyana *Lesotho* 29°30S 29°16E **97 K5**
Thabazimbi *S. Africa* 24°40S 27°21E **97 J5**
Thailand ■ *Asia* 16°0N 102°0E **82 A2**
Thailand, G. of *Asia* 11°30N 101°0E **82 B2**
Thal Desert *Pakistan* 31°10N 71°30E **84 D7**
Thame *U.K.* 51°45N 0°58W **31 C7**
Thame → *U.K.* 51°39N 1°9W **30 C6**
Thames → *Canada* 42°20N 82°25W **112 D6**
Thames → *U.K.* 51°29N 0°34E **31 D10**
Thane *India* 19°12N 72°59E **84 K8**
Thanet, I. of *U.K.* 51°21N 1°20E **31 D11**
Thanjavur *India* 10°48N 79°12E **84 P11**
Thar Desert *India* 28°0N 72°0E **84 F8**
Thargomindah *Australia* 27°58S 143°46E **98 F7**
Thasos *Greece* 40°40N 24°40E **69 D11**
Thatcham *U.K.* 51°24N 1°15W **30 D5**
Thatta *Pakistan* 24°42N 67°55E **84 G5**
Thaxted *U.K.* 51°57N 0°22E **31 C9**
The Pas *Canada* 53°45N 101°15W **108 D9**
Theale *U.K.* 51°26N 1°5W **30 D6**
Thebes *Egypt* 25°40N 32°35E **95 C12**
Thelon → *Canada* 64°16N 96°4W **108 C9**
Thermopolis *U.S.A.* 43°39N 108°13W **110 B5**
Thermopylae *Greece* 38°48N 22°35E **69 E10**
Thessalon *Canada* 46°20N 83°30W **112 B6**
Thessaloniki *Greece* 40°38N 22°58E **69 D10**
Thetford *U.K.* 52°25N 0°45E **31 B9**
Thetford Mines *Canada* 46°8N 71°18W **109 E12**
Thiers *France* 45°52N 3°33E **66 D5**
Thiès *Senegal* 14°50N 16°51W **94 F2**
Thika *Kenya* 1°1S 37°5E **96 E7**
Thimphu *Bhutan* 27°31N 89°45E **85 F16**
Thionville *France* 49°20N 6°10E **66 B7**
Thira = Santorini *Greece* 36°23N 25°27E **69 F11**
Thirlmere *U.K.* 54°32N 3°4W **26 C2**
Thirsk *U.K.* 54°14N 1°19W **26 C6**
Thlewiaza → *Canada* 60°29N 94°40W **108 C10**
Thomasville *U.S.A.* 30°50N 83°59W **111 D10**
Thompson *Canada* 55°45N 97°52W **108 D10**
Thornaby on Tees *U.K.* 54°33N 1°18W **26 C6**
Thornbury *U.K.* 51°36N 2°31W **30 C3**

Thorndon *U.K.* 52°17N 1°9E **31 B11**
Thorne *U.K.* 53°37N 0°57W **27 E7**
Thorney *U.K.* 52°37N 0°6W **31 A8**
Thornham *U.K.* 52°58N 0°35E **31 A10**
Thornthwaite *U.K.* 54°37N 3°13W **26 C2**
Thornton *U.K.* 53°52N 2°59W **27 E3**
Thornton Dale *U.K.* 54°15N 0°42W **26 D7**
Thorpe *U.K.* 52°38N 1°22E **31 A11**
Thorpe le Soken *U.K.* 51°51N 1°11E **31 C11**
Thrace *Turkey* 41°0N 27°0E **69 D12**
Thrace, Sea of *Greece* 40°30N 25°0E **69 D11**
Thrapston *U.K.* 52°24N 0°32W **31 B7**
Three Gorges Dam *China* 30°45N 111°15E **79 E11**
Threlkeld *U.K.* 54°37N 3°3W **26 C2**
Threshfield *U.K.* 54°4N 2°1W **26 D4**
Thunder B. *U.S.A.* 45°0N 83°20W **112 C6**
Thunder Bay *Canada* 48°20N 89°15W **112 A3**
Thüringer Wald *Germany* 50°35N 11°0E **64 C6**
Thurlby *U.K.* 52°45N 0°22W **27 G8**
Thurles *Ireland* 52°41N 7°49W **20 C7**
Thurmaston *U.K.* 52°40N 1°5W **27 G6**
Thursby *U.K.* 54°51N 3°2W **26 C2**
Thurso *U.K.* 58°36N 3°32W **23 E10**
Thurso → *U.K.* 58°36N 3°32W **23 E10**
Thurston I. *Antarctica* 72°0S 100°0W **55 D16**
Tian Shan *Asia* 40°30N 76°0E **78 C4**
Tianjin *China* 39°7N 117°12E **79 D12**
Tianjun *China* 38°0N 98°30E **78 D8**
Tianmen *China* 30°39N 113°9E **79 E11**
Tianshui *China* 34°32N 105°40E **78 E10**
Tiaret *Algeria* 35°20N 1°21E **94 A6**
Tibasti, Sarīr *Libya* 22°50N 18°30E **95 D9**
Tiber → *Italy* 41°44N 12°14E **68 D5**
Tiberias, L. = Galilee, Sea of *Israel* 32°45N 35°35E **86 C3**
Tibesti *Chad* 21°0N 17°30E **95 D9**
Tibet = Xizang Zizhiqu □ *China* 32°0N 88°0E **78 E6**
Tibet, Plateau of *Asia* 32°0N 86°0E **72 E10**
Tiburón, I. *Mexico* 29°0N 112°25W **114 B2**
Ticehurst *U.K.* 51°3N 0°25E **31 D9**
Ticino → *Italy* 45°9N 9°14E **68 B3**
Tickhill *U.K.* 53°26N 1°6W **27 F6**
Ticonderoga *U.S.A.* 43°51N 73°26W **113 D11**
Tideswell *U.K.* 53°17N 1°47W **27 F5**
Tieling *China* 42°20N 123°55E **79 C13**
Tierra de Campos *Spain* 42°10N 4°50W **67 A3**
Tierra del Fuego, I. Grande de *Argentina* 54°0S 69°0W **121 H3**
Tiffin *U.S.A.* 41°7N 83°11W **112 E6**
Tighina *Moldova* 46°50N 29°30E **65 E15**
Tignish *Canada* 46°58N 64°2W **113 B15**
Tigris → *Asia* 31°0N 47°25E **86 D6**
Tijuana *Mexico* 32°32N 117°1W **114 A1**
Tikhoretsk *Russia* 45°56N 40°5E **71 E7**
Tikhvin *Russia* 59°35N 33°30E **70 C5**
Tikrit *Iraq* 34°35N 43°37E **86 C5**
Tiksi *Russia* 71°40N 128°45E **77 B13**
Tilburg *Neths.* 51°31N 5°6E **64 C3**
Tilbury *U.K.* 51°27N 0°22E **31 D9**
Till → *U.K.* 55°41N 2°13W **26 A4**
Tillicoultry *U.K.* 56°9N 3°45W **25 B8**
Tillmanstone *U.K.* 51°12N 1°18E **31 D11**
Tilt → *U.K.* 56°46N 3°51W **23 J10**
Timaru *N.Z.* 44°23S 171°14E **99 J13**
Timișoara *Romania* 45°43N 21°15E **65 F11**
Timmins *Canada* 48°28N 81°25W **109 E11**
Timor *Asia* 9°0S 125°0E **83 F7**
Timor Leste = East Timor ■ *Asia* 8°50S 126°0E **83 F7**
Timor Sea *Ind. Oc.* 12°0S 127°0E **72 K14**
Tingewick *U.K.* 51°59N 1°3W **30 C6**
Tingri *China* 28°34N 86°38E **78 F6**
Tinogasta *Argentina* 28°5S 67°32W **121 E3**
Tinos *Greece* 37°33N 25°8E **69 F11**
Tintagel *U.K.* 50°39N 4°46W **29 F4**
Tintagel Hd. *U.K.* 50°40N 4°47W **29 F4**
Tipperary *Ireland* 52°28N 8°10W **20 D6**
Tipperary □ *Ireland* 52°37N 7°55W **20 C7**
Tipton *U.K.* 52°32N 2°4W **27 G4**
Tipton *U.S.A.* 41°46N 91°8W **112 E2**
Tiptree *U.K.* 51°48N 0°46E **31 C10**
Tiranë *Albania* 41°18N 19°49E **69 D8**
Tiraspol *Moldova* 46°55N 29°35E **65 E15**
Tirebolu *Turkey* 40°58N 38°45E **71 F6**
Tiree *U.K.* 56°31N 6°55W **24 A2**
Tiree, Passage of *U.K.* 56°30N 6°30W **24 B2**
Tirich Mir *Pakistan* 36°15N 71°55E **84 A7**
Tirol □ *Austria* 47°3N 10°43E **64 E6**
Tiruchchirappalli *India* 10°45N 78°45E **84 P11**
Tirunelveli *India* 8°45N 77°45E **84 Q10**
Tiruppur *India* 11°5N 77°22E **84 P10**
Tisa → *Serbia* 45°15N 20°17E **69 B9**
Tisbury *U.K.* 51°4N 2°3W **30 D3**
Tisdale *Canada* 52°50N 104°0W **108 D9**
Titchfield *U.K.* 50°50N 1°15W **30 E5**
Titicaca, L. *S. Amer.* 15°30S 69°30W **120 D3**
Titusville *U.S.A.* 41°38N 79°41W **112 E8**
Tiverton *U.K.* 50°54N 3°29W **29 F7**
Tivoli *Italy* 41°58N 12°45E **68 D5**
Tizi-Ouzou *Algeria* 36°42N 4°3E **94 A6**
Tlaxiaco *Mexico* 17°25N 97°35W **114 D5**
Tlemcen *Algeria* 34°52N 1°21W **94 B5**
Toamasina *Madag.* 18°10S 49°25E **97 H9**
Toba, Danau *Indonesia* 2°30N 98°30E **82 D1**
Toba Kakar *Pakistan* 31°30N 69°0E **84 D6**
Tobago *Trin. & Tob.* 11°10N 60°30W **120 A3**
Tobermory *Canada* 45°12N 81°40W **112 C7**
Tobermory *U.K.* 56°38N 6°5W **24 A3**
Tobol → *Russia* 58°10N 68°12E **76 D7**
Tobolsk *Russia* 58°15N 68°10E **76 D7**
Tocantins □ *Brazil* 10°0S 48°0W **120 C5**
Toddington *U.K.* 51°57N 0°32W **31 C7**
Todmorden *U.K.* 53°43N 2°6W **27 E4**
Todos os Santos, B. de *Brazil* 12°48S 38°38W **122 B3**
Toe Hd. *U.K.* 57°50N 7°8W **22 G3**
Togliatti *Russia* 53°32N 49°24E **70 D8**
Togo ■ *W. Afr.* 8°30N 1°35E **94 G6**
Tok *U.S.A.* 63°20N 142°59W **108 C5**
Tokachi-Dake *Japan* 43°17N 142°5E **81 B8**
Tokat *Turkey* 40°22N 36°35E **71 F6**

Tokelau Is. ☑ *Pac. Oc.* 9°0S 171°45W **99 B16**
Tokushima *Japan* 34°4N 134°34E **81 F4**
Tōkyō *Japan* 35°43N 139°45E **81 F6**
Toledo *Spain* 39°50N 4°2W **67 C3**
Toledo *U.S.A.* 41°39N 83°33W **112 E6**
Toledo, Montes de *Spain* 39°33N 4°20W **67 C3**
Toliara *Madag.* 23°21S 43°40E **97 J8**
Tolima *Colombia* 4°40N 75°19W **120 B2**
Tollesbury *U.K.* 51°45N 0°51E **31 C10**
Toluca *Mexico* 19°17N 99°40W **114 D5**
Tomah *U.S.A.* 43°59N 90°30W **112 D2**
Tomakomai *Japan* 42°38N 141°36E **81 B7**
Tomaszów Mazowiecki *Poland* 51°30N 20°2E **65 C10**
Tombador, Serra do *Brazil* 12°0S 58°0W **120 D4**
Tombigbee → *U.S.A.* 31°8N 87°57W **111 D9**
Tombouctou *Mali* 16°50N 3°0W **94 E5**
Tomini, Teluk *Indonesia* 0°10S 121°0E **83 E6**
Tomintoul *U.K.* 57°15N 3°23W **23 H11**
Tomsk *Russia* 56°30N 85°5E **76 D9**
Tonbridge *U.K.* 51°11N 0°17E **31 D9**
Tone → *U.K.* 50°58N 3°20W **29 F7**
Tong *U.K.* 52°40N 2°17W **27 G4**
Tonga ■ *Pac. Oc.* 19°50S 174°30W **99 D16**
Tonga Trench *Pac. Oc.* 18°0S 173°0W **99 D16**
Tongareva *Cook Is.* 9°0S 158°0W **103 H12**
Tongatapu Group *Tonga* 21°0S 175°0W **99 E16**
Tongchuan *China* 35°6N 109°3E **79 D10**
Tonghua *China* 41°42N 125°58E **79 C14**
Tongliao *China* 43°38N 122°18E **79 C13**
Tongling *China* 30°55N 117°48E **79 E12**
Tongue → *U.S.A.* 58°29N 4°25W **23 F9**
Tonk *India* 26°6N 75°54E **84 F9**
Tonkin, G. of *Asia* 20°0N 108°0E **78 G9**
Tonlé Sap *Cambodia* 13°0N 104°0E **82 B2**
Tonopah *U.S.A.* 38°4N 117°14W **110 C3**
Toowoomba *Australia* 27°32S 151°56E **98 F9**
Topeka *U.S.A.* 39°3N 95°40W **111 C7**
Topolobampo *Mexico* 25°36N 109°3W **114 B3**
Topsham *U.K.* 50°41N 3°28W **29 F7**
Tor B. *U.K.* 50°25N 3°33W **29 G6**
Torbay *U.K.* 50°26N 3°31W **29 G6**
Torne → *Europe* 65°50N 24°12E **63 D8**
Torneälven → *Europe* 65°50N 24°12E **63 D8**
Torneträsk *Sweden* 68°24N 19°15E **63 D7**
Tornio *Finland* 65°50N 24°12E **63 D8**
Toro, Cerro del *Chile* 29°10S 69°50W **121 E3**
Toronto *Canada* 43°39N 79°20W **112 D8**
Torpoint *U.K.* 50°23N 4°13W **29 G5**
Torquay *U.K.* 50°27N 3°32W **29 G6**
Torre del Greco *Italy* 40°47N 14°22E **68 D6**
Torrejón de Ardoz *Spain* 40°27N 3°29W **67 B4**
Torrelavega *Spain* 43°20N 4°5W **67 A3**
Torremolinos *Spain* 36°38N 4°30W **67 D3**
Torrens, L. *Australia* 31°0S 137°50E **98 G6**
Torrent *Spain* 39°27N 0°28W **67 C5**
Torreón *Mexico* 25°33N 103°26W **114 B4**
Torres Strait *Australia* 9°50S 142°20E **98 C7**
Torridge → *U.K.* 51°0N 4°13W **29 E5**
Torridon, L. *U.K.* 57°35N 5°50W **22 H6**
Torthorwald *U.K.* 55°6N 3°32W **25 D8**
Tortosa *Spain* 40°49N 0°31E **67 B6**
Toruń *Poland* 53°2N 18°39E **65 B10**
Torver *U.K.* 54°20N 3°6W **26 D2**
Tory I. *Ireland* 55°16N 8°14W **18 A5**
Toscana □ *Italy* 43°25N 11°0E **68 C4**
Toshka Lakes *Egypt* 22°50N 31°0E **95 D12**
Totland *U.K.* 50°41N 1°32W **30 E5**
Totley *U.K.* 53°20N 1°32W **27 F5**
Totnes *U.K.* 50°26N 3°42W **29 G6**
Totton *U.K.* 50°55N 1°29W **30 E6**
Tottori *Japan* 35°30N 134°15E **81 F4**
Toubkal, Djebel *Morocco* 31°0N 8°0W **94 B4**
Touggourt *Algeria* 33°6N 6°4E **94 B7**
Toul *France* 48°40N 5°53E **66 B6**
Toulon *France* 43°10N 5°55E **66 E6**
Toulouse *France* 43°37N 1°27E **66 E4**
Touraine *France* 47°20N 0°30E **66 C4**
Tournai *Belgium* 50°35N 3°25E **64 C2**
Tournon-sur-Rhône *France* 45°4N 4°50E **66 D6**
Tours *France* 47°22N 0°40E **66 C4**
Towanda *U.S.A.* 41°46N 76°27W **112 E9**
Towcester *U.K.* 52°8N 0°59W **31 B7**
Town Yetholm *U.K.* 55°33N 2°17W **25 C11**
Townsville *Australia* 19°15S 146°45E **98 D8**
Towraghondi *Afghan.* 35°13N 62°16E **84 B3**
Towson *U.S.A.* 39°24N 76°36W **112 F9**
Toyama *Japan* 36°40N 137°15E **81 E5**
Toyohashi *Japan* 34°45N 137°25E **81 F5**
Toyota *Japan* 35°3N 137°7E **81 F5**
Trabzon *Turkey* 41°0N 39°45E **71 F6**
Trafalgar, C. *Spain* 36°10N 6°2W **67 D2**
Trail *Canada* 49°5N 117°40W **108 E8**
Tralee *Ireland* 52°16N 9°42W **20 D3**
Tralee B. *Ireland* 52°17N 9°55W **20 D2**
Tramore *Ireland* 52°10N 7°10W **21 D8**
Tramore B. *Ireland* 52°9N 7°10W **21 D8**
Tranent *U.K.* 55°57N 2°57W **25 C10**
Trang *Thailand* 7°33N 99°38E **82 C1**
Transantarctic Mts. *Antarctica* 85°0S 170°0W **55 E12**
Transnistria □ *Moldova* 47°20N 29°15E **65 E15**
Transylvania *Romania* 46°30N 24°0E **65 E12**
Transylvanian Alps *Romania* 45°30N 25°0E **65 F13**
Trápani *Italy* 38°1N 12°29E **68 E5**
Trasimeno, L. *Italy* 43°8N 12°6E **68 C5**
Traverse City *U.S.A.* 44°46N 85°38W **112 C5**
Trawbreaga B. *Ireland* 55°20N 7°25W **18 A7**
Trawsfynydd *U.K.* 52°54N 3°55W **28 B5**
Tredegar *U.K.* 51°47N 3°14W **28 D7**

Trenton *U.S.A.* 40°14N 74°46W **113 E10**
Tres Arroyos *Argentina* 38°26S 60°20W **121 F3**
Tres Coraçôes *Brazil* 21°44S 45°15W **122 D1**
Três Lagoas *Brazil* 20°50S 51°43W **120 E4**
Três Pontas *Brazil* 21°23S 45°29W **122 D1**
Tres Puntas, C. *Argentina* 47°0S 66°0W **121 G3**
Três Rios *Brazil* 22°6S 43°15W **122 D2**
Tresco *U.K.* 49°57N 6°20W **29 H1**
Treviso *Italy* 45°40N 12°15E **68 B5**
Trevose Hd. *U.K.* 50°32N 5°3W **29 F3**
Tribal Areas □ *Pakistan* 33°0N 70°0E **84 C7**
Trichur *India* 10°30N 76°18E **84 P10**
Trier *Germany* 49°45N 6°38E **64 D4**
Trieste *Italy* 45°40N 13°46E **68 B5**
Trim *Ireland* 53°33N 6°48W **19 D8**
Trimdon *U.K.* 54°42N 1°24W **26 C6**
Trimley *U.K.* 51°59N 1°20E **31 C11**
Trincomalee *Sri Lanka* 8°38N 81°15E **84 Q12**
Trindade *Atl. Oc.* 20°20S 29°50W **52 F8**
Trinidad *Bolivia* 14°46S 64°50W **120 D3**
Trinidad *Cuba* 21°48N 80°0W **115 C9**
Trinidad *U.S.A.* 37°10N 104°31W **110 C6**
Trinidad & Tobago ■ *W. Indies* 10°30N 61°20W **115 E12**
Trinity → *U.S.A.* 29°45N 94°43W **111 E8**
Trinity B. *Canada* 48°20N 53°10W **109 E14**
Trinity Is. *U.S.A.* 56°33N 154°25W **108 D4**
Tripoli *Lebanon* 34°31N 35°50E **86 C3**
Tripoli *Libya* 32°49N 13°7E **95 B8**
Tripolitania *Libya* 31°0N 13°0E **95 B8**
Tripura □ *India* 24°0N 92°0E **85 H18**
Tristan da Cunha *Atl. Oc.* 37°6S 12°20W **52 F9**
Trivandrum *India* 8°41N 77°0E **84 Q10**
Trnava *Slovak Rep.* 48°23N 17°35E **65 D9**
Trois-Rivières *Canada* 46°25N 72°34W **109 E12**
Trollhättan *Sweden* 58°17N 12°20E **63 F6**
Trombetas → *Brazil* 1°55S 55°35W **120 C4**
Tromsø *Norway* 69°40N 18°56E **63 D7**
Tronador *Argentina* 41°10S 71°50W **121 G2**
Trondheim *Norway* 63°36N 10°25E **63 E6**
Trondheimsfjorden *Norway* 63°35N 10°30E **63 E6**
Troon *U.K.* 55°33N 4°39W **24 C6**
Trossachs, The *U.K.* 56°14N 4°24W **24 B7**
Trostan *U.K.* 55°3N 6°10W **19 A9**
Trotternish *U.K.* 57°32N 6°15W **22 G5**
Trou Gras Pt. *St. Lucia* 13°51N 60°53W **114 b**
Trout L. *N.W.T., Canada* 60°40N 121°14W **108 C7**
Trout L. *Ont., Canada* 51°20N 93°15W **108 D10**
Trowbridge *U.K.* 51°18N 2°12W **30 D4**
Troy *Turkey* 39°57N 26°12E **71 G4**
Troy *Ala., U.S.A.* 31°48N 85°58W **111 D9**
Troy *N.Y., U.S.A.* 42°44N 73°41W **113 D11**
Troy *Ohio, U.S.A.* 40°2N 84°12W **112 E5**
Troyes *France* 48°19N 4°3E **66 B6**
Trujillo *Honduras* 16°0N 86°0W **114 D7**
Trujillo *Peru* 8°6S 79°0W **120 C2**
Trujillo *Venezuela* 9°22N 70°38W **120 B2**
Truk *Micronesia* 7°25N 151°46E **102 G7**
Trull *U.K.* 51°0N 3°6W **30 E2**
Trumpington *U.K.* 52°10N 0°7E **31 B9**
Truro *Canada* 45°21N 63°14W **109 E13**
Truro *U.K.* 50°16N 5°4W **29 G3**
Tsavo *Kenya* 2°59S 38°28E **96 E7**
Tseung Kwan *China* 22°20N 114°15E **79 a**
Tshabong *Botswana* 26°2S 22°29E **97 K4**
Tshikapa *Dem. Rep. of the Congo* 6°28S 20°48E **96 F4**
Tsiigehtchic *Canada* 67°15N 134°0W **108 C6**
Tsimlyansk Res. *Russia* 48°0N 43°0E **71 E7**
Tskhinvali *Georgia* 42°14N 44°1E **71 F7**
Tsuchiura *Japan* 36°5N 140°15E **81 E7**
Tsuen Wan *China* 22°22N 114°6E **79 a**
Tsugaru Str. *Japan* 41°35N 141°0E **81 C7**
Tsumeb *Namibia* 19°9S 17°44E **97 H3**
Tsuruoka *Japan* 38°44N 139°50E **81 D6**
Tsushima *Japan* 34°20N 129°20E **81 F1**
Tuam *Ireland* 53°31N 8°51W **18 D4**
Tuamotu, Îs. *French Polynesia* 17°0S 144°0W **103 J13**
Tuapse *Russia* 44°5N 39°10E **71 F6**
Tubarão *Brazil* 28°30S 49°0W **121 E5**
Tübingen *Germany* 48°31N 9°4E **64 D5**
Tubruq *Libya* 32°7N 23°55E **95 B10**
Tubuai, Îs. *French Polynesia* 25°0S 150°0W **103 K13**
Tucson *U.S.A.* 32°13N 110°58W **110 D4**
Tucumcari *U.S.A.* 35°10N 103°44W **110 C6**
Tucupita *Venezuela* 9°2N 62°3W **120 B3**
Tucuruí *Brazil* 3°42S 49°44W **120 C5**
Tucuruí, Represa de *Brazil* 4°0S 49°30W **120 C5**
Tuen Mun *China* 22°24N 113°59E **79 a**
Tuguegarao *Phil.* 17°35N 121°42E **83 A6**
Tuktoyaktuk *Canada* 69°27N 133°2W **108 C6**
Tula *Russia* 54°13N 37°38E **70 D6**
Tulancingo *Mexico* 20°5N 98°22W **114 C5**
Tulare *U.S.A.* 36°13N 119°21W **110 C3**
Tulcán *Ecuador* 0°48N 77°43W **120 B2**
Tulcea *Romania* 45°13N 28°46E **65 F15**
Tulita *Canada* 64°57N 125°30W **108 C7**
Tulla *Ireland* 52°53N 8°46W **20 C5**
Tullamore *Ireland* 53°16N 7°31W **21 B7**
Tulle *France* 45°16N 1°46E **66 D4**
Tullow *Ireland* 52°49N 6°45W **21 C9**
Tulsa *U.S.A.* 36°10N 95°55W **111 C7**
Tulua *Colombia* 4°6N 76°11W **120 B2**
Tumaco *Colombia* 1°50N 78°45W **120 B2**
Tumbes *Peru* 3°37S 80°27W **120 C1**
Tummel → *U.K.* 56°42N 4°5W **23 J9**
Tummel, L. *U.K.* 56°43N 3°55W **23 J10**
Tumucumaque, Serra *Brazil* 2°0N 55°0W **120 B4**
Tunis *Tunisia* 36°50N 10°11E **95 A8**
Tunisia ■ *Africa* 33°30N 9°10E **95 A7**
Tunja *Colombia* 5°33N 73°25W **120 B2**
Tunstall *U.K.* 52°9N 1°27E **31 B11**
Tupaciguara *Brazil* 18°35S 48°42W **122 C1**
Tupelo *U.S.A.* 34°16N 88°43W **111 D9**
Tupiza *Bolivia* 21°30S 65°40W **120 E3**
Turfan Basin *China* 42°40N 89°25E **78 C6**
Turgutlu *Turkey* 38°30N 27°43E **71 G4**
Turin *Italy* 45°3N 7°40E **68 B2**
Turkana, L. *Africa* 3°30N 36°5E **96 D7**
Turkey ■ *Eurasia* 39°0N 36°0E **71 G6**
Türkmenabat *Turkmenistan* 39°6N 63°34E **87 B10**
Türkmenbashi *Turkmenistan* 40°5N 53°5E **87 A8**
Turkmenistan ■ *Asia* 39°0N 59°0E **87 B9**

Union City

Turks & Caicos Is. ☑ *W. Indies* 21°20N 71°20W **115 C10**
Turku *Finland* 60°30N 22°19E **63 E8**
Turnberry *U.K.* 55°18N 4°49W **24 D6**
Turneffe Is. *Belize* 17°20N 87°50W **114 D7**
Turpan *China* 43°58N 89°10E **78 C6**
Turriff *U.K.* 57°32N 2°27W **23 G13**
Tuscaloosa *U.S.A.* 33°12N 87°34W **111 D9**
Tuscany = Toscana □ *Italy* 43°25N 11°0E **68 C4**
Tutbury *U.K.* 52°51N 1°41W **27 G5**
Tuticorin *India* 8°50N 78°12E **84 Q11**
Tutuila *Amer. Samoa* 14°19S 170°50W **99 C16**
Tutume *Botswana* 20°30S 27°5E **97 J5**
Tuul Gol → *Mongolia* 48°30N 104°25E **78 B9**
Tuva □ *Russia* 51°30N 95°0E **77 D10**
Tuvalu ■ *Pac. Oc.* 8°0S 178°0E **99 B14**
Tuxford *U.K.* 53°14N 0°54W **27 F7**
Tuxpan *Mexico* 20°58N 97°23W **114 C5**
Tuxtla Gutiérrez *Mexico* 16°45N 93°7W **114 D6**
Tuz Gölü *Turkey* 38°42N 33°18E **71 G5**
Tuzla *Bos.-H.* 44°34N 18°41E **69 B8**
Tver *Russia* 56°55N 35°59E **70 C6**
Tweed → *U.K.* 55°45N 2°0W **25 C11**
Tweedmouth *U.K.* 55°45N 2°0W **26 A5**
Tweedshaws *U.K.* 55°27N 3°29W **25 D9**
Twenty *U.K.* 52°47N 0°17W **27 G7**
Twin Falls *U.S.A.* 42°34N 114°28W **110 B4**
Two Harbors *U.S.A.* 47°2N 91°40W **112 B2**
Two Rivers *U.S.A.* 44°9N 87°34W **112 C4**
Twyford *Hants., U.K.* 51°1N 1°19W **30 D5**
Twyford *Wokingham, U.K.* 51°28N 0°51W **31 D7**
Tychy *Poland* 50°9N 18°59E **65 C10**
Tydd St. Mary *U.K.* 52°45N 0°7E **27 G9**
Tyler *U.S.A.* 32°21N 95°18W **111 D7**
Tyndrum *U.K.* 56°26N 4°42W **24 B6**
Tyne → *U.K.* 54°59N 1°32W **26 C5**
Tyne & Wear □ *U.K.* 55°6N 1°17W **26 B6**
Tynemouth *U.K.* 55°1N 1°26W **26 B6**
Tyrol = Tirol □ *Austria* 47°3N 10°43E **64 E6**
Tyrone □ *U.K.* 54°38N 7°11W **19 B7**
Tyrrhenian Sea *Medit. S.* 40°0N 12°30E **68 E5**
Tyumen *Russia* 57°11N 65°29E **76 D7**
Tywardreath *U.K.* 50°21N 4°42W **29 G4**
Tywi → *U.K.* 51°48N 4°21W **28 D4**
Tywyn *U.K.* 52°35N 4°5W **28 B5**
Tzaneen *S. Africa* 23°47S 30°9E **97 J6**

U

U.S.A. = United States of America ■
N. Amer. 37°0N 96°0W **110 C7**
U.S. Virgin Is. ☑ *W. Indies* 18°20N 65°0W **115 D12**
Uaupés → *Brazil* 0°2N 67°16W **120 B3**
Ubá *Brazil* 21°8S 43°0W **122 D2**
Ubaitaba *Brazil* 14°18S 39°20W **122 B3**
Ube *Japan* 33°56N 131°15E **81 G2**
Uberaba *Brazil* 19°50S 47°55W **122 C1**
Uberlândia *Brazil* 19°0S 48°20W **122 C1**
Ubon Ratchathani *Thailand* 15°15N 104°50E **82 A2**
Ucayali → *Peru* 4°30S 73°30W **120 C2**
Uckfield *U.K.* 50°58N 0°7E **31 E9**
Udagamandalam *India* 11°30N 76°44E **84 P10**
Udaipur *India* 24°36N 73°44E **84 G8**
Uddingston *U.K.* 55°49N 4°5W **24 C7**
Údine *Italy* 46°3N 13°14E **68 A5**
Udmurtia □ *Russia* 57°30N 52°30E **70 C9**
Udon Thani *Thailand* 17°29N 102°46E **82 A2**
Udupi *India* 13°25N 74°42E **84 N9**
Uele → *Dem. Rep. of the Congo* 3°45N 24°45E **96 D4**
Ufa *Russia* 54°45N 55°55E **70 D10**
Uffculme *U.K.* 50°54N 3°20W **29 F7**
Ufford *U.K.* 52°8N 1°23E **31 B11**
Uganda ■ *Africa* 2°0N 32°0E **96 D6**
Ugborough *U.K.* 50°22N 3°53W **29 G6**
Uibhist a Deas = South Uist *U.K.* 57°20N 7°15W **22 H3**
Uibhist a Tuath = North Uist *U.K.* 57°40N 7°15W **22 G3**
Uig *U.K.* 57°35N 6°21W **22 G5**
Uinta Mts. *U.S.A.* 40°45N 110°30W **110 B4**
Uitenhage *S. Africa* 33°40S 25°28E **97 L5**
Ujjain *India* 23°9N 75°43E **84 H9**
Ukhta *Russia* 63°34N 53°41E **70 B9**
Ukiah *U.S.A.* 39°9N 123°13W **110 C2**
Ukraine ■ *Europe* 49°0N 32°0E **71 E5**
Ulaan-Uul *Mongolia* 46°4N 100°49E **78 B9**
Ulaangom *Mongolia* 50°5N 92°10E **78 A7**
Ulan Bator *Mongolia* 47°55N 106°53E **78 B10**
Ulan Ude *Russia* 51°45N 107°40E **77 D11**
Ulceby Cross *U.K.* 53°15N 0°7E **27 F8**
Ulhasnagar *India* 19°15N 73°10E **84 K8**
Uliastay *Mongolia* 47°56N 97°28E **78 B8**
Ullapool *U.K.* 57°54N 5°9W **22 G7**
Ulleungdo *S. Korea* 37°30N 130°30E **81 E2**
Ullswater *U.K.* 54°34N 2°52W **26 C3**
Ulm *Germany* 48°23N 9°58E **64 D5**
Ulsan *S. Korea* 35°20N 129°15E **79 D14**
Ulster □ *U.K.* 54°35N 6°30W **19 B9**
Ulungur He → *China* 47°1N 87°24E **78 B6**
Uluru *Australia* 25°23S 131°5E **98 F5**
Ulva *U.K.* 56°29N 6°13W **24 B3**
Ulverston *U.K.* 54°13N 3°5W **26 D2**
Ulyanovsk *Russia* 54°20N 48°25E **70 D8**
Uman *Ukraine* 48°40N 30°12E **71 E5**
Umeå *Sweden* 63°45N 20°20E **63 E8**
Umeälven → *Sweden* 63°45N 20°20E **63 E8**
Umlazi *S. Africa* 29°59S 30°54E **97 L6**
Umm al Qaywayn *U.A.E.* 25°30N 55°35E **87 E8**
Umnak I. *U.S.A.* 53°15N 168°20W **108 D3**
Umuahia *Nigeria* 5°31N 7°26E **94 G7**
Unalakleet *U.S.A.* 63°52N 160°47W **108 C3**
Unalaska *U.S.A.* 53°53N 166°32W **108 D3**
Unalaska I. *U.S.A.* 53°35N 166°50W **108 D3**
'Unayzah *Si. Arabia* 26°6N 43°58E **86 E5**
Uncía *Bolivia* 18°25S 66°40W **120 D3**
Ungava, Pén. d' *Canada* 60°0N 74°0W **109 D12**
Ungava B. *Canada* 59°30N 67°30W **109 D13**
União dos Palmares *Brazil* 9°10S 36°2W **122 A3**
Unimak I. *U.S.A.* 54°45N 164°0W **108 D3**
Union City *U.S.A.* 36°26N 89°3W **112 G3**

Uniontown   White Esk

Uniontown U.S.A. 39°54N 79°44W 112 F8
United Arab Emirates ■ Asia 23°50N 54°0E 87 F8
United Kingdom ■ Europe 53°0N 2°0W 62 E6
United States of America ■
  N. Amer. 37°0N 96°0W 110 C7
Unst U.K. 60°44N 0°53W 22 A16
Unzen-Dake Japan 32°45N 130°17E 81 G2
Upavon U.K. 51°18N 1°48W 30 D5
Upington S. Africa 28°25S 21°15E 97 K4
'Upolu Samoa 13°58S 172°0W 99 C16
Upper Heyford U.K. 51°56N 1°15W 30 C6
Upper Klamath L. U.S.A. 42°25N 121°55W 110 D2
Uppingham U.K. 52°36N 0°43W 27 G7
Uppsala Sweden 59°53N 17°38E 63 F7
Upton U.K. 53°13N 2°53W 27 F3
Upton-upon-Severn U.K. 52°3N 2°12W 30 B4
Upwey U.K. 50°39N 2°29W 30 E4
Ur Iraq 30°55N 46°25E 86 D6
Ural → Kazakhstan 47°0N 51°48E 71 E9
Ural Mts. Eurasia 60°0N 59°0E 70 C10
Uranium City Canada 59°34N 108°37W 108 D9
Uraricoera → Brazil 3°2N 60°30W 120 B3
Urbana Ill., U.S.A. 40°7N 88°12W 112 E3
Urbana Ohio, U.S.A. 40°7N 83°45W 112 E6
Ure → U.K. 54°5N 1°20W 26 D5
Urganch Uzbekistan 41°40N 60°41E 87 A10
Urmia Iran 37°40N 45°0E 86 B6
Urmia, L. Iran 37°50N 45°30E 86 B6
Urmston U.K. 53°27N 2°21W 27 F4
Uruaçu Brazil 14°30S 49°10W 122 B1
Uruapan Mexico 19°24N 102°3W 114 D4
Urubamba → Peru 10°43S 73°48W 120 D2
Uruguai → Brazil 26°0S 53°30W 121 E4
Uruguaiana Brazil 29°50S 57°0W 121 E4
Uruguay ■ S. Amer. 32°30S 56°30W 121 F4
Uruguay → S. Amer. 34°12S 58°18W 117 G5
Ürümqi China 43°45N 87°45E 78 C6
Usa → Russia 66°16N 59°49E 70 A10
Uşak Turkey 38°43N 29°28E 71 G4
Usakos Namibia 21°54S 15°31E 97 J3
Usedom Germany 53°55N 14°2E 64 B8
Ushant France 48°28N 5°6W 66 B1
Ushuaia Argentina 54°50S 68°23W 121 H3
Usk → U.K. 51°33N 2°58W 29 D6
Usolye Sibirskoye Russia 52°48N 103°40E 77 D11
Uspallata, P. de Argentina 32°37S 69°22W 121 F3
Usselby U.K. 53°26N 0°21W 27 F8
Ussuriysk Russia 43°48N 131°59E 81 B2
Ust-Ilimsk Russia 58°3N 102°39E 77 D11
Ust-Kut Russia 56°50N 105°42E 77 D11
Ústí nad Labem Czech Rep. 50°41N 14°3E 64 C8
Ústica Italy 38°42N 13°11E 68 E5
Usu China 44°27N 84°40E 78 C5
Usumacinta → Mexico 18°24N 92°38W 114 D6
Utah □ U.S.A. 39°20N 111°30W 110 C4
Utah L. U.S.A. 40°12N 111°48W 110 B4
Utica U.S.A. 43°6N 75°14W 113 D10
Utrecht Neths. 52°5N 5°8E 64 B3
Utsunomiya Japan 36°30N 139°50E 81 E6
Uttar Pradesh □ India 27°0N 80°0E 84 F12
Uttaradit Thailand 17°36N 100°5E 82 A2
Uttarakhand □ India 30°0N 79°30E 84 D11
Uttoxeter U.K. 52°54N 1°52W 27 G5
Uusikaupunki Finland 60°47N 21°25E 63 E8
Uvalde U.S.A. 29°13N 99°47W 110 E7
Uvira Dem. Rep. of the Congo 3°22S 29°3E 96 E5
Uvs Nuur Mongolia 50°20N 92°30W 78 A7
Uyuni Bolivia 20°28S 66°47W 120 E3
Uzbekistan ■ Asia 41°30N 65°0E 87 A10
Uzhhorod Ukraine 48°36N 22°18E 65 D12

V
Vaal → S. Africa 29°4S 23°38E 97 K4
Vaasa Finland 63°6N 21°38E 63 E8
Vadodara India 22°20N 73°10E 84 H8
Vadsø Norway 70°3N 29°50E 63 C9
Vaduz Liech. 47°8N 9°31E 64 E5
Váh → Slovak Rep. 47°43N 18°7E 65 D9
Vail U.S.A. 39°40N 106°20W 110 C5
Vaila U.K. 60°12N 1°36W 22 B14
Val-d'Or Canada 48°7N 77°47W 109 E12
Valdai Hills Russia 57°0N 33°30E 70 C5
Valdés, Pen. Argentina 42°30S 63°45W 121 G3
Valdez U.S.A. 61°7N 146°16W 108 C5
Valdivia Chile 39°50S 73°14W 121 F2
Valdosta U.S.A. 30°50N 83°17W 111 D10
Vale of Glamorgan □ U.K. 51°28N 3°25W 29 E7
Valença Brazil 13°20S 39°5W 122 B3
Valence France 44°57N 4°54E 66 D6
Valencia Spain 39°27N 0°23W 67 C5
Valencia Venezuela 10°11N 68°0W 120 A3
Valencia □ Spain 39°20N 0°40W 67 C5
Valencia, G. de Spain 39°30N 0°20E 67 C6
Valencia I. Ireland 51°54N 10°22W 20 E2
Valenciennes France 50°20N 3°34E 66 A5
Valera Venezuela 9°19N 70°37W 120 B2
Valladolid Mexico 20°41N 88°12W 114 C7
Valladolid Spain 41°38N 4°43W 67 B3
Valledupar Colombia 10°29N 73°15W 120 A2
Vallejo U.S.A. 38°7N 122°14W 110 C2
Vallenar Chile 28°30S 70°50W 121 E2
Valletta Malta 35°54N 14°31E 68 G6
Valley U.S.A. 53°16N 4°34W 28 A4
Valley City U.S.A. 46°55N 98°0W 110 A7
Valparaíso Chile 33°2S 71°40W 121 F2
Van Turkey 38°30N 43°20E 71 G7
Van, L. Turkey 38°30N 43°0E 71 G7
Van Buren U.S.A. 47°10N 67°58W 113 B13
Van Wert U.S.A. 40°52N 84°35W 112 E5
Vanadzor Armenia 40°48N 44°30E 71 F7
Vancouver Canada 49°15N 123°7W 108 E7
Vancouver U.S.A. 45°38N 122°40W 110 A2
Vancouver I. Canada 49°50N 126°0W 108 E7
Vandalia U.S.A. 38°58N 89°6W 112 F3
Vanderhoof Canada 54°0N 124°0W 108 D7
Vänern Sweden 58°47N 13°30E 63 F6
Vännäs Sweden 63°58N 19°48E 63 E7
Vannes France 47°40N 2°47W 66 C2
Vanrhynsdorp S. Africa 31°36S 18°44E 97 L3

Vantaa Finland 60°18N 24°56E 63 E8
Vanua Levu Fiji 16°33S 179°15E 99 D14
Vanuatu ■ Pac. Oc. 15°0S 168°0E 99 D12
Varanasi India 25°22N 83°0E 85 G13
Varangerfjorden Norway 70°3N 29°25E 63 C9
Varberg Sweden 57°6N 12°20E 63 F6
Vardø Norway 70°23N 31°5E 63 C10
Varese Italy 45°48N 8°50E 68 B3
Varginha Brazil 21°33S 45°25W 122 D1
Varna Bulgaria 43°13N 27°56E 69 C12
Vasa Barris → Brazil 11°10S 37°10W 122 B3
Västerås Sweden 59°37N 16°38E 63 F7
Västervik Sweden 57°43N 16°33E 63 F7
Vaté Vanuatu 17°40S 168°25E 99 D12
Vatersay U.K. 56°55N 7°32W 22 J2
Vatican City ■ Europe 41°54N 12°27E 68 D5
Vatnajökull Iceland 64°30N 16°48W 63 B2
Vättern Sweden 58°25N 14°30E 63 F6
Vaughn U.S.A. 34°36N 105°13W 110 D5
Vava'u Group Tonga 18°40S 174°0W 99 D16
Vega Norway 65°40N 11°55E 63 D6
Vegreville Canada 53°30N 112°5W 108 D8
Vélez-Málaga Spain 36°48N 4°5W 67 D3
Velhas → Brazil 17°13S 44°49W 122 C2
Velikiye Luki Russia 56°25N 30°32E 70 C5
Veliko Tŭrnovo Bulgaria 43°5N 25°41E 69 C11
Velikonda Range India 14°45N 79°10E 84 M11
Vellore India 12°57N 79°10E 84 N11
Velsk Russia 61°10N 42°5E 70 B7
Vendée □ France 46°50N 1°35W 66 C3
Vendôme France 47°47N 1°3E 66 C4
Venézia, G. di Italy 45°15N 13°0E 68 B5
Venezuela ■ S. Amer. 8°0N 66°0W 120 B3
Venezuela, G. de Venezuela 11°30N 71°0W 120 A2
Vengurla India 15°53N 73°45E 84 M8
Venice Italy 45°27N 12°21E 68 B5
Ventnor U.K. 50°36N 1°12W 30 E6
Ventoux, Mt. France 44°10N 5°17E 66 D6
Ventspils Latvia 57°25N 21°32E 63 F8
Veracruz Mexico 19°11N 96°8W 114 D5
Veraval India 20°53N 70°27E 84 J7
Vercelli Italy 45°19N 8°25E 68 B3
Verde → U.S.A. 33°33N 111°40W 110 D4
Verdun France 49°9N 5°24E 66 B6
Vereeniging S. Africa 26°38S 27°57E 97 K5
Verkhoyansk Russia 67°35N 133°25E 77 C14
Verkhoyansk Ra. Russia 66°0N 129°0E 77 C13
Vermont □ U.S.A. 44°0N 73°0W 113 D11
Vernal U.S.A. 40°27N 109°32W 110 B5
Vernon Canada 50°20N 119°15W 108 D8
Vernon U.S.A. 34°9N 99°17W 110 D7
Verona Italy 45°27N 10°59E 68 B4
Versailles France 48°48N 2°7E 66 B5
Vert, C. Senegal 14°45N 17°30W 94 F2
Verviers Belgium 50°37N 5°52E 64 C3
Verwood U.K. 50°52N 1°52W 30 E5
Veryan U.K. 50°13N 4°56W 29 G4
Veryan B. U.K. 50°13N 4°51W 29 G4
Vesoul France 47°40N 6°11E 66 C7
Vesterålen Norway 68°45N 15°0E 63 D7
Vestfjorden Norway 67°55N 14°0E 63 D6
Vesuvio Italy 40°49N 14°26E 68 D6
Veszprém Hungary 47°8N 17°57E 65 E9
Vianópolis Brazil 16°40S 48°35W 122 C1
Viaréggio Italy 43°52N 10°14E 68 C4
Vicenza Italy 45°33N 11°33E 68 B4
Vichada → Colombia 4°55N 67°50W 120 B3
Vichy France 46°9N 3°26E 66 C5
Vickerstown U.K. 54°6N 3°15W 26 D2
Vicksburg U.S.A. 32°21N 90°53W 111 D8
Victoria Canada 48°30N 123°25W 108 E7
Victoria China 22°17N 114°9E 79 a
Victoria U.S.A. 28°48N 97°0W 111 E7
Victoria □ Australia 37°0S 144°0E 98 H7
Victoria, L. Africa 1°0S 33°0E 96 E6
Victoria Falls Zimbabwe 17°58S 25°52E 97 H5
Victoria I. Canada 71°0N 111°0W 108 B8
Victoria Ld. Antarctica 75°0S 160°0E 55 D11
Victoria Str. Canada 69°31N 100°30W 108 B9
Victoriaville Canada 46°4N 71°56W 113 B12
Vidin Bulgaria 43°59N 22°50E 69 C10
Viedma, L. Argentina 49°30S 72°30W 121 G2
Vienna Austria 48°12N 16°22E 64 D9
Vienne France 45°31N 4°53E 66 D6
Vienne □ France 47°13N 0°5E 66 C4
Vientiane Laos 17°58N 102°36E 82 A2
Vierge Pt. St. Lucia 13°49N 60°53W 114 b
Vierzon France 47°13N 2°5E 66 C5
Vietnam ■ Asia 19°0N 106°0E 82 A3
Vieux Fort St. Lucia 13°46N 60°58W 114 b
Vigévano Italy 45°19N 8°51E 68 B3
Vigo Spain 42°12N 8°41W 67 A1
Vijayawada India 16°31N 80°39E 85 L12
Vikna Norway 64°55N 10°58E 63 E6
Vila Nova de Gaia Portugal 41°8N 8°37W 67 B1
Vila Velha Brazil 20°20S 40°17W 122 D2
Vilaine → France 47°30N 2°27W 66 C2
Vilhelmina Sweden 64°35N 16°39E 63 E7
Vilhena Brazil 12°40S 60°5W 120 D3
Vilkitski Str. Russia 78°0N 103°0E 77 B11
Villa Bella Bolivia 10°25S 65°22W 120 D3
Villa Maria Argentina 32°20S 63°10W 121 F3
Villach Austria 46°37N 13°51E 64 E7
Villahermosa Mexico 17°59N 92°55W 114 D6
Villajoyosa Spain 38°30N 0°12W 67 C5
Villarrica Paraguay 25°40S 56°30W 121 E4
Villavicencio Colombia 4°9N 73°37W 120 C2
Ville-Marie Canada 47°20N 79°30W 112 B8
Villeneuve-sur-Lot France 44°24N 0°42E 66 D4
Vilnius Lithuania 54°38N 25°19E 63 G9
Viluyu → Russia 64°24N 126°26E 77 C13
Vilyuysk Russia 63°40N 121°35E 77 C13
Viña del Mar Chile 33°0S 71°30W 121 F2
Vincennes U.S.A. 38°41N 87°32W 112 F4
Vindhya Ra. India 22°50N 77°0E 84 H10
Vineland U.S.A. 39°29N 75°2W 113 F10
Vinnytsya Ukraine 49°15N 28°30E 65 D15
Virden Canada 49°50N 100°56W 108 E9
Vire France 48°50N 0°53W 66 B3
Virgenes, C. Argentina 52°19S 68°21W 121 H3
Virgin → U.S.A. 36°28N 114°21W 110 C4

Virgin Is. (British) ☑
  W. Indies 18°30N 64°30W 115 D12
Virgin Is. (U.S.) ☑ W. Indies 18°20N 65°0W 115 D12
Virginia S. Africa 28°8S 26°55E 97 K5
Virginia □ U.S.A. 47°31N 92°32W 111 A8
Virginia □ U.S.A. 37°30N 78°45W 112 G8
Virginia Beach U.S.A. 36°49N 76°9W 111 C11
Viroqua U.S.A. 43°34N 90°53W 112 D2
Vis Croatia 43°4N 16°10E 68 C7
Visalia U.S.A. 36°20N 119°18W 110 C3
Visby Sweden 57°37N 18°18E 63 F7
Viscount Melville Sd.
  Canada 74°10N 108°0W 109 B9
Vishakhapatnam India 17°45N 83°20E 85 L13
Vistula → Poland 54°22N 18°55E 65 A10
Vitebsk Belarus 55°10N 30°15E 70 C5
Viterbo Italy 42°25N 12°6E 68 C5
Viti Levu Fiji 17°30S 177°30E 99 D14
Vitim → Russia 59°26N 112°34E 77 D12
Vitória Brazil 20°20S 40°22W 122 D2
Vitória da Conquista Brazil 14°51S 40°51W 122 B2
Vitoria-Gasteiz Spain 42°50N 2°41W 67 A4
Vittória Italy 36°57N 14°32E 68 F6
Vizianagaram India 18°6N 83°30E 85 K13
Vladikavkaz Russia 43°0N 44°35E 71 F7
Vladimir Russia 56°15N 40°30E 70 C7
Vladivostok Russia 43°10N 131°53E 77 E14
Vlissingen Neths. 51°26N 3°34E 64 C2
Vlorë Albania 40°32N 19°28E 69 D8
Vltava → Czech Rep. 50°21N 14°30E 64 D8
Voe U.K. 60°21N 1°16W 22 B15
Vogelsberg Germany 50°31N 9°12E 64 C5
Vohimena, Tanjon' i Madag. 25°36S 45°8E 97 K9
Voi Kenya 3°25S 38°32E 96 E7
Vojvodina □ Serbia 45°20N 20°0E 69 B9
Volga → Russia 46°0N 48°30E 71 E8
Volga Hts. Russia 51°0N 46°0E 71 D8
Volgodonsk Russia 47°33N 42°5E 71 E7
Volgograd Russia 48°40N 44°25E 71 E7
Volgograd Res. Russia 50°0N 45°20E 71 D8
Vologda Russia 59°10N 39°45E 70 C6
Volos Greece 39°24N 22°59E 69 E10
Volsk Russia 52°5N 47°22E 70 D8
Volta → Ghana 5°46N 0°41E 94 G6
Volta, L. Ghana 7°30N 0°0 94 G6
Volta Redonda Brazil 22°31S 44°5W 122 D2
Volzhskiy Russia 48°56N 44°46E 71 E7
Vorkuta Russia 67°48N 64°20E 70 A11
Voronezh Russia 51°40N 39°10E 71 D6
Vosges France 48°20N 7°10E 66 B7
Vostok I. Kiribati 10°5S 152°23W 103 J12
Votkinsk Russia 57°0N 53°55E 70 C9
Vratsa Bulgaria 43°15N 23°30E 69 C10
Vryburg S. Africa 26°55S 24°45E 97 K4
Vryheid S. Africa 27°45S 30°47E 97 K6
Vulcano Italy 38°24N 14°58E 68 E6
Vung Tau Vietnam 10°21N 107°4E 82 B3
Vyazma Russia 55°10N 34°15E 70 C5
Vyborg Russia 60°43N 28°47E 70 B4
Vychegda → Russia 61°18N 46°36E 70 B8
Vyrnwy, L. U.K. 52°48N 3°31W 28 B6
Vyshniy Volochek Russia 57°30N 34°30E 70 C5

W
Waal → Neths. 51°37N 5°0E 64 C3
Wabasca → Canada 58°22N 115°20W 108 D8
Wabash U.S.A. 40°48N 85°49W 112 E5
Wabash → U.S.A. 37°48N 88°2W 112 G3
Waco U.S.A. 31°33N 97°9W 111 D7
Wad Medanī Sudan 14°28N 33°30E 95 F12
Waddesdon U.K. 51°51N 0°55W 31 C7
Waddingham U.K. 53°28N 0°31W 27 F7
Waddington U.K. 53°10N 0°32W 27 F7
Waddington, Mt. Canada 51°23N 125°15W 108 D7
Wadebridge U.K. 50°31N 4°51W 29 F4
Wadhurst U.K. 51°3N 0°20E 31 D9
Wadi Halfa Sudan 21°53N 31°19E 95 D12
Wager B. Canada 65°26N 88°40W 109 C11
Wagga Wagga Australia 35°7S 147°24E 98 H8
Wah Pakistan 33°45N 72°40E 84 C8
Wahiawā U.S.A. 21°30N 158°2W 110 H15
Waigeo Indonesia 0°20S 130°40E 83 E8
Wailuku U.S.A. 20°53N 156°30W 110 H16
Wainfleet All Saints U.K. 53°7N 0°15E 27 F9
Wakayama Japan 34°15N 135°15E 81 F4
Wake I. Pac. Oc. 19°18N 166°36E 102 F8
Wakefield Jamaica 18°26N 77°42W 114 a
Wakefield U.K. 53°41N 1°29W 27 E6
Wakkanai Japan 45°28N 141°35E 81 A7
Walberswick U.K. 52°19N 1°40E 31 B12
Walbrzych Poland 50°45N 16°18E 64 C9
Walbury Hill U.K. 51°21N 1°28W 30 D6
Waldron U.K. 50°56N 0°13E 31 E9
Wales □ U.K. 52°19N 4°43W 28 C4
Walgett Australia 30°0S 148°5E 98 G8
Walker L. U.S.A. 38°42N 118°43W 110 C3
Walla Walla U.S.A. 46°4N 118°20W 110 A4
Wallaceburg Canada 42°34N 82°23W 112 D6
Wallachia Romania 44°35N 25°0E 65 F13
Wallasey U.K. 53°25N 3°2W 27 F2
Wallingford U.K. 51°35N 1°8W 30 C6
Wallis & Futuna, Ís. ☑
  Pac. Oc. 13°18S 176°10W 99 C15
Walls U.K. 60°14N 1°33W 22 B14
Wallsend U.K. 54°59N 1°31W 26 C5
Walmer U.K. 51°11N 1°25E 31 D11
Walney, I. of U.K. 54°6N 3°15W 26 D2
Walpole U.K. 50°56N 0°13E 31 A9
Walsall U.K. 52°35N 1°58W 27 G5
Walsenburg U.S.A. 37°38N 104°47W 110 C6
Walsoken U.K. 52°41N 0°11E 31 A9
Waltham U.K. 53°31N 0°7W 27 E8
Waltham Abbey U.K. 51°41N 0°1E 31 C9
Waltham Forest □ U.K. 51°35N 0°0 31 C9
Waltham on the Wolds U.K. 52°49N 0°48W 27 G7
Walton-on-the-Naze U.K. 51°51N 1°17E 31 C11
Walvis Bay Namibia 23°0S 14°28E 97 J2
Wamba Dem. Rep. of the Congo 2°10N 27°57E 96 D5
Wanborough U.K. 51°33N 1°42W 30 C5
Wandsworth □ U.K. 51°27N 0°11W 31 D8

Wanganui N.Z. 39°56S 175°3E 99 H14
Wanlweyne Somalia 2°37N 44°54E 89 G3
Wansbeck → U.K. 55°10N 1°32W 26 B5
Wantage U.K. 51°35N 1°25W 30 C6
Wanxian China 30°42N 108°20E 78 E10
Wanzai China 22°12N 113°31E 79 a
Wapakoneta U.S.A. 40°34N 84°12W 112 E5
Warangal India 17°58N 79°35E 84 L11
Warboys U.K. 52°24N 0°4W 31 B8
Ward Ireland 53°26N 6°20W 21 B10
Wardha India 20°45N 78°39E 84 J11
Wardington U.K. 52°7N 1°17W 30 B6
Wardle U.K. 53°7N 2°35W 27 F3
Ward's Stone U.K. 54°1N 2°36W 27 D3
Ware U.K. 51°49N 0°1E 31 C8
Wareham U.K. 50°42N 2°7W 30 E5
Wark U.K. 55°6N 2°14W 26 B4
Warkworth U.K. 55°21N 1°37W 26 B5
Warley U.K. 52°30N 1°59W 27 H5
Warminster U.K. 51°12N 2°10W 30 D4
Warrego → Australia 30°24S 145°21E 98 G8
Warren Mich., U.S.A. 42°28N 83°1W 112 D6
Warren Ohio, U.S.A. 41°14N 80°49W 112 E7
Warren Pa., U.S.A. 41°51N 79°9W 112 E8
Warrenpoint U.K. 54°6N 6°15W 19 C9
Warri Nigeria 5°30N 5°41E 94 G7
Warrington U.K. 53°24N 2°35W 27 F3
Warrnambool Australia 38°25S 142°30E 98 H7
Warsaw Poland 52°14N 21°0E 65 B11
Warsaw U.S.A. 41°14N 85°51W 112 E5
Warsop U.K. 53°12N 1°9W 27 F6
Warta → Poland 52°35N 14°39E 64 B8
Warwick U.K. 52°18N 1°35W 30 B5
Warwick U.S.A. 41°42N 71°28W 113 E12
Warwickshire □ U.K. 52°14N 1°38W 30 B5
Wasatch Ra. U.S.A. 40°0N 111°30W 110 B4
Wash, The → U.K. 52°58N 0°20E 31 A9
Washburn U.S.A. 46°40N 90°54W 112 B2
Washford U.K. 51°9N 3°21W 30 D2
Washington U.K. 54°55N 1°30W 26 C6
Washington D.C., U.S.A. 38°53N 77°2W 112 F9
Washington Ind., U.S.A. 38°40N 87°10W 112 F4
Washington Pa., U.S.A. 40°10N 80°15W 112 E7
Washington □ U.S.A. 47°30N 120°30W 110 A3
Washington, Mt. U.S.A. 44°16N 71°18W 113 C12
Washington I. U.S.A. 45°23N 86°54W 112 C4
Wasilla U.S.A. 61°35N 149°26W 108 C5
Wast Water L. U.S.A. 54°26N 3°18W 26 D2
Watampone Indonesia 4°29S 120°25E 83 E6
Watchet U.K. 51°10N 3°19W 30 D2
Waterbeach U.K. 52°16N 0°12E 31 B9
Waterbury U.S.A. 41°33N 73°3W 113 E11
Waterford Ireland 52°15N 7°8W 21 D8
Waterford □ Ireland 52°10N 7°40W 21 D7
Waterford Harbour Ireland 52°8N 6°58W 21 D9
Watergate B. U.K. 50°26N 5°4W 29 G3
Waterloo Canada 43°30N 80°32W 112 D7
Waterloo Ill., U.S.A. 38°20N 90°9W 112 F2
Waterloo Iowa, U.S.A. 42°30N 92°21W 111 B8
Watersmeet U.S.A. 46°16N 89°11W 112 B3
Watertown N.Y., U.S.A. 43°59N 75°55W 113 D10
Watertown S. Dak., U.S.A. 44°54N 97°7W 111 B7
Watertown Wis., U.S.A. 43°12N 88°43W 112 D3
Waterville U.S.A. 44°33N 69°38W 113 C13
Watford U.K. 51°40N 0°24W 31 C8
Watlington Norfolk, U.K. 52°40N 0°24E 31 A9
Watlington Oxon., U.K. 51°38N 1°0W 30 C6
Watrous Canada 51°40N 105°25W 108 D9
Watsa Dem. Rep. of the Congo 3°4N 29°30E 96 D5
Watseka U.S.A. 40°47N 87°44W 112 E4
Watson Lake Canada 60°6N 128°49W 108 C7
Watton U.K. 52°34N 0°51E 31 A10
Wau South Sudan 7°45N 28°1E 95 G11
Waukegan U.S.A. 42°22N 87°50W 112 D4
Waukesha U.S.A. 43°1N 88°14W 112 D3
Waupaca U.S.A. 44°21N 89°5W 112 C3
Waupun U.S.A. 43°38N 88°44W 112 D3
Wausau U.S.A. 44°58N 89°38W 112 C3
Wautoma U.S.A. 44°4N 89°18W 112 C3
Wauwatosa U.S.A. 43°2N 88°0W 112 D4
Waveney → U.K. 52°35N 1°39E 31 A12
Waver → U.K. 54°50N 3°15W 26 C2
Wawa Canada 47°59N 84°47W 112 B5
Waycross U.S.A. 31°13N 82°21W 111 D10
Wayne U.S.A. 38°13N 82°27W 112 F6
Waynesboro U.S.A. 38°4N 78°53W 112 F8
Waynesburg U.S.A. 39°54N 80°11W 112 F7
Wazirabad Pakistan 32°30N 74°8E 84 C9
Weald, The U.K. 51°4N 0°20E 31 D9
Wear → U.K. 54°55N 1°23W 26 C6
Weardale U.K. 54°44N 2°5W 26 C4
Wearhead U.K. 54°45N 2°13W 26 C4
Weaver → U.K. 53°17N 2°35W 27 F3
Weaverham U.K. 53°16N 2°35W 27 F3
Webster Springs U.S.A. 38°29N 80°25W 112 F7
Weddell Sea Antarctica 72°30S 40°0W 55 D1
Wedmore U.K. 51°13N 2°48W 30 D3
Wednesbury U.K. 52°34N 2°1W 27 G4
Wednesfield U.K. 52°37N 2°2W 27 G4
Weedon Bec U.K. 52°15N 1°5W 30 B6
Weifang China 36°44N 119°7E 79 C12
Weihai China 37°30N 122°6E 79 C13
Weipa Australia 12°40S 141°50E 98 C7
Welch U.S.A. 37°26N 81°35W 112 G7
Weldon U.K. 55°17N 1°46W 26 B5
Welford Northants., U.K. 52°25N 1°3W 30 B6
Welford W. Berkshire, U.K. 51°27N 1°24W 30 C6
Welkom S. Africa 28°0S 26°46E 97 K5
Welland Canada 43°0N 79°15W 112 D8
Welland → U.K. 52°51N 0°5W 27 G8
Wellesley Is. Australia 16°42S 139°30E 98 D6
Wellingborough U.K. 52°19N 0°41W 31 B7
Wellington N.Z. 41°19S 174°46E 99 J13
Wellington Somst., U.K. 50°58N 3°13W 30 E2
Wellington Telford & Wrekin, U.K. 52°42N 2°30W 27 G3
Wellington, I. Chile 49°30S 75°0W 121 G2
Wellington Chan. Canada 75°0N 93°0W 109 B10
Wells U.K. 51°13N 2°39W 30 D3
Wells-next-the-Sea U.K. 52°57N 0°51E 31 A10

Wellsboro U.S.A. 41°45N 77°18W 112 E9
Wellsville U.S.A. 42°7N 77°57W 112 D9
Welney U.K. 52°31N 0°15E 31 A9
Wels Austria 48°9N 14°1E 64 D8
Welshpool U.K. 52°39N 3°8W 28 B7
Welton U.K. 53°18N 0°29W 27 F8
Welwyn Garden City U.K. 51°48N 0°12W 31 C8
Wem U.K. 52°52N 2°44W 27 G3
Wembury U.K. 50°19N 4°6W 29 G5
Wemindji Canada 53°0N 78°49W 109 D12
Wemyss Bay U.K. 55°53N 4°53W 24 C6
Wenatchee U.S.A. 47°25N 120°19W 110 A2
Wendover U.K. 51°45N 0°44W 31 C7
Wenlock Edge U.K. 52°30N 2°43W 27 H3
Wensleydale U.K. 54°17N 2°0W 26 D4
Wensu China 41°15N 80°10E 78 C5
Wensum → U.K. 52°40N 1°15E 31 A11
Wenzhou China 28°0N 120°38E 79 F13
Weobley U.K. 52°11N 2°50W 30 B3
Werrington U.K. 50°39N 4°23W 29 F5
Weser → Germany 53°36N 8°28E 64 B5
West Antarctica Antarctica 80°0S 90°0W 55 D15
West Auckland U.K. 54°38N 1°43W 26 C5
West Bank ■ Asia 32°6N 35°13E 86 C3
West Bend U.S.A. 43°25N 88°11W 112 D3
West Bengal = Paschimbanga □
  India 23°0N 88°0E 85 H16
West Berkshire □ U.K. 51°25N 1°17W 30 D6
West Beskids Europe 49°30N 19°0E 65 D10
West Bridgford U.K. 52°55N 1°8W 27 G6
West Bromwich U.K. 52°32N 1°59W 27 G5
West Burra U.K. 60°5N 1°21W 22 B15
West Calder U.K. 55°51N 3°33W 25 C8
West Coker U.K. 50°55N 2°40W 30 E3
West Falkland Falk. Is. 51°40S 60°0W 121 H3
West Fen U.K. 53°5N 0°5W 27 F8
West Frankfort U.S.A. 37°54N 88°55W 111 C9
West Grinstead U.K. 50°58N 0°19W 31 E8
West Haddon U.K. 52°20N 1°3W 30 B6
West Kirby U.K. 53°23N 3°11W 27 F2
West Linton U.K. 55°46N 3°21W 25 C9
West Lulworth U.K. 50°37N 2°14W 30 E4
West Malling U.K. 51°17N 0°26E 31 D9
West Meon U.K. 51°1N 1°5W 30 D6
West Mersea U.K. 51°46N 0°56E 31 C10
West Midlands □ U.K. 52°26N 2°0W 27 H5
West Moors U.K. 50°49N 1°53W 30 E5
West Palm Beach U.S.A. 26°43N 80°3W 111 E10
West Point U.S.A. 37°32N 76°48W 112 G9
West Rasen U.K. 53°23N 0°24W 27 F8
West Seneca U.S.A. 42°51N 78°48W 112 D8
West Siberian Plain Russia 62°0N 75°0E 72 B9
West Sussex □ U.K. 50°55N 0°30W 31 E8
West Virginia □ U.S.A. 38°45N 80°30W 112 F7
West Yorkshire □ U.K. 53°45N 1°40W 27 E5
Westbourne U.K. 50°52N 0°55W 31 E7
Westbrook U.S.A. 43°41N 70°22W 113 D12
Westbury Shrops., U.K. 52°41N 2°55W 27 G3
Westbury Wilts., U.K. 51°15N 2°11W 30 D4
Westbury-on-Severn U.K. 51°50N 2°25W 30 C4
Wester Ross U.K. 57°37N 4°51W 22 G6
Westerham U.K. 51°16N 0°5E 31 D9
Western Australia □ Australia 25°0S 118°0E 98 F2
Western Ghats India 14°0N 75°0E 84 N9
Western Isles □ U.K. 57°30N 7°10W 22 G3
Western Sahara ■ Africa 25°0N 13°0W 94 D3
Westerwald Germany 50°38N 7°56E 64 C4
Westfield U.K. 50°55N 0°35E 31 E10
Westhill U.K. 57°9N 2°19W 23 H13
Westhoughton U.K. 53°33N 2°31W 27 E3
Westland Bight N.Z. 42°55N 170°5E 99 K3
Westmeath □ Ireland 53°33N 7°34W 18 D6
Westminster U.K. 39°34N 76°59W 112 F9
Westmoreland Barbados 13°13N 59°37W 114 c
Weston U.S.A. 52°51N 2°1W 27 G4
Weston U.S.A. 39°2N 80°28W 112 F7
Weston-super-Mare U.K. 51°21N 2°58W 30 D3
Westport Ireland 53°48N 9°31W 18 D2
Westray U.K. 59°18N 3°0W 23 D11
Westruther U.K. 55°45N 2°35W 25 C10
Westward Ho! U.K. 51°2N 4°15W 29 E5
Wetar Indonesia 7°48S 126°30E 83 F7
Wetaskiwin Canada 52°55N 113°24W 108 D8
Wetherby U.K. 53°56N 1°23W 27 E6
Wetwang U.K. 54°1N 0°35W 27 D7
Wewak Papua N. G. 3°38S 143°41E 98 A7
Wexford Ireland 52°20N 6°28W 21 D10
Wexford □ Ireland 52°20N 6°25W 21 D10
Wexford Harbour Ireland 52°20N 6°25W 21 D10
Wey → U.K. 51°22N 0°27W 31 D8
Weybourne U.K. 52°57N 1°9E 31 A11
Weybridge U.K. 51°22N 0°27W 31 D8
Weyburn Canada 49°40N 103°50W 108 E9
Weymouth U.K. 50°37N 2°28W 30 E4
Wha Ti Canada 63°8N 117°16W 108 C8
Whale Cove Canada 62°10N 92°34W 108 C10
Whales, B. of Antarctica 78°0S 160°0W 55 D12
Whalley U.K. 53°49N 2°24W 27 E4
Whalsay U.K. 60°22N 0°59W 22 B16
Whalton U.K. 55°8N 1°46W 26 B5
Whangarei N.Z. 35°43S 174°21E 99 H13
Whaplode U.K. 52°42N 0°3W 27 G8
Wharfe → U.K. 53°51N 1°9W 27 E6
Wharfedale U.K. 54°6N 2°1W 26 D4
Wheatley Hill U.K. 54°45N 1°23W 26 C6
Wheeler Pk. U.S.A. 38°57N 114°15W 110 C4
Wheeling U.S.A. 40°4N 80°43W 112 E7
Whernside U.K. 54°14N 2°24W 26 D4
Whicham U.K. 54°15N 3°21W 26 D2
Whimple U.K. 50°46N 3°20W 29 F7
Whipsnade U.K. 51°51N 0°32W 31 C7
Whissendine U.K. 52°43N 0°46W 27 G7
Whitburn U.K. 55°52N 3°42W 25 C8
Whitby U.K. 54°29N 0°37W 26 D7
Whitchurch Devon, U.K. 50°32N 4°9W 29 F5
Whitchurch Hants., U.K. 51°14N 1°20W 30 D6
Whitchurch Hereford, U.K. 51°51N 2°39W 30 C3
Whitchurch Shrops., U.K. 52°59N 2°40W 27 G3
White → Ark., U.S.A. 33°57N 91°5W 111 D8
White → Ind., U.S.A. 38°25N 87°45W 112 F4
White → Utah, U.S.A. 40°4N 109°41W 110 B5
White Esk → U.K. 55°13N 3°11W 25 D9

White Horse, Vale of   Zwolle

White Horse, Vale of U.K. 51°37N 1°30W 30 C5
White Horse Hill U.K. 51°34N 1°33W 30 C5
White Mts. Calif., U.S.A. 37°30N 118°15W 110 C3
White Mts. N.H., U.S.A. 44°15N 71°15W 111 B12
White Nile → Sudan 15°38N 32°31E 95 E12
White Sea Russia 66°30N 38°0E 70 A6
Whiteadder Water → U.K. 55°51N 2°25W 25 C11
Whitecourt Canada 54°10N 115°45W 108 D8
Whitefish Pt. U.S.A. 46°45N 84°59W 112 B5
Whitehall U.S.A. 44°22N 91°19W 112 C2
Whitehaven U.K. 54°33N 3°35W 26 C1
Whitehorse Canada 60°43N 135°3W 108 C6
Whitesand B. U.K. 50°21N 4°18W 29 G5
Whitewater U.S.A. 42°50N 88°44W 112 D3
Whithorn U.K. 54°44N 4°26W 24 E7
Whitley Bay U.K. 55°3N 1°27W 26 B6
Whitney, Mt. U.S.A. 36°35N 118°18W 110 C3
Whitstable U.K. 51°21N 1°3E 31 D11
Whittington Derby., U.K. 53°16N 1°26W 27 F6
Whittington Shrops., U.K. 52°52N 3°0W 27 E3
Whittlesey U.K. 52°33N 0°8W 31 A8
Whittlesford U.K. 52°7N 0°9E 31 B9
Whitwell Derby., U.K. 53°17N 1°12W 27 F6
Whitwell I. of W., U.K. 50°36N 1°15W 30 E6
Whitwick U.K. 52°45N 1°22W 27 G6
Whitworth U.K. 53°39N 2°11W 27 E4
Wholdaia L. Canada 60°43N 104°20W 108 C9
Whyalla Australia 33°2S 137°30E 98 G6
Wiarton Canada 44°40N 81°10W 112 C7
Wiay U.K. 57°24N 7°13W 22 H3
Wichita U.S.A. 37°42N 97°20W 111 C7
Wichita Falls U.S.A. 33°54N 98°30W 110 D7
Wick U.K. 58°26N 3°5W 23 F11
Wickford U.K. 51°36N 0°33E 31 C10
Wickham U.K. 50°54N 1°11W 30 E6
Wickham Market U.K. 52°9N 1°23E 31 B11
Wicklow Ireland 52°59N 6°3W 21 C10
Wicklow □ Ireland 52°57N 6°25W 21 C10
Wicklow Hd. Ireland 52°58N 6°0W 21 C11
Wicklow Mts. △ Ireland 53°6N 6°21W 21 B11
Wickwar U.K. 51°36N 2°23W 30 C4
Widdrington U.K. 55°15N 1°35W 26 B5
Widecombe U.K. 50°34N 3°49W 29 F6
Widemouth U.K. 50°47N 4°34W 29 F4
Widnes U.K. 53°23N 2°45W 27 F3
Wiener Neustadt Austria 47°49N 16°16E 64 E9
Wiesbaden Germany 50°4N 8°14E 64 C5
Wigan U.K. 53°33N 2°38W 27 E3
Wight, Isle of □ U.K. 50°41N 1°17W 30 E6
Wigmore U.K. 52°19N 2°51W 30 B3
Wigston U.K. 52°35N 1°6W 27 G6
Wigtown U.K. 54°53N 4°27W 24 E7
Wigtown B. U.K. 54°46N 4°15W 24 E7
Wilhelm, Mt. Papua N. G. 5°50S 145°1E 98 B8
Wilhelmshaven Germany 53°31N 8°7E 64 B5
Wilkes-Barre U.S.A. 41°15N 75°53W 113 E10
Wilkes Land Antarctica 69°0S 120°0E 55 D9
Wilkins Ice Shelf Antarctica 70°30S 72°0W 55 D17
Willemstad Curaçao 12°5N 68°55W 115 E11
Willenhall U.K. 52°36N 2°2W 27 G4
Willesborough U.K. 51°8N 0°56E 31 D10
Williams Lake Canada 52°10N 122°10W 108 D7
Williamsburg U.S.A. 37°16N 76°43W 112 G9
Williamson U.S.A. 37°41N 82°17W 112 G6
Williamsport U.S.A. 41°15N 77°1W 112 E9
Willingdon U.K. 50°47N 0°17E 31 E9
Williston U.S.A. 48°9N 103°37W 110 A6
Williston L. Canada 56°0N 124°0W 108 D7
Williton U.K. 51°9N 3°19W 30 D2
Willmar U.S.A. 45°7N 95°3W 111 A7
Willoughby U.K. 53°13N 0°12E 27 F9
Wilmington U.K. 50°47N 3°7W 29 F7
Wilmington Del., U.S.A. 39°45N 75°33W 113 F10
Wilmington N.C., U.S.A. 34°14N 77°55W 111 D11
Wilmslow U.K. 53°19N 2°13W 27 F4
Wilnecote U.K. 52°36N 1°39W 27 G5
Wilton U.K. 51°5N 1°51W 30 D5
Wiltshire □ U.K. 51°18N 1°53W 30 D5
Wimblington U.K. 52°31N 0°4E 31 A9
Wimborne Minster U.K. 50°48N 1°59W 30 E5
Wincanton U.K. 51°3N 2°24W 30 D4
Winchelsea U.K. 50°55N 0°43E 31 E10
Winchester U.K. 51°4N 1°18W 30 D6
Winchester Ky., U.S.A. 37°59N 84°11W 112 G6
Winchester Va., U.S.A. 39°11N 78°10W 112 F8
Wind → U.S.A. 43°12N 108°12W 110 B5
Wind River Range U.S.A. 43°0N 109°30W 110 B5
Windermere U.K. 54°23N 2°55W 26 D3
Windhoek Namibia 22°35S 17°4E 97 J3
Windrush → U.K. 51°43N 1°24W 30 C6
Windsor Canada 42°18N 83°0W 109 E11
Windsor U.K. 51°29N 0°36W 31 D7
Windward Is. W. Indies 13°0N 61°0W 115 E12
Windward Passage Caribbean 20°0N 74°0W 115 D10
Wing U.K. 51°53N 0°43W 31 C7
Wingham U.K. 51°16N 1°13E 31 D11
Winisk → Canada 55°17N 85°5W 109 D11
Winkleigh U.K. 50°50N 3°58W 29 F6
Winkler Canada 49°10N 97°56W 108 E10

Winneba Ghana 5°25N 0°36W 94 G5
Winnebago, L. U.S.A. 44°0N 88°26W 112 D3
Winnemucca U.S.A. 40°58N 117°44W 110 B3
Winnipeg Canada 49°54N 97°9W 108 E10
Winnipeg, L. Canada 52°0N 97°0W 108 D10
Winnipegosis L. Canada 52°30N 100°0W 108 C9
Winona U.S.A. 44°3N 91°39W 111 B8
Winooski U.S.A. 44°29N 73°11W 113 C11
Winsford U.K. 53°12N 2°31W 27 F3
Winslow U.K. 51°57N 0°52W 31 C7
Winslow U.S.A. 35°2N 110°42W 110 C4
Winster U.K. 53°9N 1°39W 27 F5
Winston-Salem U.S.A. 36°6N 80°15W 111 C10
Winterborne Abbas U.K. 50°42N 2°33W 30 E3
Winterthur Switz. 47°30N 8°44E 64 E5
Winterton N. Lincs., U.K. 53°39N 0°37W 27 E7
Winterton Norfolk, U.K. 52°43N 1°41E 31 A12
Winton Australia 22°24S 143°3E 98 E7
Wirksworth U.K. 53°6N 1°35W 27 F5
Wirral U.K. 53°25N 3°0W 27 F2
Wisbech U.K. 52°41N 0°9E 31 A9
Wisborough Green U.K. 51°2N 0°30W 31 D7
Wisconsin □ U.S.A. 44°45N 89°30W 111 B9
Wisconsin Rapids U.S.A. 44°23N 89°49W 112 C3
Wishaw U.K. 55°46N 3°54W 25 C8
Wiske → U.K. 54°19N 1°27W 26 D6
Witham U.K. 51°48N 0°40E 31 C10
Witham → U.K. 52°59N 0°2W 27 G8
Witheridge U.K. 50°55N 3°42W 29 F7
Withernsea U.K. 53°44N 0°1E 27 E9
Witley U.K. 51°9N 0°39W 31 D7
Witney U.K. 51°48N 1°28W 30 C6
Wittersham U.K. 51°0N 0°43E 31 D10
Wiveliscombe U.K. 51°2N 3°19W 30 D2
Wivenhoe U.K. 51°51N 0°58E 31 C10
Wkra → Poland 52°27N 20°44E 65 B11
Wloclawek Poland 52°40N 19°3E 65 B10
Woburn U.K. 51°59N 0°36W 31 C7
Woburn Sands U.K. 52°1N 0°39W 31 B7
Wodonga Australia 36°5S 146°50E 98 H8
Woking U.K. 51°19N 0°34W 31 D7
Wokingham U.K. 51°24N 0°49W 31 D7
Wolf Rock U.K. 49°57N 5°49W 29 H2
Wolfsburg Germany 52°25N 10°48E 64 B6
Wolin Poland 53°50N 14°37E 64 B8
Wollaston L. Canada 58°7N 103°10W 108 D9
Wollaston Pen. Canada 69°30N 115°0W 108 C8
Wollongong Australia 34°25S 150°54E 98 G9
Wolsingham U.K. 54°44N 1°52W 26 C5
Wolstenholme, C. Canada 62°35N 77°30W 104 C12
Wolverhampton U.K. 52°35N 2°7W 27 G4
Wolverton U.K. 52°3N 0°47W 31 B7
Wolvistan U.K. 54°38N 1°18W 26 C6
Wombwell U.K. 53°32N 1°25W 27 E6
Wŏnsan N. Korea 39°11N 127°27E 79 D14
Wonston U.K. 51°8N 1°18W 30 D6
Woodbridge U.K. 52°6N 1°20E 31 B11
Woodbury U.K. 50°41N 3°24W 29 F7
Woodhall Spa U.K. 53°10N 0°12W 27 F8
Woodhouse U.K. 53°22N 1°21W 27 F6
Woodley U.K. 51°27N 0°53W 31 D7
Woodroffe, Mt. Australia 26°20S 131°45E 98 F5
Woods, L. of the N. Amer. 49°15N 94°45W 108 E10
Woodstock N.B., Canada 46°11N 67°37W 109 E13
Woodstock Ont., Canada 43°10N 80°45W 112 D7
Woodstock U.K. 51°51N 1°20W 30 C6
Woodstock U.S.A. 42°19N 88°27W 112 D3
Wookey U.K. 51°13N 2°41W 30 D3
Wookey Hole U.K. 51°14N 2°40W 30 D3
Wool U.K. 50°40N 2°12W 30 E4
Woolacombe U.K. 51°10N 4°13W 29 E5
Wooler U.K. 55°33N 2°1W 26 A4
Woonsocket U.S.A. 42°0N 71°31W 113 E11
Wootton Wawen U.K. 52°16N 1°47W 30 B5
Worcester S. Africa 33°39S 19°27E 97 L3
Worcester U.K. 52°11N 2°12W 30 B4
Worcester U.S.A. 42°16N 71°48W 113 D12
Worcestershire □ U.K. 52°13N 2°10W 30 B4
Worfield U.K. 52°34N 2°21W 27 G4
Workington U.K. 54°39N 3°33W 26 C1
Worksop U.K. 53°18N 1°7W 27 F6
Worms Germany 49°37N 8°21E 64 D5
Wortham U.K. 52°21N 1°3E 31 B11
Worthing Barbados 13°5N 59°35W 114 c
Worthing U.K. 50°49N 0°21W 31 E8
Worthington U.S.A. 43°37N 95°36W 111 B7
Wotton under Edge U.K. 51°37N 2°20W 30 C4
Wragby U.K. 53°18N 0°17W 27 F8
Wrangel I. Russia 71°0N 180°0E 77 B19
Wrangell U.S.A. 56°28N 132°23W 108 D6
Wrangell Mts. U.S.A. 61°30N 142°0W 108 C5
Wrangle U.K. 53°3N 0°7E 27 F9
Wrath, C. U.K. 58°38N 5°1W 22 E7
Wrekin, The U.K. 52°41N 2°32W 27 G3
Wrentham U.K. 52°23N 1°40E 31 B12
Wrexham U.K. 53°3N 3°0W 28 A8
Wrexham □ U.K. 53°1N 2°58W 28 D5
Wrigley Canada 63°16N 123°37W 108 C7
Writtle U.K. 51°44N 0°27E 31 C9
Wroclaw Poland 51°5N 17°5E 65 C9

Wroughton U.K. 51°31N 1°47W 30 C5
Wroxham U.K. 52°42N 1°24E 31 A11
Wu Jiang → China 29°40N 107°20E 78 F10
Wuhai China 39°39N 106°48E 78 D10
Wuhan China 30°31N 114°18E 79 E11
Wuhu China 31°22N 118°21E 79 E12
Wuppertal Germany 51°16N 7°12E 64 C4
Würzburg Germany 49°46N 9°55E 64 D5
Wushi China 41°9N 79°13E 78 C4
Wutongqiao China 29°22N 103°50E 78 F9
Wuwei China 37°57N 102°34E 78 D9
Wuxi China 31°33N 120°18E 79 E13
Wuyi Shan China 27°0N 117°0E 79 F12
Wuzhong China 38°2N 106°12E 78 D10
Wuzhou China 23°30N 111°18E 79 G11
Wye U.K. 51°10N 0°57E 31 D10
Wye → U.K. 51°38N 2°40W 30 C3
Wylye → U.K. 51°5N 1°51W 30 D5
Wymondham Leics., U.K. 52°45N 0°43W 27 G7
Wymondham Norfolk, U.K. 52°35N 1°7E 31 A11
Wyndham Australia 15°33S 128°3E 98 D4
Wyoming □ U.S.A. 43°0N 107°30W 110 B5
Wyre → U.K. 53°52N 2°57W 27 E3
Wyre Forest U.K. 52°24N 2°24W 27 H4

X

Xaçmaz Azerbaijan 41°31N 48°42E 71 F8
Xai-Xai Mozam. 25°6S 33°31E 97 J6
Xalapa Mexico 19°32N 96°55W 114 D5
Xankändi Azerbaijan 39°52N 46°49E 71 G8
Xenia U.S.A. 39°41N 83°56W 112 F6
Xi Jiang → China 22°5N 113°20E 79 G11
Xiaguan China 25°32N 100°16E 78 F9
Xiamen China 24°25N 118°4E 79 G12
Xi'an China 34°15N 109°0E 79 E10
Xiang Jiang → China 28°55N 112°50E 79 F11
Xiangfan China 32°2N 112°8E 79 E11
Xianggang = Hong Kong □ China 22°11N 114°14E 79 a
Xiangtan China 27°51N 112°54E 79 F11
Xiantao China 30°25N 113°25E 79 E11
Xianyang China 34°20N 108°40E 79 E10
Xichang China 27°51N 102°19E 78 F9
Xigazê China 29°5N 88°45E 78 F6
Xilinhot China 43°52N 116°2E 79 C12
Ximiao China 40°59N 100°12E 78 C9
Xinghua China 32°58N 119°48E 79 E12
Xingu → Brazil 1°30S 51°53W 120 C4
Xingyi China 25°3N 104°59E 78 F9
Xining China 36°34N 101°40E 78 D9
Xinwan China 22°47N 113°40E 79 a
Xinxiang China 35°18N 113°50E 79 D11
Xinyang China 32°6N 114°3E 79 E11
Xinyi China 34°23N 118°21E 79 E12
Xique-Xique Brazil 10°50S 42°40W 122 B2
Xixiang China 22°34N 113°52E 79 a
Xizang Zizhiqu □ China 32°0N 88°0E 78 E6
Xuanhua China 40°40N 115°2E 78 C11
Xuwen China 20°20N 110°10E 79 G11
Xuzhou China 34°18N 117°10E 79 E12

Y

Y Drenewydd = Newtown U.K. 52°31N 3°19W 28 B7
Y Fenni = Abergavenny U.K. 51°49N 3°1W 28 D7
Y Gelli Gandryll = Hay-on-Wye U.K. 52°5N 3°8W 28 C7
Ya'an China 29°58N 103°5E 78 F9
Yablonovyy Ra. Russia 53°0N 114°0E 77 D12
Yacuiba Bolivia 22°0S 63°43W 120 E4
Yakeshi China 49°17N 120°44E 79 B13
Yakima U.S.A. 46°36N 120°31W 110 A2
Yakutat U.S.A. 59°33N 139°44W 108 D6
Yakutsk Russia 62°5N 129°50E 77 C13
Yala Thailand 6°33N 101°18E 82 C2
Yalong Jiang → China 26°40N 101°55E 78 F9
Yalta Ukraine 44°30N 34°10E 71 F5
Yalu Jiang → China 39°55N 124°19E 79 D13
Yamagata Japan 38°15N 140°15E 81 D7
Yamaguchi Japan 34°10N 131°32E 81 F2
Yamal Pen. Russia 71°0N 70°0E 76 B7
Yambol Bulgaria 42°30N 26°30E 69 C12
Yamethin Burma 20°29N 96°18E 85 J20
Yamoussoukro Ivory C. 6°49N 5°17W 94 G4
Yampa → U.S.A. 40°32N 108°59W 110 B5
Yamuna → India 25°30N 81°53E 85 G12
Yamzho Yumco China 28°48N 90°35E 78 F7
Yan'an China 36°35N 109°26E 78 D10
Yanbu 'al Bahr Si. Arabia 24°0N 38°5E 86 E4
Yancheng China 33°23N 120°8E 79 E13
Yangambi Dem. Rep. of the Congo 0°47N 24°24E 96 D4
Yangjiang China 21°50N 111°59E 79 G11
Yangquan China 37°58N 113°31E 79 D11
Yangtse → China 31°48N 121°10E 79 E13
Yangzhou China 32°21N 119°26E 79 E12

Yanji China 42°59N 129°30E 79 C14
Yankton U.S.A. 42°53N 97°23W 111 B7
Yanqi China 42°5N 86°35E 78 C6
Yantai China 37°34N 121°22E 79 D13
Yantian China 22°35N 114°16E 79 a
Yaoundé Cameroon 3°50N 11°35E 96 D2
Yap Pac. Oc. 9°30N 138°10E 102 G5
Yapen Indonesia 1°50S 136°0E 83 E9
Yaqui → Mexico 27°37N 110°39W 114 B2
Yaraka Australia 24°53S 144°3E 98 E7
Yarcombe U.K. 50°51N 3°5W 29 F7
Yare → U.K. 52°35N 1°38E 31 A12
Yaren Nauru 0°33S 166°55E 102 H8
Yarkant He → China 40°26N 80°59E 78 C5
Yarkhun → Pakistan 36°17N 72°30E 84 A8
Yarm U.K. 54°31N 1°21W 26 C6
Yarmouth Canada 43°50N 66°7W 109 E13
Yarmouth U.K. 50°42N 1°29W 30 E6
Yaroslavl Russia 57°35N 39°55E 70 C6
Yarrow U.K. 55°33N 3°1W 25 C9
Yarumal Colombia 6°58N 75°24W 120 B2
Yāsūj Iran 30°31N 51°31E 87 D7
Yate U.K. 51°32N 2°25W 30 C4
Yazd Iran 31°55N 54°27E 87 D8
Yazoo → U.S.A. 32°22N 90°54W 111 D8
Yazoo City U.S.A. 32°51N 90°25W 111 D8
Yealmpton U.K. 50°21N 4°1W 29 G5
Yecheng China 37°54N 77°26E 78 D4
Yelets Russia 52°40N 38°30E 70 D6
Yell U.K. 60°35N 1°5W 22 A15
Yell Sd. U.K. 60°33N 1°15W 22 A15
Yellow = Huang He → China 37°55N 118°50E 79 D12
Yellow Sea China 35°0N 123°0E 79 D13
Yellowhead Pass Canada 52°53N 118°25W 108 D8
Yellowknife Canada 62°27N 114°29W 108 C8
Yellowstone → U.S.A. 47°59N 103°59W 110 A6
Yellowstone Nat. Park △ U.S.A. 44°40N 110°30W 110 B5
Yemen ■ Asia 15°0N 44°0E 89 E3
Yenisey → Russia 71°50N 82°40E 76 B9
Yeo → U.K. 51°2N 2°54W 30 D3
Yeola India 20°2N 74°30E 84 J9
Yeovil U.K. 50°57N 2°38W 30 E3
Yerevan Armenia 40°10N 44°31E 71 F7
Yes Tor U.K. 50°41N 4°0W 29 F5
Yeu, Î. d' France 46°42N 2°20W 66 C2
Yevpatoriya Ukraine 45°15N 33°20E 71 E5
Yeysk Russia 46°40N 38°12E 71 E6
Yibin China 28°45N 104°32E 78 F9
Yichang China 30°40N 111°20E 79 E11
Yichun China 47°44N 128°52E 79 B14
Yilehuli Shan China 51°20N 124°20E 79 A13
Yinchuan China 38°30N 106°15E 78 D10
Yingkou China 40°37N 122°18E 79 C13
Yining China 43°58N 81°10E 78 C5
Yixing China 31°21N 119°48E 79 E12
Yiyang China 28°35N 112°18E 79 F11
Yogyakarta Indonesia 7°49S 110°22E 82 F4
Yokkaichi Japan 34°55N 136°38E 81 F5
Yokohama Japan 35°27N 139°28E 81 F6
Yokosuka Japan 35°20N 139°40E 81 F6
Yonago Japan 35°25N 133°19E 81 F3
Yong'an China 25°59N 117°25E 79 F12
Yongzhou China 26°17N 111°37E 79 F11
Yonkers U.S.A. 40°56N 73°52W 113 E11
Yonne → France 48°23N 2°58E 66 B5
York U.K. 53°58N 1°6W 27 E6
York, C. Australia 10°42S 142°31E 98 C7
York, Vale of U.K. 54°15N 1°25W 26 D6
Yorkshire Dales △ U.K. 54°12N 2°10W 26 D4
Yorkshire Wolds U.K. 54°8N 0°31W 26 D7
Yorkton Canada 51°11N 102°28W 108 D9
Yosemite Nat. Park △ U.S.A. 37°45N 119°40W 110 C3
Yoshkar Ola Russia 56°38N 47°55E 70 C8
Youghal Ireland 51°56N 7°52W 20 E7
Youghal B. Ireland 51°55N 7°49W 20 E7
Youlgreave U.K. 53°11N 1°40W 27 F5
Youngstown U.S.A. 41°6N 80°39W 112 E7
Yoxall U.K. 52°46N 1°47W 27 G5
Yoxford U.K. 52°16N 1°31E 31 B12
Yozgat Turkey 39°51N 34°47E 71 G5
Yr Wyddgrug = Mold U.K. 53°9N 3°8W 28 A7
Yreka U.S.A. 41°44N 122°38W 110 B2
Ystalyfera U.K. 51°46N 3°48W 28 D6
Ythan → U.K. 57°19N 1°59W 23 H14
Yu Jiang → China 23°22N 110°3E 79 G11
Yuan Jiang → China 28°55N 111°50E 79 F11
Yuanping China 38°42N 112°46E 79 D11
Yuba City U.S.A. 39°8N 121°37W 110 C2
Yucatán Mexico 19°30N 89°0W 114 D7
Yucatán Basin Cent. Amer. 19°0N 86°0W 104 H11
Yucatán Channel Caribbean 22°0N 86°30W 114 C7

Yuen Long China 22°26N 114°2E 79 a
Yueyang China 29°21N 113°5E 79 F11
Yukon → U.S.A. 62°32N 163°54W 108 C3
Yukon Territory □ Canada 63°0N 135°0W 108 C6
Yulin China 38°20N 109°30E 78 D10
Yuma U.S.A. 32°43N 114°37W 110 D4
Yumen China 39°50N 97°30E 78 D8
Yungas Bolivia 17°0S 66°0W 120 D3
Yunling Shan China 28°30N 98°50E 78 F8
Yunnan □ China 25°0N 102°0E 78 G9
Yurimaguas Peru 5°55S 76°7W 120 C2
Yushu China 33°5N 96°55E 78 E8
Yutian China 36°52N 81°42E 78 D5
Yuxi China 24°30N 102°35E 78 G9
Yuzhno-Sakhalinsk Russia 46°58N 142°45E 77 E15
Yuzhou China 34°10N 113°28E 79 E11
Yvetot France 49°37N 0°44E 66 B4

Z

Zāb al Kabīr → Iraq 36°1N 43°24E 86 B5
Zābol Iran 32°0N 67°0E 87 D10
Zabrze Poland 50°18N 18°50E 65 C10
Zacatecas Mexico 22°47N 102°35W 114 C4
Zadar Croatia 44°8N 15°14E 68 B6
Zagaoua Chad 15°30N 22°24E 95 E10
Zagazig Egypt 30°40N 31°30E 95 B12
Zagreb Croatia 45°50N 15°58E 68 B7
Zagros Mts. Iran 33°45N 48°5E 86 C7
Zāhedān Iran 29°30N 60°50E 87 D10
Zahlah Lebanon 33°52N 35°50E 86 C3
Zakynthos Greece 37°47N 20°54E 69 F9
Zalantun China 48°0N 122°43E 79 B13
Zambezi → Africa 18°35S 36°20E 97 H7
Zambia ■ Africa 15°0S 28°0E 97 G5
Zamboanga Phil. 6°59N 122°3E 83 C6
Zamora Mexico 19°59N 102°16W 114 D4
Zamora Spain 41°30N 5°45W 67 B3
Zamość Poland 50°43N 23°15E 65 C12
Zanda China 31°32N 79°50E 78 E4
Zanesville U.S.A. 39°56N 82°1W 112 F6
Zanjan Iran 36°40N 48°35E 86 B7
Zanzibar Tanzania 6°12S 39°12E 96 F7
Zaouiet Reggâne Algeria 26°32N 0°3E 94 C6
Zaoyang China 32°10N 112°45E 79 E11
Zaozhuang China 34°50N 117°35E 79 E12
Zapala Argentina 39°0S 70°5W 121 F2
Zaporozhye Ukraine 47°50N 35°10E 71 E6
Zaragoza Spain 41°39N 0°53W 67 B5
Zaranj Afghan. 30°55N 61°55E 87 D10
Zárate Argentina 34°7S 59°0W 121 F4
Zaria Nigeria 11°0N 7°40E 94 F7
Zarzis Tunisia 33°31N 11°2E 95 B8
Zaskar Mts. India 33°15N 77°30E 84 C10
Zaysan, L. Kazakhstan 48°0N 83°0E 76 E9
Zayü China 28°48N 97°27E 78 F8
Zeebrugge Belgium 51°19N 3°12E 64 C2
Zeil, Mt. Australia 23°30S 132°23E 98 E5
Zelenograd Russia 56°1N 37°12E 70 C6
Zenica Bos.-H. 44°10N 17°57E 69 B7
Zhangjiakou China 40°48N 114°55E 79 C11
Zhangye China 38°50N 100°23E 78 D9
Zhangzhou China 24°30N 117°35E 79 G12
Zhanjiang China 21°15N 110°20E 79 G11
Zhaoqing China 23°0N 112°20E 79 G11
Zhaotong China 27°20N 103°44E 78 F9
Zhejiang □ China 29°0N 120°0E 79 F13
Zhengzhou China 34°45N 113°34E 79 E11
Zhezqazghan Kazakhstan 47°44N 67°40E 76 E7
Zhigansk Russia 66°48N 123°27E 77 C13
Zhlobin Belarus 52°55N 30°0E 70 D5
Zhob Pakistan 31°20N 69°31E 84 D6
Zhongdian China 27°48N 99°42E 78 F8
Zhongshan China 22°26N 113°20E 79 a
Zhuhai China 22°17N 113°34E 79 a
Zhumadian China 32°59N 114°2E 79 E11
Zhuzhou China 27°49N 113°12E 79 F11
Zhytomyr Ukraine 50°20N 28°40E 65 C15
Zibo China 36°47N 118°3E 79 D12
Zielona Góra Poland 51°57N 15°31E 64 C8
Zigong China 29°15N 104°48E 78 F9
Ziguinchor Senegal 12°35N 16°20W 94 F2
Žilina Slovak Rep. 49°12N 18°42E 65 D10
Zimbabwe ■ Africa 19°0S 30°0E 97 H5
Zinder Niger 13°48N 9°0E 94 F7
Ziway, L. Ethiopia 8°0N 38°50E 89 F2
Zlatoust Russia 55°10N 59°40E 70 C10
Zlín Czech Rep. 49°14N 17°40E 65 D9
Zonguldak Turkey 41°28N 31°50E 71 F5
Zrenjanin Serbia 45°22N 20°23E 69 B9
Zug Switz. 47°10N 8°31E 64 E5
Zunyi China 27°42N 106°53E 78 F10
Zürich Switz. 47°22N 8°32E 64 E5
Zuwārah Libya 32°58N 12°1E 95 B8
Zvishavane Zimbabwe 20°17S 30°2E 97 J6
Zwelitsha S. Africa 32°55S 27°22E 97 L5
Zwickau Germany 50°44N 12°30E 64 C7
Zwolle Neths. 52°31N 6°6E 64 B4

Published in Great Britain in 2012 by Philip's, a division of Octopus Publishing Group Limited (www.octopusbooks.co.uk) Endeavour House, 189 Shaftesbury Avenue, London WC2H 8JY

An Hachette UK Company (www.hachette.co.uk)

Ninety-seventh edition

Copyright © 2012 Philip's

ISBN 978-1-84907-193-2 (HARDBACK EDITION)
ISBN 978-1-84907-194-9 (PAPERBACK EDITION)

Printed in Hong Kong

A CIP catalogue record for this book is available from the British Library.

Details of other Philip's titles and services can be found on our website at: www.philips-maps.co.uk

Philip's World Atlases are published in association with The Royal Geographical Society (with The Institute of British Geographers).

The Society was founded in 1830 and given a Royal Charter in 1859 for 'the advancement of geographical science'. Today it is a leading world centre for geographical learning – supporting education, teaching, research and expeditions, and promoting public understanding of the subject.

Further information about the Society and how to join may be found on its website at: www.rgs.org

PHOTOGRAPHIC ACKNOWLEDGEMENTS
Satellite images in the atlas are courtesy of the following: China RSGS p. 14tl; DigitalGlobe p. 12t; EROS pp. 8, 9t, 9bc, 9b, 14bl, 14br; ESA p. 15b; Fugro NPA Ltd (www.satmaps.com) pp. 6, 11t, 14tr, 15t, 17, 49, 88, 123, 130; GeoEye pp. 12b, 16b; NASA pp. 9tc, 10, 11bl, 11br, 13, 116; Precision Terrain Surveys Ltd p. 16t.

VENICE, ITALY

The city consists of over 100 small islands in a shallow lagoon. This image shows the largest of them, shaped like a fish and linked to the mainland by rail and road bridges. It is bisected by the sinuous Grand Canal, which flows from the train station in the north-west to St Mark's Square in the south. *(Image courtesy Space Imaging/Fugro NPA Ltd)*